ARTHURIAN TRADITION
AND CHRETIEN DE TROYES

Arthurian Tradition & Chrétien de Troyes

Roger Sherman Loomis

New York: Columbia University Press

First printing 1949
Second printing 1952

COPYRIGHT 1949 COLUMBIA UNIVERSITY PRESS, NEW YORK

PUBLISHED IN GREAT BRITAIN, CANADA, AND INDIA BY GEOFFREY CUMBERLEGE
OXFORD UNIVERSITY PRESS, LONDON, TORONTO, AND BOMBAY

MANUFACTURED IN THE UNITED STATES OF AMERICA

TO THE MEMORY OF

LOUIS CONS

LOYAL FRIEND

GALLANT SOLDIER

SENSITIVE CRITIC OF LITERATURE

LOVER OF AMERICA AND FRANCE

PREFACE

THIS BOOK was originally projected as a small volume in which the late Louis Cons was to discuss the literary art of Chrétien de Troyes and I was to give a brief account of the Celtic themes embodied in the four traditional romances—*Erec, Le Chevalier de la Charrette, Yvain,* and *Le Conte del Graal.* It was intended to accompany a series of new editions of these poems, based on the manuscripts. A text of the *Charrette,* with critical apparatus, was completed by the late Herbert K. Stone in 1938, but the war came and interrupted plans for its publication. A similar edition of *Erec,* undertaken by Professor Jean Misrahi, is now approaching completion. After the military collapse of France in 1940, Cons devoted his last energies and finally sacrificed his life for the cause of liberation. In spite of conscientious efforts to write the appreciation of Chrétien's style and workmanship which the original project called for, he did not achieve this end. In a letter written a few months before his death, Cons expressed himself with characteristic humility: "Moi, avec mes pauvres divagations sur la *manière,* je ne suis jamais assuré de ce que je fais." Without the benefit of his fine taste and critical acumen, without the feeling for the nuances of style which his range of reading in Old French literature provided, this book cannot but suffer from limitations of scope and artistic perception. It does not even pretend to deal adequately with Chrétien's personality and methods, though it may supply, in the discussion of his *matière,* some essential bases for such an account by scholars more competent than myself.

During these fourteen years my study of Chrétien's relation to the Arthurian cycle and its Celtic sources resulted in the accumulation of a much larger mass of material than I had at first anticipated. The many discoveries of scholars, besides my own, could not be properly handled within the compass of a small manual. Controversial questions, involving complicated and often unfamiliar evidence, demanded not a rapid survey but a full presentation of each case. It seemed essential to prepare the ground for these detailed arguments by rehearsing the history of the *Matière de Bretagne* up to Chrétien's time, by giving some account of the pertinent Irish and Welsh literature, and by listing and describing the typical phenomena of traditional development. Since the names of persons and places are of the greatest importance in determining the history of a tradition, it seemed well to append to the discussion of these

matters in the body of the text an onomasticon, attempting to fix, whenever possible, the derivation of each name. There must also be a summing
up of conclusions.

A fine apologia for such a study of the origins and growth of literature may be found in the Preface of Professor W. J. B. Pienaar to his
*English Influences in Dutch Literature and Justus Van Effen as Inter-
mediary* (Cambridge, 1929).

To form a true and proper estimate of a writer or of a literature, we must
obviously have all the ascertainable facts at our disposal. Among these, an
analysis of indebtedness home and foreign, its origin and extent, use and
abuse; of the forces that went to the making of great literature, may legitimately claim a place. To consider how an author combined originality and
imitation in both construction and expression, to consider the nature and extent of his original contribution, is a necessary, but much neglected, task for
which we must have all the cards on the table. Genius has eluded definition,
but we may be pardoned for wanting to see how it works. If, then, we may
discover where genius went to quarry for much of its material, what it collected and rejected and what value, if any, was added in the workshop, it
seems clear that this fascinating enquiry should be the first object of the
methodical student of literature; for upon him the onus rests of constructing
a reliable account of what happened in the making of fine literature. As regards the authors themselves, it is neither right nor fair to leave the general
reader with distorted ideas of their inventiveness. . . Instead of urging exaggerated claims of a false kind for a writer's creative capacity, a fuller consciousness of the necessary derivativeness of art may well be cultivated side
by side with reverence for genius and originality.

Since highly exaggerated notions of Chrétien's inventive powers and
constructive ability and erroneous views of the rise and spread of Arthurian romance have been asserted by his editor, Wendelin Foerster, and by
Bruce in his indispensable *Evolution of Arthurian Romance from the
Beginnings down to the Year 1300* (Baltimore, 1923), and since largely
subjective, unhistorical interpretations of Chrétien's psychology and
aesthetic procedures, based on these notions and treating him as if he
were a contemporary poet, have lately come into vogue, a corrective is
called for and has been attempted in the following pages. Of course, I am
not the first to make this effort and I have drawn largely on the findings
of three generations of scholars. Nor do I pretend to have gathered all the
pertinent evidence on so large a subject as the development of the *Matière
de Bretagne* and Chrétien's place in it. But I hope I have included most
of the relevant material and have assembled a larger body of facts and
inferences concerning the origins of Chrétien's four traditional romances
than can be found elsewhere within the covers of a single volume.

The informed reader will perceive that this book covers some of the same ground which I traversed in my *Celtic Myth and Arthurian Romance,* published twenty-one years ago (New York, 1927). I am glad of the opportunity to revise certain opinions, to correct minor errors, and to retract some prominent theses of that earlier work. The connection between the Irish Curoi and the Welsh Gwri or Gwrvan now seems to me unproved and unprovable. The origin of the Grail in a Celtic caldron of plenty or in a fertility symbol I withdraw altogether, as well as my adherence to Jessie Weston's theory that the testing of Perceval in the Grail castle was derived from a fertility rite. I regard it as impossible to trace certain Celtic sources of Arthurian romance back to a remote origin in the Eastern Mediterranean, though some striking analogies exist. In spite of these retractions, I would still maintain the three major theses of the earlier book: (1) Celtic mythology is the principal root of Arthurian tradition. (2) This tradition, originating in Ireland, Wales, and Cornwall, was passed on by professional story-tellers to the Bretons and through them to the French and Anglo-Normans. (3) Arthurian personal names are for the most part of Welsh derivation, though in many instances they have been grotesquely distorted in the process of transmission by foreign tongues and careless or puzzled scribes.

It remains to make grateful acknowledgment to the many scholars, living and dead, whose work has proved helpful and whose names appear in my text and notes. I owe a special debt to Professor W. J. Gruffydd, whose keen insight into the mind and imagination of the Welsh author has been demonstrated in several articles and in *Math Vab Mathonwy* (Cardiff, 1928). I gratefully acknowledge the assistance of my friends, Professor Kenneth Jackson of Harvard University, Professor Jean Misrahi of Fordham University, and Mr. Angus Graham of the Royal Commission on Ancient and Historical Monuments for Scotland, in their respective fields of Celtic philology, the manuscripts of Chrétien's poems, and British archaeology. The officers of the Columbia University Press by publishing this book on a remote and abstruse subject in a period of rising costs have displayed once more their devotion to the cause of learning. To the encouragement and criticism of my wife, Laura Hibbard Loomis, I am proud to owe more than words can express.

R. S. L.

Columbia University
September, 1948

CONTENTS

Book I. Backgrounds

Book II. Erec

Book III. Le Chevalier de la Charrette

Book IV. Yvain

Book V. Le Conte del Graal

Book VI. Conclusions

BOOK I. Backgrounds

Chapter I

THE MYSTERY OF THE MATIERE
DE BRETAGNE

I N THE HISTORY of medieval secular literature there is no more momentous phenomenon, no more extraordinary prodigy, no more mystifying enigma than the rise of the Arthurian legend and its spread
throughout Western Christendom in the course of the twelfth century.
As early as 1174–79 Alanus de Insulis in his commentary on Geoffrey of
Monmouth's *Prophetia Merlini* declared with astonishment:

"What place is there within the bounds of the empire of Christendom to which
the winged praise of Arthur the Briton has not extended? Who is there, I ask,
who does not speak of Arthur the Briton, since he is but little less known to
the peoples of Asia than to the Bretons, as we are informed by our palmers who
return from the countries of the East? The Eastern peoples speak of him as do
the Western, though separated by the breadth of the whole earth. Egypt speaks
of him and the Bosphorus is not silent. Rome, the queen of cities, sings his deeds,
and his wars are not unknown to her former rival Carthage. Antioch, Armenia,
and Palestine celebrate his feats." [1]

Even though we allow for a certain hyperbolic tendency in Alanus' style,
here is a sober witness to the spread of Arthur's fame from the western
to the eastern bounds of Christendom; and, as we shall see in due course,
there are many facts to corroborate his testimony.

Why this astounding interest in a British battle leader who fought the
Anglo-Saxons in the late fifth or early sixth century, a personage so obscure
that no contemporary chronicle even mentions his name? By what agency
was his posthumous renown and his legend carried to the eastern shores
of the Mediterranean? It is easy enough to understand why Charlemagne
should become the center of an epic cycle, and the existence of jongleurs
who made a living by celebrating his acts and those of the twelve peers is
well attested. Even though certain questions of origin and diffusion will
always plague students of the Carolingian cycle, there is nothing to astonish us in the phenomenon itself. Likewise, the composition of the French
romances of antiquity on the basis of classical and late Latin texts and
their vogue in the twelfth century can be easily comprehended. Yet it
was the *Matière de Bretagne,* the fantastic adventures of an alien king and
his knights of the Round Table, their faery loves, their quests and con-

[1] Alanus de Insulis, *Prophetia Anglicana Merlini Ambrosii Britanni* (Frankfort, 1608), p. 26;
(Frankfort, 1603), pp. 22 f. T. Stephens, *Literature of the Kymry* (Llandovery, 1849),
p. 421n. On date cf. R. Taylor, *Political Prophecy in England* (New York, 1911), p. 88.

quests, which achieved on the European continent an even greater vogue than the *Matière de France* or the *Matière de Rome*. Here is mystery upon mystery, riddle after riddle.

The importance of Chrétien de Troyes as the earliest of the Continental authors to exploit the vogue of Arthur in the form of long verse romances is beyond question, but the study of his work provokes many questions. Did he create these novel fictions largely out of his own imagination, with the help of some hints from Wace and some French folktales? What reliance can we place on his references to sources, written or spoken? Why does he borrow so little from the Arthurian portions of Wace's well-established chronicle? Why does he exalt to high renown persons like Erec and Lancelot who are not even mentioned by Wace? Whence did he derive the many names of demonstrably Welsh origin such as Meleagant, Giflet son of Do, Mabonagrain, and Bilis, unknown to Wace? Why does he repeatedly ignore or flout the indications of Wace, for instance, as to the character of Arthur and Keu, and as to the ownership of Escalibor? If, as some scholars even today believe, Chrétien received his chief stimulus from Wace and owed little or nothing to Celtic tradition, all this is very perplexing.

It is very perplexing, too, if we note the inconsequences and absurdities in his four poems—*Erec, Le Chevalier de la Charrette, Yvain,* and *Le Conte del Graal*—which are in large part localized in a fanciful and impossible land of dreams, and contrast them with the skillful and realistic management of his *Cliges* and *Guillaume d'Angleterre,* which would offer no problems to a twelfth-century geographer. Why these lapses from clarity and sense and verisimilitude in four out of the six romances, those four which are most typical of the Arthurian cycle as a whole? Must one charge the poet with a gross, though sporadic, carelessness, an intermittent unreason such as one usually attributes not to the logical and lucid French mind but to the erratic imagination of the Celt or to the *remanieur* of old and irreconcilable materials? This charge we must bring against Chrétien —indeed it has been repeatedly and vigorously expressed by Gaston Paris, Jessie Weston, and Zenker—if he created the four narratives out of his own head, chose his own subjects, invented, shaped, and combined his patterns of story.

Obviously this riddle should not go unsolved; obviously the origin and nature of Arthurian romance are involved in the answer; obviously it is impossible to understand the four poems or to estimate Chrétien's artistic power or his lack of it until we know whether he had sources, what was their nature, and how faithfully he followed them. No critical judgment of Chrétien's narrative art, no interpretation of his work is valid until we have an answer to this problem. To attribute to the poet himself attitudes and interests, a fertility of invention, and a disregard for sense and coherence which may not be his at all—that is to falsify the record, to under-estimate and to overestimate his achievement, and to treat him as if he lived apart from that larger and more complex phenomenon, the conquest of Christendom by the knightly legends of the Round Table.

Of course, one may find a clever journalist like Bernard De Voto assert-ing today that "Source-hunting is the most profitless of occupations"; and some scholarly writers on the Arthurian romances blandly ignore the ques-tion of traditional antecedents. Such an attitude may have its excuse, though not its justification, as a protest against a myopic absorption in problems of origin, to the exclusion of other aspects of literary art. But surely no Homeric, Biblical, or Shakespearean scholar of repute would think himself competent to discuss the *Iliad* or Genesis or *Hamlet* until he had studied what was to be known about its antecedents, even when there were great gaps in the evidence. Yet in the Arthurian field it still seems possible for scholars of eminence to ignore the question of what went before Chrétien, or to answer it by pointing to the extant Latin texts! Even among those who have concerned themselves seriously with the sources of Chrétien's *matière* there are some who enjoy great author-ity, like Foerster and Bruce, who display little or no knowledge of Celtic literature and whose reasoning is open to grave question.

It has been wisely said that the best way to understand a work of art is to watch it grow. There are aspects of Chrétien's art which one cannot fully comprehend until one perceives that the poet has gone to school to Ovid and the medieval writers on poetics.[2] There are other aspects of his art which cannot be understood and appraised until one has investi-gated with some thoroughness the development of the Arthurian legend and arrived at solidly based conclusions as to Chrétien's relation to that development. No sound interpretation of Chrétien's *matière,* his choice and handling of narrative patterns, is possible until one has studied all the pertinent evidence, internal and external, no matter in what language, no matter what its date. Then only can one form a just conception of why these fantastic tales took Europe by storm, whence and by what route they came to France, what were their early forms, and what was Chrétien's relation to them.

This book is an attempt to answer these crucial questions by a pre-liminary survey of the origin and rise of the Arthurian cycle, a discus-sion of certain basic problems such as the channels of transmission and the so-called *Mabinogionfrage,* a listing of the typical phenomena in the growth and spread of a tradition, and finally a detailed examination, epi-sode by episode, of the four poems, *Erec, Le Chevalier de la Charrette,*

[2] *Romanic Review,* XII (1921), 97 ff., 216 ff. Note Chrétien's practice of beginning with a proverb as prescribed by the textbooks. E. Faral, *Arts poétiques du XIIe et du XIIIe siècle* (Paris, 1924), pp. 58, 113, 201 f.

Yvain, and *Le Conte del Graal.* In so far as I shall succeed in my purpose, the study will make it possible to estimate with some accuracy the
extent of Chrétien's debt to Celtic tradition, to determine approximately
the form in which his stories reached him, and to appraise fairly his originality. If the result is to deprive the poet of any claim to vast inventive
powers, to the creation of a new genre largely by the exercise of a fertile
imagination, it will also relieve him of responsibility for the faults of construction and the lapses in coherence to which otherwise he would have
to plead guilty.

Of course, this work is not a pioneer effort. On the contrary, it is greatly
indebted to the researches of three scholarly generations devoted to the
disentanglement of one of the most complex webs of evidence in literary
history. To list the names of all the writers who have solved one or more
problems would occupy several pages. I shall endeavor to give credit where
credit is due when considering each specific problem, but here I shall limit
myself to naming those who have made the largest and most significant
contributions to the right understanding of the *Matière de Bretagne:*
Gaston Paris, Bédier, Zimmer, Brugger, Nutt, Jessie Weston, and Gertrude Schoepperle. All these attacked fundamental and formidable questions, and though they sometimes attacked each other and were, being
human, not infallible, they advanced the limits of our knowledge in a large
way and into obscure regions. To them my obligations are great. Furthermore, there have been elaborate investigations of *Erec* and *Yvain* in Sparnaay's *Hartmann von Aue: Studien zu einer Biographie;* of *Le Chevalier
de la Charrette* in *Lancelot and Guenevere* by Professors Cross and Nitze;
and of *Yvain* in Arthur Brown's *Iwain* and Zenker's *Ivainstudien.* These
works shed much light on Chrétien's sources and have been of immense
value to me; but they do not carry through a systematic effort to account
for every episode, motif, and proper name. This I shall attempt to do for the
four romances wherever the evidence seems to me sufficiently clear, including even a few instances, such as the rescue of Lunete from the stake and
Lancelot's defense of Guenievre against the charge of adultery with Keu,
for which a non-Celtic origin can be and will be maintained.

I shall, of course, be liable to errors of omission and commission, of
judgment and fact. I have indeed deliberately avoided a detailed refutation
of all the multitudinous hypotheses which seem to me mistaken, for to do
so would triple or quadruple the bulk of this book and would perhaps add
to the confusion in what is at best an exceedingly complicated subject. I
shall proceed on the assumption that if the evidence supports my interpretation of the facts, any contrary and inconsistent interpretation must necessarily be ruled out. This does not mean, of course, that Chrétien himself
was subjected only to Celtic influences or that his narratives are exclusively derived from any given source. He was the product of the French

civilization of his time, including its classical and Christian heritage, as his picture of customs and manners and his handling of dialogue sufficiently demonstrate. Many of his characters have several prototypes or ancestors, no one ancestor excluding the possibility of another; and many incidents are composites from several sources. Whatever the shortcomings of my treatment may be, I have not been oblivious to the fact that many strands of tradition have been intertwined in the stories which Chrétien and the other composers of Arthurian romance tell. It is this complexity which lends the subject its great difficulty and also its extraordinary fascination for those who like their puzzles to be not too simple.

Whether and in what measure I have succeeded in my undertaking, time will determine. Doubtless there will be other and better solutions offered for some of the problems. But I have the temerity to believe that most of the major mysteries and many of the minor ones are cleared up in the pages which follow, that as a result Chrétien's relation to his predecessors and successors in the development of Arthurian romance can be defined more fully and accurately than has been possible hitherto, and that at last the countless unknown Irish, Welsh, Cornish, and Breton story-tellers who contributed to the creation of the legends of the Round Table and the skillful combiner or combiners of these legends who framed the plots of *Erec* and *Yvain* may receive their just due.

Chapter II

CHRETIEN DE TROYES AND HIS TESTIMONY

THE FIRST STEP in attempting to discover the relation of Chrétien to his sources in the composition of the four poems which have been suspected of Celtic origin is to see who Chrétien was and what he says on the subject.

Presumably the poet was born at Troyes since in *Erec* (vs. 9) he calls himself "Crestiiens de Troies." The town was the focal point of several of the great trade routes of Europe, and its two great annual fairs brought merchants and entertainers from every corner of Christendom.[1] Here too was the seat of the powerful and wealthy counts of Champagne. Here or elsewhere Chrétien must have studied the trivium, for he was familiar with Ovid and the poetic manuals. Probably he took orders and may

[1] *Medieval France*, ed. A. Tilley (Cambridge, 1922), map opp. p. 202; pp. 202–6. Cf. Chrétien's *Guillaume d'Angleterre*, vss. 1986–88: "Se tu sez feire ta besoigne A Bar, a Provins ou a Troies, Ne puet estre, riches ne soies."

have been the Christianus, canon of St. Loup, mentioned in a document of 1173.[2] He may have met two clerics destined to fame in literature—Walter Map, who was hospitably entertained by Henri, Count of Champagne, in 1179, and Andreas Capellanus, chaplain of the Countess, who composed his *De Amore* in 1184-85.[3] Both of these clerics, it will be remembered, showed the pervasive influence of Arthurian fiction by incorporating tales derived from this cycle in their works.[4] Certain it is that Chrétien moved in aristocratic circles and enjoyed the patronage of two of the most prominent figures of his time—Marie, who was the spirited daughter of Louis VII of France and Eleanor of Poitou, and who became countess of Champagne by her marriage to Count Henri in 1164;[5] and Philippe, who became Count of Flanders in 1168, famed for his largess and military ardor, a cousin of Henry II of England and *de facto* regent of France between 1180 and 1182.[6] At the direction of Marie the poet undertook the composition of *Le Chevalier de la Charrette;* at the request of Philippe he wrote some 9,200 lines of *Le Conte del Graal* before he was interrupted, presumably by death. There is no reason to believe that the poet was ever attached to Philippe's court or even visited Flanders. He displays, however, in *Cliges* a familiarity with the location of Southampton, Winchester, Wallingford, Oxford, Windsor, and Shoreham, which strongly suggests that he had made a tour in southern England.

From *Cliges* we gather likewise that Chrétien had already composed the following poems: (1) a redaction of Ovid's *Ars Amatoria* and, possibly, of the *Remedia Amoris;* (2) a redaction of the Philomena episode in the *Metamorphoses;* (3) a poem on Pelops from the same source; (4) a poem on King Marc and Iseut la Blonde; (5) *Erec.* Of these 1, 3, and 4 are lost; 2 is probably identical with a portion of the *Ovide Moralisé* attributed to a "Crestiens li Gois"; 5 is the earliest extant Arthurian romance. There followed, probably in this order: (6) *Cliges,* an artificial composite, written with the intent of combining the charms of Byzantine and Breton fiction; (7) *Le Chevalier de la Charrette* (*Lancelot*), completed by Godefroy de Lagny; (8) *Yvain* (*Le Chevalier au Lion*); (9) *Guillaume d'Angleterre,* a pious narrative unrelated to the Arthurian cycle; (10) *Le Conte del Graal* (*Perceval*), left unfinished. The dates of this literary activity are hard to fix.[7] Already in *Erec* Chrétien evinced

[2] *Modern Philology,* XXXII (1935), 341 f.
[3] *Dictionary of National Biography,* XII, 994. *Speculum,* XIII (1938), 308.
[4] *Speculum,* XVI (1941), 34–56. Andreas Capellanus, *De Amore,* ed. A. Pagès (Castellon della Plana, 1929), pp. 152–61. Cf. H. Newstead, *Bran the Blessed in Arthurian Romance* (New York, 1939), pp. 141 f.
[5] On Marie cf. Andreas Capellanus, *Art of Courtly Love,* trans. J. J. Parry (New York, 1941), pp. 13–21; *Speculum,* XII (1937), 12–18.
[6] For references on Philippe cf. Chrétien de Troyes, *Conte del Graal,* ed. A. Hilka (Halle, 1932), p. 616.
[7] Cf. D. C. Cabeen, *Critical Bibliography of French Literature,* I (Syracuse, N.Y., 1947), 106 f.

knowledge of Wace's *Brut* (1155). The *Charrette* was written after Marie became a countess (1164). *Le Conte del Graal* was at least begun before Philippe went on Crusade (1190), never to return. Probably, though not certainly, the four romances with which we are concerned—*Erec, La Charrette, Yvain, Le Conte del Graal*—may be placed between 1160 and 1180.

What does Chrétien tell us of the sources of these four poems? As for *Erec*, he asserts that he is drawing "une mout bele conjointure" from "un conte d'aventure." He goes on to say: "Of Erec, the son of Lac, is the story, which those who desire to earn their livelihood by telling tales are wont to dismember and spoil in the presence of kings and counts." Taken at their face value, these statements seem to mean: (1) The story of Erec and Enide was not of the poet's own invention. (2) It was included in the repertory of professional reciters who enjoyed the hospitality of kings and counts. (3) Chrétien regarded his version as a coherent narrative (*conjointure*),[8] in contrast to the mangled and botched forms of the *conteurs*. His contempt for these reciters emerges again in *Le Conte del Graal*, where he has Guiromelant burst out ironically: "Now is it a joy and delight to me to listen to such lies; for I would as lief hear a story-teller (*fableor*) reciting (*conter*) as I do thee!" The *Erec* passage, then, attests the existence of other versions, to be heard in royal and noble courts from the lips of story-tellers, and indicates that Chrétien was well aware of the merits of coherence and rationality which this poem in large measure possesses. Thrice he refers to his source as an *estoire* (vss. 3590, 5738, 6736).

In the *Charrette* he testifies that the Countess gave him both *matière* and *san,* and that he has contributed only his labor and intelligence.[9] Again and with emphasis, then, he disclaims any credit for invention. Both the narrative material and the dominant thesis were prescribed by his patroness. In verse 468 he refers to a *conte* as his authority.

Early in *Yvain* Chrétien announces his intention to relate somewhat concerning a king (namely Arthur), "who was of such renown that people speak of him near and far; and I agree thus far with the Bretons that his name will live forever." This is significant, first, as agreeing with the statement of Alanus de Insulis that Arthur was spoken of from one end of Christendom to the other, and secondly, as referring to the Continental Bretons as peculiarly convinced of his immortal fame, to which also Alanus alludes in another well-known passage: "Go to the realm of Armorica, which is lesser Britain, and preach about the market places and villages that Arthur the Briton is dead as other men are dead, and facts themselves will show you how true is Merlin's prophecy, which says that the ending of Arthur shall be doubtful. Hardly will you escape unscathed, without

---

[8] On meaning of *conjointure* cf. Nitze in *Mod. Phil.*, XI (1914), 40–43.
[9] On this passage cf. Nitze in *Mod. Phil.*, XIV (1916–17), 14 ff.

being whelmed by curses or crushed by the stones of your hearers." [10]
In verse 2685 Chrétien cites "li contes" as the source of his information. The
concluding lines are also significant. "Thus Chrétien ends his romance
(*romanz*) of the Knight with the Lion; for never have I heard any more
of it related, nor will you hear more told, unless some one wishes to add
a lie." This passage conveys much the same impression as the lines from
Erec. The poet had heard stories of the Knight of the Lion, but he
regarded the version he followed as so good that whatever else one might
hear was false.

The dedication of *Le Conte del Graal* states that the author was putting
into rime the best tale ever told in a royal court and that Count Philippe
had given him the book which contained it. "Then Chrétien will not have
toiled in vain, who seeks and strives to rime (*rimoiier*) the best tale (*conte*)
which may be told in a royal court: this is the story of the Grail (*li contes
del Graal*), of which the Count gave him the book." As with *Erec,* it is
implied that the tale was to be heard in royal courts, but it came to him
in the form of a book. Thrice he refers to this source as a *conte* (vss. 709,
6215, 6515), four times as an *estoire* (vss. 2807, 3262, 6217, 7681). The verb
rimoiier is a crucial one. Though there has been a disposition to regard
it as meaning "to retell in verse" what was already in verse, yet even
Foerster was obliged to admit: "so heisst das wörtlich: 'ihn in Reime
umsetzen,' woraus dann folgen würde, dass dieses *livre* ungereimt, also
wohl in Prosa geschrieben war." "Nun heisst zwar *rimoiier* sicherlich
zuerst: etwas nicht gereimtes, also Prosa, in Reime umsetzen." [11] This
admittedly primary meaning of *rimoiier* seems the more likely since it
has not been demonstrated, I believe, that any early French romance in
verse represents the retelling of another romance already in verse. Moreover, we have a close parallel to Chrétien's statement in Couldrette's
Mellusine (vss. 80 f.), where the patron directs the poet: " 'You shall
put the history (*istoire*) in rime; I wish that it be rimed (*rimoyé*).' " This
surely means that Couldrette's source was in prose, and the same must be
true of Chrétien's book.

There is an interesting parallel to what Chrétien says of the Arthurian
tales in what Marie de France says of the Breton lais. She declares that
she has heard them recited: "I thought of the lais which I had heard"; "I
have heard many of them related." [12] But she has also met stories of
Tristan in written form: "Many have recited and told (*cunté e dit*) it to
me and I have found it in writing concerning Tristram and the Queen"; [13]
and she implies a written source for *Guigemar:* "At the very beginning
I will show you an adventure according to the text and the writing." These

[10] E. K. Chambers, *Arthur of Britain* (London, 1927), pp. 109 f., 265.
[11] W. Foerster, *Kristian von Troyes, Wörterbuch* (Halle, 1914), pp. 153*, 155*.
[12] Marie de France, *Lais,* ed. K. Warnke, 3d ed. (Halle, 1925), p. 4.   [13] *Ibid.,* p. 181.

lais, Marie asserts, she turned into rime: "I have rimed (*rimé*) them and made a composition"; "I undertook to bring together some lais, to put them into rime (*par rime faire*) and relate them." [14] There is, therefore, a singular harmony between Marie's relation to the Breton lais and Chrétien's relation to the Arthurian contes.

Let us review his testimony. He consistently disclaimed that he was the creator of his stories; they dealt with themes and persons already known; they had been recited before kings and counts by professionals, but in an inferior form. A written source in prose is indicated for *Le Conte del Graal* and may be presumed for the *Charrette* since it is unlikely that the Countess provided the *matière* in verse form. That the language of both oral and written sources was French goes without saying, and that Chrétien did more than merely versify the tales is equally obvious. But by his own account he did not create his plots.

How seriously should we take his testimony? The answer depends in part on whether he had any temptation to deceive and could take the risk. When he wrote for Marie and Philippe, there were motives for flattery, but was there anything to be gained by refusing credit for the story? Was it politic to assert that his patrons furnished him with his *matière* if they had done nothing of the kind? Why the references to the professional reciters if they did not exist? On these matters Chrétien deserves to be taken at his word—unless it can be shown from outside evidence that there were no *conteurs* of Arthurian tales in his time, and that there were no comparatively artistic versions of these long composite tales set down in prose. I believe that an examination of this evidence abundantly confirms Chrétien's testimony. After all, because Geoffrey of Monmouth perpetrated his notorious hoax and his book in the Breton language may never have existed, one must not put down all medieval authors as amiable liars in their citations of source, especially when they were addressing patrons who knew precisely what the facts were. Though the question, "How closely did Chrétien follow these acknowledged sources?" remains to be investigated, there is a strong presumption that what he said about them was true. He derived the main outlines at least of the four romances from tales familiar to his readers; the tales were commonly recited by professionals before aristocratic audiences; some versions were valued so highly as to be set down in manuscript in prose.

There is nothing impossible or improbable about these assertions, and when one surveys the other evidence on the circulation of the *Matière de Bretagne* in the twelfth century and examines the relation of Chrétien to the Welsh *Geraint, Owain,* and *Peredur,* his veracity is amply vindicated.

[14] Marie de France, *Lais,* p. 4.

Chapter III

THE ARTHURIAN TRADITION BEFORE CHRETIEN DE TROYES

THOUGH MUCH of what follows in this chapter is elementary knowledge for every student of the subject, certain facts seem to be unknown to, or to be rated at less than their proper value by, the authorities such as Bruce and Sir Edmund Chambers. At any rate, it is well to review briefly the available evidence outside Chrétien's poems bearing on the question whence, through what channels, and in what form Chrétien might have received his narrative materials. Let us first concern ourselves with Wales.

The historic Arthur is apparently first mentioned by name in the Welsh poem, the *Gododdin*, now assigned by experts to about the year 600.[1] The subject is a disaster which overtook British warriors of the North at the hands of the Angles. In verses 1241 and following it is said of a Briton that he glutted the ravens on the rampart of the city, "though he was not Arthur." Professor Jackson remarks: "This is perhaps the most valuable evidence yet found for the historicity of Arthur; here we have him spoken of as a famous warrior within living memory of the (supposed) date of his (supposed) death."[2]

Next comes the oft-cited passage by the South Welsh priest Nennius, composed about 800, which tells of Arthur's twelve victories over the Anglo-Saxons.[3] Arthur was not a king but a leader in battles. Two of the battle sites, the wood of Celyddon and the City of Legions, may be identified with the forest region of southern Scotland and with Chester,[4] but scholars rightly doubt whether the Anglo-Saxons could have penetrated as far to the north and west by the middle of the sixth century, and that is too late a date for Arthur's activities. Probably Nennius' list is an arbitrary compilation of places where battles, real or imaginary, had been fought.

Nennius includes in his book an account of the natural marvels of Britain, and among them are two which show that Arthur was becoming

---

[1] Edited in Welsh as *Canu Aneurin* by Ifor Williams (Cardiff, 1938). Discussed by I. Williams, *Lectures on Early Welsh Poetry* (Dublin, 1944), pp. 65–70, and by K. Jackson in *Antiquity*, XIII (1939), 25–34. A translation of certain parts by Prof. Gwynn Jones may be found in *Cymmrodor*, XXXII (1922), 4–47.   [2] *Antiquity*, XIII, 29.
[3] F. Lot, *Nennius et l'Historia Brittonum* (Paris, 1934), I, 194–96. E. K. Chambers, *Arthur of Britain*, pp. 238 f. The best studies of Arthur and the twelve battles are A. G. Brodeur, "Arthur, Dux Bellorum," *Univ. of Calif. Pub. in English*, III (1939), 237–83, and K. Jackson in *Mod. Phil.*, XLIII (1945), 44–57.   [4] *Mod. Phil.*, XLIII, 48–50.

the subject of aetiological legends.[5] One is a heap of stones called Carn Cabal; Arthur's hound Cabal left his footprint on one of these stones when the warrior Arthur was hunting the boar Troit. The cairn still gives its name to a hill in northern Breconshire,[6] and the boar hunt is described at length in *Kulhwch and Olwen.* The other marvel is the burial mound of Anir, the son of the warrior Arthur, in Herefordshire; it varied in length from six to fifteen feet. It is noteworthy that not yet is Arthur styled a king, but his name was evidently one to conjure with along the valley of the Wye.

The *Annales Cambriae,* composed about 955, record under the dates 516 and 537 Arthur's victory of Badon and his fall, together with Medraut, at the battle of Camlann.[7] There is no more reason to trust these entries than any of the previous references. The sites of Badon and Camlann are unknown, but the battle of Badon was at least a historic victory of the Britons about the year 500,[8] and Camlann was destined to inspire some of the greatest literature of the Arthurian cycle.

To the tenth century we may also ascribe a very obscure Welsh poem entitled *The Spoils of Annwn,* in which the bard Taliesin imagines himself accompanying Arthur and three shiploads of men in a raid on the faery fortress of the Chief of Annwn.[9] We find the same expedition reported in euhemerized form in *Kulhwch,* and we can detect a number of connections with ancient Welsh mythology on the one hand and with French romance on the other. In this poem for the first time Arthur appears not as a historic warrior or as the hunter of a fabulous boar, but as a central figure in a phantasmagoria of myth, as the inheritor of a rich tradition of pagan lore. In spite of the many questions to which it gives rise, it is of supreme significance in interpreting the Welsh contribution to the Arthurian legend. To the same or the next century belongs a fragmentary poem from the Black Book of Carmarthen,[10] in which Arthur gives a list of his warriors, including not only the familiar figures of Kei and Bedwyr but also the mythological personages, Mabon son of Modron and Manawydan son of Llyr. There is mention, too, of Cath Paluc, a catlike monster found also in a Welsh triad and, as the Chapalu, in French romances, as was demonstrated by Freymond in a masterly monograph.[11]

About the year 1100,[12] perhaps a decade earlier or later, there was writ-

---

[5] F. Lot, *op. cit.,* I, 216. Chambers, *op. cit.,* pp. 239 f.
[6] C. Guest, *Mabinogion,* Everyman ed., pp. 331 f. J. Rhys, *Celtic Folklore* (Oxford, 1901), II, 538 f. W. Sikes, *British Goblins* (Boston, 1881), pp. 363 f.
[7] J. Loth, *Mabinogion,* 2d ed. (Paris, 1913), II, 372. Chambers in *op. cit.,* pp. 15, 214, places the battles two years later.
[8] Brodeur, *op. cit.,* pp. 238 f., 275–78.   [9] *PMLA,* LVI (1941), 887–936.
[10] T. Malory, *Morte d'Arthur,* Everyman ed., I, xviii–xx. *Aberystwyth Studies,* VIII (1926), 54–57.   [11] *Festgabe für G. Gröber* (Halle, 1899), pp. 311 ff.
[12] On date cf. *Romanic Review,* XXXII (1941), 15 f.; J. Loth, *op. cit.,* I, 28, 39–41; *Moyen*

ten the Welsh prose love story, *Kulhwch and Olwen,* and here for the first time we have a full-scale Arthurian romance. Not only is it a work logical in structure and distinguished by charming descriptive passages and touches of humor, but also a document illustrating the magnetic power of Arthur's name. For here are brought together names, stories, and allusions from multifarious sources, from Irish saga, Brythonic myth, local folktale, and contemporary history. Here are the most valuable clues to the later Arthurian onomasticon, and here are the foreshadowings of situations and stories later utilized by the French romancers, including Chrétien, as I hope to make clear in the course of this book.

In startling contrast to the heroic portrayal of Arthur in all these sources, certain Welsh saints' lives of the second half of the eleventh century and the early twelfth century introduce him briefly in contemptible roles and contrast his power with that of the saints.[13] This hostile attitude on the part of monastic hagiographers toward the favorite of the *cyvarwyddon* (professional story-tellers) is easily understandable in view of the heathenish and immoral tales which had been absorbed into the Arthurian tradition.[14] It affords no index to Arthur's standing among the laity. The *Vita Gildae* of the Welsh monk, Caradoc of Lancarvan,[15] adopts a somewhat more favorable attitude, though Arthur is termed a "rex rebellis" (refractory, that is, to the saints) and is obliged to do penance for the slaying of Gildas' brother in battle. It is significant, moreover, that Caradoc's account of the abduction of Queen Guennuvar by Melvas forms a link between the abduction of Creiddylat as related in *Kulhwch* and the abduction of Guenievre as told by Chrétien.[16]

Such is the extant evidence on the Arthurian legend among the Welsh before Chrétien's time. Though there are important documents of later date, which will be discussed in due course, they do not force us to revise the conclusions drawn from the earlier texts. By 1100 Arthur had become the center of a great syncretic tradition in Wales, and elements of it found their way into French romance.

Next let us look at Cornwall, the home of another branch of the Brythonic peoples, close in blood and speech to the Welsh. We have no ancient Cornish literature and are obliged to rely on outside sources. Several Welsh writers assert or imply that one of Arthur's courts was at Kelliwic in Cornwall,[17] and in this seem to be reflecting a tradition of

---

Age, XLI (1931), 309; *Essays and Studies Presented to Prof. Eoin MacNeill,* ed. J. Ryan (Dublin, 1940), p. 28.

[13] *Speculum,* VIII (1933), 478–80; XIV (1939), 345–65. E. Faral, *Légende arthurienne* (Paris, 1929), I, 236–42.   [14] *Romanic Review,* XXXII, 33 f.

[15] Chambers, *op. cit.,* pp. 263 f. *Cymmrodorion Record Series,* II (London, 1901), p. 410. On Caradoc cf. *Speculum,* XIII (1938), 139–52.   [16] Cf. Chap. XXXI.

[17] Cf. Loth, *op. cit.,* II, "Index des noms propres"; F. J. Snell, *King Arthur's Country* (London, New York, 1926), pp. 29 f.; *Antiquity,* XIX (1945), 156 f.

their neighbors. Herman of Laon (or Tournai) relates in an oft-quoted passage that certain canons of Laon on a fund-raising expedition were shown, on their journey from Exeter in Devon to Bodmin in Cornwall, the seat and the oven "of that King Arthur, famed in the fables of the *Britanni*." [18] Herman also bears witness to a fracas at Bodmin between one of the canons' servants and a Cornishman who asserted that Arthur was still alive, "just as the Bretons (*Britones*) quarrel with Frenchmen over King Arthur." [19] Thus we are assured of two things: that Arthur was celebrated in the tales of the insular Britons (*Britannorum*), and that both Cornishmen and Continental Bretons (*Britones*) were ready to fight for their belief in Arthur's survival. The date of this journey was 1113.[20] Some twenty-odd years later Geoffrey of Monmouth referred to Arthur as the Boar of Cornwall, localized his birth and death in that land, and introduced in that connection Cornish names—Gorlois, Britael, Ridcaradoch, Dimilioc, and Modredus.[21] Geoffrey was probably drawing on the "fabulae Britannorum" mentioned by Herman.

Knowledge of Arthurian tales in England is first attested by William of Malmesbury in two passages of his *Gesta Regum* (1125).[22] In one of these William declared that the trifles of the Bretons (*nugae Britonum*) raved in his day about Arthur, a man worthy not to be dreamed about in false fables but proclaimed in veracious histories. In a later and equally important passage he tells of the discovery (about 1087?) in southwestern Wales of the tomb of Walwen (Gawain), the nephew of Arthur by his sister. Walwen's warlike exploits against the Saxons are mentioned, and variant accounts given of his death. William adds that Arthur's tomb was nowhere to be found, wherefore ancient ditties (*antiquitas naeniarum*) prophesied his return. The full significance of all this seems to have been appreciated only by Zimmer in his discussion back in 1891.[23] The contemporary *Britones* of the first passage must be Bretons, since Geoffrey of Monmouth says that after Cadwallader's time the Welsh were no longer called *Britones* but *Gualenses*,[24] and William himself follows this rule and uses the former word for contemporary Bretons. The form "Walwen" of the second passage betrays the same origin, since it bears little resemblance to any Welsh form. It may seem astonishing that an Anglo-Norman chronicler such as William should be in contact with Bretons and learn from them of the discovery of Gawain's tomb in western Wales. But all becomes clear if we accept, with Zimmer, Ahlström, Bédier, and Warnke,[25]

[18] Chambers, *op. cit.*, pp. 18, 184, 249.   [19] *Ibid.*   [20] *Speculum*, VIII, 455.
[21] *Romanic Review*, XXXII, 5. *Romania*, XXVIII (1899), 342; XXX (1901), 11. J. Loth, *Contributions à l'étude des romans de la Table Ronde* (Paris, 1912), pp. 63 f. *Revue celt.*, XXXVII (1917–19), 322 f.
[22] Chambers, *op. cit.*, pp. 16 f., 250.   [23] *Zts. f. franz. Sprache u. Lit.*, XIII (1891), 86–88.
[24] Geoffrey of Monmouth, *Historia Regum Britanniae*, ed. A. Griscom (New York, 1929), p. 535. *Romanic Review*, XXXII, 8.
[25] Cf. n. 23 and A. Ahlström, *Studier i den Fornfranska Lais-litteraturen* (Upsala, 1892),

the crucially important fact that after 1066 a number of important fiefs in England were held by Bretons,[26] and they would naturally welcome entertainers from their homeland. Everything goes to show that these entertainers, speaking French, found favor also with the Anglo-Normans. Their tales of impossible adventures seemed to the sober chronicler mere raving, but their report of the discovery of Walwen's tomb in Pembrokeshire (a region which, though not under Norman domination in the Conqueror's time, had received a visit from him in 1081) was worth recording. The return of professional Breton *conteurs* and singers of lais to their ancestral home in the wake of the Norman Conquest explains not only these passages in William's chronicle but much else that would be perplexing if we assumed that only the Welsh and Cornish had early legends of Arthur. Concerning these Bretons in Anglo-Norman Britain more will be said in the following chapter.

Geoffrey of Monmouth is our next important witness. Though doubtless born in what was then Wales, he resided at Oxford between 1129 and 1151 and so may be considered an Anglo-Norman rather than a Welshman at the time of his literary activity.[27] The *Prophetia Merlini,* written in 1134–35 and later incorporated in the *Historia Regum Britanniae,* besides referring to Arthur as the Boar of Cornwall, foretells his conquests, declares that his end will be doubtful, and says that he will be celebrated in the mouth of the peoples and his deeds will be food to the tellers of tales (*cibus erit narrantium*).[28] Here the novel points are the explicit references to oral diffusion and to reciters who earn a livelihood by the celebration of Arthur's deeds. This harmonizes with Chrétien's reference in *Erec* to oral recitation by professional *conteurs.*

Geoffrey's *Historia* (1136) opens with a notable passage in which he speaks of the acts of Arthur and other kings of Britain as charmingly proclaimed from memory by many peoples as if they had been committed to writing (*a multis populis quasi inscripta iocunde et memoriter predicarentur*).[29] Whatever we may think of Geoffrey's capacity for falsification—and it was great—here is a statement that was open to challenge since it concerned a matter of general knowledge. His clerical readers, ill informed doubtless about the days of Brutus, Bladud, and Belinus, were well aware of what was going on in contemporary Europe. Geoffrey was hardly so stupid as to introduce his great hoax with a patent lie. We must believe him when he says that the deeds of Arthur and other British kings

pp. 28–34; Thomas, *Tristan,* ed. J. Bédier, II (Paris, 1905), 126 f.; Marie de France, *Lais,* ed. Warnke, 3d ed., pp. xxv f.; *Romanic Review,* XXXII, 10 f.; *Journal of English and Germanic Philology,* XXIV (1925), 130.

[26] Add to the above Chambers, *op. cit.,* p. 21; Loth, *Mabinogion,* 2d ed., I, 68 f.; *Mod. Phil.,* XXII (1925), 407 ff.; A. P. Stanley, *Historical Memorials of Canterbury,* Everyman Lib., pp. 64 f.; F. M. Stenton, *First Century of English Feudalism* (Oxford, 1932), pp. 24–28.

[27] Chambers, *op. cit.,* pp. 21–24.   [28] *Ibid.,* pp. 25, 254.   [29] *Ibid.,* p. 252.

were being related in 1136 by many peoples, and that must mean outside the limits of Wales, Cornwall, and Brittany. Evidently we are approaching the time when Alanus could say that all Christendom rang with the praises of Arthur. Though Geoffrey himself doubtless contributed to this result, he did not initiate the process.

In 1141–42 Ailred, then master of the novices at the Yorkshire abbey of Rievaulx, composed his *Speculum Caritatis,* in which he represents a novice as reproaching himself because, though in his past life he had frequently been moved to tears by fables which were invented and disseminated concerning an unknown Arthur (*fabulis quae vulgo de nescio quo finguntur Arcturo*), it was almost a miracle if he could extract a tear at a pious reading or discourse.[30] Here is not only direct testimony to the familiarity of such tales in Yorkshire, but also the explanation of their vogue. They must have been told with histrionic intonations and gestures —an art naturally cultivated by professional entertainers. In fact, Peter of Blois, later in the century, speaks of the *histriones* whose tales of Arthur, Gawain, and Tristan moved their auditors to tears.[31]

Probably these *histriones* were known in southern Scotland about this time, for an anonymous *Life of St. Kentigern* (patron saint of Glasgow), written between 1147 and 1164, asserts that the father of Kentigern "is called in the tales of the minstrels (*histrionum*) Ewen son of Ulien [*sic*]." [32] This Ewen is, of course, Yvain son of Urien, of whom Chrétien was to declare not long afterwards that he had never heard any more recited concerning him than what he had embodied in his poem.

Two Anglo-Norman composers of lais attest their acquaintance with Arthurian fiction a little before or about the time when Chrétien was writing *Erec.* About 1150 Robert Biket tells the somewhat farcical incident of the chastity-testing horn in his *Lai du Cor,*[33] and asserts that the talisman was still preserved at Cirencester. It is worth noting that the personal names in this poem, though a number of them are derived from the Welsh, assume forms as remote from the Welsh as are the forms encountered in French romance. Marie de France says in *Chievrefoil* that many had told her of Tristram and the Queen and that she had found such matter also in writing.[34] And in her lai of *Lanval* she declares that her hero had a Breton name, that the Bretons tell us that this knight of Arthur's rode away with his faery mistress to Avalun, and that she has heard no man tell more of him.[35]

[30] Migne, *Patrologia Latina,* CXCV, col. 565. On date cf. *Bulletin of John Rylands Library,* VI (1921–22), 454 f., 478.
[31] Chambers, *op. cit.,* p. 267. Migne, *op. cit.,* CCVII, col. 1088.
[32] *Lives of St. Ninian and St. Kentigern,* ed. A. P. Forbes (Edinburgh, 1874), p. 245. *Romania,* XXII (1893), 506. Cf. *infra,* pp. 272, 302.
[33] Ed. F. Wulff (Lund, 1888). *Mod. Phil.,* XXXIII (1936), 232.
[34] Marie de France, *op. cit.,* p. 181.   [35] *Ibid.,* pp. 86, 112.

All this testimony from writers in England and southern Scotland indicates the presence and the activity of professional Breton reciters; they, not the Welsh or the Cornish, were principally responsible for the spread of romantic tales of Arthur and his knights throughout the Anglo-Norman world.

If we turn our attention to Brittany, we are disappointed at the total absence of any direct testimony from Bretons to the circulation of Arthurian stories. This may be accounted for, first, by the fact that the Breton *conteurs* were not writers but reciters, secondly, by the total disappearance of all early literature in the Breton tongue. But outsiders compensate for this deficiency. The Norman Wace (1155) has a reference to the Round Table, "of which Bretons tell many tales." [36] Alanus de Insulis corroborates Herman of Laon's assertion that the Bretons resented fiercely any doubt that Arthur was alive.[37] Etienne de Rouen introduces into his *Draco Normannicus* (1167–69) an imaginary correspondence between Henry II and Arthur, in which the latter is cast in the ridiculous role of supreme ruler of the Antipodes—evidently a fling at the Breton belief that Arthur lived on as a mighty potentate in the under world.[38] The internal evidence of the French romances, the localization of the youth and the last years of Tristan in Brittany, the introduction of the Forest of Broceliande in Chrétien's *Yvain*, the sprinkling of Breton place names and personal names through the Arthurian onomasticon, which we shall consider in detail at the appropriate places, combine with the evidence from England to demonstrate the familiarity of the Bretons in their own homeland with Arthurian tradition.

The troubadours of the South seem to have felt the contagion fairly early. One manuscript of Marcabrun's elegy on the death of William VIII of Poitou (1137) contains the line: "Like Arthur I shall be lost forever." [39] Bernard de Ventadour shortly after 1154 wrote that never did "Tristan l'amador" endure such anguish for "Yzeut la blonda" as did the poet for his lady, presumably Eleanor, daughter of the same William.[40]

This reference to Tristan by a troubadour attached to the house of Poitou brings up the subject of the *conteur* Bleheris, the only member of his profession whose name has come down to us.[41] From the several references to him in the literature of the twelfth century one may draw

---

[36] Wace, *Brut,* ed. I. Arnold, II (Paris, 1940), vss. 9751 f. On Round Table cf. Chap. VI.
[37] Chambers, *op. cit.,* p. 265.
[38] *Chronicles of the Reign of Stephen, Henry II, and Richard I,* ed. R. Howlett, II (London, 1885), 696–707. *Mod. Phil.,* XXXI (1933), 1–18, 113–25; XXXVIII (1941), 289–304.
[39] *Romania,* VI (1877), 123 f.
[40] K. Bartsch, *Chrestomathie provençale,* p. 63. *Mod. Phil.,* XIX (1922), 287 ff. *Revue des langues romanes,* LXV (1927–28), 238 f.
[41] On Bleheris cf. *Romanic Review,* XXXII, 16–19, and bibliography given, *ibid.,* p. 16, n. 77, particularly, *Romania,* XXXIV (1905), 100; LIII (1927), 82; *Neophilologus,* XV (1929), 30–34.

certain conclusions: (1) The name Bleheris, Breri, and so forth is surely developed from Welsh Bleddri. (2) The man in question was born in Wales and was well known there as a famous raconteur. (3) His period slightly antedated that of Giraldus Cambrensis, who was born about 1145. (4) He recited his tales before a Count of Poitou, either the famous troubadour, William VII, who died in 1127, or his son William VIII, who died ten years later. (5) Bleheris was regarded by succeeding generations as an authority on the Tristan, Gauvain, and Grail stories. (6) He must have told his tales in French. (7) If we take seriously the citations of his authority by Thomas and Wauchier de Denain, there is nothing in their poems to indicate that Bleheris' fund of stories was peculiarly Welsh, but everything points to Continental Breton tradition as the immediate source of his repertoire. (8) As the unique instance of a *conteur* whose name and fame survived him, he must have surpassed his confrères in the verve and the artistry of his recital.

The most sensational evidence for the early and wide diffusion of the *Matière de Bretagne* on the Continent comes from northern Italy.[42] Rajna long since pointed out that an Artusius appears in a document of 1114 as a brother of Count Ugo of Padua; another Artusius signed a document of 1122; I have noted still a third Artusius as a benefactor of Modena cathedral in 1125. Beginning with 1136, a certain long-lived Walwanus is named in Paduan charters. These Artusii and this Walwanus must have been christened late in the eleventh century or in the first quarter of the next. Artusius was a standard Latinization by Italians of the name Arthur when the source was French, and Walwanus is identical with the form of Gawain in one of the best manuscripts of Geoffrey's *Historia*. It is hard to explain these names unless stories of Arthur and his nephew had penetrated into the aristocratic circles of northern Italy, and rendered them illustrious.

This view is confirmed by a sculptured archivolt over the north doorway of Modena cathedral.[43] The significant points are: (1) The nearly unanimous verdict of recent art historians assigns the relief to the first decade of the twelfth century. (2) The names Artus de Bretania, Isdernus, Che, Galvagin*us,* Galvariun, Burmaltus, Mardoc, and Winlogee are incised above the figures. (3) Winlogee is plainly an intermediate form between the Breton name Winlowen and the name Guinloie, which turns up in French romance. (4) Isdernus still retains the final *n* of Welsh Edern, the son of Nudd, whereas Geoffrey's Hider filius Nucii and Chrétien's Yder fiz Nut have lost it. (5) Galvagin*us* is the earliest recorded form of Gawain and, as will be shown in a later chapter, comes closest

[42] On these names cf. *Romania,* XVII (1888), 167 ff., 356 ff.; *Romanic Review,* XXXII, 27–31.
[43] On this sculpture cf. R. S. and L. H. Loomis, *Arthurian Legends in Medieval Art* (New York, 1938), pp. 32–36, figs. 4–8. For additional discussions of date cf. *Speculum,* XIII, 221–31; *Romanic Review,* XXXII, 22–27; *Studi medievali,* N.S., IX (1936), 1 ff.

to its Welsh original. (6) Several scholars have accepted my interpretation of this carving as an illustration of the abduction of Arthur's queen, here called Winlogee, in a version which partially parallels that given in the thirteenth-century romance of *Durmart*. The conspicuous position of this profane scene in a sacred edifice can hardly be accounted for unless we presuppose that the story made a profound impression either on the sculptor or on whoever directed his work. The nomenclature, though most of the names ultimately go back to Welsh originals (Arthur, Edern, Cei, Madoc), indicates that the reciter was a French-speaking Breton.

Another curious testimonial to the Arthurian vogue in Italy dates from 1165. In that year a large mosaic pavement was laid down in the cathedral of Otranto, far to the south, and though it has been damaged by earthquakes and restorers, it contains a crude figure labeled Rex Arturus, bearing a scepter and riding a goat! [44] This extraordinary mount has received no better explanation than the frequent identification of the immortal Arthur with various Otherworld kings, and the fact that Walter Map describes one such king as riding on a very large goat.

Though the execution of this mosaic in southern Italy in 1165 and the somewhat later legends of Arthur localized about Mount Etna do not carry us to the Latin kingdoms of the East, they do prepare us to place some credence in Alanus' statement before 1179 that the renown of the British hero had reached the Holy Land.

From this survey of the rise and spread of the Arthurian legend up to and through the period of Chrétien's literary activity we can draw several large inferences.

1. As one might expect, all the earliest documents from the seventh to the end of the eleventh century come from Wales. *Kulhwch and Olwen* shows that about 1100 there existed in that country a romantic tradition which displays unmistakable connections with Nennius' reference to the hunting of the boar Troit on the one hand, and with the French romances on the other. Kulhwch's arrival and reception at Arthur's court and his meeting with the Giant Herdsman clearly anticipate Chrétien's treatment of these same subjects in *Le Conte del Graal* and *Yvain*. Two or three decades later Caradoc of Lancarvan furnished in his story of the abduction of Guennuvar a cognate form of Chrétien's *Chevalier de la Charrette*. These facts demonstrate that Wales was the birthplace and the early home of Arthurian romance.

2. Herman of Laon witnesses that in 1113 there were not only local associations of Arthur with Dartmoor and an unshakable belief in his immortality among the Cornish, but also that he was celebrated in stories of

[44] On Otranto mosaic cf. R. S. and L. H. Loomis, *op. cit.*, p. 36, figs. 9 and 9a; E. Bertaux, *L'Art dans l'Italie méridionale* (Rome, 1904), I, 488–90; *Studi medievali*, II (1906–7), 506, 510; *Mod. Phil.*, XXXVIII, 300–302.

the insular Britons. Evidently by 1100, if not before, Cornwall had its own tradition of the British hero.

3. There is practically no evidence that the Welsh communicated their tales of Arthur and his knights directly to their English-speaking or French-speaking neighbors across the border. It is obvious that the long-standing hostility between the Brythonic and Saxon peoples would render the former unwilling to pass on legends which glorified the champion of their race, and would render the latter even more reluctant to receive them. There was also a language barrier which would hamper communication between the Welsh and both Saxons and Normans. The hypothesis that the Anglo-Normans served as intermediaries in bringing the Celtic legends to the knowledge of the French must be rejected.

4. To the problem of transmission the Bretons offer the key; for they were bilingual, were akin racially to the Welsh and Cornish, were devoted to the memory of Arthur, and yet were in the closest political and cultural relations with their French-speaking neighbors, and not only had a large share in the Norman Conquest of England but also acquired great estates there. It is no wonder that whenever and wherever we get any indications as to the propagators of the *Matière de Bretagne* outside Wales and Cornwall, they point with but one exception to the Bretons. And that one exception, Bleheris, seems to have drawn on Breton traditions and must have told his enthralling tales in French. From such diverse sources as the Modena sculpture, William of Malmesbury, and Wace we gather that the Bretons were the disseminators of stories about Arthur, his Round Table, and the abduction of his queen. Their geographical range extended from southwestern Wales to the Lombard plain, and by 1170 much further.

5. Though the Bretons of the twelfth century may have inherited from their ancestors who emigrated across the Channel to Armorica in the sixth century some memories of a heroic Arthur, they were not the creators of a body of fiction independent of their Cornish and Welsh kinsmen. It will be shown in due course that certain personal names in the French romances, particularly Erec, Gauvain, and Lancelot, can best be explained as Breton substitutions for, or deformations of, Welsh forms, and the romances themselves seem to have their roots in Wales. Furthermore, such important historic figures as Yvain and Tristan, who lived respectively about 580 and 780, could not have been known to the original emigrants from Britain but must have been introduced to their Continental descendants by the Welsh or Cornish at some later period. Just what that period was is difficult to determine, but when we find a historic Tristan, lord of Vitré, recorded in the first half of the eleventh century,[45] it seems probable that the insular tradition had reached Brittany by 1000, if not

45 Pierre le Baud, *Chronique de Vitré* (bound with *Histoire de Bretagne*, Paris, 1638), p. 7. *Revue de Bretagne*, XVIII, 435–39. *Romania*, LIII, 97.

before. Of course, the Bretons embellished the Welsh stories, adapted them to French and Anglo-Norman taste, and added features of their own, but they did not create an independent legend.

6. The vast proliferation and wide circulation of Arthurian tales must be attributed in large measure to a professional class. The Welsh had their bards who composed and recited poetry (such as *The Spoils of Annwn*) and their *cyvarwyddon* who composed and recited prose tales (such as *Kulhwch and Olwen*).[46] The thirteenth-century *Dream of Rhonabwy* ends with the significant words: "This is why no one, bard or story-teller (*cyvarwydd*), knows the tale without a book." [47] Geoffrey's remarks in the *Prophetia Merlini* about the Boar of Cornwall as celebrated in the mouths of peoples and furnishing a livelihood to story-tellers, refer to such professionals and agree strikingly with Chrétien's remarks in the opening lines of *Erec*. Wace, too, speaks of the *cunteur* and the *fableur* who relate the marvels and adventures of Arthur's time and mingle falsehood and truth.[48] It must have been the emotional power of these narrators, whether Welsh or Breton, which gave them their hold on the laity, roused the antagonism of the hagiographers, and called forth the disparaging notices of William of Malmesbury and Ailred. The attitude of the poets to the *conteurs* ranged from their professed admiration for Bleheris, through the mixed praise and blame of Wace, to the contempt of Chrétien for those who spoil and mangle the plot of *Erec*.

7. The chief medium of these reciters, Welsh and Breton, was prose. The prose saga was the standard narrative form among the Celts, not the verse epic of the Germanic tribes.[49] The itinerant *conteurs* are expressly said by Wauchier to exercise their crude art "sanz rimer." [50] It must be remembered, however, that the Bretons also had their lais,[51] and some of them dealt with Arthurian themes. It is interesting to note that about 1216 Giraldus Cambrensis spoke of the "fabulosi Britones et eorum cantores"

[46] H. M. and N. K. Chadwick, *Growth of Literature*, I (Cambridge, 1932), 582–85. I. Williams, *Lectures on Early Welsh Poetry*, pp. 9 ff.
[47] J. Loth, *Mabinogion*, 2d ed., I, 377.   [48] Wace, *Brut*, ed. I. Arnold, I, lxxxv; II, 515 f.
[49] *Göttingische Gelehrte Anzeigen*, 1890, pp. 806–17.
[50] J. L. Weston, *Legend of Perceval*, I (London, 1906), 265. "Mais il sont ore maint vassal Qui fabloiant vont par ces cors, Qui les bons contes font rebors E des estoires les esloignent E des mençonges tant i joignent Que li conte tout emperissent E les bons livres en honissent; E cil qui oent e escoutent Ne sevent que bon conte coustent. Ains dient, quant cil menestrel Gisent la nuit en lor hostel E il lor font. i. poi conter D'une aventure sanz rimer, Qu'il ont toute l'estoire oie Que ja n'orront dedens lor vie; Si lor fait on mençonge acroire Et en dient la fausse estoire Et metent la mençonge avant." Cf. also *Moyen Age*, XIX (1916), 234 f.; E. Martin, *Zur Gralsage, Quellen u. Forschungen zur Sprach- u. Culturgebiete der germanischen Völker*, XLII (1880), 27 f.; *Mélanges de philologie romane dédiés à Carl Wahlund* (Macon, 1896), p. 302.
[51] On these lais cf. Marie de France, *op. cit.*, pp. xx–xlv; *Zts. f. franz. Sprache u. Lit.*, XLIX (1926), 120–53; *Mod. Phil.*, XII (1914–15), 585–644; *Revue celt.*, XXXI (1910), 413–71.

as responsible for fictions about the goddess Morganis and her transporting Arthur to the Isle of Avalon for healing.[52] There was evidently a class of Breton singers, somewhat distinct from the story-tellers, and their songs may have resembled the short allusive poems of the Welsh bards. None of these songs, however, has survived, and the extant lais in French probably have little in common with them beyond the subject matter. Since, of course, Breton songs would have been quite incomprehensible to French audiences, and since the extant lais seldom reveal a close relation to Arthurian romance,[53] it is obvious that we must not look to the Breton singers but to the Breton *conteurs* in French prose as the chief, if not the only, immediate sources of Arthurian fiction in England and on the Continent.

8. Some of these tales must have been written down and were accessible in manuscript in Chrétien's day. No such manuscript has been preserved, but this is hardly to be wondered at since not a single twelfth-century copy of Chrétien's or Marie's work has survived either. But both these authors testify to the existence of such writings, and certain name forms in Chrétien's poems show signs of scribal distortion. Such are Gomeret for Goinnet, Baudemaguz for Bran de Mangunz, Goirre for Voirre, as I hope to show in the appropriate places. Either Chrétien misread a written source or adopted a corrupt reading from such a source. Though the tales of the Breton *conteurs* were recited in French prose, can we believe that they were still in prose when first committed to writing? No wholesale generalization seems possible. The testimony of Marie de France is inconsistent. We remember that in her prologue she asserts that she has rimed the lais which she has heard, and implies therefore that there was no intermediate written form. But she introduces *Guigemar* with the statement that she is following "la letre e l'escriture," and refers in *Chievrefoil* to both oral and written forms of the Tristan story. One gets the impression that some of her lais were based on *contes* in manuscript, which she proceeded to versify. The evidence favors the view that Chrétien likewise followed prose tales in manuscript when he composed his four traditional romances. There is no indication that his sources were in verse. One cannot, perhaps, deny the possibility that Chrétien was improving an already rimed romance, but the odds are against such an interpretation of his task. When he and his contemporary Marie both speak of riming traditional narratives, the natural inference is that these were in prose; and in Chrétien's case we have good reason to believe that they were in written prose. The assertion that

[52] E. K. Chambers, *op. cit.,* p. 272.
[53] There is, of course, a relation between the lais and romances, but except in the case of *Chievrefoil* and the Tristan poems (G. Schoepperle, *Tristan and Isolt* [New York, 1913], I, 137-47), in that of *Desiré* and *Yvain,* and in that of the *Lai du Cor* and the magic horn episodes (*Speculum,* IX [1934], pp. 38-50) the relation is not close.

no one wrote French prose in the twelfth century should not be taken too seriously. Any literate person who speaks prose can write it, and the French were not a wholly illiterate people.

This review of the Arthurian tradition before and during the period of Chrétien de Troyes offers a solution for the chief mysteries that beset the student of the subject. Throughout the world's history clouds of legend have gathered about the heads of military leaders who have caught the imagination of a people. This happened to Alexander and Charlemagne, to Napoleon and Washington. For the Britons it was enough that Arthur inflicted a series of defeats on their heathen foes and staved off for a time their expulsion from what was to be England. For centuries the Welsh, the Cornish, and the Bretons firmly believed in his return, the ultimate triumph of the Red Dragon over the White, and the reconquest of England from the hated Saxon. To this racial hero the Welsh and to some extent the Cornish attached a floating mass of native traditions, together with matter derived from Ireland and the Britons of the North. This they passed on to the Bretons, who shared their passionate devotion to the memory of Arthur, and the Bretons in turn, speaking French, were able by the fire and the charm of their recitals to captivate the imagination of the non-Celtic peoples. Thus the obscure battle leader of a defeated race became the champion of all Christendom, his knights paragons of valor and chivalry, and the ladies of his court nonpareils of beauty. Geoffrey of Monmouth launched his book on the flowing tide of Arthur's prestige. The wandering *conteurs* spread his fame from Lothian to the Holy Land, and the palace of the Counts of Champagne, lying at the crossroads of western Europe, must have harbored many of them. Skilled as some were in stitching together adventure after adventure to furnish an evening's entertainment, not all of them were capable of achieving a "mout bel conjointure" out of matter so diverse and c'ten mysterious. When reduced to writing, some of the long tales revealed obvious gaps in structure, confusions in geography, inconsistencies in characterization. Yet still they retained their fascination for courtly audiences, and the demand arose for more refined and sophisticated versions, with all the charms of rime. This demand Chrétien was one of the first, if not the first, to meet with his Arthurian romances. There can be little doubt that his acknowledgments of debt to written sources are genuine, and that, whatever he may have added or altered, he reproduced to a considerable extent both the defects and the excellences of his originals. Thus only can one explain the many mystifying characteristics of his work, the many oddities which suggest that he was drawing on a body of inchoate and ultimately foreign tradition, and the exaltation of an alien king and court.

Chapter IV

SOME SPECIAL PROBLEMS

THERE ARE three problems connected with Chrétien's relation to Celtic sources which deserve special attention: (1) If the Arthurian legend developed first of all in Wales, what are we to make of the many Irish elements discovered in the French romances? (2) If the Welsh matter was not transmitted directly to the Anglo-Normans and from them to the French, how are we to explain the familiarity with certain English and Scottish localities displayed in the romances? (3) What is the relation of *Erec, Yvain,* and *Le Conte del Graal* to the Welsh prose texts, *Geraint, Owain (The Countess of the Fountain),* and *Peredur?* Not a little of the discussion devoted to Chrétien's work hinges on the answers given to these perplexing and highly controversial problems, and it may clarify much that follows if we devote a preliminary chapter to their consideration.

1. *The Irish Contribution to Arthurian Romance.*—A number of eminent scholars, to wit, Gaston Paris, Nutt, Kittredge, Arthur Brown, Cross, and Gertrude Schoepperle, have demonstrated the presence of Irish elements in the French, German, and English romances and the Breton lais. Though some claims for Irish influence have been mistaken or muddled,[1] yet no serious student, so far as I know, now denies that influence altogether. How is it, then, that these Irish motifs seeped into English and Continental literature, turning up, as we shall see, time and again in the poems of Chrétien de Troyes and elsewhere?

The bulk of the Irish materials with which we are concerned has been dated on the basis of strict linguistic tests from the eighth to the twelfth century; many of them are found in two famous manuscripts, the Book of the Dun Cow, copied about 1100, and the Book of Leinster, copied about fifty years later. The sagas which concern us may be classified roughly in three cycles: the mythological cycle, the Ulster cycle, and the Finn cycle.[2] The first deals with the doings of the Irish gods, the Tuatha De Danann. Such figures as the sea-god Manannan, the sun-god Lug, and

---

[1] My attempt to prove that Cuchulainn was a diminutive Curoi and to connect Curoi with the Welsh Gwri was unfortunate.

[2] On Irish literature cf. E. Hull, *Text Book of Irish Literature* (Dublin, London, 1906–8); *Enc. Brit.,* 11th ed., V, 614–16, 622–34; *Die Kultur der Gegenwart,* ed. P. Hinneberg, Teil I, Abt. XI, 1 (Leipzig, 1909), 78–97; H. M. and N. K. Chadwick, *Growth of Literature,* I. On Ulster cycle cf. Thurneysen, *Irische Helden- u. Königsage* (Halle, 1921) and on Finn saga cf. E. MacNeill, *Duanaire Finn,* I (London, 1908), xxiv–lix. All these may need revision in the light of T. F. O'Rahilly's *Early Irish History and Mythology* (Dublin, 1946), especially, pp. 260–85.

the lamia and prophetess, the Morrigan, are conspicuous. The chief saga of the cycle is *The Second Battle of Moytura,* dated before 908, but other sagas such as *The Voyage of Bran, The Fate of the Children of Turenn, The Adventures of Cormac in the Land of Promise,* and *The Prophetic Ecstasy of the Phantom* also introduce the ancient divinities and transport us to their lands of wonder and their faery palaces. The Ulster cycle, to judge by the extant remains, enjoyed the greatest vogue among the ruling classes. The texts date from the eighth century on, and include *The Cattle-Raid of Cooley, Bricriu's Feast, The Violent Death of Curoi, The Sick-bed of Cuchulainn, The Death of Cuchulainn,* and others. Though it has been commonly thought that the chief personages of the cycle were historic and actually lived about the beginning of the Christian era, yet even here supernatural figures play a part. Manannan, Lug, and the Morrigan again appear on the scene. Cuchulainn's father was Lug; his mother Dechtire and his uncle Conchobar are said explicitly to be gods; he himself possesses marked solar traits, and his enemy Curoi is surely no mere chief of Munster. The queen of Connaught, Medb, has been proved to be a sort of divine embodiment of the province, mated to one after another of its kings.[3] Whatever historic realities lie behind the Ulster cycle, they are mingled with mythical elements. Finally, there is the Finn cycle, developing first in Leinster by the eighth century or earlier, spreading throughout Ireland, ousting the older tales in popular favor, enjoying a great vogue among the Irish colonists in the Hebrides and the Highlands of Scotland, and attaining by a curious freak of chance a European fame through the forgeries of Macpherson. The most important text for us is *The Boyhood Exploits of Finn,* written in the twelfth century. The supernatural, though not excluded, is less prominent than in the other cycles of story.

Before being committed to writing, these cycles formed the repertory of a class of story-tellers and poets called *filid* (singular *fili*), who occupied an honorable place in Irish society from time immemorial and down through the Middle Ages.[4] The most exalted rank among the *filid* were styled "ollaves" and were qualified to recite 350 sagas by heart. The institution must go back to pagan times, for only thus can we understand the presence of so much unedifying pagan lore in the Irish sagas.

The Irish sagas which infiltrated Arthurian romance could not have passed directly from the Irish to the French. There were no direct channels of transmission except the missionaries who founded monasteries in Frankish territory in the seventh century or the scholars like Eriugena and Sedulius in the ninth, and such men would be the last to propagate the lore of Irish heathendom. Furthermore, neither the Irish nor the French

[3] *Zts. f. celt. Phil.,* XIX (1933), 352 f. On Eriu, the personification of Ireland, cf. *Eriu,* XIV (1943), 11–28.
[4] Thurneysen, *op. cit.,* pp. 66–70. H. M. and N. K. Chadwick, *op. cit.,* I, 602–15. *Mod. Phil.,* IX (1911), 121 f.

would have had the incentive and the knowledge to employ these materials for the glorification of the British Arthur and his fabulous warriors.
The Irish contribution to French romance must have been made through
some intermediate peoples. Who could these be but the Brythonic peoples
of Wales and Cornwall?

Everything goes to confirm this hypothesis. The existence of ogham inscriptions indicates the presence in western Wales of a considerable Goidelic
population between the fifth and the seventh centuries, but about 400
Cuneda, a British chieftain from near the Firth of Forth, began the conquest of these Goidels, and they were gradually expelled or absorbed among
the Brythonic settlers.[5] Naturally in the process much Goidelic tradition
would also be absorbed and blended with the ancient pagan lore of the
Britons. More important probably was the constant intercourse which
went on right down to the eleventh century between the inhabitants of
Wales and Ireland—intercourse of every kind.[6] The early literature of
Wales reveals a great debt to the neighboring island. Nennius (*ca.* 800)
knows the legendary account of the settlement of Ireland. *The Four
Branches of the Mabinogi,* dating probably from the second half of the
eleventh century, form an extraordinary amalgam of Irish stories of Lug,
Balor, Curoi, Blathnat, and others with native myths of Arawn, Riannon,
Gwri, Lleu, Bran, and Manawydan, as the masterly studies of Professor
Gruffydd have demonstrated.[7] *Kulhwch and Olwen* (*ca.* 1100) not only
lists three personages from the Ulster cycle among Arthur's warriors, but
also borrows motifs from Irish saga [8] and involves Arthur in two expeditions across St. George's Channel. Here, then, in Wales was not only the
logical place for Irish matter to mingle with British myths and hero
legends of Arthur, but also the actual place where historic conditions
favored such a mixture and where we can observe currents flowing in
from Ireland and flowing out to meet us again in French literature. It is
thus that the great Irish contribution to Arthurian romance can be fully
understood.

2. *The Hypothesis of Anglo-Norman Transmission.*—A more complicated problem is involved in the contention of some scholars, notably
Gaston Paris and M. Ferdinand Lot,[9] that the Anglo-Normans participated
in the transmission of Welsh and Cornish legends to France. We have seen
that both external testimony and the internal evidence of personal names
in Arthurian documents from the date of the Modena sculpture on down
through the thirteenth century indicate that the Bretons must have been

[5] J E. Lloyd, *History of Wales,* 3d ed. (London, New York, 1939), I, 116–21.
[6] C. O'Rahilly, *Ireland and Wales* (London, 1924), pp. 35–80. *Studies in English, Univ. of
Texas,* No. 6 (1926); No. 7 (1927). *Revue celt.,* XXXI (1910), 421 ff.
[7] *Transactions of the Hon. Soc. of Cymmrodorion,* 1912–13, pp. 72–80. W. J. Gruffydd, *Math
Vab Mathonwy* (Cardiff, 1928).   [8] C. O'Rahilly, *op. cit.,* pp. 114–22.
[9] *Romania,* XV (1886), 597; XVIII (1889), 510; XXIV (1895), 513; XXVIII (1899), 321.

the chief disseminators of the *Matière de Bretagne* on the European Continent. It has also become apparent from William of Malmesbury's references that Breton *conteurs* not only were circulating in England but were even reporting the discovery of Walwen's tomb in extreme southwestern Wales. Does this fact exclude direct passage of any considerable body of Welsh story to the English and Anglo-Normans without Breton intervention?

Two poems are significant for this question. Biket's *Lai du Cor* (*ca.* 1150), written in Anglo-Norman and displaying some acquaintance with the town of Cirencester, which is about fifty miles from the Welsh border at Monmouth, deals with what in all probability is a Welsh theme of a testing horn, and its hero was familiar to the Welsh as Caradawc Breichbras. Yet the forms of the personal names are as remote from any Welsh originals as any Continental specimens of the same names, if not more so.[10] A second witness to the same effect is the English poet Layamon, who lived about thirty-five miles from Offa's Dike and wrote his *Brut* late in the twelfth or early in the thirteenth century. Though his main source is Wace's poem, he does make additions and these might be expected to show Welsh influence. But Bruce pointed out that two proper names in these additions, Argante and Melyon, are not Welsh.[11] Only in a single instance, the love song *Annot and Johan* of the thirteenth century, did Carleton Brown find in the names Tegeu and Cradoc signs of direct communication of Welsh stories to an English poet.[12] Nothing, to my knowledge, proves that the English or Anglo-Normans were intermediaries between Welsh and Continental Arthurian fiction.

What is at first baffling and confusing, however, is that fact that certain Anglo-Norman lais and even French romances reveal an acquaintance with the geography of Wales which suggests direct communication. Marie de France's *Yonec,* for instance, correctly places the towns of Caruent and Karliun (Caerwent and Caerleon) only a short journey apart; [13] one might naturally infer that such knowledge of Monmouthshire was transmitted to Marie without Breton intervention. Yet the personal names in the same lai, Yonec and Muldumarec, resemble nothing in Welsh, and both have a termination characteristic of certain Breton names, for example Guerec. Apparently, then, we have in *Yonec* a Breton tale localized in South Wales by a Breton story-teller familiar with the region. Marie's *Lanval,* though not localized in Wales but in northern England, reveals even more clearly the same procedure. The hero's name is unknown in Welsh, and it is said specifically that "en bretanz l'apelent Lanval" (vs. 4). The form Walwain in the same lai is not Welsh, and Lanval's departure to Avalun is said

---

[10] *Mod. Phil.,* XXXIII (1936), 232.
[11] *Mod. Lang. Notes,* XXVI (1911), 65 ff. *Rev. of Eng. Studies,* X (1934), 80 f.
[12] C. Brown, *English Lyrics of the XIIIth Century* (Oxford, 1932), pp. 226 f.
[13] Marie de France, *Lais,* ed. A. Ewert (Oxford, 1944), p. 179.

to be vouched for by "li Bretun." Arthur's court is placed at Kardoel, modern Carlisle, but this localization cannot represent an old Brythonic tradition transmitted directly from the Welsh to Marie, for they called the town Cair Ligualid.[14] Kardoel is an Anglo-Norman form which could only have become known to the Bretons after the Norman Conquest.[15] Thus again we have in *Lanval* a Continental story arbitrarily fitted with an insular setting, and since the story must have been imported into England by the Bretons, it was doubtless they who were responsible for establishing Kardoel as one of Arthur's favorite seats, though possibly some local legend may have encouraged the selection.

Zimmer, who was the first to realize the significance of the name Cardoil, added the even more notable example of Caradigan, which Chrétien applied to Arthur's seat in *Erec*.[16] The Welsh always called and still call the town Aber Teivi, and it was the Anglo-Norman conquerors of South Wales who named it after the district in which it stood, and the first record of the new name appears in 1128. Though, as I shall endeavor to show in discussing *Erec,* much of the narrative matter must have come originally from Wales, yet again there are many signs of Breton manipulation, and the placing of Arthur's court at Caradigan must be due to some twelfth-century Breton visitor to South Wales, just as William of Malmesbury must have learned of the discovery of Walwen's tomb in Pembrokeshire from a Breton.

Still another cogent example of the relatively late introduction of English and Welsh place names is the "cité de Sinadon en Gales," described by Chrétien's near contemporary, Renaud de Beaujeu, in *Le Bel Inconnu.* As I have shown in *Speculum,* Vol. XXII (1947), p. 527, the Anglo-Norman Gaimar makes the first extant use of this name about 1150, and the reference can only be to the Roman fort in the Snowdon district which the Welsh called Caer Seint, near modern Carnarvon. Here again is evidence of the non-Welsh origin of even a place name in Wales and of its late introduction into the *Matière de Bretagne.* Again the presumption is, since the Welsh are ruled out and the Anglo-Normans derived their Arthurian matter from the Bretons, that the last-mentioned were the introducers of Sinadon into Arthurian toponymy.

Once it is realized that there were barriers of language and racial hostility which prevented the Welsh from sharing their heroic legends with the English and Normans,[17] this entire, somewhat roundabout process of transmitting the Welsh cycle of Arthurian tales to the Continent seems

[14] *Zts. f. franz. Sprache u. Lit.,* XIII (1891), 91.
[15] *Idem.* The *d* of Kardoel may well be due to the influence of the Breton place name Kerduel, near Lannion. Cf. F. J. Snell, *King Arthur's Country,* p. 242.
[16] *Zts. f. franz. Sprache u. Lit.,* XIII, 87 f.
[17] On the relations of the Welsh to the English and Anglo-Normans cf. *Trans. Hon. Soc. Cymmrodorion,* 1918–19, pp. 149–60.

not only plausible but inevitable. The stories themselves in large measure clustered about Arthur in Wales and Cornwall and were passed on to Armorica in the course of the ninth and tenth centuries. The personal names, too, though often transformed by the Bretons, were largely, as I hope to show, derived from insular sources. The insular place names, however, which reached the Bretons in their Continental home would have little interest for them and in a few generations would be forgotten. Only when the Breton *conteurs* flocked back to their ancestral soil after the Norman Conquest were they impelled to supply a new and an insular geography for their stories. To themselves and their Norman auditors names like Caradigan, Cardoil, and "la cité de Sinadon" meant something and added a sense of reality to the scenes enacted at these towns and castles. And when these same *conteurs* or their successors traveled back to the Continent, to Normandy, or Brittany, or Champagne, they carried with them the old stories inherited from the Welsh, now supplied with a geography extending from Galvoie (Galloway) and Loonois (Lothian) to Tintagel and St. Michael's Mount in Cornwall.

It is, then, possible to make some broad generalizations, which I believe will be amply borne out in the body of this book. The narrative materials of Arthurian romance represent in large measure an old insular tradition. The personal names are likewise, despite Breton additions and adaptations, largely derived from authentic Welsh sources. But the insular toponymy of the Arthurian romances was, for the most part, an incrustation on the old matter, made by the Breton *conteurs* traveling about England, Wales, and southern Scotland after the Norman Conquest. Only in the sense that the place names which the Bretons picked up and introduced into their romances were those current among the Anglo-Normans can one speak of an Anglo-Norman contribution to Arthurian romance. Only in the sense that these same Bretons doubtless carried on the process of elaborating and developing their tales during their sojourn in England can one speak of an Anglo-Norman stage in the development of the *Matière de Bretagne*. Paradoxically speaking, the Bretons created the Anglo-Norman stage of the legend.

That this was an important stage, however, will become clear in the course of this book. I hope to prove that the Bretons took a great interest in the castles, towns, and regions which for one reason or another they associated with the personages and the events of Arthur's reign, just as did the Welsh authors of *Kulhwch* and *The Dream of Rhonabwy*. Probably the Welsh anticipated the Bretons in identifying their mythical Isle of Glass with Glastonbury, for Caradoc of Lancarvan is the earliest to record this erroneous connection. The further step, the identification of Glastonbury with the faery Isle of Avalon, seems to have been at least known to the Bretons in England, for Giraldus testifies that it was from a "historico cantore Britone" (not a Welshman) that King Henry II learned of the spot where Arthur was buried.[18] Though it is doubtless fiction, it is surely significant fiction that, according to *Fouke Fitz Warin,* William the Conqueror learned from a *Bretoun* about the haunted ruins of Chastiel Dinas Bran, now called Dinas Bran, on the borders of Wales and Shropshire, about its foundation by King Bran, and its buried treasure.[19] This same Chastiel Bran may well have been visited by less fictitious Bretons than the one in *Fouke;* at any rate, Bran was the original of the Fisher King, and Chrétien's account of Perceval's ride along the river to the Fisher King's castle seems to show indirect acquaintance with the approach to Dinas Bran down the valley of the Dee.[20] Furthermore, Chrétien's emphasis in *Erec* on the fertility of the countryside about Caruent corresponds to the fact, and, though the possibility of coincidence cannot be ruled out, it is more likely that some real knowledge of Lower Gwent, which had been in Norman hands since shortly after the Conquest, was incorporated by a *conteur* in his tale of Erec and so eventually reached Chrétien. Carlisle, we have seen, becomes one of the favorite seats of King Arthur under its Anglo-Norman name of Cardoil, Kardoel, and so forth. One strong tradition places the mythical Castle of Maidens at Daneborc,[21] as the French called Edinburgh, while another, reflected in Wolfram von Eschenbach's *Parzival* and *La Queste del Saint Graal,* places it on the Severn.[22] Though in some instances, for example Glastonbury and Caruent, these localizations were probably invented by the Welsh, yet there can be little doubt that their introduction into French and Middle English literature was due to the Breton *conteurs* who traveled the length and breadth of Anglo-Norman Britain, eager to discover what local traditions existed about the glorious reign of Arthur, and ready to build up a romantic geography in which to place their tales of quest and adventure. This geography is the most clearly definable contribution of what we may call the Anglo-Norman stage in the evolution of the *Matière de Bretagne.*

For later generations these place names, especially as they became distorted in oral and scribal transmission, offered many fascinating puzzles and inspired many fantastic guesses. To the real place names were added others, such as Corbenic and Camaalot, originating in misreading and

18 E. K. Chambers, *Arthur of Britain,* p. 270. *Speculum,* IX (1934), 358.
19 *Fouke Fitz Warin,* ed. L. Brandin (Paris, 1930), p. 3. It must be admitted that on p. 7, l. 10, *Bretoun* means Welshman. Cf. *Zts. f. franz. Sprache u. Lit.,* XX (1898), 110.
20 *Miscellany of Studies in Honour of L. E. Kastner* (Cambridge, 1932), p. 350. The fitness of Chrétien's description to the approach to Dinas Bran which I there attributed to coincidence I would now attribute to transmission.
21 *Romania,* VIII (1879), 61.
22 Wolfram von Eschenbach, *Parzival u. Titurel,* ed. E. Martin (Halle, 1903), II, 429. M. F. Richey, *Story of Parzival and the Graal* (Oxford, 1935), p. 158. *Queste del S. Graal,* ed. A. Pauphilet, pp. 46 f. H. O. Sommer, ed., *The Vulgate Version of the Arthurian Romances* (Washington, 1908–13), VI, 34.

misinterpretation of written texts, with the result that the Arthurian geography of the Continental romancers became increasingly remote from reality, a land of dreams. But this confusion has not prevented innumerable attempts throughout the centuries to connect these tantalizing names with real places. Malory in the fifteenth century thought that Astolat was Guildford and that Joyous Garde was Bamborough or Alnwick; Leland in the next century found Camelot at Cadbury Camp in Somersetshire. Antiquaries of the eighteenth century and sentimental readers of Tennyson in the nineteenth added their conjectures. And it must be confessed that some of the learned speculations of modern scholars as to the sites of Sinadon, Camaalot, and the Green Chapel are as wide of the mark as any.

In my attempts to decipher the cryptic place names in Chrétien's four traditional poems I have profited by Zimmer's demonstration over fifty years ago, that the Bretons were the disseminators of Arthurian romance and that their insular geography, so far as it corresponds to reality, is that of Britain under the Norman domination, a Britain in which Bretons, as allies of the Normans and as kinsmen of the Welsh and Cornish, were free to travel from the Firth of Forth to Land's End. Thus, as I have already pointed out and as I hope to establish in detail, it is possible to explain not only certain of the forms assumed by the place names, but also the signs of local knowledge on the part of Chrétien which would be very hard to understand if he were drawing only on an insular tradition which reached Brittany as early as 1000 and had in the ensuing period been preserved in the memory of exclusively Continental story-tellers. Thus it becomes plausible that *Erec* should evince a hazy acquaintance with South Wales, as well as with a tradition localized at Edinburgh; that *Yvain* should preserve a legend about a fountain-fay of Lothian; that *Le Conte del Graal* in describing Perceval's approach to the Grail Castle should remind one of the approach to Dinas Bran along the valley of the Dee, and in naming the Castle of Ladies should leave a faint trace of its localization on the Severn.

3. *The Relation of Chrétien to* Geraint, Owain (The Countess of the Fountain), *and* Peredur.—For at least a hundred years it has been recognized that three of Chrétien's poems, *Erec, Yvain,* and *Le Conte del Graal,* display a marked similarity to the Welsh prose tales just mentioned. The correspondence between *Geraint* and *Erec* and between *Owain* and *Yvain* is not confined to the general outlines of the plot but extends in many instances to precise detail; *Peredur,* on the other hand, shows a much looser relationship to *Le Conte del Graal,* contains some matter similar to that in the continuations of that romance, and adds other stories unknown to the French poets. A heated controversy raged from 1889 to 1929 over

the relationship of the Welsh to the French texts,[23] and, so far as I am aware, no definitive treatment, satisfactory to all parties, has been published. Of the possible alternatives which is the correct one? Were the Welsh tales the source of Chrétien? Was Chrétien the sole source of the corresponding portions of the Welsh tales? Was Chrétien only one of the sources of the Welsh tales? Was there a common source for each of the three pairs of romances? These are the possible solutions for the famous, even the notorious, *Mabinogionfrage*—a somewhat inaccurate title, since the Welsh tales are not, strictly speaking, mabinogion.

Happily there is now agreement on certain points. Everyone recognizes that the Welsh tales are not, like *Kulhwch* and *The Dream of Rhonabwy,* of pure, or nearly pure, native inspiration, but are based in the main on French or Anglo-Norman originals. Everyone, I believe, agrees that the Welsh tales are somewhat later in date than Chrétien's poems, probably compositions of the thirteenth century.[24] There is no one now, therefore, to contend that they are the sources of Chrétien, and the first of the four alternatives is thus abandoned. But we are still left with the question whether Chrétien and the continuators of *Le Conte del Graal* were solely responsible for the similarities in the Welsh tales, whether there were other French or Anglo-Norman texts known to the Welsh authors which supplemented Chrétien and would account for the many and sometimes considerable divergences from his work, or whether Chrétien and the Welsh authors derived independently from three such lost French or Anglo-Norman texts.

There is, of course, one strong argument in favor of *Erec* and *Yvain* as the chief, if not the only, models for *Geraint* and *Owain,* and for *Le Conte del Graal* (with its continuations) as the main source of *Peredur.* A priori, the odds are against it that the Welsh redactors of French romances selected by mere chance three of the very same stories which Chrétien had used before them. The odds seem strongly in favor of the supposition that the choice was determined by the collocation of *Erec, Yvain,* and the *Graal* in some manuscript of Chrétien's works which had reached Wales and which had, perhaps through reading aloud, come to the ears of the Welsh authors.

However natural and logical this conclusion may be, it does not accord,

---

[23] In J. D. Bruce, *Evolution of Arthurian Romance* (Baltimore, Göttingen, 1923), II, 59–74, will be found a bibliography up to 1923 and a review of the controversy. To these should be added the article by Mühlhausen in *Zts. f. rom. Phil.,* XLIV (1924), 465–543, and the excellent articles by Zenker listed in J. J. Parry's *Bibliography of Critical Arthurian Literature for 1922–29* (New York, 1931), p. 53.
[24] J. Loth, *Mabinogion,* 2d ed., I, 19. "Dans ma première traduction j'avais conclu de certaines fautes du scribe du *Livre Rouge* [which contains the three Welsh romances] qu'il copiait un manuscrit plus ancien, vraisemblement de la fin du xiie ou du commencement du xiiie siècle."

in my opinion, with the detailed evidence which, as many scholars—
Edens, Zenker, Arthur Brown, and Professor Mary Williams among them
—have shown, points consistently toward the theory of a common source
as the explanation of the correspondences between the Welsh and French
romances. Furthermore, the similarity in the construction of *Erec* and
Yvain—sudden wooing and winning of a bride, marriage, estrangement,
forgiveness, and reconciliation—suggests that the sources of these poems
were the work of one man; and in that case they would naturally be bound
in one volume, and it would be no unlikely accident that manuscripts including both should have come to the attention and inspired the redactions of the French and Welsh authors. I shall not go into all the intricacies of the *Mabinogionfrage* but will present only what seem to me
the most cogent arguments.

1. Windisch made the impressive point that never does a Romance loan
word occur in the Welsh texts at the place in the narrative where Chrétien
has the same word.[25] He wrote that "die romanischen Lehnwörter der
cymrischen Erzählungen nicht aus Crestiens Dichtungen stammen. Denn
sie erscheinen nicht an denselben Stetten der Erzählung, und mehrere von
ihnen haben unverkennbar die anglonormannischen Formen." The fact
that such loan words assume Anglo-Norman forms is not very important,
since the Welsh would learn French from their neighbors and in translating from even a Continental text would tend to use Anglo-Norman loan
words. But surely the fact that such words are not found in the corresponding points in Chrétien's narratives does much to neutralize any a priori
argument in favor of Chrétien as the chief or only source of the Welsh
tales.[26]

2. The name Erec is not likely to have suggested to a Welsh redactor
the substitution of Geraint. It was probably the full form "Guerec" which
stood in the Welshman's source, not the modified form which Chrétien
used. If this probability be granted, Chrétien's poem was not the source
of *Geraint*.

3. The motivation of Erec's harsh behavior toward Enide is by no
means clear and consistent, and has provoked many and inconsistent efforts
to explain it; whereas in the Welsh tale the motive is not only explicitly
stated—suspicion of infidelity—but is also in harmony with what I hope
to show was antecedent Arthurian tradition. The inference again is that
Chrétien was not the source of *Geraint*.

4. Much the same may be said of another feature absent from *Erec*
but present in *Geraint,* namely, cutting off the stag's head and presenting

[25] E. Windisch, *Das keltische Brittannien bis zu Kaiser Arthur, Abhandlungen der philologisch-
historischen Klasse der Königl. Sächsischen Gesellschaft der Wissenschaften,* XXIX (1912),
No. VI, p. 240.
[26] Loth, *op. cit.,* I, 55 f., shows that the Welsh redactor was working from a written French
source.

it to Enid. This feature, too, seems to be in accord with what was an established formula of the *conteurs,* occurring in a Breton lai and five French romances, but it could not have been extracted from *Erec.*

5. The shabby dress which Geraint forced Enid to wear on their adventurous ride harmonizes better with his desire to humiliate and test her than does the handsome robe which Erec prescribed for Enide. Moreover, the shabby dress is paralleled in antecedent French tradition, as I hope to prove. For both reasons this feature must have been taken from some source other than Chrétien.

6. The name of Enide's father, as treated by the French and Welsh authors, is most revealing. It is introduced in the Welsh tale several times after Geraint has won the sparrow hawk, and takes the form of Nywl, Ynwl, or most frequently Ynywl.[27] Nowhere else in Welsh literature does this name occur except as that of Enid's father. Presumably, therefore, it is no genuine Cymric form but, like Gwiffret Petit and Limwris in the same mabinogi, it represents something in the French source. Two other facts are worth noting. The name Ynywl is frequently followed by the word *iarll,* meaning "count," and there is another character, Count Ynywl's nephew, who is consistently styled "y iarll ieuanc," that is, the young count.[28] We must infer that Enid's father was the old count, and his name Nywl or Ynywl, not being Welsh, was probably derived from some word or words in the French source. When we turn to *Erec,* we find nothing in the corresponding passages which could possibly have suggested Nywl or Ynywl. But at the end of the poem Chrétien does at last give his heroine's father a name, and though the manuscripts differ as to the form, one manuscript reads: "Lecon uials ot non ses pere." [29] Lecon uials can easily be analyzed as a corruption of three French words—the article *li,* the noun *cons,* the adjective *vials.* Enide's father, then, was called "the old count," exactly what we have been led to infer from the Welsh. We can now see what happened. The French source of *Erec* and *Geraint* contained a young count and an old count. The Welsh redactor correctly translated "li juenes cons" as "y iarll ieuanc." When he met the words "li uials cons," he recognized the article and the noun but failed to make out the adjective, read it as *niuls,* took it for a proper noun, cymricized it as *Nywl,* and produced "y nywl iarll." Chrétien, reading the same French tale, came across the same two personages, decided to call the younger simply "the count," and arbitrarily demoted the older to a mere vavasor. Somewhere, however, he must have read that Enide's father was called the old count, but the three words, "li cons uials," were written close together and by an odd misunderstanding he took them for a name and so wrote the

[27] J. Gwenogvryn Evans, *White Book Mabinogion* (Pwllheli, 1907), cols. 400 f.
[28] *Ibid.,* cols. 394 f., 399–401. Loth, *op. cit.,* II, 132, 136–38.
[29] *Erec,* ed. W. Foerster (Halle, 1890), vs. 6896.

line, "Et licon uials ot non ses pere." Here is definite proof that *Geraint* was not based on *Erec,* but followed, in some respects more faithfully, a common source. Once this is admitted, the argument from antecedent probability that the Welsh author or authors of *Geraint, Owain,* and *Peredur* were indebted to Chrétien for their inspiration falls to the ground. If one of the three tales is independent, the others may be.

When we examine *Yvain,* we find a similar situation. There are six signs of the independence of *Owain,* which I present here briefly, referring the reader for a fuller discussion to the section on *Yvain.*

7. The Welsh author refers repeatedly to the Hospitable Host who entertained Kynon and Owain as "the yellow man." It can be shown, I believe, that this figure goes back to the host who in *Bricriu's Feast* entertained the Ulster warriors and is there called Yellow son of White (Bude mac m-Bain) or simply Yellow (Bude). Since Chrétien does not mention this color, the author of *Owain* must have found it elsewhere.

8. As Arthur Brown made clear,[30] Chrétien's account of Yvain trapped between two portcullises in a richly painted hall, containing a bed, is absurd, for the entrances and exits of halls or bedchambers were not closed by portcullises. *Owain* lacks this absurdity, perhaps because the author was more realistic than Chrétien, but far more probably because his source was correct on this point, whereas Chrétien must have been working from a garbled version.

9. The Welsh author seems to know some things about the Lady of Noiroison which Chrétien does not mention: her walking beside a lake and her presenting Owain with the best steed in the world. It will be shown that these are traditional elements, and since they are not in *Yvain,* they presumably came from another source.

10. The title which Owain's wife bears, the Countess of the Fountain, does not occur in Chrétien's poem, yet it is almost certainly authentic. Another sign of the independence of *Owain.*

11. The Welshman, in telling of Owain's rescue of the lion, furnishes two details, not found in *Yvain,* but appearing in Neckam's version of the story. Since it is most unlikely that he turned to Neckam to supplement Chrétien, he must have used neither of these but a third source.

12. The incognito combat between Yvain and Gauvain is reserved for the end of the poem and provides an admirable climax to the hero's career, for it proves him a match for Gauvain, the paragon of knighthood, in prowess and courtesy. The corresponding battle between Owain and Gwalchmai, however, occurs shortly after Owain's marriage with the Countess of the Fountain. It is hard to see why the Welshman, if he were following Chrétien, should have transposed the scene; but it is easy to understand why Chrétien, if he were following something like the French

[30] *Romanic Review,* III (1912), 146–50.

original of *Owain,* should have made the shift for artistic purposes, and also added the preliminary story of the quarreling sisters to bring about the encounter of the two heroes.·

All this makes an impressive case for the independence of the French and the Welsh authors, their reliance on what was substantially a common original, written in the French language. Chrétien and the one or two Welsh authors treated the sources with considerable freedom as to details. Sometimes it is difficult to see any rational or artistic motive for their departures from their common original; in fact, the treatment of the "Joie de la Cort" episode in *Geraint* is so scanty that it seems based on a hazy memory rather than on direct access to the text. At other times, it is quite easy to perceive Chrétien's purposes and mannerisms in the alterations and additions. Comparison with the Welsh tales, when carried out with discrimination, can be of great value in estimating the degree of Chrétien's originality and detecting his methods of work. The common source of *Erec* and *Geraint* I shall refer to hereafter as X; the common source of *Yvain* and *Owain* (*The Countess of the Fountain*) as Y.

Peredur confronts us with a somewhat but not entirely different situation. There are whole sections which have no counterpart in *Le Conte del Graal;* the similarities are less close; there are astounding novelties, such as the presence of a bleeding head in the dish which corresponds to Chrétien's *graal.*[31] The evidence for dependence on Chrétien is much flimsier, and the evidence of a common origin for such similarities as exist in the floating traditions of Perceval and Gawain is much more obvious. For it has been pointed out by a succession of scholars that again and again *Peredur* agrees with Wolfram's *Parzival* or the Middle English *Sir Percyvelle* or the Italian *Carduino* against Chrétien.[32] No one would suspect the Welsh author of reading the German, English, or Italian poems, especially since the last two were composed a hundred years or so after his time, and it is inconceivable that the English and Continental authors could read Welsh. Only French sources, other than Chrétien, can explain the numerous agreements. Even Wolfram, who knew and used *Le Conte del Graal,* nevertheless repudiates Chrétien's authority and reveals a large debt to sources which, though sometimes close to Chrétien, must have been independent branches of the widespread tradition of Perceval and the Grail. In view of the fragility of the arguments favoring Chrétien as the fountainhead of this tradition, including *Peredur,* and in view of the massive evidence accumulated in favor of the opposed hypothesis (to which I hope to make some contributions later in this book), it seems unnecessary to discuss here the relationship of *Peredur* to *Le Conte del*

[31] *Revue celt.,* XLVII (1930), 39–62.
[32] Mary R. Williams, *Essai sur la composition du roman gallois de Peredur* (Paris, 1909), pp. 81–95. J. L. Weston, *Legend of Perceval* (London, 1906), I, 76–93. *Romanische Forschungen,* XL (1927), 251–329. C. Strucks, *Der junge Parzival* (Borna-Leipzig, 1910).

Graal. The number and the magnificent inconsistency of the extant romances of Perceval and the Grail prove that they had their origin, not in any one famous text, but in the scores of versions which the wandering *conteurs* developed about this mysterious but ever-fascinating theme. Only in the sense that both Chrétien and the author of *Peredur* drew on this reservoir of story and, for certain parts, on closely related streams of tradition, can one speak of a common source.

If this solution of the so-called *Mabinogionfrage* be correct—and I have no doubt that it is—then we are able to determine with considerable exactness the nature and content of Chrétien's immediate sources, particularly for *Erec* and *Yvain;* we are able to verify his own statements that he derived his *matière* from the *conteur* tradition and from a book; we can see that he displayed little originality (except in the *Charrette*) in the composition and shaping of his narratives, and that he deserves little blame for certain strange oversights and incoherences. If, furthermore, the answers offered above to the riddles presented by the Irish analogues and the Anglo-Norman geography are correct, then we have gone a long way toward the understanding of Chrétien's *matière.*

Chapter V

THE WAYS OF TRADITION AND METHODS OF INVESTIGATION

I F, IN THE LIGHT of the preceding chapters, it appears that the *Matière de Bretagne* is a cumulative creation, a traditional literature, what are those characteristics which one might expect to find in it? The typical phenómena of traditional development—its vagaries, its conventions, its extraordinary tenacity—have been recognized in other literatures; but some Arthurian scholars, such as Bruce and Foerster, have thought and written as if there were no such thing as Homeric and Biblical scholarship, and have tended to assume that if two texts resembled each other, it was merely necessary to establish the dates and then the earlier text must inevitably be accepted as the source of the later. Thus Chrétien was proved to be the father of all the romances of the Round Table! If eminent specialists are unaware of the attributes of a traditional literature, the average reader of Chrétien cannot be expected to be familiar with them. Indeed, some of the phenomena may well seem to him fantastic and incredible. It is necessary, therefore, to exercise the historic imagination, to ask oneself what would happen to stories, characters, and names transmitted, largely by word of mouth, for several centuries and from people to people, by a class of professional entertainers. It is necessary to realize what would be the confusions and complexities, the blunders and changes, the forgettings and suppressions, the patchings and stitchings which would eventually produce such an immense corpus of fiction as the medieval Arthurian romances.

I hoped to find somewhere an authoritative classification of these typical phenomena of a traditional literature, so that the reader would not have to rely on my word in these matters. I searched in vain,[1] and so must supply, as best I can, a list which is applicable to the Arthurian tradition. But the reader can be assured that these processes and their results are not the figments of my imagination, for most of them are the commonplaces of research in the development of the Homeric and Germanic legends. For similar conditions would, of course, produce similar results. The rhapsodes and their relation to "Homer," the scops and their relation to *Beowulf,* would offer close parallels to the Welsh *cyvarwyddon* and the Breton *conteurs* and their relation to the work of Chrétien. In all three cases the poet is the inheritor of an age-old body of stories, set in far-off times and places, preserved for generations by itinerant reciters. No wonder that the investigator in the Arthurian field discovers again and again that his problems and his solutions are much the same as those of his colleagues investigating the heroic literature of Greece and the Germanic world. I trust that the following classification may serve to introduce some clarity and order into the complex and unexpected phenomena to be dealt with in later chapters, and engender in the skeptical reader a sense that the phenomena are natural and not altogether unfamiliar.

1. *References to antecedent tradition, particularly oral.*—This is, of course, one of the most natural and obvious signs of the kind of development we have been obliged to assume for Arthurian romance. We have already examined the examples in Chrétien; Béroul rejects the version of a *conteor;* Thomas and Wauchier accept the authority of Breri-Bleheris; [2] and there are numerous other references of the same sort to previous oral and written versions. So the poet of *Beowulf* begins: "Lo! we have listened to many a lay of the Spear-Danes' fame, their splendor of old, their mighty princes, and martial deeds." The author of the *Nibelungenlied,* the traditional origin of which no one doubts, likewise begins: "Full many a wonder is told us in stories old, of heroes worthy of praise . . . now ye may hear wonders told." We cannot always take these references at their face value; Thomas's appeal to the authority of Breri may cover an original turn of his own.[3] But neither should we naively assume that, because

[1] The nearest approach to such a classification which I have been able to discover is Kaarle Krohn's *Die folkloristische Arbeitsmethode* (Oslo, Instituttet for Sammignende Kulturforkning, 1926).
[2] Béroul, *Tristran,* vss. 1265–68. Thomas, *Tristan,* ed. Bédier, II, 96. J. L. Weston, *Legend of Perceval,* I, 288.　　[3] G. Schoepperle, *Tristan and Isolt* (Frankfurt, London, 1913), I, 107 f.

Geoffrey of Monmouth could not have derived all the material of his *Historia* from his alleged source, the Breton manuscript, all citations of source in Arthurian romance are spurious.

2. *References to or summaries of incidents presumably known to the author but not related by him.*—Chrétien's references to Guigamor as the lover of Morgain la Fée and to the youthful companions of Ban de Gomeret can be filled out by consulting the lai of *Guingamor* and Wolfram von Eschenbach's account of the train of Gahmuret.[4] In the Vulgate cycle M. Lot has pointed out the numerous allusions to stories which neither the author himself nor anyone else ever tells.[5] "Le *Lancelot* fait souvent allusion à des aventures qu'il se garde de raconter, comme si le lecteur les possédait ou comme s'il avait toute facilité d'en prendre connaissance. . . . Banin doit à ses prouesses d'être admis au nombre des cent cinquante 'Chevaliers de l'Echaugette.' Qu'est-ce que cette compagnie? On ne le dit pas et même on se débarrasse de Banin en renvoyant les curieux au *Conte del commun*. L'aventure du 'Gué de la Reine' est 'la plus honorée qu'onques avenist au roi Artu.' Qu'il est donc regrettable que nous n'en sachions pas davantage!" Similarly Gilbert Murray declares that the fourth book of the *Odyssey* "consists of abridged and incomplete stories about the *Nostoi* or 'Homecomings' of Agamemnon, Aias the Less, and Menelaus. They seem to imply a reference to some fuller and more detailed original—in all probability to the series of lais called the *Nostoi* which formed one of the rejected epics." [6] The casual statement in *Beowulf*, "I have never heard tell of a worthier treasure . . . since Hama bore off to the shining city the Brosings' jewel" indicates, as Klaeber recognized,[7] the existence of a lost tale. Perhaps for the authors of the Vulgate cycle these tantalizing allusions were a deliberate deception, but for Chrétien they were not, since the stories referred to may usually be found elsewhere and in forms which preclude the notion that they are merely elaborations of the hints furnished by Chrétien.

3. *The existence of cognates.*—Practically all traditional literatures furnish variants of the same story independent of each other. The first chapter of Genesis gives one account of the creation of man and woman; the second contains another. Germanic and Anglo-Saxon epic abound in such pairs—*Waltharius* and *Waldere*, the *Völsungasaga* and the *Nibelungenlied*, the Finnsburg fragment and the Finnsburg episode. Besides these variant

[4] *Erec*, vss. 1954, 1975. *Studies and Notes in Philology and Literature*, V (1896), 221–43. *Romanic Review*, XXXVI (1945), 4–22.

[5] F. Lot, *Etude sur le Lancelot en prose* (Paris, 1918), pp. 258 f. It is possible that Lot is right in regarding these references as mere mystification, an artificial mannerism; but whence the mannerism? R. W. Chambers says in *Beowulf, an Introduction* (Cambridge, 1921), p. 299, n. 3: "There must be a background to allusions."

[6] G. Murray, *History of Ancient Greek Literature* (London, New York, 1912), pp. 37 f.

[7] *Beowulf*, ed. F. Klaeber, 3d ed. (Boston, 1936), p. 178.

narratives of a single event or series of events in which the same actors are involved, there are variant forms of the same story attached to different heroes or heroines. Beowulf's adventures with Grendel and his dam are paralleled by Grettir's struggles with the trolls. The ascent to the skies in a cage or car drawn by gryphons is ascribed to Alexander the Great, Nimrod, and the Persian king Kai Kaus.[8] Nothing is more characteristic of the Arthurian cycle than these variants of the same narrative design, derived not one from another but from some common source, near or remote. To list them would be an endless task. We have just seen that *Erec, Yvain,* and *Le Conte del Graal* are cognates on a considerable scale of the three Welsh tales. *Le Chevalier de la Charrette* is a much more remote cognate of Caradoc's account of the abduction of Guenievre. Chrétien himself tells two variant forms of the adventure of the Perilous Bed, the hero of one being Lancelot, of the other Gauvain. It seems unnecessary to illustrate further a phenomenon so obvious and so generally acknowledged. It is only necessary to emphasize the point, made over and over in our later discussion of motifs and incidents, that Chrétien did not invent them, and that one must carefully distinguish the variants which are due to borrowing from Chrétien and those which sprang from the same roots. Only the most casual of critics will assume that Chrétien is the source of all versions of the Sparrow-Hawk Contest or the visit to the Grail castle.

4. *Survival of a more archaic version in a later text.*—A moment's consideration of the ways in which traditional stories were continually changing and yet persisting in both oral and written form makes it clear that not infrequently a version which had departed far from its source happened to be written down earlier than a version more faithful to the original. Traditional literature, therefore, can furnish plentiful examples of this confused chronological relationship, the seemingly later story antedating the composition of the seemingly earlier story. Murray pointed out that the "rejected epics" of the Troy cycle were worked into final shape much later than our Homer, yet their matter is often very old and sometimes represents the sources of Homer.[9] The thirteenth-century *Grettissaga,* as Professor Lawrence has shown,[10] preserves the original form of the story of the fight with the trolls much better than the seventh- or eighth-century *Beowulf* so that it may even be used to explain obscure incidents and descriptions in the Anglo-Saxon. In Arthurian romance we have two excellent examples of this topsy-turvy sequence. The fourteenth-century *Gawain and the Green Knight* retains many more details of the ancient Irish motif of the Beheading Test from which it derives than does the version in *Le Livre de Caradoc,* which antedates the English

[8] *Burlington Magazine,* XXXII (1918), 136.　　　　[9] Murray, *op. cit.,* p. 47.
[10] W. W. Lawrence, *Beowulf and Epic Tradition* (Cambridge, Mass., 1928), pp. 178–87.

poem by at least a hundred and fifty years.[11] The development of the motif of the Perilous Bed follows an exactly inverse order from that of the texts in which it is preserved.[12] The fourteenth-century romance, *Artus de la Petite Bretagne,* is the latest of the texts but comes closest to the original Irish concept of a seat in a revolving fortress since it represents the enchanted castle as turning on an axis, carrying the bed with it. In Wolfram von Eschenbach's *Parzival* (*ca.* 1205) the castle has become stationary, but the bed rolls about on wheels; in Chrétien's *Conte del Graal* (*ca.* 1175) both castle and bed are stationary, but the bed is equipped with wheels; finally, in *Le Chevalier de la Charrette,* the earliest version of all, no trace is left of the original concept of a revolving fortress. Again and again we shall find in late romances, such as Malory's Book of Gareth, that original features of Celtic tradition, partially or wholly obliterated in Chrétien's narrative, have survived. Except in those cases where actual borrowing can be demonstrated, the chronological sequence of the texts tells nothing as to which text comes closest to the original form of the tradition.

5. *Conflation.*—When two or more variants of the same story or scene or motif were current, sooner or later they would tend to fuse, to combine in one version. This process, called conflation, is familiar to every student of myth, heroic legend, folktale, epic, and sacred scripture. Conflation on a large scale is represented by the Gospel of Matthew, which combines the Gospel of Mark with another source called Q. On a smaller scale the process is represented in the *Odyssey* by the slaying of the suitors. Gilbert Murray says: "In our present version Odysseus begins with the bow, uses up all his arrows, puts down the bow, arms himself with spear and shield and helmet, which Telemachus has meanwhile brought. What were those fifty desperate men with their swords doing while he was making the change? Nearly all critics see here a combination of an old Bow-fight with a later Spear-fight." [13] The *Matière de Bretagne* furnishes a neat illustration in *Gawain and the Green Knight,* to which both versions of the Beheading Test in *Bricriu's Feast* have contributed.[14] There is not, so far as I have been able to discover, any example as clear or as demonstrable in the four romances of Chrétien. One, perhaps, is that blend of the testing of the heroes of Ulster by Curoi as the storm-giant on the plain with the testing of the same heroes by Terror son of Great Fear which, as I shall attempt to show in due course,[15] is responsible for the adventures of Calogrenant and Yvain with the Hospitable Host and at the Storm-making Spring. The two Irish tales, though somewhat similar and though dealing

[11] G. L. Kittredge, *Study of Gawain and the Green Knight* (Cambridge, Mass., 1916), pp. 32–34.
[12] R. S. Loomis, *Celtic Myth and Arthurian Romance* (New York, 1927), pp. 165–75.
[13] Murray, *op. cit.,* p. 39.   [14] *PMLA,* XLVII (1932), 316 f., 324 f.
[15] *Infra,* pp. 278–80,

with the same personages, are not exactly variants of the same story and so do not provide in their blending a perfect instance of conflation. Better examples may be found in *Le Conte del Graal,* where the damsel bearing a *graal* and the damsel bearing a *tailleor* seem to be doublets, and where the Rich Fisher has been suspected of identity with his infirm father.[16] Since in most accounts of the visit to the Grail Castle we have but one maiden with a vessel and but one Maimed King, the doubling of these figures is best explained on the theory that two versions have been combined.

6. *Contamination.*—When two or more distinct stories are welded into one indissoluble unit, we have what is called contamination. This is, of course, one of the universal practices of the narrative artist, whether primitive savage or modern novelist, and it seems hardly necessary to give proof of its prevalence. A beautiful example from medieval literature is the lai *Sir Orfeo,* which blends the classical Orpheus myth with similar though wholly independent Celtic tales of the abduction and rescue of a queen. Chrétien is full of these contaminations. The *Charrette* combines versions of the abduction of a woman by force with versions of the winning of a woman from her husband by a ruse. The mysterious visit of Lancelot to the cemetery in the same romance owes its lack of sense to the inextricable entanglement of two wholly different stories. His strange adventure in the castle of the amorous hostess is apparently a blend of Pwyll's visit to Arawn's palace and Cuchulainn's visit to Curoi's fortress. In *Yvain* the adventures at the fountain are compounded from at least four different sources, and the helpful-lion episodes seem to blend a late development of the Androcles tradition with an Irish saga of a helpful dog-headed horse. Many incidents in which women are concerned betray signs of contamination by the tales which had grown up about Morgain la Fée. To continue the list would merely tire the reader's patience, and he will need all of it when he comes to the disentanglement of these complex stories and their even more complicated relationships. For it is this complexity which, together with the lacunae in our evidence, has baffled and to some extent completely thwarted the proper interpretation of Arthurian romance.

7. *Inconsistency.*—When either conflation or contamination takes place, some inconsistency or some improbability, tantamount to inconsistency, is likely to remain unless the combiner is unusually wary and skillful. Take, for example, the slaying of the suitors by Odysseus, already cited as an example of awkward conflation. Or take the wall about the Greek camp in the *Iliad;* it was built in the last year of the war or the first; it is there or not there. As Murray remarks, "It is pretty clear that there were two versions of the fighting extant, one in which the camp was unfortified, and one in which it was provided with a wall and moat. And brilliant

16 Cf. *infra,* pp. 389, 432 f.

episodes are borrowed from one or the other as the minstrels pleased." [17]
Beowulf states on one page that the Danes were heathen, and on the next
shows them listening to a scop chanting a poem on the Creation. In the
opening lines of the *Chanson de Roland* Marsile complains that he has
no army left him fit to give battle, but within a few days he has assembled
400,000 warriors! But strangely enough, among these thousands Blancan-
drin, who has played so notable a role in the earlier *laisses,* is never mentioned.[18] Such flaws and lapses are, of course, characteristic of Arthurian
romance. M. Lot has drawn attention to a great number in the Vulgate
cycle; [19] they stare at one from many pages of Malory's *Morte d'Arthur,*
and no one can doubt that in this instance they are attributable to the
variety of his sources. Critics of all schools have recognized them in the
work of Chrétien. Gaston Paris called attention to the inconsistency of
the *Charrette* as to the frontiers of the realm of Goirre; [20] Lancelot seems
to be within Baudemaguz' kingdom before he has crossed the sword
bridge which he must traverse in order to enter it. Foerster also admitted
"die grosse Menge von Lücken, dunkeln Rätseln, Geheimniskrämereien
und geradezu von Ungereimtheiten und selbst Verkehrtheiten" in the
same romance.[21] Some of these discrepancies must be due to the conjunction of irreconcilable variants. In *Yvain* we discover the hero making
his way from Carduel (Carlisle) to the Forest of Broceliande without
crossing the Channel—a blunder due, as we shall see later, to the combination of a tale localized in Lothian with the famous legend of the
Breton spring of Berenton. There can be little doubt that failure to reconcile conflicting stories is one of the chief causes for the inconsistencies
which characterize the *Matière de Bretagne.*

8. *Harmonizing the conflicts of tradition.*—Story-tellers could not escape noticing the disharmonies in the *données* with which they worked,
and the more intelligent and conscientious could not but try to remove
them in their retellings. We read in the Book of Leinster (*ca.* 1150): "He
is no *fili* who does not synchronize and harmonize all the stories." [22] The

---

[17] Murray, *Rise of the Greek Epic,* 3d ed. (Oxford, 1924), p. 243.
[18] R. Fawtier, *La Chanson de Roland* (Paris, 1933), pp. 51–53. Prof. Raymond Weeks has
shown that the inconsistencies in the *Chanson d'Aliscans* were due to conflation. *Studies and
Notes in Philology and Literature,* V, 127–50.
[19] F. Lot, *Etude sur le Lancelot,* pp. 215–57. Cf. p. 257, n. 3: "Des négligences du même
ordre se rencontrent naturellement chez les prédécesseurs et les successeurs du *Lancelot* en
prose. Les 'manifold discrepancies' de Chrétien de Troyes ont été signalés à plus d'une reprise
(voy. J. L. Weston, *Lancelot,* p. 44, note 1). Robert de Boron dans l'épisode de l'amour
d'Hélène, sœur de Gauvain, pour Lancelot [*read* Perceval] amorce une aventure qui avorte
complètement (*Perceval* dans Weston, II, 18; Hucher, I, 424). Wauchier et Pseudo-Wauchier
sont remplis d'obscurités et de contradictions (voy. Heinzel, *loc. cit.,* p. 32–35)."
[20] *Romania,* XII (1883), 483.
[21] Chrétien de Troyes, *Karrenritter,* ed. W. Foerster (Halle, 1899), p. lxxxiii.
[22] E. O'Curry, *Lectures on the Manuscript Materials of Ancient Irish History* (Dublin, 1861),
p. 583. H. M. and N. K. Chadwick, *Growth of Literature,* I, 169.

Anglo-Norman poet Thomas states that he knows many versions of the legend of Tristan, and that it has been his effort to harmonize them.[23] He uses an expression "en uni dire," which Bédier translates "donner au milieu de variantes contradictoires de la légende un récit logique et cohérent." [24] We find an explicit avowal of this procedure in the Dutch romance of *Morien*: "Herein doth the adventure tell of a knight who was named Morien. Some of the books give us to wit that he was Perceval's son, and some that he was son to Agloval, who was Perceval's brother. . . . Now we find it written for a truth that Perceval and Galahad alike died virgin knights in the Quest of the Holy Grail; and for that cause I say of Perceval that in sooth he was not Morien's father, but rather was Morien his brother's son." [25] The author of the *Huth Merlin* knew of Morgain la Fée both as a hideous and as a ravishingly beautiful woman, and reconciled the two traditions ingeniously and amusingly by asserting that her beauty lasted until she took up enchantment, and then the Devil entered into her and she became loathsome except to those bespelled by her.[26] In the *Charrette* the abduction of Guenievre by ruse and the abduction by force have been somewhat clumsily combined by distributing the roles: Keu tricks Arthur into permitting him to ride away with the Queen, and Meleagant then forcibly abducts her from Keu.[27] We have seen how "Homer" harmonized the Bow-Fight and the Spear-Fight versions of the slaying of the suitors by the unrealistic device of letting one follow the other.

9. *Mythological elements.*—In the literature of any pagan people and even in the literature of peoples who have emerged from paganism one is almost certain to encounter evidences of that poetic science which we call myth—attempts to account for the mysteries of Nature, the passions of man, and the usages and achievements of society by means of stories. After a while the personages of myth became so real that tales were woven about them, not to explain anything but merely to entertain. So widespread and so well known is this phenomenon that no illustrations seem necessary except from the field of our immediate inquiry. We saw in the last chapter that a number of the Irish sagas center about or introduce the Tuatha De Danann—Lug, Manannan, Mider, the Dagda, the Morrigan, and so forth. Cuchulainn, the chief hero of the Ulster cycle, may not have been a deity, but he was a rebirth of the sun-god Lug and acquired solar traits.[28] Many stories tell of human beings who visit the Other World, which may be conceived as an isle of beautiful women, or a revolving fortress, or a splendid palace abounding in every luxury and supplied with inexhaustible meat and ale. The oldest Welsh prose tales, *The Four Branches,* have

[23] Thomas, *Tristan,* ed. Bédier, I, vss. 2107–56.   [24] *Ibid.,* II, 451.
[25] *Morien,* trans. J. L. Weston (London, 1901), p. 18.
[26] *Huth Merlin,* ed. G. Paris, J. Ulrich (Paris, 1886), I, 166.
[27] Cross and Nitze, *op. cit.,* pp. 49 f.   [28] R. S. Loomis, *Celtic Myth,* pp. 47 f.

not only absorbed a number of Irish myths [29] but have also blended them with stories in which figures of the old British pantheon appear—Bran and Manawydan, sons of Llyr; Arawn, leader of the Wild Hunt; his enemy Havgan, the embodiment of summer, as his name meaning "Summer-white" indicates. In *Kulhwch* and the Arthurian poem in the Black Book of Carmarthen there is mention of Mabon and his mother Modron, whose names scholars agree in deriving from the Apollo Maponos and the Matrona of Gallo-Roman inscriptions. It is highly significant that both the tale and the poem assign Mabon and the old sea-god Manawydan to a place among Arthur's warriors or comrades in adventure. Naturally, Celtic mythology finds its way into Arthurian romance. I shall endeavor to show that Lug and the Morrigan have their descendants, and it has long been noted that Cuchulainn has bequeathed several of his roles to Gauvain. Gauvain possesses the solar trait of waxing and waning in strength with the rising and the setting of the sun. Many stories, like the Irish, relate visits to Otherworld abodes, turning castles, castles of maidens, castles where every desire for food and drink is satisfied. The wounded sea-god Bran of the mabinogi appears as the languishing Fisher King, Bron. The hospitable leader of the Wild Hunt, Arawn, appears as the Green Knight, the huntsman who entertained Gawain.[30] Arawn's enemy, "Summer-white," who fought an annual battle by night at a ford, turns up as Gasozein, clad in white, fighting successive combats with Arthur and others by night at a ford. The enchanters Mabon and Mabuz doubtless go back to Mabon, while Mabuz' mother, queen of an isle of women, where no one grew old, must have inherited much from Modron. As for Chrétien, the abduction and deliverance of Guenievre has long been recognized as a myth; the enchanted garden of Mabonagrain is obviously a supernatural domain, and Mabonagrain himself a counterpart of Mabon; the complex of events concerned with the Grail is charged with mythological meanings. As Ker perspicaciously put it:

"Whether in the Teutonic countries, which in one of their corners preserved a record of old mythology, or in the Celtic, which allowed mythology, though never forgotten, to fall into a kind of neglect and to lose its original meaning, the value of mythology is equally recognizable, and it is equally clear that mythology is nothing more than Romance. Everything in the poets that is most enthralling through the mere charm of wonder, from the land of the Golden Fleece to that of the Holy Grail, is more or less nearly related to mythology." [31]

10. *Fading.*—Stories which have been transmitted by word of mouth for generations or centuries tend to lose sharpness of outline; the colors fade; the specific becomes generalized; certain features are forgotten alto-

[29] C. O'Rahilly, *Ireland and Wales*, pp. 103–11. W. J. Gruffydd, *Math Vab Mathonwy.*
[30] *Journ. of Eng. and Germ. Phil.*, XLII (1943), 170–76.
[31] W. P. Ker, *Dark Ages* (New York, 1904), p. 47.

gether. So obvious and inevitable is this development that the wonder is that many stories, on the contrary, have retained their pristine form with extraordinary fidelity through many centuries. It seems unnecessary, therefore, to prove that traditional narratives do sometimes fade and lose their distinctive details with the result that the latest versions are scarcely recognizable with any certainty, unless proper names or the survival of intermediate forms establishes a connection. I will restrict myself to pointing out two examples of fading in the *Matière de Bretagne*. A few pages back I pointed out that Chrétien's description of Lancelot's nocturnal adventure in the castle of the Perilous Bed really represents the last development of a theme traceable back to Cuchulainn's nocturnal adventure in Curoi's fortress, and I shall deal with the evidence more fully when I come to discuss the incident in the chapters on *Le Chevalier de la Charrette*. By comparing Chrétien's version in this poem with his own fuller version in *Le Conte del Graal* and the far fuller version in *Artus de la Petite Bretagne* we can perceive how many of the distinctive details have been lost, and the loss seems to be due not so much to any deliberate omission, but to failures of memory or indifference on the part of the *conteurs* through whose hands the story passed. Another example of fading is Chrétien's rather commonplace account of Erec's encounter with five knights near a ford. In my discussion of this episode I hope to show that here, too, an elaborate story pattern found in *Le Lai de l'Espine* has undergone a gradual loss of distinctive details, a process traceable through an intermediate stage in Malory's Book of Gareth. Again no rational motive seems to be responsible for the successive omissions (though possibly some may be ascribed to a realistic tendency), but the fading of the original pattern into mere commonplace seems due rather to the faulty memory of the transmitters.

11. *Rationalization.*—Though the supernatural elements in a given tradition may simply fade out through lapses of memory or neglect, they may also be deliberately suppressed or be given a rational turn by incredulous or realistic redactors. A few examples from Celtic and Arthurian story may suffice. The old Irish concept of a revolving fortress, which I take to have its origin in the revolving dome of heaven, occurs without excuse or explanation in *Bricriu's Feast,* but in Keating's *History of Ireland* it has become a magic wheel in motion at the door of the fortress.[32] The same rationalizing process is carried even further in Wirnt von Gravenberg's *Wigalois,* where the revolving wheel at the entrance to an enchanter's castle is driven by water power.[33] A frank expression of this rationalistic tendency is found in a manuscript of the *Vulgate Lancelot;*[34] it is explained that many fools called Arthur's sister "Morgain la déesse," but

[32] G. Keating, *History of Ireland*, ed. P. S. Dinneen, II (Dublin, 1905), 223.
[33] P. Piper, *Höfische Epik* (Stuttgart, 1892–95,), II, 229.   [34] *Speculum*, XX (1945), 200.

that was only because she, though a mere woman, knew much of sorcery and haunted the deep forests and springs by day and night. M. Lot comments at length on this tendency of the author of the Vulgate cycle: [35] "L'auteur a une tournure d'esprit tout à fait euhémeriste. Il ne croit pas, ou ne veut pas qu'on croie, à la réalité du lac enchanté où la fée a transporté Lancelot: ce lac n'est qu'une apparence, un mirage." Chrétien does not indulge in these excursuses justifying the marvelous to the reason of his readers. He either leaves the supernatural without explanation or defense, or he eliminates it; or rather, it had already been eliminated by his predecessors. Gauvain's experience in attempting to cross the Water Bridge, as Professor Hibbard detected,[36] is simply a burlesque rationalization of the descent to the subaqueous palace of a god. Mabonagrain, the wondrously tall knight in vermeil arms, puts up a fierce fight against Erec until the hour of *none* is past, and then his strength and breath fail him. This is surely a euhemeristic development of that supernatural trait, the increase of strength till midday or *none,* which is ascribed to three other formidable knights in red arms—Escanor, Graysteel, and the Red Knight of the Red Laundes. These are but two instances of the suppression of the marvelous in Chrétien's work, and we must be prepared to find many more. Indeed, the detailed study of the poems will reveal that rationalization was one of the most potent influences exerted upon them by Chrétien's predecessors.

12. *Modernization.*—The reduction, elimination, or rationalization of the supernatural was not the only method by which the Breton *conteurs* and the French romancers adapted the fantastic tales of the Arthurian cycle to the tastes of their auditors and readers. Like the narrative artists of every age, they felt bound to bring their stories up to date by introducing contemporary customs, manners, ethical standards, costumes, and architectural settings. In the Bible we see the anthropomorphic tribal god of the Hebrews, who walks in the garden of Eden and wrestles with Jacob and inspires deceit and vengeance, gradually being replaced by a lofty spiritual conception of deity. In the Homeric poems we see the partial supplanting of older methods of fighting, older styles of armor, older household arrangements by later. Murray points out examples of moral refinement.[37] "In the *Great Eoiai* the married pair Alkinous and Arete are undisguisedly brother and sister: our *Odyssey* explains elaborately that they were really only first cousins. . . . A version of the slaying of Hector followed by Sophocles in his *Niptra* made Achilles drag his enemy alive at his chariot wheels. That is the cruder, crueler version. Our poems cannot suppress the savage insult, but they have got rid of the torture." Simi-

[35] F. Lot, *op. cit.,* p. 272.   [36] *Romanic Review,* IV (1913), 167, n. 2.
[37] Murray, *History of Ancient Greek Literature,* pp. 40 f.

larly in *Beowulf* scholars have recognized a partial adaptation of old heathen beliefs and practices to the new Christian faith. Pagan cremation coexists with Christian burial; Almighty God is supreme over the blind Wyrd; the concluding lines celebrate the hero as "to men the mildest and of men the kindest, to his folk the gentlest." So the wild fables of Celtic heathendom have been brought into some conformity with the ways and ideals of twelfth-century romance. Chrétien clothes his knights and ladies in the latest fashion; they dwell in castles equipped with drawbridges and portcullises; they frequent tournaments. Gauvain is a paragon of chivalry, magnanimity, and courtesy; Lancelot and Guenievre obey the rules of *amour courtois;* Perceval, unlike his ultimate prototypes Cuchulainn and Finn, is instructed by his mother in the rudiments of the Christian faith. Though here and there a trace of the more barbarous world from which the romances emerged remains, such as the heads on stakes in Mabonagrain's garden and the custom mentioned in the *Charrette* (vss. 1323-28) that permitted a knight to do what he would with a damsel won by force of arms, yet, on the whole, Chrétien's world is that of twelfth-century France.

13. *Misinterpretation.*—When a tradition has been handed down from one generation to another and from one race to another, misunderstandings are inevitable and sometimes these misunderstandings can have momentous consequences. A notorious example is furnished by the horns which spring from Moses' forehead in medieval and Renaissance art owing to the ambiguity of the Hebrew verb which could mean either to sprout horns or to shed rays. A similar blunder is probably responsible for Nennius' statement that at the battle of Castellum Guinnion Arthur bore the image of the Virgin Mary "super humeros suos"—a strange encumbrance; the explanation seems to be that in Old Welsh the word for shoulder was *iscuid* and the word for shield was *iscuit*.[38] A thirteenth-century interpolation in Nennius asserts that fragments of this very image were still preserved at Wedale, that is Vallis Doloris, six miles from Melrose;[39] and modern writers have identified this place with Stow in the valley of Gala Water, where the church and a spring near by are dedicated to St. Mary.[40] This is but one of many proofs that Lothian was busy in forming local associations with Arthur in the twelfth and thirteenth centuries. Bruce cites another tradition based on misunderstanding.[41] There was a

[38] T. Malory, *Morte d'Arthur*, Everyman ed., I, xii f.
[39] F. Lot, *Nennius et l'Historia Brittonum*, I, 195, n. 8.
[40] *Merlin*, ed. H. B. Wheatley, Part III, lxxvi f. F. J. Snell, *King Arthur's Country*, p. 213. On identification of Mons Dolorosus with Melrose cf. Chap. XV.
[41] J. D. Bruce, *Evolution of Arthurian Romance*, I, 90 f. The name of Arthur's father, Uther, Gertrude Schoepperle Loomis showed to be due to a misunderstanding of the gloss "mab uter." *Vassar Mediaeval Studies*, ed. C. F. Fiske (New Haven, 1923), pp. 4 f.

Welsh hero Caradawc who was distinguished by the epithet Breichbras, "Arm-strong." Breichbras was mistaken for the French words *Brief-bras,* and a very romantic story was concocted to explain how Caradoc acquired a short arm. There can be little doubt that the tragic loves of Tristan and Iseut were profoundly influenced by the supposition, entirely mistaken, that the hero's name had something to do with French *triste*. Actually it was derived from Pictish Drustan through Welsh Drystan, Trystan.[42] The most curious and momentous of all the misinterpretations in the Arthurian cycle was due to the total unfamiliarity of the French with a sacred drinking horn. There was such a horn in Welsh tradition, the horn of Bran, the euhemerized sea-god, which provided instantly whatever food or drink one desired. The French words for "the horn" in the nominative case were *li cors*. Since *c* and *t* were almost or quite indistinguishable in many manuscripts and since the French were familiar with bovine images as objects of pagan worship, two romances, *Perlesvaus* and *Fouke Fitz Warin,* describe castles whose pagan inhabitants worshiped a *tor* (bull) of metal which provided them with great abundance of riches or of whatsoever they desired.[43] On the other hand, *li cors* could mean "the body" and its miraculous provision of meats and drinks could be interpreted as the wonder-working power of a saint's body. To pious souls the words would almost inevitably suggest "Corpus Domini," the Eucharist, for many legends were current concerning its marvelous power to feed and sustain life. This natural misconception, as Professor Newstead and I have shown, was fraught with far-reaching consequences.[44] It has long been recognized that Bran himself became the Bron or the Maimed King of the Grail romances. His horn was responsible for the constant association of both the King and the Grail with the Eucharist. It explains many of the mysteries of that most mysterious legend. It may well be questioned whether any other blunder in literary history has had so stupendous and fructifying an influence on the imaginations of men.

14. *Fusion of characters.*—The blending of two or more characters into one is a phenomenon which every student of myth and legend is bound to meet sooner or later. This fusion may occur because of identity or similarity of names. Thus about 1200 we find a Latin text, *Vitae Duorum Offarum,* in which an exploit of Offa, king of the Continental Angles in the fourth century, is attributed to Offa of Mercia in the eighth.[45] Most scholars believe that the legend of St. Brigit combined some historical facts with pagan traditions of a Brigit who was daughter of the god

[42] Bruce, *op. cit.,* I, 178 f.

[43] *Miscellany of Studies in Romance Languages and Literatures in Honour of L. E. Kastner,* pp. 342–50. H. Newstead, *Bran the Blessed in Arthurian Romance* (New York, 1939), pp. 86–106.   [44] Newstead, *op. cit.,* pp. 86, 92–95. *Speculum,* VIII (1933), 430 f.

[45] L. A. Hibbard, *Mediaeval Romance in England* (New York, 1924), p. 30. A legend of Rogier was attached to Ogier. Cf. *Romanic Review,* I (1910), 3–8.

Dagda and was worshiped by the *filid*.[46] It is probable, as I shall point out in my discussion of Perceval, that his story represents a blend of the legend of a mythical Pryderi with that of a historical Peredur—a blend due to the similarity of names. Far more common is the fusion of characters because of a resemblance, close or remote, in nature or function. Mythologies are full of these syncretic personalities. Zeus, Aphrodite, Hermes, and the rest of the Greek pantheon are composite figures, each embodying a score of divine prototypes of the Hellenic world and attracting their various legends. We have the testimony of such authorities as Windisch and Professor Robinson that in Gaul the mother-goddesses, the Matres or Matronae, were combined with other female deities,[47] such as the Parcae, the Nymphae, and the Lamiae. Matrona's Brythonic descendant, Modron, seems to have blended her personality and her story with those of the Irish lamia, the Morrigan,[48] and thus eventually gave rise to the multiple personality, Morgain la Fée. Morgain in turn seems to have attracted to herself every type of tale current among the Breton *conteurs* which had to do with a fay, with the result that her saga became a mass of inconsistencies. Miss Paton puts it mildly when she remarks that "we find her manifesting her power in a wide range of capacities."[49] Mark Twain's Connecticut Yankee, who had made Morgain's personal acquaintance, put the matter more forcefully: " 'I have seen a good many kinds of women in my time, but she laid over them all for variety.' " In the later pages of this book I hope to produce cogent evidence for the multiple origin of this Queen of Faerye and her pervasive influence on the *Matière de Bretagne*. Sometimes the fusion of two characters is indicated by the telescoping or the coalescence of two names. Chrétien's Guingambresil, as I shall show in my discussion of the figure, has inherited the names of Guingamor and Bercilak and the role of the latter as the challenger of Gawain at Arthur's court. Coalescence of characters is one of the complicating and baffling factors in the formation of Arthurian story, but, once understood and accepted, it elucidates many mysteries.

15. *Fission of characters.*—Quite as common a development in the *Matière de Bretagne* is the splitting of one original character into two or more; it explains in large measure the proliferation of personages who fill the pages of the Vulgate cycle. So far as I am aware, no other tradition exemplifies the process on so grandiose a scale. However, in certain mythologies something of the sort has been observed. Bréal may be quoted:

[46] J. F. Kenney, *Sources for the Early History of Ireland*, I (New York, 1929), pp. 357 f. For similar phenomena cf. P. Saintyves, *Saints Successeurs des dieux* (Paris, 1907), 303–12.
[47] E. Windisch, *Das keltische Brittannien bis zu Kaiser Arthur*, p. 103. Hastings, *Encyclopaedia of Religion and Ethics*, IV, 409. A. Maury, *Croyances et légendes du moyen age* (Paris, 1896), p. 10.
[48] *Revue celt.*, XII, 128. *PMLA*, LVI (1941), 6.
[49] L. A. Paton, *Fairy Mythology of Arthurian Romance* (Boston, 1903), p. 7.

"Le soleil, par exemple, est nommé dans les védas de plus de vingt façons différentes. . . . Il est tour à tour le Brillant (*Surya*), l'Ami (*Mitra*), le Généreux (*Aryaman*), le Bienfaisant (*Bhaga*), Celui qui nourrit (*Pushan*), le Créateur (*Tvashtar*), le Maître du Ciel (*Divaspati*), et ainsi de suite. . . . Mais, une fois que le premier âge de l'humanité fu passé, l'époque suivante, étonnée, chercha à mettre de l'ordre dans ce chaos. Elle supposa que tant d'appellations ne pouvaient appartenir à un seul objet, et elle commença à distinguer *Mitra* de *Surya, Bhaga* de *Tvashtar, Divaspati* d'*Aryaman*." [50]

Professor Macurdy notes the same development in Hellenic mythology.

"Like many of the Sun and Moon epithets, this one [Hyperion] becomes a relative of the divinity in question, in this case the father of the Sun. . . . Again Titan, at Titane, is called brother of the Sun. . . . Perhaps the most famous son of the Sun who was developed from an epithet is Phaethon, whose story all the world knows. The epithet appears once in the *Iliad* and once in the *Odyssey* to mark the sun in his brightness, and in the twenty-third book of the *Odyssey* it has become a name for a steed of Dawn. . . . The subject is inexhaustible." [51]

Various causes operated to produce fission in the legends of the Celts. John MacNeill writes: "It is surely most probable that every Nuadu to whom the *filidh* assign a remote prehistoric place in the pedigrees . . . is but a reappearance of Nuadu Silverhand." [52] Again he says:

"I take it, that no matter how often each name occurs, it is the name of the same mythological ancestor, e.g., that Eochu Cenn Mairc (the horse-headed), Eochu Cenn Reithi (the ram-headed), Eochu Mumo (of Munster), etc. are all one and the same Eochu of Irish mythology. . . . The supposition that many names occurring in a pedigree are synonyms of a single personage of mythology calls up a difficulty. How does it come about that this person is represented as his own son, grandson, or remoter descendant? Before attempting an answer let me say that this phenomenon undoubtedly takes place. In one pedigree Lugh, son of Ethniu, is both an ancestor and a descendant of Fergus, not only his own name but his mother's occurring twice in the line of descent." [53]

Phillimore pointed out that in a Welsh genealogy Amalech son of Aballac is simply a doublet of his father, due to scribal corruption.[54] The list of Arthur's warriors in *Kulhwch* contains two Gweirs, sons of Llwch,[55] and since brothers do not ordinarily bear the same name, the Gweirs were probably one and the same. Llwch's epithet, Llawwynnyawc, seems to have split off and become a separate character in the altered form Llenlleawc.[56] When these and other Welsh names passed on to the Bretons and from

---

50 M. Bréal, *Mélanges de mythologie et de linguistique* (Paris, 1877), pp. 12 f.
51 R. S. Loomis, *Celtic Myth*, p. 96.
52 J. MacNeill, *Celtic Ireland* (Dublin, London, 1921), p. 55.
53 *Ibid.*, pp. 61 f. Similar phenomena have been noted by W. Perrett, *Story of King Lear*, *Palaestra*, XXXV (Berlin, 1904), p. 5, and M. Ashdown, *Mod. Lang. Rev.*, XVII (1922), 123.
54 *Cymmrodor*, IX (1888), 170, n. 5.   55 J. Loth, *Mabinogion*, 2d ed., I, 276.
56 *PMLA*, LVI (1941), 914-16.

them to the French, the possibilities of multiplication were enormously
increased since they underwent, first, the hazards of pronunciation by
foreign tongues and assimilation to foreign names, and secondly, the
even worse peril of mangling by bewildered scribes. Bruce understated
the case when he remarked: "New characters occasionally come into existence through the failure of subsequent writers to recognize that the new
names are merely manuscript corruptions of old ones." [57] Thus we find
Percevaus and Pellesvaus listed as separate knights in *Escanor;* Gareth and
Gaherys are brothers in Malory's seventh book. Professor Newstead has
pointed out many figures whose names and histories are derived from
the Welsh Bran the Blessed—Bron, Braus or Ban de Gomeret, Gahmuret,
the Fisher King, and so forth. [58] The Welsh Mabon reappears in the romances as Mabon, Mabuz, and Mabonagrain. One could go on indefinitely.
Another cause for the multiplication of characters was the difficulty of
reconciling the stories told about a given personage. Professor Malone has
demonstrated that from a very early period Hrethric, son of the Danish
king Hrothgar, was presented from two very different angles. [59] "The
logical Icelanders therefore made two persons of him." It is generally
thought that Giraldus Cambrensis distinguished two Merlins, Merlinus
Ambrosius and Merlinus Silvester, because of the differences between
Geoffrey of Monmouth's account of the prophet in the *Historia Regum
Britanniae* and that in the *Vita Merlini*. [60] No personage in the Arthurian
cycle was the subject of such multifarious traditions as Morgain la Fée, and
none developed into such a variety of characters. Arthur's sister was evidently reputed to be the wife of Loth, Urien, and Neutres. [61] Since the
same woman could not have three husbands at once, the author of the
Huth Merlin gives Arthur three sisters, leaving the first nameless, assigning to the second the name Morgue (a back formation from Morgain),
and to the third the name Morgans. [62] The first sister, the wife of Loth,
is in other romances called Morcades or Morgause. [63] It seems fairly obvious that Morgans, Morgue, and Morgause are but three forms of the
same name and that they served conveniently as an escape from the
dilemma created by the variety of Morgain's marital relations. The same
expedients were forced on other authors by the gross inconsistency between the legends which painted the fay as a lustful, treacherous woman
and those which portrayed her as charming and faithful. Legends of the
first sort must have made her name so notorious that story-tellers were
reluctant to apply it to the heroine of legends of the second sort; conse-

---

[57] *Mod. Phil.,* XVI, 347. [58] Newstead, *op. cit.*

[59] *PMLA,* XLII (1927), 285 f.

[60] *Speculum,* XVIII (1943), 271–74. *Annales de Bretagne,* XV (1899–1900), 333–35.

[61] Paton, *op. cit.,* p. 143. In *PMLA,* XLV (1930), 441 f., I pointed out that Neutres or
Nentres represented a corruption of "Urien reis."

[62] *Huth Merlin,* I, 120. [63] Paton, *op. cit.,* pp. 138, 141.

quently, they frequently left her anonymous. If it were not for a reference in Chrétien's *Erec* to Morgain as the *amie* of Guigamor, we should not realize that the anonymous fountain-fay of *Guingamor* was a form of the enchantress. Close study reveals that many another lovely but nameless lady inherited her role from Morgain, as I shall endeavor in later pages to prove. Sometimes the lady's title will afford a clue to her original identity. She may be the Countess of the Fountain or Dame Lyones, titles which Morgain seems to have acquired as a water-nymph or as the wife of King Loth of Lothian. Sometimes an entirely new name, such as Galiene in *Fergus* or Tryamour in *Sir Launfal,* has been arbitrarily applied to the heroine, but still a study of the narrative pattern reveals that it is a reflection of some of the more attractive traditions concerning the many-sided fay. Though we shall see that other ladies prominent in Celtic story —Blathnat, the Sovranty of Erin, Liban, Fand, Riannon, Gwenhwyvar— have their descendants in Arthurian romance, most of the heroines of that cycle have inherited something from the great syncretic tradition about Morgain la Fée. That tradition is not only the most notable example of the fusion of many supernatural personalities into one, but also the most amazing instance of the fission of one personality into many.

16. *The transformation of proper nouns.*—We have just observed that the corruption of names accounts in part for the multiplication of characters. And anyone who has examined the variant readings of a single name in the manuscripts of Chrétien is forced to realize that the possibilities of scribal corruption are almost infinite and are subject to no fixed laws. Neither is the development of names transmitted from one people and language to another a matter of phonological certainties. Professor Tatlock speaks of the "infinite transformations, accidental and deliberate, of proper names in early literature and popular tradition." [64] R. W. Chambers remarked:

"It is true that in dealing with the native words of a language, the presumption is that such words will only change in accordance with phonetic law. But this does not apply to legendary and foreign geographical names which as they pass from mouth to mouth undergo transformations which are the result, not of phonetic law but of mere error. Are we to account phonetically for every letter in such a change as Stafford for Oxford through an intermediate Asquesufforch, in Berners' Froissart?" [65]

Miss Paton also bears testimony on this point:

"We may as well acknowledge the fact that no fay nor mortal was ever more elusive or erratic in career than is a proper name in mediaeval literature, and that with the multitudinous opportunities for a misunderstanding in an oral

[64] J. S. P. Tatlock, *Scene of the Franklin's Tale Visited* (London, Chaucer Society, 1914), p. 68.
[65] R. W. Chambers, *Widsith* (Cambridge, 1912), p. 160.

or a misspelling in a written source, theories as to its domestication on foreign soil according to strict phonological conventions 'gang aft agley.' " [66]

To be sure, some of the commonest names, such as Artus, Gauvain, Lancelot, Perceval, Keu, Guenievre, were standardized early, and can usually be recognized at once, but even these are found in strange forms. And the less familiar names underwent almost every conceivable metamorphosis. In spite, however, of the unpredictable irregularity of these corruptions certain common phenomena may be observed. Some Welsh names adopted by the Bretons were assimilated to more familiar names. Llenlleawc became Lancelot under the influence of Lancelin; Breton Ivan and Brien were substituted for Owain and Bran.[67] In two instances, at least, Welsh names which happened to be identical with common nouns, Llwch and Llew, were translated into French as Lac and Lion.[68] When the French *contes* came to be written down and were copied and recopied, the usual scribal errors occurred, such as the confusion of *c* and *t*, of *u, n,* and *v,* of medial *s* and *l.* Initial *B* and *G,* as Bruce and M. Lot have noted,[69] were sometimes interchanged and led to such distortions as Beaumayns from Gauvains, Balaain from Galaain, Genewis from Beneis.[70] The loss of an initial letter in transcription is not uncommon; thus Morgain's name, which is sometimes written Morgant, takes the form Argante in Layamon's *Brut.*[71] The syllable *es* is prefixed, perhaps to add dignity,[72] to a few names, so that we have side by side Calibor and Escalibor, Cavalon and Escavalon. There are compound names, Brangemuer, Mabonagrain, Guingambresil. Since there are no uniform laws for the development of Celtic sounds transmitted to the French and Anglo-Normans or for graphic errors in the copying of manuscripts and since the possibilities of corruption in both stages are almost infinite, one should not be too skeptical of seemingly far-fetched equations. Neither, however, should one throw caution to the winds. I have in the past enumerated five criteria which may serve as safeguards in the equation of names,[73] criteria which are actually in common use by scholars and which I trust will commend themselves to the good sense of my readers as I submit them here. (1) A demonstrated possibility of transmission. (2) A detailed or sustained similarity in nature or activities of the persons named. (3) A correspondence in their relationships to identifiable characters. (4) Intermediate forms between the two names. (5) A reasonable explanation for the development of the name. Not

[66] Paton, *op. cit.,* p. 152.   [67] *PMLA,* LVI, 915, 921. *Romanic Review,* XXXII, 36.
[68] Loomis, *Celtic Myth,* pp. 94 f. *Romania,* LIV (1928), 518. *PMLA,* XLV (1930), 432–38.
[69] F. Lot, *Etude sur le Lancelot,* p. 148n. *Mod. Phil.,* XVI, 347.
[70] *PMLA,* LIV (1939), 659–65. Loomis, *Celtic Myth,* pp. 251 f. Note that the Pant von Genewis of the *Lanzelet* is the Ban de Benoic of the *Vulgate Lancelot,* and that the latter name is a corruption of Bran le Benoit. Cf. Newstead, *op. cit.,* p. 157.
[71] *Mod. Lang. Notes,* XXVI (1911), 65 ff.   [72] *Mod. Phil.,* X (1913), 449 f.
[73] *PMLA,* XLV, 418.

all of these criteria need to be met, of course, in order to establish with practical certainty that a transformation of one form into another has occurred, and indeed the first criterion is already satisfied by the evidence that Welsh Arthurian tradition did spread through Brittany to France and Anglo-Norman Britain and was disseminated in both oral and written forms. If the equation meets two other tests, including 2 or 3 and 4 or 5, it should commend itself to our acceptance. In dealing with Arthurian nomenclature in this book I have endeavored to avoid the extremes of timidity and temerity, neither blinking the fact that the most erratic transmogrifications did take place, nor recklessly propounding guesses without adequate support.

This completes our survey of the typical phenomena to be observed in a body of narrative cultivated over a long period of time and among many peoples, both in spoken and written forms. To understand them is to understand the ways of tradition and the evolution of Arthurian romance.

Kittredge declared that Chrétien's Arthurian poems stand at the end of a long course of development,[74] and all the facts that we have noted confirm his dictum. Naturally, then, the problems involved in the analysis and the history of his work are complicated, and the task of tracing portions of it back to Celtic sources is not easy. It is, therefore, desirable to explain and, if possible, to justify the methods of investigation which I have employed.

The first step is to isolate the various elements which make up a romance. No single principle can be applied in determining what constitutes an isolable element. Sometimes it is a particular figure, such as Guenievre or Yvain, whose history deserves separate treatment; sometimes it is an object such as the Round Table or the sword Escalibor. Sometimes it is an adventure which bears only a tenuous relation or none at all to what goes before and after. Sometimes it is a more complex group of incidents which reveal on examination that they belong together. There is no chemical formula which will serve in the analysis of a poem into its component parts. To a large extent the process of isolating incidents must be conditioned by later steps, by the discovery of comparable incidents and probable sources. The analysis of a poem is valid if it meets the pragmatic test: does it work? does it succeed in separating out the various strands of tradition?

The second step in the investigation of an incident or complex of incidents or a personal history or a motif is to make a careful and wide search (with the aid of previous studies) for parallels. The search may extend not only through Arthurian romance, but also through the Breton lais and even the *chansons de geste,* some of which borrowed heavily from the

[74] G. L. Kittredge, *Study of Gawain and the Green Knight,* p. 241.

Matière de Bretagne. No analogue should be neglected merely because of its late date, since we have seen that the period of composition is no safe index to the antiquity of the material. Neither should an analogue be rejected offhand because, along with resemblances, there are marked differences from Chrétien's version. Variations of all kinds must be expected.

The third step is to determine as far as possible from a study of the variant versions what details are original. Here, again, no rule of thumb can be applied. Sometimes, though not always, the fullest version will be found to contain a large amount of traditional material which has faded out of the others. Supernatural elements are likely to be old, and so too are those features which crop up in cognate versions. By applying one or all of these criteria it is usually possible to discover the rough outlines of the original design. Sometimes in this process one discovers that more than one pattern has been used by Chrétien, certain features occurring in one set of analogues, others in another set, still others in a third set. Thus we detect a case of contamination.

The fourth step is to look for a parallel or parallels in Irish and Welsh literature and folklore and in the survivals of Breton tradition. Particular caution must be exercised in regard to Irish and Gaelic folktales recorded after 1600, since some of them have demonstrably borrowed from French or English Arthurian romance.[75] The work of Nutt and Professor Reginald Griffith on the Irish origins of the Perceval story is vitiated by too ready an acceptance of these late tales as representatives of ancient sagas and by too ready an assumption that these hypothetical sagas were the sources of Arthurian romance. But apart from these suspect Irish and Gaelic tales and apart from the Welsh tales of *Geraint, Owain,* and *Peredur,* which are redactions of French or Anglo-Norman romances, it can generally be assumed that if a correspondence exists between a Celtic and an Arthurian motif or story-pattern, it is the Celtic which represents the older tradition. The validity of the correspondence as proof of a relationship should, of course, be tested by the number of corresponding details, their distinctiveness, and their arrangement. At this stage also it may be possible to detect the fusion of two or more separate stories or personages in Chrétien's poem by the discovery that two or more Celtic stories have been laid under contribution.

When the first four steps have been taken and have led with a considerable degree of certainty to the surviving representatives of the Celtic *matière* from which Chrétien ultimately drew, then one can sometimes take a fifth and final step. That is to trace the history of an episode or motif from its Celtic origin to its incorporation in Chrétien's work, by studying the relations between the variant forms, by noting the evidence of names and places, by watching the play of motives in the various redac-

[75] *Beihefte zur Zts. f. rom. Phil.,* LXX (1921), 41–83. *Mod. Phil.,* XLII (1945), 197–211.

tors, and by interpreting these observations in the light of the general history of Arthurian romance. It has been my experience, and I trust it will be the reader's, that when sufficient material exists, such a reconstruction can frequently be made. The gap between Chrétien's poems and Celtic antiquity can be bridged.

There is, of course, nothing essentially new about these methods of treating the *Matière de Bretagne;* they have been employed by my predecessors in this field and many of my conclusions have been anticipated. If I have attained some new and some surer results, it has only been by surveying as fully as I could the intricate and involved process of legend-making, by canvassing the field and related fields even more widely for pertinent evidence, by discarding mistaken prepossessions, and by following the *via media* between excessive temerity and excessive caution. The rest of this book will give the reader an opportunity to judge for himself the validity of my reasoning and the soundness of my conclusions.

BOOK II.   Erec

Chapter VI

THE ROUND TABLE

CHRÉTIEN mentions the Round Table thrice,[1] each time as an institution or fellowship. He introduces Erec as a member: "he belonged to the Round Table." Later the poet undertakes to give a roll call of the membership, some fifty-odd in all. In *Le Conte del Graal* the Queen of the Castle of Ladies asks Gauvain if he is one of those of the Table Round, "who are the most esteemed in the world."

A few years before, Wace made the first surviving reference to the Table as an object in the familiar lines describing the twelve years of peace which followed Arthur's first conquests.

"For his noble barons, of whom each thought himself the best and each regarded himself as superior, and none would admit inferiority, Arthur made the Round Table, of which Bretons tell many tales. There the vassals sat all in knightly wise and all equal; at the table they sat on an equality and were equally served. None of them could vaunt that he sat higher than his peer; all were seated within, and there was none outside." [2]

Three points should be noted: The Bretons were credited with telling many yarns about the Table. Arthur's purpose in establishing it was to preserve equality among his vassals so that none could boast of a more honorable position than his fellow. It was an actual table. Wace makes two other allusions to the Table but in the sense of a fellowship.[3]

Robert de Boron, according to the prose redaction of his *Merlin,* told quite a different story.[4] The Table was made not by or for Arthur but at the instigation of Merlin for King Uter. There were places for fifty knights besides the King, and an empty seat corresponding to the place which Judas had occupied at the Last Supper. In the prose redaction of Robert's lost *Perceval* (the *Didot Perceval*) we learn of Perceval's occupying this seat, with the result that the dire enchantments of Britain began.[5] *La Queste del Saint Graal* (followed by Malory) gives us the famous scenes of the occupation of the Siege Perilous by Galaad, clad in vermeil arms, of his display of prowess in a tournament, and of the evening meal at the table when all were served by the Grail, veiled in white samite.[6]

[1] *Erec,* vss. 83, 1689. *Conte del Graal,* vs. 8125.
[2] Wace, *Brut,* ed. I. Arnold, II, vss. 9747–60.   [3] *Ibid.,* vss. 10285, 13269.
[4] *Huth Merlin,* ed. G. Paris, J. Ulrich, I, 94–98. H. O. Sommer, *Vulgate Version,* II, 53–55. Cf. also *Huth Merlin,* II, 61–68.
[5] *Didot-Perceval,* ed. W. Roach (Philadelphia, 1941), pp. 147–51. Cf. *Speculum,* VIII (1933), 420 f., 427 f.; R. S. Loomis, *Celtic Myth,* pp. 218–22.
[6] *Queste del S. Graal,* ed. A. Pauphilet, pp. 4–15. Sommer, *Vulgate Version,* VI, 5–13.

Dr. Laura Hibbard Loomis has put forward the highly plausible view that Wace, in emphasizing the equalitarian function of Arthur's Round Table, and Robert, in connecting it with the Table of the Last Supper, were inspired by the fact that there was actually shown to pilgrims at Jerusalem a marble round table, declared to be that at which Christ supped with His apostles on the night of His betrayal.[7] It was seen by Saewulf in 1102; it must have been seen also by Bretons who visited the holy places after the conquest of Jerusalem. No wonder that this most sacred of all tables should have been in the minds of authors when they wrote about the other round table. No wonder that Wace associated the latter with the idea of equality since, according to St. Luke, Christ Himself had rebuked His apostles at the Last Supper, when they quarreled among themselves as to which of them should be accounted the greatest, and had said: "He that is greatest among you, let him be as the younger; and he that is chief, as he that doth serve." [8] No wonder, Robert elaborated the notion that Uter's table was modeled on that at which the Savior Himself had supped with His apostles. There can be little doubt that from the time of Wace the famous table of Arthur's fellowship was colored by association with the even more famous round table which had been seen by many at Jerusalem. And since among the Crusaders and pilgrims were Bretons, and since Wace specifies that Bretons told tales of Arthur's table, may not the association have come first from them?

But was there nothing besides these sacred traditions and this sacred object to inspire the *conteurs?* Was there no substratum of Celtic legend? There are some violent discords in the stories which the romancers relate about the Round Table which are a little difficult to explain if they were working freely with a concept derived from the Scriptures. Why should the place corresponding to that of Judas be so holy that only the purest of knights, a Galaad, was worthy to fill it? Why does Perceval's taking the same seat bring about the enchantments of Britain? Evidently the Siege Perilous motif was something foreign to the Christianized concept of the Table, and, as we shall see in our examination of Lancelot's adventure in the cemetery, it had its origin in an Irish tale of Lug's taking the seat of the sage at the court of King Nuada.[9]

This being so, perhaps the Round Table itself was another Celtic tradition. But there is one formidable obstacle to the acceptance of this possibility; neither the Irish nor the Welsh sat at their meals about a large banqueting table, either rectangular or circular in shape. Giraldus Cambrensis, in fact, declared of his countrymen that their houses were not furnished with tables.[10] Even the Welsh word *bwrdd,* which occurs in

---

[7] *Mod. Lang. Notes,* XLIV (1929), 511–15.   [8] Luke 22:24–26.
[9] *Speculum,* VIII, 419 f.   [10] Giraldus Cambrensis, *Descriptio Cambriae,* Chap. X.

The Dream of Maxen and *Owain*,[11] is a borrowing from Anglo-Saxon. Arthur's list of his treasured possessions in *Kulhwch* contains nothing of the kind.[12] Therefore, the Round Table *as such* could not have been taken over by the Bretons from the Welsh.

Nevertheless, there was a characteristic feature of Celtic custom which I believe was the nucleus of the Breton and French tradition. Long since, scholars observed that it was the habit of Celtic warriors to sit in a circle at individual tables about the bravest.[13] Posidonius, about 90 B.C., testified to the practice among the Gauls. Irish sagas show that it prevailed among the Irish in the eighth and later centuries of the Christian era. According to *Bricriu's Feast*, the royal couch of Conchobar stood in the banqueting hall of Bricriu's palace; "twelve other couches were set up around him, destined for the twelve chief warriors of Ulster." [14] It should be noted, furthermore, that the plot of this whole saga revolves around a quarrel which sprang up in the same hall concerning the assignment of the "Champion's Portion," in other words, a quarrel over precedence. It is of great significance, therefore, that both the seating of twelve warriors about a leader at a feast and the quarrel about precedence should reappear in the *Matière de Bretagne*, the latter in specific connection with Arthur's Round Table.

In three romances of the Grail and in one other we find a table set for thirteen. According to Robert de Boron's *Joseph*,[15] God instructed Joseph of Arimathea to seek out a table like that of the Last Supper, to place Bron, the Rich Fisher, beside him, and to set the Grail on the board. Joseph obeyed the divine command, the seats at the table were all filled, save for the one vacant place of Judas, and all who sat received the accomplishment of their desires from the Holy Vessel. Years after, Joseph was instructed by an angel to commit the vessel and all (*et tout*) [16] to the charge of the Rich Fisher, Bron, and Bron departed with these things, including apparently the table, to the Occident. Thus we find in *Perlesvaus* [17] that when Gauvain was entertained at the Fisher King's castle, somewhere in Britain, he was led into a hall and there found twelve knights, who though they were over a hundred years old seemed less than forty. "They seated Sir Gavain for the repast at a right rich table of ivory, and

---

[11] J. Gwenogvryn Evans, *White Book Mabinogion*, cols. 180, 227.

[12] J. Loth, *Mabinogion*, 2d ed., I, 258 f.

[13] *PMLA*, XX (1905), 260. *Studies and Notes in Philology and Literature*, VII (1900), 183 ff.

[14] D'Arbois de Jubainville, *L'Epopée celtique*, p. 83. *Feast of Bricriu*, ed. G. Henderson (London, 1899), pp. 3, 5.

[15] Robert de Boron, *Roman de l'Estoire dou Graal*, ed. W. A. Nitze (Paris, 1929), vss. 2487–2566.   [16] Vs. 3380.

[17] Ed. W. A. Nitze (Chicago, 1932–37), I, 118 f. On the number of knights cf. variant readings of mss. Br and P for l. 2414; also *Perlesvaus*, II, 266.

then sat down around him." While they were eating, a damsel passed through the hall, bearing the Holy Grail. It is obvious that this table with seats for thirteen in the castle of the Fisher King is the same table, made in the likeness of the table of the Last Supper, which had been entrusted to Bron by Joseph of Arimathea, together with the Grail. It is noteworthy that Gauvain saw the image of a child in the midst of the Grail, for this same feature along with other elements of the tradition is reflected in *La Queste del Saint Graal*.[18] There we learn that twelve knights, including Galaad, assembled in the palace of the Maimed King and were welcomed by him. In his presence the twelve knights beheld the vision of a child descending into the mass-wafer contained in the Grail. They seated themselves at a table of silver and were served with the holy vessel by the wounded Christ Himself, who declared to them that just as the Apostles had eaten with Him at the Last Supper, so did the knights eat with Him at the table of the Grail, for they were like in number to the Apostles while He Himself was the thirteenth. A purely secular version of the same basic tradition may be found in the *Vulgate Lancelot*.[19] King Brangoire ordained a great tourney; Bohort distinguished himself above all the other knights, was clad in red samite, took his place with twelve knights at a table of honor, and was served with spices by King Brangoire's daughter.

That the three accounts of the Grail table are related goes without saying. Let it be noted particularly that Bron, the Rich Fisher, of Robert's *Joseph,* the Fisher King of *Perlesvaus,* who is suffering from a strange malady, and the Maimed King of the *Queste* are surely identical. If there be any doubt, there is the witness of the *Didot Perceval* that the languishing Grail King was called Bron.[20] The fourth account of a table with thirteen places must represent the same basic tradition. For King Brangoire must be the same as King Bron; Bohort, who took his seat at the table clad in red corresponds to Galaad, who wore red arms and took his seat, clad in vermeil sendal, at the Grail table; Brangoire's daughter, who served the thirteen knights with spices, recalls the Fisher King's daughter in Manessier, who was the Grail Bearer.[21] The common basis for the four accounts must be the Welsh legend of Bran the Blessed, who was wounded in the foot and whose company journeyed from place to place, feasting and growing no older in appearance though they tarried at Gwales, an island off western Wales, for eighty years.[22] These are evidently the traditions which meet us in Arthurian romance as Bron's languishment, his journey with his company to the Occident, the youthful

---

[18] *Queste,* ed. Pauphilet, pp. 267–71. Sommer, *Vulgate Version,* VI, 188–91.

[19] Sommer, *op. cit.,* IV, 264–70. Cf. *Mod. Lang. Rev.,* XXIV (1929), 420–23; H. Newstead, *Bran the Blessed in Arthurian Romance,* pp. 51–54.

[20] *Didot-Perceval,* ed. Roach, pp. 305 f.

[21] C. Potvin, *Perceval le Gallois* (Mons, 1866–71), V, 158.

[22] Loth, *Mabinogion,* 2d ed., I, 144–48. Cf. Newstead, *op. cit.,* pp. 19 f., 36–46, 168–72.

appearance of the aged knights in the Fisher King's hall, and their feasting. There is, of course, no table of Bran mentioned in the mabinogi for reasons already noted, and there are other discrepancies; but only a strong Welsh tradition that the wounded King Bran held his miraculous feasts, with twelve warriors in a circle about him, can account for the persistent association of a table set for thirteen with Bran's Arthurian counterparts.

The ancient Celtic custom of placing the king or chief in the midst of his feasting warriors and the specific number of those warriors recorded in *Bricriu's Feast* and, inferentially, in the Welsh traditions of Bran must therefore be the underlying elements in the Arthurian concept of a table set for thirteen. The same Celtic elements must also underlie the concept of Arthur's Round Table. For this table too, according to the *Didot Perceval* (Modena ms.), had thirteen seats,[23] of which one was left vacant in memory of Judas' seat, and was duly occupied by a knight in red arms, Perceval. Evidently the Celtic traditions which shaped the tables of Bron and Brangoire also determined the form of Arthur's famous Table Round.

Even more cogent as evidence for the Celtic origin of the Round-Table concept is the fact, brought out by Arthur Brown,[24] that the very same dining hall in which King Conchobar sat with his twelve warriors around him was the scene of a quarrel over precedence like that which Layamon tells us arose over the question of precedence in Arthur's hall. Let me quote from *Bricriu's Feast* certain pertinent selections.

"The half of the palace was set apart for Conchobar and his retinue of valiant Ulster heroes; the other half for the ladies of Ulster attending on Mugan . . . wife of King Conchobar." Egged on by Bricriu, the charioteers of Loegaire, Conall, and Cuchulainn claim the Champion's Portion for their respective masters. The three warriors arose, "donned their shields and seized their swords. At one another they hewed till the half of the palace was an atmosphere of fire. . . . Great alarm gat hold upon the palace; the valiant heroes shook; Conchobar himself and Fergus mac Roig got furious on seeing the injury and the injustice of two men surrounding one. . . . There was no one among the Ulstermen who dared separate them till Sencha spake to Conchobar: 'Part the men,' quoth he. Conchobar and Fergus intervened, and the combatants immediately let drop their hands to their sides." [25]

Compare this with the scene described by Layamon.[26]

King Arthur held his Yuletide festivities at London, and the nobles and their sons and womenfolk came from far and near. There was much envy, for one accounted himself high, the other much higher. Arthur sat down at the tables and beside him Wenhaver, his Queen, and then the earls, barons, and knights

[23] Ed. Roach, pp. 142, 146. [24] See note 13 above.
[25] D'Arbois de Jubainville, *op. cit.*, pp. 89–92. *Feast of Bricriu*, ed. Henderson, pp. 13–17. Cf. similar quarrels described by Posidonius. *PMLA*, XX, 262 f.
[26] Vss. 22736 ff. Gervase of Tilbury also connects Round Table with Cornwall. Ralph of Coggeshall, *Chronicon Anglicanum*, ed. J. Stevenson (1875), p. 436.

in order. They were served with meat according to their rank. Presently there were angry blows. A young man, son of Rumaret, King of Winet [Gwynedd], counseled the King to retire with the Queen to his chamber, and, seizing three knives, he felled seven of the quarrelsome thanes. Arthur returned with a hundred armed knights to the hall, and threatened dire punishment to any future offenders. Then "it saith in the tale" that he went to Cornwall and caused a marvelous table to be made by a carpenter, which had three remarkable properties: it could seat sixteen hundred; it was arranged that the high should be even with the low; it could be carried with Arthur wherever he wished to ride. The result was that all were satisfied; "none might boast there of other kind of drink than his comrades who were at the board had. This was the same board that Bretons boast of, and say many sorts of lies about Arthur the King."

The case for the derivation of Layamon's story from some such Celtic tale as that in *Bricriu's Feast* was so strong that even the hypercritical Bruce accepted it.[27] And one peculiar attribute of the table as described by Layamon, though not paralleled in Irish or Welsh literature, must have some traditional basis in Celtic marvel, and that is its amazing portability, considering the fact that it could accommodate sixteen hundred persons. In the Provençal romance of *Jaufré*,[28] whose author naturally could not have read Layamon's *Brut,* we read that a fay who finally announced herself as "la fada del Gibel" and who was therefore Morgain [29] rose with all her retinue and her baggage train from a fountain and had a huge tent set up which extended for half a league. Within, a magnificent banquet was served to ladies and knights and squires, and at its conclusion the fay presented Jaufré with the tent, saying that a single cart could contain it and all its equipment.[30] Surely this possession of Arthur's sister, in which hundreds of persons could feast and which could be packed in a single cart, must be akin to Arthur's table, at which hundreds could feast and which could be carried with him wherever he rode. That a Provençal poet writing for a king of Aragon about 1225 and a country priest of the Severn valley should be familiar with curiously kindred traditions is significant for the homogeneity and the wide dissemination of the *Matière de Bretagne*. It also confirms the view that Layamon obtained the additions to his version of Wace not immediately from the neighboring Welsh but from a developed French body of legends.[31]

Thus our examination discloses that the history of the Round Table passed through seven stages. (1) It originated in the Celtic seating arrangement in a banquet hall—a king on his couch, with twelve chief warriors on their couches around him. (2) A Welsh form of this tradition must

[27] J. D. Bruce, *Evolution of Arthurian Romance,* I, 87.

[28] *Jaufré,* ed. H. Breuer (Göttingen, 1925), vss. 10346–10676.

[29] L. A. Paton, *Fairy Mythology of Arthurian Romance,* p. 250, n. 1. A. Graf, *Miti, leggende e superstizioni del medio evo* (Turin, 1893), II, 308, 312.

[30] Vss. 10547–49.   [31] Bruce, *op. cit.,* I, 85.

be inferred, according to which the gigantic King Bran sat in his palace or in a tent, with twelve warriors in a circle about him. (3) The tradition was transferred to Arthur. (4) The Bretons, who used tables and knew of the circular table at Jerusalem, which served Christ and His twelve apostles, invented two round tables with thirteen places, assigning one to Bron, the Fisher King, and the other to Arthur. (5) For various reasons the number of seats at Arthur's table was increased to fifty, one hundred and fifty, or even sixteen hundred. (6) Other originally Celtic tales, such as the quarrel for precedence and the Siege Perilous, were attracted and attached to the tradition. (7) Perhaps under the influence of the religious orders of knighthood, such as the Templars, the Round Table became the symbol of a chivalric fellowship. Pope Urban at the Council of Clermont in 1095 enjoined on all noble youths the duty of defending the oppressed, the widow, and the orphan, and of protecting women of high birth.[32] Likewise Malory declared that all the knights of the Table Round swore each year "never to do outragyousyte nor mordre and alweyes to flee treason; also by no meane to be cruel but to gyve mercy unto hym that asketh mercy upon payn of forfeture of their worship and lordship of kyng Arthur for evermore, and alweyes to doo ladyes, damoysels, and gentylwymmen socour upon payne of dethe." [33]

Such, in brief, was the history of the Round Table in literature. But the legend also made an impact on life. The glamor of King Arthur's mythical order lasted as long as the age of chivalry and served as the model of many a renowned fellowship; the Order of the Garter had its origin in Edward III's vow to found a Round Table as Arthur had done: "mensam rotundam inciperet eodem modo et statu quo eam dimisit dominus Arthurus." Tournaments which were called "tables rondes" and which followed the supposed ceremonial and practices of Arthur's days are recorded from 1223 to 1345, and were held in places as far apart as Cyprus, Prague, Saragossa, and Falkirk in Scotland.[34] Even in the reign of Elizabeth a society of archers existed at London who styled themselves Knights of the Round Table.[35]

Possibly the circular board which hangs to this day in the hall of Winchester Castle and which Caxton cited as proof of Arthur's historic reality was a relic of some unchronicled festival of this sort.[36] It was known to the chronicler Hardyng in the middle of the fifteenth century. Probably

[32] R. L. Kilgour, *Decline of Chivalry* (Cambridge, Mass., 1939), p. xviii.
[33] Malory, *Morte d'Arthur*, Bk. III, chap. 15.
[34] *Mediaeval Studies in Memory of A. K. Porter* (Cambridge, Mass., 1939), I, 82–87. Cf. also *Speculum*, XVI (1941), 109–20; XIX (1944), 389–420; XX (1945), 204–11; L. Keeler, *Geoffrey of Monmouth and the Latin Chroniclers* (1946), pp. 15 f., 131–37.
[35] C. B. Millican, *Spenser and the Table Round* (Cambridge, Mass., 1932), pp. 54–64.
[36] *Ibid.*, pp. 156 f. R. S. and L. H. Loomis, *Arthurian Legends in Medieval Art*, pp. 40 f., Fig. 18.

it was painted with the design it still bears in 1486, for in that year a royal prince was born at Winchester and christened Arthur, and the twenty-four names of knights inscribed round the periphery reveal indebtedness to Malory's *Morte d'Arthur,* published in 1485. Suspended from the wall, the table bears concrete testimony to the spell which the legends exercised over the minds of medieval men.

Chapter VII

THE STAG HUNT

VERSES 27–124, 279–341, 1751–1843

At Eastertide Arthur held high court at Caradigan. Before the assemblage of nobles and ladies broke up, the King announced that he would observe the custom of hunting the White Stag. Whoever could slay it had the right to kiss the fairest maiden. Though warned of the disputes which the custom would provoke, the King insisted on the customary chase, and was himself successful in killing the stag. Before he bestowed the kiss, however, the Queen persuaded him to delay until the third day, when Erec had promised to return from avenging an insult to the Queen. On Erec's arrival he brought with him his affianced bride, the lovely Enide. Arthur adjudged her the fairest of the damsels and with the consent of all gave her "the kiss of the stag."

THE ROMANCE of Erec and Enide, up to the marriage of the two, consists of a series of episodes which, whatever their original purport, have been skillfully recast in order to bring out the supreme beauty and *franchise* of Enide. This purposeful artistry may be clearly observed in the adaptation of the chase of the white stag and the bestowal of the kiss. Even Guenievre, whom one might expect to be jealous of a rival beauty, proclaims that Enide is "the most lovely (*jante*) of the maidens that are here and of those throughout the world," and all the courtiers agree that she deserves "the kiss of the stag."

The skeptical Bruce conceded that the stag hunt "reminds one irresistibly of the marvelous white doe in *Guigemar,* which, as we have seen, is, no doubt, of Celtic origin." [1] Certainly the Welsh often conceived the animals of the Other World as white. [2] There is a strange text explaining that the Battle of Goddeu was occasioned by a white roebuck and a whelp. [3] "They

---

[1] J. D. Bruce, *Evolution of Arthurian Romance,* I, 109 f.

[2] J. Rhys, *Celtic Folklore, Welsh and Manx* (Oxford, 1901), I, 143, 146.

[3] W. F. Skene, *Four Ancient Books of Wales* (Edinburgh, 1868), I, 205. C. Guest, *Mabinogion* (London, 1849), II, 347 f.

came from Annwn [4] [the land of the gods], and Amathaon ap Don [5] brought them. Therefore Amathaon ap Don and Arawn, king of Annwn, fought." In the mabinogi of *Pwyll* Arawn appeared with a pack of shining white hounds.[6] In the mabinogi of *Manawydan* Pryderi pursued a pure white boar into an enchanted castle, where it disappeared.[7]

Though we may search vainly in early Welsh sources for any parallels to Chrétien's account of the chase of the white stag, Arthur's outstripping the other huntsmen at the death, and his bestowal of a kiss on Enide as the fairest lady of the court, we may obtain some light on earlier stages of the tradition from Wauchier's continuation of *Le Conte del Graal* and in the Breton lai of *Tyolet,* which must derive from a common remote source. Wauchier's long tale may be thus summarized.[8]

A fay (a pupil of Morgain's) rises from the moat of an enchanted castle, and when Perceval demands her favors, she makes the condition that he bring her the head of a white stag in the park near by, and gives him a white brachet with which to track it. Perceval with the help of the hound overtakes and decapitates the stag, and is returning with the head and the hound when he is robbed of both. After sundry adventures, he recovers them and, on presenting these tokens of his success, he is granted the satisfaction of his desires by the fay.

A roughly similar plot is found in *Tyolet.*[9]

A king's daughter arrives at Arthur's court and announces that she will wed the knight who cuts off the white foot of a shining stag. When Tyolet, after others have defaulted, undertakes the task, she gives him a white brachet to lead him to the stag. Guided by the hound, Tyolet finds his prey, and cuts off its foot, but is robbed of the tokens of his success and only after various difficulties wins the princess as his reward.

Variations on the same story occur in the *Didot Perceval,* the Dutch *Lancelot, Peredur,* the *Huth Merlin,* and Malory.[10] None of these could possibly

---

[4] On meaning of Annwn cf. *PMLA,* LVI (1941), 891–98.

[5] On Amathaon cf. J. Rhys, *Lectures on the Origin and Growth of Religion as Illustrated by Celtic Heathendom,* 2d ed. (London, 1892), pp. 89 f.; W. J. Gruffydd, *Math Vab Mathonwy,* 148; J. Loth, *Mabinogion,* 2d ed., I, 300n.   [6] Loth, *Mabinogion,* 2d ed., I, 84.

[7] *Ibid.,* I, 159. For a similar adventure cf. *Guingamor* in Marie de France, *Lais,* ed. K. Warnke, 3d ed., pp. 238–46; C. Potvin, *Perceval le Gallois,* IV, vss. 28916 ff.

[8] Potvin, *op. cit.,* IV, vss. 22392 ff., 27004 ff., 27715 ff., 29907–30554. Note that the fay professes to have been in the service of Morgain la Fée, that she has built a castle beside a river, and that she rises out of the river itself. This story is discussed in L. A. Paton, *Fairy Mythology of Arthurian Romance,* pp. 157 f., 230 f.; J. L. Weston, *Legend of Perceval,* I, 107–17.

[9] *Romania,* VIII (1879), 45–50. For comment cf. Weston, *Legend of Lancelot du Lac* (London, 1901), pp. 32–39; Paton, *Fairy Mythology,* pp. 171 f.; *Romanische Forschungen,* XL (1927), 471 ff.

[10] *Didot-Perceval,* ed. W. Roach, pp. 167–71, 212–18; comment on pp. 52–56. *Roman van Lancelot,* ed. W. J. A. Jonckbloet ('s Gravenhage, 1846–49), II, vss. 22271–23126; comment in Weston, *Legend of Lancelot,* pp. 30–39. Loth, *Mabinogion,* 2d ed., II, 114–17; comment in Paton, *Fairy Mythology,* pp. 157 f., 231 f. *Huth Merlin,* ed. G. Paris, J. Ulrich, II, 77–137; comment in Paton, *op. cit.,* pp. 229–33; *PMLA,* XLIII (1928), 438–41. Malory, *Morte d'Arthur,* Bk. III, chaps. 5–15.

have been inspired by *Erec,* and must be offshoots from an early Breton *conte.* The essential features were: a fay offers her love on condition that the hero pursue a white stag with the aid of a white hound which she provides; the hero cuts off the stag's head; he is robbed of it; he finally recovers it and receives the fay's love as his reward.

Of this *conte, Geraint* seems to have preserved one feature which has been suppressed by Chrétien: Arthur cuts off the stag's head and presents it to Enid.[11] *Erec* retains only the core of the plot and modifies it: whatever knight of Arthur's court succeeds in killing the white stag is entitled to kiss the fairest damsel. Evidently the gory gift of the stag's head seemed inappropriate to the refined taste of Chrétien, and he substituted the kiss. Both *Erec* and *Geraint* concur in simplifying the old tale, and adapting it to the purpose of demonstrating Enide's beauty. The credit for this artistic adaptation must go to the author of their common source, X.

Chapter VIII

EREC, SON OF LAC

M. FERDINAND LOT showed long since that the name Erec was developed from the Breton Guerec, borne conspicuously by a Count of Nantes, son of Alain Barbe-Torte, in the tenth century.[1] This may possibly have something to do with the fact that Chrétien placed the coronation of his hero at Nantes; but the odds are against this supposition, for since nothing is said of the coronation in the Welsh *Geraint,* this linking of Erec with Nantes was probably, as many scholars think,[2] Chrétien's own invention; and furthermore Nantes appears as Arthur's, not Erec's, seat.

Though the name of Erec is Breton and was suggested by the historic Guerec, we must look elsewhere for an explanation of his father's name, Lac, and of his father's realm of Destregales. Though there has been much controversy about this word,[3] there should be little doubt that it means South Wales. The scribes, of course, did not know this, for they give such variants as Dentregales and Doutregales,[4] and Chrétien himself

---

[11] Loth, *Mabinogion,* 2d ed., II, 139
[1] *Romania,* XXV (1896), 588. Cf. Loth, *Mabinogion,* 2d ed., I, 56.
[2] Loth, *op. cit.,* I, 56 f. *Zts. f. franz. Sprache u. Lit.,* XLIV (1916–17), 158 f. *Zts. f. rom. Phil.,* XLVIII (1928), 131–33. W. Foerster, *Kristian von Troyes, Wörterbuch,* p. 56. H. Sparnaay, *Hartmann von Aue, Studien zu einer Biographie* (Halle, 1933), I, 111 f. G. Cohen, *Chrétien de Troyes et son œuvre* (Paris, 1931), pp. 154 f. *Romanic Review,* XVI, 46–50.
[3] J. D. Bruce, *Evolution of Arthurian Romance,* II, 70, n. 12.
[4] *Erec,* ed. W. Foerster (Halle, 1890), vss. 1874, 3881, variants.

apparently took the initial *D* to be the preposition *de* with elided vowel. But there never was a region known as Estregales or Outregales, whereas M. Lot pointed out fifty years ago, and Windisch and Zenker have recognized,[5] that there are strong reasons for equating Destregales with South Wales. (1) The Welsh regularly called this portion of their country Deheubarth,[6] meaning the right (hand) part, and in French *destre* means right and *Gales* means Wales. (2) Giraldus Cambrensis Latinizes this Welsh expression: "Sudwalliam, id est, Australem Walliam, quae Cambrice Deheubarth, id est, Dextralis Pars, dicitur."[7] (3) According to ms. A, verse 2315, Lac, King of Destregales, sojourned at his castle of Caruent, and Caerwent is in Deheubarth.[8] (4) Renaud de Beaujeu seems to have had an inkling of the truth when he wrote in *Le Bel Inconnu,* verses 5573 and following: "And the mighty duke of North Wales (Norgales) was there, and Erec of Estregales." Since Estregales means nothing, whereas Destregales means something and corresponds to the "Dextralis Pars" of Giraldus, it seems hypercritical to doubt that Erec's realm was South Wales.

But how did a prince with a Breton name come to be heir to, and later king of, this realm? I believe the answer is: Guerec, son of Lac, was a Breton-French substitution for Welsh Gweir, son of Llwch,[9] and Gweir was confused with Gwri, prince of South Wales. This hypothesis is supported by the following points:

1. The muster roll of Arthur's warriors in *Kulhwch* mentions two brothers, Gweir Gwrhyt Ennwir and Gweir Baladyr Hir,[10] probably one person with two epithets, Gweir of Trusty Valor and Gweir of the Long Spear, since brothers are not likely to bear the same name.

2. These Gweirs were sons of Llwch; and *llwch,* as a common noun, meant "lake" and would be translated into French as *lac.* Thus Gweir, son of Llwch, might, as a result of substitution and translation, become Guerec, son of Lac.

3. The name Llwch is also given in *Kulhwch* as Lloch, and this form,

[5] *Romania*, XXV, 7 ff. E. Windisch, *Keltische Brittannien bis zu Kaiser Arthur*, p. 260. R. Zenker, *Zur Mabinogionfrage* (Halle, 1912), pp. 95 f. Note that Hartmann von Aue consistently calls the land of Erek's father Destregales.

[6] J. E. Lloyd, *History of Wales*, 3d ed. (London, 1939), I, 256 ff.

[7] Loth, *op. cit.*, II, 367. [8] Lloyd, *op. cit.*, I, 273.

[9] Some scholars have assumed that Erec is a substitution for the name Geraint, borne by the hero of the Welsh tale corresponding to Chrétien's poem. Cf. Loth, *op. cit.*, I, 56; Zenker, *op. cit.*, p. 89; Windisch, *op. cit.*, pp. 174–76; *Etudes celtiques*, II (1937), 220–22. Though there seem to have been three historic kings or princes of Devon and Cornwall named Geraint, and one of them is mentioned in the Black Book of Carmarthen, where his men and Arthur's seem to be regarded as fighting side by side at the battle of Llongborth (*Idem;* Loth, *op. cit.*, II, 121n.; Windisch, *op. cit.*, pp. 175 f.; Malory, *Morte d'Arthur*, Everyman ed., I, xvi f.), Erec was not the ruler of Devon or Cornwall, and Geraint was the son of Erbin, not of Lac. The conclusion to be drawn is that the Welsh author of *Geraint* substituted this name, familiar to him through native tradition, for the Breton name Guerec, which he found in his source. [10] Loth, *op. cit.*, I, 276.

according to Joseph Loth,[11] became Loth in the French romances. Llwch is described as "from the other side of the extreme sea," [12] and both Lac and Loth were kings of Orcanie,[13] the Orkney Isles, which Nennius described as lying "in extremo limite orbis Brittanniae." [14]

4. King Loth had a son Guerehes, and one of the adventures of Guerehes, son of Loth, as will be seen,[15] offers a significant parallel to the ride of Erec, son of Lac, with Enide.

5. King Loth had another son Guahries or Gaheries, the Gareth of Malory, and Gareth's adventures offer many significant and unique parallels with those of Erec, as will be seen in due course.[16]

6. The objection that the Gweirs are said to be uncles of Arthur—brothers of his mother, whereas, on the contrary, Arthur was the uncle of Guerehes and Gaheries, being the brother of their mother, is not very cogent. First, we never read elsewhere of any brothers of Ygerne. Secondly, it is easy to see that, in the confused state of the list of Arthur's warriors,[17] the relation of the Gweirs to Arthur might have been reversed. Compare the passage in *Kulhwch* with a similar passage in the *Didot Perceval*. The former runs: "Gweir Gwrhyt Ennwir and Gweir Baladyr Hir, uncles of Arthur, brothers of his mother, sons of Llwch Llawwynnyawc from the other side of the extreme sea." [18] The latter passage, also included in a list of Arthur's warriors, runs: "Mordres, the nephew of Arthur . . . and Guirres his brother, and Garries and Gavains. And these four were sons of King Lot of Orchanie; and King Arthur was their uncle." [19] Here, except for the addition of Mordred and Gauvain, and the reversal of the relationship to Arthur, much the same statements are made about Guirres and Garries as are made about the two Gweirs. This similarity can hardly be fortuitous, especially since we shall be able to explain the addition of

---

[11] *Ibid.*, I, 264, n. 3. *Revue celt.*, XVI (1897), 84. E. T. Griffiths, *Chantari di Lancelotto* (Oxford, 1924), p. 186. *PMLA*, XLVIII (1928), 386 f. Note that in the *Vulgate Lancelot* (H. O. Sommer, *Vulgate Version*, III, 269 f.) there was a King Lohoz, whose son according to ms. D was named Gaher.

[12] J. Gwenogvryn Evans, *White Book Mabinogion*, col. 466: "Llwch Llawwynnyawc or tu draw y vor terwyn." Prof. W. J. Gruffydd suggested to me that *terwyn* represents the noun *terfyn*, meaning end, extremity, *w* being substituted in certain mss. for *f*. Cf. J. Strachan, *Introduction to Early Welsh* (Manchester, 1909), p. 3 (d). Prof. Jackson writes me that he prefers the meaning "raging," and refers me to *Canu Llywarch Hen*, ed. I. Williams, pp. 148, 241. Perhaps there has been some confusion between the two meanings.

[13] Sommer, *op. cit.*, I, 280; II, 72, 94; VII, 15, 37, 146. *Huth Merlin*, ed. G. Paris, J. Ulrich, I, 119. Malory, *Morte d'Arthur*, Bk. I, chaps. 2, 8, etc. For Loth's connections with Lothian and Ireland cf. Chaps. XV, XXVI.

[14] Faral, *Légende arthurienne*, III, 6 f.   [15] Cf. Chap. XVII.

[16] Cf. *infra*, pp. 86, 127–29. On name Gareth cf. *PMLA*, LIV (1939), 659 f.

[17] Note the corruption of the Irish names. Loth, *op. cit.*, I, 261 f. C. O'Rahilly, *Ireland and Wales*, pp. 114 f.

[18] Loth, *op. cit.*, I, 276. Strangely enough, the same relationship to Arthur is predicated of two other figures in the list (*ibid.*, I, 271), Llygatrudd Emys and Gwrbothu Hen. Cf. A. W. Wade-Evans, *Welsh Christian Origins* (Oxford, 1934), p. 102.

[19] *Didot-Perceval*, ed. W. Roach, p. 140.

Gauvain, and since Mordred is elsewhere said to be the son, not of Loth, but of Arthur.

7. The prominence of Erec and Gareth as heroes of romance is best accounted for by the confusion of Gweir, son of Llwch, with another person listed in *Kulhwch* among 'Arthur's warriors, Gware Gwallt-euryn; [20] for this name is admittedly another form of Gwri Gwallt-euryn, and Gwri was the baptismal name of the youthful hero of *The Four Branches of the Mabinogi*.[21] Such confusions between persons of somewhat similar names is a familiar phenomenon in Welsh. Llyr is confused with Lludd, Mabon with Madawg.[22] Even St. Cadawc was credited with the aphorisms of Dionysius Cato for no better reason than the resemblance in their names.[23] Gweir and Gware, both warriors of Arthur, could thus coalesce into one person.

8. The inconsistency in the tradition which makes Loth and Lac kings of Orcanie in certain prose romances, and which makes Lac king of Destregales in *Erec,* may be accounted for by the hypothesis that whereas Llwch is said to be from the other side of the extreme sea, his son Gweir became confused with Gwri, whose father reigned over Dyved, southwestern Wales, and who, under his sobriquet Pryderi, became ruler over all South Wales.[24]

9. The hypothesis that Gweir, the original of Erec, King of Destregales, came to be identified with Gwri, ruler of South Wales, gains color from the fact that Chrétien had some authentic information about the region. As was pointed out above, he knew that it contained Caruent, and, more than that, he knew that Caruent was the center of a fertile district. Though Foerster's text gives Carnant, and though two places, Ros Carnant and Kelli Carnant, have been discovered in Cornwall and South Wales respectively,[25] neither had any importance. But ms. A gives Caruent, and Caerwent in Monmouthshire has three claims on our attention. First, it enjoyed·such renown that Gaimar (*ca.* 1150) mentions Karrewein, together with Karliun and "la cité de Snauedun," as the three famous cities of Wales.[26] Secondly, it was known to the Bretons, who were trans-

[20] Loth, *op. cit.,* I, 278.
[21] Prof. Gruffydd, in his *Math Vab Mathonwy,* pp. 324–27, shows that the *Four Branches* form the saga of Pryderi.
[22] Loth, *op. cit.,* II, 273, n. 1; 318, n. 1.   [23] *Ibid.,* II, 290, n. 1.
[24] *Ibid.,* I, 81 f., 174. On the cantrevs of Dyved and South Wales cf. Lloyd, *op. cit.,* I, 256–81.
[25] *Romania,* XXV (1896), 9. *Revue celt.,* XIII (1892), 503.
[26] Geffrei Gaimar, *Estorie des Engles,* ed. T. D. Hardy, C. T. Martin (London, 1888), I, 285. It is interesting to note that the same three cities appear together as Cair Segeint, Cair Legeion guar Uisc, and Cair Guent in the Nennian list of the 28 Cities of Britain. Faral, *Légende arthurienne,* III, 57. On this list cf. Prof. Jackson's article in *Antiquity,* XII (1938), 44–55. On identity of Cair Segeint with "la cité de Snauedun" cf. *infra,* p. 115, n. 43. The three cities owed their renown to the imposing Roman remains. On those at Caerwent cf. *Archaeologia,* LXII (1910), Part I, 1–20; LXIV (1912–13), 447–52. On those at Cair Segeint (near Carnarvon) cf. *Cymmrodor,* XXXIII (1923); *Archaeologia Cambrensis,* LXXVII (1922), 258–326.

mitters of Welsh matter to the Anglo-Normans and French, for Marie de France, in her lai of *Yonec*,[27] makes Caruent the home of the lord of the district, and he journeys towards Caerleon on Usk, which is about ten miles from Caerwent. Thirdly, Gwri, under his sobriquet of Pryderi, obtained possession of the seven cantrevs of Morganhwc, in which Caerwent lies.[28] Fourthly, Chrétien dilates on the fertility of the district about Caruent, and this corresponds to the facts. He writes: "Never did he [Erec] see a castle better situated; it was rich with forests, meadows, vines, tilled fields, rivers, and orchards . . ." [29] Sir John Lloyd remarks of Gwent Iscoed: "It was famed for its fertility; the renown of the wheat and the bees of Maes Gwenith [the Field of Gwenith, a few miles north of Caerwent] . . . passed for a proverb throughout the whole of Wales." [30] Can it be wholly fortuitous that Gwri came to rule over Deheubarth, including Caerwent and the fertile district around it, while (Gu)erec inherited the land of Destregales, including the castle of Caruent, surrounded by meadows, vineyards, farms, and orchards?

10. The association of Erec with Destregales is not the only instance in Chrétien's poem where an authentic Welsh local association has been preserved. One of the guests at Erec's wedding was a King Ban or Braus de Gomeret (vs. 1975). Professor Newstead has shown,[31] and the evidence will be reviewed later in this book,[32] that this personage is no other than the King Bran who is the principal figure in the second of *The Four Branches of the Mabinogi*. Bran holds court at several places in Gwynedd, including Aberffraw, the royal seat of North Wales.[33] Gwynedd would be written in French Goinet or Goinnet, and this might easily be misread, as M. Lot pointed out,[34] Gomeret. Thus it appears that Chrétien's text, in spite of its corruptions, retains two local associations found in *The Four Branches,* that of Bran with Gwynedd and that of Gwri with Deheubarth.

To sum up, the hypothesis of a coalescence of Gweir son of Llwch, with Gwri, lord of South Wales, whose career forms the connecting link be-

---

Caerwent is probably the Carnavent where according to Pseudo-Wauchier Arthur held court and which is described as "en la marche de Gales et de la terre de Bretagne," an accurate description of Caerwent if one takes Bretagne to mean England. Cf. J. L. Weston, *Legend of Perceval*, I, 236, and map at end of Vol. 2 of Lloyd's *History*.

[27] Marie de France, *Lais,* ed. Warnke, 3d ed., pp. 123 f., 142, 265; ed. A. Ewert, pp. 82, 94 f., 179. Cf. Brugger in *Zts. f. franz. Sprache u. Lit.,* XLIX (1927), 411–14.

[28] Loth, *op. cit.,* I, 174. Lloyd, *op. cit.,* I, 275, 279.

[29] *Erec,* vss. 2318–28. The phrasing may have been influenced by Wace. M. Pelan, *L'Influence du Brut de Wace* (Paris, 1931), pp. 34 f.

[30] Lloyd, *op. cit.,* I, 278 f. Loth, *op. cit.,* II, 271. J. Rhys, *Celtic Folklore,* II, 503–06.

[31] H. Newstead, *Bran the Blessed in Arthurian Romance,* pp. 155–63; *Romanic Review,* XXXVI (1945), 3–26.

[32] Cf. Chap. LX.   [33] Loth, *op. cit.,* I, 121, 124, 134; II, 368.

[34] F. Lot, *Etude sur le Lancelot,* pp. 147, n. 8. Cf. *infra,* pp. 348 f.

tween *The Four Branches,* explains a mass of facts concerning Erec, including the name of his father, his connection with Destregales, and the parallels between his adventures and those of Guerehes and Gareth, sons of Loth. And the reader will discover that there is much other evidence pointing to this same equation of Gweir and Gwri.[35] The objection that no story told of either of these Welsh figures corresponds to Chrétien's poem is invalid for the reason that we have no love story of Gweir or Gwri and no *enfances* of Erec. Our means of comparison are limited to the family relationships of Gweir and the local associations of Gwri, and these amply justify the conclusion that in the person of Erec are fused the two Welsh figures of Gweir and Gwri.

Since in the preceding paragraphs we have entered on the highly significant subject of the toponymy and local associations of *Erec,* it may be well to consider what the other place names of Britain reveal and how far they confirm the views expressed in Chapter IV. Some of the places I am unable to identify with any certainty—Montrevel, Robais, Peneuris—though I offer some suggestions at the end of this book. Others, if my interpretation is correct, belong to the dreamland which the *conteurs* and scribes created out of Brythonic mythology, such as Avalon, "l'Isle de Voirre," Limors, Brandigan, and Lalut.[36] Tintaguel is, of course, the romantic castle in Cornwall, rendered famous by the Tristan legend and by Wace's *Brut,* but through what channel Chrétien had knowledge of it is difficult to say. The mention of Escoce, that is, Scotland, particularly the part north of the Firth of Forth,[37] betrays by the fact that it is the kingdom of Anguisseaus that Chrétien was here drawing on Wace.[38] Other Scottish place-names seem rather to have been transmitted by those *histriones* who we saw in Chapter III were known to the author of the *Life of St. Kentigern* before 1164 as telling tales of Yvain. These *conteurs* would be responsible for Yvain de Loenel (scribal corruption of Loeneis, i.e. Lothian),[39] Galvoie (Galloway), and Danebroc (Edinburgh).[40] Likewise, probably professional entertainers who catered to the Anglo-Norman nobility furnished the names Carduel (Carlisle) and Evroic (York), for these are Norman, not Welsh, forms.[41] The same is true of Caradigan in Wales.[42] Arthur's knight, Yvain de Cavaliot, bears the name of a contem-

[35] Cf. Chap. XXI.   [36] Cf. Index.
[37] *Mod. Lang. Rev.,* XX (1925), 160. *Mod. Phil.,* XXVI (1928), 7 f.
[38] *Erec,* vs. 1970. *Brut,* ed. Le Roux de Lincy (Rouen, 1836–38), vs. 10519. M. Pelan, *op. cit.,* p. 25.
[39] *Erec,* vs. 1707. *Mod. Phil.,* XXXVIII (1941), 270–86. Cf. *infra,* p. 316.
[40] On Danebroc cf. Chap. XV.
[41] *Zts. f. franz. Sprache u. Lit.,* XIII (1891), 91. Evroic is based on Anglian Eoforwic, not on Welsh Caer Ebrauc.
[42] *Ibid.,* p. 87. *Göttingische Gelehrte Anzeigen,* 1890, 526 ff. Lloyd, *op. cit.,* II, 401, n. 2. *Romania,* XXX (1901), 19.

porary of Chrétien's, Owein of Cyveilioc, a Welsh chieftain and poet, friendly to the Anglo-Normans, who did not come into the limelight until 1160.[43] Both the personal and the place-name, therefore, must have been transmitted by some visitor to England shortly before the composition of *Erec*. Rotelan, too, recognized by scholars as the important fortress of Rudlan in North Wales, was much in the news after 1157,[44] and probably owes its mention by Chrétien to that fact. All this goes to confirm Zimmer's claim that the Breton *conteurs,* traveling about Britain after the Conquest and returning to recite their tales on the Continent, were chiefly responsible for the place-names of French Arthurian romances, since these names are linked to or mingled with such personal names as Yvain and Erec, which are Breton.[45]

Besides these comparatively recent accretions, there may be two instances of much older local associations current among the Welsh. Ban's kingdom of Gomeret and Erec's kingdom of Destregales are derivable, as we have seen, from Bran's connection with Gwynedd and Gwri's connection with South Wales; and these connections are recorded in the eleventh century and may be far more ancient. It is possible, therefore, that their persistence in French romance may be due not to any arbitrary fancies of Breton *conteurs* in the twelfth century but to local Welsh traditions of considerable antiquity. They must have been carried to France, however, by the Breton *conteurs* and so have reached the author of X and Chrétien.

The author of *Geraint* found the place names in X not to his taste. Being familiar with southeastern Wales, he substituted Caerleon for Caradigan, localized the stag hunt in the Forest of Dean, and the sparrowhawk contest at Cardiff; and having identified the hero with the historic Geraint, king of Cornwall, he made him ruler over that land instead of Destregales.

[43] *Mod. Phil.*, XXXVIII, 268. *Dict. Nat. Biog.*, XIV, 1289. Lloyd, *op. cit.*, II, 487–553. Giraldus Cambrensis, *Opera* (Rolls Series), VI, 144 f. *Fouke Fitz Warin,* ed. L. Brandin, p. 26.

[44] Rotelan is the reading of ms. B for vs. 1335. Cf. *Erec,* grosse Ausgabe, vss. 1335, 1882, for variants. On identification of Rotelan with Rudlan cf. Bruce, *Evolution of Arthurian Romance,* II, 71; R. Zenker, *Zur Mabinogionfrage,* p. 87. There was another Rudlan on the River Teivi in Cardiganshire, and it is interesting to observe that Gwri (alias Pryderi) had a palace there, mentioned in the mabinogi of *Math* (Loth, *op. cit.,* I, 179; Lloyd, *op. cit.,* I, 260). One is tempted to think that this is the Rotelan which Erec promised Enide's father, since it is actually in South Wales. But the northern Rudlan was much more celebrated. Cf. Lloyd, *op. cit.,* II, 494 ff.   [45] For Yvain as a Breton form cf. *infra,* p. 273.

Chapter IX

THE AFFRONT TO THE QUEEN

VERSES 67-274

When King Arthur and his knights set out from Caradigan for the chase of the White Stag, the Queen followed after with a damsel, both mounted on palfreys. Erec, the handsome and brave knight, armed only with a sword, overtook them and escorted them to the wood. As the chase had passed out of sight and hearing, the three paused. An armed knight, named Yder son of Nut, accompanied by a damsel and a dwarf, rode past. Guenievre sent her damsel to summon the knight to her, but the dwarf halted the damsel and struck her on the hand with a scourge. The Queen then despatched Erec on the same errand, and he too received a blow from the dwarf which scarred his face. Rather than provoke a quarrel with the armed knight by punishing the dwarf, Erec discreetly rode back to the Queen, telling her that he would follow the knight, obtain arms, avenge, if possible, his disgrace, and return by the third day to Caradigan.

TO UNDERSTAND the original form of this adventure it is important to notice that the departure of Arthur and his household to hunt the White Stag forms the prelude to an attack on the Queen's escort not only in *Erec* and *Geraint* but also in Ulrich von Zatzikhoven's *Lanzelet* and in *Durmart le Gallois*. Ulrich doubtless derived some of his details from Chrétien through the intermediate *Erek* of Hartmann von Aue, but other features, it will appear, must have come from elsewhere. Let me summarize Ulrich's story.[1]

Lanzelet and other knights are approaching Kardigan when they learn bad tidings from a youth. King Arthur and his household had set out to chase the White Stag with intent to maintain the custom of bestowing the kiss on the fairest maiden, a custom established by Utpandragon. The Queen had accompanied them. Valerin, an old lover of hers, surprised the party, wounded Arthur, and carried her off.

The localization near Kardigan, the mention of the "wizen hirz," the corrupt form Utpandragon disclose the generally recognized influence of Hartmann's *Erek* on *Lanzelet*.[2] But the imparting of the news by a youth

---

[1] P. Piper, *Höfische Epik* (Stuttgart, 1892–95), II, 190.
[2] G. Ehrismann, *Geschichte d. deutschen Lit. bis zum Ausgang d. Mittelalters*, II Teil, 2 Bd. (Munich, 1935), p. 6.

and the abduction of the Queen by a former lover are features which occur, not in Hartmann, but in *Durmart le Gallois*.[3]

Durmart was riding near Arthur's court at Glastonbury when he learned sad news from a *valet*. Arthur and his knights had departed the day before for the chase. The Queen, a handmaid, and her unarmed escort, Ydier fiz Nu, had been left far behind. Suddenly an armed knight, Brun de Morois, had ridden up to them, plucked Ganievre from her palfrey and set her before him on his horse. When Ydier had seized the bridle, Brun had struck him down from his palfrey and ridden away. Brun had been a lover of the Queen for several years. Ydier, being unarmed, could do no more than follow after till he reached the castle of the abductor.

Let us first observe that, for the common features, the French author of *Durmart* could not well have drawn on the Swiss *Lanzelet,* nor could *Lanzelet* for chronological reasons have drawn on *Durmart;* [4] there must have been, therefore, a common source in which Arthur's hunting expedition formed a sort of prelude to the abduction of his Queen. Next, it is highly significant that the *Durmart* account of the abduction reflects a tradition which in a more complicated form is represented on the Modena archivolt, dated early in the twelfth century,[5] over fifty years before the composition of *Erec*. It now seems agreed that the sculpture illustrates a Breton *conte* dealing with the abduction of Arthur's Queen, and it parallels the *Durmart* version in depicting Isdernus (Ydier, of course) as wearing no armor and leaning backwards as if about to fall from his horse. Thirdly, this old tradition must have influenced the composer of X, for we find marked correspondences between *Durmart* and *Erec*—Arthur's hunt; the separation of the Queen, her handmaid, and her unarmed escort from the rest of the hunting party; the appearance of an armed knight; the violence done to the unarmed escort; his riding after the attacker.

Much becomes clear if we realize that this incident in *Erec* is a deliberate transformation of a story about the abduction of Guenievre.[6] The hunt of the White Stag was retained as a prelude; the forcible seizure of the Queen by the felon knight has been reduced to a scourging of her handmaid by his dwarf; Erec having superseded Ydier as the Queen's escort, the latter's name was transferred to the felon knight. This arbitrary transference furnishes the answer to a puzzle: When scholars agree that Ydier fiz Nu played a creditable role in early Arthurian tradition and there are signs that he anticipated Lancelot as the favored lover of the Queen, why

[3] *Durmart le Gallois*, ed. E. Stengel (Tübingen, 1873), vss. 4185 ff.

[4] J. D. Bruce (*Evolution of Arthurian Romance*, II, 224) dates *Durmart* in the second quarter of the 13th century, which is too late for it to influence *Lanzelet*.

[5] R. S. and L. H. Loomis, *Arthurian Legends in Medieval Art*, pp. 32–35. *Romanic Review*, XXXII (1941), 22–27.

[6] For studies of this favorite theme cf. G. Schoepperle, *Tristan and Isolt*, II, 528–40; T. P. Cross and W. A. Nitze, *Lancelot and Guenevere*, pp. 20–62.

is he guilty in *Erec* of the grossest discourtesy—to use no harsher term—
to the same exalted lady? In view of the evidence from *Durmart* it is plain
that Ydier was originally the Queen's escort, but the author of X, having
assigned the part to Erec and, needing a name for the unchivalrous knight,
casually and in defiance of tradition, called the latter Yder. But Chrétien
preserves vestiges of the earlier and authentic tradition, listing a "rois
Ydiers" and an "Yders del Mont Dolereus" (doubtless doublets of Yder
fiz Nu) among the honored members of Arthur's court.[7]

The Celtic sources of the abduction of Guenievre and their mythical
significance will be reserved for treatment in Chapters XXXI and XLIV,
below.

Chapter X

THE DWARF, THE FAIR HOSTESS, AND
THE PROVISION OF ARMS

VERSES 125–1080

*While escorting the Queen, Erec met Yder, his damsel, and a dwarf, and
received a blow from the dwarf. Being unarmed, he rode after them with
intent to procure arms and avenge the insult. He came to the dwelling
of a white-haired vavasor, who extended him a hospitable welcome and
promised to lend him new arms and a horse. Erec fell in love with the
vavasor's beautiful daughter, Enide, and asked for her hand in marriage.
This the old man promptly and joyfully granted, and the maiden herself
was glad of her betrothal, knowing that Erec was valiant and courteous.
The next morning she laced on him the new armor provided by her father, had his horse brought, and presented him with shield and lance. In
the contest for the sparrow-hawk, prize of beauty, Erec not only avenged
the insult he had received from Yder but also championed successfully the
beauty of the vavasor's daughter.*

THE DWARF, one may notice, had no share in the abduction story out
of which the insult to Guenievre developed, nor does he appear in
any of the many other forms of that story. Yet he was not a picturesque invention of Chrétien's. Together with the knight and the damsel,
he forms a trio of riders which reappears several times in Arthurian
romance. Later in the same poem this trio is formed by Erec, Enide, and
Guivret, and similar trios meet us in *Le Bel Inconnu, Libeaus Desconus,*

[7] Vss. 313, 1724. On an early tradition of Yder cf. E. Faral, *Légende Arthurienne*, II, 452–57;
Yder, ed. H. Gelzer (Dresden, 1913), p. liv; *PMLA*, XVIII (1903), 496 ff.

Carduino, Malory's Book of Gareth, and, of course, in the familiar opening of Spenser's *Faerie Queene.* It was surely a traditional feature.

The dwarf's striking the hero is paralleled elsewhere in romance; for
instance, in the Tertre Devée episode and Gauvain's visit to King Pelles'
castle in the *Vulgate Lancelot.*[1] A more violent form of the same motif is
provided by the occasions when a hero, unarmed, was attacked and ignominiously overthrown by a dwarf knight, as Carahes was by the Petit
Chevalier in Pseudo-Wauchier's continuation of *Le Conte del Graal.*[2] That
these are all variants of one basic tradition will become apparent later in
our study of Guivret.[3]

Why is the dwarf introduced at this point in *Erec?* The answer lies
in the role which a dwarf with a scourge plays in two romances, for in
both he serves to introduce adventures somewhat resembling those of
Erec—the entertainment by a beautiful hostess, a consequent love affair,
and the provision of arms. The dwarf, then, serves as a link between Erec's
encounter with Yder and his meeting with Enide. The first of these
analogous tales is in Chrétien's *Charrette.*[4]

A mounted dwarf with a scourge induces Lancelot to follow him into an ambush. Lancelot is captured and placed in the custody of the wife of Meleagant's
seneschal. Hearing of a great tournment to be held, he persuades his hostess to
provide him with a horse and arms, and she permits him to attend the tournament, on condition that he return to his prison and grant her his love. Incognito,
he proves the victor in a two-day assembly, and returns faithfully to his prison.
Meanwhile Gauvain has organized a search for him.

As Webster pointed out,[5] this tale has the same origin as the Pluris adventure in Ulrich von Zatzikhoven's *Lanzelet.*[6]

A mounted dwarf with a scourge drives Lanzelet away from the castle of Pluris.
Later the hero returns to the castle, overthrows the hundred knights who guard
it, and is accepted as her spouse by the Queen of Pluris. But she keeps him under
strict watch and takes away his armor. Walwein and three other knights set out
to release him. He finally obtains the Queen's permission to arm and joust with
them, on a promise to return. He breaks his pledge and escapes.

A comparison of these tales with *Erec* shows the following elements
common to two or more of them: (1) A mounted dwarf with a scourge
beats the hero. (2) The hero follows him to the dwelling of a beautiful
lady. (3) The lady falls in love with him, and he becomes her knight.
(4) Though he is in the lady's custody, she permits him to go forth to
a joust on condition that he return. (5) She gives the unarmed hero

[1] H. O. Sommer, *Vulgate Version,* IV, 344; V, 237. Cf. Chap. XXX.
[2] C. Potvin, *Perceval le Gallois,* IV, 36–41.   [3] Cf. Chap. XX.
[4] *Karrenritter,* ed. W. Foerster, vss. 5077–5101, 5187–5256, 5443–6078. For a full discussion
cf. Chap. XLII.
[5] *Harvard Studies and Notes in Philology and Literature,* XVI (1934), 208 f.
[6] P. Piper, *Höfische Epik,* II, 173, 187, 190.

arms. (6) He is victorious in combat. (7) He is the object of a search by Gauvain and others. Of these seven features which seem to have belonged to the underlying plot, *Erec* preserves all but 4 and 7.

Yet though this plot accounts for the appearance of the insolent dwarf in *Erec* and offers a rough parallel to the subsequent events, there are too many unexplained discrepancies. The formula provides no counterpart to the white-haired vavasor, Enide's father, his hospitality, his bestowal of his daughter on Erec, and his offer of arms. On the other hand, Erec is no unwilling captive; he does not obtain Enide's consent to ride out to martial adventure on a promise to return; he is not the object of a search by Gauvain. We may properly suspect some new influence which would account for the marked variations from the formula of the insolent dwarf and the amorous jaileress. Can we not discover a plot which affords a closer parallel to the experiences of Erec in Enide's home?

Such a parallel exists in the Middle English poem, *Libeaus Desconus,* and the parallel extends to the sequel, the so-called sparrow-hawk episode. For reasons which will become apparent later, it is desirable to include in our summary not only the parallel to *Erec* but also the preceding circumstances.[7]

A damsel, Elene, appears at Arthur's court with a dwarf, and demands aid for her mistress. Libeaus volunteers and sets out with the damsel and the dwarf. As they are resting one night in a wood, Libeaus is roused by the dwarf, mounts, arms, and leaving his companions, spies two giants, one clasping a maiden. The maiden cries out for help, and Libeaus drives his spear through the first giant. The second attacks Libeaus, kills his horse, breaks his shield, but is finally decapitated, "as it is found in the French book." The rescued maiden discloses that she is Violette, the daughter of a hoary-headed earl. The giants had beset her father's castle and seized her as she was playing. Libeaus, Violette, Elene, and the dwarf then ride on to the earl's castle. In gratitude the earl offers his daughter in marriage to her rescuer, and though the offer is refused, provides him with new arms and a noble steed. Libeaus departs with Elene and the dwarf. The adventure of the sparrow-hawk follows immediately.

Here, be it observed, are four correspondences with *Erec:* (1) the hero's arrival at the castle of a white-haired nobleman; (2) the nobleman's offer of his daughter in marriage to the hero on slight acquaintance; (3) the nobleman's gift of new arms and a horse to the hero; (4) the sequel of the sparrow-hawk adventure. The most marked variation from *Erec,* the hero's refusal of the maiden, is of course to be explained by the main plot of the English poem, which required that Libeaus accomplish his errand and finally marry Elene's mistress. One might easily jump to the conclusion, since the English poem was composed about 150 years later than *Erec,*[8]

---

[7] *Libeaus Desconus,* ed. M. Kaluza (Leipzig, 1890), vss. 109–276, 589–753.
[8] *Libeaus* is dated 1325–50 by J. E. Wells, *Manual of the Writings in Middle English* (New Haven, 1926), p. 70.

that it is indebted to Chrétien for the four parallels listed; and this conclusion might be fortified by the fact that *Erec* contains at a later point in the narrative [9] an encounter with giants somewhat similar to that in *Libeaus*. Erec and Enide are riding through a forest; they hear the cries of a damsel in distress; Erec leaves his wife to go to the rescue; he learns that two giants have seized the damsel's lover; he overtakes the giants, slays them, and restores the lover to his lady; he then rejoins Enide. It seems a plausible conjecture that, indirectly at least, the author of *Libeaus* derived from *Erec* the common elements: the trio of knight, dwarf, and damsel, the rescue from giants, the hoary host, his lovely daughter, his gift of arms, and the sparrow-hawk adventure.

But this conjecture will not stand scrutiny, and has in fact been rejected by Paris and Schofield.[10] That it does not apply to the sparrow-hawk episode will be shown in the next section. Its application to the other parallels between *Erec* and *Libeaus* is ruled out by the evidence of the two following stories. The first occurs in *Le Livre d'Artus,* a prose romance of the thirteenth century.[11]

A damsel appears at Arthur's court with a dwarf, and demands aid for her mistress. Gauvain volunteers; the damsel sets out on the return journey; Gauvain after some preparation follows, with his squire Eliezer. As he is riding through a forest, he hears the cries of a woman, arms himself, and leaving Eliezer, rides to the rescue. He sees one of the fairest of maidens in the clutches of a giant and two other Saxons standing near by. Gauvain drives his spear through the first giant. The others attack him, only to be slain in their turn. The rescued maiden reveals that she is the daughter of a king, and later it appears that her name is Floree. The giants had seized her while she was under the escort of a forester. Gauvain and Floree ride towards the point where he had left Eliezer. Gauvain asks the maiden whether she has ever loved, and she, not knowing the identity of her rescuer, replies that she is enamored of Gauvain, whom she has never seen. She also informs him that she has a rival for Gauvain's affections, the sister of Guingambresil. Meanwhile Eliezer has killed five Saxons. Accompanied by the squire, Gauvain brings Floree to her father's castle. Here he is warmly welcomed by the king, Alain, but preserves his incognito. He proceeds on his way, performs feats of arms, and accomplishes his mission. On his return to King Alain, Floree seeks him out, "come cele cui amors traveilloit molt forment," and they are united in love. Gauvain has a similar affair with Floree's rival, Guingambresil's sister. For this reason Guingambresil hates Gauvain and conspires with his cousins against him. Eventually Gauvain's two lady-loves are married, though not to Gauvain.

[9] Vss. 4306–4577. Discussed in Chap. XXIII.
[10] *Romania*, XX (1891), 300. *Studies and Notes in Philology and Literature*, IV (1895), 152.
[11] Sommer, *Vulgate Version*, VII, 74–77, 84–90, 108–15, 274–80. For another form of the Floree story cf. Froissart, *Meliador,* ed. A. Longnon (Paris, 1895–99), vss. 4775–5204.

The second story is to be found, suprisingly enough, in *Floovant,* a *chanson de geste* of the last quarter of the twelfth century.[12]

Floovant, followed at a great distance by his squire Richier, is riding through a wood when he hears the cries of a maiden whom three Saracens are attacking. He runs the first through with his spear, cuts down the second, and puts the third to flight. The maiden reveals that she is the daughter of King Flore, and later we learn that her own name is Florete. Florete and Floovant mount and ride toward her father's castle. Meanwhile Richier meets the surviving Saracen and kills him. A series of irrelevant incidents follows until Floovant, accompanied by his squire, brings Florete to her father's castle. Here he is warmly welcomed by the king, but preserves his incognito. He performs prodigies of valor against the Saracens, and a Saracen princess, Maugalie, falls in love with him. On his return to King Flore, Florete seeks him out, barefooted and disheveled, and begs for a kiss. When he refuses, she expresses her jealous hatred of Maugalie. Floovant conquers a Saracen town and captures Maugalie. King Flore then offers him a part of his lands and his daughter, Florete, but receives a noncommittal answer. Her brothers hate Floovant and conspire with the Saracens against him. The rivalry of Florete and Maugalie is continued until the eventual marriage of Florete to Richier and of Maugalie to Floovant.

We are at last in a position to draw a number of important conclusions.

1. *Floovant* and *Le Livre d'Artus* tell two versions of the same story, including not only the rescue of Floree or Florete from the giants and her restoration to her royal father, but also the motifs of the love-rivalry between the two heroines and the hostility of the brother or brothers of one of them toward the hero.

2. Though *Floovant* gives the earlier of the two versions, it cannot be the source of *Le Livre d'Artus,* first, because in general the *chansons de geste* borrowed from the *Matière de Bretagne* rather than vice versa; [13] secondly, because there are in *Le Livre d'Artus* none of the characteristic features of the *chansons de geste* such as one would expect to find if the story of Floree were borrowed from *Floovant;* [14] thirdly, because the story of the rescue from giants in *Erec* and *Geraint* tends to show that this was a stock motif of the *Matière de Bretagne* before the date of *Floovant;* and fourthly, because the amatory relationship between Gauvain and

[12] *Floovant,* ed. S. Andolf (Uppsala, 1941), pp. lxxxix–xcv, 10–70. For other influences on this epic cf. *ibid.,* pp. xlii–li; K. Voretzsch, *Introduction to Study of Old French Literature* (New York, 1931), p. 186.

[13] *Romanic Review,* XXXII (1941), 19–22. *Mod. Phil.,* XXV (1928), 331–54. Le Roux de Lincy, *Livre des légendes* (Paris, 1836), pp. 254–56. L. A. Paton, *Fairy Mythology of Arthurian Romance,* pp. 74–80, 114–17. C. Voretzsch, *Die Composition des Huon von Bordeaux* (Halle, 1900), pp. 123–38. Cf. *infra,* pp. 129 f., 136–38, 315.

[14] A typical feature of the *chansons de geste* which occurs in *Floovant* but has no counterpart in the *Livre d'Artus* is the Saracen princess who falls in love with a French hero and delivers him and his companions from prison. Cf. *PMLA,* XXIX (1914), 341–58; A. Dickson, *Valentine and Orson* (New York, 1929), p. 241.

Floree, presented by *Le Livre d'Artus,* is reflected in the *Matière de Bretagne* in several different ways [15] which show that it was a traditional Arthurian feature and could not have been based on the story of Floovant and Florete.

3. Therefore the tale of the rescue of Floree from the giants in the forest, her restoration to her father, and his offer of Floree to Gauvain in marriage (which has been suppressed in the *Livre d'Artus* but preserved in *Floovant*) must have antedated *Floovant;* and since it probably inspired the giants episode in *Erec* and *Geraint,* may well have antedated their common source X.

4. This tale of Floree must have been the ultimate source of the parallel incidents in *Libeaus Desconus,* not only because of this parallelism but also because her name would account for the name of her counterpart in *Libeaus,* Violette, and the name of her counterpart in *Le Bel Inconnu,* Clarie. The floral connotation of Floree suggested Violette; scribal corruption produced Clarie.

This ancient tale, it seems certain, bequeathed to *Libeaus Desconus* the following features: the rescue of Violette from the giants, her restoration to her father, his offer of Violette to Gauvain's son on slight acquaintance, and his gift of arms. In *Libeaus* this tale leads up to the sparrow-hawk episode; likewise in *Erec* the latter part of the same tale introduces the sparrow-hawk episode. Since *Erec* cannot be the source of this combination in *Libeaus,* it seems probable that the combination already existed before X was composed, and therefore furnished to the author of X his materials for Erec's entertainment by the white-haired vavasor, the sudden mutual love of Erec and Enide, the betrothal sanctioned by her father, the provision of arms, the offer of a steed, and the sparrow-hawk episode.

The author of X displayed no small ingenuity when he used the traditional dwarf with the whip as a means of connecting his modification of the abduction of Guenievre with the traditional visit to the venerable noble and his lovely daughter, and its sequel, the sparrow-hawk episode. An episode in which, as we have seen, the hero traditionally lacked weapons to protect Guenievre is thus neatly attached to an episode in which the hero traditionally obtained weapons from a white-haired, noble host, and thus he is enabled both to avenge the insult to the Queen and to win a beautiful bride. By skillful changes, omissions, and dovetailing, the author of X succeeded in the difficult task of making a coherent, well-motivated narrative out of four distinct patterns—the abduction of Guenievre, the insolent dwarf, the venerable host and his beautiful daughter, and the sparrow-hawk contest. He was an artist of a high order.

Was any of this material Celtic in origin? That the dwarf was derived

15 J. L. Weston, *Legend of Gawain* (London, 1897), p. 46. *Zts. f. franz. Sprache u. Lit.,* XVIII (1895), 50, n. 2 R. S. Loomis, *Celtic Myth,* pp. 22, 228.

from the mythology of Wales will become apparent when we come to consider Guivret in Chapter XX. The influence of the famous Irish love story of Cuchulainn and Blathnat on Arthurian romance will be demonstrated several times in these pages,[16] and is probably responsible for the liaison between Gauvain and Floree, since Gauvain is frequently the counterpart of Cuchulainn, as in *Gawain and the Green Knight*,[17] and since Floree probably owes her name to Blathnat, "Little Flower." [18] But nothing closely resembling the deliverance of Floree from the giants and her restoration to her father can I discover anywhere in early Irish or Welsh literature. Quite possibly this is no peculiarly Celtic theme, but was a *lieu commun* of story-tellers, which was picked up by the Breton *conteurs* and grafted upon the Arthurian cycle. A form of it seems to be preserved in Geoffrey of Monmouth's story of the giant of Mont St. Michel.[19] As for the sparrow-hawk adventure, I shall endeavor to show in the next chapter that it is a Breton development of Welsh material.

Chapter XI

THE SPARROW-HAWK ADVENTURE

VERSES 393–1080

When Erec took lodging with the hospitable vavasor, the latter's exquisitely beautiful daughter, Enide, appeared and took charge of the knight's horse. After the evening repast the vavasor informed his guest that on the morrow there was to be an award of a sparrow hawk. Whoever wished to gain it must have a mistress fair, prudent, and without coarseness. If he wished to claim for her the title of fairest, she must step forward and lift the bird from its silver perch. Erec also learned that Yder had twice in successive years claimed the sparrow-hawk for his mistress without challenge, and that probably he would be successful in doing so once more. Erec asked the vavasor for the privilege of championing Enide's claim to the prize as his betrothed, and the old man agreed. In the presence of the count who ruled the town and a great multitude Erec disputed the right of Yder's mistress to the sparrow-hawk and claimed that Enide was the fairest. Thereupon a prolonged fight ensued and Erec came out the victor. When he rode away with his affianced bride to Arthur's court, she played with the prize bird.

[16] Cf. Chaps. XXIX, XXX, XXXVI, LXII.
[17] Weston, *op. cit.*, pp. 17, 95. *PMLA*, XLVIII (1933), 1002–27.
[18] *Journ. of Engl. and Germ. Phil.*, XLII (1943), 156–69.
[19] E. Faral, *La Légende arthurienne*, III, 254–57. Faral (*ibid.*, II, 286–89) inclines to the view that Geoffrey did not invent the story, "mais l'a recueillie des lèvres ou du livre d'un autre."

THOUGH *Libeaus, Erec,* and *Geraint* agree in prefixing to the adventure of the hawk or falcon the introductory matter of the venerable host, his fair daughter, and the gift of arms, yet there are nine analogues of the hawk adventure which have no such introduction. These analogues are found in Andreas Capellanus' *De Amore,* the Italian *cantare, Bruto di Brettagna* (based directly on Andreas), the Austrian *Wigalois,* the French *Le Bel Inconnu, Durmart le Gallois, Le Chevalier du Papegau, Meraugis de Portlesguez, Vulgate Lancelot,* and the English Book of Gareth by Malory.[1] No thorough study of the relationships of these twelve variants has been made,[2] and none will be attempted in this book, but we shall try to discover what we can as to their traditional basis.

First, it is worth observing that a number of facts point toward Morgain la Fée as the heroine of the adventure. In Malory's Book of Gareth [3] Dame Lyones, who dwells with Gryngamor in the Isle of Avylyon and is therefore to be identified with Morgain, whose *ami,* according to *Erec,* was Guigamor or Guingomar, lord of Avalon,[4] held a tourney of which she herself was to be the prize if the victor was a bachelor; if a wedded man, his wife was to receive a gerfalcon. Gareth by his prowess won the lady. In *Meraugis* the heroine of the sparrow-hawk contest was the daughter of the King of Cavalon,[5] and one remembers that Morgain was the daughter "Regis Avallonis." [6] In *Le Chevalier du Papegau* the damsel whose beauty is vindicated by the award of the bird was the sister of Morgaine la Fée.[7] In *Le Bel Inconnu* the winner of the sparrow hawk was the daughter of a king and the sister of King Agolans, and her name was Margerie.[8] It seems clear, in the light of the other indications, that these un-Arthurian names have been substituted for Avalon and Morgain. Thus four widely differing analogues of the sparrow-hawk episode in *Erec* concur in hinting that Morgain was the original heroine.

[1] Andreas Capellanus, *De Amore,* ed. A. Pagès, pp. 152 f., 157–61. *Fiore di leggende,* ed. E. Levi (Bari, 1914), pp. 201–12. Wirnt von Gravenberc, *Wigalois,* ed. J. M. N. Kapteyn (Bonn, 1926), vss. 2349–3285. Renaud de Beaujeu, *Le Bel Inconnu,* ed. G. P. Williams (Paris, 1929), vss. 1497–1842. *Durmart le Gallois,* ed. E. Stengel, vss. 2010–768. *Chevalier du Papegau,* ed. F. Heuckenkamp (Halle, 1896), pp. 5–12. Raoul de Houdenc, *Meraugis de Portlesguez,* ed. M. Friedwagner (Halle, 1897), vss. 157–394. H. O. Sommer, *Vulgate Version,* IV, 335–38. Malory, *Morte d'Arthur,* Bk. VII, chap. 26. There are, besides, a number of translations of Andreas which include the hawk story. Cf. *Art of Courtly Love,* trans. and ed. J. J. Parry (New York, 1941), pp. 213–15.

[2] The following may be consulted: W. H. Schofield, *Studies on the Libeaus Desconus* (Boston, 1895), pp. 25–32, 164–70; *Giornale storico della letteratura italiana,* Supplemento 16 (1914), p. 153; *Chevalier du Papegau,* pp. xxxiii–xxxix; *Zts. f. franz. Sprache u. Lit.,* XLIV (1916–17), 141–43; H. Sparnaay, *Hartmann von Aue, Studien zu einer Biographie,* I, 70–72.

[3] Malory, Bk. VII, chap. 26.

[4] *Erec,* vss. 1954–57. For further evidence on the identity of Lyones and Morgain cf. Chaps. XV, XXXVI, LI, LXXII.

[5] *Meraugis,* vss. 37–43.

[6] L. A. Paton, *Fairy Mythology,* p. 46.

[7] *Chevalier du Papegau,* p. 11.

[8] *Bel Inconnu,* vss. 1825–35.

This suggestion is corroborated in still a different way by the version of Andreas Capellanus,[9] which may be dated about 1185.[10]

A Briton knight met in a forest a lone damsel sitting on a caparisoned steed. She was most beautiful and had preternatural knowledge of his errand, for she informed him that his lady had imposed as a condition of her favor that he should win a hawk in Arthur's palace and prove in combat that he enjoyed the love of a more beautiful damsel than did any other knight. He agreed to undertake the adventure if the lone damsel would allow him to fulfill the condition by claiming the enjoyment of her love. She consented to grant him his desire, gave him the kiss of love, and bestowed on him her own steed, declaring that it would take him to his destination. After surmounting various trials of his prowess, the Briton knight won the hawk and returned to find the damsel at the same place. She rejoiced over his victory, gave him thirteen kisses, and dismissed him with the promise that as often as he sought her alone in that place, she would always be with him.

Certain inferences seem to be justified. The damsel of wondrous beauty, "met in forest wide," possessed of preternatural knowledge, was surely a fay. There are strong hints that she was more to the hero than merely a helpful adviser. Though not explicitly his mistress, she allowed him to claim the enjoyment of her love, declared that he would obtain from her whatever he desired, gave him the kiss of love, promised him, seductively, her company alone in the forest, and moreover addressed him as "carissime." [11] Andreas has made a perfunctory effort to disguise a passionate relationship between the knight and the fay because, otherwise, he would involve the hero in a double and a diabolic love. For if the knight really enjoyed the embrace of the fay as well as aspiring to the love of another lady, he would violate one of the laws which he found inscribed in Arthur's palace, dictated by the King of Love himself: "No one can be bound by a double love." [12] Moreover, in clerical eyes a faery mistress could be no other than a devil.[13] But in spite of these motives for obfuscation, Andreas has left it pretty clear that the solitary fay in whose name the Briton knight won the hawk was his paramour and the real heroine of the story.

Light is shed on her identity by the parallel in the Middle English lai of *Sir Launfal*.[14] Launfal comes on the daughter of the King of Faerye in a forest. She too grants him her love, bestows on him her own horse, and promises that if he wishes her company at any time, he need only go to a secluded place and she would come to him. Though it would seem

[9] *De Amore*, ed. Pagès, pp. 152 f., 157–61. [10] *Speculum*, XIII (1938), 304–08.
[11] *De Amore*, p. 159. [12] *Idem*.
[13] J. A. MacCulloch, *Medieval Faith and Fable* (London, 1932), Chap. III.
[14] *Middle English Metrical Romances*, ed. W. H. French, C. B. Hale (New York, 1930), pp. 352–59. This parallel has been noted by Sparnaay, *op. cit.*, I, 70 f.

that her prohibition to speak of her beauty stood in direct contradiction to the willingness of Andreas' fay to permit such a boast, the English poet has retained a trace of the tradition followed by Andreas. For Launfal was explicitly challenged to combat by Sir Valentyne "fore love of hys [Launfal's] lemman, Yf sche be any gantyle woman, Courteys, fre, other hende." [15] Launfal's acceptance of this challenge meant, of course, that he asserted his possession of such a paramour. Even on this point, therefore, the English lai and Andreas' tale are not completely divergent; both faery mistresses permitted public acknowledgment of their love. The role of Launfal's mistress thus parallels in certain striking ways that of Andreas' fay. Now though the former is said to have her home in the "jolyf ile, Olyroun," Kittredge proved that Olyroun is a substitution for Avalon; [16] all the variant versions, Marie de France's *Lanval, Sir Landeval,* and *Sir Lambewell,* support Avalon against Olyroun. And though *Sir Launfal* puts us off the track by naming the faery mistress Tryamour—a name for which there is no support elsewhere—we know that the most famous lady of Avalon, the daughter of King Avallo, was Morgain la Fée. Thus we are led to surmise that Launfal's mistress and her counterpart in Andreas' book, the faery heroine of the hawk adventure, were originally Morgain.

Both, be it remembered, gave their own steeds to their lovers, and these steeds proved their excellence in combat. This is a highly significant matter, for the gift of a remarkable horse to her lover or protégé was one of the characteristic acts of Morgain. In the *Roman de Troie,*[17] which antedates *Erec* by several years at least, Benoit testifies that Morgain la Fée loved Hector and presented him with "the very fairest horse on which a mortal man ever mounted, the best, the swiftest, the strongest, and the largest; so fair a creature was never born." In *Floriant et Florete* Morgain calls herself the love and the mistress (*amie et drue*) of her foster son, the hero, and bestows on him the handsomest destrier in the world.[18] In *Lanzelet* it is an anonymous Queen of Meydelant who brings up the hero and gives him arms and a fleet, spirited horse,[19] but her island home of maidens reveals such a likeness to the island home of Morgen and her eight sisters

---

[15] *Middle English Metrical Romances,* p. 363.

[16] *American Journal of Philology,* X (1889), 13 f.

[17] Benoit de Ste.-Maure, *Troie,* ed. L. Constans (Paris, 1904), I, vss. 8023–33. Cf. *Speculum,* XX (1945), 183–87.

[18] Ed. Harry F. Williams (Ann Arbor, London, 1947), vss. 786 f., 2523 f. This is not the only instance where Morgain or some other fay appears both as a foster mother and a mistress of the hero. Cf. Paton, *op. cit.,* p. 194n.; *Fiore di leggende,* ed. E. Levi, pp. 63–72. Note also the very amorous interest which the Dame du Lac takes in her foster son Lancelot. Cf. Sommer, *Vulgate Version,* III, 86–90. In *Diu Krone* (ed. Scholl [Stuttgart, 1852], vss. 24517–20) Keii implies that the Lady of the Sea was Lanzelet's mistress (as well as his foster mother).

[19] P. Piper, *Höfische Epik,* II, 171 f.

in the *Vita Merlini*[20] that there can be little doubt the Queen of Mey-delant is the famous fay. Her shining castle of gold and her role seem to identify her, moreover, with the chief of the nine sorceresses of the Shining or Transparent Castle, Caer Loyw, who instructs the youthful Peredur in chivalry and on his departure equips him with arms and a steed.[21] Thus, not only by the similarity of their roles to that of Morgain in *Floriant and Florete,* but also by their relation to the nine sisters[22] of the *Vita Merlini,* the Queen of Meydelant and the chief sorceress of the Shining Castle betray their identity and demonstrate how consistently Morgain was reputed to have given her favorites a marvelous horse. And in our study of *Le Chevalier de la Charrette* we shall discover more evidence to the same effect. Thus by another route we arrive at the conclusion that the heroine of the sparrow-hawk adventure was a fay, the most celebrated of all. It was no coincidence that Malory's Book of Gareth, *Meraugis, Le Chevalier du Papegau,* and *Le Bel Inconnu* pointed in the same direction. Indirectly but with singular unanimity the prototype of Enide in this episode is identified as Morgain.

[20] Geoffrey of Monmouth, *Vita Merlini,* ed. J. J. Parry, *University of Illinois Studies in Lang. and Lit.,* X (1925), vss. 908 ff. E. Faral, *Légende arthurienne,* III, 334. Both are isles of maidens; both are marvelously fertile; in both one may live for over a hundred years.

[21] Loth, *Mabinogion,* 2d ed., II, 75 f. Though Loth interpreted Kaer Loyw as Gloucester, that being an ancient and still common interpretation, yet actually it means "shining or transparent fortress." *Loyw* is a regularly lenated form of the adjective *gloyw,* "shining," after a feminine noun. Its attachment to Gloucester seems to be an instance of the tendency to pin mythical names on to real places because of fanciful etymologies. Thus the mythical *Caer Wydyr,* "Fortress of Glass," mentioned in one of the earliest Welsh Arthurian texts, was identified with Glastonbury. Cf. *PMLA,* LVI (1941), 891, 926. Likewise, the mythical *Gwlad yr Haf,* "Land of Summer," was identified with Somerset. Cf. *Journ. of Eng. and Germ. Phil.,* XLII (1943), 176, n. 92. The same mistaken ingenuity went into the identification of Kaer Loyw with Gloucester. As early as the time of Nennius (a. 800), the name of the city, called by the Romans Glevum, had been converted by the Welsh into Cair Glovi, supposedly founded by an imaginary Glovus or Gloiu. This latter form seems the more authentic since the Nennius passage reproduced the Welsh of ms. Jesus College 20: "Gloyw gwalltir, y gwr hwnnw awnaeth ar ymyl Hafren tref ac oe enw y gelwir y Gaer loew," "Gloyw of the Long Hair; that man built on the bank of the Severn a city, and from his name it is called the Fortress of Gloew." The mythical "Shining Fortress" had therefore been identified with Gloucester as early as 800 merely because of the similarity in sound between Caer (G)loyw and Caer Gloui. On this subject cf. *Nennius et l'Historia Brittonum,* ed. F. Lot, I, 189, n. 3; *Bulletin of the Board of Celtic Studies,* XI (1941), 44; E. Faral, *Légende ar-thurienne,* II, 160; III, 140; *Cymmrodor,* XLII (1930), 137–40; and Chap. LXXVIII. In *Kulhwch* (c. 1100) Kaer Loyw is understood as Gloucester since it lies on a salmon river. Cf. Loth, *op. cit.,* I, 326–28. But in *Peredur* it evidently retained its original meaning since it was the home of the sorceress who trained Peredur and presented him with arms and a horse, whereas the Queen of Meydelant, who did the same for Lanzelet, lived in a castle all of gold, like a star. Cf. Ulrich von Zatzikhoven, *Lanzelet,* ed. K. A. Hahn (Frankfurt, 1845), vss. 224 f.; *Speculum,* XX, 188, n. 2.

[22] For groups of nine fays in Celtic mythology cf. *Medieval Studies in Memory of G. Schoep-perle Loomis* (New York, Paris, 1927), p. 275; *Studies and Notes in Philology and Lit.,* VIII (1903), 97n.; W. G. Wood-Martin, *Traces of the Elder Faiths of Ireland* (London, 1902), I, 135; *PMLA,* LVI (1941), 890, 907.

Two versions of the episode agree with Andreas by introducing the heroine as a solitary damsel on horseback whom the hero encounters by chance, and one of them furnishes interesting details as to her steed. In both *Le Bel Inconnu* and *Wigalois*,[23] as in Andreas' book, the hero meets a most beautiful rider, who informs him of the sparrow-hawk (or parrot) adventure and whose beauty he undertakes to champion in combat. Though in neither of these poems does the damsel present her horse at once to the hero, yet in *Wigalois* there is a second horse, one of the prizes of the contest, and this she bestows on the hero after he has won it for her.[24] There has evidently been a duplication of the damsel's steed, for in no other version of the episode is a horse mentioned, together with a bird, as a prize of the contest, and both the horses in *Wigalois* have manes as red as blood or cinnabar.[25] The prize horse is furthermore described as white as a swan and has one red ear—very significant features, as we shall presently see. A "Saxon" with red beard and hair, who wears red armor in combat, has wrongfully seized the horse and the popinjay and has given them to his ladylove, so that Wigalois is obliged to fight him to win back the prizes for the beautiful rider. And she, as we have just noted, gives the strangely colored animal on parting to Wigalois.

It seems fairly certain that the prize horse in *Wigalois* owes its existence to a mistaken duplication of the beautiful rider's own horse, and therefore the Austrian romance preserves in muddled form the same motif as that found in Andreas' work and in *Bruto*—the fay's gift of a steed to the hero. That this motif was Celtic is disclosed by the peculiar coloring of the prize horse, its white body, red mane, and red ear; for we meet with animals similarly colored not only in the *Matière de Bretagne* but also in Welsh and Irish texts. In *Owain* Kynon was provided, on leaving the Hospitable Host, with a palfrey whose mane was bright red.[26] In the Breton *Lai de l'Espine* a knight in red arms appeared regularly on St. John's eve at a ford, mounted on a white steed with red ears.[27] In *Partonopeus de Blois,* a romance full of borrowings from the *Matière de Bretagne,* the hero received from a lady "a white horse whose ear was the color of blood." [28] In *Tristan als Mönch* the hero received from an enamored queen a steed with red ears, and Gawan's horse in Wolfram's *Parzival* had ears of the same hue.[29] The eleventh-century Welsh mabinogi of *Pwyll* describes the hounds of Annwn, the Other World, as white with

[23] *Bel Inconnu,* vss. 1525–1644. *Wigalois,* vss. 2356–607.
[24] *Wigalois,* vss. 3234–54.
[25] Vss. 2400–2402, 2543–46. On other strangely colored horses cf. Chaps. XX, XXII.
[26] Loth, *Mabinogion,* 2d ed., II, 15.
[27] *Zts. f. rom. Phil.,* XVII (1893), pp. 249 f. Cf. *infra,* p. 131.
[28] *Partonopeus de Blois,* ed. G.-A. Crapelet (Paris, 1834), II, vss. 7709 f. *PMLA,* LXI (1946), 938 f.
[29] *Sitzungsberichte K. B. Akad. Wissenschaften zu München,* phil.-hist. Klasse, 1895, pp. 337 f. Wolfram, *Parzival,* 339, 29.

red ears.[30] In the Irish *Lay of Oisin in the Land of Youth* a red-eared, white hound is seen pursuing a fawn over the waves.[31] Two Irish sagas mention cows similarly colored,[32] and there is no doubt of their unearthly nature. We may rest assured, then, that the horse which Wigalois won for the beautiful rider and which she presented to him at parting was a creature from the Celtic faery world.

This evidence accords with our earlier conclusion that the original heroine of the sparrow-hawk adventure was Morgain la Fée, who of all the figures of Arthurian romance most patently belongs to Celtic mythology, and is referred to as *goddes, gotinne, dea, déesse,* and *dwywes.*[33] For some of her traits and roles, as Miss Paton and Zenker have demonstrated,[34] she was indebted to the Irish goddess Morrigan. Even more directly and profoundly was she indebted to the Welsh goddess Modron, her immediate prototype. The identity of Morgain and Modron is proved by the fact that Morgain was the daughter of Avallo or Avaloc and the mother of Ivain by the mortal, King Urien, whereas Modron was the daughter of Avallach and the mother of Owein by the mortal, King Urien.[35] Celtic mythologists are agreed that the name Modron is derived from Matrŏna, a goddess whose worship was widespread among the Continental Celts and who gave her name to the River Marne.[36] Modron, according to *Kulhwch and Olwen,* was also the mother of Mabon, the Apollo Maponos of Romano-British inscriptions,[37] and this fact explains why the Queen of Meydelant in *Lanzelet,* whom we have identified with Morgain, was the mother of Mabuz[38]—a name which is easily recogniz-

---

[30] J. Loth, *Mabinogion,* 2d ed., I, 84. Cf. M. Trevelyan, *Folklore and Folk-Stories of Wales* (London, 1909), p. 47.

[31] Micheal Cuimin, *Lay of Oisin on the Land of Youth,* ed. John O'Daly (Dublin, n.d.), p. 17. P. W. Joyce, *Old Celtic Romances* (Dublin, 1920), pp. 389, 392 f.

[32] R. Thurneysen, *Irische Helden- u. Königsage,* pp. 286, 311. A. H. Leahy, *Heroic Romances of Ireland* (London, 1906), II, 138. Cf. also K. Meyer, A. Nutt, *Voyage of Bran* (London, 1895), I, 71, 75.

[33] Loomis, *Celtic Myth,* p. 192. *PMLA,* LVI, 907. Hartmann von Aue, *Erek,* vs. 5161. *Roman van Lancelot,* ed. W. J. A. Jonckbloet, II, p. lxix.

[34] Paton, *Fairy Mythology,* pp. 148–66. *Zts. f. franz. Sprache u. Lit.,* XLVIII (1925–26), 82–92.

[35] On the relationships of Morgain cf. E. K. Chambers, *Arthur of Britain,* pp. 257, 266; Paton, *Fairy Mythology,* p. 46; *Huth Merlin,* ed. G. Paris and J. Ulrich, I, 201 f. On relationships of Modron, cf. Loth, *Mabinogion,* 2d ed., II, 284; *Aberystwyth Studies,* IV (1922), 105. Cf. also *Romanic Review,* XXIX (1938), 176 f.

[36] Hastings, *Encyclopedia of Religion and Ethics,* III, 292. J. Rhys, *Hibbert Lectures,* 2d ed. (London, 1892), pp. 28 f. T. Gwynn Jones, *Welsh Folklore* (London, 1930), p. 17. *Cymmrodor,* XLII (1930), 140. *Celtic Review,* III (1906), 48. J. A. MacCulloch, *Religion of the Ancient Celts* (Edinburgh, 1911), p. 123. *Cambridge Medieval History,* II, 477. On Matrona, cf. *infra,* p. 269.

[37] J. A. MacCulloch, *Religion of Ancient Celts,* p. 123. *Romania,* XXV (1896), 276, 284. S. Baring-Gould, J. Fisher, *Lives of the British Saints* (London, 1911), III, 392. *Cymmrodor,* XXVIII (1918), 198 f.; XLII (1931), 140. E. Hübner, *Inscriptiones Britanniae Latinae* (Berlin, 1873), nos. 218, 1345.   [38] Piper, *Höfische Epik,* II, 181.

able as a Norman or Anglo-Norman nominative form, based on Mabon. As we proceed in our investigation of other episodes in Chrétien's romances, we shall meet additional proofs of Morgain's intimate connection with Brythonic mythology and its developments in Welsh and Breton faery lore.

Since the faery heroine of the sparrow-hawk story was identified at an early stage with Morgain, and since the horses with which she is connected in *Wigalois* reveal their Celtic origin, is there reason to believe that the story itself goes back to Wales? No Welsh text independent of French influence connects a hawk or falcon with fays or Otherworld adventures. But there is evidence that the Bretons, at least, made this association. Lanval's mistress from Avalon, whom we have recognized as Morgain, and Desiré's faery mistress in another Breton lai both rode into a royal court to claim their lovers, carrying on their fists a sparrow hawk.[39] In the lai *Sir Orfeo* the ladies of a faery cavalcade bore each a falcon.[40] The motif persists in the romances. The mistress of Ille d'Or, in *Le Bel Inconnu,* was clearly a supernatural personage, and Guinglain met her returning from sport, carrying a sparrow-hawk and attended by a cavalcade of dames, knights, and maidens bearing various birds of prey.[41] In the Swiss *Lanzelet* the daughter of the enchanter Malduc, a maiden so wise that only Femurgan surpassed her, rode out from her father's castle with a sparrow hawk on her fist.[42] In *Diu Krone* a damsel who rescued Gawein from drowning carried the same bird, and—*nota bene*—was followed by a hound, half red, half white.[43] These facts, combined with the six versions of the sparrow-hawk adventure which point to Morgain as the traditional heroine, indicate that among the Bretons at least there was a strong association between "the hardy sperhauk, the quayles foo," and the equestrian fays, particularly Morgain.

We have testimony, moreover, to the existence of legends concerning castles of sparrow hawks where unearthly ladies dwelt, and though these legends are not localized in Celtic lands, there is reason to suspect Breton influence, perhaps Breton origin. Gervase of Tilbury, early in the thirteenth

---

[39] Marie de France, *Lanval*, vs. 579. *Lays of Desiré, Graelent, and Melion,* ed. E. M. Grimes (New York, 1928), p. 72. The English *Sir Launfal* substitutes a gerfalcon. French and Hale, *Middle English Metrical Romances*, p. 377.

[40] Vs. 305. *Middle English Metrical Romances,* p. 332.

[41] Renaud de Beaujeu, *Le Bel Inconnu,* ed. G. P. Williams (1929), vss. 3936–41, 3993 f.

[42] Piper, *op. cit.,* II, 192.

[43] Heinrich von dem Türlin, *Crone,* ed. Scholl, vss. 14458–64. There is probably some connection between this fay equipped for falconry and the Damoiselle Cacheresse. Cf. L. A. Paton, *Fairy Mythology,* pp. 228–47; *PMLA,* XLV (1930), 438–40. On the fay's rescue of Gawain from drowning cf. similar incidents in *Graelent* and *Il Bel Gherardino. Lays of Desiré* etc., ed. Grimes, pp. 99 f. *Fiore di leggende,* ed. E. Levi, pp. 18 f. Other solitary equestrian ladies appear in Arthurian romance carrying sparrow-hawks. Cf. Sommer, *Vulgate Version,* V, 212, 404. Raoul de Houdenc, *Vengeance Raguidel,* ed. M. Friedwagner (Halle, 1909), vss. 3783–87.

century, tells of a "castrum de Esperver" in the kingdom of Arles, whose mistress, when forced to stay for the consecration of the Host, flew off through the air—a sure proof of her unearthly nature [44] and a point of resemblance to Morgain and her sisters who could fly with wings. Perhaps related to this tale is that found in two versions of the Melusine legend, a pseudo-historical romance about the origins of the house of Lusignan.[45] I give a summary of the fuller version, composed by Jean d'Arras between 1387 and 1394, which contains several typical Arthurian details.[46]

A young king of Armenia hears of an enchanted castle in that country where strange adventures await anyone who arrives there two days before St. John's day and keeps vigil over a sparrow-hawk for three days and nights. He enters the castle on the appropriate date and is welcomed by a venerable man in white. Within he finds the sparrow-hawk on its perch and a glove near by. The old man explains that if the adventurous knight does not fall asleep, the lady of the castle will appear on the fourth day and grant him whatever he desires, except her own person, but that if he sleeps, he will have to stay in attendance on the lady the rest of his life, in ease and enjoyment. The king, left alone, partakes sparingly of the noble foods and drinks set out on a table. Then he studies the mural paintings, of which there are many. He remains awake, and at sunrise of the fourth day a lovely lady enters and asks him to name his desire. When he demands the lady herself in marriage, she angrily reveals that she is Melior, his aunt, sister of the fay Melusine, and therefore within the forbidden degrees of consanguinity. When the king attempts to seize her, she vanishes. He is then beaten by an invisible agency and expelled from the castle.

The localization of the castle in Armenia is due in all probability to the fact that a scion of the house of Lusignan became king of Little Armenia (ancient Cilicia) in 1342, and the *Melusine* romance is consecrated to the fortunes of that family. The name of the faery lady, Melior, was perhaps purloined from the faery heroine of the twelfth-century romance, *Partono-*

[44] Gervase of Tilbury, *Otia Imperialia*, ed. F. Liebrecht (Hannover, 1856), pp. 26, 126. Cf. *Gesta Romanorum*, trans. C. Swan, tale 160; Walter Map, *De Nugis Curialium*, Dist. IV, cap. 9; H. Weber, *Metrical Romances* (Edinburgh, 1810), II, 5-12; Wolfram von Eschenbach, *Parzival*, trans. W. Hertz, 7th ed. (1927), pp. 474 f.
[45] The best study of the history of the Melusine legend is that of L. Hoffrichter, *Die ältesten französischen Bearbeitungen der Melusinensage, Romanistische Arbeiten*, XII (1928). He seems to be in error when he assumes that the story of the sparrow-hawk castle was taken from Mandeville's *Travels* into the common source of Jean d'Arras and Couldrette (p. 33). On the contrary, it was the connection of the Lusignan family with Armenia which led to the localization of the castle there. Hoffrichter's dating of the common source of the Melusine romances should therefore be changed to a *terminus a quo* of 1342, the date when Guy de Lusignan became King of Armenia, and a *terminus ad quem* of 1371, the latest possible date for the *Travels*. For bibliography of Melusine legend cf. A. Van Gennep, *Manuel de folklore français* (Paris, 1938), IV, 651.
[46] Jehan d'Arras, *Melusine* (Paris, 1854), pp. 412-19. For the other version, dated 1401, cf. Couldrette, *Mellusine*, ed. F. Michel (Niort, 1854), vss. 5765-6138. A Middle English trans. of Jehan was edited by A. K. Donald for the E.E.T.S. (London, 1895), and the adventure is related on pp. 363-68.

peus de Blois. But eight details of the narrative betray Breton or Arthurian influence. The limitation of the adventure at the bespelled castle to the period before St. John's Day seems to reflect the same tradition as the annual encounter on St. John's Eve at the Perilous Ford, described in *Le Lai de l'Espine.*[47] The venerable man recalls a number of similar figures met by the hero in the castles of Arthurian romance.[48] The table spread with delicacies in the empty hall of a castle is another commonplace feature.[49] The sparrow hawk on its perch, together with a glove, reminds us, first, of Andreas Capellanus' account of the hawk on its perch in the splendid palace of Arthur, accessible only to one who has the hawk's gauntlet, and, secondly, of a sparrow hawk's perch in the magnificent castle of the faery mistress of Ille d'Or, as described in *Le Bel Inconnu.*[50] The vigil test by which a knight finally succeeds in winning a lady where others had failed occurs in the Breton lai of *Doon,* and is localized in "le chastel as puceles." [51] The mural paintings in Melior's castle are paralleled in the palace of Arthur and Morgain la Fée, as described by Guillem Torella and Jean d'Outremeuse.[52] The knights constrained to dwell the rest of their lives in Melior's castle, attending on her and lacking no delights, have their counterparts in the victims of Morgain's enchantments.[53] The ejection of the hero by invisible agency from the bespelled castle recalls Gauvain's experience in the perilous palace of Corbenic.[54] Moreover, earlier in the history of Melusine we learn that Melior and her sister fays had been brought up in the isle of Avalon. Whoever it was who composed the original romance of Melusine was steeped in the Arthurian tradition. Did he follow, so far as the faery elements were concerned, some authentic Breton *conte,* or did he make a pastiche from various authentic traditions? This question we shall probably have to postpone forever, but at least there can be no doubt that the conception of

[47] *Zeits. f. rom. Phil.,* XVII (1893), 246–54. For uncanny observances on St. John's Eve, cf. P. Sébillot, *Paganisme contemporaine chez les peuples celto-latins* (Paris, 1908), Index s.v. *Jean;* E. Hull, *Folklore of the British Isles* (London, 1928), Index s.v. *Midsummer Eve;* W. C. Hazlitt, *Faiths and Folklore* (London, 1905), II, 346–50, 410. Cf. *infra,* p. 276.
[48] E.g. Eurain, King of Brandigan, who explains the perils of the Joie de la Cort to Erec.
[49] Cf. *infra,* p. 229.
[50] Andreas Capellanus, *De Amore,* ed. Pagès, pp. 157 f. Renaud de Beaujeu, *op. cit.,* vss. 4582–86, 4868, 4904. On perch for hawks cf. T. Wright, *Volume of Vocabularies* (1857), I, 100.
[51] *Romania,* VIII (1879), 61 f. The sleep which overcomes Doon is paralleled in *Jaufré,* vss. 3059–3732.
[52] R. S. and L. H. Loomis, *Arthurian Legends in Medieval Art,* pp. 24 f. M. Mila y Fontanals, *Poetes catalans* (Paris, 1876), p. 16. Jean d'Outremeuse, *Myreur des Histors* (Brussels, 1877), IV, 51 f., 57. These two independent descriptions of the murals in Morgain's palace may reflect the same tradition as the curious story in the *Vulgate Lancelot* of Lancelot's adorning the walls of Morgain's castle with scenes from his amour with Guenievre. Sommer, *Vulgate Version,* V, 216 ff.
[53] Cf. for example the Val Sans Retor. Sommer, *op. cit.,* IV, 117.
[54] *Ibid.,* IV, 347.

a castle of a sparrow-hawk, whose mistress was Morgain la Fée or one of her sisters, was no mere figment of the imagination.

Chrétien's account of the sparrow-hawk contest and its eleven analogues in romance reveal on close scrutiny that they constitute merely one group in a much larger class of *contes* concerned with a testing talisman which is displayed, usually in Arthur's court, and which serves to prove the hero and his lady-love superior to all others. The talisman may be a cup, a horn, a glove, or a mantle.[55] Particularly significant is the analogy which Andreas' version of the meeting with the fay and the winning of the hawk presents to a story which Wauchier de Denain relates concerning Gauwain's meeting with a fay and his winning of a silver shield. Wauchier, who seems to know what he is talking about, asserts that this story was told by the famous *conteur* Bleheris to the Count of Poitiers, and that would mean that it was older than 1137.[56] Let us first observe how similar Chrétien's account of the sparrow-hawk is to Wauchier's account of the shield. In *Erec* we read (vss. 565-77):

"For in the presence of all the people there will be set on a perch of silver a very beautiful sparrow-hawk. . . . Whoever wishes to win the sparrow-hawk must have a lady-love fair and wise, without baseness. If there is a knight so bold as to wish to defend the worth and the renown of the fairest maiden, let him cause his lady to lift the hawk from the perch before all those assembled."

Compare the lines of Wauchier concerning the silver shield.

"No knight deserves to take it or carry or hang it from his neck unless he has intelligence, force, vigor, generosity, nobility, and honor, and at the same time a fair lady-love, who is loyal and true, and who loves him as her own heart."[57]

The sparrow-hawk and the shield have this property, then, in common, that they rightly belong only to a knight who has an *amie* "bele et sage sans vilenie." Turning to Wauchier's story of the silver shield,[58] let us observe how in the main it approximates Andreas' story of the winning of the hawk.

Gauwain, riding through a forest, comes on a solitary and most beautiful damsel, sitting beside a spring, who promptly grants him her love. Her brother, a dwarf who guards the talismanic shield, appears on the scene, hospitably entertains Gauwain, and, bearing the shield, accompanies him to a tourney held by King Arthur. There Gauwain enters the fray incognito, and, though there is no direct

---

[55] The cup and glove tests occur in Heinrich von dem Türlin's *Krone*, vss. 918-3189, 22990-24719. The horn and mantle tests are discussed in O. Warnatsch, *Der Mantel*, "Germanistische Abhandlungen," II (Breslau, 1883); F. J. Child, *English and Scottish Popular Ballads* (Boston, 1882-98), I, 265 ff.; *Mod. Phil.*, X (1913), 289-99; Paton, *Fairy Mythology*, pp. 104-23; *Speculum*, IX (1934), 38-50; *Zts. f. celt. Phil.*, I (1896-97), 305; *Archaeologia Cambrensis*, ser. 3, IX (1863), 7-40.

[56] *Mod. Lang. Notes*, XXXIX (1924), 319-29. *Romania*. LIII (1927), 82-92. *Romanic Review*, XXXII (1941), 16-19.

[57] C. Potvin, *Perceval le Gallois*, V, vss. 31805-11.   [58] *Ibid.*, vss. 31596-32838.

statement that it is by virtue of the beauty and loyalty of his faery love, he is able to bear the shield and to discomfit all of Arthur's knights. He returns to the damsel, who welcomes him with joy. But soon afterwards he departs, leaving her to lament his attractiveness to other women.

This story, though enriched by much additional detail, parallels Andreas' narrative in the following points: a knight rides at adventure, meets in a forest with a solitary and beautiful damsel, promptly wins a claim to her love, demonstrates in the presence of Arthur her superiority in beauty and his superiority in arms, brings back in triumph the talisman which belongs only to a knight with a lovely and loyal *amie,* is welcomed by the damsel of the forest, and promptly leaves her. The most notable difference, of course, is the prominence of the dwarf, who is as big as a child of seven years, takes the shield to be contested for in the presence of Arthur, and himself overthrows Sir Kay. Highly significant for the kinship of the hawk and shield stories with the other Arthurian accounts of testing talismans is the fact that in *Le Chevalier du Papegau* [59] it is a dwarf who brings the bird to be contested for by Arthur, and in *Diu Krone* [60] it is a dwarf, as big as a child of six years, who brings the magic cup which tests fidelity in love to Arthur's court and overthrows Kay in combat. Evidently, then, these stories of talismanic birds, shields, and drinking vessels either borrowed from each other freely at an early stage, or they were regarded as branches of one original tradition, with certain common features.

The same conclusion is suggested by the frequency with which Morgain la Fée is concerned, not only, as we have had reason to suspect, with the sparrow-hawk adventure, but also with the shield and horn tests. To be sure, the solitary damsel of the forest introduced by Wauchier is called Tanree,[61] but this name seems to have no support from the analogues, whereas her counterpart in Andreas is to be identified, as a fay and a horse-giver, with Morgain. Wauchier's damsel is discovered sitting beside a spring, like the faery mistress of Guingamor in the lai of that name, and Guingamor's *amie,* according to Chrétien, was Morgain. It is probably no mere accident that in the *Prose Tristan* Morgain sends a shield to Arthur's court under circumstances recalling Wauchier's story.[62]

[59] *Chevalier du Papegau,* p. 7.

[60] *Diu Krone,* vss. 946–50, 3028–41. It may also be significant for the kinship between the shield, horn, and mantle stories that Wauchier's dwarf not only guards the talismanic shield but also blows an ivory horn, whereupon vallets appear bringing two silken mantles for his sister, one of them particularly rich. Cf. H. Newstead, *Bran the Blessed in Arthurian Romance,* pp. 111–14, for confusion between blast horn and drinking horn.

[61] Potvin, *op. cit.,* IV, vs. 32094. The Edinburgh ms., f. 194, reads "tauree"; Montpellier ms., f. 216, reads "tencree."

[62] Löseth, *Roman en prose de Tristan* (Paris, 1891), sections 190–92; Malory, *Morte d'Arthur,* Bk. IX, chaps. 40–43; *Tavola Ritonda,* ed. F. L. Polidori (Bologna, 1864–65), chaps. lxxx, lxxxii.

Tristan comes by chance to Morgain's castle and is there entertained. On the morrow the faery queen shows him such favor as to arouse the jealousy of her paramour. She consents, however, to Tristan's departure on condition that he carry a shield of hers to a tournament held by King Arthur. He does so; the shield, on which the figures of Arthur, Guenievre, and Lancelot are portrayed, arouses great attention. The King wonders who the unknown knight may be. Tristan vanquishes the knights of the Round Table and departs.

We seem to have here, attached to Tristan, Wauchier's tale of the amorous fay and the talismanic shield which enables the hero to vanquish incognito the champions of Arthur's court; [63] and it is no longer surprising to observe that the amorous fay is explicitly Morgain.

Hitherto Morgain has appeared, anonymously or under a pseudonym, as a damsel whose beauty entitled her lover or champion to the award of the hawk or popinjay or shield. But in this tale from the *Prose Tristan* we meet her under her own name in the sinister role of one who sends by emissary an object designed to bring shame on King Arthur and his court. There are several variants of this formula in which the malignant phase of Morgain's nature is emphasized. One variant is likewise found in the *Prose Tristan* and its derivates,[64] and represents her as sending a knight to Arthur's court with an enchanted horn from which no faithless wife can drink without exposure of her frailty and which, like the shield, will serve to reveal Guinevere's love for Lancelot. Another variant in a German Shrovetide play attributes the sending of the horn to the Queen of Cyprus, who, since she is Arthur's sister, must be Morgain.[65] Two variants of the theme substitute for the testing horn a mantle which will fit only a faithful wife. In *Le Mantel Mal Taillé* the sender is Morgain; [66] in *Lanzelet* the mantle is brought to Arthur's court by a messenger from Lanzelet's foster mother, the Queen of Meydelant,[67] whom we have already identified with Morgain. This persistent association of Morgain with the testing shield, horn, and mantle cannot be due to accident. It must be due to tradition.

This tradition was probably current in Wales even before it was linked to Morgain. In several lists of the Thirteen Treasures of the Isle of Britain a mantle with precisely the property described in the Arthurian

---

[63] Miss Paton (*Fairy Mythology*, p. 135) rightly remarks of this incident: "It possibly points to a tradition in which she [Morgain], like the Petit Chevalier [the dwarf knight in Wauchier], owned a shield of the earlier type that would more directly betray the guilty lovers."
[64] Paton, *op. cit.*, p. 105.
[65] *Ibid.*, pp. 108 f. Warnatsch, *Der Mantel*, pp. 66 f. The association of Morgain with Cyprus is probably a variation on the familiar identification of Avalon with Sicily. Cf. Paton, *op. cit.*, pp. 250–52; E. G. Gardner, *Arthurian Legend in Italian Literature* (London, 1930), 12–15; A. Graf, *Miti, Leggende e superstizioni del medio evo*, II, 303 ff.; P. S. Barto, *Tannhaüser and the Mountain of Venus* (New York, 1916), pp. 13–16; *Mod. Lang. Notes*, LII (1937), 414–16; R. S. and L. H. Loomis, *Arthurian Legends in Medieval Art*, pp. 24 f.
[66] Legrand d'Aussy, *Fabliaux ou contes* (Paris, 1829), I, 126 ff. Cf. Paton, *op. cit.*, pp. 119–21.
[67] Piper, *Höfische Epik*, II, 188 f.

tales is found.[68] Edward Jones translated from one of the lists as follows:

"The Mantle of Tegau Eurvron: no one could put it on who had dishonoured marriage; nor a young damsel who had committed incontinence; but it would cover a chaste woman from top to toe." [69]

Professor Robinson translated from another list as follows:

"The mantle of Tegau Eurvron, which would not serve anyone who had violated her marriage or her virginity; and for the woman who remained true to her husband it would reach to the ground, and to the one who had violated her marriage it would not reach to her lap; and for this reason there was envy against Tegau Eurvron." [70]

Jones also states, though without citation of source, that Tegau Eurvron had three rarities, which befitted none but herself; and these were her mantle, her golden goblet, and her knife.[71] The fact that the earliest manuscripts to mention Tegau's mantle are of the sixteenth century has induced a certain reluctance on the part of scholars to assert the priority of the Welsh tradition over the Continental and English poems which deal with the theme of the testing mantle and horn, of which the earliest, *Le Lai du Cor,* belongs to the middle of the twelfth century.[72] It is natural, moreover, to suspect that Jones took his mantle, goblet, and knife from the English ballad of *The Boy and the Mantle,*[73] since it describes Craddock's wife (who of course is identical with the wife of Caradawc, Tegau Eurvron) as triumphantly vindicating her chastity by means of a mantle, a horn, and a knife. But so far as I am aware, Jones, though quite uncritical, has never been convicted of fobbing off English material as Welsh; and moreover, he mentions as his second talisman not a horn but a golden goblet, and this he could not have derived from any English or French version of the chastity test. Only in *Diu Krone* does a cup take the place of the enchanted horn,[74] and Jones certainly did not take a trip to Germany to consult the manuscripts of the then unprinted romance. The Welshman's integrity and his significant variation from *The Boy and the Mantle* combine to prove that he was recording native tradition—

[68] Manuscripts containing the lists are Peniarth, 51, 60, 77, and 179 at the National Library of Wales, Aberystwyth. Versions have been printed in Y *Brython,* 1860, pp. 372 f., in E. Jones, *Bardic Museum* (London, 1802), pp. 47–49, and in Y *Greal* (London, 1805), p. 188. The earliest, Peniarth 51, dated by the Librarian of the National Library, *ca.* 1460, contains the Mantle of Tegau, but it has been added in a later hand. Peniarth 60 and 77 also contain it, but these are sixteenth-century mss.   [69] Jones, *op. cit.,* p. 49.

[70] Carleton Brown, *English Lyrics of the Thirteenth Century,* p. 226. It is interesting to note that Tegau was known for her truth and Cradoc for carving the roast at court, even among Englishmen on the Welsh border. Such knowledge of Welsh stories through direct contact seems to be wholly exceptional.   [71] Jones, *op. cit.,* p. 49, n. 13.

[72] *Lai du Cor,* ed. H. Dörner (Strassburg, 1907).

[73] F. J. Child, *English and Scottish Popular Ballads,* I, 265 ff. H. C. Sargent, G. L. Kittredge, *English and Scottish Popular Ballads* (Boston, New York, 1904), pp. 46–49. This ballad had been published by Bishop Percy in his *Reliques* in 1765.   [74] Vss. 1073 ff.

the tradition which lay behind the whole group of horn and mantle tests in French, English, and German. Warnatsch was right in declaring: "Celtischer Boden ist die Heimat beider Arten der Probe. Ihre literarische Gestaltung erlangten sie jedoch erst in der altfranzösischen Poesie, der Erbin celtischer Ueberlieferungen." [75]

We are thus led to infer that the motif of the talismanic mantle and horn originated in Wales. In its purest form the tale merely recounted how the talisman was produced at Arthur's court and put to shame all the ladies except Caradawc's wife, Tegau Eurvron. Other objects, such as a shield or a glove, seem to have obtruded themselves into the pattern. With the shield came the notion of a combat involving the hero. One offshoot of the tradition replaced Tegau, renowned for her chastity, by Morgain, famed for her beauty. In Brittany, curiously enough, the fay's own hawk or falcon became the testing talisman and the prize of victory. Morgain's reputation, however, was so bad that her name was suppressed and her identity disguised. Thus in Chrétien's poem she has yielded her place as heroine of the sparrow-hawk adventure to Enide. But the essence of the motif is preserved in the lines:

> Qui l'esprevier voudra avoir,
> Avoir li covandra amie
> Bele et sage sanz vilenie.

Erec and *Geraint* present only a late development of the Welsh stories of a talisman which tested the virtue and beauty of ladies, but to this general category the versions of the sparrow-hawk adventure belong.

Let me summarize briefly the points which emerge from this discussion.

1. Six of the twelve tales in which a hawk or other bird is the prize of womanly beauty and virtue and knightly valor indicate Morgain la Fée as the original heroine.

2. The white body and red ear of the horse which appears, together with the bird, as a prize in *Wigalois* suggests Celtic influence.

3. In Breton lais and Arthurian romances faery ladies appear with sparrow hawks or falcons on their fists. One of these, Lanval's faery mistress from Avalon, was doubtless Morgain, and another is compared with Femurgan.

4. We have no proof that the association of these birds with fays goes back to the Welsh stage of the *Matière de Bretagne,* and therefore the sparrow-hawk adventure may be an innovation of the Bretons.

5. If so, it is a novel variation on an older narrative formula, represented in Arthurian romance, in which a shield, a horn, or a mantle serves as a test of women's virtue and men's valor. The relationship of the hawk adventure to this formula is shown by the similarity between Andreas

[75] Warnatsch, *Mantel,* p. 58. Prof. Cross in *Mod. Phil.,* X, 289 ff., offers evidence that these tests are Celtic.

Capellanus' form of the hawk episode and Wauchier's tale of the shield, and also by the persistence with which Morgain is connected with these testing shields, hawks, horns, and mantles.

6. Since the drinking vessel and the mantle are mentioned in Welsh records which, though late, seeem to be independent of foreign influence, the basic formula was probably Welsh. Tegau Eurvron, the wife of Caradawc Breichbras,[76] was in Wales the traditional heroine, and this tradition carried over into *Le Lai du Cor, Le Livre de Caradoc,* and *The Boy and the Mantle.*

7. When in course of time the tradition was also attached to Morgain, probably by the Bretons, important developments took place. As the noble Queen of Meydelant in *Lanzelet,* she sent the mantle to Arthur's court to prove the beauty and fidelity of her foster son's wife, Iblis. As the fay of the spring in Wauchier, she enabled her lover Gauvain to carry the magic shield to victory over Arthur's knights by virtue of her loyalty and devotion. As the mounted fay in Andreas' tale, she gave the Briton knight her steed and sent him as her lover to win the faery hawk at Arthur's court. But Morgain's reputation was, to say the least, dubious; many unpleasant stories were in circulation about her. Her name was, therefore, frequently suppressed or altered; her sending the mantle, the horn, or the shield to Arthur's court, as in *Le Mantel Mal Taillé* and the *Prose Tristan,* came to be attributed to her malignant hatred of Arthur and Guinevere. In *Erec* and in *Geraint,* a new heroine, the lovely and virtuous Enide, took the place of the enchantress as the winner of the sparrow hawk.

Chapter XII

ENIDE

THE ORIGIN of the name Enide is an enigma. M. Lot first maintained and some other scholars have agreed that Enide represents a Welsh common noun *enid,* meaning a wood lark.[1] But Professor Kenneth Jackson, kindly responding to an inquiry of mine, writes that the dictionaries of Silvan Evans and Pugh, on which this interpretation rests, are "very poor sources for lexicographical material." The latest dic-

---

[76] On Caradawc and Tegau cf. *Romania,* XXVIII (1899), pp. 214–31, 568–78. Lot's assertion (pp. 576–78) that the story of Caradoc's wife with the golden breast is of Scottish origin seems to rest on the feeble argument that analogues have been found in a modern Gaelic folktale and in the Child ballad No. 301, "The Queen of Scotland." A close study of the latter shows that the amorous Queen of Scotland is no other than Morgain, sometimes represented as wife of King Loth of Lothian, famous for her painted chamber.

[1] *Romania,* XXX (1901), 21.

tionaries do not recognize the word. The author of *Geraint* calls the lady Enyt, Enit, or Enyd,[2] and the name occurs in later Welsh literature.[3] But the source of these later allusions is pretty clearly *Geraint,* and that in turn must have derived Enyd from the same French text which gave Chrétien "Enide." So there seems to be no reliable authority for a Welsh common noun *enid* or a native Welsh name Enyd. None of the onomastic counterparts of Erec (Guerehes, Gareth, Gaheries) is ever involved with a lady called Enide or anything of the sort. The daughter of King Pelles, called in most manuscripts of the *Vulgate Lancelot* Amide, Amite, and so forth, is called in one manuscript Enite, but she bears no resemblance to Erec's bride, and the same is true of a damsel, Elidia, in Ulrich von Zatzikhoven's *Lanzelet.*[4] Renaud de Beaujeu has in his *Bel Inconnu* an Elie who accompanies Guinglain on his adventures, somewhat as Enide accompanies Erec, but Elie seems to be a corruption of Elene, the name borne by her counterpart in *Libeaus Desconus.*

We should not overlook, however, two ladies in Arthurian romance whose names and histories evince a partial similarity to those of Erec's bride. Idain, in Raoul de Houdenc's *Vengeance Raguidel,* appears bearing a sparrow-hawk on her fist,[5] whereas Enide rides with the sparrowhawk which Erec won for her. Idain's temporary lover, Gauvain, suspects on good grounds her fidelity, and consequently forces her to ride ahead of him;[6] so Erec suspects Enide's love and therefore obliges her to ride ahead of him. Riding in this manner, Gauvain and Idain come to the court of Baudemagus and there Gauvain defeats a dwarf;[7] riding similarly, Erec and Enide meet with Guivret, the dwarf, and Erec defeats him. Now Idain, as Friedwagner inferred, is the oblique case of Ide. A somewhat completer counterpart to Enide is Ade in Ulrich's poem. Lanzelet is riding with his temporary wife Ade, when they are met by Walwein, who tries to persuade them to come to Arthur's court;[8] just so, Erec is riding with Enide when they are met by Gauvain, who tries to persuade them to come into Arthur's presence. Lanzelet and Ade arrive at Schatel le Mort, where all who enter lose their courage and strength, and where Lanzelet is promptly struck lifeless by the lord of the castle;[9] similarly, Erec and Enide arrive at the castle of Limors, Erec in a lifeless condition. I hope to prove at later points in our inquiry that both these correspondences are not accidental, but are rooted in a common tradition,[10]

[2] J. Gwenogvryn Evans, *White Book Mabinogion,* p. 205, col. 409.

[3] Loth, *Mabinogion,* 2d ed., II, 121, n. 2.

[4] *Mod. Phil.,* V (1908), 293, n. 1. *Lanzelet,* ed. K. A. Hahn (Frankfurt, 1845), vs. 7990.

[5] Raoul de Houdenc, *Vengeance Raguidel,* ed. M. Friedwagner, vss. 3786, 4475. Note that Idain appears with Morgain as a fay in *Enfances Garin de Monglane,* ed. O. Bisinger (1915), pp. 57 f.   [6] Raoul de Houdenc, *op. cit.,* vss. 4769-87.

[7] *Ibid.,* vss. 4786-831.   [8] P. Piper, *Höfische Epik* (Stuttgart, [1892-95]), II, 177 f.

[9] *Ibid.,* II, 181.   [10] Cf. Chaps. XXI, XXIV.

and the same is probably true of the correspondences between Enide and Idain (originally Ide). Cognate tales were apparently told about Ade, Ide, and Enide, but this conclusion does not clarify the origin of the three names.

Though we may never know whence and why our heroine got her name, we have already seen and shall discover repeatedly in the following pages that she (as well as Ade) inherited her part from Morgain la Fée. This may seem at first a fantastic doctrine. Enide, the meek maiden and model wife, patterned after the lascivious and vengeful enchantress? The apparent absurdity of the notion is doubtless the reason why no scholar has heeded the evidence which points again and again to this conclusion. But if anything is consistent about the legends of Morgain la Fée it is their inconsistency. No figure of the Arthurian cycle was more changeful than she. In the *Huth Merlin* and Malory she hates her brother Arthur and plots his murder; in the *Vita Merlini* and Layamon's *Brut* she heals his wounds on her faery island.[11] She may be the virgin daughter of King Avallo, as in the *Gesta Regum Britanniae*,[12] or a Venus of lust as in many scenes in the Vulgate cycle. She may be old and ugly or supremely beautiful.

The reason for these astounding contradictions in the character of Morgain, as has already been suggested, is that from a very early period her Welsh prototype attracted to herself almost every variety of story concerned with a fay.[13] These legends were naturally as inconsistent as the traditions which attached themselves to the mythological personages of antiquity or to the fairy folk of popular belief. Even the Yahveh of the Jews was not always a model character. Up to a certain stage in the development of mythologies and other forms of fiction, the human mind does not require logic and is at home in chaos. The world of the supernatural is inexplicable, and one is not startled by anything a god or a fay may do. But the time comes when reason asserts itself; the systematizers, the euhemerists, the apologists appear. Gradually the mass of conflicting traditions is brought into harmony; the grossest incongruities are eliminated; the lesser are rationalized. But seldom is the process wholly complete and satisfactory. And this was the case with the legends of Morgain la Fée.

She appears twice in *Erec* under her own name, as the *amie* of Guigamor, lord of Avalon, and as the maker of a medicinal plaster, which she gave her brother Arthur. There was nothing in these brief allusions to jar the reader. Morgain was well established in tradition as lady of the faery isle and as a skillful healer. But it is noteworthy that in the lai of *Guingamor* the author has left the faery mistress of the hero without a name,

[11] *Romanic Review*, III (1912), 190. *Review of Eng. Studies*, X (1934), 81.
[12] L. A. Paton, *Fairy Mythology*, p. 46.   [13] *Speculum*, XX (1945), 183–203.

even though she must have been, according to Chrétien's testimony, Morgain. Very likely the motive for this omission was to avoid a clash with other traditions which represented her as the wife or *amie* of sundry other men. When some other romancer undertook to weave a long and realistic narrative out of the Morgain tradition, if he was a man of intelligence, he had to perform three operations: (1) He had to eliminate obvious traces of the fay and the enchantress, else his heroine would be suspected of diabolic connections. (2) He had to modify or expunge the stories which represented her as treacherous or overlustful. (3) He had to give her a name which had no such unpleasant associations. It will be clear before our study of *Erec* is completed that this is just what the author of Chrétien's source, X, must have done, and done with remarkable success. But the renaming of his heroine had already been done before him, since we have just seen that in the analogous stories from *La Vengeance Raguidel* and *Lanzelet* the lady is called Idain or Ade. But what the immediate original of Enide, Idain, and Ade was called, there seems to be no way of telling.[14]

Chapter XIII

ENIDE'S RAGGED GARMENT

When Erec was invited to take lodging with the hospitable vavasor, his wife and daughter appeared, the latter clad in an old robe (chainse),[1] *worn through at the elbows. After Erec won the prize of the sparrow-hawk for the damsel, now his affianced bride, he refused the offer of a handsome robe for her to wear on her presentation at Arthur's court, and insisted that she should ride with him alone, dressed just as she was. Thus Enide arrived at the castle of Caradigan in her humble robe with both sleeves ragged at the elbows.*

THERE IS substantial agreement between *Erec* and *Geraint* regarding Enide's shabby robe,[2] and therefore the motif was in the common source X. Both extant narratives agree in motivating Erec's humiliating command that his betrothed ride with him to court in her mean garb by his desire that she should receive a new robe from no less a person

[14] It should, of course, be understood that, whatever the immediate prototype of these three figures was called, the names Ade and Ide existed independently. They were not new coinages of the romancers, but were borne by aristocratic ladies of contemporary society.
[1] On meaning of *chainse* cf. E. R. Goddard, *Women's Costume in French Texts of the Eleventh and Twelfth Centuries* ("Johns Hopkins Studies in Romance Literatures and Languages," VII, Baltimore, 1927), pp. 69 ff.　[2] Loth, *Mabinogion,* 2d ed., II, 131, 137, 143.

than the Queen herself. And the Queen's enthusiastic bestowal of a jeweled and furred *bliaut* and mantle on Erec's destined bride affords proof of her gratitude to the hero and of the heroine's charm. That the motif possesses dramatic and picturesque value is shown by the fact that Tennyson in his poetic rendering of *Geraint* focuses interest on Enid's faded silk dress and its role in the vicissitudes of her romance. All this bears testimony to the ingenuity and artistic sense of the author of X.

But though Erec's refusal to allow his betrothed to ride to court in worthy costume is felicitously accounted for, his refusal at the same time of the Count's offer to send a company of knights to escort them on the road is not explained. Of course, one can imagine motives for refusing an honorable escort; lovers do not enjoy company, for instance. Still one is tempted to ask whether the basic explanation of all this does not lie once more in tradition. Was there a story of Erec's riding with Enide in her shabby gown, without escort of any kind—a story in which the situation seems more completely understandable? This is just what we do find later, not precisely in *Erec,* but in *Geraint.*[3]

Geraint a second time commanded that Enid ride with him alone, again clad in a mean dress. This time the meanness of her attire is consistent with Geraint's desire to punish her for her aspersions on his strength and for her suspected infidelity. The absence of any retinue is likewise natural since an escort of knights would prevent him from demonstrating his individual prowess. When we deal with this later, well-motivated ride,[4] we shall find that it certainly had a traditional basis, and that the well-worn dress in *Geraint* was a part of the tradition. Enide's ride to Arthur's court in her old white *chainse* must therefore be a sort of doublet of her later adventurous journey with her jealous husband. Let us see how the author of X came to incorporate two variants of the same situation in his romance.

The picture of Erec in glittering mail and of Enide in her shabby garment, which the composer of X must have derived from his sources, evidently so impressed his imagination that he was not content to use it only in its traditional narrative setting. Where else could he employ it? There was Erec's triumphant return to Arthur's court with his newly affianced bride. What then of the old dress? It could not be explained by anger and jealousy on Erec's part. The characteristic independence and ingenuity of the author found the felicitous solution: none but the richest of robes, received from the hands of Guenievre herself, was worthy of Enide's beauty; so the old gown had to be worn till the Queen could supply a new and splendid one.

Chrétien, reading X, doubtless appreciated this freshly motivated version of Enide's ride and made much of its sentimental possibilities. But when,

---

[3] *Ibid.,* II, 153.   [4] Cf. Chap. XVII.

later in the narrative, he came upon her again wearing (as in *Geraint*) the same or another humble garment, he seems to have disliked the repetition and ineptly altered Erec's instructions, with the result that we find the angry hero ordering his wife to wear her loveliest robe and to ride her best palfrey[5]—an odd method of humiliating her! Surely the Welsh tale has preserved the original tradition in representing Enid, the victim of her husband's offended pride and jealous suspicions, as wearing not her best but her worst gown.

Chapter XIV

ENIDE'S COUSIN

VERSES 1353–1423

After Erec's victory in the sparrow-hawk contest, a female cousin of Enide's insisted on presenting Enide with a piebald (ver) *palfrey. "Birds which fly through the air do not travel more swiftly than the palfrey; but it is not too lively and is such as befits a maiden. . . . Whoever rides it is not distressed, but moves more easily and softly than if he were in a boat." Erec, addressing the damsel somewhat startlingly as "ma douce amie," accepted the animal on behalf of Enide. When the maned* (crenu) *palfrey was brought by a squire, Erec approved it heartily and ordered it to be stabled beside his destrier.*

THERE ARE several strong hints that this incident is a *rifacimento* of the now-familiar motif of the fay's gift of her horse to her lover. It is surprising to find Erec addressing Enide's cousin, after so slight an acquaintance, as "ma douce amie," [1] and this recalls the fact that in Andreas' book the Briton knight addressed the fay who gave him her steed as "carissime." [2] Moreover, though the palfrey is ostensibly a gift to Enide, it is Erec who accepts it on her behalf, it is stabled with his own horse, and only 900 lines later is any mention made of Enide's riding it.[3] One is led to surmise that, like Andreas' fay and Launfal's mistress, Enide's cousin should have bestowed her steed on the hero. There is a suggestion in the words *ver* and *crenu* applied to the animal that there was something distinctive about its coloring and its mane, since we know from *Wigalois* that a faery horse was likely to have a white body, a long red mane, and red ears.[4] That the palfrey was of Celtic breed is manifested by passages

---

[5] *Erec*, vss. 2580–83.   [1] *Erec*, vs. 1403. Note that in vs. 1433 Erec's *amie* is surely Enide.
[2] *De Amore*, ed. Pages, p. 159.   [3] *Erec*, vs. 2307.
[4] Cf. *supra*, p. 90. Note, however, that *vair* and *crenu* are adjectives frequently applied to horses which have nothing supernatural about them. Cf. *Romanic Review*, X (1919), 325 f., 350–52; F. Bangert, *Tiere im altfranzösischen Epos* (Marburg, 1885), p. 52.

in *Le Lai du Trot* and the mabinogi of *Pwyll,* where we find unearthly ladies mounted on horses distinguished by preternatural celerity and smoothness of motion. The Breton lai describes a cavalcade of lovely ladies issuing from a forest. "They had palfreys entirely white, which carried them so gently that if a person sat upon one and if he did not see the palfrey moving, he would surely think that it was standing still; and yet they moved far more fleetly than one would gallop on the tallest Spanish horse." [5] This was a true Celtic tradition, for in *Pwyll* Riannon rides a white steed with similar uncanny motion. "They saw a woman coming, mounted on a pale-white, large, fine horse. . . . It seemed to all who saw it that the horse moved at a slow, even pace." [6] A squire was sent on the swiftest horse in the palace to summon the lady. "He put spurs to his mount, but the more he struck it, the further was she from him. She kept the same pace she had at starting." [7] The palfrey of Enide's cousin was indubitably, then, a faery creature. Orthodox Arthurian tradition prescribed that she should give it to the hero, and of this original destination Chrétien has retained certain traces. But he or the author of his source may well have doubted the suitability of a lady's mount for a knight, and so violated precedent by making Enide the recipient.

Who was this anonymous cousin of Enide, the possessor of the palfrey? Was she Morgain and therefore a sort of doublet of Enide herself? As giver of the faery steed, she seems to fill the part of Morgain; as one whom Erec addressed as "ma douce amie" she seems to share his affection with Enide. And if she is to be identified with Mabonagrain's mistress, who was likewise Enide's cousin, there are many features in her story which equate her with the great enchantress.[8] But there are a few indications that reveal her as a composite figure, Morgain and Niniane, the Lady of the Lake, blended into one.

For Morgain was not the only fay to present her protégé with a horse. Twice Lancelot's foster mother in the *Vulgate Lancelot,* the Dame du Lac, gave him a steed when he was about to leave her. On the first occasion the animal is thus described: "large, strong, of proved celerity and boldness, and it was all white like new-fallen snow." [9] Its swiftness recalls the palfrey of Enide's cousin; its swiftness and whiteness recall the faery horses described in *Le Lai du Trot* and in *Pwyll.* That these are not accidental resemblances is demonstrated by a number of facts. (1) The Dame du Lac, who gave Lancelot this exceedingly fleet white horse, is according to many sources the fay Niniane.[10] (2) In the *Huth Merlin* Niniane rode into Arthur's hall "with the greatest speed that she could extract from her pal-

[5] *Romanic Review,* XXVI (1935), 318, vss. 99–107.   [6] Loth, *Mabinogion,* 2d ed. I, 93.
[7] *Ibid.,* I, 95.   [8] Cf. *infra,* pp. 178–82.
[9] H. O. Sommer, *Vulgate Version,* III, 118; IV, 155 f.
[10] *Ibid.,* III, 374; V, 65. Paton, *Fairy Mythology,* pp. 201, 221 f., 234, 239 f.

frey;"[11] and Malory, probably on the authority of another manuscript, adds that the palfrey was white.[12] (3) The circumstances under which Niniane appeared in the *Huth Merlin* [13] vividly recall those under which Riannon appeared in *Pwyll*.[14] Both King Arthur and Pwyll, Prince of Dyved, sat surrounded by their courtiers. Both Niniane and Riannon rode up on swift white steeds. Two boys (*enfants*) were sent in pursuit of a stag and a hound which had preceded Niniane, and Pwyll sent a youth (*macwy*) to pursue Riannon. King Pellinor was sent after Niniane, and Prince Pwyll himself rode finally after Riannon. (4) Niniane was "one of the fairest damsels who had ever entered the court of King Arthur"; [15] of Riannon it is said that all the maidens and ladies Pwyll had ever seen were ugly in comparison with her.[16] (5) In the printed Merlin of 1528 we read that Nymanne (that is, Niniane) "is a Chaldean name which means in French '*rien nen* feraye.' " [17] Either this statement is sheer non-sense since there is no reason why Niniane should be called "I will do nothing with it" in Chaldean or any other language,[18] or it harks back to a not wholly unreasonable effort to interpret a name which sounded like "rien nen," and that is about as close as one could get in French to Welsh Riannon. Niniane, with all its variants, must be a scribal corruption for some such form as Rianon—a corruption which anteceded the Vulgate cycle.

The evidence thus shows that Enide's cousin was patterned largely after Niniane, "la Dame del Lac." This may provide a clue as to the name of the town where this cousin was dwelling when she presented Enide with the marvelous palfrey, for, some thousands of lines later, we are told that it was Lalut.[19] So far as I am aware, no town of this name is mentioned elsewhere in Arthurian romance, and no convincing explanation has been put forward.[20] Either it is a mystery, or it is a corruption of "le

[11] *Huth Merlin*, ed. G. Paris, and J. Ulrich, II, 77. The fay's name is given as Niviene on p. 136.
[12] Malory, *Morte d'Arthur*, ed. Sommer, I, 104.   [13] *Huth Merlin*, II, 77–80.
[14] Loth, *op. cit.*, I, 92–98.   [15] *Huth Merlin*, II, 77.
[16] Loth, *op. cit.*, I, 96.   [17] Paton, *Fairy Mythology*, p. 245.
[18] *Ibid. PMLA*, XLV (1930), 440. For a similar etymology which reposes on tradition cf. H. Newstead, *Bran the Blessed in Arthurian Romance*, pp. 89 f.
[19] Vs. 6320. The name also occurs in vss. 6249, 6251. Variants are "laluth," "lalit," "jalut," and "lelit." The ending -*ut* is confirmed by rime with *reconut*.
[20] Prof. Mary Williams has suggested that it is a corruption of Llanllwch (*Etudes celtiques*, II [1937], 236–38), and the resemblance is tempting. But I know of no instance where a place so insignificant as this was adopted into Arthurian nomenclature. Moreover, I am un-able to accept the identification of Bleddri ab Cadivor, the overlord of the territory in which Llanllwch lay, with the Bleheris who according to Giraldus Cambrensis and Wauchier was a *fabulator* or *conteur*. Though both were Welshmen, there was a social chasm which forbids identification. Note the contemptuous tone in which Chrétien (*Erec*, vss. 20–22; *Conte del Graal*, ed. A. Hilka, vss. 8676–80), Wauchier (J. L. Weston, *Legend of Sir Perceval*, I, 265), Wace (E. K. Chambers, *Arthur of Britain*, p. 103), and Béroul (*Tristan*, vss. 1265–68) refer to the *conteor* and *fableor*. If even poets looked down on the professional tale-tellers, it is hardly conceivable that Giraldus would have referred to a great lord like Bleddri ab Cadivor as "famosus ille fabulator."

lac." It is worth noting that Niniane brought up Lancelot in her palace "dedens le lac," and on his departure presented him with a marvelous horse,[21] and that Enide's cousin, modeled after Niniane, dwelt at Lalut, and on Enide's departure bestowed on her a marvelous palfrey. This is not proof, of course, that Lalut is a corruption of "le lac," but that is the sort of thing that happened. On other pages we shall discover that the castle of Corbenic is simply a corruption of "cor beneit," that is, "blessed horn"; that the water-girt realm of Goirre is really "l'isle de voirre"; and Professor Newstead has demonstrated that King Ban's city of Benoic owed its name to the corruption and misunderstanding of Bran le Benoit, Bran the Blessed.[22] It would be nothing abnormal if Niniane's lake should have developed into the town of Lalut.

Chapter XV

THE TOURNEY IN THE PLAIN BELOW DANEBROC

VERSES 2129–2270

After the wedding of Erec and Enide, a tourney was arranged to take place between the towns of Evroic and Danebroc. Gauvain was to head the knights of the Round Table on one side, while Meliz and Meliadoc were to head those on the other. A month later the assembly was held in the plain below Danebroc. The knights of the Round Table drove their opponents back to the gates of the castle on the first day. Erec distinguished himself on this and the following day, so that all agreed that he had won the honors of the tournament.

THERE IS HARDLY a clue in this highly conventional account of a tourney to indicate that it represents anything more than an effort to display Erec's prowess once more. Yet there may be something in the localization which is not accidental but traditional. Though the assembly is arranged to take place between York (Evroic) and Edinburgh (Danebroc, Daneborc, Tenebroc),[1] it is actually held near the latter town. Now Edinburgh was early identified as the Castle of Maidens, and the Castle of Maidens was later celebrated in romance as the site of several famous tourneys.[2]

[21] H. O. Sommer, *Vulgate Version*, III, 15, 118. Cf. also *ibid.*, p. 84.
[22] H. Newstead, *Bran the Blessed in Arthurian Romance*, pp. 86–106.
[1] Cf. variants for vss. 2131, 2137. On the identity of Danebroc with Edinburgh cf. *Zts. f. franz. Sprache u. Lit.*, XX, 130 f.; XXVIII, 27, n. 48; XLIV, "Referate," 91 ff.
[2] On the Castle of Maidens in the romances cf. *Perlesvaus*, ed. Nitze and others, II, 295–97; *Elucidation*, ed. A. W. Thompson (New York, 1931), p. 63. Wauchier tells quite a different

Geoffrey of Monmouth inspired this identification, even though he did not actually make it in his *Historia* (*ca.* 1136). There he stated: "Ebraucus founded moreover the city Alclud in Scotland (*Albania*) and the city of Mount Agned, which is now named the Castle of Maidens (*Castellum Puellarum*), and the Dolorous Mount (*Montem Dolorosum*)." [3] Ebraucus, the wholly imaginary eponymous founder of York (Old Welsh Ebrauc),[4] is thus credited with founding three other towns, all presumably in Scotland. The first is certainly Dumbarton (Old Welsh Alt-Clut) on the Clyde.[5] But nobody knows where Mount Agned, referred to by Nennius as the site of one of Arthur's victories over the Saxons, actually was,[6] or what place (if any) Geoffrey had in mind in speaking of Mons Dolorosus.[7]

It is a striking fact, however, that in 1142 and subsequently, King David I of Scotland, who had hitherto dated certain of his charters at "Edenburge," used as an alternative "Castellum" or "Castrum Puellarum." [8] Now in the preceding year, 1141, David had joined forces with Robert, earl of Gloucester, one of the most powerful nobles of England, in supporting the cause of David's niece, Matilda, against King Stephen.[9] For months King David had been in contact with Earl Robert at London, Oxford, and Winchester; and Robert, we know, was a lover of books, was one of the dedicatees of Geoffrey of Monmouth's opus, and possessed a copy.[10] One can reasonably suppose that during those months Robert spoke of the sensational new "history," with its many references to Scotland. One can even surmise that he introduced King David to Geoffrey at Oxford,[11] and that the canny chronicler assured the King that Mons Agned was the

story from the rest (Potvin, *Perceval le Gallois*, IV, 210–27), and I have shown in *Romania*, LIX (1933), 560–62, that this is ultimately derived from the visit of Maelduin to the Isle of Women. On places called Maiden Castle cf. R. E. M. Wheeler, *Maiden Castle, Dorset* (Oxford, 1943), pp. 8–11.

[3] *Historia Regum Britanniae*, ed. A. Griscom, p. 259; ed. E. Faral (*Légende arthurienne*, III), p. 97. It is amazing to note that M. Faral (*ibid.*, II, 98), Prof. A. B. Hopkins (*Influence of Wace on the Arthurian Romances of Crestien de Troyes* [Menasha, 1913], p. 142), and Dr. Blenner-Hassett (*Speculum*, XVII, 1942, p. 250) all ignore the case of Montem Dolorosum and treat it as if it were a second title of Mons Agned. The last mentioned also errs in stating (*ibid.*, p. 253) that "Mons Agned is clearly Edinburgh Rock."

[4] Faral, *Légende arthurienne*, III, 49, 57.

[5] J. Loth, *Mabinogion*, 2d ed., II, 276, n. 1. *Antiquity*, XII (1938), 49. *Zts. f. franz. Sprache u. Lit.*, XLVI (1924), 415–18.

[6] Prof. Jackson gives the best and latest study of Mons Agned in *Mod. Phil.*, XLIII (1945), 52 f.
[7] It has been identified, without any good reason, with Stirling and with Arthur's Seat, a mountain near Edinburgh. Cf. A. O. Anderson, *Early Sources of Scottish History* (Edinburgh, 1922), II, 275, n. 6.

[8] A. C. Laurie, *Early Scottish Charters Prior to A.D. 1153* (Glasgow, 1905), pp. 112, 123, 146.
[9] Anderson, *op. cit.*, II, 202. R. Howlett, *Chronicles of the Reigns of Stephen, Henry II, and Richard I* (Rolls Series), III, 75–83.

[10] E. K. Chambers, *Arthur of Britain*, pp. 41–44, 55, 261. Faral, *op. cit.*, II, 14–28. Both these should be corrected by Prof. Hammer's article in *Quarterly Bulletin of the Polish Institute of Arts and Sciences*, Jan., 1944, pp. 524–29.

[11] Geoffrey lived at Oxford; Robert and David were with Matilda at Oxford for some time in the summer of 1141. Geoffrey refers to the events of this summer in his *Vita Merlini* (ed. J. J. Parry, vss. 1485–97, and p. 124).

royal fortress of Edinburgh. Certain it is that in the following year the Scottish king adopted Castellum Puellarum as an official designation of Edinburgh castle.

This procedure seems to have started among the Scots a mania for discovering in the pages of Geoffrey or in the romances the supposedly ancient titles of Scottish towns, castles, and other places. There is good evidence that by 1171 the abbot of Melrose, David's foundation, was curiously known as the abbot of Mons Dolorosus,[12] and about 1220 Guillaume le Clerc, the French author of *Fergus,* who knew southern Scotland well,[13] identifies Mont Dolerous with the mountain of Melrose, and locates on it a castle overhanging a deep river.[14] My friend, Angus Graham, of the Royal Commission on Historical Monuments for Scotland, graciously points out to me that this must refer to the ridge overhanging the Tweed in the parish of Melrose, where in the twelfth century the ruins of the great Roman fort of Trimontium would have been conspicuous. Moreover, Guillaume was familiar with Edinburgh as "le Castiel as Puceles," localized many scenes of his Arthurian romance at Roxburgh, Jedburgh, Dunnottar Castle, and so forth, and made his heroine "la dame de Lodien (Lothian)." [15] The lai of *Doon* explicitly tells us that Daneborc (Edinburgh) was called "le chastel as puceles" because of a beautiful and proud virgin, the mistress of that country, who dwelt there with her maidens; [16] and we are given a romantic story of how the virgin was won and then deserted by Doon. In 1365 Froissart learned at Stirling that the fortress had been called Sinaudon in the days of King Arthur, and had been a resort of the knights of the Round Table.[17] He was inspired by this sort of thing to invent more romantic names for places in and outside Scotland, and in his Arthurian *Meliador (ca.* 1385) he called Roxburgh Mon-

[12] According to Anderson, *op. cit.,* II, 275, the *Chronicle of Holyrood Abbey* notes the death of William, abbot of Mons Dolorosus, under this year. Anderson is puzzled by this entry, but supposes that the reference is to a certain William, who was abbot of Holyrood as late as 1168. But on Anderson's p. 268 we find that in 1170 William, third abbot of Melrose, resigned the pastoral charge. If he did so on account of illness or old age, it is natural to read of his death in the following year.

[13] *PMLA,* XLIV (1929), 263 f. *Miscellany of Studies in Romance Languages and Literatures in Honour of L. E. Kastner,* pp. 94–107.

[14] *Fergus,* ed. E. Martin (Halle, 1872), pp. xxi, 121. On Mont Dolereus cf. *Zts. f. franz. Sprache u. Lit.,* XLIV, "Referate," 96–98; A. B. Hopkins, *op. cit.,* p. 143, n. 19; *Conte del Graal,* ed. Hilka, p. 718. On the Roman fort and its site cf. J. Curle, *A Roman Frontier Post and Its People, the Fort of Newstead in the Parish of Melrose* (Glasgow, 1911). A 13th century interpolation in two Nennius mss. calls Wedale the Vallis Doloris, places it six miles to the west of Melrose (presumably Stow on the Gala Water), and says, that there were preserved fragments of an image of the Virgin which Arthur had carried in the battle of Guinnion. F. Lot, *Nennius et l'Historia Brittonum,* I, 195, n. 8.

[15] *Fergus,* pp. xix–xxii, 106, 180. *Mod. Lang. Rev.,* XX (1925), 158–60.

[16] *Romania,* VIII (1879), 61.

[17] Froissart, *Œuvres,* ed. Kerwyn de Lettenhove (Brussels, 1867), II, 313. There is no evidence whatever that this was an ancient name for Stirling. For the real identification of Sinaudon cf. *infra,* n. 43.

chus, Melrose "la Blanche Lande," and Chepstow Montrose.[18] In a document of 1368 Dumbarton is called "Castrum Arthuri." [19] Some of these fanciful namings were used by the wholly uncritical Glennie in his *Arthurian Localities* to prove that the historic Arthur had actually belonged to southern Scotland; and even the formidable critic, Dr. Brugger, accepted Sinaudon as an early name of Stirling, though every bit of evidence before 1365 tells against him.[20]

One can feel sure that Geoffrey was in part the inspirer of this fashion by localizing the "Castellum Puellarum" and the "Mons Dolorosus" in Scotland. But one may well inquire whether he himself was not inspired by an antecedent *conteur* tradition. For scattered through Arthurian literature are the vestiges of two traditions: according to one Morgain la Fée was the lady or queen of Lothian; according to the other she dwelt with her maidens in a very strong fortress, the Castle of Maidens. The evidence will be presented later in this book.[21] Combine these two traditions, and the inference is almost inescapable that Edinburgh, the chief fortress of Lothian, was the "Castellum Puellarum" or "le chastel as puceles." Naturally, one cannot prove that the equation had been made before Geoffrey's time (in fact, he did not make it himself), but similar inferences had been made. William of Malmesbury (*ca.* 1125) asserted that Walwen (Gawain) reigned over Walweitha (Galloway),[22] doubtless because of the similarity in the names. It is quite on the cards, therefore, that a Breton *conteur,* catering to the French-speaking nobility of the Scottish Lowlands, let us say in the first quarter of the twelfth century, decided that the legendary King Loth was the eponymus of Lodien,[23] that his paramour and wife, Morgain, was the Lady of Lothian, and that ergo her famous Castle of Maidens was no other than the fortress of Edinburgh. If this could happen after Geoffrey's time, it could happen before; and the new discovery could reach the ears of the inquisitive "historian," who thereupon with characteristic effrontery introduced the "Castellum Puellarum" among the foundations of Ebraucus in Scotland. If Geoffrey met the King of Scots in 1141, he could have assured him that Mons Agned and Castellum Puellarum were simply ancient names for his own royal residence on the Castle Rock.

[18] Froissart, *Meliador,* ed. A. Longnon, S.A.T.F. (1899), III, 331, 340 f.
[19] W. F. Skene, *Four Ancient Books of Wales,* I, 55 f.
[20] *Zts. f. franz. Sprache u. Lit.,* XLVI (1924), 410–14. W. C. Mackenzie, *Scottish Place-Names* (London, 1931), p. 81.   [21] *Infra,* pp. 112–16, 302–5, 451–57.
[22] Chambers, *op. cit.,* p. 250. Brugger (*Zts. f. franz. Sprache u. Lit.,* XXXIII [1908] "Referate," 59 f.) and Bruce (*Evolution of Arthurian Romance,* I, 21n.) agree that the connection of Walwen with Walweitha is "eine gelehrte Erfindung," and are of course right.
[23] Geoffrey of Monmouth actually makes a connection between Loth and Lodonesia. Cf. Faral, *Légende arthurienne,* III, 225, 237. Like the connection of Walwen with Walweitha, this is of course factitious, and in no way disposes of the theories advanced elsewhere in this book as to Loth's original connection with Ireland or his later connection with the Orkneys.

To be sure, much of this is speculation, but not wholly idle speculation. That Breton entertainers were welcomed in Scotland and responded by giving a Scottish coloring to their productions seems clear from the lais of *Doon, Desiré,* and *Gurun* (the last preserved only in a Norse translation). Professor Magoun has shown convincingly that *Gurun* reflects in some detail a historic insurrection of the men of Moray in 1116, and both the hero and heroine are said to be nigh kin to the King of Scotland.[24] Evidently the Tweed was no barrier to the Breton minstrels, any more than to other propagators of Anglo-French culture.

It is in the light of this fact that we must interpret the extraordinarily persistent association of Morgain in one or another of her guises with Edinburgh and its general neighborhood. The number and variety of these associations prove them to be deeply rooted, and since Chrétien's *Yvain,* as we shall see in our discussion of Laudine, provides an instance, they must go back to the middle of the twelfth century, at the very least. We shall see at the same time that the lai of *Desiré* offers strong evidence that its anonymous heroine was Morgain, and the setting is the land of Calatir, which the latest scholarship identifies with the district of Calder, just west of Edinburgh.[25] The lai of *Doon* not only, as we have noted, identifies Daneborc with the Castle of Maidens, but also furnishes evidence that the mistress of Daneborc was originally Morgain, for in several ways she suggests identity with Morcades, the paramour and later the wife of Loth, King of Lothian. Morcades, according to *Le Conte del Graal,*[26] dwelt in a castle with five hundred dames and damsels. Morcades, according to *Les Enfances Gauvain,*[27] bore a son out of wedlock and sent him away with a ring as a recognition token. So also did the mistress of Daneborc in *Doon.*[28] Morcades' son, Gauvain, according to the *Vulgate Merlin,*[29] met his father in battle, overthrew him, and only when his father asked his name, did mutual recognition follow. *Doon* tells much the same story of the son of the mistress of Daneborc.[30] It is clear that the name Morcades is simply a variation on Morgain, and that therefore the Lady of Daneborc, the mistress of the Castle of Maidens, was originally Morgain. *La*

[24] *Studia neophilologica,* XIV (1942), 1–24. If, as Prof. Magoun contends, the original lai of *Gurun* was "put together in French octosyllabic couplets not many years after 1118," it is one of the earliest documents in the history of the *Matière de Bretagne* and displays a precocious interest in affairs of love.

[25] *Lays of Desiré, Graelent, and Melion,* ed. E. M. Grimes, p. 48. Anderson, *op. cit.,* I, 234. W. S. Watson, *History of Celtic Place-Names in Scotland* (Edinburgh, 1926), p. 105.

[26] Weston, *Legend of Perceval,* I, 193.   [27] *Romania,* XXXIX (1910), 19–23.

[28] *Romania,* VIII, 63.   [29] Sommer, *Vulgate Version,* II, 317.

[30] *Romania,* VIII, 63 f. It is also striking that, as was noted above (pp. 93 f.), the vigil test which the Lady of Daneborc imposed (*Romania,* VIII, 61 f.) was also imposed by the faery lady Melior, who had been brought up in the isle of Avalon. Moreover, Doon's supernatural swift horse Baiart (*ibid.*) seems identical with the *cheval faé* Baiart, which Maugis d'Aigremont obtained by following the instructions of the faery Oriande, who is certainly modeled after Morgain. Cf. *Maugis d'Aigremont,* ed. F. Castets (Montpellier, 1893), pp. 30–56.

Mort Artu, though it does not place Morgain's castle at Taneborc, puts it less than two days' journey away, and though knights are mentioned as present in the castle, only damsels serve Arthur with a sumptuous repast and only damsels attend him to his bedchamber.[31] Here again is a Castle of Maidens belonging to Morgain, and it is in the general vicinity of Edinburgh.

Equally striking evidence to the same effect is afforded by an elaborate story in *Le Livre d'Artus,* of which the significant elements are these: [32]

A certain enchantress, the Queen of Danemarche, fearful for her son's safety, surrounded a garden with a wall of air and there entrapped the knights of Arthur. As each knight entered, a *pucele* offered him an apple, and if he ate, he lost all desire and power to leave, for he found in the garden all the delights of the world. Finally the enchantments were ended. We learn that the castle where the Queen of Danemarche dwelt was called "li Chastiaus des Puceles" because of the maidens in the adjoining garden.

First, it should be observed (and has been observed by Miss Paton) [33] that this enchanted garden bears a marked resemblance to the Val Sans Retor established by Morgain, which was also enclosed by a wall of air and where Arthur's knights were held captive, enjoying all delights in company with their *amies.*[34] Moreover, the motive of the Queen of Danemarche in establishing this enclosure is precisely that which impelled the Queen of Meydelant in *Lanzelet* to construct the Schastel Mortel,[35] namely the protection of her son; and the Queen of Meydelant, we know, was Morgain.[36] The apples offered by the *puceles* of the Queen of Danemarche are evidently of the same species as that which Ogier ate in the Isle of Avalon, for after eating it Ogier dwelt there with Morgain for two hundred years in such delights as no earthly being can imagine.[37] Manifestly, the Queen of Danemarche in *Le Livre d'Artus* has taken over, lock, stock, and barrel, the traditions linked to Morgain la Fée, including her residence in the Castle of Maidens. And it is easy to see how she came to be Queen of Danemarche: Danemarche was simply more familiar to the author of *Le Livre d'Artus* than Daneborc, "le chastel as puceles." If we take the evidence from *Doon* and *Le Livre d'Artus* which links Morgain to Edinburgh, and add the evidence from *Desiré* and *Yvain* (to be developed in a later chapter) which links her to Calder and Lothian, there can be hardly a doubt that this was a widespread tradition and an old one.

I can think of no reason why these many traditions should cluster about Edinburgh and the surrounding district except that at an early date, say about 1100, Morgain was joined in love and marriage to Loth, the sup-

[31] *Mort le Roi Artu,* ed. J. Frappier (Paris, 1936), pp. 44–47.
[32] Sommer, *Vulgate Version,* VII, 170, 246, 268, 298, 312–19. On this story cf. Chap. XXIV.
[33] L. A. Paton, *Fairy Mythology,* pp. 82–84.
[34] Sommer, *Vulgate Version,* IV, 117–23.   [35] P. Piper, *Höfische* Epik, II, 181.
[36] Cf. *supra,* pp. 91 f.   [37] Paton, *op. cit.,* p. 76.

posed eponymus of Lothian.[38] Once she had been recognized by certain early *conteurs* as lady or queen of Lothian, and her Castle of Maidens had been fixed at Edinburgh, the association survived for centuries in spite of the many conflicting associations with the Isle of Avalon, Mount Etna, and so forth, all the more easily, of course, since her name was often suppressed. It is understandable, moreover, why Loth, whose name was presumably responsible for Morgain's connection with Lothian, dropped out of these stories. Morgain had an array of lovers and at least one other husband, Urien. These rivals simply crowded Loth out, except in those stories where he appears as the husband of Morcades, Morgades, or Morgause— *Le Conte del Graal, Les Enfances Gauvain, Le Chevalier as Deus Espees, Diu Krone,* and Malory's *Morte d'Arthur*.[39]

Whether this explanation be true or not, the fact remains that in 1142 Edinburgh was officially recognized as the Castellum Puellarum. Word of this would get abroad, and the *conteurs* would hear of it (even if they had not been the first to make the identification themselves). Since Chrétien placed his tournament at Danebroc, it is pertinent to note that three romances describe a tourney at the Castle of Maidens and give signs of following an established tradition. One of these accounts, supplied by the *Vulgate Lancelot*,[40] is of no concern to us except as witnessing the existence of a notion that the place was appropriate for a passage of arms. Another account, given in the *Prose Tristan,* reveals traces of a standard pattern.[41]

The hero appears incognito, with a black shield, at the tourney in a plain surrounding the "château aux Pucelles." He carries all before him, retiring at the

[38] This seems to be the most plausible explanation since it brings into harmony four facts: (1) Loth is frequently styled King of Lothian; (2) five romances give Loth's wife the name Morcades or Morgause; (3) various legends connected with Morgain are localized in or near Lothian; (4) Morgain's Castle of Maidens was identified with Edinburgh. Dr. Blenner-Hassett's statement (*Speculum,* XVII, 1942, p. 253) that this romantic epithet "no doubt reflects the connection of the place with some female religious establishment in early times" is unsupported by any proof that there was ever a nunnery at Edinburgh, and is wholly out of accord with the romances; for never is a Castle of Maidens a nunnery. Dr. Brugger in his learned discussion of the subject (*Zts. f. franz. Sprache u. Lit.,* XLIV, "Referate," 95 f.) suggests that Geoffrey of Monmouth supposed that Edinburch was an aphetic form of Meideneburch, and translated this hypothetical form into Latin. This involves two hazardous assumptions: (1) that Geoffrey identified Mons Agned with Edinburgh; (2) that, though no Englishman ever seems to have imagined that Edinburgh stood for Meideneburch, the Normanized Welshman made this far-fetched guess. W. J. Watson's assertion in his *History of Celtic Place-Names,* p. 156, that there was some connection with St. Monenna and her maidens is open to the same objection as Dr. Blenner-Hassett's view. The saint did not establish a nunnery at Edinburgh. An early attempt to explain the name is found in *Chronicon de Lanercost,* ed. J. Stevenson (Edinburgh, 1839), p. 179.

[39] Paton, *op. cit.,* pp. 138, n. 6, 141. Malory, *Morte d'Arthur,* Bk. I, chap. 2. *Li Chevaliers as Deus Espees,* ed. W. Foerster (Halle, 1877), vss. 2944 f. F. H. von der Hagen, *Denkmale des Mittelalters,* Heft I (Berlin, 1824), p. 12. Potvin, *Perceval le Gallois,* V, vs. 30851 (Montpellier ms.). J. D. Bruce, *Historia Meriadoci and De Ortu Walwanii,* pp. xlv, xlvii, n. 1.

[40] Sommer, *op. cit.,* IV, 229-31.

[41] E. Löseth, *Roman de Tristan en prose* (Paris, 1890), pp. 94-109.

end of each day to the forest, where he is tended by his squire. Gaheriet is also present, incognito. The King of Scotland, Aguisant, plays a prominent part. All agree that the knight with the black shield deserves the prize, and are grieved when he disappears.

The third account, and probably the earliest in date, occupies several hundred lines in Renaud de Beaujeu's *Le Bel Inconnu* and is most important.[42]

Arthur proclaims the tournament at the instance of Blonde Esmerée, who wishes to lure her beloved, Guinglain, away from the enchantress of the Ille d'Or and marry him. The assembly is held in the plain outside the Castiel as Puceles, near Valedon. Guinglain arrives incognito and carries all before him, but is recognized by his shield. The King of Scotland, Aguizans, plays a prominent part. All agree that Guinglain deserves the prize. Arthur gives him Blonde Esmerée as his wife. The pair are wedded with great ceremony at "la cité de Sinaudon (or Senaudon)" in Wales,[43] and are crowned king and queen.

Nothing in the narrative indicates that the Castle of Maidens was at or near Edinburgh, but two remarkable cognates support this localization. One occurs in Guillaume le Clerc's *Fergus*.[44]

Arthur proclaims the tournament to lure Fergus out of hiding, and it is held in the plain below Gedeorde (Jedburgh in Lothian). Fergus appears incognito with his shining shield and carries all before him, but retires each night to the forest. The Dame de Lodien arrives and requests Arthur to give her the knight with the shield as her husband. Gavain fetches Fergus, and the King bestows on the youth the hand of the Dame de Lodien. The pair are wedded with great ceremony and crowned king and queen. Two *puceles* from a castle near by are specially summoned to the nuptials.

[42] Ed. G. P. Williams (Paris, 1929), vss. 5055–6246.
[43] "La cité de Sinaudon" in Wales is surely the chief city of Snowdonia, namely Caer Seint. There are three reasons for this conclusion. First, Geffrei Gaimar, who was a sober chronicler according to his lights and no romancer, writing in England shortly before 1150, asserted (*Estorie des Engles,* ed. T. D. Hardy, C. T. Martin, I, 285): "En Wales ot plusur citez, Ke mult furent renomez; Cum Karrewein e Karliun E la cité de Snauedun." We recognize Caerwent (cf. *supra,* pp. 73 f.) in Karrewein, Caerleon in Karliun. There must therefore have been a third renowned city known in the twelfth century as "la cité de Snauedun." Secondly, there is ample evidence from the eleventh century onward that the English called the great mountain range in northwest Wales Snaudun or Snaudon (*Anglo-Saxon Chronicle,* sub anno 1095; Bruce, *Historia Meriadoci,* pp. xxv, 1, 15); even more pertinent is the fact that in a ms. of about 1200 the whole district about Snowdon, Guinodocia or Gwynedd, is equated with Snaudune (*Vitae Sanctorum Britanniae,* ed. A. W. Wade-Evans, Cardiff, 1944, pp. 232, 246). The most important city of this region was Caer Seint. Thirdly, the ruins of the Roman fort of Segontium (known as Caer Seint or Seiont) were the center of legends, reported by Nennius (Chap. 25) and the authors of *Branwen* and the *Dream of Maxen* (Loth, *Mabinogion,* 2d ed., I, 134, 220 f.). The ruins were responsible for the description of Sinadon in *Le Bel Inconnu* (vss. 2775–2808) as a Cité Gaste; and the fact that in the *Dream of Maxen* the *kaer* at the mouth of the river Seint is the residence of the supremely beautiful maiden Elen (Loth, *op. cit.,* I, 216 f. 222, 224) may possibly be connected with the fact that *Libeaus Desconus* (ed. M. Kaluza, vss. 121–26) calls the supremely beautiful maiden who guided the hero to Sinadoun Elene. Cf. *Speculum,* XXII (1947), 520–33.   [44] Pp. 177–89.

It is important to observe that in this striking parallel with *Le Bel In-connu,* the lady who is prize of the tournament is the Lady of Lothian, and that though there is no mention of the Castle of Maidens or of Edinburgh, the passage of arms takes place in the region of which Edinburgh is the capital, and maidens are summoned from a castle in Lothian to the wedding.

Proof that correspondences between the *Tristan, Le Bel Inconnu,* and *Fergus* are not merely accidental is furnished by Malory's Book of Gareth,[45] which describes a tournament corresponding significantly with not merely one but all three versions.

The assembly is proclaimed by Dame Lyones (Lyones is Malory's form for Loenois, Lothian) [46] at the instance of King Arthur, who wishes to lure Gareth from hiding. The assembly takes place at the Castle Perilous beside the isle of Avylyon. Gareth appears incognito and carries all before him. King Agwysaunce and the King of Scotland are among the participants. Gareth is recognized, but retires into the forest. Gawain goes to fetch him and after some time brings him to King Arthur. Arthur bestows Dame Lyones on Gareth, and the wedding is celebrated with great solemnity at Kynkenadon (elsewhere called "Kynke Kena-donne upon the sondes that marched nyghe Walys").[47]

This narrative corresponds to the *Prose Tristan* not only in the general pattern but also in the presence of Gareth (Gaheriet) incognito, the participation of King Agwysaunce, and the hero's retiring to the forest. It agrees with *Le Bel Inconnu* in the participation of King Agwysaunce; it apparently reflects the same tradition in that Avylyon and Valedon, both variations on Avalon,[48] are near the scene of the tournament, and the weddings of Gareth and Guinglain take place respectively at a city and castle called Kynke Kenadonne near Wales and at "la cité de Sinaudon (Senaudon)" in Wales.[49] Malory also agrees with Guillaume le Clerc in regarding the heroine as Lady of Lothian, in motivating the tourney as an effort to lure the hero into the limelight, and in representing him as retiring to the forest after the day's hurly-burly, being sought out and brought to Arthur by Gawain. Add to these the links between the *Prose Tristan, Le Bel Inconnu,* and *Fergus,* and there can be no doubt that the common original dealt with a tournament held by Arthur at the Castle of Maidens,

---

[45] *Morte d'Arthur,* ed. H. O. Sommer, I, 254–63, 268–70.   [46] Cf. Chap. LI.

[47] Malory, *op. cit.,* I, 213.

[48] Valedon seems to be a corruption of Avalon under the influence of Sinaudon. There can be no doubt that the isle of Avylyon was introduced because Morgain was not only Lady of Lothian but also queen of Avalon, the isle of maidens.

[49] Malory (or his source) apparently had a form Cenadon before him, took the initial for a hard *c*, and substituted K. Note his transformation of Corbenic into Carbonek (*op. cit.,* II, 713, 717). A similar blunder is noted in *PMLA,* XXXIX (1924), 138: "Bocas in cent nouellys witnessyth the same" was transcribed as "Bocase in kent witnesith the same"! I suspect that "Kynke" is a corruption of *cité*. This might have been misread as *cice,* owing to the similarity of *c* and *t* in ms., and *k*'s might have been substituted for *c*'s as in Kenadonne.

that is, Edinburgh, for the hand of the heiress of Lothian, and with the ensuing nuptials.

Though Chrétien has nothing of the elaborate plot connected with the tourney at the Castle of Maidens, it seems probable, since there are other marked parallels between the romances of Gareth and Erec, that his localization at Danebroc, "le chastel as puceles," of Erec's feats of prowess after his marriage preserves a vestige of a well-established tradition. It is not hard to perceive why the author of X expunged all other traditional details of the tournament at the Castle of Maidens, since he had already employed the sparrow-hawk adventure as the means by which his hero won a bride. He was too intelligent to follow this by another adventure in which Erec achieved a new bride, the Lady of Lothian.[50] Unwilling to dispense with a well-known theme altogether, especially since tournaments had become so fashionable as spectacles and testing grounds of prowess by the second half of the twelfth century that he could not afford to omit it, he nevertheless was compelled to cut out the features which did not harmonize with his previous narrative. He (and perhaps Chrétien after him) performed the operation with such thoroughness that only the telltale name Danebroc remained. The Welsh redactor of X went even farther, dropping the incident completely and merely remarking: "Thereafter Geraint loved the tournament and hard encounters, and from all he emerged victorious." [51]

It may well be remarked that the theme of a tournament could not, as such, be Celtic, and even in France such martial sports had not been known for more than a hundred years.[52] I would suggest that the theme of a tournament held at the Castle of Maidens is an adaptation to twelfth-century fashions of an older story pattern of which a number of examples are to be found in Arthurian romance—the deliverance of the Queen of the Castle—or the Isle, or the Land—of Maidens from her oppressors.[53] The hero wins the battle or the single combat and sometimes weds the Queen or has an amour with her. There is no prima-facie difficulty in maintaining a Celtic derivation for this romantic theme. I shall discuss it in connection with Perceval's deliverance of Blancheflor,[54] and hope to demonstrate that in that instance, as well as in the story of Gareth's deliverance of Dame Lyones, the ultimate sources are Irish and Welsh. And to that chapter I would refer the interested reader.

[50] Ulrich von Zatzikhoven's *Lanzelet* and the anonymous *Peredur* are glaring examples of unintelligent concatenation, with the result that the heroes acquire a series of mistresses and brides.
[51] Loth, *op. cit.*, II, 145.
[52] A. Schultz, *Das höfische Leben zur Zeit der Minnesinger*, ed. 2 (Leipzig, 1889), II, 107.
[53] For example, J. D. Bruce, *Historia Meriadoci*, pp. 89–92; *Perlesvaus*, ed. Nitze, I, ll. 3888–4000; *Sir Perceval of Galles*, ed. J. Campion, F. Holthausen (Heidelberg, New York, 1913), vss. 1125–1744; *Queste del Saint Graal*, ed. A. Pauphilet, pp. 47–50.
[54] Chap. LXVI.

Chapter XVI

EREC'S AMOROUS INDOLENCE

VERSES 2434–2577

Erec returned with his bride from Arthur's court to Caruent, and there was welcomed by his father Lac and all the nobles of Destregales. He was so passionately in love with Enide that he abandoned the pursuit of arms and avoided tournaments, and often it was past midday before he left his wife's embraces. There was much murmuring among his knights and squires at Erec's unmanly indolence, and echoes of this reached the ears of Enide. She was blamed for holding her husband "lacié et pris," a recreant from knightly deeds.

IT IS a little surprising to find that Chrétien, who has hitherto treated his hero as a paragon of knightly prowess, should rather suddenly inform us that after his return to his own land he abandoned himself to uxorious dalliance, often lying abed till after noon and earning the reputation of a complete "slacker." It is also surprising to find him, the model lover, proud of his beautiful wife, suddenly taking violent umbrage at her for telling him what he admitted to be true, and forcing her to undergo perils and humiliation. Of course, such changes in character do take place in reality. Was it an instinct for realism, a sense that impeccable heroes do not exist, which led the author of X (from whom Chrétien took over these novel developments in Erec's character) to invent the motif of his hero's recreancy from the ways of chivalry and the incidents which flow from it? Or was he following what has hitherto been his habit—treating with ingenuity and naturalism traditional themes?

So far as Erec's sloth is concerned, no final answer seems possible, but there are several reasons for supposing that once more we are dealing, not with invention, but with freely adapted tradition. We have already observed that in the sparrow-hawk episode Enide acted the part formerly assigned to Morgain. It will appear in the next few pages that Erec's sudden display of anger at Enide and the trials to which he subjected her are likewise based on a tale of which the original heroine was Morgain. If, therefore, in the interim between these two phases of Erec's relation to Enide, he rather unaccountably becomes a victim of her charms, yields himself to sloth, and leads people to remark that Enide holds him "lacié et pris," [1] lost to honor, it behoves us to inquire whether Morgain had a similar effect on her lovers.

[1] *Erec*, vs. 2563.

That is just what we do find. It was one of the many contradictions of Morgain's nature that, though in one group of tales she equipped her favorite with horse and arms and sent him forth to heroic deeds, in another group she held him enthralled in a bower of ease and idleness. And in this, of course, she is copied by Enide. She plays in one act the role of Gloriana, the Faery Queen, the inspirer of chivalry, who sends her knights out to glorious adventure; in another act she is Acrasia, "that wanton lady, with her lover loose, Whose sleepy head she in her lap did soft dispose." [2] Indeed, it is recognized that Morgain is the literary ancestress of Alcina, Armida, and Acrasia.[3]

This aspect of Morgain displays itself in at least five stories. We noted a few pages back that she established the Val Sans Retor and kept many lovers, including her own faithless Guiomar, in blissful idleness.[4] Much the same story is found in *Claris and Laris,* though no lovers of Morgain are specifically mentioned.[5] She also caused Ogier le Danois to be wrecked near the Isle of Avalon, restored his youth, and made him forget his past; and he spent with her two hundred years in such delight that they seemed to him to be but twenty.[6] Another form of this authentic tale is told in *Le Bastard de Bouillon,* with the same emphasis on oblivion of the past and the supernatural lapse of time.[7] In two other versions the fay is anonymous but can readily be identified with Morgain. In the first the lover is Guingamor,[8] who, as we learn from *Erec,*[9] was Morgain's *ami* and lord of Avalon, and he lives with her three hundred years though it seems but three days. In the second tale, related by Wauchier, the fay dwells significantly in Avalon and keeps her knightly lover in an enchanted castle for ten years without martial adventure.[10] We shall have occasion to return to this legend of Morgain as the Acrasia of Arthurian romance in our consideration of the "Joie de la Cort" episode. There can be no doubt of its vogue with the *conteurs.*

It is very likely, then, though not a demonstrable fact, that Enide's adoption of a similar sinister role was suggested by the Morgain tradition, after which so much of her story was patterned. Once more the author of X seems to be revamping old motifs; once more he is careful to expunge any features that would throw discredit on his heroine. Enide, like Morgain, holds her lover "lacié et pris," but, unlike her prototype, exerts her spell

[2] E. Spenser, *Faerie Queene,* Bk. II, Canto xii, st. 76.
[3] P. Rajna, *Fonti dell'Orlando Furioso,* 2d ed. (Florence, 1900), p. 166. I. E. Rathborne, *Meaning of Spenser's Fairyland* (New York, 1937), pp. 211–17. Ariosto recognized similarity of Morgana and Alcina (*Orlando Furioso,* Canto VI, st. 38).
[4] Sommer, *Vulgate Version,* IV, 117–23. Cf. *supra,* p. 113.
[5] *Claris et Laris,* ed. J. Alton, *Bibliothek d. literarischen Vereins in Stuttgart,* CLXIX (Tübingen, 1884), pp. 97–112.   [6] Paton, *Fairy Mythology,* p. 76.
[7] *Bastars de Buillon,* ed. A. Scheler (Brussels, 1877), pp. 119–32.
[8] Marie de France, *Lais,* ed. K. Warnke, 3d ed., pp. 247–50.
[9] *Erec,* vss. 1954–57.   [10] C. Potvin, *Perceval le Gallois,* IV, pp. 239–45.

involuntarily, and all legitimate blame for Erec's uxorious sloth rests on his shoulders. This hypothesis affords at least a possible explanation for Erec's unexpected recreancy. It also would justify M. Roques's view [11] that Enide presents an antithesis to Mabonagrain's mistress, who *willfully* bound her lover by his promise to live with her in her enchanted *vergier*.

Chapter XVII

EREC'S HARSH TREATMENT OF ENIDE

VERSES 2473-3769

One morning, as Enide lay beside Erec in bed, she wept because she was the occasion of his shameful inactivity. He awoke to notice her tears and to hear the words, "What an evil hour it was for thee! (Con mar i fus!)" Though she denied the words, he drew from her the admission that she had been lamenting that people called him recreant from his duty and blamed her for the change. Erec at once acknowledged that she and they were right, but instructed her to don her best dress and order her palfrey. He himself called for his arms and his steed. After commending Enide to his father's loving care in case he should not return alive, he set out with her on a journey as chance would dictate. He ordered her to ride ahead of him and on no account to speak to him unless spoken to. On several occasions when she was moved to warn him of imminent peril, he sternly rebuked her for disobedience.

THOUGH ONE of Erec's motives in setting forth on his perilous journey with Enide is clearly his desire to vindicate his knightly reputation, and though it is natural that he should wish his bride to accompany him and witness his mighty strokes, yet his sudden adoption of a harsh and masterful attitude toward his beloved wife hardly seems the behavior of a just and generous man. Chrétien does not expound this matter with his usual lucidity in psychological matters. Erec admits that Enide and the courtiers are right in charging him with neglect of arms; [1] he adopts the course which she recommends [2] and sets out to silence the charge by his deeds; he entrusts her, in case he should not return, to his father's loving protection and requests that she be given half his royal domains. [3] These are the reactions of a rational being and of a husband who respects his wife's judgment and believes in her loyalty. Yet he addresses her as if she were guilty of a grave fault, commands her to ride some distance

---

[11] *Romania*, XXXIX (1910), 379 ff.
[2] Vss. 2566-68.
[1] Vss. 2576 f.
[3] Vss. 2725-31.

ahead of him, and forbids her to speak until spoken to.[4] He even declares that he hates her.[5] And she on her part thrice accuses herself of folly and pride,[6] though her only fault has been to tell Erec what he needed to know and what he has admitted to be true. Moreover, it transpires in the course of their adventures that he has doubted her love, and at last he reveals that he has been testing her and is now assured that she loves him perfectly.[7] Yet Chrétien has mentioned nothing which would engender such hatred and suspicion in the mind of the rational and devoted husband that Erec seems to be.

Scholars have offered the most varied solutions of the difficulty.[8] Professor Nitze, granting the inconsistency of Erec's behavior, believes it to be good psychology.[9] "It is only natural that Erec, wounded in his pride, should turn against the cause of his dishonor, blameless as Enide really is. In such moments of tension the best of men will not be just." This interpretation one might readily accept if an examination of analogous stories did not show that once more the answer to the puzzle lies in tradition. Professor Sparnaay [10] has made out a good case for the theory that we have here an incomplete fusion of two traditional rides of a knight with a damsel: one in which the hero's purpose is to demonstrate his prowess to the damsel who doubts it; the other in which the knight's purpose is to humiliate and punish his wife whom he suspects of infidelity. The fusion may have been suggested by the fact that in both traditions the damsel rides some distance ahead of the knight. At any rate, it is not difficult to prove that these two distinct stories existed and that both contributed to the motivation and the incidents of Erec's adventurous ride with Enide.

In this chapter let us consider the evidence that Erec's harshness was motivated in earlier tradition by his doubt of her fidelity. Not only does Chrétien imply that his hero questioned Enide's love, but in *Geraint* the suspicion is put down in so many words.[11] The hero is alarmed by overhearing Enid's self-blame for his loss of glory, but "another thought distressed him, that it was not through solicitude for him that she had spoken thus, but through pondering on her love for another man and desiring to be rid of himself." Geraint voices this suspicion to Enid. "'Shame be

[4] Vss. 2768–75.   [5] Vs. 3004.
[6] Vss. 2589–610, 3108–18, 4623–69.   [7] Vss. 3767 f., 4920–25.
[8] For some examples cf. *Romanic Review*, V (1914), 115 ff.; VI (1915), 434 ff.; IX (1918), 1 ff.; X (1919), 26 ff.; J. D. Bruce, *Evolution of Arthurian Romance*, II, 59–62; *Zts. f. franz. Sprache u. Lit.*, XLIV (1916–17), 146–48; *Zts. f. rom. Phil.*, XLVIII (1928), 123–28; XL (1919–20), 85–87; *Germanisch-romanische Monatschrift*, XVIII (1930), 292–301; *Zts. f. franz. Sprache u. Lit.*, Supplement, *Behrens Festschrift* (1929), 219–21; *Archivum Romanicum*, XVIII, 443 ff.; *Romania*, XX (1891), 163 f.
[9] *Mod. Phil.*, XI (1914), 448.
[10] H. Sparnaay, *Hartmann von Aue, Studien zu einer Biographie*, I, 78–101.
[11] Loth, *Mabinogion*, 2d ed., II, 153.

to me if thou return hither until thou knowest whether I have lost my strength as utterly as thou hast said, and if thou shalt be as free from care as thou wast to desire to be alone with the man of whom thou wast thinking.'" In *Geraint,* moreover, as we have noted, the hero commands his wife to put on her worst dress in preparation for the ride.

That the Welsh version has preserved in the jealousy motive and the shabby dress two authentic features which are absent from *Erec* is borne out by the marked parallelism between *Geraint* and the episode of the Proud Knight of the Glade in Chrétien's *Conte del Graal.*[12]

Perceval's first adventure after leaving his mother's forest abode was to enter a most beautiful tent, surmounted by a golden eagle, to force a damsel lying within to accept his kisses, and to help himself to food and drink. Soon after his departure, the damsel's lover returned from hunting (*del bois*), found her in tears, saw signs of a recent visitor, and refused to believe that she had not entertained a rival. He declared that her horse should not be fed nor should she change her dress, but she must follow him till he could avenge himself on his rival. Some time later Perceval met with the same damsel, pale and in a ragged gown, mounted on a bony and trembling nag. She recognized him, reproached him, and warned him to flee. Her lover, the Proud Knight of the Glade, now rode up in a fury, and when Perceval admitted that he had been the occasion of suspicion, a combat followed. Perceval won; his adversary promised to make amends to his innocent mistress and betook himself to Arthur's court.

The resemblance to the situation in *Geraint* is obvious: the weeping woman, the suspicious and angry lover, the command to wear her oldest garment, her riding far in front of him. A second remarkable analogue has hitherto been overlooked; it is found in the *Vulgate Lancelot.*[13]

In the course of a long series of adventures, Guerehes [14] came to four tents. In the first he helped himself to food and drink; in the fourth he found a damsel sleeping, took off his clothes and lay with her in the darkness, without observing a sleeping knight in the same bed. When the knight awoke and found a rival in his place, he dragged his innocent wife out of bed and threatened vengeance. Guerehes in turn awoke and killed the knight. After the interment of the body, he forced the lady to ride with him against her will. He slew a knight who defied him. The damsel spied four knights ahead and warned Guerehes, but he overthrew them all. The episode ends with the lady's taking the veil at a nunnery.

It seems quite unnecessary to point out that the Proud Knight story and the Guerehes story were not based on *Erec* or on X, and presumably no Continental Frenchman could have read *Geraint.* These later versions go back ultimately to the same *conte* of the jealous lover and his humiliated

---

[12] *Percevalroman,* ed. A. Hilka (Halle, 1932), vss. 635–832, 3691–4001.

[13] H. O. Sommer, *Vulgate Version,* V, 29–32.

[14] Though ms. Brit. Mus. Add. 10293 gives Gaheries as the name for part of this episode, Sommer (*op. cit.,* V, 9, n. 6) points out that the form Guerehes is correct, and he is confirmed by the *Dutch Lancelot.* Cf. J. L. Weston, *Legend of Lancelot du Lac,* pp. 227 f.

lady which the author of X employed. It is clear that the Proud Knight version has preserved a coherent and well-motivated sequence of events. It is natural under the circumstances for the Proud Knight to suspect his mistress's fidelity; it is therefore natural for him to drive her forth on his quest for vengeance on his supposed rival. This, then, was probably the original form. The Guerehes version is garbled since the author has made the rival lover kill the angry husband and then take over the husband's role of forcing his wife to ride with him. In X, though Erec's conduct was probably ascribed in part, as in *Geraint*, to suspicion of Enide, yet the scene which supplied grounds for suspicion was absent; and so Chrétien, finding Erec's doubts unwarranted by anything in his source, deleted them. Hence all our mystification as to Erec's motives.

Another fact which tends to show that suspicion of Enide's loyalty was the original cause of Erec's behavior is to be found in Raoul de Houdenc's *Vengeance Raguidel*.[15] Gauvain, having been convinced with good reason that his mistress, Ydain, was ready to desert him for a rival, obliges her to ride ahead of him, just as Erec treats Enide. *Geraint, Le Conte del Graal,* and *La Vengeance Raguidel* then agree in representing a jealous knight as adopting this mode of punishment for his suspected mistress or wife. It is this evidently stereotyped situation which explains much in Erec's harsh conduct toward Enide.

Can we, as with the other traditional plots, discover the identity of the original actors? Who was the damsel of the tent whose part Enide has acquired? Who was the Proud Knight of the Glade, whom Erec has supplanted? The evidence is not conclusive but it is consistent. Once more there is reason to believe that Enide's prototype was Morgain. The Proud Knight seems to go back to Arawn, King of Annwn, whose wife may well have been Modron, the original of Morgain. Let me elaborate.

A suggestion that the damsel of the tent was Morgain occurs in *Sir Launfal*.[16] Here too, as in Perceval's adventure, the hero came to a very rich tent with a golden eagle on the top, found a beautiful lady reclining on "a bed of prys," kissed her, and had his fill of meat and wine; and this lady, we know, was the daughter of the "Kyng of Fayrye"; Kittredge proved that her home was the isle of Avalon; [17] the gift of her own horse to Launfal suggests an equation with Morgain.[18] It seems plausible, therefore, that Perceval's encounter with the damsel of the tent is an artistic variation on the traditional meeting with Morgain la Fée; Perceval, the mannerless simpleton, is represented as taking by force the favors and the hospitality which the fay willingly bestowed on Launfal.

This view gains support from the fact that Perceval forcibly wrests from

15 Vss. 4769-87.
16 French and Hale, *Middle English Romances*, pp. 354-57, vss. 262-345.
17 *American Journal of Philology*, X, 13 f.
18 Cf. *supra*, pp. 87-89, and *PMLA*, LXI (1946), 929 f.

the damsel of the tent her ring, and there are many traces of a tradition that Morgain was in the habit of giving her favorites a magic ring. In the lai of *Desiré,* which presents many analogies to *Sir Launfal* and belongs to the same group of tabu stories,[19] the hero finds a fay lying on a couch in the forest, wins her love, and on parting is presented by her with a ring which will vanish when he reveals their amour.[20] Not only is her role similar to that of the fay in *Launfal,* but she also bears her lover a beautiful son and daughter, just as Modron, the original of Morgain, bears a beautiful son and daughter to Urien.[21] *La Pulzella Gaia* is another analogue of *Launfal.*[22] Galvano, riding at adventure in the woods, comes upon a serpent which transforms itself into a lovely maiden, enjoys her love, and on parting is presented by her with a ring which will lose its power if he divulges their amour. She is the daughter of the Fata Morgana. In the Middle English romance of *Eglamour* the King of Sidon offers his daughter, who bears the suggestive name of Organata, to the hero, and on his refusing she gives him a ring which would protect his life on water or land.[23]

There are other instances. When Morgain had brought Ogier to the isle of Avalon to be her lover, she put a ring on his finger which restored his youth, and when it was removed, he became an old man.[24] We have already recognized the same fay in the foster mother of Lanzelet, the Queen of Meydelant; and in Chrétien's *Charrette* Lancelot's foster mother gave him a ring which contained a stone of such virtue that no enchantment could hold him.[25]

In the fourteenth-century *cantare* of *Lionbruno* we discover a fay who, though her name is Aquilina, is obviously a composite of Morgain in her various roles, including that of bestowing a ring on her protégé-lover.[26] Like Morgain in the *Vita Merlini* she can fly through the air on wings,[27] and like a certain fay from Avalon in the *Didot Perceval* she assumes the form of a bird;[28] like Morgain in the *Bataille Loquifer* she transports

[19] *Lays of Desiré, Graelent, and Melion,* ed. E. M. Grimes, pp. 12–26.

[20] *Lays,* ed. Grimes, pp. 52–57, vss. 175–268.

[21] Loth, *Mabinogion,* 2d ed., II, 284; I, 284, n. 4. *Aberystwyth Studies,* IV (1922), 105.

[22] *Lays,* ed. Grimes, p. 16. E. G. Gardner, *Arthurian Legend in Italian Literature,* pp. 242–47. *Fiore di leggende,* ed. E. Levi, pp. 32–36. Cf. Margot-la-Fée's daughter in P. Sébillot, *Folk-lore de France,* III, 289.

[23] *Thornton Romances,* ed. J. O. Halliwell (London, 1844), pp. 146 f., vss. 601–621. Note · in connection with the name Organata the frequency with which Morgain lost the first letter of her name. Cf. *Mod. Lang. Notes,* XXVI, 65 ff.; *Review of Eng. Studies,* X (1931), 81; *Speculum,* XX (1945), 183–85.

[24] L. A. Paton, *Fairy Mythology,* pp. 76–78.

[25] *Charrette,* ed. W. Foerster (Halle, 1899), vss. 2347–62.

[26] *Fiore di leggende,* pp. 63–72.

[27] Geoffrey of Monmouth, *Vita Merlini,* vss. 922–25. Faral, *Légende arthurienne,* III, 334. Cf. also Hartmann von Aue, *Erek,* ed. M. Haupt, 2d ed. (Leipzig, 1871), vss. 5177 f.; *Prophecies de Merlin,* ed. L. A. Paton (New York, 1926), I, 416.

[28] *Didot-Perceval,* ed. Roach, pp. 200–02.

her future lover through the air to her palace; [29] like the fay of the tent in *Lanval,* whose home is in Avalon, she gives the hero her love, confers on him the magic power to have whatever riches he desires, puts him under a tabu not to reveal their amour, and when he boasts of it, comes at the last moment with her maidens to save his life.[30] It is not probable that mere chance led the author of *Lionbruno* to unite in one personage Morgain, Lancelot's foster mother, and Lanval's mistress, the faery damsel of the tent. Probably he found his plot ready-made; probably it was constructed when a single fay, Morgain, was recognized as the center of all these traditions.

Altogether, then, the testimony of the romances points to Morgain as the prototype of the Lady of the Tent, not only in *Lanval* and *Launfal,* but also in *Le Conte del Graal,* and Perceval's snatching the ring from her and placing it on his own finger before his departure was a deliberate comic alteration of the persistent theme that Morgain placed a magic ring on the finger of her favorites at parting.

When we try to discover the identity of the Proud Knight of the Glade we come to a conclusion which is happily harmonious with our inferences about the lady of the tent. Chrétien says that the Proud Knight, when he discovered his *amie* weeping, was returning "del bois," [31] an expression which was commonly employed in the sense of "from the hunt." [32] This interpretation agrees with Guiglain's meeting with the Proud Knight of the Glade in *Le Bel Inconnu.*[33] The latter appears as a huntsman in a woolen coat, horn in hand, riding after a stag with a pack of hounds. One of these, a fair white brachet with black ears, is seized by Guiglain's companion, and Guiglain refuses to give it up to the huntsman. Later, as in *Le Conte del Graal,* there is a combat; the hero is victorious and sends the Proud Knight of the Glade to Arthur's court. The circumstances of their first meeting correspond remarkably with the opening scene in the mabinogi of *Pwyll.*[34] Arawn, king of Annwn, appears as a huntsman in a woolen coat, horn in hand, riding after a stag with a pack of hounds, all with shining white bodies and red ears. They run down the stag in a glade. Pwyll, the hero, tries to beat them off and sets his own hounds on the quarry. Arawn angrily reproaches him for thus molesting his hounds. The quarrel is settled amicably, however. The Welsh parallel to *Le Bel Inconnu* seems sufficiently exact,[35] especially the interference with the

[29] Paton, *Fairy Mythology,* p. 50. Le Roux de Lincy, *Livre des Légendes,* pp. 248 f.

[30] Marie de France, *Lais,* ed. Warnke, 3d ed., pp. 86–112.

[31] *Percevalroman,* ed. Hilka, vs. 783.

[32] *Ibid.,* vs. 6056. Marie de France, ed. Warnke, p. 283. Chrétien, *Charrette,* vs. 2029.

[33] Renaud de Beaujeu, *Bel Inconnu,* ed. G. P. Williams (1929), vss. 1276–490.

[34] Loth, *Mabinogion,* 2d ed., I, 84 f.

[35] Other Arthurian parallels to this scene in *Pwyll* occur in *Didot-Perceval,* ed. Roach, p. 213; C. Potvin, *Perceval le Gallois,* IV, vss. 27008–11, 27116–27317; *Libeaus Desconus,* ed. Kaluza, vss. 1057–1296; P. Piper, *Höfische Epik,* II, 214 f. Cf. W. H. Schofield, *Studies in Libeaus*

white hound or hounds, with colored ears, which provokes the huntsman's anger; and it explains how the huntsman came to be known as the Proud Knight of the Glade, since it was in a glade that Arawn displayed a haughty resentment at Pwyll's behavior.

The mabinogi does not tell us any story of Arawn's wife which corresponds closely to that of the Lady of the Tent, but it does tell us that she was ravishingly beautiful and that during her husband's absence she received into her bed the hero, Pwyll.[36] Both were, however, completely innocent, she because Pwyll had assumed her husband's form, he because he rejected her embraces, and all was done with Arawn's full connivance. There is therefore in the mabinogi no suspicious and enraged husband and no driving of the suspected wife forth in ragged garb to accompany her husband on his mission of vengeance. But the very compromising situation in which the proud huntsman's wife was involved during his absence might well have given rise to just such a sequel. In fact, there is preserved in the Dutch *Lancelot* an incident which evidently derives from *Pwyll* and which shows that the huntsman's wife had acquired a reputation for infidelity.[37]

Walewein, riding through a forest, heard the cry of hounds in pursuit of a stag, and presently saw a pack of tiny white dogs. He took one of them up with intent to give it to the Queen when their master, a dwarf, appeared on the scene and reproached him for his conduct. The newcomer announced that he was king of the country and transformed Walewein into his own shape. He invited him to his castle, and there Walewein learned that the huntsman's wife was in disgrace because she had been discovered in the arms of a vile servant.

Compare this with the incident in the mabinogi.

Pwyll, riding through a forest, heard the cry of hounds in pursuit of a stag, and presently saw a pack of white dogs. He was driving them off their quarry when their master appeared on the scene and reproached him for his conduct. The newcomer announced that he was a king of Annwn and transformed Pwyll into his own shape. He sent Pwyll to his palace, and there, as we know, Pwyll was received into the queen's bed.

There can be no doubt that the Welsh story is the indirect source of the Dutch, and little doubt that the ambiguous situation in the former has developed into a scandal. It confirms our suspicion that the wife of the supernatural huntsman of Welsh tradition had become in Arthurian romance notorious for her lechery. If further proof is necessary, we can find it in *Gawain and the Green Knight,* where likewise we have a super-

---

Desconus (Boston, 1895), pp. 32–35, 171–74. Cf. discussions of Guingambresil and Guiromelant below.   [36] Loth, *Mabinogion*, I, 87 f.

[37] *Roman van Lancelot,* ed. W. J. A. Jonckbloet, II, vss. 12663–812. Cf. Dr. R. E. Bennett's article in *Speculum,* XIII (1938), 68 f. The famous dwarf king of Welsh tradition (see Chaps. XX, LXXV) has been arbitrarily substituted for Arawn, the leader of the Wild Hunt. On both these figures and their confusion with Arthur cf. *Mod. Phil.,* XXXVIII (1941), 289–302.

natural huntsman whose wife plays the wanton.[38] And all this evidence
is in harmony with the conclusion we have already reached that the prototype of these amorous ladies was the celebrated light-o'-love, Morgain la
Fée. No wonder that Erec was suspicious of Enide's loyalty since she bears
a historic affinity to Morgain. This motivation of Erec's harsh behavior,
so dimly discernible in Chrétien's poem, is correctly and clearly expressed
in *Geraint* and the analogous episode in *Le Conte del Graal*. Thus Sparnaay's interpretation is in part vindicated.

Chapter XVIII

EREC AND THE ROBBERS

VERSES 2795–3085

*As Enide rode silently ahead of Erec on their strange journey, three knights
who lived by robbery spied them. One of them, determined to have Enide's
palfrey as his booty, spurred against Erec. Enide warned her husband of
the robbers, only to receive a rebuke for disobeying his command of silence. However, he met the first knight and killed him, wounded the
second, and unhorsed the third, and turned over their three mounts to
Enide. Proceeding on their way, Erec and his wife were observed by five
other knights bent on plunder, who began to divide up among them the
horses as their prospective spoils. Again Enide warned Erec, and again
earned his reproach. The hero took on each of the five robbers, vanquished
them all, and hurled one into a ford where he was drowned. The five
horses Erec handed over to Enide, to drive along with the other three.*

SPARNAAY's thesis that the confused motivation of Erec's ride with
Enide is due to the fusion of two traditional rides of a knight and a
lady, one motivated by the knight's suspicion of his lady's fidelity and
his desire to humiliate her, and the other motivated by the knight's deire to
vindicate his prowess to a lady who doubts it, has thus been demonstrated
so far as the first motive is concerned. It now remains to show that the
thesis also holds good for the second motive. Sparnaay, following Philipot
and Meyer-Lübke,[1] noted that Erec's adventurous journey with a damsel
who has cast doubt on his valor and his encountering three robbers are
paralleled in *Le Bel Inconnu*.[2] But there is very little similarity in the
circumstances, except that in both tales the robbers observe the chivalrous

[38] *Journ. of Eng. and Germ. Phil.*, XLII (1943), 170–83.
[1] *Romania*, XXV (1896), 294. *Zts. f. franz. Sprache u. Lit.*, XLIV (1916–17), "Abhandlungen," 149.
[2] H. Sparnaay, *Hartmann von Aue, Studien zu einer Biographie*, I, 104.

practice of attacking one at a time, and the first of the three is killed.[3]
Since these features are not found in the Middle English *Libeaus Desconus*,[4]
derived from the same source as *Le Bel Inconnu*, and since Schofield has
proved that the latter was greatly indebted to Chrétien's poem,[5] it is quite
possible that these specific resemblances are due to borrowings from *Erec*.
Sparnaay would have found a closer and more significant analogue to
Erec's fight with the robbers in Malory's Book of Gareth,[6] which I have
shown elsewhere [7] must rest on a source antecedent to Chrétien. Let me list
the correspondences in parallel columns.

1. Erec's valor has been questioned by Enide.
2. Enide rides ahead and Erec follows.
3. Erec overcomes two robbers and then a third who flees.
4. Enide warns Erec of five knights who bar his way.
5. Erec defeats them, including one whom he hurls into a ford and drowns.

1. Gareth's valor is questioned by Lynet.
2. Lynet rides ahead and Gareth follows.
3. Gareth overcomes three thieves and then three others who flee.
4. Lynet calls attention to two knights who bar Gareth's way.
5. Gareth defeats them, including one whom he hurls into a ford and drowns.

Another indication of a common source may perhaps be seen in the fact
that the names of the heroes, Erec and Gareth, have a common origin in
the alternative forms of the Welsh hero's name, Gwri and Gware.[8]
Though this correspondence may be fortuitous, yet the others surely are
not. Gareth's adventure cannot be derived from Erec's for two reasons.
First, there are too many signs that the Book of Gareth follows the tradition of the Damoisele Maudisante, which lies behind certain episodes in
Le Bel Inconnu, Libeaus Desconus, Wigalois, and *Le Chevalier de la
Cote Maltaillié* [9]—a tradition which cannot possibly be derived from
Erec. Secondly, in this tradition the motives of the hero and heroine are
perfectly clear and consistent, whereas those of Erec and Enide are strangely
ambiguous. It is therefore easy to explain the obscurity in Chrétien's poem
by Sparnaay's theory of contamination, whereas it is difficult to see how
Erec's adventurous ride with Enide could have evolved into the story of
Gareth's ride with Lynet.

Sparnaay then was right. The adventure with the robber knights was
borrowed by the author of X from a *conte* of the Damoisele Maudisante

---

[3] *Erec*, vss. 2795–924. Renaud de Beaujeu, *Bel Inconnu*, ed. G. P. Williams (1929), vss. 953–
1234.   [4] *Libeaus Desconus*, ed. M. Kaluza, vss. 481–582.
[5] W. H. Schofield, *Studies on the Libeaus Desconus*, pp. 60–106, 112–34.
[6] Bk. VII, chaps. 5, 6.   [7] *PMLA*, LIV (1939), 656–64.
[8] Cf. Chap. VIII and *PMLA*, LIV, 656–68.
[9] On this tradition cf. Schofield, *op. cit.*, pp. 6–13. The story of La Cote Male Taillée, Breunor
le Noir, occurs in Malory, Bk. IX, chaps. 1–9, and is derived from the *Prose Tristan*.

type, of which Malory's Book of Gareth is the closest representative and which supplied the five features listed above.

The basic framework of the Damoisele Maudisante romances seems to go back to *The Sickbed of Cuchulainn,* an Irish saga containing linguistic forms of the ninth century; [10] at least, the Book of Gareth offers a general parallel,[11] and *Le Bel Inconnu* may preserve in the name of the hero Guiglain the name of the Irish hero Cuchulainn. But within this framework many incidents of independent origin have been fitted. The fight with the robbers is one of these, and its origin may be determined with remarkable clarity.

The clues are found in *Erec* and the Book of Gareth. Both texts, as we have seen, place the second encounter with the knights at a ford. Chrétien, moreover, mentions, before both encounters, the robber knights gloating over the prospect of capturing steeds and harness, and emphasizes the ironic overturn of their hopes when Erec captures their own mounts instead. Likewise, Malory relates [12] that immediately after the encounter at the ford Gareth comes to a black hawthorn; there a dialogue ensues with a knight who threatens to deprive him of horse and harness; Gareth declares: "Hors ne harneys getest thou none of my," and after slaying the knight takes possession of his horse. The significance of these features in *Erec* and the Book of Gareth becomes apparent when one realizes that a combat at a ford was one of the stock motifs of the *Matière de Bretagne;* [13] that in seven instances, besides those mentioned, the victor possesses himself of the horse of his antagonist or antagonists; [14] and that in three of these the motif is connected with a hawthorn or a blackthorn.[15] By no possibility could all these versions of the combat at the ford be derived from *Erec;* in fact, everything goes to show that Chrétien has given us a severely realistic version of what was one of the most uncanny themes in Arthurian romance.

A thorn tree was a thing of magic. Under a flowering *aube espine* in the Forest of Broceliande Viviane enchanted Merlin, as, following the *Vulgate Merlin,*[16] Matthew Arnold has described and Burne-Jones has painted the scene. In *Maugis d'Aigremont,* which owes much to Arthurian tradition, the infant hero was left beneath "l'espine à la fee," and we are

---

[10] Thurneysen, *Irische Helden- und Königsage,* p. 415.
[11] Cf. *infra,* pp. 296 f.   [12] Bk. VII, chaps. 6, 7.
[13] Meager treatments of the subject occur in Schofield, *op. cit.,* pp. 12–14; J. L. Weston, *Legend of Sir Perceval,* II, 204–10; J. R. Caldwell, *Eger and Grime* (Cambridge, Mass., 1933), pp. 119 f.; *Didot-Perceval,* ed. W. Roach, pp. 70–73.
[14] Caldwell, *op. cit.,* pp. 284 f. H. O. Sommer, *Vulgate Version,* IV, 216 f. *Didot-Perceval,* ed. Roach, pp. 195–202. *Zts. f. rom. Phil.,* XVII (1893), 246–55. P. Piper, *Höfische Epik,* II, 264 f. *Historia Meriadoci and De Ortu Walwanii,* ed. J. D. Bruce, pp. 86–88. Renaud de Beaujeu, *Bel Inconnu,* vss. 321–514. In *Libeaus Desconus* the seizure of the horse has been transferred to the battle with the kinsmen of the ford-knight (vss. 508–10).
[15] *Didot-Perceval,* p. 196. *Zts. f. rom. Phil.,* XVII, 249 f. Piper, *Höfische Epik,* II, 264.
[16] Sommer, *Vulgate Version,* II, 452.

told that Oriande, who later became the hero's faery mistress, was wont to rest there when she passed by.[17] In one manuscript of *Sir Degarre*, a princess, leaving her handmaids asleep under a hawthorn tree, is ravished by a faery knight.[18] Sir Cawline in the ballad met the Eldridge King at midnight at a thorn.[19] Folk superstition among the Irish and Welsh preserved similar beliefs;[20] to cut down a hawthorn brought on the vengeance of the fairies. If a thorn alone was magical, much more was a thorn beside a spring[21] or stream. Beside springs fays awaited their human lovers;[22] beside a ford, where hounds mysteriously barked, Modron, the daughter of the King of Annwn, was discovered and ravished by Urien.[23] We have the combination of ford and hawthorn in Béroul's *Tristan*,[24] where there is mention of "le Gué Aventuros, et iluec a une aube espine." In *Rigomer* there is casual mention of a Gué de Blance Espine, where "Morge li fee" and many dames and damsels assembled.[25] In Irish folklore a whitethorn, growing on the banks of streams, was considered to be the haunt and peculiar abode of the fairies.[26] Such an eerie spot was the scene, evidently, of three versions of the combat at the ford. In *Diu Krone* Gasozein rides by night in midwinter near the ford of Noirespine. In the *Didot Perceval* the defender of the Gué Perellos is the son of the Queen of the Noire Espine. In *Le Lai de l'Espine* the hero fights with an Otherworld knight at the Gué de l'Espine, near which a thornbush grows.

These last two texts make it clear why the capture of the opponent's steed is a recurrent element in the fight at the ford; the steed is a supernatural creature. In the *Didot Perceval* the hero finally discomfited the defender of the ford and allowed him to depart on foot. The latter had not gone far when he was carried away with the greatest rejoicing in the world, and he disappeared together with his horse, which Perceval had

[17] *Maugis d'Aigremont*, ed. F. Castets, pp. 23, 26. Cf. Gerbert de Montreuil, *Continuation de Perceval*, ed. M. Williams, I (Paris, 1922), 78–80.
[18] *Sir Degarre*, ed. G. Schleich (Heidelberg, 1929), vs. 74, ms. R.
[19] Sargent and Kittredge, *English and Scottish Popular Ballads*, p. 115.
[20] E. Hull, *Folklore of the British Isles* (London, 1928), pp. 134 f. M. Trevelyan, *Folklore and Folk-Stories of Wales*, pp. 106, 149. For similar English and Scottish beliefs cf. *Folklore*, XVII (1906), 172 f.; C. Hole, *English Folklore* (1940), pp. 87, 132.
[21] J. Rhys, *Celtic Folklore, Welsh and Manx*, I, 332–62. M. A. Courtney, *Cornish Feasts and Folklore* (Penzance, 1890), pp. 32 f. W. G. Wood-Martin, *Traces of the Elder Faiths of Ireland*, II, 81, 88, 96, 156.
[22] *Lays of Desiré, Graelent, and Melion*, ed. E. M. Grimes, pp. 15, 20–23, Marie de France, *Lais*, ed. Warnke, 3d ed. (1925), pp. 247 f. Cross and Slover, *Ancient Irish Tales*, pp. 83 f., 93–95. Potvin, *Perceval le Gallois*, IV, 240; V, 38.
[23] *Aberystwyth Studies*, IV, 105. T. Gwynn Jones, *Welsh Folklore and Folk-Custom*, p. 107. That the woman was Modron is proved by a triad in Loth, *Mabinogion*, 2d ed., II, 284. For Irish examples of faery ladies met at fords cf. *Mod. Phil.*, XII (1915), 604–7.
[24] Vs. 1320. Cf. Guillaume le Clerc, *Fergus*, vs. 252.
[25] *Mervelles de Rigomer*, ed. W. Foerster (Dresden, 1908), I, vss. 9433–39.
[26] Wood-Martin, *op. cit.*, II, 156.

attempted to retain. In *L'Espine* the mysterious knight of the ford was mounted on a white horse with red ears; after the conflict the hero led it to his lady-love under the thorn tree. He then fought with two other knights, and one of them informed him that the captured steed was the swiftest and best for jousting, but that it would be lost if the bridle was removed. The hero returned with his love and the supernatural horse to his father's court. The animal served him well and long, till one day the damsel removed the bridle and the animal vanished.

These two versions of the ford combat, in the *Didot Perceval* and *Le Lai de l'Espine,* show that Gareth's encounter at the river passage, his fight near a hawthorn tree, and his seizure of the vanquished knight's horse constitute a single tradition.

Moreover, both versions offer strong evidence that the tradition was born in Wales. The spectral knight in the lai rode on a white horse with red ears, and we have already had occasion to observe [27] that in the mabinogi of *Pwyll* the hounds of Annwn, the Other World, had white bodies and red ears—a belief which survived for centuries in Welsh folklore.[28] It is therefore pertinent to remark that this same steed, which the hero of the lai captured and then lost through the removal of the bridle, seems to reappear in a modern Welsh folktale as a *ceffyl-dwr,* or water horse.

"A man once caught a Ceffyl-dwr on the shores of Carmarthen Bay, and afterwards tried to break the creature in. By means of an artfully contrived bridle he led the animal home, and used it as a cart horse. But one day the bridle became unfastened, and the Ceffyl-dwr darted with the cart and driver into the sea, and was never afterwards seen." [29]

Both the coloring of the faery steed in *L'Espine* and its disappearance, then, strongly suggest that its original home was in South Wales.

The episode of the ford combat in the *Didot Perceval* is even more strongly saturated with Welsh matter.[30] Here too, as we have just seen, there is a horse, captured at a ford and carried away mysteriously. And here there is an extraordinary parallel with the episode in *Pwyll*,[31] which we studied in the last chapter and which is localized in southwest Wales. Let us recall that in the French romance Urbain, the defender of the ford, is vanquished by Perceval, reveals that he has been dwelling in an invisible castle near by with a faery mistress, and urges Perceval to defend the ford for a year in his stead. In the mabinogi Arawn, the King of Annwn, after his defeat at the ford, gives over to Pwyll the enjoyment of his palace near by and his wife, on condition that at the end of a year Pwyll will meet another king from Annwn, Havgan, in combat at the

[27] Cf. *supra,* pp. 90 f. [28] M. Trevelyan, *op. cit.,* p. 47.
[29] *Ibid.,* p. 64. A similar story is recorded from County Clare: R. Giddings, *Lovely Is the Lee* (New York, 1945), pp. 30 f. [30] *Mod. Phil.,* XLIII, 63–71. [31] Loth, *op. cit.,* I, 85 f.

ford. Though the sequel offers no parallel to the *Didot Perceval,* it does present one notable similarity to *L'Espine* and *Diu Krone:* the fight takes place by night.

In another place [32] I have developed with some fullness the thesis that *Pwyll* has preserved to us in this episode a seasonal myth which had a considerable influence not only on *L'Espine* and the *Didot Perceval* but also on several other romances, including *Gawain and the Green Knight.* The King of Annwn whom Pwyll encountered at the end of a year at a ford bore the name Havgan, which means "Summer White." [33] On this figure the fourteenth-century poet Dafydd ap Gwilym sheds some light, for he represents Haf, "Summer," as a prince, who departs to his own land of Annwn to escape the gales of winter.[34] What of Havgan's victory over Arawn, the huntsman clad in gray wool and mounted on a gray horse? We read in a collection of Welsh folklore: "In some parts of Wales it was stated that Arawn and his *Cwn Annwn* (Hounds of Annwn) hunted only from Christmas to Twelfth Night, and was always accompanied by a howling wind." "In Glamorgan, Brecon, and Radnor Arawn, the master of these hounds, rides a grey horse and is robed in grey." "Stories about the Brenin Llwyd, the Grey King, or Monarch of the Mist, were told in most of the mountainous districts. . . . He was represented as sitting among the mountains, robed in grey clouds and mist." [35] Arawn is evidently the Wild Huntsman of European folklore, whom Tylor, Grimm, and Mogk have recognized as a genius of the storm,[36] and particularly the storms of winter.

In fact, the annual combat at the ford as related in *Pwyll* was a conflict between Summer and Winter. The basic concept survived in the form of folk ritual down into the nineteenth century. It was recorded in 1909 in the words of an aged Welshman.

"When I was a boy, two companies of men and youths were formed. One had for its captain a man dressed in a long coat, much trimmed with fur, and on his head a rough fur cap. He carried a stout stick of blackthorn and a kind of shield, on which were studded tufts of wool to represent snow. His companions wore caps and waistcoats of fur decorated with balls of white wool. These men were very bold, and in songs and verse proclaimed the virtues of Winter, who was their captain. The other company had for its leader a captain representing Summer. This man was dressed in a kind of white smock decorated with garlands of flowers and gay ribbons. On his head he wore a broad-brimmed hat trimmed

[32] *Journ. of Eng. and Germ. Phil.,* XLII (1943), 170–78.
[33] J. Rhys, *Studies in the Arthurian Legend* (Oxford, 1891), p. 281.
[34] For Welsh text and free English translation cf. Dafydd ap Gwilym, trans. H. I. and D. Bell (London, 1942), pp. 252–59. See also T. Gwynn Jones, *Welsh Folklore and Folk-Custom,* p. 154.   [35] M. Trevelyan, *op. cit.,* pp. 53, 48, 69.
[36] J. Grimm, *Teutonic Mythology,* trans. Stallybrass (London, 1883), III, 918–48. H. Paul, *Grundriss der germ. Philol.,* 2d ed., III (Strassburg, 1900), 333–37. E. B. Tylor, *Primitive Culture,* 6th ed. (London, 1920), I, 362.

with flowers and ribbons. In his hand he carried a willow-wand wreathed with spring flowers and tied with ribbons. All these men marched in procession, with their captain on horseback heading them, to an appropriate place. This would be some stretch of common or waste land. There a mock encounter took place, the Winter company flinging straw and dry underwood at their opponents, who used as their weapons birch branches, willow-wands and young ferns. A good deal of horseplay went on, but finally Summer gained the mastery over Winter. Then the victorious captain representing Summer selected a May King and the people nominated a May Queen, who were crowned and conducted into the village." [37]

Similar seasonal customs were enacted in the Isle of Man, in England, and on the Continent.[38] The concept of an annual combat on the first of May is reflected in the brief account in *Kulhwch and Olwen* of the repeated encounters of Gwynn, King of Annwn, and Gwythyr,[39] which will require our attention again in connection with *Le Chevalier de la Charrette.* Thus we see that the combat at the ford between Havgan and Arawn is but one form of a widespread myth of the yearly struggle between Summer and Winter.

It is a far cry from this Welsh myth to the realistic encounter of Erec with the robbers, but the tradition is so well represented in the *Matière de Bretagne* that the links of connection can be established through *L'Espine,* the *Didot Perceval,* and Malory's Book of Gareth. We can have no better illustration of the fading of Celtic mythology into a commonplace adventure of romance. The ancient tale, stripped of its original significance, but retaining the ford, the hawthorn, and the seizure of the horse, was introduced into the Damoiselle Maudisante framework as a means of demonstrating Gareth's prowess to a damsel who questioned it. The author of X completed the process of removing all traces of eerie supernaturalism from the encounter at the ford.

Chapter XIX

COUNT GALOAIN'S BOAST

VERSES 3209–61

A squire in the service of Count Galoain met Erec and Enide after they had spent the night in the open, provided them with cakes, wine, and cheese, and rode back to the town to bring news to his master, the Count,

[37] Trevelyan, *op. cit.,* p. 25.
[38] Grimm, *op. cit.,* II, 758–68. J. G. Frazer, *Golden Bough,* 3d ed., IV, 254 ff. W. Hone, *Every-Day Book* (London, 1838), I, 358 f. E. K. Chambers, *Mediaeval Stage* (Oxford, 1903), I, 173.   [39] Loth, *op. cit.,* I, 331 f.

of their approach. He reported that Erec was very courteous and the handsomest man he had ever seen. Galoain replied: "I believe that he is not more good-looking than I." The squire stoutly maintained Erec's superiority in form and feature, and Galoain set out to verify the report.

THIS INCIDENT seems to be a variation on one of the commonplaces of Arthurian romance, which occurs in *Diu Krone, De Ortu Walwanii, Rigomer, Hunbaut,* Gerbert's continuation of *Le Conte del Graal, Arthur and Gorlagon, King Arthur and King Cornwall,* the Dutch *Lancelot,* and *L'Atre Périlleux.*[1] The usual formula tells how a self-complacent king is challenged on some point of pride by his wife or *amie* and is much incensed, but sets out to determine the facts.[2] Only one of these versions, the Dutch *Lancelot,* resembles *Erec* in that the issue is one of good looks.[3] A certain lord, Morilagan,[4] asked his mistress whether she knew of any man so fair and so good a knight as he.[5] When she asserted that Walewein (Gawain) was a handsomer and better knight, Morilagan punished her, but was later vanquished by Walewein. In five other versions (*Diu Krone, De Ortu Walwanii, Rigomer, Hunbaut, L'Atre Périlleux*) it is a question of martial might alone. It seems likely, then, that the Dutch *Lancelot* has combined two versions of the boast, one which involved prowess, the other which involved comeliness. It is the latter which is represented by Galoain's vaunt.

One must not overlook the fact that in *Erec* it is Galoain's superior

[1] Heinrich von dem Türlin, *Diu Krone,* ed. Scholl, vss. 3356–5080. *Mervelles de Rigomer,* ed. W. Foerster, I, 470–82. *Historia Meriadoci and De Ortu Walwanii,* ed. J. D. Bruce, pp. 85–87. *Perceval le Gallois,* ed. C. Potvin, VI, 251. *Studies and Notes in Philology and Literature,* VIII (Boston, 1903), 150 f. F. J. Child, *English and Scottish Popular Ballads,* I, 283 ff. *Roman van Lancelot,* ed. W. J. A. Jonckbloet, II, vss. 18826–19106. *L'Atre Périlleux,* ed. B. Woledge (Paris, 1936), pp. 216 f. *Hunbaut,* ed. Stürzinger and Breuer (Dresden, 1914), pp. 2–5. Discussions of this motif from various angles are to be found in Child, *op. cit.,* I, 274 ff.; *Englische Studien,* XXXVI (1906), 337 ff.; A. Dickson, *Valentine and Orson,* pp. 83 f.; *University of Michigan Publications, Language and Literature,* VIII (1932), 27–37.

[2] The formula also occurs in the *Pèlerinage Charlemagne* and *Morkinskinna.* Cf. M. Schlauch, *Romance in Iceland* (Princeton and New York, 1934), p. 164. Both must have derived it more or less directly from an Arthurian *conte.* Cf. discussion below.

[3] In the cognate *Pèlerinage Charlemagne,* as we shall see, the king boasts of his handsome appearance, as well as his might as a conqueror. Since this is the earliest French form of the motif, and is based on an even earlier Arthurian *conte,* it seems certain that long before Chrétien's *Erec* the issue of superiority in physical appearance had entered the traditional formula of the boast.

[4] It should be noted that whereas in the Dutch *Lancelot* Morilagan punishes his *amie* by forcing her to sit in a well, in *La Pulzella Gaia (Fiore di leggende,* ed. E. Levi, p. 43) a similar punishment is visited upon the *amie* of Galvano by Morgana, and in Malory, Bk. XI, chap. 1 there is a story, which Miss Paton (*Fairy Mythology,* p. 100, n. 1) has shown to be related, and in which Morgan le Fay is said to have punished a lady by placing her in a boiling bath to await the coming of a knight to deliver her. Evidently the name Morilagan is a confused reminiscence of Morgan. Another evidence of confusion lies in the fact that whereas Morilagan is lord of the land of Swerte Montanie (vs. 18854), which in French would be "noire montaigne," in the analogous tale in *L'Atre Périlleux* the damsel is placed in "une noire fontaine" (ed. Woledge, p. 218, vs. 191).   [5] Ed Jonckbloet, Bk. III, vss. 18858 f.

beauty which is questioned, whereas in the Dutch *Lancelot* it is Walewein's. Not only are the names nearly homophonous, but there is much
to support the view that Gawain was an indispensable figure in the
formula of the boast. In *De Ortu Walwanii* Arthur asserts his superiority
in arms to all other knights, and when the Queen denies it, he goes forth
and is overwhelmingly defeated by Walwanius. In *Diu Krone,* which supplies a version notably similar, the role of Walwanius is taken by Gasozein
de Dragoz, and since a Gasoain d'Estragot turns up in the *Vulgate Lancelot,*[6] we may feel certain that the *z* of Gasozein is unauthorized and may
well suspect that the *s* represents a misreading of *l;* in short, Gasozein not
only plays the part of Walwanius, but owes his name to a corruption of
Galoain. In *L'Atre Périlleux,* which offers a detailed parallel to the Dutch
Lancelot, when King Brun's *amie* asserts the superiority of the knights of
the Round Table over her lover, it is Gavain who vindicates her by de-
feating Brun. In *Rigomer* the situation is altered, but still Gauvain's
prowess is involved; Arthur asserts that Gauvain is the best knight, and
the Queen says that she knows one equally good, meaning Lancelot.
King Arthur and King Cornwall and *Arthur and Gorlagon* both represent Gawain as accompanying his uncle on an expedition to a foreign
king's court, prompted by the Queen's disparaging remarks about her husband. In *Hunbaut,* when Arthur is told that there is a king who does
not acknowledge his sovranty, it is Gauvain whom he sends to demand
submission. Gerbert de Montreuil is the only author who does not assign
Gawain a conspicuous part in the boast formula.

This is not the only argument for the hypothesis that in bragging of
his beauty Galoain has taken over a tradition attached to Gawain. We have
already observed that in the Dutch *Lancelot* the superior beauty of Walewein is asserted and challenged, and have noted the phonetic similarity
of this name to Galoain. The *Vulgate Lancelot* bears witness to the physical perfections of Gawain.[7] "It is true that Sir Gauvain was the handsomest knight of all his brothers. . . . He was the handsomest knight in
body and right well shaped in his limbs, and was not too large nor too
small, but of right fair stature." And one of the scribes who copied *Erec*
may have had a suspicion of Galoain's real identity, for he spells the name
Galuain,[8] a recognizable form of Gawain. Putting all these facts together,
we can hardly resist the conclusion that the author of X, with characteristic freedom, introduced in Galoain's boast a traditional motif, not realiz-

[6] Sommer, *Vulgate Version,* III, 119. Since this Gasoain and Gasozein both fought a fierce
duel with Gawain, it is not likely that the names could have been derived from Chrétien's
Erec, where though ms. B mentions a Gorsoein d'Estrangot and ms. P a Gasauens de Tranglot, there is no word of such a duel. All three romances must derive the name ultimately
from some common ms. source. On Gasozein cf. *Zts. f. franz. Sprache u. Lit.,* XXVIII (1905),
"Abhandlungen," 38–46.   [7] Sommer, *Vulgate Version,* IV, 358.
[8] Ed. Foerster (Halle, 1890), vs. 3129, table of variants.

ing, of course, that Galoain was the same character whom he had already introduced into his romance as Gauvain. Neither did Chrétien suspect their original identity.

Can we trace the formula of the boast back into Celtic literature? It is possible to show: first, that the earliest appearance of the formula in French literature occurs in a poem which contains many Irish motifs, and thus renders plausible the Irish origin of the formula; secondly, that an intermediate stage is furnished by the appearance of the formula in a Welsh setting, attached to a king of South Wales; thirdly, that this Welsh version is obviously related to an elaborate Irish version, which explains the outstanding features of the Arthurian treatment. The case for Celtic origin seems a good one if these three arguments are sound.

First, turning our attention to *Le Pèlerinage Charlemagne,* we note, as Kittredge and Professor Reinhard have done before us,[9] that in the opening scene we have a good example of our formula, and since the *Pèlerinage* probably belongs to the second quarter of the twelfth century [10] this is the earliest occurrence in French literature. Some scholars may hastily decide that the Arthurian versions are mere adaptations. But this can hardly be. For not one of the many Arthurian parallels to this, as to other features of the *Pèlerinage,* contains the slightest vestige of the Carolingian and ecclesiastical character of the poem as a whole or a single detail of the boasting scene which would betray this *chanson de geste* as the source. Medieval story-tellers were seldom experts in removing the telltale marks of origin. That all the Arthurian poets who used the formula of the boast should have been particularly cautious and expert in this regard is a preposterous supposition. We are forced to conclude that the *Pèlerinage,* except for the portions concerned with the relics, was a rifacimento of an Arthurian *conte.* This view is reinforced by the detection by Dr. Laura Hibbard Loomis and Professor Cross of several Irish motifs in the *Pèlerinage,*[11] as would be natural if there had been borrowing from the *Matière de Bretagne.* And the presence of these Irish motifs lends plausibility to the Celtic origin of the boasting scene which opens the *chanson de geste.*[12]

Charlemagne, in the presence of his dukes and barons, proudly asks his wife: "Lady, have you ever seen a king beneath the sky whose sword so well became him or whose crown sat so well on his head? I will conquer yet more cities with my lance." She unwisely replied: "I know another who is more comely when he wears his crown among his knights." The emperor was wroth and demanded

[9] *Studies and Notes in Philology and Literature,* VIII, 212, n. 4. *University of Michigan Publications, Lang. and Lit.,* VIII, 29 f.
[10] J. Coulet, *Etudes sur l'ancien poème français du voyage de Charlemagne* (Montpellier, 1907), p. 70.   [11] *Mod. Phil.,* XXV (1928), 331 ff.
[12] *Karls des grossen Reise nach Jerusalem und Constantinopel,* ed. E. Koschwitz (Leipzig, 1923), vss. 1–52.

the name of this king, threatening to cut off her head if she lied. She answered: "I have heard many a word concerning King Hugon the Strong; he is emperor of Greece and Constantinople. . . . There is no knight so handsome from here to Antioch. No baronage was ever like to his, save yours." Charlemagne then declared that he would learn the truth and set out for the East.

There is reason, accordingly, to surmise that this scene came into the *Pèlerinage* ultimately from a Celtic source.

In the second place, Walter Map gives a version of the formula in his *De Nugis Curialium* and attaches it to a King of South Wales.[13]

The King of Deheubarth,[14] seated with his household at a banquet, boasted: "There is no province or kingdom under heaven from which I cannot easily carry off booty and return without a battle, for who can withstand me and my mighty following?" A member of his household, Triunein, replied that the King of Brecknock was so preeminent in his own valor and in that of his men that no other king could carry off booty from him on a clear day. Thereupon the King of Deheubarth ordered Triunein to be bound and cast into prison, but relented and allowed him to lead an expedition against the King of Brecknock to test the truth of his assertion.

We have already had evidence that the geography of *Erec* is largely that of Deheubarth and that Erec's combat at the ford can be traced back through *Le Lai de l'Espine* to legends localized in Carmarthenshire and Pembrokeshire.[15] Here we have the formula of the king's boast linked to the King of Deheubarth, which included those counties.

Thirdly, Professors Reinhard and Schlauch have noted [16] the resemblance between the king's boast in the *Pèlerinage* and a curious Irish tale, preserved in a form of the thirteenth or fourteenth century, though the tradition must go back in part to the eleventh,[17] namely, "The Journeys of the Tuath Luchra (the Dwarf People) and the Death of Fergus." As the title suggests, this tale consists of two parts. The first part bears a most obvious likeness to Map's story of the King of Deheubarth, and the second part accounts for the intrusion of the taunting queen into the Arthurian formula of the king's boast.[18]

In the first part, Iubdan, king of the Lilliputian folk, the Lupracan, seated with his household and his queen at a banquet, bragged: "Have you ever seen a king that was better than myself? Horses or men of battle have you ever seen better than they who tonight are in this house? I give my word that it would be a hard task to take out of this house tonight either captives or hostages, so surpassing

---

[13] Walter Map, *De Nugis Curialium*, Div. II, Chap. 11. *Ibid.*, trans. Tupper and Ogle (London, 1924), p. 92.
[14] Map says that this means North Wales, but as Tupper, p. 331, remarks, the author is nodding here.   [15] Cf. *supra*, pp. 73–76, 131.
[16] *University of Michigan Pub., Lang and Lit.*, VIII, 29–37. M. Schlauch, *Romance in Iceland*, p. 164, n. 34.   [17] R. Thurneysen, *Irische Helden- und Königsage*, pp. 540 f.
[18] *Ibid.*, pp. 542–47. Cross and Slover, *Ancient Irish Tales*, pp. 471–87.

are its heroes and men of battle." A member of his household, Esirt, then declared: "I know of a province in Ireland, one man of which could take hostages and captives from all four battalions of the Lupracan." King Iubdan then ordered Esirt to be seized, but relented and allowed him to go to Emain Macha to bring back some proof of his assertion. Later Iubdan himself went to test the might of the Ulstermen, and returned after great humiliations. In the second part, Fergus, king of Ulster, was disfigured by a water monster in Dundrum Bay. His queen, during a quarrel, taunted him with his wry mouth and suggested that he revenge himself. Fergus went to the bay and killed the monster, but was himself fatally wounded.

Both parts, one may observe, have an element in common: a king, whose pride is offended by criticism, takes up the challenge to his honor and meets with misfortune. In the first part it is Iubdan's superiority in arms which is called in question; in the second, it is Fergus' physical beauty which is the subject of his wife's taunt. Telescoping the two stories would be natural, and it would account for the main features of the boast formula as we find it in the *Pèlerinage* and in Arthurian romance. Let me list them. (1) Quarrel between king and queen: *Pèlerinage, Diu Krone, De Ortu Walwanii, Rigomer, King Arthur and King Cornwall, Arthur and Gorlagon, L'Atre Périlleux*. (2) King's physical attractions impugned by woman: *Pèlerinage*, Dutch *Lancelot*. (3) King's assertion of his superiority in arms challenged by a woman: Dutch *Lancelot, De Ortu Walwanii, Rigomer, L'Atre Périlleux*. (4) Long journey to the court of rival: *Pèlerinage, Arthur and Gorlagon, King Arthur and King Cornwall, Hunbaut*. (5) Humiliating outcome for the boastful king: *De Ortu Walwanii*, Dutch *Lancelot, L'Atre Périlleux*. These versions of the boast have been affected, of course, by other narrative patterns; for example, the *Pèlerinage* and *Arthur and Gorlagon* have incorporated many other Irish motifs,[19] and *De Ortu Walwanii* and *Diu Krone* have absorbed the Welsh combat at the ford.[20] Taking into account these contaminations, we need not be surprised at the various forms which the king's boast has taken. But underlying them all we recognize the composite Irish tale of *The Journeys of the Tuath Luchra and the Death of Fergus*. There lies the ultimate source of Count Galoain's boast.

For the rest of Galoain's part in the story I have been unable to discover any traditional basis. Possibly this is pure invention on the part of the author of X; possibly he was reworking some tale in which Gawain played a caddish role, as in Malory's story of Pelleas and Ettard.[21]

---

[19] Cf. *supra*, n. 11.   [20] Cf. *Journ. of Eng. and Germ. Phil.*, XLII (1943), 171–78.
[21] Malory, *Works*, ed. E. Vinaver (Oxford, 1947), I, 163–71; III, 1351–56).

Chapter XX

GUIVRET AND HIS SISTERS

VERSES 3663–3930, 4939–5446, 6411–67

After their escape from Galoain and his men, Erec and Enide were pass-
ing by a tower and were espied by a very small knight, who armed him-
self and rode fiercely against Erec. There was the usual desperate battle,
and after six hours Erec forced his tiny opponent to surrender. The latter
revealed himself as Guivret le Petit, a rich and powerful ruler of Irish
vassals. On learning Erec's identity, he became his sworn friend and prom-
ised his aid in case of need. Some days later, after Erec's flight from Limors,
he was riding again with Enide when he was encountered by Guivret.
It was dark and Erec was so feeble from his wounds that the little King
hurled him to the ground without recognizing him. But on discovering
that it was Erec, Guivret had him cared for that night in a tent and pro-
vided him with pasties and wine from six casks. The next day the three
proceeded to a castle called Penevric or Pointurie, and there the dwarf
king's sisters, skilled in medicine, washed Erec's wounds and applied
plasters until he recovered wholly. When he announced his intention to
seek Arthur's court, Guivret offered to accompany them and before their
departure presented Enide with a palfrey of a sorrel color, with a head
part white, part black, with a green stripe between. When the trio neared
the castle of Brandigan, Guivret warned Erec of its perils. Finally all three
were welcomed by Arthur and Guenievre and were persuaded to remain
at court.

No PERSONAGE in *Erec* offers better credentials as a creation of the
Celtic fancy than the dwarf king Guivret, even though the author
of X stripped him of many of his most uncanny attributes. Zenker
made an illuminating study of the spirited and loyal monarch,[1] and showed
that he had much in common, first, with Wauchier's Petit Chevalier,
whom we have seen in Chapter XI to be a traditional figure, and secondly,
with the famous Auberon of *Huon de Bordeaux,* whose Arthurian affini-
ties have been generally recognized.[2]
    Let us see what links connect Guivret with Wauchier's dwarf knight
who guarded the talismanic shield. Both display incredible prowess in

[1] *Zts. f. franz. Sprache u. Lit.,* XLVIII (1925–26), 30–37.
[2] Paton, *Fairy Mythology,* pp. 114–30. C. Voretzsch, *Composition des Huon von Bordeaux,*
pp. 123–38. E. Brugger, *Illuminated Tree in Two Arthurian Romances* (New York, 1929),
p. 28. *Mod. Lang. Rev.,* XX (1925), 158. *Zts. f. rom. Phil.,* LIV (1934), 74 ff.

arms.[3] Both, when the hero has been engaged in combat, provide a lodge (or tent), food, and drink.[4] Both are lords of great castles.[5] Both have a sister or sisters to whose care the hero is committed.[6] Both accompany him to Arthur's court.

More telling are the resemblances between Guivret and Auberon. Both are dwarfs who have large armies at their command.[7] Both go singly to meet the hero when he trespasses on their domains.[8] Both promptly become his friends, swear to come to his aid when he is in need, and do so.[9] Both tell him of the perils of a certain castle and advise him to pass it by.[10] Both are most generous with gifts.[11] Both are welcomed by Arthur to his court.[12]

The relationship between the three dwarfs is clinched by the resemblances between Auberon and Wauchier's Petit Chevalier. Auberon's domain consists of a forest forty leagues long; Wauchier's dwarf calls himself "li Chevaliers Petis del castel de la forest grande."[13] Both are marvelously beautiful.[14] Both are as small as a child of five or seven years.[15] Both possess a talisman (escu, hanap) by which the hero and others are tested.[16] Both have a horn to summon their retainers.[17] Both display great prowess in a tournament before King Arthur.[18]

The traditional nature and activities of Guivret were recognized by the Welsh author of *Geraint*, for he noted that the Cymry called him the Little King.[19] In fact, two Welshmen of the twelfth century recorded stories of dwarf kings which recall certain aspects of Guivret. Giraldus Cambrensis[20] told of a boy from the neighborhood of Swansea who was led to the land of the dwarfs and was received most hospitably by the king. The inhabitants were models of honor and truth, and deeply resented human treachery. A significant point, though not recorded of Guivret, is the fact that these pigmies rode on horses as small as greyhounds. Walter Map[21] knew a legend of a diminutive king, who ap-

[3] *Erec*, vss. 3680–822. Potvin, *Perceval le Gallois*, V, vss. 31729 ff.

[4] *Erec*, vss. 5127–67. Potvin, vss. 32617–27.   [5] *Erec*, vss. 5187 f. Potvin, vss. 31889–31916.

[6] *Erec*, vss. 5190–5225. Potvin, vss. 31682–31875, 32729–79.

[7] *Erec*, vss. 4960–68. *Huon de Bordeaux*, ed. F. Guessard and C. Grandmaison (Paris, 1860), p. 101.   [8] *Erec*, vs. 3771. *Huon*, p. 98.

[9] *Erec*, vss. 3890–3917, 5953–71. *Huon*, pp. 104, 111, 134, 198.

[10] *Erec*, vss. 5387–5446. *Huon*, pp. 136 f.

[11] *Erec*, vss. 5212–17, 5316–58. A. Graf, *I Complementi della chanson d'Huon de Bordeaux*, I, *Auberon* (Halle, 1878), vss. 2179–2245.

[12] *Erec*, vss. 6462 f., 6503–9. Graf, *Auberon*, vss. 2206–11.

[13] *Huon*, p. 94. Potvin, V, vss. 32087 f.   [14] *Huon*, p. 94. Potvin, vss. 31665–69.

[15] *Huon*, p. 102. Potvin, vs. 31697.   [16] *Huon*, pp. 110, 303 f. Potvin, vss. 31800–31829.

[17] *Huon*, p. 97. Potvin, vss. 31744–55.

[18] Graf, *Auberon*, vss. 2212–47. Potvin, vss. 32484–32513.

[19] Loth, *Mabinogion*, 2d ed., II, 168.

[20] *Opera*, ed. J. F. Dimock, VI (London, 1868), 75. Cf. *Mod. Phil.*, XXXVIII (1941), 294 f.

[21] Map, *De Nugis Curialium*, ed. M. R. James (Oxford, 1914), p. 13. *Ibid.*, trans. Tupper and Ogle (London, 1924), pp. 15–18. Cf. *Mod. Phil.*, XXXVIII, 301 f.

peared, riding on a goat, to an ancient British sovereign, Herla, made a friendly compact with him, brought his own servants to cater at Herla's wedding with gold and crystal vessels, guided him to his own land, and showered him with gifts, including horses. Map's emphasis on the dwarf king's presence at a wedding and his provision of food and drink in splendid vessels from a far-off land suggests comparison with another Welsh figure, Gwiddolwyn Gorr (the Dwarf), whose magic bottles could keep a drink warm even though borne from the East to the West and which were required in preparation for the nuptials of Kulhwch and Olwen.[22] It is highly probable that Gwiddolwyn is the original of the dwarf king Gleodalen, whom Chrétien mentions among the wedding guests of Erec and Enide.[23]

Ireland, too, had its Lilliputian king, as we have just seen in the very saga of *The Journeys of the Tuath Luchra,* which influenced the Arthurian formula of the king's boast. Like the dwarfs of Giraldus' tale, Iubdan is "of truthful utterance."[24] Like them, he possesses a miniature steed, as small as a hare.[25] Most significant is the fact that this animal had a pure crimson mane, four green legs, a gold-colored body, and a gold-encrusted bridle;[26] for not only have we met in the *Wigalois* version of the sparrow-hawk adventure two strange horses with red manes,[27] but we may now observe that the horse which Guivret presented to Enide had a gold-colored (*sors*) body, a golden bridle, and a green stripe on its head.[28] This palfrey is as surely Celtic as the dappled one which Enide had received earlier in the story from her cousin. So too was the donor of the palfrey, whom the Welsh called the Little King.

But the author of *Geraint,* though he recognized the Little King as a personage familiar to his countrymen, found the name "Gwiffret Petit" foreign; it was used by the French and Saxons.[29] So far as I am aware, Guivret appears with the epithet "petit" or as a dwarf only where the influence of *Erec* is demonstrable.[30] Guivret's counterpart, Auberon, does not derive his name from the Celts.[31] Wauchier leaves his Chevalier Petit

[22] Loth, *Mabinogion,* 2d ed., I, 309.
[23] *Erec,* ed. Foerster (Halle, 1890), vs. 2005, ms. H.
[24] Cross and Slover, *Ancient Irish Tales,* p. 475.   [25] *Ibid.,* p. 476.
[26] *Ibid.,* p. 477.   [27] Cf. Chap. XI.
[28] *Erec,* vss. 5322–34. On this and similar many-colored horses cf. *Zts. f. franz. Sprache u. Lit.,* XLVIII, 37–41; *Revue des langues romanes,* LXV (1927–8), 213.
[29] Loth, *Mabinogion,* II, 168.
[30] Wauchier (Potvin, *Perceval le Gallois,* V, vs. 31374) has "Guiviers li petis," but the passage draws clearly on *Erec.* There is a dwarf-king Givreiz in *Lanzelet* (P. Piper, *Höfische Epik,* II, 188), but its author certainly used Hartmann's *Erek.*
[31] Auberon probably derived his name from the famous dwarf Alberich of Germanic romance. Cf. C. Voretzsch, *op. cit.,* Chap. 7, especially p. 265, n. 2. Another example of borrowing a Germanic name and applying it to a similar figure in Brythonic folk-tradition is found in Map's story of Herla, which is plainly Brythonic in its content but which assigns to the Wild Huntsman a name etymologized out of Hellequin, a Germanic word containing, as all scholars

anonymous, and so do Giraldus and Map their pigmy monarchs. But surely, though the Welsh did not call the Little King Gwiffret or anything like it, they did not leave him nameless.

There is reason to suppose that Guivret had two Welsh dwarfs as prototypes. One slender thread of connection leads us to Gwiddolwyn Gorr, mentioned above. Guivret rides with Erec and Enide to the scene of their last adventure and gives warning of its perils, much as the dwarf in *Libeaus Desconus* rides with Gingelein and Elene and warns the hero of the perils of the sparrow-hawk adventure.[32] Likewise, Guivret provides pasties and wine for Erec in his need, much as the dwarf in *Libeaus Desconus* serves Gingelein and Elene "of al that nede was." [33] Now this dwarf is called Teodelain,[34] and one is reminded of Chrétien's dwarf king Gleodalen. The corruption of the name may easily be due to the common loss of the initial letter in manuscript transmission,[35] and to the mistaking of *l* for *t*. Gleodalen, in turn, seems to be descended from Gwiddolwyn the dwarf in *Kulhwch*. All this may be merely a series of coincidences. But if it is not, then Guivret has inherited a bit of the legend of Gwiddolwyn, and his casks full of good wine may be the very *botheu* (bottles) of the Welsh dwarf.[36]

Since there can be no doubt of the tendency in Arthurian tradition to blend two or more similar personages, it is quite possible that Guivret has also inherited the role of another dwarf who appears as Gleodalen's overlord in Chrétien's list of the guests at Erec's marriage, namely Bilis or Belin.[37] Bilis, who is introduced as King of the Antipodes and of the dwarfs and as a very noble man, can hardly be other than Giraldus' pigmy monarch, who dwelt in the lower hemisphere and whose probity was of the highest. Bilis is in turn identifiable with Pelles, King of the "Basse Gent," in *Perlesvaus*,[38] for *basse* evidently refers to stature, as in *Meraugis:* "la noif est haute et li nains bas." [39] Pelles is the hero's hermit uncle, and in the *Didot Perceval* this uncle inhabited a house of which the door was

---

agree, the element *Hölle*. Cf. W. Map, *De Nugis Curialium*, trans. Tupper and Ogle, pp. 15–18, 233 f., 322 f.; O. Driesen, *Ursprung des Harlekin* (Berlin, 1904); G. Cohen in *Yale Romanic Studies*, XXII (1943), 21. Another example of this fusion of Germanic nomenclature with Brythonic tradition is found in Adam de la Halle's *Jeu de la Feuillée*, where Morgue (i.e. Morgain la Fée) chooses for her lover Hellekin, "le grigneur prinche qui soit en faerie." Cf. A. Rambeau, *Die dem Trouvere Adam de la Hale zugeschriebene Dramen* (*Ausgaben u. Abhandlungen aus dem Gebiete der romanischen Philologie*, LVIII, 1886), p. 91, vss. 758 f.; p. 92, vss. 827–30.

[32] *Erec*, vss. 5367–5492. *Libeaus Desconus*, ed. M. Kaluza, vss. 751–804.
[33] *Erec*, vss. 5146–69. *Libeaus Desconus*, vss. 478–80.
[34] *Libeaus Desconus*, vss. 145, 508. Cf. Kaluza's note, p. 139.
[35] J. D. Bruce, *Evolution of Arthurian Romance*, II, 131n.
[36] *Erec*, vs. 5151. *White Book Mabinogion*, ed. J. Gwenogvryn Evans, col. 482.
[37] *Erec*, vss. 1993–2011.
[38] *Perlesvaus*, ed. Nitze and others, I, ll. 37 f.
[39] Raoul de Houdenc, *Meraugis de Portlesguez*, ed. M. Friedwagner, vs. 1424.

so low (*bas*) that it behoved Perceval to bend down on entering.[40] Therefore, though it is not explicitly stated, Pelles, as well as his people, was
unusually short. When we consider how much Chrétien makes of Guivret's
giving shelter to the wounded Erec and of the healing ministrations of
Guivret's sisters, we cannot ignore the fact that the author of *Perlesvaus*
makes much of Pelles' giving shelter to the sick hero in a hermitage and
of the ministrations of Pelles' female cousin.[41] When Perlesvaus felt well
again, he sallied forth armed, met Lancelot in a fierce combat, was severely
wounded, and again "the damsel, who was very wise, cared for the
wounds of the knights." This was a traditional story of King Pelles and
his kinswomen, for the same situation occurs in the *Vulgate Lancelot* with
the parts of Lancelot and Perceval reversed.[42] Here it is Lancelot, the hero
of the romance, who was wounded and tended by a hermit in his hermitage, was recognized and given shelter by King Pelles and his daughter,
was healed of his madness by the Grail (of which Pelles' daughter had
been the bearer),[43] and on being cured engaged in a fierce battle with
Perceval.

We have, then, two dwarf kings, Bilis and Pelles, and the latter resembles Guivret. Furthermore, the character Pelles is curiously involved and
confused in the prose romances with King Pellinor,[44] and it is not to be
overlooked that a dwarf by the name of Belinor turns up in *Escanor*
(vs. 19254) presenting the marvelous steed Gringalet to a knight, much
as Guivret presented the beautiful palfrey to Enide. The signs then point
to Pelles or Pellinor or Belinor as the original of Guivret.

The explanation of all this—and of much else in the *Matière de Bretagne,*
as we shall eventually see—lies in the mythical Welsh personage Beli,
who was euhemerized as King of Britain and who acquired the title
Mawr, meaning "the Great." [45] The name Beli, plus the Old French
nominative ending *s,* gave Bilis and Pelles; plus the epithet *Mawr,* it suggested Belinor and Pellinor. In fact, the correct *m* (instead of *n*) is retained in one occurrence of the name Belinor, so that we have Belimor,[46]
than which there can be nothing closer to Beli Mawr.

Unluckily no story of Beli has reached us, but a web of evidence (parts
of which will be found later in this book) leaves no doubt that he was a
euhemerized pigmy king of the Other World. If any considerable part of
the Welsh traditions about him had survived, there would have been no

[40] *Didot-Perceval,* ed. W. Roach, p. 181.   [41] *Perlesvaus,* I, 90, 118, 139, 142.
[42] Sommer, *Vulgate Version,* V, 398–406.
[43] *Ibid.,* II, 159; V, 108. It is noteworthy that in the texts which call the Grail King Pelles
the Grail Bearer shows signs of derivation from Morgain—her infatuation for Lancelot, her
summery isle of joy, the healing power of her vessel. In other texts the Grail Bearer shows no
such affinity, and can be derived confidently from Eriu. Cf. Chaps. LXVIII, LXXI.
[44] *Mod. Phil.,* XVI (1918), 337–46. Needless to say, I am not convinced by Bruce's explanation of this confusion.   [45] *PMLA,* LVI (1941), 920–24, especially notes 190, 191.
[46] *Mort Artu,* ed. J. Frappier, p. 113, n. 14, ms. R.

mystery as to the relationship of Bilis, Pelles, Belinor, Auberon, Wauchier's Petit Chevalier, and Guivret. All these dwarfs of French romance, despite certain other strains of influence, were descended from Beli.

Four of them had kinswomen who deserve further scrutiny. Wauchier's Petit Chevalier had a sister, "who in beauty resembled a fay," and we have already observed that she reveals in several ways a common origin with Morgain. According to *Huon*, Auberon was the son of Morgain; [47] according to the fourteenth-century *Ogier*, he was her brother.[48] According to *Huon*, Auberon possessed a horn whose sound would cure the sick; [49] according to the Prologue to *Huon*, this horn belonged to Morgain.[50] Several facts tend to show that the healing horn of Morgain was not a blast horn but a drinking horn. John of Garland explicitly declared: "cornu est equivocus." [51] In some romances blast horn and drinking horn are confused,[52] and Morgain is said to possess a magic drinking horn.[53] The fay Loospine in *Eger and Grime* gave the wounded Eger a grass-green drink from a horn, "and all was soft that erst was sore." [54] At any rate, the testimony is clear: Auberon had a faery mother or sister, Morgain, who possessed a healing horn. In *Perlesvaus*, we remember, King Pelles' female cousin, "who was very wise," twice tended and cured the hero in the hermitage of "li Rois de la Basse Gent." In the *Vulgate Lancelot* the hero was first healed of a wound in a hermitage and then cured of madness in King Pelles' castle of Corbenic (= Cor Beneit, "Blessed Horn")[55] by the magic of the Grail; and King Pelles' daughter had been keeper of the Grail.[56] Furthermore, by her hopeless passion for Lancelot, her jealous rivalry with Guenievre, her dwelling with her damsels for a time in the Isle of Joy, where there was no winter so severe that they could not carole every day,[57] she betrays her kinship and her original identity with Morgain, who likewise nursed a hopeless passion for Lancelot, provoked the jealous rivalry of Guenievre, and dwelt with her sisters in the isle of Avalon, where "no snow or winter or excessive summer rages." [58] Finally, Chrétien himself suggests a parallelism between the sisters of Guivret and Morgain.[59] The sisters "know much about curing wounds." In their brother's castle they took charge of Erec and repeatedly applied an *antret* (plaster) to his wounds; so that in a fortnight he felt no pain.

[47] *Huon*, p. 104.
[48] J. Dunlop, *Geschichte der Prosadichtungen*, trans. F. Liebrecht (Berlin, 1851), pp. 141, 535, n. 20.
[49] *Huon*, p. 97.   [50] Graf, *Auberon*, vss. 1221-26, 1459-65.
[51] A. Schultz, *Das höfische Leben zur Zeit der Minnesinger*, 2d ed., I, 382, n. 1.
[52] H. Newstead, *Bran the Blessed in Arthurian Romance*, pp. 111-14.
[53] Paton, *Fairy Mythology*, p. 105.   [54] *Eger and Grime*, ed. Caldwell, pp. 202 f.
[55] Newstead, *op. cit.*, pp. 86-95. Cf. *infra*, pp. 173 f., 431 f.
[56] Cf. *supra*, n. 43. On this damsel cf. *Mod. Phil.*, XVI, 338 f.; F. Lot, *Etude sur le Lancelot*, pp. 109-12.   [57] Sommer, *op. cit.*, V, 403.
[58] Paton, *Fairy Mythology*, pp. 45 f.   [59] *Erec*, vss. 5114, 5201, 5205.

Now earlier in the poem Erec's wounds had been treated by the application of an *antret* of special virtue which Arthur's sister Morgue had supplied, and Arthur had proposed a rest of a fortnight to accomplish the cure.[60]

We could hardly ask for more various but still consistent proofs that the dwarf king of Arthurian tradition had a kinswoman famed for her healing powers, and that she was originally Morgain. The family relationships of the two faery figures may differ from romance to romance, and the modes of healing may range from Grail magic to prosaic emplastration. But that the tradition existed is sure. Once more, the profound influence of the legends of Morgain la Fée on the matter of *Erec* is established.

The Welsh prototypes of Pelles and Morgain, namely, Beli and Modron, were related, but not as father and daughter or brother and sister. Beli was the father of Avallach and therefore the grandfather of Modron.[61] But since all three were immortal and all were living in the time of King Arthur, it would be natural for the generations to become mixed, and though Morgain remained the daughter of Avaloc,[62] her relation to the dwarf king, whose original was Beli, became hopelessly muddled. She is the cousin of Pelles in *Perlesvaus,* the daughter of Pelles in the *Vulgate Lancelot,* the sister of Wauchier's Petit Chevalier, the sister or mother of "le petit roi faé," Auberon, and one of the sisters of the Little King, Guivret.

One little mystery remains to be cleared up. The dwarf potentate introduced himself to Erec with the words: " 'I am king of this land. My liegemen are Irishmen (*Irois*), and there is no one there who does not pay me tribute.' " How did this Welsh figure, whom Erec encountered on his adventurous ride in Britain, happen to be the overlord of Irishmen? The answer lies in one of those characteristic misreadings which are responsible for other baffling features of Arthurian romance. Let us look at what Chrétien had previously said of that other noble dwarf king, Bilis: "For splendor and for lordship Bilis brought in his retinue two kings (*rois*) who were dwarfs and who held their land from him." [63] Evidently Bilis was overlord of other kings (*rois*). Even more striking is the fact that when a noble dwarf appeared to Herla in Map's story, he announced himself as follows: " 'I, king of many kings and princes, of an innumerable and infinite people, have been sent by them and gladly come to thee.' " [64] He too was overlord of other kings. Something of this kind Chrétien or the author of X must have found in his source, but mistaking *rois* for *irois* he made Guivret overlord of the Irish.[65]

---

[60] Vss. 4218–38.

[61] J. Rhys, *Studies in the Arthurian Legend,* pp. 336 f. Loth, *Mabinogion,* 2d ed., II, 284, 336.

[62] *Romanic Review,* XXIX (1938), 176 f. Paton, *op. cit.,* p. 46. E. K. Chambers, *Arthur of Britain,* p. 266.   [63] *Erec,* vss. 2001–04.

[64] Walter Map, *De Nugis Curialium,* ed. M. R. James, p. 13.

[65] For another case of confusing *rois* and *irois,* cf. *infra,* p. 152, n. 40.

Chapter XXI

GAUVAIN AND KEU

VERSES 3931–4211

King Arthur arranged to spend a few days hunting in a forest and had his tents and pavilions pitched. Keu took without permission Gauvain's steed, shield, and lance, and riding at a gallop met Erec and Enide. He attempted to lead Erec by force to see the King and Queen, but Erec refused to go and in the ensuing encounter threw Keu to the earth. When Keu returned ignominiously to Arthur and reported his meeting with so redoubtable a knight, the King sent Gauvain to request the stranger to come to him. Gauvain, "who was full of great nobility (franchise)," performed his errand in the most courteous fashion, but still Erec refused to accompany him. Gauvain then sent a message secretly to Arthur to move his tents to a point on the road which Erec was traveling, and did his best to delay Erec meanwhile. When in due course Erec, Enide, and Gauvain arrived at the spot where Arthur had now pitched his camp, Erec recognized that he had been outwitted by Gauvain's intelligence (grant san), and revealed his identity. All three then proceeded to Arthur's tent, and both Erec and his wife were received with embraces and kisses.

THOUGH Gauvain had already been introduced several times by Chrétien, this is the first incident in which he played an important part. It behoves us, therefore, to investigate this most prominent figure of the *Matière de Bretagne*. Chrétien, in enumerating the knights of the Round Table, assured us that "Gauvain ought to come first of all the good knights"; [1] and all the earliest Continental and English documents confirm this testimony. When sculptured under the name Galvaginus over the north portal of Modena cathedral, [2] he was distinguished above the other knights accompanying Arthur by the decoration on his shield and by his position in the forefront of the attack. We find a Walwanus recorded as living near Padua in 1136, and there can be little doubt that the man had been named for Arthur's nephew at least fifteen years earlier. [3] In 1125 William of Malmesbury mentioned Walwen as "a warrior most celebrated for valor." [4] Geoffrey of Monmouth assigned him a prominent role in his *Historia,* and Wace added two laudatory passages in his *Brut*. The first runs: "He was valorous and of great moderation

[1] *Erec*, vss. 1691 f.
[2] R. S. and L. H. Loomis, *Arthurian Legends in Medieval Art*, pp. 32–35; figs. 6, 7.
[3] *Romania*, XVII (1888), 362; *Romanic Review*, XXXII, 27.
[4] E. K. Chambers, *Arthur of Britain*, p. 250.

(*mesure*); he was not given to pride or excess. He wished to perform more than he said and to give more than he promised." [5] In the second passage he is coupled with Hoel. "Two such vassals had not lived before them. Never in the age that had passed were there two such barons in virtue or courtesy or renown of knighthood." [6] So firmly established was the conviction of Gauvain's invincible prowess that the Austrian poet, Wirnt von Gravenberg, asserted in his *Wigalois* that he would never have believed that Gawein was defeated by King Joram unless the squire who told him the tale had vouched for its truth.[7] To be sure, we have observed that, disguised under the name Galoain, the hero plays a less gracious part than that ordinarily assigned him,[8] but it is obvious that Chrétien did not recognize the boastful count as Gauvain. Moreover, though we shall discover in dealing with *Le Chevalier de la Charrette* that Chrétien used Gauvain as a foil for Lancelot and rendered him somewhat absurd; and in our discussion of *Le Conte del Graal* it will appear that Gauvain's character was blackened in some of the late romances; [9] yet in each instance an intelligible motive for this debasement of the *preux chevalier* can be detected. There can be no doubt that Gauvain was the nonpareil of Arthur's knights in the early stages of Arthurian tradition on the Continent and in England.

It is hardly conceivable, therefore, that he had no prototype among the warriors of Arthur's household recorded in Welsh literature. It was held by some scholars of an earlier generation that this prototype was Gwalchmei son of Gwyar,[10] who is listed in *Kulhwch* among Arthur's warriors, and who is thus described: "He never returned home from a mission without accomplishing it; he was the best man afoot and the best on horseback; he was the nephew of Arthur, the son of his sister and his cousin." [11] The description, of course, fits Gauvain, and Gwalchmei plays the part in *Geraint, Owain,* and *Peredur* which Gauvain plays in *Erec, Yvain,* and *Le Conte del Graal*. But it is now generally conceded that the three Welsh romances were not the sources of the corresponding poems of Chrétien, and therefore Bruce declared that the name Gwalchmei did not belong to the native Welsh Arthurian tradition but was merely substituted for French Gauvain.[12] Bruce's reversal of the relationship between the two names proposed by earlier scholars is corroborated by six facts. (1) Such. attempts by the Welsh to reproduce French names unknown to native

[5] Wace, *Brut*, ed. I. Arnold, II, vss. 9859–62.   [6] *Ibid.*, vss. 12762–66.
[7] *Wigalois*, vss. 20,15 ff. W. H. Schofield, *Studies on Libeaus Desconus*, p. 221. *Hist. litt. de la France*, XXX, 32.
[8] Cf. Chap. XIX.   [9] Cf. *infra*, pp. 399–407.
[10] A. Nutt, *Studies on the Legend of the Holy Grail* (London, 1888), p. 225. J. Rhys, *Studies in the Arthurian Legend*, p. 13. E. Windisch, *Das keltische Brittannien bis zu Kaiser Arthur*, p. 172. Even Chambers, as late as 1927 (*op. cit.*, p. 151), subscribed to this view.
[11] Loth, *Mabinogion*, 2d ed., I, 288.
[12] Bruce, *Evolution*, I, 192. Cf. R. S. Loomis, *Celtic Myth*, pp. 37, 62.

Arthurian tradition did occur. For example, in a certain triad we find Galaath, son of Lawnselot dy Lac, and Bort, son of King Bort.[13] (2) Gwalchmei, after being mentioned and described in *Kulhwch,* drops out of the story; he is not assigned a single one of the many missions undertaken by Arthur's warriors.[14] (3) His name, if it means anything, signifies "Hawk of May"[15] and is hardly appropriate for Gauvain, who is never likened to a hawk or connected with the month of May. (4) It is not easy to see how the name Gwalchmei, if it passed from the Welsh to the French, acquired the final *n* of Gauvain, still less the three syllables of Galvagin, the earliest Continental form of Gauvain. (5) Gauvain is never represented, in the vast French literature of Arthurian romance, as the son of anyone whose name resembles Gwyar, the father (or mother)[16] of Gwalchmei. He is always the son of Loth. One is therefore obliged to suspect that Gwalchmei was a name substituted by the Welsh for the French form Galvain, because of similarity in sound. Evidently tales of the Arthurian cycle were being circulated in French by the end of the eleventh century, and, backed by the prestige of French military prowess and culture, some of them filtered back into Wales.[17] It was in this way that the author of *Kulhwch* might have come to know of Arthur's great nephew, Galvain, preeminent in the Continental tradition. He felt bound to introduce him into his list of Arthur's warriors and gave him a name which was a rough Welsh approximation to Galvain; perhaps he knew of some Gwalchmei who was the son of Gwyar. But since none of the tales of Galvain which he may have heard fitted into his scheme, he merely introduced Gwalchmei with some compliments and then dismissed him. However tentative this explanation of the appearance of Gwalchmei in *Kulhwch* may be, it remains certain that he is an unsatisfactory prototype or original for Gauvain.

[13] Loth, *op. cit.,* II, 285. No one would pretend that these names are anything but Welsh adaptations of the French forms Galaat, Lancelot du Lac, and Bohort.

[14] It may also be significant that he is not mentioned in the early poem in the Black Book of Carmarthen (copied about 1175) which supplies a list of Arthur's warriors. Cf. E. K. Chambers, *op. cit.,* pp. 64–66; or Malory, *Morte d'Arthur,* Everyman ed., I, xviii–xx.

[15] Rhys, *Studies in the Arthurian Legend,* p. 13. Windisch, *op. cit.,* p. 172.

[16] *Cymmrodor,* XXIV (1913), 258. *Speculum,* I (1926), 344–46.

[17] Loth, *op. cit.,* I, 40. *Trans. of Hon. Soc. of Cymmrodorion,* 1919–20, pp. 57–61. In connection with this early reflux of Arthurian tradition from the Continent into Wales it might be well to note the passage in the Iolo mss. about the return of Rhys ap Tewdwr from Brittany in 1077, bringing with him the system of the Round Table to Wales, where it had been forgotten, and restoring it in regard to minstrels and bards, as it had been at Caerleon on Usk under Emperor Arthur. Of the Iolo mss. Prof. Gruffydd said in *Math Vab Mathonwy,* p. 203n. "I refer to this much suspected source with all due reserve, but it may be safely stated that a large portion of the information given in the Iolo mss. goes back directly or indirectly to genuinely ancient sources." And this passage from Iolo is discussed by Prof. Watkin in *Trans. of Hon. Soc. of Cymmrodorion,* 1919–20, p. 5. Moreover, is it likely that the patriotic Iolo would have concocted a story to the discredit of Wales or have fancied a situation so harmonious with evidence of which he knew nothing?

Since there must have been such a prototype and since Gwalchmei will hardly do, let us scan the muster roll of Arthur's warriors again. One name arrests our eyes, Gwrvan Gwallt-avwyn.[18] It suggests, on the one hand, some connection with Gwri Gwallt-euryn, the youthful hero whose career under this name and under his sobriquet of Pryderi runs through *The Four Branches of the Mabinogi,* and who, it is hoped, has been sufficiently identified as the Welsh prototype (along with Gweir) of Gauvain's brothers, Gurehes and Gareth.[19] On the other hand, the epithet Gwallt-avwyn raises an echo in our minds; can it be the trisyllabic original of Galvagin, the earliest form of Gauvain? Is this sobriquet the answer to our riddle? Ten arguments show that not only does this Welsh name offer the only solution to the problem of Gauvain's origin, but it also elucidates some of the most obscure matters of the Arthurian onomasticon.

1. Gwrvan Gwallt-avwyn is probably some sort of alternative or substitution for Gwri Gwallt-euryn. Sir John Morris-Jones wrote me on Dec. 16, 1927, as follows: "Gwrvan Gwallt Avwyn suggests Gwri Wallt Eurin, who also appears in the [*Kulhwch*] list as *Gwarae Wallt Eurin* in the White Book [of Rhydderch], and as *Gware Gwallt Euryn* in the Red Book [of Hergest]. . . . It appears to me as if the two old names *Gwri* and *Gwrvan* had been mixed up, or that Gwri's epithet has been applied to Gwrvan." We have already seen reason to believe that Gwri or Gware was confused with Gweir,[20] and that such substitutions did occur is proved by the triads, where two versions of one triad give Mabon and Madawg respectively, and two versions of another give Llyr Lluyddawc and Lludd Llurugawc.[21] In view of such facts no one can deny that Gwrvan Gwallt-avwyn may have been an alternative form of the name Gwri Gwallt-euryn, borne by the hero of *The Four Branches.*

2. The epithet Gwallt-avwyn, Morris-Jones wrote me, "means no doubt 'with hair like reins.'" It was perhaps intended to suggest long, streaming tresses. But I am now inclined to accept a suggestion made to me over twenty years ago by the late Canon Robert Ellis Jones, of the Cathedral of St. John the Divine, New York City, namely, that *avwyn* is a scribal error for *advwyn,* meaning "bright, fair." [22] Thus Gwallt-advwyn would be almost the equivalent of Gwallt-euryn, "Golden Hair," and renders plausible the identity of Gwrvan with Gwri. Gwri, too, might have been called Gwallt-advwyn.

3. Since Gwri's birth, upbringing, and youthful precocity are related in

---

[18] Loth, *op. cit.,* I, 277.
[19] Cf. Chap. VIII.
[20] *Ibid.*
[21] Loth, *op. cit.,* II, 273, 318.
[22] J. Lloyd-Jones in *Geirfa Barddoniaeth Gynnar Cymraeg,* the most recent authority on early Welsh, gives under the form *aduwyn* (the *u* represents *v*) the meanings "gwych, hardd," and *gwych* has the meanings of "splendid, gorgeous, brilliant," and *hardd* the meanings "handsome, beautiful." Spurrell's *Welsh-English Dictionary,* 10th ed., under the modern spelling *addfwyn,* gives as obsolete meanings "goodly, fine, fair."

the first of *The Four Branches of the Mabinogi;* since this same *Branch,* as we know,[23] furnished to Arthurian romance one of the most influential narrative patterns—the combat at the ford—and also, as we shall see,[24] contains the rash boon motif prominent in the *Charrette;* since Gwri is frequently referred to as a *mab,* "boy," thus justifying the title *Mabinogi,* "a tale of boyhood and youth," [25] there could be no fitter person to be the prototype of an Arthurian hero. As a matter of fact, Gwri is easily recognizable among Arthur's warriors in the *Kulhwch* list as Gware Gwallt-euryn.[26]

4. The parallels between Gwri and Gauvain are not a few, even though Gwri's history has been crossed with that of Pryderi,[27] and Gauvain's legend has been contaminated by some form of the Pope Gregory legend.[28] Gwri is characterized as "the most agreeable, the most comely, the best endowed with every good accomplishment of any one in the kingdom." [29] Needless to say, Gauvain was a paragon of fine manners, good looks, and martial prowess. Both Gwri and Gauvain were born under circumstances which brought shame to their mothers; both were discovered as foundlings, swaddled in a rich cloth, and their gentle birth was recognized; both were baptized, one as Gwri Gwallt-euryn, the other as Gauvain or Walwanius; both, after a precocious boyhood in charge of foster parents, were given in charge to a prince or emperor; both, after this ruler's decease, inherited his dominions.[30]

5. The confusion between the names Gwri, Gware, Gwrvan Gwallt-a(d)vwyn, and Gweir son of Llwch explains the fact that King Loth had four sons, namely, Gurehes, Guahries, Agravain (a metathesized form of Gwrvan), and Galvagin.[31] The terminal *s* in the first two names represents the French nominative ending, and the *h* is silent. A closer approxi-

[23] Cf. Chap. XVIII. Cf. also *Mod. Phil.,* XLIII, 64–69; *Journ. of Eng. and Germ. Phil.,* XLII (1943), 170–81.   [24] Cf. *infra,* p. 203.
[25] *Trans. of Hon. Soc. of Cymmrodorion,* 1912–13, pp. 39 f. C. O'Rahilly, *Ireland and Wales,* pp. 101–03. I. Williams, *Pedeir Keinc y Mabinogi* (Cardiff, 1930), pp. xlii–liii. This meaning is proved by the fact that in ms. Peniarth 14 an apocryphal account of Christ's childhood is entitled *Mabinogi Iesu Grist.*
[26] Loth, *op. cit.,* I, 278, 333. Lady Guest, in the Everyman edition of the *Mabinogion,* p. 322, and Prof. I. Williams, in *Pedeir Keinc,* p. 151, take it for granted that Gware is Gwri.
[27] Cf. *infra,* p. 341.
[28] I still believe that the theory set forth in my *Celtic Myth and Arthurian Romance,* pp. 331–38, that the Welsh Gwri tradition was affected by the Coptic tale of the grandson of King Armenios, and thus gave rise to the pious legends of Pope Gregory and St. Albanus, as well as to the Arthurian stories of Gauvain and Galobrun, offers the best explanation of the facts.   [29] Loth, *op. cit.,* I, 116.
[30] *Ibid.,* 106–16. J. D. Bruce, *Historia Meriadoci and De Ortu Walwanii,* pp. xxxvii–l, 55–59. *Perlesvaus,* ed. Nitze and others, I, 307 f.; II, 327 f. *Romania,* XXXIX (1910), 1 ff.
[31] The form Guahries is found in ms. Bib. Nat., fr. 12577 (J. L. Weston, *Legend of Perceval,* I, 248n.). A form Gwarehes is recorded in *Joseph of Arimathie,* ed. W. W. Skeat (E.E.T.S., XLIV), p. 71, along with Walwanus, Agraneyns, and Geheries. Cf. also the forms in Sommer, *Vulgate Version,* IV, 358 f., the remarks of Jessie Weston in her *Legend of Lancelot,* p. 159, n. 1, and those of Bruce in *Mod. Phil.,* XVI, 347.

mation of the four French forms to the Welsh could hardly be expected.

6. The hypothesis that Gware Gwallt-euryn, "Golden-Hair," was the original of Guahries (oblique case Guahriet) explains the fact that Malory's Gareth was recognized at a tournament by his hair. We read of the Welsh hero: "he was given the name of Gwri Wallt Euryn [Golden Hair] because the hair on his head was as yellow as gold." [32] Malory states concerning Gareth: "the kyng sawe by his here [hair] that it was the same knyght. 'But byfore he was in so many colours and now he is but in one colour, that is yelowe.' " [33]

7. The identity of Gwri or Gware with Gareth and Gauvain(s) is shown by the fact that Gareth enjoyed the sobriquet Beaumayns, which must be the result of a misreading of Gauvain(s). The initials B and G were sometimes interchanged,[34] and Beaumayns, which combines a masculine singular adjective with a feminine plural noun, can hardly be anything but a crude attempt, probably by an Anglo-Norman,[35] to give meaning to Gauvain(s), correctly recognized as an epithet but incorrectly read as Bauuains.

8. The Bretons regarded Gauvain as a sobriquet, for we find in a Breton document of about 1120 the name Rainaudus Gauvain.[36]

9. The Welsh form Gwallt-a(d)vwyn accounts for the three syllables of the earliest recorded form of Gauvain—Galvagin.

10. The development of the name Gauvain from the epithet Gwallt-a(d)vwyn is matched very significantly, as we shall see in Chap. XXVI, by the development of the name Lancelot from the epithet Llawwynnawc.

The hypothesis set forth above accounts for the prominence of Gauvain, the story of his birth and boyhood, the form of his name and those of his brothers, and the fact that he was the son of Loth. As I wrote twenty years ago, "When a key which at first sight may seem rather queer and complicated actually fits into such a complex structure of facts, and throws the bolt, then it should not be discarded until another key, as good or better, can be produced." [37]

The same hypothesis explains still another noteworthy fact about Gauvain, his relationship to the Irish champion Cuchulainn. It has often been pointed out by previous investigators, and it will be seen again and again in the following pages, that Arthurian romance laid under contribution the sagas of the Ulster cycle—*The Sickbed of Cuchulainn, Bri-*

---

[32] Loth, *op. cit.*, I, 110. The epithet Gwallt-euryn also seems to have split off from the name Gwri or Gware, since it offers the only plausible explanation of the name Galvariun (by assimilation to Galvagin), which appears on the Modena archivolt.

[33] Malory, *Morte d'Arthur*, ed. H. O. Sommer, I, 262.   [34] *PMLA*, LIV (1939), 659.

[35] *Ibid.*, 659 f. F. J. Tanquerey, in *Recueil de lettres anglo-françaises* (Paris, 1916), p. lv, notes "le nombre considérable de cas pour lesquels l'accord ne se fait pas entre l'adjectif et le nom. . . . Une irrégularité du même genre accouple un singulier et un pluriel."

[36] H. Morice, *Mémoires pour servir de preuves à l'histoire de Bretagne*, I, col. 541.

[37] *Celtic Myth*, p. 66.

criu's Feast, and *The Violent Death of Curoi;* and in many of these instances the part of Cuchulainn has been taken over by Gauvain. Now it is hardly a coincidence that, as Rhys observed sixty years ago, the Welsh counterpart of Cuchulainn is Gwri, the very personage whom we have come to recognize as the Welsh prototype of Gauvain. Let me quote Rhys:

"In Gwri we have a sort of parallel to Cuchulainn and Lleu. Gwri's rapid growth recalls both Lleu and Cuchulainn, in common with whom he was also remarkable for his golden hair. . . . The allusion also to the colt born at the time of Gwri's own birth deserves especial notice, as it has its counterpart in the story of one of the obscure incarnations of Lug before he was born Setanta or Cuchulainn." [38]

Dechtere, sister of King Conchobar of Ulster, was present at the birth of an unnamed child of Lug, at the same time that a mare gave birth to two colts. These colts were kept as a present for the child, but he sickened and died. Dechtere herself then became pregnant by Lug and bore the son later to be nicknamed Cuchulainn; and Lug charged her to present the colts to him. To quote again from Rhys:

"The coincidence with the birth-story of Gwri is not seriously lessened by the colts being two in the one story and only one in the other, as that is a consequence of the fact that a man who fights on horseback in the Mabinogion would be made to ride forth in a chariot drawn by two horses in the epic tales of Ireland."

The connection between Cuchulainn and Gauvain through the intermediate Gwri or Gweir is established by the fact that Cuchulainn was the son of the Irish god Lug Lonnbemnech (later form Lugh Loinnbheimionach),[39] Gweir was the son of Llwch or Lloch Llawwynnyawc, and Guahries and his brother (or rather his alter ego) Gauvain were sons of Loth, who, according to the best reading of *Erec,* verse 1737, was an "Irois." [40]

Finally, this hypothesis shows through what intermediary the famous solar characteristics of Cuchulainn were transmitted to Gauvain. Not to go into this subject fully,[41] let us observe that the name Gauvain was derived,

---

[38] J. Rhys, *Lectures on the Origin and Growth of Celtic Heathendom,* 2d ed., pp. 501–03. Cf. also Baudis in *Folklore,* XXVII, 49.

[39] *Rev. Celt.,* XII (1891), 127. E. Hull, *Cuchullin Saga in Irish Literature* (London, 1898), pp. lvi f.

[40] Foerster, in his large edition of *Erec* (Halle, 1890), gives the line as "Ne Bravaïns ne Loz li rois." The treatment of Bravaïns as trisyllabic is unnatural and forced; nowhere else, so far as I am aware, do Arthurian names terminating in *-ain* split the diphthong into two vowels. Furthermore, two mss. supply the needed extra syllable, reading "li irois," instead of "li rois." The former deserves preference as the *lectio difficilior.* On these two grounds, then, one should prefer "li irois."

[41] Cf. my *Celtic Myth,* p. 47. Though in the same book, pp. 55–66, I attempted to elaborate a thesis that the name Curoi was represented in Welsh by Gwri, and that Gwrvan and Gwrnach Gawr (the Giant) meant Little and Big Gwri, I have long since come to the conclusion that there is too little supporting evidence and too many difficulties to put it forward again. I still

through the form Galvagin, from an epithet Gwallt-a(d)vwyn, meaning probably "Bright Hair"; that Gwri was distinguished by his golden hair, and bore the sobriquet "Gwallt-euryn"; and that Cuchulainn not only had a crown of hair, like the shining of yellow gold, but also was capable of withdrawing the hair into his head so that he appeared shorn, while a drop of blood stood at the root of each hair.[42] As Rhys suggested,[43] this seems to be a grotesquely physiological description of the sun, withdrawing its rays as it approaches the horizon and turning blood-red. More obvious is the solar significance of Cuchulainn's becoming on two occasions a "crimson wheelball from his crown to the ground."[44] Gauvain, so far as I am aware, never undergoes these remarkable metamorphoses—and one can well understand why the trait was suppressed—but in many passages we read of his increasing in might till midday or *none*, and then declining.[45] This characteristic remains as a testimony to his descent from Cuchulainn, the semidivine hero of a heliolatrous people.[46]

Thus the hypothesis outlined above, however complicated it may seem, harmonizes with a multitude of facts precisely because of that complication. It harmonizes also with the theory advanced on an earlier page as to the Welsh antecedents of Erec. It provides the links between Cuchulainn, hero of the Ulster cycle, Gwri, hero of *The Four Branches,* and Gauvain, the best knight of Arthur's fellowship and the hero of many a romance. Objections, to be sure, there may be,[47] but none sufficient to outweigh

---

believe, however, that in the modified form set forth in *PMLA*, XLIII (1928), 384–96, there is a good deal to be said for it.

[42] D'Arbois de Jubainville, *Epopée celtique*, p. 100. "La fureur lui fit faire d'affreuses grimaces, une goutte de sang brilla à la racine de chacun de ses cheveux; il s'arracha les cheveux, le sommet de son front parut chauve." Cf. for English translation and Irish text *Feast of Bricriu*, ed. G. Henderson (London, 1899), pp. 32 f., where the references to Cuchulainn's imitating the motion of a millstone and his fiery vigor may also have solar significance. [43] Rhys, *Lectures*, p. 438.

[44] J. Dunn, *Ancient Irish Epic Tale, Tain Bo Cualnge* (London, 1914), pp. 70, 78. Another possibly solar attribute of Cuchulainn was his concern with wheels, which were solar symbols among the Celts. He had five golden wheels on his shield (*ibid.*, p. 196; Cross and Slover, *Ancient Irish Tales*, pp. 164, 270 f.; *Journ. of Eng. and Germ. Phil.*, XLII, 168 f.; Windisch, *op. cit.*, pp. 87, 200 f.). [45] *Mort Artu*, ed. J. D. Bruce (Halle, 1910), pp. 287 f.

[46] On sun worship in Ireland cf. my *Celtic Myth*, pp. 39–44; *Etudes celtiques*, III (1938), 46–58.

[47] It is, of course, embarrassing that the crucial epithet Gwallt-avwyn should occur only once in extant Welsh literature, and then attached to the seemingly obscure Gwrvan. But there are two facts which should serve to rebut this objection. The first is the extraordinary paucity of the Welsh literature which survives. There is no reference to Trystan in Welsh literature before *The Dream of Rhonabwy* (13th century), a mere name in a list, and yet he had already become as imposing and famous a figure as Gauvain on the Continent. The almost total silence of the extant remains on the subject of Gwrvan Gwallt-a(d)vwyn does not therefore prove that he was an insignificant personage. A second point is that Gwrvan was a figure of sufficient importance to appear prominently as Gorvain in *Meraugis* and *Hunbaut,* and successively corrupt forms of the name Gorvain (Gornain, Gosnayn, Gosenain, and Osenain) occur in the Vulgate cycle (cf. Sommer, *Vulgate Version*, Index of Names and Places).

the extraordinary amount of corroborative evidence. As the Welsh prototype of Gauvain, there is no other candidate who can offer one tithe the number of credentials as does Gwri Gwallt-euryn, otherwise called Gwrvan Gwallt-a(d)vwyn.

To return to the incident summarized at the head of this section, both here and in *Le Conte del Graal* [48] we find a hero meeting with Keu, refusing to accompany him to Arthur and unhorsing him, and then, at the request or through the contrivance of Gauvain, consenting to accept the King's hospitality. Since the same situation occurs in *Geraint,* it could not have been invented by Chrétien. Somewhat modified, it was used by Pseudo-Wauchier. The episode was seemingly devised to set off the *courtoisie* of Gauvain against the churlishness of Keu.

At a very early stage in the development of these characters they displayed antithetic traits. We have seen that in the mabinogi of *Pwyll* Gwri was "the most agreeable, the comeliest, the best endowed with every good accomplishment of anyone in the kingdom." By contrast, when the youthful Kulhwch demanded entrance to Arthur's hall in the midst of a feast, and Arthur declared: "It is a grievous thing to leave a man like him in the wind and the rain," Kai inhospitably exclaimed: "By the hand of my friend, if you would follow my counsel, you would not violate the laws of the court for him." [49]

In the hands of the Breton *conteurs* these opposed characters were accentuated: Keu became the typical quarrelsome braggart; Gauvain was held up to admiration, not only as the handsomest and most puissant of knights, but also as the most gracious and courtly of speech.[50] Apparently it occurred to some *conteur* to create an incident in which this contrast could be dramatically displayed. He seized on a situation of which we have a good example in the Swiss romance of *Lanzelet.*[51] The exploits of the young son of King Pant having reached the ears of Arthur and filled him with admiration, Walwein is sent to invite the promising youth to the court, and on meeting him employs his arts of gracious persuasion. But in vain. The proud youth forces Walwein into a prolonged combat on horse and afoot, and it is not till some days later that Lanzelet is brought into the presence of the King. This basic episode the hypothetical *conteur* altered in accordance with his purpose. Keu is the first to summon the hero to Arthur's presence. The youth resents Keu's crusty language, and when the seneschal resorts to force, hurls him from his saddle. Gauvain

---

[48] Vss. 4274–4578.

[49] Loth, *op. cit.,* I, 256 f. *Zts. f. franz. Sprache u. Lit.,* XLVII (1924–5), 225 f.

[50] *Mod. Lang. Notes,* XLIII (1928), 215–22. Note the jest on this subject at the expense of an ignorant minstrel in *Les Deux Bourdeurs Ribauds,* who thus boasts of his repertoire: " 'Ge sai des romanz d'aventure, De cels de la Reonde Table, Qui Sont a oir delitable. De Gauvain sai le malparlier, Et de Quex le bon chevalier.' " E. Faral, *Mimes français du XIIIe siècle* (Paris, 1910), p. 96.   [51] P. Piper, *Höfische Epik,* II, 177 f.

is then sent to invite the proud youth and succeeds in accomplishing by
courtesy what Keu had failed to achieve by churlish speech and violence.
This little lesson in chivalric manners evidently found favor and passed
into the repertoire of other *conteurs* and into the French romances.

The reflux of Arthurian stories into Wales brought both the tradition
of Gauvain's persuasive powers and this example of their effectiveness into
Welsh literature. Gwalchmei is mentioned in the triads as one of the
three golden-tongued knights of Arthur's court.[52] "They were three wise
men, so noble, so pleasant, so eloquent in their speech that it was difficult
to refuse them whatever they desired." Another triad calls him one of the
three best men toward guests and strangers.[53] We have an example of
his gracious eloquence in a series of late *englynion* which are thus introduced:

"Here are *englyns* between Trystan, the son of Tallwch, and Gwalchmai the
son of Gwyar, after Trystan had been absent three years from Arthur's Court,
in displeasure, and Arthur had sent eight-and-twenty warriors to seize him, and
bring him to Arthur, and Trystan smote them all down, one after another, and
came not for any one, but for Gwalchmai with the Golden Tongue." [54]

The author of X seems to have known both the earlier form of this tradition in which even Gauvain is rebuffed by the young hero, as in *Lanzelet,*
and also the later development in which Gauvain is successful in bringing
him before Arthur. At any rate, in *Erec* the hero stubbornly refuses Gauvain's invitation and in *Geraint* he actually comes to blows with Gwalchmei. But Gauvain is not only a model of manners but also a man of
"mout gran san." [55] He meets Erec's rebuff by a stratagem, and secretly
sends word to the King to move his tents so that Erec cannot avoid meeting him and accepting his hospitality. Already the author of X conceived
of the ideal knight as one in whom *san* was added to *proesce* and *courtoisie.* He anticipated the author of *Gawain and the Green Knight* in his
rounded and realistic portrayal of a medieval hero.

[52] Loth, *op. cit.,* II, 289.   [53] *Ibid.,* II, 291.
[54] C. Guest, *Mabinogion,* Everyman ed., p. 375. J. Rhys, *Studies in the Arthurian Legend,*
pp. 278–81. In the *Ystoria Trystan,* which exists in mss. as early as the 16th century, this
poetic dialogue is affixed to a Tristan tradition which must go back to a very much earlier
stage before the reflux of French romance into Wales. Cf. *Romania,* LIII (1927), 92–95;
Thomas of Britain, *Romance of Tristram and Ysolt,* trans. by R. S. Loomis, 2d ed. (New
York, 1931), pp. xiii–xviii.
[55] *Erec,* vs. 4112.

Chapter XXII

LE GUINGALET

VERSES 3942–4087

King Arthur, the Queen, and his barons resorted to the forest for some days of recreation. Gauvain tied his horse, "le Guingalet," outside a tent while he went inside to rest. Keu took the steed and Gauvain's lance and shield, and galloped off. He met Erec and Enide, engaged in a combat with Erec, and was thrown to the earth. Erec was about to lead away the steed when Keu informed him that it belonged to Gauvain. Erec then restored the horse to Keu and Keu rode back to tell his misadventure to the King. Gauvain mounted "le Guingalet," with instructions from the King to bring the stranger knight back with him.

CHRÉTIEN again introduces Gauvain's steed under similar circumstances in *Le Conte del Graal*.[1] In both poems the word Guingalet is treated as a common noun, modified by the article or the possessive pronoun. Certain manuscripts of both poems give the alternative form "le gringalet," a word which in later French and Provençal usage seems to mean "homme chétif" or "cheval maigre et alerte." [2] In neither poem are we vouchsafed any information about the animal, its qualities, or its history.

A number of later romances mention Gauvain's steed, and three of them supply interesting facts about it. Wolfram von Eschenbach calls the animal Gringuljet or Gringulet; it was given to Gawan by Orilus, the husband of the lady of the tent; it had come from Montsalvatsch, the Grail Castle; it had red ears.[3] We have already seen that red-eared horses are an authentic Celtic feature,[4] and that the hero of *Le Lai de l'Espine* won in combat a supernatural white horse with red ears. The *Vulgate Merlin* tells how Gauvain acquired his famous mount from King Clarion of Northumberland,[5] who "rode upon Le Gringalet, a horse which was so named by reason of its excellence." If *gringalet* had in the thirteenth century its later significance of "weakling," the name could have been applied to Gauvain's destrier only in an ironic sense, as, for instance, in Thomas's *Tristan*,[6] the tall Breton knight is called Tristan the Dwarf.

[1] Ed. Hilka, vss. 6209, 7136, (ms. S) vs. 7429. Cf. Hilka's note on p. 736, with its references. For references to other romances cf. *Histoire Littéraire*, XXX, 36 f.
[2] *Zts. f. franz. Sprache u. Lit.*, XIII (1891), 25. F. Mistral, *Dictionaire provençal-français*, II, 98.   [3] Wolfram, *Parzival*, 339,26–340,1.
[4] Cf. *supra*, pp. 92 f., 131.   [5] H. O. Sommer, *Vulgate Version*, II, 339, 341.
[6] Ed. J. Bédier (Paris, 1902), I, vss. 2185, 2208.

The *Merlin* continues significantly: "For the tale tells that even after a run of ten leagues his flanks and his sides would not heave, nor would the hide of his crupper or shoulder sweat." When Gauvain meets Clarion alone, and "sees the horse pawing the earth and eager to go, he coveted it greatly in his heart and said that if he had such a horse, he would not give it away for the best city in Arthur's possession." In the succeeding encounter, Gauvain hurled Clarion from his saddle and seized "le Gringalet." Rejoining his father and brothers, he announced: "'I have won such a horse that I would never exchange it for the castle of Glouchedon.'"

The romance of *Escanor* by Gerard d'Amiens gives the fullest account of the steed.[7] Gauvain in the course of a battle overthrew Escanor le Grant, his inveterate enemy, and seized the horse on which the latter was mounted. The animal belonged, however, to Escanor's nephew, Escanor le Bel, to whom it had been sent by the supremely lovely fay Esclarmonde, enamored of his prowess. It was called "le Gringalet," and was "of great strength and handsome and tireless and powerful." After Gauvain had won the horse, however, he discovered that it would not eat and was pining away. While he was at a loss for a remedy, a lovely damsel in a red robe, a chaplet of peacock feathers on her head, arrived in the company of a dwarf, and offered, on conditions, to work a cure. Her name was Felinete. She withdrew a bag of powder from the horse's ear, its appetite returned, and Gauvain was rejoiced.

Earlier in the poem [8] we gain some significant information about the fay Esclarmonde, who had been the original owner of the steed and had bestowed it on Escanor le Bel. She had made for another favorite, Briant des Illes, a chamber elaborately painted with scenes from the Troy legend and a marvelously rich bed, "just as the tale affirms." [9] She had learned the art of necromancy from Virgil. Though *Escanor* was not composed till about 1280 and is very prolix, there is reason to believe that, in part at least, the poet was following old traditions which are extant only in cognate forms. The fay Esclarmonde, the pupil of Virgil, was apparently modeled after Morgain la Fée, the pupil of Merlin.[10] The elaborately painted chamber which she created is one of the stock features of Morgain's palaces, as we learn from the *Vulgate Lancelot, La Faula,* and *Le Myreur des Histors,*[11] and yet it is inconceivable that Gerard derived the notion from any of these texts. Esclarmonde's gift of the marvelous

---

[7] Ed. H. Michelant (Tübingen, 1886), pp. 507 f., 527-36.
[8] *Ibid.*, pp. 411-27.   [9] *Ibid.*, vs. 15840.
[10] L. A. Paton, *Fairy Mythology*, pp. 61 f.
[11] Cf. *supra*, p. 94; R. S. and L. H. Loomis, *Arthurian Legends in Medieval Art*, pp. 16 f., 24 f.; Sommer, *op. cit.*, V, 216 ff.; M. Mila y Fontanals, *Poetes catalans*, p. 16; Jean d'Outremeuse, *Myreur des Histors*, IV, 57. Cf. the embroidered curtains with scenes from the Troy and Aeneas legends in Morgain's bark, described in *Floriant and Florete*, ed. F. X. Michel (Edinburgh, 1873), vss. 843 ff.

steed, "le Gringalet," to Escanor le Bel must reflect the same tradition as Morgain's gift of the marvelous steed Galatee to Hector of Troy, mentioned by Benoît de Ste. Maure about 1160.[12] The mysterious naming of Hector's war-horse after a Greek sea-nymph clears up when one realizes that it merely represents an attempt to classicize the gift of "le Gringalet" by Morgain to the Arthurian knight Estor.[13] Likewise, Esclarmonde's gift of "le Gringalet" to Escanor is simply a variation on the well-known motif of Morgain's gift of a horse to one of her favorites, which we have met before,[14] and which I have elsewhere traced back to Ireland.[15]

When we open the question whether "le Gringalet" is a French substitute for Guingalet, and whether the latter is based on a Welsh original,[16] we are able to progress little beyond the point reached by Zimmer in his able discussion of 1891.[17] He pointed out that the Black Book of Carmarthen, copied about 1175, contains this triad: "The three spirited steeds of the Isle of Britain: Guyneu Goduff Hir, the horse of Kei; Ruthir Ehon Tuthbleit, the horse of Gilberd son of Kadgyffro; Keincaled, the horse of Gualchmei."[18] It is very natural, of course, to assume that this triad preserves an old tradition, and that the original of Gauvain's Guingalet is Gwalchmei's Keincaled, which is good Welsh for "handsome and hardy."[19] But Zimmer called attention to two suspicious facts,[20] and there is still another. The Welsh author of *Geraint,* though presumably working from the same source as that which Chrétien used in his *Erec,* has no Keincaled to correspond to Guingalet, and it would seem that he rejected the name as unfamiliar. Moreover, the owner of the second horse bears not a Welsh but a French name, Gilbert,[21] and this throws doubt on the sources of the triad as representing native Welsh tradition. Likewise, we have just seen that the name Gwalchmei is not the original of Gauvain, but a Welsh substitute for French Galvain. Therefore, two out of the three elements in the triad betray in the names Gilberd and Gwalchmei that they have been borrowed from French-speaking people, and Keincaled may well be a substitute for French Guingalet.

Nevertheless, the possibility that Guingalet is of Welsh derivation is not

---

[12] Benoit, *Roman de Troie,* ed. L. Constans, I, 434 f. Cf. *Speculum,* XX (1945), 183–91.
[13] Cf. *Speculum,* XX, 202, n. 4.   [14] Cf. Chaps. XI, XIV.
[15] *Speculum,* XX, 191 f.
[16] For discussions cf. *Romania,* XX (1891), 150; R. Zenker, *Zur Mabinogionfrage,* pp. 101 f.; E. Windisch, *Das keltische Brittannien bis zu Kaiser Arthur,* pp. 269 f.; Loth, *Mabinogion,* 2d ed., II, 228, n. 6.   [17] *Zts. f. franz. Sprache u. Lit.,* XIII (1891), 18–26.
[18] *Ibid.,* p. 18. Loth, *op. cit.,* II, 228.
[19] Zimmer (*Zts. f. franz. Sprache,* XIII, 19) translates "schönausdauernd." Loth (*loc. cit.*) translates "beau" "dur." Windisch (*op. cit.,* p. 270) translates "schön" "hart." On the meaning of *calet* cf. *Cymmrodor,* XXVIII (1918), 192.
[20] *Zts. f. franz. Sprache u. Lit.,* XIII, 19—21.
[21] Even though Zimmer's identification of the Gilberd of the triad with Gilbert "filius Ricardi," active in the Norman conquest of Cardiganshire, may not be accepted, yet the name is still certainly French.

ruled out. Possibly the Black Book triad simply restored the original Welsh form. Another Welsh etymology for Guingalet, suggested by Professor Tolkien,[22] is also possible, namely, Old Welsh *guin-calet,* meaning "white and hardy." This compound, to be sure, is nowhere recorded in Welsh literature,[23] but there are three arguments in its favor: (1) it approximates more closely the sound of Guingalet than does Keincaled; (2) Guingalet had red ears, and according to the testimony of *Le Lai de l'Espine, Wigalois,* and *Partonopeus* [24] a horse with red ears should have a white body; (3) the history of these white horses with red ears offers some correspondence to that of Guingalet, for the remarkable steeds in *L'Espine* and *Wigalois* are won by the hero in combat, and those in *Wigalois* and *Partonopeus* are presented by a lady to the hero. I am strongly inclined to believe, therefore, that Guingalet is derived from Old Welsh *guin-calet,* meaning "white and hardy," and aptly descriptive of the many supernatural white horses of Celtic and Arthurian romance.[25] "Le Gringalet" would then be merely a popular and inappropriate word, substituted for Guingalet. Whether this hypothesis be correct or not, it seems certain that Benoît de Ste. Maure, telling of Morgain's gift of the steed Galatee to Hector, and Gerard d'Amiens, telling of Esclarmonde's gift of the steed, "le Gringalet," to Escanor,[26] and Wolfram von Eschenbach, revealing that Gringulet had red ears, preserve interesting vestiges of a tradition concerning Gauvain's famous steed, antedating Chrétien and seemingly unknown to him.

[22] *Sir Gawayn and the Green Knight,* ed. J. R. R. Tolkien and E. V. Gordon (Oxford, 1925), pp. 90 f. "Gryngolet is more probably of Celtic origin, though the Welsh form Keincaled appears to be only a late reformation of the French Guingalet under the influence of a false etymology (Welsh *kein* 'fair'; *kaled* 'hard'). The French Guingalet, Gringalet (with intrusive *r,* as often in the French treatment of Celtic or Germanic *w*) point rather to a name beginning (*g*)*w*-, probably Welsh *Gwyngalet* 'white-hard.' "

[23] It is interesting to note, however, that Kulhwch is required to obtain Guyn Mygtwn (or Mygdwn), "le cheval de Gweddw, aussi rapide que la vague, pour chasser le Twrch Trwyth sous Mabon." Later we read that Arthur obtained the horse, and finally that Mabon son of Modron rode Gwynn Mygdwn in pursuit of the boar, Twrch Trwyth, as far as the Severn, spurred his stallion, and snatched the razor from the boar's head. Cf. Loth, *op. cit.,* I, 312, 332, 343; J. G. Evans, *White Book Mabinogion,* cols. 483, 496, 504. Nothing is known about Gweddw, but his stallion is swift as the wave and bears a name meaning, according to Loth (*op. cit.,* I, 343, n. 1), "blanc, à la crinière brune."   [24] Cf. *supra,* p. 90.

[25] *Ibid. Speculum,* XX, 189. Cross and Slover, *Ancient Irish Tales,* p. 440. P. W. Joyce, *Old Celtic Romances* (Dublin, 1920), pp. 385 f.

[26] The name Escanor is not properly Arthurian, but is a borrowing from the *Matière de France.* Cf. E. Langlois, *Table des noms propres* (Paris, 1904), s.v. *Esquanors.*

Chapter XXIII

THE RESCUE OF CADOC OF CARDUEIL

VERSES 4308–4579

As Erec was riding with Enide through a forest, he heard the cry of a damsel in distress. Leaving his wife, he came upon the damsel and learned that her lover, Cadoc of Cardueil, had just been dragged away by two giants. Erec spurred after the giants and discovered them beating Cadoc, whom they had bound to the back of a nag. He ran the first giant through with his lance, and despatched the other with his sword. Then he restored Cadoc to his ladylove and returned to Enide.

As WAS SHOWN in an earlier chapter,[1] this incident seems to be a variation on a stock narrative pattern—the rescue of Floree or Florete from the giants—which occurs in *Floovant, Le Livre d'Artus, Le Bel Inconnu, Libeaus Desconus, Wigalois,* and *Carduino.*[2] In the last four romances, the hero is riding with a lady through a forest; in all six he hears the screams of a woman; in all but one he leaves his squire to go to the rescue and finds two giants attacking a maiden; and of course in all he overcomes the giants. No Celtic source for this commonplace adventure has been discovered, but it must have been familiar to the Breton *conteurs,* and a form of it was used by Geoffrey of Monmouth in his story of the giant of Mont St. Michel.

The author of X took over this banal incident but with a marked difference; it is the damsel's escort whom the giants attack and whom the hero rescues from their clutches. This character Chrétien called Cadoc de Cardueil.[3] Was this by arbitrary choice?

Let us note some very curious facts. In *Le Livre d'Artus* Floree was carried off by giants while under the escort of a forester;[4] in the *Vulgate Lancelot* Uther's chief forester is named Do de Carduel.[5] In *Wigalois* the anonymous damsel was abducted by giants from Karidol[6] (the regular German form of Cardoil). In *Le Bel Inconnu* the damsel, Clarie, whose name we concluded was a substitution for Floree, was abducted by a

---

[1] Chap. X.
[2] On this incident in the last four romances cf. W. H. Schofield, *Studies on the Libeaus Desconus,* pp. 18–24.
[3] Vss. 4515, 4574. This is the reading of ms. P in both verses. It is supported by A (carboil), E (quarbroil), for vs. 4515, and by C (cabruel), VA (cabriel), E (quarbroil) for vs. 4574. Foerster's reading Tabriol is certainly a corruption.
[4] Sommer, *Vulgate Version,* VII, 85, l. 23.   [5] *Ibid.,* II, 102, ll. 19 f.
[6] Wirnt von Gravenberc, *Wigalois,* ed. J. M. N. Kapteyn, vss. 2080–82.

giant from her father's garden;[7] according to *Le Livre d'Artus* Doon of Kardoil had a daughter, Lore or Lorete,[8] who must be the same as Ulrich Fuetrer's Floreis zu Karidol.[9] Here, then, is a remarkable agreement among these various texts to the effect that the damsel rescued from the giants was named Floree or Florete, and that she was somehow connected with Do de Cardoil.

Moreover, the story of Lore, daughter of Doon de Kardoil, as found in *Le Livre d'Artus*,[10] though it involves no abduction by giants and Doon plays no conspicuous part, does recall here and there the story of Floree's adventures and the rescue of Cadoc of Cardueil. Lore and Guenievre, escaping from the city of Kardoil, wander in a forest under the escort of loyal knights, and see fifty Saxons sitting down at an outdoor feast. While the knights attack the Saxons, the Queen and Lore release Gaheriet, whom the Saxons have tied to a sumpter horse. Of course, the number of personages has been multiplied and the whole incident has been worked into the scheme of a pseudo-historical war with the Saxons, which dominates much of *Le Livre d'Artus;* yet one seems to hear echoes of Gauvain's rescue of Floree in the forest, Wigalois' rescue of a damsel near Karidol, Libeaus' rescue of Violette from two giants, one of whom was preparing a roast boar for an outdoor feast,[11] Erec's rescue of Cadoc of Cardueil, whom two giants had bound hand and foot. The author of *Le Livre d'Artus* has shuffled about his materials and effectively hidden their origin, but careful scrutiny reveals that his inspiration came from a version of the giants episode in which the scene was laid in a forest near Cardoil; Floree, daughter of Do of Cardoil, was the heroine; and a knight, mounted on a nag and tied hand and foot, was released by the hero. It is a legitimate conclusion that such a tale was the remote source of Chrétien's episode of the rescue of Cadoc of Cardueil. (The tale was not, of course, the same as that which had already been used by the author of X and which led on from the rescue of Floree to the arrival at her father's castle, the offer of the damsel in marriage, the provision of arms, and the sparrow-hawk adventure, though the two tales were akin.) Cadoc of Cardueil, for alliterative reasons, has replaced Do of Cardoil, and has become, probably for romantic reasons, the lover instead of the father of the distressed damsel.

Though I am unable to suggest any reason why Do became connected with Cardoil or Cardueil (the city which we now know as Carlisle), or with Lore or Floree, or with the episode of the giants, it is possible to dis-

---

[7] Renaud de Beaujeu, *Bel Inconnu,* ed. G. P. Williams (1929), vss. 892–97.
[8] Sommer, *Vulgate Version,* VII, 206 f.
[9] R. Zenker, *Ivainstudien, Beihefte zur Zts. f. rom. Phil.,* LXX (1921), 209.
[10] Sommer, *Vulgate Version,* VII, 206–10.   [11] *Libeaus Desconus,* ed. Kaluza, vss. 613–96.

cover whence his own name was derived. One form of the name given
in *Le Livre d'Artus* is Doon. Here and elsewhere Do is the father of
Giflet; again and again we hear of "Giflet fils Do." [12] There is an obvious connection with the Welsh figure, Gilvaethwy son of Don.[13] It
was natural, of course, for the inheritors of Welsh legend to assume that
Don was Giflet's father. But in the mabinogi of *Math* it is plain that Don
was a woman: "He [Math] could not make a circuit of the country, but
Gilvathwy, son of Don, and Eveydd, son of Don, his nephews, sons of his
sister, and the house host with them, made it in his place." [14] Three other
sons of Don were Gwydion, the magician, Govannon, the smith god, and
Amaethon, the plowman god.[15] A shadowy figure, Don was evidently a
mother goddess of the Welsh, corresponding to the Irish Dana.[16] The
Arthurian Do or Don, father of Giflet and Lore, has undergone a strange
metamorphosis, from an ancient Brythonic goddess into the castellan of
Carlisle and the chief forester of Uterpandragon!

Chapter XXIV

THE ADVENTURE AT LIMORS

VERSES 4580–4935

*Overcome by loss of blood after his battle with the giants, Erec fell sense-
less from his horse. Enide, thinking him dead, reproached herself as the
cause and was about to commit suicide when Count Orguilleus de Limors
came on the scene with his retinue. He took her to his castle of Limors
and caused the lifeless body of Erec to be conveyed to the hall and laid
out on a litter. He then forced Enide to undergo a marriage ceremony
with him. At supper she refused to eat and drink in the presence of her
dead lord and declared she would never submit to the Count. Suddenly
Erec regained consciousness, drew his sword, and clove the Count's skull,
while the courtiers fell into a panic at the spectacle, crying out, "Flee, flee!
Behold the dead man!" Erec and Enide made good their escape.*

---

[12] He is mentioned three times in *Erec* and in Biket's *Lai du Cor*, which is even earlier than
Erec. His name underwent curious corruptions. In *Libeaus* he appears as Giffroun le fludus, le
frendous, Ile ffredicus, le frondeus, etc. (vss. 796, 817, 961)—the knight who contests the
gerfalcon with Libeaus. In the Provençal *Jaufré*, ed. H. Breuer, he is the hero Jaufré, son of
Dovan. In Wolfram's *Parzival* he is Jofreit fis Idol.
[13] W. J. Gruffydd, *Math Vab Mathonwy*, pp. 204 f. For the story of Gilvaethwy cf. *ibid.*,
pp. 3–12; Loth, *Mabinogion*, 2d ed., I, 176–88.
[14] Loth, *op. cit.*, I, 176.   [15] Gruffydd, *op. cit.*, pp. 56 f., 145, 148, 196–203.
[16] J. A. MacCulloch, *Religion of the Ancient Celts*, pp. 103 f. I. Williams, *Pedeir Keinc y
Mabinogi*, p. 253.

EREC'S EXPERIENCE at the castle of Limors brings him at last the conviction of Enide's love and fidelity. Chrétien's narrative is eminently realistic and dramatic; nothing happens but what might have happened in a twelfth-century castle, and the episode serves admirably as a climax to the series of trials to which the heroine's faith is subjected. But Chrétien has preserved a few clues to the original content and meaning of the adventure, a content and meaning very different from those apparent in the poem. One is tempted by the strange name, "chastel de Limors," to examine an episode in the Swiss *Lanzelet*.[1]

The hero, his wife Ade, and a squire arrived before a castle known as Schatel le Mort. It was the dwelling of one Mabuz, son of Lanzelet's foster mother, the Queen of Meydelant. For his protection she had bespelled the place so that all who entered lost their courage and strength, and Mabuz had taken more than a hundred knights and killed some of them. When Lanzelet entered Schatel le Mort, Mabuz dragged him from his horse so that he lay as if dead. The squire led the grief-stricken Ade away. Lanzelet, though revived, gave no thought to food and drink and would not eat with the other prisoners at table. After a fortnight, however, Mabuz forced him to depart, promising that he would kill no prisoners for a year. Once outside the castle, Lanzelet recovered his full strength and rode away to his great battle with Iweret.

Though this tale differs in many ways from the episode in *Erec,* three notable similarities appear. Schatel le Mort corresponds to "chastel de Limors." Erec is rendered lifeless before he is brought to the castle; Lanzelet is rendered lifeless as he enters the castle. Enide refuses to eat; Lanzelet gives no thought to food and drink. These resemblances might seem accidental if we did not possess in *Le Livre d'Artus* a much more elaborate form of the same basic story.[2]

Oriles fell in love with the Countess of Limos, who refused him her favor until he had vanquished Gauvain. Oriles set out in search of Gauvain. His mother, alarmed for his safety, established three enchantments. One was a strange cry, issuing from the air, which caused all who heard it to fall to the earth as if dead. The second consisted of two barking giants. The third was a garden, attached to her castle, from which no one could escape who ate of the apples in it. Some time later the Countess de Limos brought her suitor, Oriles, to the spot where Gauvain awaited him. In the course of the ensuing fight, Oriles in cowardly fashion ran away. His men, lying in ambush, came to his rescue, but Gauvain alone carried on the battle, and as midday passed, his strength doubled and the enemy gave way before him. A party of knights came to his aid, and Oriles, badly mauled, fled to the forest. The Countess of Limos gave her love to Gauvain. After a few

[1] P. Piper, *Höfische Epik,* II, 181 f.
[2] H. O. Sommer, *Vulgate Version,* VII, 170 f., 265–67, 298, 312–18. Oriles seems to be identical with "li Orguelleus Faé" in *L'Atre Périlleux,* whose mistress has promised him her love if he would slay Gavain, and who boasts that he has fulfilled the condition but is vanquished by that hero. Cf. *L'Atre Périlleux,* ed. B. Woledge, vss. 5017–6408.

days Gauvain set out for the orchard which Oriles' mother "had by necromancy enclosed around with air." [3] On his way he slew the barking giants. Sagremor put an end to the second enchantment of the fatal cry, and then entered the orchard. There he found several knights of the Round Table who had eaten of an apple and so lost all desire to continue their quests, for they found in the orchard "all the joys of the world." [4] Sagremor and later King Arthur rejected the apple and were obliged to battle with ten knights. A damsel summoned Gauvain to their aid, and the three slew the knights of the orchard and ended the enchantment. All were now free to leave and went to the tower where Oriles' mother dwelt. They found the aged enchantress seated in state and forced her to leave the land. Her castle was called "le chastel as puceles."

On analysis this story reveals itself as a highly conflate form of the same story we have found in *Lanzelet.* Instead of one hero and one enchantment there are three heroes and three enchantments. Whereas the coward knight, Mabuz, is met by Lanzelet within the enchanted castle established by his mother and is forced to abandon his custom for a year, his counterpart, Oriles, encounters Gauvain under quite different circumstances, and the ending of his mother's spells is brought about by different means. Nevertheless, *Lanzelet* and *Le Livre d'Artus* still have in common the enchantress who is queen of a castle of maidens and who devises for her son's protection a place where all who enter lose the will or the power to leave; the many knights who have succumbed; the hero who rejects the food of the place; his combat with the son of the enchantress; his termination of the wicked custom. In both versions there are signs of confusion. Lanzelet succumbs at first to the spell of Schatel le Mort and is consequently overpowered by Mabuz; and yet, quite inconsistently, he renews his strength, obliges Mabuz to abandon his evil practices, and departs. Thus he plays the double role of victim and victor. Confusion also appears in the Oriles story since, though the Countess of Limos is ostensibly the *amie* of Gauvain, she imposes on Oriles the task of killing him and summons her suitor to the combat. It is therefore a plausible guess that originally the Countess of Limos was Oriles' lady, and that Oriles was the Count of Limos.

At any rate, it can hardly be an accident that in the *Lanzelet* we have the Schatel le Mort and its cowardly lord, in the *Livre d'Artus* "la comtesse de Limos" and her cowardly suitor, Oriles, and in *Erec* "le conte Orguilleus de Limors." The article being consistently masculine singular—le Mort, Li-mors—we are confronted with the probability that Schatel le Mort

[3] Sommer, *op. cit.,* VII, 268, l. 41.
[4] *Ibid.,* p. 312. On eating food of the Other World cf. Hartland, *Science of Fairy Tales,* pp. 38–48, 155; W. Y. E. Wentz, *Fairy-Faith in Celtic Countries* (Oxford, 1911), pp. 47, 68, 127, 219, 275 f.; Stith Thompson, *Motif-Index of Folk-Literature* (Bloomington, 1932), I, 394 f.; C. Guest, *Mabinogion,* Everyman ed., p. 311; *Romania,* XXV (1896), 271 f.; W. Bottrell, *Traditions and Hearthside Stories of West Cornwall,* 2nd Ser. (Penzance, 1873), p. 98; A. W. Moore, *Folklore of the Isle of Man,* p. 41; *Folklore,* II, 183 ff.

meant the Castle of the Dead Man. Now it is at least curious that the Bretons, who had much to do with the shaping of the Arthurian romances, apply this title, *ar Maro,* which literally means the Dead One, to Death himself.[5] If, then, Schatel le Mort is presided over by Death personified, we can understand why Lanzelet lost all his strength and lay as if dead when he entered the castle, and why the familiar motif of the fatal effects of eating the food of the Other World has been introduced both in this story and more logically in the parallel tale of Oriles. This concept of the Castle of Death seems to have been quite foreign to the medieval Welsh,[6] but it appears in the Breton lai of *Sir Orfeo* and in the Chastel Mortel of *Perlesvaus*.[7] Probably its occurrence in *Lanzelet, Le Livre d'Artus,* and *Erec* is due to a Breton modification of an earlier Celtic visit to some divine abode.

According to this interpretation, Mabuz of Schatel le Mort, Oriles, and Count Orguilleus de Limors would be personifications of Death. Can we reconcile this view with other aspects of their character? Mabuz, as we have seen, derived his name ultimately from Apollo Maponos of Romano-British inscriptions.[8] And if Mabuz was originally a Celtic Apollo, it would explain the odd fact that his counterpart in *Le Livre d'Artus,* Oriles, was called "le Vermeil Chevalier," [9] and that his other counterpart in *Erec,* Mabonagrain, as we shall presently see, was also clad in "armes vermoilles." [10] For among the Celts red was a solar color.[11] Moreover, the knights of Oriles gave ground as soon as midday was passed, and Mabonagrain wearied after the hour of *none*.[12] That these details are not meaningless is shown by the fact that three knights in medieval romance, Escanor, Graysteel, and the Red Knight of the Red Laundes, combine significantly red arms with the solar trait of increasing in strength till midday or *none* and then declining.[13] There seems to be a gross incongruity between the sun, giver of life and joy, and Death, which deprives mortals of both. Is the dual character of Mabuz and Oriles a sample of mere muddlement or does it spring from a genuine mythical fusion?

[5] J. Rhys, *Lectures on the Origin and Growth of Religion,* ed. 2, p. 659.
[6] *PMLA,* LVI (1941), 891–98.   [7] *Ibid.,* p. 898.
[8] Cf. *supra,* p. 46.   [9] Sommer, *op. cit.,* VII, 170, ll. 7–10.
[10] *Erec,* vs. 5899. On Mabonagrain and Mabon in the *Matière de Bretagne* cf. *supra,* p. 91, *infra,* pp. 175–77, and *Zts. f. franz. Sprache u. Lit.,* XLVI (1923–24), 265–74, 439 f.; XLVII (1924–25), 73; W. H. Schofield, *Studies on the Libeaus Desconus,* pp. 45–52, 125–27.
[11] R. S. Loomis, *Celtic Myth,* p. 46. *Nuovi studi medievali,* II (1925), 290 f. W. F. Skene, *Four Ancient Books of Wales,* I, 529. F. Sébillot, *Folk-lore de France,* I, 36.
[12] Sommer, *op. cit.,* VII, 267, l. 4. *Erec,* vss. 5998–6001.
[13] *L'Atre Périlleux,* ed. Woledge, vss. 1516 f., 1560–69. W. H. French, C. B. Hale, *Middle English Metrical Romances,* pp. 675, 699 f., 701. Malory, *Morte d'Arthur,* Bk. VII, chaps. 15, 17. Cf. J. L. Weston, *Legend of Gawain,* pp. 12 f.; Raoul de Houdenc, *Meraugis de Portlesguez,* ed. M. Friedwagner, vss. 3075–91; *Mort Artu,* ed. J. D. Bruce, pp. 287 f.; C. Potvin, *Perceval le Gallois,* III, 334; *Romania,* XXIV (1895), 323 f.; *Zts. f. franz. Sprache u. Lit.,* XVII, 107, 120; *PMLA,* LIV (1939), 663.

Such a fusion was not only possible but seems to have been familiar to the medieval Celts. As to its possibility, we read in Pauly-Wissowa: "Helios ist als echter Gott der Toten aufgepasst worden." [14] In Irish mythology Donn of the Fallen Teeth (*Detscorach*) is accepted by the best authorities as the god of death, and in *The Destruction of Da Derga's Hostel* (ninth century) three uncanny riders from his land appear, clad in red and riding red horses, and declare that though they are alive they are dead. [15] Much more satisfying, though later, evidence comes from Map's *De Nugis* (*ca.* 1181). [16] The dwarf king, who is one of the prototypes of Guivret, possessed a glowing face and a red beard, his pigmy subjects were so brightly garbed that they were like the sun before the other stars, and his subterranean palace, approached through a cave in a cliff, was like that of the sun as described by Ovid. So much for the solar aspect of this Otherworld king. His character as King of the Dead is suggested by his sending his guests from his palace with the warning that they should not dismount from their horses until a hound which he had given them should leap to the earth, and by the fact that those who disregarded this injunction changed at once to dust. [17] Map's story also contains the familiar motif of the supernatural lapse of time in fairy-land. [18] The tale was probably collected in Brittany [19] (though localized in England) and presents some astonishing analogies with a folktale which was collected by Luzel from Breton peasants seventy years or more ago. In all versions of the folktale a woman is married to a supernatural bridegroom, who takes her away to his land, and who regularly departs from his home at sunrise and returns at sunset; [20] in one version his castle is "le château du Soleil-Levant." [21] Yet on the other hand, two tales call him a dead man, and another calls him "le Trépas," Death himself. [22] Here, in the plainest terms we find the same dual concept suggested in Map's legend, and there is further evidence of affinity between the modern folktale and the twelfth-

[14] Pauly-Wissowa, *Real-Encyclopädie*, new ed., VIII, col. 77.

[15] Thurneysen, *Irische Helden- und Königsage*, p. 635, n. 2. *Sitzungsberichte der preussischen Akademie der Wissenschaften*, 1919, pp. 537 ff. Cross and Slover, *Ancient Irish Tales*, pp. 101 f.

[16] Ed. M. R. James (Oxford, 1914), pp. 13 f. Trans. Tupper and Ogle (London, 1924), pp. 16–18. On this story cf. *Mod. Phil.*, XXXVIII (1941), 300 f.; *PMLA*, LVI (1941), 894 f., 917 f.

[17] Cf. Cross and Slover, *Ancient Irish Tales*, pp. 455 f., 595; A. C. L. Brown, *Iwain* (*Studies and Notes in Philology and Lit.*, VIII, Boston, 1903), p. 41; Marie de France, *Lais*, ed. K. Warnke (1925), p. 254.

[18] Hartland, *Science of Fairy Tales*, chaps. VII–IX.

[19] Note that the name Herla is not Welsh. Cf. Map, *De Nugis Curialium*, trans. Tupper and Ogle, pp. 233, 322 f. Map included in his work three Breton narratives, Dist. IV, chaps. 8, 13, 15; trans. Tupper and Ogle, pp. 218, 233, 237 ff.

[20] *Revue celt.*, II (1873–5), 289–320. Luzel, *Contes populaires de Basse-Bretagne*, I, 3–65.

[21] *Rev. celt.*, II, 299. Luzel, *op. cit.*, I, 17. Cf. *ibid.*, pp. 70 f.

[22] *Rev. celt.*, II, 291, 297, 303. Luzel, *op. cit.*, I, 3, 14, 32. Le Braz reports the modern Breton belief that the soul of a dying man flies to the Land of the Setting Sun. F. J. Snell, *King Arthur's Country*, p. 66.

century tale. In one or more of the modern variants we discover the subterranean entrance through a rock to the Other World,[23] the resplendent palace,[24] and the motif of the supernatural lapse of time.[25] Since, then, there must have been a continuous tradition linking Map's probably Breton legend with the modern Breton tale, and since in both the sun is personified and equated with Death, we are justified in concluding that the same equation which we have detected in *Lanzelet* and *Le Livre d'Artus* was no mere accidental blunder; it arose out of the strangely vital paganism of twelfth-century Brittany.

Further scrutiny of this Breton mythology explains one feature in the adventures of Erec and Enide at Limors which neither *Lanzelet* nor *Le Livre d'Artus* accounts for: Enide is wedded to the lord of the castle, and Erec delivers her from his power. It is not to be overlooked that in all variants of the Breton folktale the heroine becomes the bride of the solar king of the dead. A far older and more primitive version of the same theme is preserved in the Middle English *Sir Orfeo,* based doubtless on a Breton lai, in which the classical myth of Orpheus has been skillfully combined with the Breton myth.[26]

The king of the Other World, wearing a crown of neither silver nor gold but as bright as the sun, appeared in a dream to the mortal queen Heurodys, and the next day carried her off to his realm. Her husband Orfeo sought her for ten years and more. One day catching sight of her among a troop of riders, he followed them through an opening in a rock and presently came to a castle, shining like the sun. Within he found many folk who had met death in various ways, lying as if asleep, and saw the king and queen of the land enthroned in dazzling clothes. Orfeo gained leave to take his beloved Heurodys back with him, but when he returned to his home no one recognized him.

Evidently this lai of *Orfeo* illustrates once more the fusion of god of the dead and the solar divinity which we have detected in Arthurian romance and Breton tradition. Once more, as in Map's legend and the modern folktales, this mythical figure dwells in a shining palace reached by entering the side of a rock and following a subterranean passage; and in the failure of the folk to recognize Orfeo on his return there is a reminiscence of the supernatural passage of time. Once more, as in the folktales, the faery king takes a mortal woman with him to the realm of the dead, and years after her brother or husband comes to deliver her. Though in *Orfeo* Heurodys does not wed the Plutonian Apollo, it is easy to see that she was destined to be his bride, as she is in the modern Breton analogues.

[23] *Rev. celt.,* II, 291 f., 314. Luzel, *op. cit.,* I, 4 f., 54.

[24] *Rev. celt.,* II, 292, 304, 314. Luzel, *op. cit.,* I, 5, 33, 55.

[25] *Rev. celt.,* II, 302, 318 f. Luzel, *op. cit.,* I, 24, 64.

[26] French and Hale, *Middle English Metrical Romances,* pp. 323–41. Cf. L. A. Hibbard, *Mediaeval Romance in England,* pp. 195–99; *Mod. Lang. Notes,* LI (1936), 28–30.

Returning to *Erec,* we may now feel confident that Enide's enforced marriage to the Count of Limors was not invented by the author of X, but was derived from a Celtic form of the Persephone myth. The episode at the castle, though stripped of its supernatural features and drastically remodeled, still preserves in the name Chastel de Limors, the lifeless body of Erec, Enide's wedding, her refusal to eat, and her deliverance by Erec vestiges of the original macabre tale.

There are several other vestiges of this Breton tradition of the King of the Dead or his cavalcade. Map twice repeats the tale of a knight of Brittany who discovered his deceased wife among a throng of women in a lonely valley, seized her, and brought her back to live with him.[27] Andreas Capellanus has a scene, based on a Breton lai, of a meeting with the God of Love and bands of horsewomen, who describe themselves as belonging to the "exercitus mortuorum." [28] Huon de Méry describes himself in the *Tornoiement Anticrist* as meeting in the Forest of Broceliande, beside the storm-making spring, "un Mor de Mortaigne," later referred to regularly as Li Mors, who seems to be not so much a Moor as a personification of Death, since he is leader of the knights of hell.[29] In *Diu Krone* the Grail King tells Gawein that he and his folk are dead.[30] In *Wigalois* Count Hojir von Mannesvelt, a knight with red hair and beard, accoutred in red arms, has a grisly image of Death painted on his shield.[31] The hero of *Amadas et Ydoine* engages in a nocturnal combat with a spectral knight who has come to carry off the body of Ydoine from her tomb.[32] Some at least of these stories illustrate the vitality of the legends about Death which must have been current in Brittany in the twelfth century, as they were still in the nineteenth.

Chapter XXV

THE "JOIE DE LA CORT"

VERSES 5367–6410

Riding with Enide and Guivret, Erec approached a strongly fortified town on an island cut off by a deep, roaring stream, and was informed that it belonged to King Eurain, was called Brandigan, and was plentifully sup-

[27] Map, *De Nugis Curialium,* Dist. II, chap. 13; Dist. IV, chap. 8; trans. Tupper and Ogle, pp. 97, 218.
[28] Andreas Capellanus, *De Amore,* ed. A. Pages, pp. 47 f.; trans. J. J. Parry, pp. 75 f. On relation to *Lai du Trot* cf. *Romanic Review,* XXVI (1935), 313–21.   [29] Vss. 215 ff.
[30] Heinrich von dem Türlin, *Krone,* ed. Scholl, vss. 29532–34.
[31] Wirnt von Gravenberc, *Wigalois,* ed. J. M. N. Kapteyn, vss. 2841 f., 2997–99.
[32] *Amadas et Ydoine,* ed. J. R. Reinhard (Paris, 1926), vss. 5339–6461.

plied with fruit, wheat, and wine, but none of the knights who had visited it ever came back, because of a perilous adventure called the "Joie de la Cort." Nevertheless Erec and his companions entered and the townsfolk ominously foretold his death on the morrow, for none had ever come to claim the "Joie de la Cort" who had not met death. King Eurain insisted on entertaining the strangers in his palace. That night they had in abundance all that heart desires. Though warned by his royal host, Erec proceeded the next morning to a garden outside the town, surrounded by an impenetrable wall of air. Both summer and winter it bore flowers and fruit, but whoever wished to carry away the fruit could not find his way out until he had restored the fruit to its place. The garden contained every singing bird to gladden men, and medicinal herbs in abundance. Attended by Eurain and his people, Erec rode in and saw stakes, each impaling a man's head, except the last which supported only a blast horn. This stake, Eurain said, was reserved for Erec's own head, but great renown would be his who succeeded in blowing the horn. From this point Erec went on alone till he descried a surpassingly lovely woman lying on a couch beneath a sycamore. A very tall knight in vermeil arms challenged him and a combat ensued, lasting till none. Erec, victorious, compelled the Red Knight to relate his history. He was the nephew of Eurain, and had pledged his word to his mistress never to leave the garden until he was worsted in combat. The heads on stakes were those of his victims. When he was released from his vow, all those of the court would rejoice—hence the name "Joie de la Cort." His name was Mabonagrain, but none had ever known it before in any land where he had been. Erec must now blow the horn, for then the Joy would begin. As Erec did so, all far and near made merry and Erec himself was well fed with joy and served to his heart's desire. Only Mabonagrain's mistress moaned and wept, but was comforted by Enide, who turned out to be her cousin. When all returned to the castle from the garden, the vassals had assembled from the country round, and for three whole days the rejoicing lasted. Erec then departed with Enide and the dwarf king to Arthur's court at Robais.

OF THIS ELABORATE NARRATIVE Gaston Paris remarked in *Romania*, Volume XX (1891), page 154: "Il est assurément impossible d'imaginer quelque chose de plus absurde, de plus incohérent et en même temps de moins intéressant que ce récit, allongé d'ailleurs par le poète à grand renfort de détails inutiles et raconté avec une fatigante prolixité. Il est clair qu'on se trouve en présence d'un vieux conte mal transmis, que le poète francais ne comprenait plus et qu'il a rendu encore plus inintelligible en essayant de l'expliquer."

Though one is entitled to disagree with Paris' appraisal of the story's interest, scholars have generally agreed that it is a patchwork of traditional motifs, some of them Celtic in origin.[1] The studies of Philipot and Professor Newstead have been particularly serviceable in illuminating the complicated relationships of the episode.[2] And I hope to show that almost every feature can be accounted for by the coalescence of two famous themes—the visit to the castle of Bran and the release of Mabon from captivity. These two distinct traditions are responsible for the many disharmonies in Chrétien's narrative.

Professor Newstead has shown that the king of Brandigan, his island fortress, and his reception of Erec display both directly and indirectly his relationship to King Bran in the mabinogi of *Branwen*. The King of Brandigan, like Bran, was famous for his hospitality; and his guests, like the followers of Bran, feasted by night in a royal hall on an island supplied with abundance.[3] Compare Chrétien's lines: "Whatever heart desires and craves they had in plenty that night. . . . But the joyous entertainment (*bele chiere*) surpasses all,"[4] with the description of the hospitality of the Noble Head in the island of Gwales: "That night they were there in the midst of plenty and joy."[5] Like King Baudemaguz, whose name will later be shown to contain a corrupt form of Bran, the King of Brandigan dwells in an island fortress, separated from the land by a very deep, broad, and roaring water;[6] Baudemaguz' land is one whence no one returns, and the castle of Brandigan is equally fatal;[7] Baudemaguz' son fights Lancelot in an ever green glade beside a sycamore and is vanquished,[8] just as the King of Brandigan's nephew is vanquished by Erec in an ever blossoming *vergier* beside a sycamore. The King of Brandigan also resembles the Fisher King, whose name the *Didot Perceval* gives as Bron,[9] in that both are notable for their lavish hospitality, their wealth, and the perils encountered in their castles.[10] When we take up the discussion of Baudemaguz in *Le Chevalier de la Charrette* and the Fisher King in *Le Conte del Graal*,[11] the descent of these figures from the Welsh Bran will become patent. The same ancestry must hold good for the King of Brandigan.

Of course, Chrétien thought of Brandigan as a castle, but Professor Newstead has noted that Wauchier, more correctly, understood it as the

---

[1] J. D. Bruce, *Evolution of Arthurian Romance*, I, 109. A. C. L. Brown, *Iwain*, pp. 135 f. *Romania*, XXV (1896), 275. *Zts. f. franz. Sprache u. Lit.*, XLVIII (1926), 49.

[2] *Romania*, XXV, 258 ff. *PMLA*, LI (1936), 13 ff. H. Newstead, *Bran the Blessed in Arthurian Romance*, pp. 106-20.

[3] J. Loth, *Mabinogion*, 2d ed., I, 124, 132, 148-50. Cf. Newstead, *op. cit.*, pp. 19 f.; *PMLA*, LVI (1941), 904 f.   [4] *Erec*, vss. 5584-88.

[5] Loth, *op. cit.*, I, 148.

[6] Chrétien, *Chevalier de la Charrette*, vss. 3024-27. *Erec*, vss. 5374 f.

[7] *Charrette*, vss. 645, 1948, 5439. *Erec*, vss. 5436 f.

[8] *Charrette*, vss. 7005-10, 7095-7107.   [9] *Didot-Perceval*, ed. W. Roach, p. 150.

[10] For these perils cf. R. S. Loomis, *Celtic Myth*, pp. 159-64; *Bulletin of the Board of Celtic Studies*, II (1925), 180 f.   [11] Cf. Chaps. XL, LXVIII.

name of a king: "at the court of King Brandigan"; "in the castle of King Brandigain, the grandfather of Sir Gauwain." [12] Probably, then, the employment of the name Brandigan as that of a place was due to a misunderstanding of some such ambiguous phrase as "le castiel Bran," in which Bran might be taken as the name either of the castle or its owner. Once mistaken for a place name, it probably acquired the termination -igan by analogy with "le chastel de Caradigan." [13]

The identification of the King of Brandigan with the Fisher King, Bron, is helpful in elucidating the mysterious title of the adventure which took place near his castle, "la Joie de la Cort." Scholars are agreed that Chrétien himself seems hardly to have understood the phrase, though he does offer the lame explanation that the court of the king will have joy when Erec, after his victory over Mabonagrain, has sounded the horn, suspended in the enchanted garden.[14] We evidently have references to the same tradition in the Elucidation, prefixed to Le Conte del Graal, which provides two passages concerning the joy produced by the discovery of "the court of the Rich Fisher." It behooves the knights of the Round Table to search "until God will grant them to find the court, whereby the joy will come with which this land will be resplendent." [15] "Sir Gauwain found it [the court] at the time when Arthur reigned, and was in truth at the court. Farther on you will be told of the joy which he obtained there, whereby all the kingdom was advantaged." [16] Again there is reference to the great wealth which prevailed throughout the land, among both rich and poor, when "the court (la cors) was discovered." [17] Compare the verses which describe Erec's achieving the adventure of "la Joie de la Cort." When Erec has blown the horn (cor), "the King is glad and his people likewise. . . . No one ceases or rests from making joy and singing. . . . The tidings fly throughout the land that the affair has reached this outcome. Then there was nothing to restrain all from coming to the court. . . . With joy was Erec well fed (peuz) and well served to his heart's desire." [18]

Of course, the author of the ironically named Elucidation and other romancers give a report of the finding of the Fisher King's court which is very different from Erec's experiences at Brandigan, but this need not disconcert us. It will become clear, when in due course we examine the second main theme which has been worked into the "Joie de la Cort" episode, that it has displaced or overlaid much of the characteristic matter of the visit to Bran's castle. We may therefore confidently equate the court of the King of Brandigan with that of the Rich Fisher; both courts are found by knights of the Round Table; both kings enjoy great wealth

---

[12] Potvin, Perceval le Gallois, IV, vss. 22378, 30321 f.
[13] Caradigan is repeatedly mentioned in Erec as Arthur's seat.
[14] Vss. 6121–24, 6147.   [15] Elucidation, ed. A. W. Thompson, vss. 206–8.
[16] Ibid., vss. 225–30.   [17] Ibid., vss. 107–12.   [18] Erec, vss. 6165–91.

and feast their guests lavishly; in both instances the successful termination of the adventure brings great joy to all the inhabitants of the land. This common tradition clarifies in part the mysterious "Joie de la Cort." As the title of the adventure Chrétien uses the phrase somewhat loosely, just as, earlier in the poem,[19] he employs the phrase "li beisiers del cerf" elliptically to designate the kiss which the slayer of the stag was entitled to bestow on the fairest woman.

Though there can be no doubt that for Chrétien and the author of the *Elucidation* the word *cort* (nom. *corz* or *cors*) meant a court and nothing more, there are numerous reasons for suspecting that both poets are drawing upon a tradition concerned with a horn (nom. *corz* or *cors;* obl. *cor*). Even though the gender was different, confusion was likely, for even in the *Elucidation* itself "le court" occurs.[20] Moreover, drinking horns were evidently unfamiliar to the French of the twelfth and thirteenth centuries, and so the word *corz* was likely to be taken in some other sense. This unfamiliarity with drinking horns is attested by the fact that they are not mentioned in the nearly fifty thousand lines comprised in *Le Roman de Troie* and *Le Roman de la Rose,* and by the fact that though the horns possessed by Auberon and "la Pucelle au Cor d'Ivoire" are said to satisfy hunger and thirst,[21] they perform this function by their sound, as if the authors of *Huon de Bordeaux* and the continuation of *Le Conte del Graal* did not recognize them as drinking vessels. The Welsh, on the contrary, used horns at their banquets,[22] and it is therefore of great significance, considering the Welsh origin of the Brandigan episode and of the corresponding matter in the *Elucidation,* that among the Thirteen Treasures of the Isle of Britain there is listed the Horn of Bran: "the drink and the food that one asked one received in it when one desired." [23] Is it possible that the *cort* of the King of Brandigan and the *cort* of the Rich Fisher, alias Bron, represent misunderstandings of the magic horn of Bran?

When one turns to *Erec* for an answer to this question, one notes certain curious circumstances. It is Erec's blast upon the horn which ends the enchantment and produces the consequent joy.[24] Shortly afterwards, "with joy was Erec well fed (*peuz*) and well served to his heart's desire." [25] One suspects that "la Joie de la Cort" should be "la Joie del Cor," and that the *cor* had something to do with Erec's being so happily fed and served according to his desire. When one turns to the *Elucidation,*

---

[19] *Erec,* vss. 1819, 1845.   [20] *Elucidation,* vs. 220.
[21] *Huon de Bordeaux,* ed. Guessard and Grandmaison, p. 97. Newstead, *op. cit.,* p. 112.
[22] Loth, *Mabinogion,* 2d ed., I, 251, n. 3; 306, 319. *Transactions of the Hon. Soc. of Cymmrodorion,* 1940, p. 182. For Irish horns cf. *Romanische Forschungen,* XLV (1931), 72–77.
[23] National Library of Wales, ms. Peniarth 77, p. 214. "Corn Bran galed or gogledd; y ddiod ar bwyd a ofynid a gaid ynddo pan i damunid." On this list cf. *PMLA,* LVI, 910–13.
[24] *Erec,* vss. 6144–47. Mabonagrain says: "Fors de ceanz issir ne doi Tant que le cor aiiez soné; Mes lors m'avroiz desprisoné Et lors comancera la Joie."   [25] *Erec,* vss. 6190 f.

one finds even stronger hints that the *cort* of the Rich Fisher in origin was a horn of plenty. It made the land resplendent (*resplendissoit*) with many things, including food (*viandes*).[26] It is coupled with the Grail as if both were objects of quest: "Truly the court (*la cours*) and the Grail were found;"[27] and as we learn from the Vulgate cycle it was a function of the Grail also to supply the worthy with such food (*viandes*) as they desired. "Piere, a kinsman of Josephes, bore the holy vessel through the rows [of people]. Then the rows were filled with all the good foods (*viandes*) which the heart of man could imagine."[28] "Thus as it [the Holy Grail] passed before the tables, they were instantly filled at each seat with such food (*viande*) as each desired."[29] The coupling of the *cors* and the Grail becomes all the more significant when one notes that the same Welsh list of the Treasures of the Isle of Britain contains not only the feeding horn of Bran but also a magic dish (*dysgl*), the equivalent of French *graal*:[30] "whatever food was wished thereon was instantly obtained.".[31] Here, then, is a neat explanation for (1) the coupling of *cors* and *greaus* in the *Elucidation;* (2) the fact that the *cors* made the land resplendent with food; (3) the fact that it belonged to the Rich Fisher, Bron.

Another connection of the horn of plenty with traditions of the Grail and the Fisher King is to be found in the Vulgate *Queste,* where the Grail castle is called "le chastel de Corbenic," and the name is said to mean in Chaldean "most holy vessel (*saintisme vaissel*)."[32] Here, apparently, is a reminiscence of the fact that the castle contained a most holy vessel, the Blessed Horn (*corbeneit*).[33] In this castle dwelt the Maimed King, wounded in the legs,[34] whom the romancers identified with the Rich Fisher, and whom a number of scholars have recognized as the Welsh Blessed Bran, wounded in the foot in battle.[35] Certainly at the castle of Corbenic the Grail heroes were entertained as hospitably as was Erec at the castle of Brandigan. Bishop Josephes announced to Galaad after the sacring of the mass: " 'Thou shalt be fed (*repeu*) with the noblest food (*viande*) and the best of which ever knight partook.' "[36] Again, Christ

---

[26] *Elucidation*, vss. 100–106. The Grail was apparently credited with supplying forms of wealth other than food. Cf. P. S. Barto, *Tannhäuser and the Mountain of Venus*, pp. 11 f.

[27] *Elucidation*, vss. 386 f.   [28] Sommer, *Vulgate Version*, I, 250.

[29] *Ibid.*, VI, 13.

[30] *Speculum*, VIII (1933), 430. On the meaning of *graal* cf. *Mod. Phil.*, XIII (1916), 681 ff.

[31] Edward Jones, *Bardic Museum*, p. 48. Although Jones gives a tablecloth as an alternative to the *dysgl*, no other list which I know agrees; all those in the National Library mention the *dysgl* without alternative.   [32] Sommer, *op. cit.*, I, 288.

[33] That there was a testing horn in Arthurian tradition which was called "li cors beneiz" is vouched for by the following mss. of *Conte del Graal*, the readings of which were kindly given me by Prof. Roach: ms. Edinburgh, f. 101*b*: "Ce cor qui Beneoiz a non"; ms. Montpellier, f. 111*c*: "Cest cor qui Beneiz a non"; ms. Bib. Nat. fr. 1429, f. 143*a*: "Cest cor qui Beneoiz a non." It is very significant that, as Prof. Cross has noted (*Mod. Phil.*, X, 292, n. 4), this horn resembles the Grail in that it will not serve the unworthy.

[34] Sommer, *op. cit.*, VI, 188, 191.   [35] H. Newstead, *Bran the Blessed*, pp. 6, 36, n. 21.

[36] Sommer, *op. cit.*, VI, 190.

himself declared to the twelve knights: " 'The knights of this place and many others have been fed (*repeu*) with the grace of the Holy Vessel. . . . Now hold and receive the noble food (*viande*) which you have so long desired.' " [37] If it be objected that there is here no mention of a *cors*, but only of the dish (*escuele*) from which Christ ate the lamb at the Last Supper, the answer is not difficult. For it is precisely Christ's body (*cors*) with which the twelve were fed. Though the word *cors* is not used, the *Corpus Christi* is specifically mentioned. The Lord gave to Galaad "his Savior (*son Salveor*)," and likewise to the others: "there was none of them to whom it did not appear that a piece in the semblance of bread was placed in his mouth." [38] This, then, is the "cors beneiz" after which the castle was named; the pious author of the *Queste* or his source has very naturally interpreted it, not as "blessed horn," but as the body of the Lord. There is even a trace in the *Queste* of the joy which ensued on the discovery of the *cort* of the Rich Fisher in the *Elucidation* and of the joy which followed the blast of the horn in *Erec*. When Galaad, Perceval, and Boors were about to leave the castle of Corbenic, they were assured by those who had feasted with them: " 'Sirs, wit ye well that we have never had such great joy as that which we have now had.' " [39]

In *La Queste del Saint Graal*, therefore, we meet with many of the very motifs and the very words which in the *Elucidation* were associated with the *cors* of the Rich Fisher: the knights of the Round Table who seek the castle of Corbenic; the provision of *viandes;* the combination of the *escuele* (equivalent of *graal*) with the mass wafer (equivalent of *cors*); the joy which followed the finding of the Maimed King's court. And as for *Erec*, the very words which are there applied to the hero of "la Joie de la Cort" and the blower of the *cor* might apply to the heroes of Corbenic: "With joy was Erec well fed and well served to his heart's desire."

One could point to several other instances of the association of the Grail with the Horn of Bran in one or another of its disguises, but since Professor Newstead has covered the matter fully in her book,[40] it will suffice to mention only a few. *Sone de Nansai* tells us that the body (*cors*) of the Fisher King reposed in a holy vessel and was exhibited together with the Grail. Moreover, "the abbot was supplied with holy bodies (*de sains cors fu l'abbés garnis*), and he has served them right well." [41] One may suspect that behind this curious remark lay the statement that the abbot, who was lord of a Grail castle, was well supplied by the *saint cor* of the Fisher King, and it had served him right well. According to *La*

---

[37] Sommer, *op. cit.*, VI, 190.   [38] *Ibid.*   [39] *Ibid.*, p. 192.

[40] Newstead, *op. cit.*, pp. 86–134. The confusion on the subject of the *cors* of the Fisher King was increased by the fact that, as we shall see in our discussion of this personage in the *Conte del Graal*, there was actually a tradition of his death and of his body lying in the Grail castle awaiting vengeance.

[41] *Sone de Nansai*, ed. M. Goldschmidt (Tübingen, 1899), vss. 4927–29.

Queste del Saint Graal, Perceval came to an abbey, found there a wounded king lying in bed, Mordrain by name, who had never tasted earthly food (*viande*) for hundreds of years but is fed only with "li cors Jhesucrist." [42] This passage evidently corresponds to and illuminates the famous passage in Chrétien's *Conte del Graal* where Perceval's Hermit Uncle explains how the Fisher King's father is kept alive in the Grail castle. " 'The holy man sustains and solaces his life with a single mass wafer (*oiste*) which is brought to him in this Grail. So holy a thing is the Grail and so spiritual that he needs no more to preserve his life than the wafer which comes in the Grail.' " [43]

Various are the forms in which the magic *cors* of Bran appears—as the sacred Host (*li cors Jhesucrist*), as the body (*cors*) of the Fisher King, as the court (*cors*) of the Rich Fisher, as the horn (*cors*) in the garden of Brandigan—but their repeated association with the Grail, with the Fisher King, called Bron in the *Didot Perceval,* and with feeding, supplying, or serving should leave little doubt as to their origin.

Such doubts as may remain as to this interpretation of the "Joie de la Cort" may be removed by the consideration of the second main theme which has been amalgamated with the theme of Bran's hospitality and his magic horn. For it is in this second complex that we find the answers to certain haunting questions: Why does the hospitable king bear the name Eurain instead of some recognizable form of the name Bran? Why does the horn, if it is a drinking vessel, appear, not in the hall of the king, but in the perilous *vergier?* What connection have Mabonagrain and his *amie* with King Eurain? We shall see that not only has this second pattern been superimposed on the Bran complex, thus obliterating wholly many of the characteristic features of the visit to the Fisher King's palace, but it has also affected to some extent the features that have been retained, giving us a misleading name for the hospitable king, changing the whole character of the disenchantment motif, and causing the horn to be suspended from a stake in the garden.

In this second complex Mabonagrain is the outstanding figure; and already in our examination of the Limors episode we have seen that he has his counterparts in Mabuz and Oriles, and if this be so, his original would be the Romano-British Apollo Maponos. It is clear, then, why he wears red arms and why his strength fails after the hour of *none*—a combination of solar characteristics attached to three other redoubtable and uncanny knights in medieval romance. Nor is any explanation required for the tabu against carrying fruit out of the enchanted garden. "The fruit had such a property that it could be eaten within [the garden]; the danger lay in carrying it outside; for whoever wished to carry any outside never

[42] Sommer, VI, 60.
[43] Chrétien, *Conte del Graal,* ed. Hilka, vss. 6422–28. Cf. Chap. LXXV.

would return to the door and never would issue from the garden until he had put the fruit back in its place." [44] This manifestly is a form of the tabu against eating the food of the Other World which so tenaciously clings to Schatel le Mort, the castle of Limors, and the enchanted *vergier* of Oriles' mother. Mabuz, Orguilleus de Limors, and Oriles are unquestionably, then, the cognates of Mabonagrain.

Other cognate personages were identified by Philipot. Even the Welsh confused the mythical name Mabon with the common personal name Madawc, for whereas one triad lists Mabon son of Modron as one of the three famous prisoners of the Isle of Britain, another triad substitutes Madawg son of Modron.[45] It is therefore understandable that Mabonagrain's abhorrent custom of affixing to stakes the heads of the knights whom he had conquered was also practised by Maduc le Noir in *Le Vengeance Raguidel* and *Le Livre d'Artus,* and by Malgiers le Gris in *Le Bel Inconnu.*[46] This motif, as Schofield and Professor Taylor have shown, was characteristically Celtic;[47] it occurs in *Kulhwch,*[48] in many Irish and Gaelic folktales, and in the Arthurian romances. That its attachment to Mabonagrain, Maduc, and Malgiers is no accidental similarity is proved by the fact that each of these sinister personages stands in a subordinate position to a lady—as a lover bound unwillingly by a promise, as a feudal liegeman,[49] or as a rejected lover;[50] and furthermore, Maduc le Noir was in the habit of setting out abundant food in his castle so that an errant knight, on entering, would be tempted to remove his helm to eat, whereupon Maduc would treacherously attack him and impale his head on a stake.[51] This practice must be a rationalization of the danger which attended eating the food of the Other World,[52] the familiar motif attached to the dwellings of Mabuz and Mabonagrain.

It is Mabonagrain who also furnishes the clue to the name of the King of Brandigan, Eurain or Uirain.[53] For in Pseudo-Wauchier's continuation of *Le Conte del Graal* there are two brief but significant passages: "the fair son of King Urain, who was called Mabounain"; "with the fair

---

[44] *Erec,* vss. 5748–54. [45] Loth, *Mabinogion,* 2d ed., II, 267, 318.
[46] Raoul de Houdenc, *Vengeance Raguidel,* ed. M. Friedwagner, vss. 622–25. Sommer, *Vulgate Version,* VII, 143. Renaud de Beaujeu, *Bel Inconnu,* ed. G. P. Williams (1929), vss. 1956–2004.
[47] *Studies and Notes in Philology and Lit.,* IV, 175–79; VIII, 137, n. 1. *Romanic Review,* IX (1918), 21 ff.
[48] Loth, *Mabinogion,* 2d ed., I, 346. [49] Sommer, VII, 143, l. 15.
[50] Renaud de Beaujeu, *op. cit.,* vss. 2005–37. [51] Sommer, VII, 143, ll. 26–36.
[52] A further rationalization of the motif appears in *Libeaus Desconus,* where we read that Maugis, the counterpart of Malgiers in *Le Bel Inconnu,* treacherously attacked Gingelain while he was drinking from his helmet to quench his thirst. Cf. *Libeaus,* ed Kaluza, vss. 1435–41. As Kaluza pointed out (p. cl), the motif was probably influenced by the Auchinleck *Guy of Warwick.*
[53] *Erec,* grosse Ausgabe, vs. 6070, ms. H gives *Uirains.* The rime with *main* in vs. 5567 makes it certain that Chrétien's form ended in *-ain(s).* Cf. similar deformation of Urien by exigencies of rime in *Tyolet* (*Romania,* VIII, 49): "Gauvain le baise et Uriain, Keu et Evain, le filz Morgain."

son of King Enrain." [54] In the second passage the Montpellier manuscript substitutes Urien for Enrain. Light begins to shine on the mystery of Chrétien's nomenclature, for if Mabonagrain was really the son of Urien, there would be a correspondence with Welsh tradition. Modron was the mother not only of Mabon, as we know, but also the mother of Owain by Urien.[55] If the father of Mabon was unknown—and no Welsh text gives his name—what more natural than to assume that Mabon's father was the lover of Mabon's mother, Urien? In the absence of any information to the contrary, it would be an almost inevitable conclusion. It would explain why Pseudo-Wauchier, who certainly did not derive his information from *Erec,* makes Urain, Enrain, or Urien the father of Mabounain. And though Chrétien gives a more corrupt form of the tradition, we may well believe that King Eurain represents the Welsh King Urien, so far as his name and his kinship to Mabonagrain are concerned. This view is not inconsistent with the belief that his lordship of the castle of Brandigan, his island domain, and his hospitality are derived from the Welsh King Bran, for Eurain is a composite figure, just as the whole "Joie de la Cort" adventure is a composite pattern.

We have already discovered several reasons for equating Mabonagrain with the Welsh Mabon son of Modron; there are more. Mabonagrain was held in captivity (*an prison*) for years; he could not be released until he had been vanquished in combat; no one outside the land knew his name.[56] There are curious parallels in the history of Mabon. He was long incarcerated in Caer Loyw; he could be released "only by combat and battle"; [57] each of the three oldest animals, when questioned as to his whereabouts, replied: " 'I have never heard speak of the man about whom you inquire.' " [58] The most remarkable analogy, however, is this: Mabonagrain was held captive by a damsel whose prototype, we shall see, was the Dame du Lac, and the Dame du Lac brought up Lancelot in a beautiful mansion, below which ran a river full of fish, instructed him in the duties of knighthood, and on his departure gave him a horse.[59] Likewise, Mabon was held captive in Caer Loyw, "the Shining Fortress," below which ran a salmon river, and which was the abode of a sorceress who schooled Peredur in the use of arms and on his departure gave him a horse.[60] Of course, it would be easy to point out differences between the imprisonment of Mabon and that of Mabonagrain, but surely these should not weigh too heavily in the balance. The astonishing thing is that there should be as much resemblance when the intervals of space and time be-

[54] Potvin, *Perceval le Gallois,* III, vss. 16305 f., 19659.
[55] Loth, *Mabinogion,* 2d ed., II, 284. Owain and Mabon are mentioned in an ancient Welsh poem. Cf. *Cymmrodor,* XXVIII (1923), 198 f.   [56] *Erec,* vss. 6052–78, 6090–97, 6132–36.
[57] Loth, *Mabinogion,* 2d ed., I, 326–28.   [58] *Ibid.,* I, 323–25.
[59] Sommer, *Vulgate Version,* III, 22, 114 f., 118.
[60] Loth, *Mabinogion,* 2d ed., I, 326; II, 75 f. On Caer Loyw and its identification with Gloucester on the Severn cf. *supra,* p. 89, n. 21.

tween the two traditions and the vagaries of oral circulation are considered.

As for the element -*agrain*, it may well be the name of Mabon's brother which has been compounded with his own. Such compounds are not unknown to the romancers, for Pseudo-Wauchier explains that King Brangemuer derived his name from those of his father and mother: "For this reason his name was divided in two." [61] Other examples of names compounded from those of two separate characters are Baudemaguz and Guingambresil, which will be analyzed later in this book. Now in *Libeaus Desconus* there are two brothers, Maboun and Irain, both enchanters, dwelling in the same castle, who engaged Gingelain together in combat and were both overcome by him.[62] The similarity in nature and role probably led to confusion and then to fusion; Mabon and Irain may thus have become Mabonagrain. This hypothesis is essentially the same as that put forward by M. Lot and Philipot and adopted by Bruce.[63] It accords with a recognizable practice of the French poets. There is, I believe, no other so plausible.

Let us now examine Mabonagrain's mistress and her role. She is, of course, Enide's cousin, and we have already discovered that another female cousin of Enide's was modeled after Niniane and her Welsh original Riannon. Perhaps this cousin also, though Chrétien differentiates the two, may have the same antecedents. Support for this equation of Mabonagrain's mistress with Niniane is furnished by the similarity between the wall of air which enclosed her garden [64] and that with which Niniane surrounded her lover, Merlin. The wizard declared: " 'There is no tower in the world so strong as that in which I am locked; and yet there is no wood, iron or stone in it, but by enchantment it is enclosed with air and nothing more. . . . I cannot issue forth nor can any one enter, save only her who has done this to me and who, when she pleases, keeps me company here.' " [65] This sort of enclosure has been influenced by a legend of Virgil, reported by Neckam: "How is it that the said prophet fortified and surrounded his garden, moveless air taking the place of a wall?" [66] But it was probably suggested originally by the magic mist which, according to Irish legend, concealed the palaces of the gods, such as that of Manannan in *The Adventures of Cormac in the Land of Promise*.[67] Another indirect connection between Mabonagrain's mistress and Niniane is suggested by the melodious birds of the enchanted *vergier*. "Under

[61] Potvin, *Perceval le Gallois*, IV, vss. 21857–71. Cf. Newstead, *Bran the Blessed*, pp. 122–24.
[62] *Libeaus Desconus*, ed. Kaluza, vss. 1777–2127.
[63] Bruce, *Evolution of Arthurian Romance*, I, 109, n. 16. These scholars take the second element to be a corruption of Evrain, the name of the second enchanter in *Le Bel Inconnu*. But Evrain is probably a substitution suggested by *Erec*.
[64] *Erec*, vss. 5739–45.   [65] Sommer, *Vulgate Version*, II, 461.
[66] Alexander Neckam, *De Naturis Rerum*, ed. T. Wright (London, 1863), p. 310. Cf. J. W. Spargo, *Virgil the Necromancer* (Cambridge, Mass., 1934), pp. 60, 61, 65, 67, 68.
[67] T. P. Cross, C. H. Slover, *Ancient Irish Tales*, p. 504.

heaven there is no flying bird, agreeable to man, which did not sing there to please and delight him and of which one could not hear many of every kind." [68] In Welsh tradition it would appear that the three birds of Riannon were famed for their enchanting song. Bran the Blessed told his followers that they would be seven years banqueting at Harlech. " 'The birds of Riannon will sing for you.' " And when the men arrived there and settled down to a prolonged feast, "three birds came to sing them a song compared with which all others which they had heard were unpleasing." [69] In one manuscript of *Kulhwch* and in a triad there is also mention of these birds.[70] Of course, it is impossible to assert categorically that the many songsters of Mabonagrain's garden are descended exclusively from the three birds of Riannon, for similar choirs were heard in the wonderlands of Irish romance, particularly the three birds which Clidna gave to Taidg to accompany him on his voyage.[71] Nevertheless, since Riannon is the prototype of Niniane, it is likely that her birds are akin to those which warbled so ravishingly in the garden of Mabonagrain's mistress.

But though we may feel satisfied that the enchantress of the garden was related to Niniane, we cannot overlook certain signs of the pervasive influence of Morgain. Although the two fays are usually distinct personalities and are even opposed to each other,[72] they inherited some common traditions. Both were instructed in magic by Merlin.[73] Furthermore, whereas in the *Vulgate Lancelot* the hero was reared and presented with a horse by the Dame du Lac, Niniane, according to *Lanzelet* the same hero was brought up and presented with a horse by the Queen of Meydelant, the mother of Mabuz, whom for several reasons we have identified with Morgain. Thus, although the melodious birds seem to point to Niniane as the mistress of the bespelled garden, the mention of medicinal herbs [74] points rather to Morgain. "There is not to be found as far as the earth extends any spice or root which avails for healing but it had been planted there [in the *vergier*] and grew in plenty." Rarely is Niniane credited with a knowledge of curative plants, whereas Morgain is renowned for her skill in their use. One is reminded at once of the verses on the Isle of Apples in the *Vita Merlini:* "The ground of its own accord produces everything instead of merely grass." Of the nine sisters who rule there, the chief is most skilled in the healing art. "Morgen is her name, and she has learned what useful properties all the herbs contain, so that she can cure sick bodies." [75]

[68] *Erec*, vss. 5755–59.   [69] Loth, *Mabinogion*, 2d ed., I, 145, 147 f.
[70] *Ibid.*, I, 97, n. 1; 307, n. 2.
[71] A. C. L. Brown, *Iwain*, pp. 84–91. S. H. O'Grady, *Silva Gadelica* (London, 1892), II, 394 f.
[72] L. A. Paton, *Fairy Mythology*, pp. 195–200.   [73] *Ibid.*, pp. 205–8, 213, 226n.
[74] *Erec*, vss. 5760–64.
[75] Ed. J. J. Parry (Urbana, 1925), vss. 914–21. Cf. also *Erec*, vss. 5746 f.: "Et tot esté et tot

The same tendency to confuse the two enchantresses is doubtless responsible for the fact that the two completest analogues to Erec's adventures in the orchard assign the part of Mabonagrain's mistress either to Morgain or to one who manifests in certain specific details that she is Morgain. The first of these analogues, long since recognized by Philipot, is that of the "Val Sans Retor" in the *Vulgate Lancelot.*[76] Morgain established an enchanted valley, "all closed about with air." Here she confined many knights, including her lover, Guiomar; and here they enjoyed whatsoever could delight the body of man. Lancelot entered the valley, came to a garden, discovered the enchantress lying on a beautiful couch, overcame the knights who opposed him, thus put an end to the spell, and was thanked by Morgain's lover for his deliverance. Morgain, however, was furious. The parallel with Erec's experiences in the *vergier* needs no laboring. Equally obvious is the relationship to the adventures of the enchanted orchard in *Le Livre d'Artus.* And in view of the already demonstrated kinship of the stories about Mabonagrain, Oriles, and Mabuz,[77] and the presence of the coward-knight motif in the latter two, it is perhaps worth noting that in the "Val Sans Retor" there is a "chevalier coars," who ran away from Lancelot, as Oriles and his knights fled before Gauvain. We need have no hesitation, then, in recognizing in the "Val Sans Retor" episode an authentic branch of the Mabon tradition, a branch unlike the Mabonagrain story in that there is no contamination by the Welsh Bran complex.

An even more elaborate parallel to the Mabonagrain story, likewise unaffected by the Bran complex, is one hitherto, I believe, neglected—Gareth's encounter with the Red Knight of the Red Laundes in Malory's seventh book.[78]

Gareth, accompanied by a damsel and a dwarf, comes before the castle of the Lady Lyones beside the isle of Avylyon, where she dwells with her brother Gryngamor.[79] The next morning he rides toward the place of combat, sees many knights who have been defeated by the Red Knight of the Red Laundes hanging from trees, and is told that the same fate awaits him if he is vanquished. An ivory horn hangs from a sycamore tree, and Gareth blows it to summon his adversary, who appears on the scene in red arms, mounted on a red horse. They fight till the hour of *none* (by which Malory meant midday), the might of the Red Knight increasing till he has seven men's strength. Finally after evensong Gareth beats the Red Knight down and is about to slay him. But the Red Knight pleads excuse for hanging his victims that he once loved a fair damsel, who wished to be avenged on Lancelot or Gawain, and made him promise to put all knights whom he overcame to a villainous death. (An earlier passage shows that

iver I avoit flors et fruit meur," with the lines in the *Gesta Regum Britanniae* (Paton, *op. cit.,* p. 46) descriptive of Avalon: "Ver tepet eternum. Nec flos nec lilia desunt   Nec rosa nec viole."
[76] Sommer, *Vulgate Version,* IV, 117–23.   [77] Cf. Chap. XXIV.
[78] Malory, *Morte d'Arthur,* ed. H. O. Sommer, I, 234–40.   [79] *Ibid.,* p. 255.

the fair damsel was Dame Lyones.) [80] Gareth accepts his excuse and pardons him.

The analogies with the "Joie de la Cort" adventure can be easily picked out: the hero accompanied by damsel and dwarf, the island castle, the ignominious exhibit of slain knights, the sycamore tree, the blast horn, the red knight whose strength reaches its maximum at the hour of *none,* his surrender, his excuse that his cruel custom had been imposed on him by his ladylove. The absence of any trace of the Bran complex makes it pretty clear that Malory did not derive this episode even indirectly from Chrétien. The ultimate source of both must have been an early form of the story of Mabon's enchantment by his faery love and his deliverance.

In that earlier source Dame Lyones must have played the part of Mabonagrain's mistress since the Red Knight of the Red Laundes, Mabonagrain's counterpart, declares that Lyones is his lady and that for her he has done many strong battles, and alleges his promise to a former ladylove as an excuse for hanging the knights. A glance at this counterpart of Mabonagrain's mistress reveals that she is Morgain under an alias. She is the lady of a castle in the isle of Avylyon, and dwells there with her brother Gryngamor. In *Erec* itself we read that Guigamor "was lord of the isle of Avalon; of him we have heard it said that he was the lover of Morgain la Fée." [81] Obviously, since Lyones was destined to be the bride of Gareth, she could not be represented as the paramour of Gryngamor, and on a later page we shall see why she was converted into his sister.[82] Moreover, it is worth noting that she is consistently called, not simply Lyones, but Dame Lyones or Lady Lyones. For Malory uses precisely the same word Lyones as the name of Tristram's native land,[83] and also omits on occasion the preposition *of* or *de,* as in the case of Lady Lyle of Avelione,[84] so that a place name becomes a personal name.[85] There is therefore excellent reason to suppose that Dame Lyones represents "la Dame de Loenois." Loenois has been proved by Dr. Brugger to be the Latin Lodonesia, the modern Lothian; [86] and we have seen in connection with the tourney of Danebroc that Morgain was regarded in one body of Arthurian tradition as Lady of Lothian. Malory, in fact, introduces her as Morgause, Queen of Lothian.[87]

Of course, it may be objected that if Malory's Dame Lyones and Queen Morgause were both Morgain, there would be a duplication of the same character and Gareth would be guilty of incest by marrying his own mother. But surely by this time it has become manifest that the intro-

---

[80] Malory, ed. Sommer, I, 237.
[81] *Erec,* vss. 1954–57. The form Guigamor is given by ms. E. [82] *Infra,* pp. 364 f., 368 f.
[83] Malory, ed. Sommer, I, Bk. VIII. [84] *Ibid.,* I, 81.
[85] Cf. King Cornwall (*English and Scottish Popular Ballads,* ed. H. C. Sargent and G. L. Kittredge, pp. 52, 54). [86] *Mod. Phil.,* XXII (1924), 159 ff.
[87] Malory, *Morte d'Arthur,* ed. Sommer, I, 37 f., 88, 233, 268.

duction of the same original character in more than one role and under more than one name in a given romance is a characteristic phenomenon of the Round Table cycle, which could be illustrated by many recognized examples.[88] No one played more diversified parts than Morgain, and so long as these were narrated separately as short and simple *contes,* she could be the faery mistress or the tender foster mother or the malevolent sorceress or the efficient leach or the great queen without involving the author in violent contradictions or grotesque absurdities. But when the *contes* were stitched together into long romances, then appalling confusion would have arisen unless the authors, deliberately or accidentally, had assigned the inconsistent roles to separate characters. Nevertheless, they usually remained faithful to tradition to the extent that they preserved a few telltale marks of identity. Thus Dame Lyones, as lady of Lothian and as dwelling in the isle of Avylyon with Gryngamor, reveals that one of her prototypes was Morgain.

We see, then, that two analogues of the "Joie de la Cort" adventure, namely, the "Val Sans Retor" and the Red Knight of the Red Laundes episodes, assign the part of Mabonagrain's mistress either explicitly to Morgain or to one who shows signs of her derivation from that lady. And so the faery cousin of Enide's is a composite character, displaying on the one hand her affinity to Niniane, the Dame du Lac, and on the other her affinity to Morgain la Fée.

It must have occurred to the perspicacious reader that the occurrence of the blast horn, suspended from a sycamore tree, in the account of Gareth's combat with the Red Knight of the Red Laundes makes it necessary to reconsider that feature in the "Joie de la Cort" episode. Though there is a difference in the function of the two horns in that Gareth blows the one in order to summon the Red Knight to combat, whereas Erec blows the other to announce his victory over a knight in red arms, yet the surrounding circumstances are so much alike that the horns must have sprung from one tradition. And this raises the question whether this was the tradition of Bran's horn of plenty after all; for there is no evidence that the Bran complex had any influence on Malory's story of the Red Knight of the Red Laundes, and there is considerable evidence to connect Morgain with a blast horn and a drinking horn. Is it not likely, then, that the horn in the enchanted *vergier* over which Mabonagrain's mistress presided was the horn of Morgain rather than the horn of Bran? Or is it possible that, as the episode of the "Joie de la Cort" is a blending of the Bran and the Mabon-Morgain traditions, so the horn is a blending of the two famous horns of Bran and Morgain?

We have twice had occasion to note that Morgain possessed a horn

[88] *Mod. Phil.,* XVI (1918), 347 f. *PMLA,* LIV (1939), 667.

with magic powers: [89] it could serve as a test of virtue by spilling its contents over the unworthy; it could heal the sick and wounded. In the German Shrovetide play it served both as blast and drinking horn.[90] In *Auberon* it is definitely a wind instrument and its sound could be heard by all Morgain's vassals and would summon twenty thousand armed men.[91] In *Le Bastard de Bouillon* we discover what is apparently the same blast horn under circumstances which are reminiscent of the "Joie de la Cort" episode.[92]

Hue de Tabarie and twelve Christian princes sailed beyond the Red Sea to the land of Arthur and Morgain, whence no galley had ever returned. As they landed and rode on, Hue was separated from his companions by a cloud, and after wandering for a day and a night discovered a pavilion in which a horn was suspended. An inscription informed him that only a knight supreme in valor could blow it. When he made the essay, the blast could be heard for half a league, and the scattered princes were able to join him. They tried to sound the horn but in vain. Arthur and Morgain appeared on the scene, and Arthur declared that Hue had conquered the horn. No one had entered the land for two hundred years. All followed Arthur to the noblest *vergier* in the world. "Never did God create an herb . . . which one would not find in the garden." There a thousand fays were disporting themselves. Losing all desire to return to their homes and wives, the princes remained five years. Hue demonstrated his sovereign prowess once more by entering another *vergier* guarded by two golden automata with flails.[93] When the princes departed, they could not believe that they had spent five years in *faerie*.

Without much difficulty one recognizes here characteristic features of the "Val Sans Retor" and the enchanted *vergier* in *Erec*, not to mention other kindred traditions. And when we observe that the horn serves as a test of prowess and also summons knights from a distance and is a prominent feature in Morgain's land of *faerie*, there can be no doubt that this is the traditional horn of Morgain. Its influence on the same motif in *Erec* is beyond dispute.

[89] Cf. *supra*, pp. 97, 144.

[90] H. Newstead, *Bran the Blessed in Arthurian Romance*, pp. 111 f.

[91] *I Complementi della chanson d'Huon de Bordeaux*, ed. A. Graf, I, vss. 1209, 1459 ff.

[92] *Li Bastars de Buillon*, ed. A. Scheler, pp. 119–32. In two other romances we can recognize Morgain as an anonymous fay with her blast horn. In the *Vulgate Lancelot* (ed. Sommer, IV, 306–8) we find the following characteristic features: a combative dwarf, a rich pavilion, a most beautiful damsel within, who provoked thoughts of love, a knight of Arthur's court imprisoned by her, an ivory horn which the damsel dares the hero to blow, a big knight in red arms who answers the challenge and who is her *ami*, a combat between the hero and the red knight. In Pseudo-Wauchier (J. L. Weston, *Legend of Perceval*, I, 13; *Romanische Forschungen*, XLV, 92) there is a forest full of songbirds, a damsel on a mule with an ivory horn, at whose sound a hundred or more attendants appear and spread a picnic dinner under an oak. Very significant is the damsel's statement concerning the horn (ms. B.N. fr. 12577, f. 66*v*): "Que ja li homs quil [*sic*] lait o soy   Naura ne fain ne froit ne soi   Ja ni ert en si estrange leu." It is evidently a feeding horn like that of Auberon. Cf. Newstead, *op. cit.*, pp. 112 f.

[93] Cf. Paton, *Fairy Mythology*, pp. 131, 168; Loomis, *Celtic Myth*, pp. 174 f.; *Mod. Phil.*, X (1913), 516.

But before we conclude that the motif is thus completely explained, let us recall the title of the adventure, "la Joie de la Cort," and the repeated emphasis on the joy produced by the blast of the horn. There is no such emphasis on the joy produced by the blast in any of the accounts of Morgain's talisman; there is just such an emphasis in the *Elucidation* on the joy which follows the discovery of the Fisher King's *cort*. And we have seen good reason for the view that both these joys reflect traditions connected with the horn of plenty in the court of the Fisher King. In fact, it seems likely that the presence of the horn in both the Morgain and the Bran legends prompted the author of X to combine the two in the "Joie de la Cort" episode.[94] This common element, therefore, may be responsible for placing the mist-girdled orchard of Niniane-Morgain beside the island fortress of Brandigan, for making the "Val Sans Retor" an annex of Corbenic.

Though the presence of this and other common elements is the probable cause for dovetailing together the traditions of Bran, Urien, Mabon, and Morgain, it is an interesting coincidence that all four figures appear in close proximity elsewhere, namely, in the toponymy and the local legends of Denbighshire. Just north of Llangollen rises sharply the grassy hill crowned with the ruins of a castle called Dinas Bran, the Fortress of Bran, which I showed some years ago to be a traditional site of the Grail castle.[95] Just north of this is Ruabon Mountain, and Ruabon derives from Rhiw Vabon, the Hill of Mabon.[96] Not many miles further north is the parish of Llanferres and the ford where Urien met the daughter of the King of Annwn, ravished her, and begat Owein son of Urien.[97] She can hardly be other than Morgain, the mother of Ivain by Urien—Morgain in her role as a water-fay awaiting her lover. This collocation within a space of twelve miles of the sites associated with the very personages who are represented in the "Joie de la Cort" episode by King Eurain of Brandigan, Mabonagrain, and his mistress is, of course, a coincidence; but it is a happy reminder of the fact that these figures were once very much alive in the imaginations of the Welsh and that they played their parts in some of the most romantic landscapes of Wales, the land of "hut a'r lledrith."

[94] Perhaps the similarity of Morgain's island paradise of Avalon to the delectable isle of Bran and the fact that both Morgain and Bran were given to holding Arthur's knights in captivity may have aided the fusion. Cf. Newstead, *op. cit.*, pp. 16, 138, 147.
[95] *Miscellany of Studies in Romance Languages and Literatures in Honour of L. E. Kastner*, pp. 342 ff. For other mythic and Arthurian traditions in this region cf. Newstead, *op. cit.*, p. 23; F. J. Snell, *King Arthur's Country*, p. 183; *Journal of British Archaeological Association*, 1878, p. 426; T. Pennant, *Tour in Wales* (London, 1784), I, 401; W. Sikes, *British Goblins*, pp. 79 f.; J. Rhys, *Celtic Folklore*, I, 238; *Zts. f. celt. Phil.*, III (1901), 133; *Celtic Review*, IV (1907–8), 258; *Aberystwyth Studies*, VIII (1926), 71n.
[96] W. J. Gruffydd, *Math Vab Mathonwy*, p. 179, n. 2. S. Baring-Gould and J. Fisher, *Lives of the British Saints*, III, 391, n. 1.
[97] *Aberystwyth Studies*, IV, 105. T. Gwynn Jones, *Welsh Folklore and Folk-Custom*, p. 107.

BOOK III.   Le Chevalier de la Charrette

Chapter XXVI

LANCELOT DU LAC

IN CONSIDERING the name and personality of Erec, son of Lac,[1] we saw that there was much evidence that his Welsh prototype was Gweir, son of Llwch, one of Arthur's warriors mentioned in *Kulhwch and Olwen.* Llwch also was one of Arthur's warriors, and apparently a prominent one. He is mentioned in the *Kulhwch* muster roll as Lloch Llawwynnyawc,[2] and again in the Black Book of Carmarthen he appears as a companion of Arthur under the name Lluch Llauynnauc.[3] *The Spoils of Annwn,* a poem perhaps as old as A.D. 900, describes a raid by Arthur and his men on an island fortress to carry off the magic caldron of the Chief of Annwn, and we have the obscure lines: "The sword of Lluch Lleawc was lifted(?) to it, And in the hand of Lleminawc it was left."[4] It would seem as if the name and epithet which appear together in *Kulhwch* and the Black Book poem were here separated, Lluch being the name and Lleminawc the epithet. In *Kulhwch,* as Rhys pointed out,[5] this very expedition of Arthur's to secure the caldron is related in somewhat euhemerized form, and Llenlleawc Wyddel takes the place of Lluch Lleminawc. "Llenlleawc the Irishman seized Caletvwlch, brandished it, and slew Diwrnach and all his host."[6] This Irish Llenlleawc also seems to have been a notable figure, for, besides performing his exploit, he is twice listed in the *Kulhwch* muster roll.[7] Since he fills the place of Lluch Lleminawc as the brandisher of a sword, his name is evidently another deformation of the epithet attached to Llwch in *Kulhwch* and detached from Lluch in *The Spoils of Annwn.*

Two inferences are to be made: (1) Llwch was according to the oldest Welsh traditions one of Arthur's distinguished warriors. (2) There was an extraordinary uncertainty as to the precise form of his epithet.

Why this uncertainty? Perhaps it arose from the attempts by the Welsh to find substitutes for an ill-understood foreign name. The fact that Llenlleawc was an Irishman furnishes a clue. Among the great figures

---

[1] Cf. Chap. VIII.   [2] J. Gwenogvryn Evans, *White Book Mabinogion,* col. 461.
[3] Evans, *Facsimile of Black Book of Carmarthen* (Oxford, 1888), f. 47*v*. W. F. Skene, *Four Ancient Books of Wales,* II, 51. Malory, *Morte d'Arthur,* Everyman ed., I, p. xix.
[4] Malory, *op. cit.,* I, p. xxiii. *PMLA,* LVI (1941), 890. "Lleawc" may be an adjective formed from *lleu,* "light," and would mean "shining."
[5] J. Rhys, *Studies in the Arthurian Legend,* p. 10. Malory, *op. cit.,* I, p. xxv.
[6] Evans, *White Book Mabinogion,* cols. 498 f. Loth, *Mabinogion,* 2d ed., I, 334 f. Cf. *PMLA,* LVI, 906 f. Caletvwlch is the Welsh name of Arthur's famous sword, Excalibur. Cf. Chap. LXXIII.   [7] Evans, *White Book Mabinogion,* cols. 464, 466.

in Irish mythological saga was the god Lug,[8] whose name, as pronounced during the Old and Middle Irish periods, would closely approximate Welsh Lluch; in fact, one of the spellings in *The Second Battle of Moytura* is Luch.[9] Lug's legend profoundly influenced the mabinogi of *Math,* as Professor Gruffydd demonstrated, and left its imprint on *Kulhwch.*[10] It also furnished, as we shall see in due course,[11] certain features of Lancelot's visit to the cemetery, and even more clearly affected the coming of Galaad to Arthur's court in *La Queste del Saint Graal.* There is every reason, therefore, to believe that Irish traditions about Lug were familiar in Wales, and since a number of other Irish personages can be recognized among Arthur's warriors in the *Kulhwch* list,[12] it is entirely probable that Lug was the original of Lluch Lleminawc and Llenlleawc the Irishman.

This hypothesis is confirmed in several ways. Lug had an epithet given as Lonnbemnech in *The Second Battle of Moytura* and as Loinnbheimionach in *The Fate of the Children of Turenn.*[13] This cognomen, meaning "of the mighty blows," though not common, was in use at least as early as the eleventh century, to which Flower attributed the extant redaction of *The Second Battle.*[14] It is easy to see how the Welsh, finding it incomprehensible, made various substitutions—Lleminawc, Llenlleawc, and Llawwynnawc.[15]

Moreover, not only was Arthur's warrior, Llenlleawc, described as an Irishman, but Llwch also turns up in Arthurian literature as a Hibernian. The best reading of verse 1737 in *Erec* mentions "Loz li Irois" among the knights of the Round Table.[16] Geoffrey of Monmouth, as everyone knows, makes much of a great war which took place between Arthur and Lucius Hiberus. Professor Hammer informs me that two manuscripts of the *Historia Regum Britanniae*[17] give Lucius Hibernus or Hibernius—readings which, though having no authority, suggest that Hiberus is a corruption of Hibernus, Irishman. This suggestion is borne out by the fact that Arthur's war with Lucius Hiberus resembles in eight respects Arthur's war with King

---

[8] R. S. Loomis, *Celtic Myth,* pp. 46 f. *Proceedings of the Royal Irish Acad.,* XXXIV (1918), C, 141–43. *Revue archéologique,* IVe série, XXIV, 205 ff. W. J. Gruffydd, *Math Vab Mathonwy,* Index, *sub* Lugh, Lugnassad, Lugus.

[9] Prof. O. J. Bergin, one of the most eminent of Irish scholars, kindly informed me that the final *g* in Lug had throughout the Old and Middle Irish periods the sound of *g* in German *Tage. Revue celt.,* XII (1891), 127.

[10] Gruffydd, *op. cit.* C. O'Rahilly, *Ireland and Wales,* pp. 117–19.

[11] *Infra,* pp. 234–36.   [12] O'Rahilly, *op. cit.,* pp. 114, 115, n. 3. *Revue celt.,* XLI, 489.

[13] *Revue celt.,* XII (1891), 127. E. Hull, *Cuchullin Saga,* pp. lvi f.

[14] R. Flower, *Catalogue of Irish Mss. in British Museum,* II (London, 1926), 319. Prof. V. Hull dates the saga in the 9th century (*Zts. f. celt. Phil.,* XVIII, 1930, 80).

[15] Llyminawc occurs as a proper name in *Book of Taliesin,* poem XLVII, and seems to be an adjective meaning "very keen, sharp, intense" or "leaping." Cf. Owen's *Dictionary* (1803). Llawwynnawc, meaning "of the white hand" (Loth, *Mabinogion,* 2d ed., I, 264, n. 3), was probably influenced by Lug's famous epithet Lamfada, meaning "of the long hand."

[16] Cf. *supra,* p. 152, n. 40.

[17] Lincoln Cathedral, No. 98, f. 91*v,* and Cambridge Univ. Lib., Mm. 5. 29, f. 93*r.*

Loth as related in the *Huth Merlin*. (1) The campaign against Lucius is immediately preceded by a reference to Arthur's triumph over Ritho, who had demanded Arthur's beard to add to those of other kings whom he had slain.[18] Likewise, the conflict with Loth is preceded by Arthur's war with Rion, who had demanded Arthur's beard to join with those of other kings.[19] (2) Geoffrey says of Lucius: "Being in the flower of early youth, he possessed much audacity, vigor, and honor."[20] In the Huth manuscript Merlin describes Loth to Arthur as one who will be "the best knight whom you know in your realm, even of those who wear a crown."[21] (3) According to Geoffrey, Arthur learns that Lucius' camp is not far away and sends two consuls and Walwanius with a message bidding him leave Gaul; Lucius refuses; Walwanius starts a fight and rides away with his companions.[22] According to the *Merlin,* Arthur learns that Loth's host is not far away and sends two knights with a message bidding Loth to submit; Loth refuses; the knights ride back.[23] (4) Lucius divides his force into twelve armies, each commanded by a king, duke, or senator.[24] Likewise Loth had twelve allied kings.[25] (5) According to both accounts,[26] there is a preliminary battle with Lucius' or Loth's allies, in which Walwanius and Balaain [27] respectively distinguish themselves; the Britons are hard pressed, but receive reinforcements and win the day; Lucius and Loth respectively are disturbed by this defeat, but nevertheless resolve to attack. (6) According to both accounts,[28] Arthur wields Caliburnus (Escalibor) with great effect. (7) When in the final battle Lucius and Loth fall, their armies flee and are pursued with great slaughter.[29] (8) Both accounts agree that Arthur has the bodies of his warriors honorably interred, and also those of the enemy.[30]

It is, of course, not credible that this series of parallels is due to chance; it is hardly credible that the author of the *Huth Merlin* based his account of Arthur's war with Loth on Geoffrey's or Wace's narrative of Arthur's war with Lucius without betraying in some concrete detail his indebted-

[18] Faral, *Légende arthurienne*, III, 257. Geoffrey of Monmouth, *Historia Regum Britanniae,* ed. A. Griscom, p. 473.
[19] *Huth Merlin*, ed. G. Paris and J. Ulrich, I, 202, 212 f.
[20] Faral, *op. cit.*, III, 271. Geoffrey of Monmouth, *op. cit.*, p. 492.
[21] *Huth Merlin*, I, 246.
[22] Faral, *op. cit.*, III, 258. Geoffrey of Monmouth, *op. cit.*, pp. 474 f.
[23] *Huth Merlin*, I, 247–49.
[24] Faral, *op. cit.*, III, 267 f. Geoffrey of Monmouth, *op. cit.*, pp. 486 f. On the sources from which Geoffrey derived the names of these twelve commanders cf. *Speculum*, VI (1931), 206–220. Prof. Tatlock is, of course, mistaken about Lucius Hiberus.
[25] *Huth Merlin*, I, 262 f.
[26] *Ibid.*, I, 250–57. Faral, *op. cit.*, III, 259–64. Geoffrey of Monmouth, *op. cit.*, pp. 475–81.
[27] For the original identity of Gauvain and Balaain cf. R. S. Loomis, *Celtic Myth*, pp. 250–52.
[28] Faral, *op. cit.*, III, 272 f. Geoffrey of Monmouth, *op. cit.*, pp. 492 f. *Huth Merlin*, I, 253 f.
[29] Faral, *op. cit.*, III, 273. Geoffrey of Monmouth, *op. cit.*, 494 f. *Huth Merlin*, I, 260 f.
[30] Faral, *op. cit.*, III, 274. Geoffrey of Monmouth, *op. cit.*, 495.

ness. The similarities must be accounted for by the theory of a common source. The emperor Lucius Hiberus and King Loth had the same origin, doubtless in Llwch Llawwynnawc, alias Llennlleawc the Irishman. Llwch and its alternative form Lloch account for the names Lucius and Loth; "the Irishman" explains the Hiberus and the fact that Chrétien called Loth "li Irois."

How does all this bear on Lancelot? The fact is that the name and the history of Lancelot du Lac fit neatly into the jigsaw puzzle formed by the names of Llwch Llawwynnawc, Lucius, and Loth. Llwch was surely numbered among the warriors of Arthur; so was Lancelot. Llwch, we know, could be and was translated into French as Lac,[31] since the Welsh noun *llwch* means lake. It was natural for Bretons or Frenchmen to assume that Lac was not the hero's name but rather referred to the place of his birth or upbringing. Llawwynnawc or Llenlleawc would then be taken for the true name, and by assimilation to the name Lancelin, recorded in Brittany as early as 1034 and 1069,[32] it became Lancelot.

It is highly significant as a confirmation of these relationships that Lancelot not only resembles Llawwynnawc, Llenlleawc, and Loth as prominent among Arthur's warriors, but also resembles Loth in being involved in a great war with his suzerain. Moreover, this conflict between Lancelot and Arthur, as related in *La Mort Artu,* reveals a notable similarity to that between Lucius and Arthur. According to both narratives, Arthur crossed the sea with a great host and landed in France;[33] Gauvain or Walwanius was the outstanding champion on Arthur's side and engaged in an indecisive single combat with Lancelot or Lucius.[34] In the French romance "le roi Lyon" brought succor to Lancelot;[35] in the Latin history the emperor Leo was expected to bring succor to Lucius.[36] According to

---

[31.] Cf. Chap. VIII.
[32] *Zts. f. franz. Sprache u. Lit.,* XIII (1891), 43 ff.; XIV (1894), 180. H. Morice, *Mémoires pour servir de preuves à l'histoire ecclésiastique et civile de Bretagne* (Paris, 1742–46), I, 432.
[33] Faral, *op. cit.,* III, 252–54. Geoffrey of Monmouth, *op. cit.,* pp. 465–69. Sommer, *Vulgate Version,* VI, 317 f. *Mort Artu,* ed. J. Frappier (Paris, 1936), p. 143. The localization of both campaigns in France is probably due to the confusion between Gales (Wales) and Gaule (Gaul). Geoffrey (*op. cit.,* p. 474; Faral, II, 258) refers definitely to Lucius' invasion of *Gallia.* The author of *La Mort Artu* distinguished Gaule from Lancelot's realm and city of Gaunes (ed. Frappier, pp. 157, 180), but many mss. show confusion between the two (ed. Frappier, p. 134, n. 45). It seems obvious that Gaunes is a ghost name, due originally to a misreading of Gaulles. Gaulles in turn was doubtless a more or less deliberate substitution for Guales, in accord with the effort to make Lancelot a French hero, as Geoffrey's *Gallia* was a substitution for Guallia. That the confusion between Gales and Gaule did occur is proved by Sommer, *op. cit.,* I, 293, n. 10, and the statement in a ms. of Wace's *Brut* (Bib. Nat., fr. 375, f. 219r) that Franche and Cambrie are both equivalent to Gales. The underlying Welsh tradition, I suspect, represented Llwch Llawwynnawc as invading Wales from Ireland and being met and conquered by Arthur.
[34] Faral, *op. cit.,* III, 271 f. Geoffrey of Monmouth, *op. cit.,* pp. 491 f. Sommer, *op. cit.,* VI, 338–43. *Mort Artu,* pp. 170–77.   [35] *Mort Artu,* p. 147.
[36] Faral, *op. cit.,* III, 263. Geoffrey of Monmouth, *op. cit.,* p. 481. On Leo and Lyon cf. R. H. Fletcher, *Arthurian Material in the Chronicles* (Boston, 1906), p. 85, n. 2; Loomis, *Celtic Myth,.*p. 347; Gruffydd, *Math Vab Mathonwy,* pp. 60–62; *PMLA,* XLV (1930), 432–38.

both accounts, the war was soon followed by news of Modred's treason, and Arthur returned to Britain.[37]

To complete the case for the original identity of Lancelot and Loth, there are four parallels between them. (1) In *La Mort Artu* Lancelot carried off Guenievre from Arthur; he incurred the mortal hatred of Gauvain, and after his return to his kingdom engaged in a duel with his old friend.[38] In the *Vulgate Merlin* we read that Loth attempted to carry off Guenievre from Arthur; in the midst of the battle Gauvain arrived and fought with Loth in single combat.[39] (2) Both Lancelot and Loth begat sons in clandestine affairs.[40] (3) The ladies involved seem to have been originally the same. Loth's paramour was Morcades, whose name was a variation on Morgain;[41] Lancelot's paramour was King Pelles' daughter, whom on an earlier page we traced back to Morgain.[42] (4) The sons of Lancelot and Loth by Morgain were Galaad and Gauvain, and there is considerable evidence that Galaad was a sublimated Gauvain.[43] Needless to say, Lancelot and Loth had long been differentiated and their stories had developed on very divergent lines. Still the links remain, and a further link is provided by a certain King Orcans in *L'Estoire del Saint Graal,* who resembles Loth in that his chief city was Orcanie, and who, like Lancelot, challenged all comers to joust with him beneath a pine on an island.[44] These multifarious points of similarity between Loth and Lancelot cannot all be accidental; they must be due to a common origin in the Welsh Llwch Llawwynnawc.

Lancelot, to be sure, is never connected with Ireland as was Loth. But, curiously enough, a certain Lanceor turns up in the *Huth Merlin,* who is a "chevalier d'Irlande."[45] He set out from Arthur's court in pursuit of Balaain when the latter rode off, engaged him in combat, and was killed. His role, therefore, parallels that of Lancelot in Malory's Book of Gareth, for Lancelot set out from Arthur's court in pursuit of Beaumayns when the latter rode off, engaged him in combat, and was worsted.[46] Lanceor

---

[37] Faral, *op. cit.,* III, 274 f. Geoffrey, *op. cit.,* pp. 496 f. *Mort Artu,* pp. 184–87. Sommer, *op. cit.,* VI, 348–51.

[38] *Mort Artu,* pp. 98–100, 141, 158–79. Sommer, *op. cit.,* VI, 280–82, 316 f., 328–43.

[39] Sommer, *op. cit.,* II, 300, 315–18.

[40] *Ibid.,* V, 109–11. J. D. Bruce, *Historia Meriadoci and De Ortu Walwanii,* p. xlv.

[41] Cf. *supra,* p. 112.   [42] Cf. *supra,* pp. 142–45.

[43] Loomis, *Celtic Myth,* pp. 250 f.

[44] Sommer, *op. cit.,* I, 273–77; V, 403–6. Cf. *Mod. Lang. Rev.,* XXIV (1929), 425–27.

[45] *Huth Merlin,* I, 223, n. 1; 225 f. *Roman de Balain,* ed. M. D. Legge (Manchester, 1942), pp. 15–24. The tragic ending of the adventure was demanded by Balaain's special character as a fated knight. Cf. Prof. Hibbard in *Medieval Studies in Memory of G. Schoepperle Loomis,* pp. 175–86.

[46] Malory, *Morte d'Arthur,* Bk. VII, chap. 4. The fact that both Balaain and Beaumayns represent developments from Galvain strengthens the parallel. Cf. Loomis, *Celtic Myth,* pp. 250 f.; *PMLA,* LIV (1939), 656–68. There is another curious hint of Lancelot's original connection with Ireland in *L'Estoire del Saint Graal* (Sommer, *op. cit.,* I, 293), where we read of his grandfather, also named Lancelot, as follows: "cil sen parti de gaule & ala en la grant bertaigne & prinst a feme la fille au roy dirlande. si ot la terre qui ot esté a son pere & en fu

must owe his name and his brief role to Lancelot, and he was a knight of Ireland—probably a vestige of the same tradition that was attached to Loth, Lucius, and Llenlleawc. In view of all this dovetailing evidence one can hardly doubt that the Welsh ancestor of Lancelot was Llwch, alias Llenlleawc the Irishman, and his ultimate ancestor was the Irish god, Lug.

It may be objected that there is little direct parallelism between Lancelot and his Celtic forebears. As for his relation to Llwch or Llenlleawc, one may reply that we know almost nothing about Llwch except that he was a warrior of Arthur's from beyond the extreme (?) sea and the father of Gweir, and we know almost nothing of Llenlleawc except that he was a warrior of Arthur's and an Irishman; yet these facts are in accord with the traditions of Lancelot's cognate, Loth, who was at the same time an Irishman and King of Orcanie and the father of Gaheries. It must be admitted that Lancelot's connections with Lug are slight and, but for the intermediate connection with Llwch, would be unconvincing; yet they are at least worth mentioning. A gloss informs us that Lug had a red color on him from sunset to morning—doubtless a reference to the redness of the sun as it approached the western horizon and rose from the east.[47] So Lancelot in Chrétien's poem bore red arms at the tourney of Noauz; in the *Vulgate Lancelot* he bore a red shield at the tourneys of Godosaire, Camaalot, and Peningue, at the assembly outside the town of Malehot, and in *La Mort Artu* at the tourney of Guincestre.[48] Both Lug and Lancelot (not to mention Loth) begat in secret and illicit union sons destined to high renown, Cuchulainn and Galaad.[49] Lug's arrival at the court of King Nuada, related in *The Second Battle of Moytura,* supplied certain features of Lancelot's cemetery adventure in the *Charrette,* as will be shown in Chapter XXXVII. Though these correspondences may be ascribed to accident, it cannot be said that there is nothing in common between Lancelot and Lug.

---

rois." Although this implies, of course, that Lancelot, the elder, returned to Gaul to inherit his father's land, yet it possibly reflects a statement that he inherited the land of his father-in-law, the King of Ireland.

[47] *Revue celt.,* XII, 127: "A red color used to be on him from sunset to morning." Cf. Skene, *Four Ancient Books,* I, 529: "No one knows whence the bosom of the sun is made ruddy." Sébillot, *Folklore de France,* I, 36: F. M. Luzel, *Contes populaires de Basse-Bretagne,* I, 69–73, 99–107. In other countries red is a solar color. Cf. *Gests of Alexander of Macedon,* ed. F. P. Magoun (Cambridge, Mass., 1929), p. 190: "solem rubicundum"; Chrétien, *Yvain,* vss. 427 f.: "plus vermauz Que n'est au matin li solauz"; Froissart, *Poésies,* ed. A. Scheler (1871), II, 238 f.: "le soleil . . . Sa couleur n'est pas dyasprée, Mes sanguine . . . Et vermauls com vermeille Rose"; Tylor, *Primitive Culture,* 6th ed. (London, 1920), I, 342, 345 f.; J. Grimm, *Teutonic Mythology,* II, 721.

[48] Vss. 5518 f. Sommer, *Vulgate Version,* III, 117, 214; V, 172–81, 283. *Mort Artu,* ed. Frappier, pp. 9, 13 f.

[49] D'Arbois de Jubainville, *L'Epopée celtique en Irlande,* pp. 33–38. Cross, Slover, *Ancient Irish Tales,* pp. 134–6. Cf. Sommer, *op. cit.,* V, 109–11.

After all, however, it must be acknowledged that the history of Lancelot, as we find it in the Arthurian romances, has drawn heavily on other legends besides those of Lug and Llwch. The translation of the latter name by the French-speaking Bretons as Lac must be responsible for the artificial association of Lancelot with the Dame du Lac, Niniane. She was apparently celebrated as the foster mother and instructress of a hero, the son of King Ban of Benoic and the Queen of Great Sorrows; at least, this is the role she plays in the *Vulgate Lancelot*.[50] Lancelot might thus have acquired the *enfances* of another hero whom there is some reason to identify with Perceval, for Professor Newstead demonstrated that King Ban may be equated with Perceval's father, and the Queen of Great Sorrows with Perceval's mother, whose sorrowful heart (*cuer dolent*) is mentioned in the *Bliocadran Prologue,* and who is called Herzeloyde in *Parzival*.[51] Lancelot's epithet "du Lac," the result of a mistaken etymology, seemingly provided him with royal parents and a happy childhood in the enchanted *manoir* of his foster mother, the Dame du Lac.

At some period Llwch and his French counterparts underwent the fate of every prominent Arthurian knight; they became involved with Morgain la Fée in one or another of her characteristic roles. Her role as the baffled temptress is reflected in the *Vulgate Lancelot,* where she repeatedly offers her love to the hero in vain; and in the *Charrette* she seems to be a prototype of the unnamed amorous hostess on whom Lancelot turned his back. The same tradition, combined with the additional motifs of the gift of a steed and the three days' tournament, appears in the *Lancelot* as the affair with the Dame de Malehot, in the *Charrette* as the affair with the wife of Meleagant's seneschal. It may be suspected, not without reason, that Morgain was also the original of the lovesick maidens in the Vulgate cycle whom Lancelot spurned, and of Ade who provided Lanzelet with horses and arms for the three days' tournament. Morgain appears in quite a different role as Morcades, Loth's mistress and Gauvain's mother, and as King Pelles' daughter, Lancelot's mistress and mother of Galaad. Evidently, then, in the Breton stage of his history, if not earlier, Lancelot became entangled with the ubiquitous and forthputting fay.

What of that other, that immortal tradition, which forever unites Lancelot's name with that of Guenievre? Does it go back to the Celts? Was it a late development? Did Chrétien invent it? There is no trace of it before the *Charrette*. Nothing that we know of Lug or Llwch exactly corresponds; nor did Lucius Hiberus or King Loth ever plant horns on the brows of Arthur. The *Lanzelet* shows acquaintance with many love affairs of its hero and represents Ginover as fickle of fancy, but there is no inkling of any guilty passion between the two. On the contrary, there is evidence

[50] Sommer, *op. cit.,* III, 13–16, 33, 111–18.   [51] *Romanic Review,* XXXVI (1945), 3–26.

that according to early traditions the Queen was enamored of Yder and Gauvain,[52] not Lancelot. Many of Lancelot's adventures in the *Charrette* are elsewhere, as we shall see, attached to Gauvain. In fact, the *Charrette* suggests that Gauvain was a traditional liberator of the Queen, since it is he who escorts her back to Arthur and is at first credited with her deliverance.[53]

Eminent scholars, such as Paris and Professor Nitze,[54] have concluded that it was Chrétien who first made Lancelot the favored lover of Guenievre, and it must be admitted that all the facts are on their side, except, perhaps, the handling of the situation by Chrétien himself. I find it hard to believe that the poet was introducing an idea altogether novel to his readers. To be sure, he withholds the hero's name until verse 3676, but this seems to be a characteristic mannerism of his rather than an exceptional procedure in the case of Lancelot.[55] When at last Guenievre reveals the name of her lover, the damsel to whom she reveals it exhibits no astonishment but is rather filled with joy, believing that Lancelot will derive new strength in his fight with Meleagant from the sight of the Queen. This reaction of the damsel—her lack of surprise and her assumption of some more than ordinary relationship between Lancelot and her mistress —seems to me significant for the response which Chrétien expected of his audience. Apparently, the concept of Lancelot as the Queen's devoted knight was no novelty to them. Though it seems most unlikely that this idea was old or widely known, it seems also unlikely that Chrétien was the first to introduce it to the courtly circle of Marie de Champagne. Yet the evidence is not decisive. Perhaps the Countess decided that the new *san* required a new lover; perhaps the poet took the initiative. I surmise that he had a precedent, but I cannot affirm it.

We are now in a position to sketch the history of the Lancelot legend, so far as the sometimes fragmentary evidence permits. Of the original Irish traditions about Lug two possibly, and one certainly, have left vestiges in Arthurian romance. Lug's red color *may* be reflected in Lancelot's habit of appearing incognito in red arms; Lug's begetting a glorious son *may* be the ultimate root of Lancelot's begetting Galaad; Lug's arrival at the court of Nuada, it will be shown, contributed features to Lancelot's adventure at the cemetery. As for Llwch Llawwynnawc, there must have been a Welsh tradition of his war with Arthur, for it has come down to us in the three forms of Arthur's wars with Loth, Lucius, and Lancelot. At the same time, as we glean from *Kulhwch* and the Black Book, Llwch

---

[52] R. S. Loomis, *Celtic Myth*, pp. 7–9. Bruce, *Historia Meriadoci*, pp. 87 ff. Sommer, *op. cit.,* II, 321. Wolfram von Eschenbach, *Parzival*, sec. 645. Girard d'Amiens, *Escanor*, vss. 7343 f.
[53] Vss. 5320–37. Cf. J. L. Weston, *Legend of Gawain*, pp. 69 f.
[54] *Romania*, XII, 516. Cross and Nitze, *Lancelot and Guenevere*, p. 66.
[55] In *Conte del Graal* Perceval is not named until vs. 3575 (Hilka's edition). In *Erec* Enide is not named until vs. 2031.

(alias Llenlleawc) was known as one of the foremost of Arthur's warriors. In either the Welsh or the Breton stage two somewhat inconsistent traditions must have sprung up as to his loves. One linked him to Morgain as the begetter of her son in a clandestine union, and thus gave rise to the stories of Loth's intrigue with Morcades and Lancelot's affair with King Pelles' daughter. The other represented him as repulsing the lustful overtures of Morgain, and of this there are several instances in the *Vulgate Lancelot*.[56] Still later, when Llwch was introduced to the French, he became Lancelot du Lac, and so acquired a foster mother and a protectress in the Dame du Lac, and with her the whole story of his upbringing, instruction, and equipment with a marvelous horse and a magic ring.[57] Evidently, by this time he had attracted to himself many miscellaneous adventures, such as we find in the Swiss *Lanzelet*. It was shortly before Chrétien's time, so far as we can judge (if it was not an innovation by Chrétien himself) that Lancelot supplanted Yder and Gauvain as the favorite or lover of Guenievre, and took over, as we shall see, certain incidents of the Tristan legend. So great, however, was the prestige of *Le Chevalier de la Charrette* that thenceforth his devotion to the Queen became the focal point of his life.

The notion, once widely held, that Lancelot was unknown to the Welsh and was a newcomer in the *Matière de Bretagne* is surely erroneous. Indeed, he goes much farther back in Celtic tradition than Arthur himself. Not only is it assured that his ancestor Lug was a deity of importance among the Irish, but most authorities hold that a certain divine Lugos gave his name to the fourteen towns in Gaul which were called Lugdunum and to Luguvallium or Lugubalia (modern Carlisle) in Britain.[58] The ultimate prototype of Lancelot may well be one of the most illustrious of the Celtic gods, whose cult extended from the Pyrenees to the plains of Meath. Only Morgain la Fée, descended, as we have seen, from the Celtic mother- and water-goddess Matrona, can claim as ancient and illustrious an origin.

[56] *Speculum*, XX (1945), 186 f.
[57] The stealing of the infant Lancelot by the fay who plunged with him into the lake reflects the same belief recorded by J. Rhys in 1901 (*Celtic Folklore, Welsh and Manx*, I, 33). A Welsh woman, when a child in the Snowdon region thirty or forty years before, was often warned by her mother "not to go far away from the house when there happened to be thick mist on the ground, lest they [she and her brothers and sisters] should come across the *Tylwyth Teg* [the fairies] dancing and be carried away to their abode beneath the lake." It is noteworthy that in *Lanzelet*, though the infant hero is not carried under the surface of a lake, there is a lake near the spot where he is abducted (vs. 169), and the fay comes with a mist (*dunst*, vs. 181).
[58] *Revue archéologique*, XXIV, 205. E. Windisch, *Das keltische Brittannien bis zu Kaiser Arthur*, pp. 99 f. *Proceedings of the Royal Irish Academy*, XXXIV (1917-19); C, 141-43. J. Rhys, *Lectures on the Origin and Growth of Religion*, 2d ed., pp. 419 f. John MacNeill, *Celtic Ireland*, p. 57.

Chapter XXVII

GUENIEVRE

CHRÉTIEN's Guenievre is, of course, identical with Geoffrey of Monmouth's Guenhuvara [1] and the Welsh Gwenhwyvar. It has been proposed that she goes back ultimately to Finnabair, [2] daughter of King Ailill and Queen Medb of Connaught, who appears in *Bricriu's Feast, The Cattle Raid of Cooley,* and *The Cattle Raid of Fraech*. [3] But this seems most doubtful, first, because Gwenhwyvar means "white phantom," whereas Finnabair probably means "fair eyebrow"; [4] and secondly, because there is nothing in common between Guenievre and Gwenhwyvar on the one hand and Finnabair on the other, except that Guenievre and Finnabair were of royal birth and all three seem to have had more than one lover.

Whether there was any historic Gwenhwyvar and whether she was the wife of Arthur, the "dux bellorum" mentioned by Nennius, no man can say. She does not make her appearance in Welsh literature till some five hundred years after Arthur is mentioned in the *Gododdin,* and then she is scarcely more than a name. Arthur excepts her from his promise of a gift to Kulhwch, along with his sword, his spear, his ship, his shield, his mantle, and his knife; and she heads the list of the golden-torqued daughters of Britain in the same tale. [5] The Red Book of Hergest (fourteenth century) contains three triads which mention her. [6] One attributes the battle of Camlann (Arthur's fatal battle with Modred) to the blow which Gwenhwyvach (her sister) gave her. Another lists among the three costly expeditions of the Isle of Britain that which Medrawt (Modred) made when he went to the court of Kelliwic in Cornwall, consuming all the food and drink, dragging Gwenhwyvar from her royal chair, and striking her. A variant of this triad adds that Medrawt committed adultery with her. This would seem to be the same tradition which Geoffrey gives of Modred's unhallowed union with Guenhuvara during Arthur's absence. [7]

---

[1] The Bern ms. reads Guenhuuaram, the third *u* standing for *v*. Geoffrey of Monmouth, *Historia,* ed. A. Griscom, p. 445n.

[2] R. Thurneysen, *Die Irische Helden- und Königsage,* p. 95. *Zts. f. celt. Phil.,* XX (1936), 136 f. A. C. L. Brown, *Origin of the Grail Legend* (Cambridge, Mass., 1943), pp. 336–38. Loth, *Mabinogion,* 2d ed., I, 260n.

[3] Thurneysen, *op. cit.,* Index s.v. *Finnabair.* T. P. Cross and C. H. Slover, *Ancient Irish Tales,* pp. 267, 270. A. H. Leahy, *Heroic Romances of Ireland,* II, 6–56. D'Arbois de Jubainville, *L'Epopée celtique en Irlande,* pp. 110–18, 124.

[4] T. P. Cross and W. A. Nitze, *Lancelot and Guenevere,* p. 58, n. 1.

[5] Loth, *Mabinogion,* 2d ed., I, 259, 283.

[6] *Ibid.,* I, 259, n. 2; II, 246 f., 250. On versions of these triads cf. *Aberystwyth Studies,* VIII (1926), 65 f., 69 f.

[7] Geoffrey of Monmouth, *op. cit.,* p. 496. Faral, *Légende arthurienne,* III, 274.

The other triad from the Red Book lists three Gwenhwyvars, all wives of Arthur, apparently in the effort to reconcile three traditions as to the name of Gwenhwyvar's father. The third lady is said to be the daughter of Ocrvan Gawr, and it is this tradition which Davydd ab Gwilym followed in a passage, to be discussed in Chapter XXXI, which speaks of Melwas as entering the house of the Giant Ogurvan's daughter at Caerleon.[8] There are two very different versions of a poetic dialogue in which the names of Gwenhwyfar and Cai are found,[9] but the interpretation is extremely difficult. Finally, there is a Welsh saying: "Gwenhwyfar daughter of Ogrfan Gawr, naughty young, more naughty later." [10]

Though the treatment of Arthur's queen in extant Welsh literature is surprisingly scanty and obscure, yet the Welshman, Caradoc of Lancarvan, gives in his *Vita Gildae* a Latin version of her abduction by Melvas, ruler of the Summer Country,[11] and thus testifies to the antiquity of the main theme of Chrétien's *Charrette*. Even earlier, moreover, is the evidence of the Modena archivolt which proves that a variant of the abduction story was known to a Lombard sculptor as early as 1106.[12] Here Arthur's queen is labeled Winlogee, as she is called Guendoloena in *De ortu Walwanii*,[13] both forms developed from the Breton name Winlowen or Wenlowen,[14] which had been substituted for the less euphonious Gwenhwyvar. These facts, plus the existence of many versions of the abduction in Arthurian romance,[15] render it certain that, despite the paucity of the records in Welsh, Gwenhwyvar had been from an early time "a lady very much subject to the misfortune of being run away with." [16]

Chrétien's portrait of the lady is highly favorable. In *Erec* and *Cliges* all is admiration. Though her rebuke of Keu in *Yvain* is couched in language which we should regard as hardly ladylike, Chrétien must have thought it no more than was due to the occasion. In *Le Conte del Graal* Gauvain delivers an eloquent panegyric on the Queen: "Since the time when God made the first woman from the side of Adam, there has been

[8] J. Rhys, *Studies in the Arthurian Legend*, p. 65. Cf. Chap. XXXI.
[9] For the Welsh texts and suggested translation cf. *Speculum*, XIII (1938), 39–42. Prof. Mary Williams' interpretation is highly speculative, but she has done service in pointing out (p. 38) that the title given to the poem, the assignment of speeches, and the mention of Arthur have little authority. These cautions should be kept in mind in reading the translations of one version given by Rhys (*op. cit.*, pp. 57 f.) and by Prof. Gwynn Jones (*Aberystwyth Studies*, VIII, 58 f.). Cf. also Cross and Nitze, *op. cit.*, p. 59, n. 3.
[10] Rhys, *op. cit.*, p. 49. Loth, *op. cit.*, I, 260n.   [11] Cf. Chap. XXXI.
[12] R. S. and L. H. Loomis, *Arthurian Legends in Medieval Art*, pp. 32–36; pls. 4–8. *Romanic Review*, XXXII (1941), 22–27. Cross and Nitze, *op. cit.*, Frontispiece, pp. 22 f.
[13] J. D. Bruce, *Historia Meriadoci and De Ortu Walwanii*, pp. 85–87.
[14] A. de la Borderie, *Histoire de Bretagne* (Rennes, Paris, 1898), II, 280. J. Loth, *Chrestomathie bretonne* (1890), p. 147. On the name Winlogee cf. *PMLA*, XLIII (1928), 419–21.
[15] Cross and Nitze, *op. cit.*, pp. 21–29. G. Schoepperle, *Tristan and Isolt*, II, 528–40. Sommer, *Vulgate Version*, IV, 157–60; VII, 65.
[16] E. K. Chambers, in *Arthur of Britain*, p. 213, quotes a schoolgirl to this effect.

no lady so renowned, and well she deserves it. Just as a wise teacher instructs little children, so my lady the Queen teaches and instructs every one." [17] Though Chrétien may have had his own private opinion of her conduct in the *Charrette*, as he had his opinion of Iseut's, which he did not hesitate to express in *Cliges*, yet he allows only expressions of praise to escape him regarding Lancelot's paramour. The romantic literature of the Middle Ages maintains this sympathetic attitude toward the erring Queen, with the exception of the lais of the *Lanval* group. *La Queste del Saint Graal*, with its strong monastic coloring, naturally condemns Lancelot's sin in vigorous terms, yet there is not a harsh word for his partner. The chroniclers, however, beginning with Wace, adopt on the whole a very different attitude toward Guinevere and pave the way for Tennyson.

Chapter XXVIII

ARTHUR

WE HAVE SEEN in our survey of the Arthurian tradition before Chrétien de Troyes that the British battle leader acquired various attributes, attracted many legends, was viewed in different lights. And before the close of the Middle Ages he was destined to assume still other roles and forms. Originally he was the historic champion of the Britons in their desperate struggle with the Saxons. Popular tradition came to associate his name with cairns and cromlechs, Roman ruins and crumbling castles.[1] He survived in the isle of Avalon or in the deep recesses of Mount Etna or in the caverns of the Welsh hills.[2] He became king of the pigmy people of the Antipodes, or he led the Wild Hunt by moonlight on the forested slopes of the Mont du Chat.[3] The Cornish and Breton folk regarded him as a Messiah and awaited the day when he would return to reconquer their ancestral home from the Saxons.[4] Welsh hagiographers might ridicule and vilify him, but Geoffrey of Monmouth made him a model potentate and a great conqueror on the pattern of Charlemagne and Alexander. *La Mort Artu* presented him in the role of tragic hero, the victim of inexorable doom, brought about by his in-

[17] Ed. Hilka, vss. 8176–98.
[1] E. K. Chambers, *Arthur of Britain*, pp. 183–95. F. J. Snell, *King Arthur's Country, passim.*
[2] L. A. Paton, *Fairy Mythology*, pp. 25–47, 250 f. J. Rhys, *Celtic Folklore*, II, 458–66, 492–97. Snell, *op. cit.*, pp. 208, 214–17. A. Graf, *Miti, leggende e superstizioni del medio evo* (Turin, 1893), II, 303–59.   [3] *Mod. Phil.*, XXXVIII (1941), 289–304. Chambers, *op. cit.*, p. 278.
[4] R. H. Fletcher, *Arthurian Material in the Chronicles*, pp. 100–102, 120, 145, 165, 167, 188, 190, 202, 207, 230.

cestuous begetting of Modred,[5] and thus gave the Arthuriad the somber majesty of an *Oedipus Rex.*

Strange to say, of all these multifarious characters assumed by Arthur not one is reflected or anticipated in the pages of Chrétien. There is no word of the Saxon wars, of quarrels with the saints, of Modred and his treachery. Though Arthur is a king over kings and lord of widespread territories, he is no conqueror.[6] There is no trace of the Breton hope or the sleeping hero in the cave or the phantom huntsman or the Maimed King; no reference to the long sojourn in Avalon.

To be sure, one may admit the influence of Geoffrey of Monmouth and Wace on the portrayal of Arthur in *Erec* and *Yvain,* for though in these poems the King is no victorious opponent of the Saxons and conqueror of foreign lands, he is a mighty monarch and his court includes a few names traceable to the *Brut.*[7] But it would seem that the concept of Arthur which Chrétien took over from X and Y was rather that created by the Breton *conteurs.* The portrait of the adventurous, liberal, hospitable, just, and courteous king is precisely what one would expect to emerge from the patriotic imaginations of these kinsmen of King Arthur, responding to the courtly idealism of the twelfth century. And the adventures in which Arthur himself participates remind one of *Kulhwch and Olwen* rather than the *Historia Regum Britanniae.* The hunt of the White Stag, we have seen, is admittedly Celtic and recalls the prominence and prowess of Arthur in the hunting of the Twrch Trwyth. In *Yvain* Arthur vows to spend the night before St. John's day at the perilous spring and fulfills his oath. This too is an adventure of which the Celtic nature and the Breton setting has been widely recognized. The consistently noble and adventurous character which Arthur bears in *Erec* and *Yvain* may be ascribed in the main to the Breton *conteurs.*

It is surprising and perplexing, therefore, to find that the *Charrette* and *Le Conte del Graal* present us with quite a different personage. In both poems Arthur is something of a poltroon; in the latter he is a cuckold, deceived by his wife and her splendid lover. The *Charrette* opens with Meleagant's insolent boast that he holds Arthur's subjects in captivity and his challenge to any knight of Arthur's court to fight for the possession of Guenievre. All this Arthur takes lying down, and it is left for Gauvain and Lancelot to undergo ignominies and dangers to bring the Queen back. In the *Graal* also Arthur helplessly accepts the affronts of the Red Knight, whom a mere boy was able to kill with his javelin. Yet, at the same time,

---

[5] *Medieval Studies in Memory of G. Schoepperle Loomis,* pp. 197–208. R. S. Loomis, *Celtic Myth,* pp. 339–41. J. Frappier, *Etude sur la Mort le Roi Artu* (Paris, 1936), pp. 169, 203.
[6] A possible exception is the reference in *Conte del Graal,* ed. Hilka, vss. 850–52, to Arthur's victory over Rion, King of the Isles.   [7] Anguisseaus, Cadorcaniois, Cadoalanz.

it is evidently a great and coveted distinction to belong to Arthur's court. What is responsible for this belittlement of the great king and hero, for this union of a Jekyll and a Hyde in one frame?

I suspect that two forces have been at work: one, narrative technique; the other and stronger, tradition. The writer of a biographical romance early learns that if his hero is to occupy the center of the stage, rivals, even though they may be greater men, must be pushed into the background. Gauvain, who evidently enjoyed the reputation in the early twelfth century of being the mightiest of Arthur's knights, was repeatedly obliged, as in the *Charrette* itself, to yield first place to the hero of a given poem. So when Lancelot was selected as the hero of a poem on the abduction of Guenievre, not only Gauvain but also Arthur had to play a secondary part. This demotion or debasement of one character in order to exalt another is a common bit of political as well as literary technique.

But it is hardly likely that this process would have gone to the extreme of depicting Arthur as a spiritless cuckold if another and more powerful force had not been operative, namely, a traditional narrative pattern. Gertrude Schoepperle and Professor Cross have shown that a certain formula, akin to that employed in the *Charrette,* recurs in Irish and Welsh literature:[8] A mortal king is required by a haughty stranger to give up his wife, and, being bound by a rash promise, the king has to submit meekly when the stranger takes her away. Usually in these Celtic versions the king manages to win her back by force or ruse. But it would seem that a development of this tradition represented the king and the members of his court as not only helpless to prevent the departure of the queen but also unable to bring about her rescue. That this was an early-established formula is indicated by its presence in three Tristan romances (Thomas, the Berne *Folie Tristan,* and the Prose *Tristan*),[9] for it is generally agreed that the Tristan story was already famous before the middle of the twelfth century. Here the king's part is taken by Mark; he grants a boon to a baron from Ireland; the stranger demands Iseut; Mark at first refuses, but is bound by his oath, and none of his men offers resistance; Iseut is taken away; Tristan returns to Mark's court, discovers what has happened, and brings his mistress back by means of a trick.

A contemptible role is fitting enough for Mark, and one may presume that the formula of the helpless and pusillanimous king, as thus elaborated, was first attached to him. So strong was the force of tradition that when the formula was transferred to Arthur, all his prestige as gallant knight and unmatched conqueror did not save him from being degraded to the level of the poltroon and cuckold Mark. Certainly Chrétien himself did not of his own initiative besmirch the character of Arthur, whom he had

---

[8] G. Schoepperle, *Tristan and Isolt,* II, 422–29, 528–40. T. P. Cross and W. A. Nitze, *Lancelot and Guenevere,* pp. 32–61.   [9] Schoepperle, *op. cit.,* II, 420–22.

exalted in *Erec* and of whom he had written in *Cliges:* "Since God created the first man, no king who believed in God has been born equal to
you in power." [10] The poet must have taken over the unflattering portrait
from his source, and that source in turn seems to have borrowed it from
some version of the Tristan legend. In Chapter XLI we shall have occasion to note the influence of that legend on other episodes of the *Charrette*.

Le Conte del Graal furnishes a similar instance of the debasement of
Arthur.[11] The Red Knight comes before the King, claims his lands,
snatches up the royal cup, spilling the contents over the Queen, rides
off, and sends back an insulting challenge to Arthur to yield his lands
or dispatch someone out to fight for them. Arthur is reduced to a mourn-
ful and helpless silence, and it is left for the boy Perceval to take vengeance.
This is another case where the technique of promoting the hero of a particular romance at the expense of established reputations has combined
with a traditional formula to demote Arthur to a humiliating role. The
formula, as we shall see in Chapter LXII, is again one of the variants of
the Celtic abduction theme and can be traced back to Curoi's abduction
of Blathnat.

In all the romances of the Round Table there are few instances, if any,
which illustrate the tenacity, the rigidity, of narrative formulae more
clearly than the handling of Arthur in the *Charrette* and *Le Conte del
Graal*. The violent disharmony between the supine behavior attributed to
him in the scenes we have been considering and the prodigious reputation
he enjoyed as a warrior was of no concern to the authors whom Chrétien
followed. The formula called for a *roi fainéant*. If it clashed with the
principle of consistent characterization, so much the worse for that principle. Chrétien's intelligence must have been offended by such jarring discords, but he had to obey meekly the behests of Marie de Champagne and
Philippe de Flandres.

Chapter XXIX

KEU'S DEMAND AND HIS OVERTHROW

VERSES 84–269

*While Arthur was holding high court at Camalot on Ascension Day, a
knight, fully armed, appeared before him and challenged him to entrust
the Queen to the escort of one of his knights. In a wood outside the castle
the stranger would await the Queen and her escort, and would determine
by battle whether he would surrender to Arthur the captive knights and*

---

[10] *Cliges*, vss. 344–46.   [11] *Conte del Graal*, ed. Hilka, vss. 865–1119.

ladies whom he held. Keu, hearing the challenge, demanded permission to leave the court. The King was grieved and implored him to stay, but in vain. Guenievre then tried her arts of persuasion on the seneschal, and finally throwing herself prone at his feet she won from him the promise to remain at court if Arthur would grant him a boon. Much relieved, the King agreed to do whatever Keu wished. Thereupon Keu demanded the right to escort the Queen to the forest. The King was bound to keep his rash promise, and reluctantly gave his wife into Keu's charge. She declared that Keu displayed pride, presumption, and folly, but rode away with him. No one expected her to come back alive. By Gauvain's advice, however, the King and his knights rode out to the wood and met Keu's horse running wild, with bloodstained stirrup-leathers and a broken saddlebow. The stranger knight and the Queen had vanished. Later we learn that his name was Meleagant.

Keu's role in the opening scenes of the *Charrette* is of a composite nature. The seneschal is held in such high esteem that Arthur is willing to give anything to keep him at court. On the other hand, he is guilty of an outrageous demand and is considered no match for the stranger. The high valuation set by Arthur on his services doubtless reflects the same tradition as to his valor which Geoffrey of Monmouth records in his *Historia* and which can be traced back to Welsh sources. For in the old poem preserved in the Black Book of Carmarthen and in *Kulhwch and Olwen* Kei is presented as one of the greatest of Arthur's warriors.[1] The latter text, however, gives a hint of his churlishness, for he advises Arthur not to admit the youthful Kulhwch during a banquet, and receives Arthur's rebuke.[2] It is this aspect of Kei's character which we know was so accentuated in the French romances,[3] and which is here awkwardly combined with the tradition of his high standing at Arthur's court.

The motif of the rash boon, as we have just seen,[4] was also derived from Celtic tradition. It occurs several times in Irish, Welsh, and Arthurian story, and is regularly linked to the abduction of a queen from her consort and her subsequent recovery. In *The Adventures of Cormac in the Land of Promise*[5] the sea-god Manannan comes to the palace of Tara and obtains from King Cormac the granting of three boons. The third boon is King Cormac's wife. Manannan disappears with the lady, but Cormac follows him, comes to his magnificent fortress, is hospitably entertained, learns that his queen has not seen the face of a man since her abduction, and the next morning finds himself back at Tara with his wife. In another

---

[1] E. K. Chambers, *Arthur of Britain*, pp. 63–66. Loth, *Mabinogion*, 2d ed., I, 286, 319–21, 330 f.
[2] Loth, *Mabinogion*, 2d ed., I, 256 f. *Zts. f. franz. Sprach u. Lit.*, XLVII (1924–25), 225 f.
[3] Cf. Chap. XXI.   [4] Cf. Chap. XXVIII.
[5] Cross and Slover, *Ancient Irish Tales*, pp. 503–7.

tale [6] Mongan, King of Ulster, is forced by a similar rash promise to yield his wife to the King of Leinster, but before she departs, she obtains from her abductor the assurance that he will not claim her body for a year. By means of a ruse Mongan wins her back at the end of that time. According to the Welsh mabinogi,[7] Pwyll, Prince of Dyved, makes a rash promise to a noble youth named Gwawl, who then demands Pwyll's bride. She obtains from Gwawl the respite of a year, and when he returns at the expiration of that time, Pwyll contrives to outwit him and wins back his bride. In Thomas's *Tristan* [8] an Irish baron, who has long been in love with Iseut, comes to King Mark's court and obtains from him the promise of a boon. He then demands the Queen and takes her to his ship, but before he is able to enjoy her love, Tristan comes and by means of a ruse delivers her.

There can be no doubt that the rash-boon motif was a common feature of the famous Celtic abduction stories. In the *Charrette* it is transferred from the abductor to Keu; for it is Keu, not Meleagant, who obtains from Arthur the promise of any gift he may ask, and then demands the guardianship of the Queen.

The reason for this transfer is the desire to combine the rash boon with another form of the abduction story in which the stranger knight carries off the queen by force [9]—a proceeding which would be unnecessary if he had already won her by guile. The closest parallel to the forcible abduction as we find it in the *Charrette* is supplied by *L'Atre Périlleux*.[10]

A handsome knight rides into Arthur's hall, seizes a damsel whom he has long loved, and rides off with her, announcing that he will proceed so slowly that anyone who wishes to may overtake him before he reaches a wood near by and dispute her possession. Keu follows him, and of course is unhorsed and badly injured. Gavain delays out of courtesy till the banquet is over, then sets out in pursuit and comes upon Keu's horse with its saddle broken and reins torn. He proceeds on his way, and is able to prevent the abductor from sleeping with the damsel on two successive nights. He learns that the abductor carries a red shield and that his strength increases till the hour of *none,* and then gradually wanes with the setting of the sun.[11] Finally the two knights meet in combat. Gavain kills his opponent's horse with his opponent's spear, is able to snatch back his sword which had become wedged in his adversary's shield,[12] and finally slays him.

[6] A. Nutt and K. Meyer, *Voyage of Bran* (London, 1895), I, 58 ff. M. Joynt, *Golden Legends of the Gael* (Dublin, n.d.), II, 10–19.

[7] Loth, *Mabinogion,* I, 98–104.   [8] Thomas, *Tristan,* ed. Bédier, I, 168–175.

[9] Cf. Chap. IX.   [10] Ed. B. Woledge, pp. 5–78.

[11] *Ibid.,* vss. 1516 f., 1560–68. Cf. *supra,* p. 153.

[12] This is probably a variation on the exchange of swords which takes place in the midst of the fight between Gareth and the Red Knight with the waxing and waning strength. Malory, *Morte d'Arthur,* Bk. VII, chap. 17; ed. H. O. Sommer, I, 238. "And at somtyme they were so amased that eyther took others swerd in stede of his owne."

The roles of the abductor, Keu, and Gavain in the first part of this story correspond markedly to those of Meleagant, Keu, and Gauvain in the opening scenes of the *Charrette,* except that there is no trace of the rash boon. This is significant, for we can identify the Irish source of this episode in *L'Atre Périlleux;* it is the famous abduction of Blathnat by Curoi, and her rescue by Cuchulainn, as a résumé will make clear.[13]

Curoi comes to the court of Ulster and carries off the maiden Blathnat, whom he has long desired. Cuchulainn pursues him, but is shamefully defeated. But after a year's delay he again sets out to recover the damsel, engages in combat with Curoi, and slays him with his own sword. From other sources we learn that Curoi had certain curious solar traits.[14]

This Irish tale has been preserved in several versions which attest its popularity, and has left its imprint on many Arthurian abduction stories, including the abduction of Guenievre in *Durmart* which we have noticed in our study of *Erec.* Thus while the rash-boon motif in the *Charrette* is derived from one well-known Celtic type of abduction story, the humiliating defeat of Keu at the hands of the abductor is derived from the defeat of Cuchulainn by Curoi.

Chapter XXX

THE SHAMEFUL CART AND THE PERILOUS BED

VERSES 306–542

Gauvain, riding in pursuit of the Queen's abductor, came on signs of a fight in which several knights had been engaged and found the horse which he had lent Lancelot lying dead. Presently he overtook Lancelot himself, walking fully armed behind a cart, such as was employed in those days to expose criminals to public derision. A dwarf was driving the cart and told Lancelot to get in if he would have news of the Queen. Torn between Reason, which counseled him to avoid the shame of the cart, and Love, which bade him mount at once, Lancelot took two steps before deciding. Then he leaped in. Gauvain followed the cart on horseback. Proceeding on their way, they passed through a town, where young and old shouted taunts at the knight in the cart and asked the dwarf of what crime the knight had been guilty. Beyond the town, Gauvain fol-

---

[13] R. S. Loomis, *Celtic Myth,* pp. 12–15. Cf. *Journ. of Eng. and Germ. Phil.,* XLII (1943), 156–58; *Miscellany Presented to Kuno Meyer* (Halle, 1912), pp. 26–33.
[14] Cf. the next chapter.

lowed the cart to a tower, and there both knights alighted and were sumptuously entertained at supper by the chatelaine. When the evening was advanced, the damsel showed her guests three beds made up in the hall, one of them more richly appointed than the others. Though she warned Lancelot that he would pay dearly for his presumption, he insisted on occupying this bed. At midnight a lance with a flaming pennon descended from the rafters and grazed Lancelot's side. He put out the fire, removed the lance, and lay down again to sleep. At daybreak, when the two knights had dressed, the damsel had mass celebrated for them as if nothing had happened.

T HE ADVENTURES of the cart and of the bed both betray in Chrétien's handling the characteristic unreason of traditional matter. Gaston Paris remarked of the first: "La charrette elle-même est inexpliquée: qui était ce nain qui la conduisait? quel interêt avait-il à contraindre Lancelot à un acte déshonorant? comment la reine a-t-elle connu cette aventure? nous ne l'apprenons nulle part." [1] Jessie Weston perceived a similar inconsequence in the second incident. "The maiden of the castle warns them [Gauvain and Lancelot] against sleeping in a certain bed; whoever does so will scarce escape with his life. Lancelot braves the adventure, but the next morning when he is found safe and well, the lady expresses no surprise." [2] Chrétien was evidently following blindly his *matière,* the bungling narrative of some inexpert compiler. Now the incidents of the cart and the bed appear in conjunction, though in reverse order, in what seems to be a fuller and more authentic form supplied by the *Vulgate Lancelot.*[3] Let us see whether this version provides any clues as to their origin and meaning.

Gauvain, having been welcomed at the Grail castle, Corbenic, sees a tall knight borne in by servants, and learns that it is the king. A most beautiful maiden brings in a vessel in the form of a chalice, and all are served with good viands except Gauvain. After the repast he is left alone in the hall. A dwarf with a rod enters, addresses him with insults, tries to strike him, and predicts that he will not depart without shame. A damsel now appears and warns him not to lie on a very rich bed unless he is armed. Gauvain, after arming himself, sits on the bed and at once with a hideous noise a lance with a flaming point smites him through the shoulder, and is withdrawn by an unseen agency. After some eerie visions, he engages in a desperate combat with a knight and swoons away. Thunder and lightning follow. The maiden with the Grail restores Gauvain's body to health. After her departure, he is seized by many persons and bound fast to a cart in the courtyard. In the morning an old woman with a whip drives the cart through the town. "When the minstrels see the knight in the cart, they follow after, jeering and shouting, and they throw plenty of dung, old shoes, and mud. Thus they

---

[1] *Romania,* XII (1883), 483.   [2] J. L. Weston, *Legend of Lancelot,* p. 43.
[3] Sommer, *Vulgate Version,* IV, 343–47.

escort him with great ignominy out of the town with all the muck that they can find."

Here there has been some intrusion of Grail themes since the magic castle has been identified with Corbenic. The Maimed King and the damsel with her discriminating and healing vessel are easily recognizable as belonging to this branch of tradition, and the threatening and combative dwarf is probably King Pelles himself.[4] But in spite of this additional matter, we can without difficulty perceive the resemblance of the narrative to Chrétien's two episodes. Though differently arranged, the following common features occur: the hero's ride in the cart of shame; the hooting crowd; a damsel who provides hospitality in a castle; a damsel who warns against lying in a bed; the fiery lance descending on the hero in the middle of the night.

It does not seem likely that the author of the *Vulgate Lancelot* has filched these materials from Chrétien, and for two reasons: first, there are not those close similarities which appear in the passages of the *Lancelot* certainly based on the *Charrette;* [5] and secondly, there is a greater rationality and coherence in the series of Gauvain's successive humiliations than in the disconnected adventures of Lancelot. It seems fairly safe, therefore, to conclude that both accounts of the Perilous Bed and cart incidents go back through several intermediate stages to a common source, and that the *Vulgate* account better preserves the original order and concatenation.

This inference is justified by the fact that when the two incidents are studied, the Perilous Bed adventure can be traced back with certainty and the cart adventure with probability to tales found in the Irish saga *Bricriu's Feast,* the generally acknowledged source of much other Arthurian matter. In order to perceive the relationship between the Perilous Bed story and the Irish saga, it is necessary to summarize the most elaborate French form of the story as it is given in the fourteenth-century romance, *Artus de la Petite Bretagne.*[6]

The Princess Florence possessed an enchanted castle. A magician, who loved and served her, foretold the coming of a knight who would surmount the perils of the castle and win its mistress. She promptly fell in love with the unknown knight, and sent the magician to the castle to watch his progress from the battlements. Artus, the hero of the prophecy, and his squire Baudoin forced their way into the castle, and Artus alone entered a chamber where there was a rich bed, fatal to all but the destined knight. Two lions in succession attacked Artus and

---

[4] Cf. Chap. XX and *PMLA*, LVI (1941), 921–24.
[5] F. Lot, *Etude sur le Lancelot,* pp. 383–417. *Le Roman en prose de Lancelot du Lac, Le Conte de la Charrette,* ed. G. Hutchings (Paris, 1938), pp. lii–lviii.
[6] Summary based on ms., *Livre de Petit Artus,* in New York Public Library, folios 18*r*, 21*v*, 50*r*, 52*v*–61*v*. A description of this ms. was published by the Library in 1928, with halftones of five illuminated pages. Cf. R. S. Loomis, *Celtic Myth,* pp. 172–76; *PMLA*, XLVIII (1933), 1000–1018.

were slain. He then killed a giant clad in a serpent's hide, wielding an ax. Weary from his wounds, he then lay on the bed. Swords mysteriously hurtled about him and a lance of fire struck the bed, but Artus leapt aside. The palace began to turn like a wheel, but Artus clung to a stationary image. When all was quiet once more, he was led to the magician and greeted by him as the sovereign knight of the world. He supped luxuriously at the expense of Florence.

This tale should be compared with the testing of Cuchulainn at Curoi's fortress as narrated in *Bricriu's Feast*.[7]

Cuchulainn and two rival heroes of Ulster went to Curoi's fortress in order that Curoi might judge which of them best deserved the sovranty among the warriors of Ireland. When they arrived, Curoi had departed, but knowing beforehand that they would come, he had counseled Blathnat, "Little Flower," concerning them, and she served them with refreshing drinks and prepared excellent beds. Each was to take his turn for a night watching the fortress till Curoi returned. Every night the fortress revolved. Each of Cuchulainn's rivals took the seat of watch, only to be attacked by an enormous giant and hurled out of the fortress. When Cuchulainn took his seat of watch, he was assailed in turn by three troops of nine unearthly foes and by a water monster; and he despatched them all. The giant, whom Cuchulainn addressed as "bachlaig" (herdsman), approached and hurled branches at the hero, but was forced to surrender and to concede to him the sovranty of Ireland's warriors. Blathnat had known full well of the plight of her lover, Cuchulainn, and so apparently did Curoi, for on his return he also accorded the sovranty to Cuchulainn.

The French and the Irish narratives present the following parallel features: the magician's foreknowledge of and solicitude concerning the hero's coming; his absence from the scene of testing; his knowledge, despite his absence, of the hero's victory; the turning castle; the hero's arrival with one or two companions; his taking the seat of watch; the flying missiles; the combat with monsters, followed by a fight with a giant; the magician's declaration of the hero's sovranty in prowess; the interest of the lady of the fortress in the hero's fate; her provision for his entertainment; her floral name. If any doubt remain as to the connection between the Irish saga and the Perilous Bed episode in *Artus de la Petite Bretagne*, it must vanish before these further considerations: (1) The giant who attacked Cuchulainn must have been Curoi, for not only does he concede the sovranty to Cuchulainn in almost the same terms as does Curoi, but also, as Arthur Brown observed, "If the giant is not Curoi, how can he promise the sovranty, inasmuch as Cuchulinn is sworn to abide by the decision of Curoi?"[8] (2) The identity of the giant with Curoi is supported by

[7] *Feast of Bricriu*, ed. G. Henderson (London, 1899), pp. 100–13. H. D'Arbois de Jubainville, *L'Epopée celtique en Irlande*, pp. 135–42. T. P. Cross and C. H. Slover, *Ancient Irish Tales*, pp. 272–76.
[8] A. C. L. Brown, *Iwain*, p. 55n. Prof. Hulbert, in *Mod. Phil.*, XIII (1915), 438, says: "The giant whom Cuchulainn overcomes at Curoi's fort is undoubtedly Curoi." So also D'Arbois, *op. cit.*, p. 140n.

the application of the same word *bachlach* (herdsman) to both.[9] (3) It is further supported by the fact that whereas the attacking giant in *Artus* is clad in a hide and wields a great sharp ax, so does Curoi wear a hide and wield a great sharp ax in the next episode of the Irish saga, "The Champion's Covenant." [10] (4) It is finally supported by the fact that, whereas in *La Mule sans Frein* of Paien de Maisières [11] we discover a situation paralleling that in *Artus*—a revolving castle, a bed on which the hero reclines, two lions which attack him in succession, a meal with the lady of the castle—we find, in place of the attacking giant with his hide and ax, a *vilain* with an ax who carries out the Beheading Test with the hero—the very role which Curoi plays in the "Champion's Covenant." [12] Thus, while the author of *Bricriu's Feast* betrays in his way the identity of the attacking giant of the turning castle with Curoi, the combined evidence of *Artus* and *La Mule sans Frein* reveals their identity in another way. The origin of the Perilous Bed theme in the visit of Cuchulainn to Curoi's fortress could hardly be more completely demonstrated.[13]

It is of interest and importance to observe that though Chrétien's version of this stock theme lacks many of the original features preserved in *Artus,* it retains three reminiscences of the Irish source which *Artus* lacks: the hospitality which the lady of the castle shows the knights on the evening of their arrival; the three beds, which suggest that originally there had been three knights to occupy them; the testing of the hero by night. If we add these three features of the Perilous Bed adventure as given by Chrétien to those we have enumerated above from the *Artus* version, the total of correspondences with the visit to Curoi's fortress is fifteen.

There is no room for doubt, then, that the Perilous Bed adventure goes back ultimately to an Irish story preserved in a text of the eighth century. There can be little doubt, moreover, that the Irish story contains some very primitive mythical conceptions; for, as I pointed out twenty years ago, Curoi mac Dairi possesses the combined traits of a sun and storm divinity. We have abundant evidence, including the testimony of St. Patrick and of Bishop Cormac, that heliolatry prevailed among the pagan Irish.[14] We have the concordant witness of such authorities as Jastrow, A. B. Cook, Montelius, and Déchelette that sun and lightning were regarded by early peoples as identical or correlated forces.[15] On examination Curoi proves

[9] *Feast of Bricriu,* ed. Henderson, p. 108, l. 11; p. 128, ll. 11 f.
[10] *Ibid.,* p. 117. D'Arbois, *op. cit.,* pp. 143 f. Cross and Slover, *op. cit.,* p. 277.
[11] Paien de Maisieres, *La Damoiselle à la Mule,* ed. B. Orlowski (Paris, 1911), vss. 429–947.
[12] For comparison of Beheading Test in *Bricriu's Feast* and the *Mule sans Frein* cf. *ibid.,* pp. 92–107; G. L. Kittredge, *Study of Gawain and the Green Knight,* pp. 10–14, 42–45.
[13] *PMLA,* XLVIII, pp. 1002–7, 1011–18. Loomis, *Celtic Myth,* pp. 159–75.
[14] Loomis, *op. cit.,* pp. 41–44. *Etudes celtiques,* III (1938), 46 ff. *Kilkenny Archaeological Journal,* Ser. B, I (1868–69), 308. P. W. Joyce, *Origin and History of Irish Names of Places* (Dublin, 1875), Ser. II, Chap. 14.   [15] Loomis, *op. cit.,* pp. 45 f.

to have this dual nature.[16] When the three rival heroes of Ulster came to his fortress to be judged, he had gone on a journey to the east, and his home, as we know, revolved as fast as a millstone every night during his absence. When he returned, it was morning. One is reminded of a passage in an Anglo-Saxon astronomy: "The heaven locketh up in its bosom all the world, and it turneth ever about us, swifter than any mill-wheel. . . . It is all round and solid and painted with stars." [17] It is evident that Curoi's dwelling is the celestial dome, which visibly revolves about the pole by night during the sun's absence on a journey to the east.[18] When in the "Champion's Covenant" [19] Curoi entered the royal hall of Ulster, Duach taunted him with claiming the function of illuminating the house; "only you are more likely to set fire to the house than to give light to the household." Curoi replied: "However tall I may be, the whole household shall have light, and yet the house shall not be burned." Evidently Curoi brought light but not burning—a trait which recalls an old Highland Scottish signet ring, incised with a solar circle and rays and bearing the motto, "Luceo non uro." He went on to boast that lighting of houses was not his only art; he had journeyed to Africa, Asia, Scythia, Greece, the Orkney Isles, and the Pillars of Hercules—as far, then, as the limits of the known world. The solar characterization of Curoi is full and consistent. On the other hand, he wore in this very scene a dark gray mantle and is elsewhere referred to as the man in the gray mantle; [20] the creaking of his hide and the crash of his ax was like the loud noise of a wood on a stormy night; [21] his approach was heralded by the rolling up of a dark cloud of mist; [22] he himself is referred to as a *Scath*, "Shadow"; [23] the ax which he carried is in many mythologies a lightning weapon.[24] These facts, then, suggest that Curoi had his dark and stormy aspect. The same dual concept which is embodied in Curoi can be detected in his adversary Cuchulainn and in the god Lug.[25]

It is startling to realize that the various French versions of the Perilous Bed adventure have not only retained many of the grotesque and strange features of the visit to Curoi's fortress, such as the revolving castle, but

---

[16] *Feast of Bricriu*, ed. Henderson, pp. 101, 103, 109, 111. Cross and Slover, *op. cit.*, pp. 273, 275 f.

[17] O. Cockayne, *Leechdoms, Wortcunning, and Starcraft of Early England* (Rolls Series), III, 233.

[18] Cf. similar conception of sky in J. Hertel, *Die Himmelstore im Veda und im Awesta* (Leipzig, 1924), pp. 41, 44.

[19] *Feast of Bricriu*, ed. Henderson, p. 118. *Zts. f. celt. Phil.*, III, 423. Cross and Slover, *op. cit.*, p. 277. Kittredge, *op. cit.*, p. 11.

[20] *Feast of Bricriu*, p. 46, l. 5, "arit odor"; p. 116, l. 12, "brat dub lachtna." R. Thurneysen, *Irische Helden- und Königsage*, pp. 441, 443, 445.

[21] *Feast of Bricriu*, pp. 127, 129.   [22] *Ibid.*, pp. 45, 49. D'Arbois, *op. cit.*, pp. 106–8.

[23] *Feast of Bricriu*, pp. 102 f. D'Arbois, pp. 136–40.

[24] J. Déchelette, *Manuel d'archéologie préhistorique*, II, 482. C. Blinkenberg, *Thunder Weapon in Religion and Folklore* (Cambridge, 1911). Arthur B. Cook, *Zeus* (Cambridge, 1914–40), II, 505 ff.   [25] Loomis, *Celtic Myth*, pp. 46–49.

have preserved in some respects more faithfully than the Irish account its mythical import. In *Artus* when the hero seats himself on the bed there is a great darkness, a wild wind, and peal after peal of thunder. Then a lance of blazing fire descended from on high toward the bed. In the *Vulgate Lancelot*,[26] when Gauvain sat on the bed, he heard the most hideous voice that he had ever known, and he thought that it was the voice of a devil. Straightway he saw issuing from a chamber a lance of which the point was all ablaze. Later,[27] after his combat with a knight, the palace began to tremble and the window-shutters to slam, and it began to thunder and lighten and to storm violently. The same romance gives us an account of Bohort's nocturnal experiences in the castle of Corbenic,[28] and this agrees with the *Artus* version that as soon as the hero lay on the bed, the tempest began. There was a terrific crash; a high wind banged the window shutters; a long lance with a burning head came toward Bohort "like a flash of lightning." This is, of course, the same lance which according to Chrétien's meagre narrative barely missed Lancelot and set the bed afire. The astonishing fact is that the Irish story merely tells us that the gigantic shadow, Curoi, hurled oaken branches or stakes at the Ulster warriors. It is the French romances which have preserved for us the wind, the slamming windows, the thunder, and the fiery lance which betray the presence of the storm-god. Lancelot's adventure on the Perilous Bed is a survival of Irish myth.

Let us return to the subject of the humiliating ride in the cart, and let us note that, unlike Lancelot, Gauvain in the *Vulgate Lancelot* does not step into the shameful vehicle of his own volition, but after his fight in the Grail castle is dragged out by unseen persons, is tied fast to a cart and driven through the streets amid the derisive cries of the minstrels and showers of mud and old shoes. This recalls another scene, described earlier in the *Vulgate Lancelot*,[29] and characterized by that unreason typical of traditional material far removed from its source.

A dwarf, driving a cart, approaches Arthur's palace at Camaalot. The occupant of the cart is an unknown knight, whose hands are bound behind his back and whose feet are tied to the shafts. When Arthur asks the dwarf what wrong the knight has done, he receives the enigmatic reply: "As much as the other." No wonder that the King did not know what the answer meant. When he now inquires of the knight how he may be delivered, he is informed that another knight must volunteer to take his place. Arthur says that that may not be, and the dwarf drives away with his unfortunate passenger. "From every side old shoes and mud were thrown at them." Somewhat mysteriously, when the royal court is seated for dinner, the cart reappears, and the unknown knight descends from it and tries to take a seat among the fellows of the Round Table. But he is thrust away by the knights, then by the squires, and has to make his exit. Gauvain, mindful

---

[26] Sommer, *Vulgate Version*, IV, 344.   [27] *Ibid.*, IV, 346.   [28] *Ibid.*, V, 298.
[29] *Ibid.*, IV, 215–17. *Le Roman en Prose,* ed. G. Hutchings, pp. 100–104.

that Lancelot once rode in such a vehicle of shame, joins the stranger, much to the King's chagrin. It is even more disastrous to the King's pride when the stranger soon afterwards, mounted on one of the royal steeds, overthrows five knights of the Round Table. Once more the dwarf returns with the cart, this time occupied by the Damsel of the Lake. She reproaches Arthur for failing to deliver the unknown knight of the cart, reveals that he is Bohort, her foster son, and declares that henceforth all carts are to be honored for Lancelot's sake.

The irrationality and inconsequence of this narrative are glaringly patent. The reader is never told why or by whom Bohort was thus bound to the wagon. Though none of Arthur's knights undertakes to liberate him, he is nevertheless free to leave the vehicle, return to the court, borrow one of Arthur's horses, and overthrow several knights at a ford. When the cart appears again, it is occupied by the Damsel of the Lake, how or why one never learns. In all probability, then, we are faced with traditional matter, torn from its original context, fitted into a new setting, and awkwardly elaborated to glorify Lancelot and to point the moral that external humiliations do not derogate from knightly honor. But there seems to be some basic relation between this episode and Gauvain's ignominious ride since both Bohort and Gauvain are tied to the shafts of a cart, and both are hooted at and pelted with mud and old shoes as they are driven through the streets.

Perhaps the Irish saga which has shed so much light on the origins of the Perilous Bed theme may shed some light on that of the Shameful Cart. The three rivals for the Champion's Portion, we have seen, are sent on two occasions to be judged by Curoi mac Dairi, on another occasion to be judged by Yellow son of Fair, and it is one of these testings which furnished the pattern for the Perilous Bed adventure. On still another occasion the rivals are sent to Ercol for the same purpose.[30] Successively the Ulster warriors engage in combat with Ercol and his horse, and Loegaire and Conall are put to flight. Cuchulainn's horse kills Ercol's, "and Cuchulainn ties Ercol himself behind his chariot with him till he reached Emain Macha," the royal palace of Ulster. Cathbad, the druid, chants a poem:

> It is Cuchulainn who deserves [the Champion's Portion];
> He has waged with Ercol a good, victorious conflict.
> The strong, envious warrior is bound
> Behind the tail of the peerless chariot.

Certain points should be noted. (1) This incident appears in the same saga and belongs to the same category of testings as does the visit to Curoi's fortress, the source of the Perilous Bed episode. (2) It resembles the story of Gauvain's ignominious ride in the cart since it deals with a vanquished warrior, tied to a wheeled vehicle. (3) It resembles the story

[30] *Feast of Bricriu*, pp. 85–89. D'Arbois, pp. 125–30.

of Bohort's ignominious ride in the cart since it deals with a warrior, tied to a wheeled vehicle and thus driven in disgrace before a royal household. If these resemblances are merely fortuitous, it is a very remarkable coincidence. The probabilities favor the supposition that the Shameful Cart motif and the Perilous Bed motif are linked together in Chrétien's *Charrette* and in Gauvain's humiliating experience at Corbenic because they are ultimately derived from the same type of story.

Proceeding on this supposition, let us endeavor to explain the development of the Irish story of Ercol's ignominious experience into Chrétien's story of Lancelot's experience in the cart. The warriors of the Ulster cycle rode to battle in chariots, like the Homeric heroes, and a victor would naturally tie his defeated enemy to his chariot to transport or drag him in triumph to the royal court. This is what we find in the story of Cuchulainn's discomfiture of Ercol. When a narrative tradition of this sort was transmitted to peoples who knew nothing of war chariots, the vehicle, as Professor Cross suggested,[31] might easily become a cart. The ignominy involved in the previous defeat and the present plight of the bound warrior would be associated with the vehicle itself, since Chrétien and the author of the *Vulgate Lancelot* were apparently familiar with tumbrels, employed to expose criminals to the insults of the multitude.[32] Accordingly, this concept of the cart would call up a vivid picture of a condemned man, driven through the streets, exposed to the jibes and the missiles of the rabble, and this picture might survive in the mind of a storyteller, even when he forgot or chose to forget the introductory scene of defeat and the binding of the defeated warrior to the cart. Thus the original features which have survived in the story of Gauvain's humiliating adventure at Corbenic and make it comprehensible would be stripped away, and we would have left what we find in the *Charrette*—a knight sitting in a cart, driven through the streets of a town and jeered by old and young as a malefactor.

But why, one may ask, is the driver of the shameful cart a dwarf, instead of the victorious knight whom we should expect? The answer to this question is suggested by the story of Gauvain. For it will be remembered that before Gauvain endured the perils of Corbenic and was finally driven away in the cart, he had been attacked by a dwarf, identifiable as the lord of the castle, King Pelles. Though the *Vulgate* text makes little of the struggle and Gauvain is represented as easily disarming the dwarf,

[31] T. P. Cross and W. A. Nitze, *Lancelot and Guenevere*, p. 54, n. 1. Note a curious parallel in the description of the defeated king of the Arverni, Bituitus, when brought in triumph to Rome. "Nihil tam conspicuum in triumpho quam rex Bituitus, discoloribus in armis argenteoque carpento, qualis ipse pugnaverat." D'Arbois de Jubainville, *La Civilisation des Celtes et celle de l'epopée homérique* (Paris, 1899), pp. 329 f.

[32] *Charrette*, vss. 323–46, 414–21. Sommer, *Vulgate Version*, IV, 215: "Li roys demande au nain que li chevaliers a forfait."

yet Pseudo-Wauchier tells a cognate story in which the dwarf is the victor and the hero is obliged to depart from the castle, mocked by the towns-folk and pelted with offal.[33] The importance and the probable authenticity of this incident in Pseudo-Wauchier are attested by its many congeners in Arthurian romance, which Professor Newstead and Dr. R. E. Bennett have pointed out.[34] In summarizing it I omit many details in order that its kinship to the story of Gauvain's misadventures at Corbenic may be apparent.

Carahes wanders through a very splendid but seemingly deserted castle, sees three richly decorated beds in a chamber and sits on one of them, laying aside helm and shield. He then passes on to another chamber where stands the largest bed ever seen, with a silken coverlet. He finds in a garden a tall wounded knight, lying on a couch in purple robes, fed from a hanap by a damsel. (This is evidently the Grail King, and this is the Grail castle.) A handsome dwarf, "le Petit Chevalier," attacks Carahes with a dart, overthrows him and places his foot on his neck. Carahes yields and is permitted to depart on condition that he return in a year. As he rides away through the streets, the tradesmen mock him and shower him with offal. "Never was any man so humiliated since the world was established."

This tale is certainly related to the shaming of Gauvain in the *Vulgate Lancelot:* both narratives have the wounded lord of the castle; the beau-tiful damsel who serves from a vessel; the mysterious rich bed; the ag-gressive dwarf; the shameful departure. There was evidently for both a remote common source, with the Grail castle setting, the Perilous Bed adventure, the humiliating defeat of the hero by a dwarf, his ignominious departure in a cart driven by the dwarf. The author of the *Lancelot,* taking over some form of this tradition, played down the dwarf combat and gave prominence to the Perilous Bed theme, while Pseudo-Wauchier conversely played down the Perilous Bed and gave prominence to the dwarf combat. Both retain the jeering and pelting crowd, but the *Vulgate* author sub-stituted an old woman for the victorious dwarf as driver of the cart, and Pseudo-Wauchier omitted the cart altogether. It is in the *Charrette* (as well as in the Bohort episode) that we find, oddly enough, the insolent dwarf, the cart, and the mocking crowd which formed a consistent pic-ture in the common source of Pseudo-Wauchier and the *Vulgate Lance-lot.* Chrétien, however, retained nothing of the preliminary defeat of the hero; the invincible Lancelot could not be thus disgraced, least of all at the hands of a pigmy knight. If he entered the cart, it must have been of his own volition, and Chrétien chose to make this act a solemn symbol of Lancelot's dedication to love's service.

---

[33] C. Potvin, *Perceval le Gallois,* IV, 33–45. For similar scenes cf. Tobler-Lommatzsch, *Altfr. Wörterbuch,* II, 75, s.v. çavate.
[34] H. Newstead, *Bran the Blessed,* pp. 70–76. *Speculum,* XVI (1941), 43–50.

To recapitulate, the episodes of the Shameful Cart and the Perilous Bed are based ultimately on two ancient Irish story patterns, represented by the humiliation of Ercol by Cuchulainn, and the triumph of Cuchulainn over the storm-giant in Curoi's fortress. These Irish formulae were combined with the Welsh formula of the humiliating defeat of a hero by the handsome dwarf, Beli, in the castle of the Maimed King, Bran. The combination, with some changes and additions, is still discernible in the *Lancelot* and in Pseudo-Wauchier. In the *Charrette* the elements have been so garbled and shuffled and adapted to Chrétien's dominating purpose that only the closest examination of their analogues reveals their origin and meaning.

It may be possible to suggest other explanations for this or that element in Chrétien's story of the Shameful Cart and the Perilous Bed, as Gaston Paris, Professors Cross and Nitze, and Dr. Krappe have done,[35] but I know of no other which fits the whole complex of facts.

Chapter XXXI

MELEAGANT THE ABDUCTOR

VERSES 641–47

After Lancelot and Gauvain had left the tower of the Perilous-Bed adventure, they encountered at a crossroad a damsel, who vouchsafed the following information. The abductor of the Queen was a tall and powerful knight, named Meleagant, son of the King of Goirre.

I T HAS BEEN SHOWN in Chapter XXIX that the abduction of Guenievre, particularly the rash-boon motif and the ignominious overthrow of Keu by the abductor, owed much to Irish sagas. It will be remembered that in two of these stories there is a year's interval between the loss of the lady and her recovery, and this feature recurs significantly in what has long been recognized as a fairly close cognate of Chrétien's narrative, a passage in Caradoc of Lancarvan's *Vita Gildae* (written before 1136),[1] which I here translate.

"Gildas . . . came to Glastonbury (*Glastoniam*) . . . while Melvas was reigning in the summer land (*aestiva regione*). . . . It [Glastonbury] was therefore besieged by the tyrant Arthur with a countless host because his wife Guennuvar had been raped and stolen by the aforesaid evil king, and had been carried thither

---

[35] *Romania*, XII (1883), 514. Cross and Nitze, *op. cit.*, p. 54, n. 1; pp. 70 f. *Revue celt.*, XLVIII (1931), 94.
[1] On date cf. *Speculum*, XIII (1938), 139–52; XIV (1939), 350–53. Cf. also on the Melvas story, G. Schoepperle, *Tristan and Isolt*, II, 530 ff.; *Romanic Review*, XXXII (1941), 6 f.

by reason of the refuge afforded by its inviolate site and the reeds, river, and marsh which protected it. The recalcitrant king [Arthur] had been seeking the queen for about a year and at last heard that she was there. He moved thither the armies of all Cornwall and Devon; a battle was arrayed between the enemies. Seeing this, the abbot of Glastonbury, accompanied by a cleric and Gildas the Wise, went between the battle lines and advised his king Melvas peacefully that he should restore the stolen woman. She who should have been restored was restored as a sign of peace and good will." [2]

The lapse of a year between the abduction and the finding of Guennuvar suggests the influence of the famous Irish story of the abduction of Blathnat and Cuchulainn's year-long search for her. But the characters are new and their names are Welsh, Guennuvar and Melvas representing Gwenhwyvar and Melwas. These personages are, of course, identical with Chrétien's Guenievre and Meleagant, and scholars are agreed that Caradoc has given us an ecclesiasticized variant of the main plot of the *Charrette*.

The name Meleagant has probably been influenced by the Meleager of Ovid [3] or the *Roman de Thèbes*. Caradoc's form, Melvas, is merely a graphic variant of Welsh Melwas, which, as Zimmer and Rhys believed,[4] is a compound of *mael* (prince) and *gwas* (youth). Twice in Welsh poetry of the fourteenth century there is reference to Melwas's love for Arthur's queen.[5] Davydd ab Gwilym, referring to a window before which the poet-lover stands, has a passage which Rhys translated as follows:

> May I die! if it was not of magic make
> A window of this the very counterpart. . . .
> That was the one at Caerleon of yore,
> Which entrance gave of old to Melwas—
> Driven by over-love without love's fears,
> The dire plague and pain of mighty passion—
> At the house of Giant Ogurvan's daughter.

The daughter of Ogurvan (or Gogfran),[6] we know, was Gwenhwyvar. Davydd ab Edmwnt wrote, according to Rhys' translation:

> Alas that a bachelor's sigh avails not
> For me to invoke the art of Melwas;
> The thief, that, by magic and illusion
> Took the fair one to the world's end:
> To the green wood that juggler went

[2] The Latin text is given by Schoepperle, *loc. cit.;* E. K. Chambers, *Arthur of Britain,* pp. 263 f.; *Monumenta Germaniae Historica, Chronica Minora Saeculorum IV–VII,* Vol. III, 107; *Cymmrodorion Record Series,* II (London, 1901), p. 410.
[3] *Metamorphoses,* viii, 299 ff. Of course, Chrétien was familiar with Ovid.
[4] *Karrenritter,* ed. Foerster, p. xxxviii. Rhys, *Arthurian Legend,* p. 51. Lot's interpretation of the name as Prince of Death has been refuted by K. Meyer in *Sitzungsberichte der preussischen Akademie der Wissenschaften,* 1919, p. 546, n. 1.
[5] On these Welsh passages cf. Rhys, *op. cit.,* pp. 65–67; Cross and Nitze, *Lancelot and Guenevere,* p. 47, n. 2.   [6] This is the form in the Welsh text given by Rhys, *loc. cit.*

To the leafy rampart of a bough—
And to climb tonight aloft like him,
That is what I could wish to do.[7]

It is hard to relate these passages to the stories told by Caradoc and Chrétien, but an edition of Davydd ab Gwilym's poems published in 1789 contains a note, probably written by William Owen, which is more satisfying.

"He [Melwas] dressed himself in leaves, to lie in wait for Gwenhwyfar and her attendants, who, according to custom, was to come on May morning to gather birch for garlands to welcome summer: by means of that disguise he ran away with her."[8]

There is a curious correspondence between this account and the story of Guinevere's abduction given in Malory's Book XIX. The Queen and her attendant knights and ladies rode a-Maying in the woods and fields near Westminster, and were all "bedasshed with herbys, mosses and floures in the best maner and fresshest," when Mellyagraunce and 160 men attacked them and carried off the Queen. Moreover, in the Austrian romance, Der Pleier's *Garel*,[9] composed between 1260 and 1280, it was "im meien an dem phingestage" (in May on the day of Pentecost)[10] that Meljakanz appeared in a flowery plain before the wood of Briziljan (Broceliande), demanded that Arthur yield up his queen, and rode away with her.

What is the relation between these three witnesses, Owen, Malory, and Der Pleier, who assign the abduction to a May festival? Zimmer,[11] followed by others, was confident that Owen certainly knew Malory's book, and that, recognizing the identity of Melwas and Mellyagraunce, the Welsh editor made up his note on the former from some suggestions in *Le Morte d'Arthur*. But this hypothesis is full of loopholes. Why did Owen transfer to Melwas the leafy garb which Malory assigned to the Queen's party? Why did he omit so much information about Mellyagraunce? How did Der Pleier also hit on a May festival as an appropriate date? It seems that we must explain the triple correspondence either by accident or by a common stock of tradition, for certainly Der Pleier could not have known Malory or Owen.

The case for tradition is strengthened if we look back to Caradoc's story in the *Vita Gildae* and observe that it presents analogies to a Welsh abduction tale in which May Day is conspicuous. This tale is briefly given in *Kulhwch*.

[7] Rhys, *op. cit.*, p. 67.   [8] Cross and Nitze, *op. cit.*, p. 62.
[9] Ed. M. Walz (Freiburg, 1892), vss. 1 ff. On transference of May festival to Whitsuntide cf. E. K. Chambers, *Mediaeval Stage*, I, 172 f.
[10] Even Chrétien sets the time of the abduction on Ascension Day, which usually falls in May.
[11] *Karrenritter*, ed. Foerster, pp. xxxiv–xxxvii.

"Kreiddylat, daughter of Lludd of the Silver Hand, went away with Gwythyr son of Greidawl. Before he slept with her Gwynn son of Nudd came and took her away by force. Gwythyr son of Greidawl mustered a host and came to fight with Gwynn son of Nudd, and Gwynn won the victory. . . . Arthur, hearing of this, came to the North, summoned Gwynn son of Nudd, released the noble captives, and made peace between him and Gwythyr son of Greidawl. This is the peace which was made. The maid was to remain in her father's house, inviolate by both sides, and Gwynn and Gwythyr were to fight every Mayday till the Day of Judgment, and he who won the victory on the Day of Judgment would take the maid." [12]

From a later Welsh text we discover that Gwynn son of Nudd was a king of Annwn and the faery folk, and had his castle at Glastonbury.[13]

Accordingly, both the *Vita Gildae* and *Kulhwch* contain these elements in common: the abduction of a wife by a king who had a castle at Glastonbury; the assembling of an army by the outraged husband; and the settlement of the dispute by a third party. Though in *Kulhwch* the abduction itself is not said to have occurred on May Day, yet the combat over the abducted damsel was to be repeated yearly on that date, as if it were an anniversary. Malory, Der Pleier, and Owen then agree that Arthur's queen was stolen on some day in the month of May, whereas Malory and the author of *Kulhwch* agree that there was a fight over a stolen lady on May Day. William Owen, it seems clear, did not borrow his account of the abduction of Gwenhwyvar from Malory, but preserved, in an unfortunately meager form, the old Welsh tradition which also came down through the channels of Arthurian romance to Der Pleier and Malory —the tradition that the Queen was seized by Melwas during a May festival. Chrétien, too, seems to have been heir to this tradition, for it was during the Feast of the Ascension, which usually falls in May, that Meleagant made his insolent appearance at Camalot.

This is a matter of high significance. The first of May was an important seasonal date among the Celts—the beginning of summer, as November first was the beginning of winter.[14] We have already seen in connection with Erec's fight with the robber knights that on May Day in South Wales, even as late as the nineteenth century, there was a folk ritual corresponding to the annual combat between Gwynn and Gwythyr for the abducted Kreiddylat.[15] Young men, divided into two companies to represent the forces of Winter and Summer, engaged in a sham battle. Finally Summer gained the mastery, and the people selected a May Queen.

[12] Loth, *Mabinogion*, 2d ed., I, 331 f.   [13] *Ibid.*, I, 314n. *PMLA*, LVI, 893 f.
[14] E. Hull, *Folklore of the British Isles*, pp. 248-60.
[15] M. Trevelyan, *Folklore and Folk-Stories of Wales*, p. 53. For similar customs cf. Hull, *op. cit.*, pp. 251 f.; J. G. Frazer, *Golden Bough*, 3d ed., IV, 254 ff.; J. Grimm, *Teutonic Mythology*, trans. Stallybrass, II, 758-69; W. Hone, *Every-Day Book*, I, 358 f.; *Cymmrodor*, XXII (1910), 2.

The captain of the Summer forces "was dressed in a kind of white smock decorated with garlands of flowers and gay ribbons. On his head he wore a broad-brimmed hat trimmed with flowers and ribbons. In his hand he carried a willow-wand wreathed with spring flowers and tied with ribbons." Let us remember that Caradoc's Melvas, the abductor of Guennu-var and the counterpart of Gwynn, who yearly fought for the possession of Kreiddylat every first of May, was ruler of the *aestiva regio,* the Summer Country, and that Owen's Melwas dressed himself in leaves on May morning to lie in wait for Gwenhwyfar. The persistence of these seasonal suggestions can hardly be explained away, and further evidence will accumulate to reinforce them before we finish with the role of Meleagant in Chrétien's poem. From Caradoc of Lancarvan, from Der Pleier, from Malory, from William Owen the testimony is consistent. The abduction of Guenievre by Meleagant goes back to a Welsh seasonal myth, in which Melwas as King of the Summer Country vanquished the King of Winter on May morning, and bore away with him to the end of the world the Giant Ogurvan's daughter.

Chapter XXXII

THE LAND OF GOIRRE

VERSES 641–47, 6132–56

The damsel whom Lancelot and Gauvain met at the crossroad informed them that Guenievre had been carried off by Meleagant, son of the King of Goirre, to the realm whence no stranger returns. The name of the king was Baudemaguz. The land was accessible only by perilous bridges, one under and the other over water. Later Chrétien tells us that Lancelot was imprisoned in a tower which stood on an island lying in an arm of the sea near Go(i)rre.

WHAT WAS this land of Goirre? What was the sea-girt tower near by? From three sources we learn that Meleagant was lord of an "isle of glass." An obscure Welsh poem mentions "Melwas o ynys wydrin," "Melwas from the Glass Island." [1] Chrétien himself in *Erec* writes thus of Maheloas, whose name is almost a phonetic equivalent of Welsh Melwas, and who is generally recognized as identical with Meleagant:

"There came Maheloas, a mighty baron, the lord of the Isle of Glass (*Voirre*). In this island no thunder is heard, no lightning strikes nor storm rages, no toad or serpent abides there, and it is neither too hot nor wintry." [2]

[1] *Speculum,* XIII (1938), 39.   [2] *Erec,* vss. 1946–51.

This is obviously the same tradition which is reflected in Caradoc of Lancarvan's account of the abduction of Guenievre. For Melvas reigned in the summer country (*aestiva regio*), and his fortress where he held the queen, was at Glastonia, the name of which is thus interpreted:

"Glastonia was in ancient times called Ynisgutrin and is still so called by the Britanni who live there; *ynis* in the Britannic language is *insula* in Latin, and *gutrin* indeed is glass. But after the coming of the English and the expulsion of the Britanni (that is, the Welsh), it was renamed Glastigberi in succession to its first name; that is, *glas* in English is *vitrum* in Latin, *beria* is *civitas;* thence Glastiberia, namely, *Vitrea Civitas.*" [3]

Scholars are agreed that this is a false etymology of the name Glastonbury,[4] since it is certain that the Saxon Glaestingabyri has nothing to do with the word glass, but means the town of the Glaestings. This equation of Ynisgutrin, later Welsh *ynys wydrin,* with the marsh-encircled town in Somersetshire is therefore but another instance of that mistaken ingenuity which equated the fabulous Caer Loyw, "Shining Fortress," where Mabon was imprisoned and where Peredur received his training in arms from the nine sorceresses, with Gloucester, which Nennius in the ninth century called Cair Gloiu.[5]

The identification of the Isle of Glass with Glastonbury was all the more convincing because, as Chrétien's description of the *Isle de Voirre* shows, it was a realm where there was never storm or wintry weather, and Glastonbury lay in *Somer*setshire. Even to this day the Welsh call the county across the Bristol Channel *Gwlad yr Hav,* "the Land of Summer," though a trace of the original elysian meaning of the phrase survives.[6] But, of course, the equation of the *aestiva regio* with Somersetshire is as purely fantastic as the connection of the mythical *insula vitrea* with Glastonbury, for the county is named after the Sumorsaete, a Saxon tribe.

It seems plain that Caradoc brought Guennuvar to Glastonia as the captive of Melvas because Melvas was lord, not only of a summer country, but also of the Ynisgutrin or Insula Vitrea, just as Melwas in the Welsh poem came from *ynys wydrin,* and just as Maheloas was lord of the Isle de Voirre. Now since everyone admits that these persons are no other than Meleagant, and since Meleagant was prince of the water-girdled realm of Goirre (this form is supplied by ms. A, vs. 643), one is justified in wondering whether Goirre is not a corruption of Voirre, due to the substitution of G for V. Exactly this substitution did take place in

[3] E. K. Chambers, *Arthur of Britain*, p. 264. Bruce, *Evolution*, I, 198, n. 12.
[4] *Perlesvaus,* ed. Nitze and others, II, 58. Chambers, *op. cit.,* p. 123. Bruce, *op. cit.,* I, 198 f. *Zts. f. franz. Sprache u. Lit.,* XX (1898), 98 f. *Romania,* XXIV (1895), 329. F. J. Snell, *King Arthur's Country,* p. 69. On Glastonbury traditions cf. also J. Armitage Robinson, *Two Glastonbury Legends* (Cambridge, 1926); Robinson, *Somerset Historical and Archaeological Essays* (London, 1921), pp. 1 ff.
[5] Cf. *supra,* p. 89, n. 21.   [6] J. Rhys, *Studies in the Arthurian Legend,* pp. 345 f.

the fifteenth century prose version of *Erec,* where instead of "isle de voirre" we find "isle de guerre." No other *satisfactory* explanation of the name Goirre (or Gorre) has ever been offered,[7] and we shall see later more evidence in support of this view.

Is the land of Goirre the land of the dead as some scholars have been led to believe by the phrases which Chrétien uses: "the realm . . . from which no stranger returns," "the land . . . from which neither serf nor man of gentle blood comes forth," "the realm whence no man escapes," "whence no man is wont to return"? [8] There is good reason to equate Baudemaguz, King of Goirre, with the King of Brandigan in *Erec,* and of the latter's castle likewise we read that "no man returned who went to seek adventure there," and again, "no man could escape thence alive." [9] Do these recurring clauses mean that Goirre is "the undiscovered country from whose bourn no traveler returns"? Is Hamlet's soliloquy a safe guide to the interpretation of Chrétien? We know from our study of the castle of Limors in *Erec* that the concept of the Other World as a land of the dead was known to the Bretons and filtered into Arthurian romance. But in the *Charrette* I am unable to discover any sure sign of this tartarean nature. On the contrary, far from being a land whence no one returns, it is a land from which everyone returns alive and happy—Lancelot, Keu, Gauvain, Guenievre, and all the captives of Logres. If ever anyone conceived of the land over which Baudemaguz reigned as a *Totenreich,* all vestiges of the concept have been effectively obliterated. The explanation of the phrases which have so misled scholars [10] is that it was apparently customary to emphasize the perils which attended the visits of adventurous knights to the uncanny castles of romance by asserting that no one had returned alive. Just such phrases occur in *Kulhwch and Olwen.* Of the *kaer* of Yspaddaden Penkawr it is said: "No one has ever come to make this request who has returned alive." [11] The *kaer* of another giant, Gwrnach Gawr, has an equally bad reputation: " 'No one has ever lodged in this castle who has come forth alive.' " [12] There is nothing to prove

[7] Rhys's suggestion that Goirre was the peninsula of Gower has no sound basis, since he produces no evidence that this was a French form for Welsh Gwanas Gwyr, nor does it appear that the Welsh or any other people attributed to this region the character of the Other World or connected it with Melwas. Rhys, *op. cit.,* pp. 329 f. Prof. Cross's statement (Cross and Nitze, *Lancelot and Guenevere,* p. 53) that Gower is near Bath is hardly accurate according to medieval conceptions of distance. By the road which crosses the Severn at Gloucester the distance is about 140 miles. Brugger's derivation of Gorre from Strathmore is, of course, accepted by no one.

[8] Vss. 645, 1916, 1948. On this subject cf. *PMLA,* LVI (1941), 895–99.

[9] Vss. 5436 f., 5463.

[10] *Romania,* XII (1883), 508. *Karrenritter,* ed. W. Foerster (1899), pp. lix–lxxi. Rhys, *Arthurian Legend,* pp. 328 f. *Revue celt.,* XLVIII (1931), 105.

[11] Loth, *Mabinogion,* 2d ed., I, 291.

[12] *Ibid.,* p. 318 f.

that Yspaddaden or Gwrnach were personifications of death. The formula means no more than what it says.

If, then, the identification of Melvas's *insula vitrea* with Glastonbury was due to a mistaken etymology, if the identification of Goirre with the peninsula of Gower is a baseless and improbable guess, if the realm whence no stranger returns was not Hamlet's "undiscovered country," what then was the essential nature of Meleagant's land?

The description of Maheloas' "Isle de Voirre," quoted above, shows that it was a land of perennial spring. Fuller details are furnished by the romance of *Sone de Nansai*.[13] The island formerly ruled by Baudemagus and Meleagant was very beautiful and square in shape. Four palaces stood at the four corners. In the midst was a fountain, gushing forth from a horn of gilded copper. The island was connected with the shore half a league away by a causeway and a sword-bridge, where many heads had been cut off when Meleagant was lord. This description, as Bruce pointed out,[14] bears a significant resemblance to that of the "land whence no one returns" in the *Historia Meriadoci*.[15] That island, too, was of equal length and breadth and was approached by a narrow causeway; it contained four castles, a hall of beautiful workmanship, and a garden of divers trees and fruits. The narrow approach was defended by the redoubtable Gundebald, who had abducted the emperor's daughter, as Meleagant had abducted Guenievre. The connection with Meleagant, the recurrence of the phrase, "the land whence no man returns," the sword-bridge, and the abduction motif serve to identify these islands with the water-girdled land of Goirre, and an investigation of other motifs in the *Charrette* will reveal, as we proceed, the basic and authentic kinship of these traditions of the island paradise.

The source of these conceptions we may trace back to Wales. From two old Welsh poems in the *Book of Taliesin* we can form a composite picture of Kaer Siddi, "the Fortress of the Fays."[16] It was on an island of the sea and contained a fountain. Since the fortress was also known as Kaer Pedryvan and Kaer Wydyr,[17] it must have been four-cornered and made of glass. Neither old age nor disease afflicted those who dwelt there. Its immortal inhabitants included the sea-god Manawydan son of Llyr and probably his brother Bran, "the Noble Head."[18] At any rate, it will appear in Chapter XL that the name of Meleagant's father, Baudemaguz,

---

[13] *Karrenritter*, ed. Foerster, pp. xlix–li. *Sone de Nausay,* ed. M. Goldschmidt (Tübingen, 1899), vss. 17131–17203. Cf. *PMLA*, LVI, 933–35.
[14] J. D. Bruce, *Historia Meriadoci*, pp. xxxiv f.
[15] *Ibid.*, pp. 43 f.
[16] *PMLA*, LVI, 889–91, 902.
[17] *Ibid.*, pp. 925–29.
[18] *Ibid.*, pp. 902–05.

can best be explained as a corrupt compound of these two names of Welsh divinities. The land of Goirre in its pristine nature was a glass fortress on an island of the sea, the elysian abode of the gods.

We shall return to the subject in considering the transparent prison of the Dame de Malehot in the *Vulgate Lancelot* and the Castle of Ladies in *Le Conte del Graal*.[19]

Chapter XXXIII

THE WATER BRIDGE

VERSES 651–71, 693–700, 5116–47

The damsel who informed Lancelot and Gauvain that Guenievre had been carried off to the land of Goirre went on to say that one could not enter that land except by two passages. One was called the "Pont Evage," and consisted of a bridge a foot and a half in width, which lay beneath the surface of the water so that there was as much water above it as below it. Gauvain chose to follow the road which led to this bridge. Several days later, when nothing had been seen or heard of him, a search was made at the water bridge at the instance of Lancelot, and Gauvain was discovered, still wearing hauberk and helm and rising and sinking in the stream. In attempting to cross the bridge he had fallen off. By means of poles and hooks the half-drowned knight was dragged out and his body was emptied of water. As soon as he recovered consciousness, he asked for news of the Queen and learned of her deliverance by Lancelot.

PROFESSOR HIBBARD's remarks regarding the *Pont Evage* deserve quotation: "This bridge seems directly reminiscent of the concept of an Otherworld lying beneath water. Although such a concept is not exclusively Celtic, one of the frequent episodes of old Irish story is that of a hero going by way of an under-water passage to a Land of Marvel. . . . The sword bridge and the one beneath the water are so closely connected, it seems probable that they are derived from the same kind of material." [1] Miss Hibbard cited several examples from Irish legend of a hero who reached the Other World by plunging beneath the waters. The oldest is found in *The Adventures of Laeghaire Mac Crimhthainn*,[2] where we read that after Fiachna, one of the faery folk, had asked the warriors of Connaught to help him recover his wife from Goll, a king of the fort of Magh Mell, Laeghaire and fifty warriors followed him on this errand. Fiachna "goes before them down under the lake, while they go after

---

[19] Cf. Chaps. XLII, LXXVIII.   [1] *Romanic Review*, IV (1913), 167, n. 2.
[2] *Speculum*, XVII (1942), 381–85.

him." Goll and his army were massacred. When Laeghaire attacked the fort, the woman was surrendered and returned to her husband.

Whether by coincidence or not, here is a parallel to Gauvain's plunging under the waters surrounding the castle of Baudemaguz in order to help in the rescue of a woman stolen from her husband. That Gauvain did not succeed in making his way across the Pont Evage and had to be extracted from the water, half drowned, is to be explained plausibly by the fact that he had to play a secondary role to the hero Lancelot.

Stronger evidence in favor of the general interpretation of the Water Bridge as a rationalized and burlesqued passage to a subaqueous world was first suggested by Jessie Weston [3] and later developed by Professor Newstead.[4] The *Reductorium Morale* of Pierre Bercheur (who died in 1362) contains a most provocative passage, of which Jessie Weston remarked: "This fourteenth-century reference is noteworthy as testifying to the considerable mass of Arthurian romance which has perished, a fact which must be borne in mind when the argument, so dear to some scholars, *ex silentio,* is brought forward." [5] The passage runs:

"What shall I say of the marvels which occur in the histories of Galvagnus and Arthur? Of which I will mention only one, namely of the palace which Galvagnus, when by chance drawn under the water, discovered, where he found a table spread with eatables and a chair placed ready. But he did not see any door by which he might depart. When he became hungry and wished to eat, suddenly the head of a dead man appeared in the platter, and a giant was lying on a bier near the fire. When the giant arose and struck the palace with his head, and the head [on the platter] called out and forbade the repast, he [Galvagnus] never dared to eat of the food. But after many marvels he escaped, but he knew not how he escaped." [6]

A hundred years ago Madden observed with acumen: "Berchorius here evidently refers to the prodigies seen by Gawayne at the palace of the Graal." [7] Since Madden's time much evidence has accumulated to identify this subaqueous palace with the Castle of the Grail. Professor Mary Williams pointed out that the severed head in the platter reappears in the Castle of Wonders, visited by Peredur under circumstances corresponding to those of Perceval's visit to the castle of the Fisher King.[8] She also asserted that the same tradition was to be found in the account of the feasting of Bran's

[3] J. L. Weston, *Legend of Gawain,* p. 74.
[4] H. Newstead, *Bran the Blessed,* pp. 140–42. Gawain is also nearly drowned in a river which he attempted to cross, according to Heinrich von dem Türlin's *Krone,* ed. G. H. F. Scholl, vss. 14407–57. An incident of obviously Arthurian inspiration tells how Reinbrun, in crossing a river to an Otherworld palace, sinks below the waters, according to *Gui de Warewic,* ed. A. Ewert (Paris, 1933), II, vss. 12341–62.   [5] Weston, *Legend of Gawain,* p. 75, n. 1.
[6] The Latin text is given by Newstead, p. 76.
[7] F. Madden, *Syr Gawayne* (London, 1839), p. xxxii.
[8] M. R. Williams, *Essai sur la composition du roman gallois de Peredur* (Paris, 1909), pp. 46 f.

followers in the presence of his head, as related in *Branwen*. Another some-what muddled form of Bercheur's story is given by Pseudo-Wauchier, who tells how Gauvain, after passing two fays at a spring, entered the mysterious castle of Bran de Lis, and saw a hundred heads of boars on grails (*graaus*).[9] Professor Newstead has assembled the pertinent facts,[10] and they all point toward the identification of Bercheur's underwater palace with the castle of the Fisher King, the fortress of Bran, son of Llyr, "the Sea."

As all authorities have recognized, the Celts believed the blissful abodes of the gods to be hidden from the eyes of normal man in a wide variety of places—behind a wall of mist, under ground, beyond a river, on a remote island, beneath a lake, under the sea. Bran, the sea-god, though in the euhemeristic stages of his legend he might have his seat at Aberffraw or Harlech or Dinas Bran or the isle of Grassholm,[11] would surely be credited with an appropriate home beneath the waves. As inheritor of the legends of Bran, Brangorre has his Chastel de la Marche, alias Dinas Bran; [12] Bron, the Fisher King of the *Didot Perceval,* languishes "en ces illes d'Irlande en un des plus biaus lius del monde"; [13] the King of Brandigan and Brandus des Illes have their island castles. The castle of Baudemaguz can be approached both by a bridge over a deep and turbulent river and by a bridge under water. The latter, as the passage from Bercheur shows, is related to the fact that Bran's palace was sometimes thought of as beneath the sea.

Webster made it clear that some predecessor of Chrétien attempted to give the passage of Gauvain to the sea-god's home a realistic coloring by suggesting in his description of the water bridge the underwater causeways which led to the "crannogs" or lake dweller's fortresses, common in Scotland and Ireland.[14] This modification of the old concept in the direction of realism Chrétien seems to have carried even further in the direction of burlesque. The scene where Lancelot's liegemen fish out the half-drowned Gauvain with poles is deliberate farce.

[9] C. Potvin, *Perceval le Gallois,* III, vss. 16676–16766. Trans. by J. L. Weston, *Sir Gawain and the Lady of Lys* (London, 1907), pp. 27–29.   [10] Newstead, *op. cit.,* pp. 70–85.
[11] *Ibid.,* pp. 14, 19, 23.   [12] *Ibid.,* pp. 52–55.   [13] *Didot-Perceval,* ed. W. Roach, p. 306.
[14] *Mod. Lang. Rev.,* XXVI (1931), 69–73. For an example in Wales cf. J. Rhys, *Celtic Folklore,* I, 73.

Chapter XXXIV

THE SWORD BRIDGE

VERSES 672–77, 3017–55

Of the two passages to the land of Goirre the more dangerous was the Sword Bridge. Lancelot, after parting from Gauvain and encountering various adventures, came to a black and raging stream. The bridge which spanned it was a sword as long as two lances, fixed at each end in a tree trunk. At the farther side there appeared to be two lions tied to a great rock. Removing the mail from his hands and feet, Lancelot crept across the sword, which was sharper than a scythe and cut his hands, knees, and feet. When he reached the other bank of the stream, he looked for the lions, but he did not see so much as a lizard.

THE SAFEST WAY to ascertain the origin of the Sword Bridge is surely not to point out a general resemblance to infernal bridges in apocalyptic or visionary literature,[1] but to examine its Arthurian affiliations and then discover, if possible, a source which answers to this Arthurian complex. The specific group of facts connected with the Sword Bridge are these:

The sword bridge leads to the fortress of King Baudemaguz. The name of Baudemaguz contains, as we shall presently see,[2] the element Bran in a corrupt form. If so, since we discovered in *Erec* that Bran, son of Llyr, was the original of the Fisher King,[3] and since we shall discover in *Le Conte del Graal* much other evidence to the same effect, there should be some correspondence between the fortress of Baudemaguz and that of the Fisher King; and there is. In *Le Conte del Graal* and in *Perlesvaus,* the castle of the Fisher King is equipped with one or more perilous bridges. In the former romance [4] the bridge rises under Perceval as he is leaving and his horse is compelled to leap to the farther bank in order to escape injury. In the latter romance [5] there are three bridges, of which the first is not a foot wide, is called "the Bridge of the Eel (*Anguille*)," and rises automatically behind the hero; and the third is guarded by a ferocious-looking but actually harmless lion. Is this variety of bridges attached to the castles of Baudemaguz and the Fisher King merely the whimsy of the French romancers? Or is there a source for them, Celtic or otherwise?

[1] *Romanic Review,* IV (1913), 172–84. Prof. Hibbard concludes (p. 184): "Chrétien's bridge is totally unlike any form of the soul bridge to which allusion has yet been made; it is much more nearly like the fairy bridges of old Irish story."   [2] Cf. Chap. XL.
[3] Cf. Chap. XXV.   [4] *Conte del Graal,* ed. Hilka, vss. 3402–9.
[5] *Perlesvaus,* ed. Nitze, I, 114 f.

In the Irish *Training of Cuchulainn* the Bridge of the Cliff by which the hero reaches the island of Scathach combines the features of the various bridges just noted.[6] "When one sprang upon it, it was narrowed till it was as narrow as a hair, and it was as sharp as a blade-edge and as slippery as an eel's tail. At another time it would rise so that it was as high as a mast." Here, then, is a bridge which combines the properties of sharpness, narrowness, and automatic elevation, and which well deserves to be called "le Pont de l'Anguille." This group of correspondences did not occur by chance. And since we have already seen that several characteristic features of the *Charrette* are of Irish origin, it is natural to assume that the sword bridge is derived from *The Training of Cuchulainn*.

But there is an objection. The Irish story, according to Thurneysen,[7] is a fifteenth-century composition, and cannot therefore in its surviving form be the source of a twelfth-century poem. But the objection loses much of its force when it is realized that *The Training of Cuchulainn* is a *remaniement* of an older story incorporated in *The Wooing of Emer*,[8] and that the *Wooing* was composed as early as the eighth century.[9] In one version the bridge leading to Scathach's isle is a narrow rope;[10] in another it rises.[11] In these earlier stages of the tradition, therefore, the Bridge of the Cliff already possessed two of the four properties attributed to it in the fifteenth century. There is a balance of probability, therefore, that the author of *The Training of Cuchulainn* found the other two properties—blade-like sharpness and eel-like slipperiness—in earlier traditions concerning the Bridge of the Cliff—traditions as old perhaps as the tenth century.

The most reasonable hypothesis by which we may account for the remarkable similarity between the Bridge of the Cliff and the bridges attached to the castles of Baudemaguz and the Fisher King is this: Before the year 1000 the dangerous bridge which Cuchulainn crossed to reach the isle of Scathach was credited by Irish *filid* with one or more of four marvelous properties. The thinness alone appears in the eleventh-century version of *The Wooing of Emer,* the rising alone in the later version; all four traits occur in the fifteenth century redaction, *The Training of Cuchulainn*. Passed on to the Welsh, this concept of the perilous bridge was connected with the island abode of Bran, son of Llyr. Though we have no Welsh text to corroborate this conclusion, it is difficult otherwise to understand how all four properties of the Bridge of the Cliff should also cling to the bridges which led to the castles of Baudemaguz and the Fisher King, figures whom on quite other grounds we are led to identify with the Welsh Bran.

[6] *Revue celt.,* XXIX (1908), 119. R. Thurneysen, *Irische Helden- und Königsage,* p. 398.
[7] Thurneysen, *op. cit.,* p. 396.
[8] D'Arbois de Jubainville, *Essai d'un catalogue* (Paris, 1883), p. clii.
[9] Thurneysen, *op. cit.,* p. 382.   [10] *Ibid.,* p. 389.   [11] *Ibid.,* p. 389, n. 4.

Two other features of the Sword Bridge may be plausibly accounted for by Irish tradition. Professor Hibbard pointed out [12] that one of the feats of the famous lover Diarmaid was to place two forked poles upright, fix a sword, edge upward, between them, and then thrice measure the sword by paces from the hilt to the point.[13] This may well be the "blade feat," which Cuchulainn learned on the isle of Scathach,[14] and which might very naturally coalesce with the crossing of the narrow bridge to the same island. Certainly, the fixing of the sword in the forked poles seems to correspond to Chrétien's assertion that the *Pont de l'Epée* was fixed in two tree trunks on opposite sides of the river. Another feature possibly derived from Irish saga is the two phantom lions, for in Version III of *The Wooing of Emer* the glen crossed by the rising bridge was filled with spectral monsters.[15]

Chapter XXXV

THE COMBAT AT THE FORD

VERSES 734–940

On his way to the Sword Bridge Lancelot reached a ford in the midst of a plain. It was guarded by a knight, accompanied by a damsel on a palfrey. Three times the guardian of the ford called to Lancelot across the water, forbidding him to pass over. But Lancelot was deaf, lost in contemplation of his lady. His steed, however, leapt into the ford and began to drink. The guardian knight charged at him and knocked him into the river. Lancelot, recovering himself, remonstrated and seizing his opponent so roughly forced him to concede a joust on even terms, with the result that it became the turn of the ford knight to take a bath. The fight continued. Lancelot was the victor, but at the plea of his opponent granted him his life, and at the prayer of the damsel permitted him to go free.

WE HAVE ALREADY OBSERVED in connection with Erec's victory over the robber knights that a ford combat was among the stock features of the *Matière de Bretagne*.[1] But Lancelot's encounter with the nameless knight at the water passage lacks the most distinctive details of the formula. There is no thorn tree near by; there is nothing uncanny about the knight or his steed; Lancelot does not lead the animal away. The only interest which Chrétien seems to have found in the episode is that it permitted him to display Lancelot's absorption in thoughts of love, illustrating one of the cardinal doctrines of *amour courtois*, and

[12] *Romanic Review*, IV, 187.   [13] Cross and Slover, *op. cit.*, p. 386.   [14] *Ibid.*, p. 168.
[15] Thurneysen, *op. cit.*, p. 389, n. 3.   [1] Cf. Chap. XVIII.

his magnanimity toward a vanquished foe. Two details of the ford-combat tradition, however, Chrétien seems to have preserved: Lancelot's horse was drinking at the ford when his master was challenged; the guardian of the passage had a damsel in his company. Both these details occur in the version of the ford adventure in the *Didot Perceval*,[2] and this version, which we saw was steeped in Welsh mythic lore,[3] is not likely to have borrowed them from the *Charrette*. The correspondences lend a slight plausibility to the view that Chrétien and the *Didot Perceval* had a remote common source for the ford combat.

Chapter XXXVI

THE AMOROUS HOSTESS

VERSES 946–1292

After parting from the guardian of the ford, Lancelot met a fair damsel, who without ado offered him lodging on condition he would lie with her. He accepted, though with reluctance, and accompanied her to her home. A drawbridge was lowered to let them pass in, but no servitors met them as they rode into the hall. Lancelot dismounted and his hostess provided him with a mantle. A table was laid ready with lighted candles, and the two, after washing their hands, sat down to eat and drink. Throughout all this no person was visible. After their repast, when Lancelot sought the damsel to keep his promise, he heard her cry out and spied her in a room about to be assaulted by a knight. Two other knights and four serjanz, armed with axes, stood at the door, barring his way to her. With extraordinary agility Lancelot dodged their blows, caught up one of the axes, placed himself between her bed and the wall, and dared them to attack. The damsel then calmly dismissed the knights and serjanz, who belonged to her household, and they obeyed. Then she lay down on a bed in the hall, and Lancelot, true to his promise, took his place beside her. But his heart was still faithful to Guenievre, and he turned his back and uttered no word. Finding him cold to her charms, the amorous damsel politely took leave and retired to her own chamber.

B OTH Foerster and Kittredge have recognized the gross ineptitude of this episode.[1] Nothing could be more fatuous than to represent Lancelot, who is ready to undergo any humiliation or peril for the

---

[2] Ed. Roach, pp. 195 f. Cf. also Wauchier's version, C. Potvin, *Perceval le Gallois*, IV, 134–40.
[3] Cf. Chap. XVIII and *Mod. Phil.*, XLIII (1945), 63–71.
[1] *Karrenritter*, ed. W. Foerster, p. 370. Kittredge, *Study of Gawain and the Green Knight*, pp. 263 f. Kittredge's explanation of the story is valueless since he failed to analyze the elements. Cf. *PMLA*, XLVII (1932), 337; *Journ. of Eng. and Germ. Phil.*, XLII (1943), 149–84.

Queen's sake, as agreeing to enter the bed of a strange woman rather than forego the comfort of a night's shelter. It is even more preposterous that this offence, which compromised his fidelity to the Queen far more than his momentary hesitation to mount the cart, is never held against him by the sensitive dame. The episode on the face of it is a stereotype which Chrétien has failed to reconcile either with common sense or the *san* of his romance.

On analysis it proves to be an unique combination of three motifs: (1) a visit to an empty castle, where a table is spread with food; (2) an assignation which is interrupted by one or more men with axes; (3) a hospitable chatelaine, whose seductions are resisted by the hero.

The first motif is fairly common, occurring, for instance, in the Brandelis adventure in *Le Conte del Graal,* the *Vengeance Raguidel, Historia Meriadoci,* and Andreas Capellanus' *De amore.*[2] That this feature is of Celtic origin can hardly be questioned since it appears in *The Voyage of Maelduin,*[3] of which the text is of the eleventh century at latest. "The voyagers landed [on an island], and went through the whole house without meeting anyone. But they saw in one large room an ornamented couch . . . and in each of the other rooms was a larger one . . . and there was a cup of crystal on a little table before each couch. They found abundance of food and ale, and they ate and drank till they were satisfied."

In several versions of the visit to the empty castle a gigantic intruder suddenly makes his appearance and attacks the hero, and it is probably this sequel which has suggested amalgamation with the second traditional motif, a visit to a castle where the hero and an amorous chatelaine are interrupted in their love-making by the attack of one or more men armed with axes. One form of this second motif is elaborated in Chrétien's *Conte del Graal.*[4]

Gauvain meets the King of Cavalon out hunting and is sent by him to his castle with a message to the chatelaine, the King's sister, that she show as much love to the stranger as she ever showed to any knight. The lady proves to be very beautiful and is disposed to follow her brother's instructions, so that presently she and Gauvain are kissing and making great joy. They are attacked by the townsfolk and by certain *vilains* armed with axes and *jusarmes* (long-handled axes). The lovers defend themselves, oddly enough, by hurling large chessmen, and are finally rescued by the arrival of the King of Cavalon and his vassal, Guingambresil.

[2] Potvin, *Perceval le Gallois,* III, 253 f. Raoul de Houdenc, *Vengeance Raguidel,* ed. M. Friedwagner, vss. 713 ff. *Historia Meriadoci,* ed. Bruce, pp. 33–35. Andreas, *De Amore,* ed. A. Pagès, p. 155. For other examples cf. *Revue celt.,* XXXI (1910), 463, n. 1.
[3] P. W. Joyce, *Old Celtic Romances* (1920), pp. 124 f. On the influence of the Irish *imrama* on Arthurian romance cf. *Romania,* LIX (1933), 557.
[4] Ed. Hilka, vss. 5706–6087. On this episode cf. Chap. LXXII and *PMLA,* XLVIII (1933), 1024–9.

Another form of the motif is preserved in Malory's Book of Gareth.[5]
The hero, who is nicknamed Beaumayns, is welcomed by Gryngamor and his
sister, Dame Lyones, to his castle in the isle of Avylyon.[6] The lady is very beautiful. Beaumayns falls head over heels in love with her, and she, with her brother's
encouragement, reciprocates his advances. Kisses are followed by an assignation
in bed. The lovers are interrupted by a knight with a gysarme in his hand and
many lights about him. Beaumayns smites off his head, but Dame Lyones' sister
restores it to his shoulders, and he departs whole. A second assignation between
Beaumayns and Lyones is likewise interrupted when the knight with the gysarme enters, a great light shining before and behind him. Again Beaumayns decapitates him and hews his head into many pieces. And again Lyones' sister
restores the mysterious intruder and he departs.

That these two stories are fundamentally the same is shown by the following common elements: the host who is lord of Cavalon or of a castle
in the isle of Avylyon; his commending the hero to his sister's love; the kissing and embracing; the attack by one or more men with axes; the names
Gryngamor and Guingambresil.[7] It is significant that both tales suggest
the same origin for the motif of the attack. For the *vilains* with their
jusarmes recall the *vilain* with his *jusarme* who proposes the beheading
test to Gauvain in *Le Mule Sans Frein*,[8] and who replaces his head after
Gauvain has cut it off and reappears the next day intact. Now the original
of this *vilain,* as Kittredge proved beyond peradventure,[9] was Curoi mac
Dairi, who appeared with his ax in the guise of a *bachlach,* or churl, at
the court of Ulster, proposed the Beheading Test, and, though his head
was cut off, was able to replace it and to reappear the next day intact.[10]
The knight who assailed Beaumayns with his gysarme likewise suggests
the same Irish origin, for he, like Curoi, submits to decapitation, resumes
his head, and returns intact later. Furthermore, there are details in this
story of Beaumayns which clinch its connection with the sagas of Curoi.
For both Beaumayns and Cuchulainn vainly endeavor to prevent the
restoration of the ax-bearer's head by chopping it in pieces.[11] Besides,
whereas Beaumayns' assailant is accompanied by a mysterious light blazing about him, Curoi replies to the taunt that he will burn the house down,
with the words: "However tall I may be, the whole household shall have
light, and yet the house shall not be burned." [12] Malory has evidently preserved in his description of the knight with the gysarme a trace of Curoi's
solar nature.[13] It is most important for our particular episode to note that

[5] Bk. VII, chaps. 20–23. Ed. Sommer, I, 244–50. Cf. *PMLA*, XLVIII, 1000–1007, 1021–23.
[6] The location of the castle is given in Malory, ed. Sommer, I, 255.
[7] On the relation of these names cf. *PMLA*, XLVIII, 1021–27.
[8] Paien de Maisières, *Damoisele à la Mule,* ed. B. Orlowski, vss. 504–633.
[9] Kittredge, *op. cit.,* pp. 44 f. Kittredge's genealogy is, of course, quite mistaken. Cf. *PMLA.*
XLVIII, 1004.   [10] Kittredge, *op. cit.,* pp. 10–13.   [11] *Ibid.,* p. 13.   [12] *Ibid.,* p. 11.
[13] Loomis, *Celtic Myth,* p. 49. *PMLA,* XLVII (1932), 321–23; LVI (1941), 892.

Curoi not only appears as a *bachlach* with an ax to propose the Beheading Test, but also in the form of a *bachlach* attacks Cuchulainn by night in his own fortress.[14] More than that, on this occasion Curoi's wife has been entertaining Cuchulainn and his companions with special care at Curoi's request, and Zimmer and Miss Buchanan [15] have shrewdly surmised that Blathnat's hospitality towards her lover Cuchulainn went considerably beyond the provision of refreshing drinks and good beds. Can there be any reasonable doubt that the ultimate original of the four *serjanz* who attacked Lancelot by night with *haches* in the midst of his affair with the amorous chatelaine was Curoi, with his dreaded ax, who attacked Cuchulainn by night in the fortress where he was being entertained by his mistress Blathnat?

The chaste behavior of Lancelot, however, remains to be accounted for, since there is no such scruple to be observed in the behavior of Beaumayns and Gauvain in the castles of Gryngamor and the King of Cavalon, nor is it at all likely that Cuchulainn was ever so self-restrained in his relations with Blathnat. Of course, one might guess that Chrétien arbitrarily altered the tradition rather than permit Lancelot to violate his fidelity to Guenievre. But this surmise is demonstrably mistaken, for everything goes to show that a third traditional motif has been injected into the story, that of the hospitable chatelaine whose seductions are resisted by the hero. The surviving Celtic form of this motif we have already met in the mabinogi of *Pwyll*,[16] and may be briefly summarized as follows:

Pwyll meets Arawn, King of Annwn, out hunting. Arawn sends Pwyll to his palace on the understanding that Pwyll will share his wife's couch. Arawn's wife makes Pwyll welcome and feasts him, but when that night they go to bed, "he turns his face towards the bedside and his back towards her. From that time till the morning he said to her not one word."

Now it may be coincidence that Lancelot's hostess also feasts him and that when finally he comes to her couch, his behavior is thus described: "He takes good heed not to touch her, and, keeping his distance, turns his back on her and says not a word. . . . Never does he look at her or in any other direction." [17] But there cannot be accident in the fact that this episode in *Pwyll* has also left its imprint on the two versions of the liaison interrupted by men with axes which we have just examined. Pwyll's meeting with Arawn, King of Faerye, as he goes hunting obviously parallels Gauvain's meeting with the huntsman King of Cavalon; and the subsequent reception of Pwyll by Arawn's hospitable wife parallels the reception

[14] *PMLA*, XLVIII, 1005 f. *Feast of Bricriu*, ed. G. Henderson, pp. 101–15. Notice that on p. 108 the *scath* who attacked Cuchulainn is addressed as "bachlaig" and is thus further identified with Curoi, the *bachlach*.
[15] *Sitzungsberichte d. Kön. preuss. Akad. d. Wiss.*, 1911, I, 205. *PMLA*, XLVII, 326 f.
[16] Loth, *Mabinogion*, 2d ed., I, 81–88.   [17] *Karrenritter*, vss. 1228–34.

of Gauvain by the King of Cavalon's sister. Moreover, in the course of our study of *Erec* [18] we discovered that Arawn's wife was the original of Morgain, the fay of Avalon. This, of course, explains why the huntsman, counterpart of Arawn, who sent Gauvain to his castle was King of Cavalon, and why Beaumayns' analogous adventure took place in a castle in the isle of Avylyon. We have seen,[19] moreover, that the amorous Dame Lyones was originally the Lady of Lothian, Morgain. The presence of Gryngamor is explained likewise by the fact that he was "sire d'Avalon" and the lover of Morgain.[20] Finally, we know that a persistent tradition represented Lancelot as spurning the blandishments of Morgain.[21] It is no freak of chance, therefore, that Lancelot's chaste conduct in the castle of the amorous hostess resembles so closely the conduct of Pwyll with Arawn's wife, who was the Welsh original of Morgain.

Chapter XXXVII

THE CEMETERY

VERSES 1841–1966

Accompanied by his amorous hostess of the night before, Lancelot came to a monastery (mostier) and a cemetery beside it. While the damsel remained outside, an old monk led the knight into the cemetery and showed him many beautiful tombs, on which were carved the names of those destined to be buried in them: "Here Gauvain will lie, here Looys and here Yvain." One marble sarcophagus was larger and richer than the rest, and on Lancelot's inquiry the monk declared that it would require the strength of seven men to raise the lid of stone, and that he who succeeded in doing so would set free the captives in the land whence neither serf nor noble could issue forth. Lancelot easily performed the feat and was assured by the astonished monk that the tomb was destined for him who would liberate the captives from the realm whence no one escaped. Lancelot departed without revealing his name. While the damsel was mounting her palfrey to follow him, the monk begged her to reveal the name of her escort, but she had to confess her ignorance.

---

[18] Cf. Chap. XVII.   [19] Cf. *supra*, pp. 86, 181.   [20] *Erec*, vss. 1954–57.
[21] Cf. *supra*, p. 195. Another possible link with Morgain is found in the extraordinary employment by Gauvain and the sister of the King of Cavalon of chessmen as missile weapons (*Conte del Graal*, ed. Hilka, vss. 6000–11). For in Wauchier's continuation of *Le Conte del Graal* Perceval enters a mysterious castle, is mated by automatically moving chessmen. A richly dressed maiden rises from the moat beside the castle, and Perceval becomes violently enamoured of her, as Gauvain does of the King of Cavalon's sister. We learn later that she has built the castle, is over a hundred years old, has been trained by Morgain la Fée and has received the chessboard and chessmen as a gift from her. Cf. J. L. Weston, *Legend of Perceval*, I, 107 f., 111; *PMLA*, L (1935), 25–35; *Didot-Perceval*, ed. Roach, pp. 52–56.

THE ADVENTURE of Lancelot among the tombs is one of the many which leave the reader mystified. No wonder that Lancelot asked: "What purpose do these tombs here serve?" and the monk's reply, that Lancelot had read the inscriptions and therefore knew what they said, is hardly enlightening. Why and by whom were these sepultures prepared with such foresight for knights of the Round Table? Who had anticipated the arrival of the deliverer of the captives in the land of Goirre and considerately built for him a magnificent tomb? Is it a felicitous notion that this deliverer should be faced with a reminder of his mortality? A clue to the original form and purport of this episode was discovered by Webster, who called attention to a parallel adventure in Ulrich von Zatzikhoven's *Lanzelet*.[1]

The hero, on his way to the encounter with the formidable Iweret, comes to the little monastery of the Sorrowful Fief. The abbot receives him hospitably and tells him that Iweret is the overlord of the monastery and causes all those whom he slays to be buried there. Lanzelet goes on to his fight with Iweret and kills him. The inmates of the monastery bring a bier and inter the body. As Lanzelet rides away with Iweret's daughter, a maiden on a white mule meets them, brings the hero greetings from his foster mother, the Queen of Meydelant, and tells him his name.

Webster rightly commented on the burial of knights at the monastery: "Therefore there probably were tombs, though they are not mentioned." [2] Thus an earlier and fuller form of Ulrich's story would present the following parallels with Chrétien: the hero, Lancelot; his arrival at a "mostier"; a friendly monk, who acts as his informant; tombs destined for the knights of the Round Table; a damsel who is much concerned about Lancelot's name. In this earlier version Lancelot would see the tombs of his hapless comrades, inscribed with their names, and an empty tomb awaiting him in the event of his defeat. The situation would make sense and would supply an artistically ominous prelude to the fearsome combat with Iweret.

We do not need for the support of this view to rely on any hypothetical reconstruction, for, transferred to another hero, the required formula for the tomb adventure is found in *Les Merveilles de Rigomer*.[3] It may thus be summarized.

Cliges, riding at adventure, sees a cemetery and a chapel. Within the chapel he discovers thirty sarcophagi, each containing a corpse. Another sarcophagus awaits the body of an apparently lifeless knight, and still another is being carved by four masons. Cliges alights at a hall near by, and is told by two youths that the cemetery is called "Astres Maleïs," and that every stranger knight is slain

[1] *Harvard Studies and Notes*, XVI (Cambridge, 1933), 206 f. Cf. Piper, *Höfische Epik*, II, 182–85. [2] *Loc. cit.*, p. 206, n. 16.
[3] Ed. W. Foerster, I (Dresden, 1908), vss. 9136–9490.

and placed in a sarcophagus. His own awaits him. After a sumptuous meal in the hall with knights and ladies, Cliges is conducted to the body of the lifeless knight in the chapel, and draws out a lance. Whereupon the knight comes to life, and a fierce battle ensues. Finally Cliges plunges the shaft of the lance into his antagonist's heart, and the body is placed in the sarcophagus intended for Cliges.

It becomes obvious that Chrétien's version of the cemetery episode has lost the poignant meaning of the story as we find it in *Lanzelet* and the *Merveilles*. Foreign and discordant matter has been introduced, and the combat, to which the sight of the tombs should form a prelude, is omitted.

Less direct but still cogent evidence for this interpretation of the adventure is supplied by a comparison between Lanzelet's fight with Iweret and Erec's fight with Mabonagrain.[4] In both the hero is given warnings and lengthy instructions by a venerable host; the scene of the combat is an ever-blossoming wood, filled with healing herbs and singing birds; the fight takes place near a conspicuous tree; the antagonist bears red arms; a lovely maiden is present; and, needless to say, the hero is victorious. Now just as Lanzelet's venerable host informs him that all Iweret's victims have been buried in the monastic precincts, and, as we have been led to infer, points out their tombs, including one for the hero himself, so Erec's venerable host, Eurain, makes it clear that the heads on stakes are those of Mabonagrain's victims and that the empty stake awaits Erec's head.[5] Can there be a doubt that the adventure at the cemetery originally served the same artistic purpose as the convention of heads on stakes which occurs so frequently in Arthurian romance?—it sent thrills of anticipatory terror down the spines of the hearers or readers. The gruesome array of heads, as we know, was surely a Celtic motif,[6] and the array of tombs would seem to have developed from it as an effective, though less repulsive, variation.

But a number of features in Chrétien's cemetery episode still remain without explanation. Why do the inscriptions on the tombs indicate that they are yet to be occupied by knights of the Round Table, when we should expect all but one to be filled with bodies of the slain? Whence comes the motif of lifting a slab of marble as a test of prowess? Why is the hero recognized as the deliverer of captives from bondage? Why is there such curiosity as to his name? None of these features is accounted for by Lanzelet's visit to the monastery of the Sorrowful Fief, nor is there any close and repeated correspondence with any other of the many tomb and cemetery episodes in Arthurian romance.[7]

[4] Piper, *op. cit.*, II, 182–85. *Erec*, vss. 5547–6007.   [5] *Erec*, vss. 5774–814.
[6] Cf. *supra*, p. 176.
[7] For references to other tomb and cemetery adventures cf. L. H. Loomis in *Mod. Lang. Rev.*, XXVI (1931), 408, n. 3; *Perlesvaus*, ed. Nitze and others, II, 220 f., 306–09. Mrs. Loomis offers strong evidence to show that the story of the tombs of Chanaam and his brothers, which begins in the *Estoire del S. Graal* (Sommer, *Vulgate Version*, I, 266–68), is carried on in the

Miss Marian Speyer pointed out [8] the source of all these features in the tradition of the Siege Perilous, of which a late version appears in *La Queste del Saint Graal*.[9]

On the morning of Pentecost all the empty seats at the Round Table are found to be inscribed with the names of their rightful occupants: "Here ought such a one to sit." There is also a large empty seat, the Siege Perilous, with an inscription saying that it is to be filled that day. The inscription is then covered over with a cloth. Later, when Arthur and the companions of the Round Table have all taken their places, Galaad enters in vermeil arms under the escort of an old man. The latter announces that this is the Knight Desired, through whom the marvels of this and strange lands will come to an end. He leads Galaad to the Siege Perilous, lifts the cloth, and reveals the letters: "Here is the seat of Galaad." The young knight sits down and provokes great curiosity as to his identity. Gauvain proclaims that God has sent him "to deliver our land from the great wonders and strange adventures which have so often and so long taken place." Galaad then undertakes to draw a sword from a marble block, which Gauvain and Perceval have tried to do in vain. On the pommel there is lettering to the effect that only the best knight can draw forth the sword; but Galaad with ease extracts it from the marble block. A damsel on a palfrey declares that Lancelot is no longer the best knight in the world.

Here are counterparts for many features of the cemetery episode in the *Charrette,* including those hitherto unexplained, namely: the empty seats inscribed with the names of those destined to occupy them; the larger empty seat, of which the occupant's name is concealed, but which is destined for one who is to be the deliverer of his people; the entrance of the hero under the escort of an old man; the revelation that the larger seat is to be occupied by him; the marked curiosity as to his identity; the accomplishment of a feat of strength involving a huge stone; the damsel on a palfrey, who declares that no man living is his equal. These seven features, though somewhat modified and re-arranged, are recognizable in Chrétien's story of Lancelot's visit to the cemetery. The blending of two such originally dissimilar traditions as those represented by Lanzelet's visit to the monastery of the Sorrowful Fief and Galaad's adventure of the Siege Perilous was probably suggested by the fact that in both traditions the hero enters under the escort of an old man and sees the names of Arthurian knights inscribed, among them his own. Because of this accidental resemblance some audacious *conteur* or romancer produced the combination which Chrétien found in his *matière,* and which was probably as unsatisfying to him as it is perplexing to us.

Miss Speyer strengthened her hypothesis by showing further that the

Vulgate Lancelot (*ibid.,* IV, 339–41), and is abruptly concluded in the *Queste* (*ibid.,* VI, 184), derives from Irish traditions of standing stones.
[8] *Romanic Review,* XXVIII (1937), 195 ff.
[9] Sommer, *op. cit.,* VI, 5–11. *Queste del Saint Graal,* ed. A. Pauphilet, pp. 4–13.

coming of Galaad to Arthur's court was based on the ancient Irish legend of the coming of Lug to the court of Nuada, as related in *The Second Battle of Moytura,* and by showing that on three points wherein Chrétien's tale of Lancelot among the tombs differs from the tale of Galaad's coming, it reproduces the Irish legend.[10] The relation between the Galaad and the Lug episodes is assured by the fact that though they have followed divergent paths for centuries they retain in common the assembled court, the empty seat awaiting a worthy occupant, the arrival of a youth "with a red color on him," [11] his taking the seat, the demonstration of his superior strength by means of a stone, the recognition by the warriors that this is their destined leader, the king's relinquishing his couch to the stranger, the demand that each warrior should undertake a task, the list of warriors who do so. It is highly significant that Lug does not extract a sword from a stone [12] but raises and throws a stone which required fourscore oxen to move, much as Lancelot raises a slab requiring the strength of seven mighty men to lift. Again it is significant that Lug is shown by the stone test to be the hero who could deliver the Tuatha De Danann from the bondage which they suffered from the Fomorians, while Lancelot is proved by the stone test to be he who "will bring forth the men and women who are captives in the land"—a closer approximation than we find in the Galaad story. Finally, it is probably not an accident that whereas the name Galaad bears no relation to that of Lug, Lancelot's name is derived through the Welsh Llauynnauc or Lleminawc from Lug's epithet Loinnbheimionach. Thus the ultimate derivation of Lancelot's stone-lifting feat from that of Lug is scarcely open to doubt.

The hypotheses of Webster and Miss Speyer, though seemingly inconsistent, are not so in reality. They are complementary and between them account for nearly everything in Lancelot's visit to the cemetery.

[10] *Romanic Review,* XXVIII, 199–203. For French translation of *Second Battle of Moytura* cf. H. D'Arbois de Jubainville, *L'Epopée celtique en Irlande,* pp. 418–22; for most accurate translation (in German) cf. *Anthropos,* XXVI (1931), 445 ff. For English trans. cf. Cross and Slover, *Ancient Irish Tales,* pp. 35–37.
[11] R. S. Loomis, *Celtic Myth,* p. 46. For red as a solar color cf. p. 192.
[12] On this motif, which the author of the *Queste* substituted for the stone-lifting, cf. E. Willson, *Middle English Legends of Visits to the Other World and Their Relation to the Metrical Romances* (Chicago, 1917), p. 3.

Chapter XXXVIII

THE PASSAGE OF THE BRETESCHE

VERSES 2206-50

On his way to the Sword Bridge Lancelot arrived before a bretesche, *or wooden tower, where there was always a man on guard. A knight issued from it, accompanied by "serjanz qui tenoient haches tranchanz." Lancelot unhorsed him, and the servants deliberately avoided striking Lancelot with their axes. So the hero passed on his way.*

SEEING the role which *serjanz* with *haches* played in the episode of the Amorous Hostess, one is justified in suspecting here again a traditional motif.

In the twelfth century it is pretty clear that *bretesche* meant a wooden tower of defense.[1] Let me quote from Wace's *Roman de Rou* (1160-74): "Entor out bretesches levées, Bien planchies et kernelées." [2] Now in the Arthurian sculpture at Modena cathedral, carved early in the century, a castle is represented, with a central donjon, a surrounding wall, a moat, and two *bretesches,* well made of boards and battlemented.[3] Before one of them stands a churl, brandishing a sort of pick, apparently ready to defend the entrance against Arthur and his warriors. Several facts make it likely that the sculpture is related to Lancelot's adventure at the *bretesche.*

It depicts a version of the abduction and rescue of Arthur's Queen—the main theme of the *Charrette.*[4] Though it depicts the defender of the *bretesche* as a *vilain,* not as a *serjant,* we have just seen that the *vilains* who attacked Gauvain in the King of Cavalon's castle correspond to the *serjanz* who attacked Lancelot in the castle of the amorous chatelaine, and it seems probable that *serjanz* have likewise replaced *vilains* in the adventure of the *bretesche.* At the same time we saw that one original attacker with an ax had been multiplied to four, and a similar multiplication seems probable here. One might reasonably guess that, as on the Modena archivolt, the original warder of the *bretesche* was a single churl wielding an ax.

This conjecture is rendered plausible by the Welsh evidence. In one of

[1] H. Schumacher, *Das Befestigungswesen in der altfranzösischen Literatur* (Göttingen, 1906), p. 12. The word also had the meaning of a projecting wooden gallery on a wall. *Ibid.,* p. 45. C. Enlart, *Manuel d'archéologie française,* deuxième partie (2d ed.; Paris, 1932), II, 540, 542.
[2] Wace, *Roman de Rou,* ed. H. Andresen (Heilbronn, 1877-79), II, vss. 4327 f.
[3] R. S. and L. H. Loomis, *Arthurian Romances in Medieval Art,* pp. 32-34, Fig. 8. On date cf. also *Romanic Review,* XXXII (1941), 22-26.
[4] R. S. and L. H. Loomis, *op. cit.,* pp. 34 f. Nitze and Cross, *Lancelot and Guenevere,* p. 23.

the oldest of Arthurian texts, a poem in the Black Book of Carmarthen,[5] we find a certain gatekeeper (*porthawr*), who refuses entrance to Arthur and his warriors, including Kei and Lluch Llauynnauc, the original of Lancelot du Lac [6]—a situation which reminds us somewhat of the scene on the Modena sculpture, where the churl defends the *bretesche* against Arthur and his warriors including Che. The gatekeeper of the Welsh poem is called Glewlwyd Gavaelvawr, that is "Bold-Gray of the Mighty Grasp." [7] Now Glewlwyd, according to *Kulhwch,* enters Arthur's hall and declares that though he has been in Great and Little India, in Europe and Africa and the islands of Corsica, and was present when Arthur conquered Greece, he has never seen a man to equal Kulhwch.[8] Now it can hardly be a coincidence that according to *Bricriu's Feast* Curoi entered the hall of the King of Ulster in a gray mantle, and the might of his grasp may be inferred from the fact that each finger was as thick as another person's wrist.[9] He declared that though he had been in Europe, Africa, Asia, Greece, and the islands of Gades, he had never found a man to keep faith with him.[10] Curoi, then, like Glewlwyd Gavaelvawr is a bold, gray man with a mighty grasp and he uses the same formula under somewhat similar circumstances. It is a fair conjecture that Glewlwyd is a Welsh counterpart of Curoi. If we substitute Curoi, the churl with his great ax, for Glewlwyd in the role of a gatekeeper, refusing entrance to Arthur and his warriors including Kei, we have a picture amazingly close to that presented by the sculptor at Modena. For here is a churl, brandishing a pick-like weapon, before the entrance to a castle, defending it evidently against Arthur and his warriors, including Che. It is not likely that such a similarity can be due to chance alone.

Accordingly, we may well believe that the figure of Curoi, with his gray mantle, his mighty hands, his formidable ax, was known in Wales as Glewlwyd Gavaelvawr, as well as by other names. He acquired a new role as a *porthawr,* or gatewarden, sometimes guarding his own house, as in the Black Book poem, sometimes guarding Arthur's palace, as in *Kulhwch.* On one occasion the Bold Gray Man of the Mighty Grasp stood at the gate of his own house, denying entrance to Arthur, Kei, and the original of Lancelot. This is evidently the legend which was caught up into the miscellany of incidents connected with the abduction and rescue of Arthur's Queen. It was reflected with some clarity in the Modena

[5] Malory, *Morte d'Arthur,* Everyman ed., I, pp. xviii–xx.   [6] Cf. Chap. XXVI.
[7] C. Guest, *Mabinogion,* ed. A. Nutt (London, 1904), p. 373. On the importance of the gate-keeper or porter in a Welsh royal household cf. A. W. Wade-Evans, *Welsh Medieval Law* (Oxford, 1909), p. 178.
[8] *Mabinogion,* ed. Nutt, p. 105. Loth, *Mabinogion,* 2d ed., I, 255 f.
[9] *Feast of Bricriu,* ed. Henderson, p. 117. Note that the word translated "dun" is *lachtna,* which Dineen, *Irish-English Dictionary* (new ed.; Dublin, 1927) explains as "grey, dun." H. D'Arbois de Jubainville, *L'Epopée celtique en Irlande,* pp. 143 f.
[10] *Feast of Bricriu,* ed. Henderson, p. 119. D'Arbois de Jubainville, p. 145.

sculpture, and very obscurely in the combat of Lancelot with the ax-bearing *serjanz* at the *bretesche*.

Chapter XXXIX
LANCELOT'S FAERY FOSTER MOTHER

VERSES 2347–62

After passing the bretesche, *Lancelot rode on, accompanied by two youths. A man invited them to spend the night at his house, and when they followed him into a castle a gate was lowered behind them, and as they still pursued, a portcullis dropped in front of them. They thought themselves victims of enchantment. So Lancelot looked at the finger ring which had been given him by the fay who had nurtured him in his infancy, and which had the virtue of freeing the wearer from spells. Gazing at it, he perceived that he and his companions were not confined by any magic art, and drawing their swords, they hacked their way out of the tower.*

WE HAVE ALREADY SEEN in the lengthy discussion of Erec's treatment of Enide that one of the stock motifs attached to Morgain la Fée was her gift of a magic ring to her foster son or lover.[1] We can now, since we have recognized Morgain in Dame Lyones,[2] add another example in the ring which Lyones gave to Gareth and which had the triple virtue of increasing her own beauty, enabling him to change the color of his arms, and preserving him from loss of blood.[3] We shall later discover still another instance, Laudine's present to Yvain of a ring which, so long as he was a true lover, preserved him from prison and loss of blood. The particular form of the tradition which Chrétien employed in his cursory reference to the ring bestowed on Lancelot by his faery foster mother is given most fully in the *Vulgate Lancelot*,[4] where we read that the Dame du Lac, on the departure of the young hero from her home, placed on his finger a ring with the assurance that it had "the power to reveal and make visible all enchantments."

The fact that Lancelot in the present episode employed the talisman when trapped between two lowered gateways suggests that we have here a reminiscence of a far fuller and evidently traditional scene in *Yvain*, where the son of Urien is trapped likewise between two portcullises in a

[1] Cf. *supra*, pp. 123 f.   [2] Cf. *supra*, pp. 86, 181.
[3] Malory, Bk. VII, Chap. 27. Ed. Sommer, I, 257 f.
[4] Sommer, *Vulgate Version*, III, p. 123, ll. 31–42.

gateway and escapes from his peril through the potency of a ring given him by Lunete.[5] Chrétien's handling of the situation in the *Charrette* is so casual and unrealistic that we may surmise that he is retelling a feeble and garbled form of the adventure which he was later to find in the source of *Yvain*.

Chapter XL

BAUDEMAGUZ

VERSES 3156–4083

King Baudemaguz of Goirre was watching from a strong tower as Lancelot crossed the Sword Bridge. He was a man of strict scruples, courtesy, and loyalty. He endeavored to dissuade his son Meleagant, who stood beside him, from contesting the possession of the Queen against Lancelot and urged him to receive the unknown knight with courtesy. When Meleagant refused to do so, Baudemaguz rode down to meet Lancelot, offered him ointment for his wounds, and promised him the use of excellent arms and a horse when he was recovered and ready to meet Meleagant in battle. That night the King sent a surgeon to treat Lancelot's wounds and the next day again tried to persuade his son to make peace, but in vain. When the battle went against his son, Baudemaguz arranged for the deliverance of the Queen and a truce. Keu informed Lancelot that Baudemaguz had shown him also every kindness and had carefully guarded the Queen from any molestation by Meleagant. In other scenes Baudemaguz maintains the same character of friendliness and honor toward Lancelot and Guenievre and the same opposition toward his son's folly and violence.

VARIOUS EXPLANATIONS have been offered of the name and the personality of Baudemaguz,[1] but only one, I believe, has an abundance of corroborative facts in its favor.[2] A study of these facts reveals that the first syllable Bau- must be a corruption of the name Bran, in part· at least through scribal error. For *u* and *n* are frequently indistinguishable, and MS E, verses 3157 and 5158, furnishes an illustration in the form Bondemaguz. The omission of *r* is exemplified by variants of the name of a Saxon king, found in manuscripts of the Vulgate cycle: Brannague,

---

[5] *Yvain*, vss. 900–1143.
[1] Rhys, *Arthurian Legend*, pp. 344 f. *Zts. f. franz. Sprache u. Lit.*, XXVIII, "Abhandlungen," 12. A. B. Hopkins, *Influence of Wace on the Arthurian Romances of Crestien de Troies*, p. 57. A. C. L. Brown, *Origin of the Grail Legend*, p. 436.
[2] *Romania*, LXIII (1937), 383 ff. H. Newstead, *Bran the Blessed*, pp. 135 ff.

Bannagues, Branmague, Bamague, Bonegue; [3] and other instances could be supplied. Not only could Bran become Bau, but it is astonishing to find that again and again parallels occur between Baudemaguz and persons whose names contain the element *Bran*.

We have already seen that the King of Brandigan in *Erec* is one of these. He dwells in an island fortress, only to be entered across "a very deep, wide, and roaring water." [4] So Baudemaguz dwells in a fortress cut off by "the treacherous, violent and roaring water . . . perilous and deep." [5] From the castle of Brandigan "no man returned who sought adventure there," and again, "no man could escape thence alive." [6] From the realm of Baudemaguz "no stranger returns," "no man escapes." The King of Brandigan's nephew fights Erec beside a sycamore in an ever-blossoming *vergier*. [7] King Baudemaguz' son fights his last battle with Lancelot beside a sycamore in an ever-green glade. [8] Both kings are very hospitable, and seem, oddly enough, to favor the heroes against their own son and nephew respectively.

There are more striking resemblances between Baudemaguz and other figures whose names contain the element *Bran*. Brandus des Illes, whose name easily resolves itself into Bran, dus des Illes, resembles Baudemaguz in that he is lord of an island fortress and holds captive many knights of Arthur's household, destined to be released by Lancelot; [9] and of this fortress too we read: "No errant knight came there who did not die or suffer imprisonment."

Baudemaguz also resembles King Brangorre in the *Vulgate Lancelot*. In the latter part of the *Charrette* Baudemaguz held a very joyous court. "It was the day of his birth, and therefore he celebrated it with a great and full attendance. Folk of many sorts had come there with him in numbers. The palace was all crowded with knights and maidens." [10] According to the *Vulgate Lancelot* [11] Baudemagus held court on the anniversary of his coronation and caused all his great barons to assemble. He had tents pitched in a meadow by reason of the great heat. Now the same text, in an earlier passage,[12] tells how King Brangorre held a great tournament on the octave of his coronation at the Chastel de la Marche, and a thousand knights and many damsels gathered there. Afterwards the King had two pavilions pitched for a banquet because of the great heat. The associa-

---

[3] Sommer, *Vulgate Version*, Index, p. 17.   [4] *Erec*, ed. Foerster (1890), vss. 5374 f.

[5] *Karrenritter*, vss. 5023–27.   [6] *Erec*, vss. 5436 f., 5463.   [7] *Erec*, vss. 5746.f., 5880 ff.

[8] *Karrenritter*, vss. 7005 ff. A curious corroboration of Meleagant's being originally a son of Bran is furnished by a 14th-century Italian ms. which tells "quomodo preliaverunt lancelotus de lachu et malgaretes regis groonç filius." A. Graf, *Miti, leggende e superstizioni del medio evo*, II, 356. Gardner (*Arthurian Legend in Italian Literature*, p. 16) says that Malgaretes is obviously the Meleagant of Chrétien's poem, and in view of the common substitution of initial *G* for *B* it is also obvious that Groonç is a corruption of Brons.

[9] Newstead, *op. cit.*, pp. 146–50.   [10] Vss. 6254–61.

[11] Newstead, p. 143.   [12] Sommer, *op. cit.*, IV, 259, 264.

tion of King Brangorre with a border castle and his holding a feast in tents were not mere figments of the French author's imagination. According to *Fouke Fitz Warin,* Chastiel Bran, now Dinas Bran, on the border of Wales, was once called "the Old March"; [13] and according to the mabinogi of *Branwen* King Bran and his brother Manawydan banqueted in pavilions; "Blessed Bran could never be contained within a house." [14] The Welsh tale thus explains the banqueting in tents by Bran's gigantic size,[15] and it is obvious that this was too absurd for the French romancers and a new and prosaic explanation was devised for the pavilions of Baudemagus and Brangorre: they served as a shelter from the heat.

All these correspondences between Baudemaguz, the King of Brandigan, Brandus des Illes, and Brangorre suggest a common derivation from Welsh legends of Bran, son of Llyr, the gigantic king of the Island of the Mighty. We have already found reason in our study of the "Joie de la Cort" episode to believe that Bran was the original of the Fisher King, whom the *Didot Perceval* calls Bron. And no tradition of French romance is more persistent than that the Fisher King was wounded and awaited the coming of a knight to heal him. If we find this same tradition linked to Baudemaguz, it should establish solidly the conclusion that he is descended from the Welsh Bran and owes to this fact the first syllable of his name. In the *Vulgate Lancelot* [16] Gauvain discovers in a white abbey a sick knight, who turns out to be Baudemagus, wounded in combat. Gauvain offers to stay with him till he is well, but the King refuses to grant the request. A few pages later we read that Lancelot discovers in the castle of a wounded knight, who can be cured only by the best knight in the world, another wounded knight, who turns out to be King Baudemagus. The King welcomes Lancelot with great joy and readily accepts his apology for not staying with him till he is well. Lancelot departs, praying that God may restore his health. Is it not manifest that all this is a more or less deliberate variation on the stereotyped formula of successive visits to the castle of the wounded King Bran, who is awaiting deliverance from his malady, and that King Bran is represented by Baudemagus?

In connection with this account of Baudemagus as a wounded knight visited by Lancelot, it should be noted that his chief city, according to the *Vulgate Lancelot,* was called Gaion or Gaihom,[17] and that his son, who dwelt with him in that city, was, of course, Meleagant. It can scarcely be a mere chance, therefore, that in the same romance there appears an aged knight named Traan, who was healed of his wounds by Lancelot and who long after entertained him hospitably, and that the name of Traan's castle

[13] *Fouke Fitz Warin,* ed. L. Brandin, p. 3. Cf. Newstead, pp. 23, 95–106; C. Oman, *Castles* (London, 1926), pp. 225–27.   [14] Loth, *Mabinogion,* 2d ed., I, 124.
[15] *Ibid.,* I, 137 f. For reflections of Bran's size in Arthurian romance cf. Newstead, pp. 71–77.
[16] Sommer, *op. cit.,* V, 219 f., 224 ff. Cf. *ibid.,* VI, 22 f.   [17] *Ibid.,* IV, 199.

was "li gays chastiaus," and the name of his son who lived with him there was Melyant.[18] That Melyant is a variant form of Meleagant is shown by Heinrich von dem Türlin's calling the abductor of Ginover "Milianz"[19] and by further considerations which will be brought out in the discussion of Melians de Lis in Chapter LXXIV. Baudemagus, the wounded knight, corresponds then to Traan (presumably a corruption of Bran), Gaion to Gai, Meleagant to Melyant.

Another link between Baudemaguz and the Arthurian counterparts of Bran is the fact that his tomb is of rare magnificence. According to *La Queste del Saint Graal*,[20] Lancelot, after departing from the Grail Castle, came to a white abbey and there beheld a very rich tomb, and approaching it perceived that it was of such fine workmanship that he knew a mighty prince lay within. He read the inscription: "Here lies King Baldemagus of Gorre . . ." He wept and made great dole for love of the King and tarried another day before departing. Shortly afterwards, we read,[21] Galaad "came to the entry of Gorre as adventure led him, until he came to the abbey where Lancelot had been and where he found the tomb which burned so marvelously." Though the author goes on to explain that this was the tomb of Symeu, yet the passage just quoted would lead one to believe that it was the tomb of Baudemaguz, King of Gorre, which Lancelot had found in an abbey.[22] Compare this with what we learn in *Perlesvaus* of the tomb of the Fisher King.[23] In a chapel of the Grail Castle it lay before the altar; "the sepulchre was very rich, crusted with precious stones." A priest and a knight informed Perlesvaus that "every night there was great brilliance of candles there, and they knew not whence they came save from God." Professor Newstead has demonstrated[24] that one of the most persistent traditions regarding the other descendants of Bran is the sanctity of their sepulchres; Ban de Benoic, Bliocadran, Gahmuret, and the Fisher King in *Sone de Nansai*—all of whom she successfully derives from Bran—were interred in holy places. It is surely a remarkable fact that Ban de Benoic was entombed in a rich monastery on a very high hill,[25] Baudemaguz was buried in a rich tomb in a white abbey,[26] and Bran the Blessed caused his head to be buried in the White Hill in London.[27]

There is a formidable array of parallels, therefore, between Baudemaguz

[18] *Ibid.*, IV, 95.   [19] J. L. Weston, *Legend of Gawain*, p. 80n.
[20] Sommer, VI, 184.   [21] *Ibid.*, VI, 185.
[22] Malory, *Morte d'Arthur*, Bk. XVII, chap. 18, says specifically that it was the tomb of King Bagdemagus.   [23] *Perlesvaus*, ed. Nitze, I, 269.
[24] *Romanic Review*, XXXVI (1945), 3-29.
[25] Sommer, III, 12, l. 30, "un moult haut tertre"; p. 16, ll. 14-25.
[26] Too much stress cannot be laid on the "blanche abeie," since of course it means a Cistercian abbey and, as M. Pauphilet showed, the author of the *Queste* has at least four other specific references to houses or monks of this order. Pauphilet, *Etudes sur la Queste del St. Graal*, pp. 54 f.   [27] Loth, *op. cit.*, I, 145, 149.

and the Arthurian counterparts of Bran—the King of Brandigan, Brandus des Illes, Brangorre, the Maimed King, Traan, the Fisher King in *Perlesvaus* and *Sone de Nansai,* Ban de Benoic, Bliocadran, and Gahmuret. Evidently the first element in the name Baudemaguz represents a scribal corruption of Bran.

If *Bau-* is a corruption of Bran, the second syllable probably is the preposition *de,* inserted through some misunderstanding—a hypothesis which gains support from the fact that a certain King Branmague appears in the *Vulgate Merlin,*[28] and his name looks like a compound of *Bran* and *Mague*(s). Such unwarranted insertions of *de* did occur, for the forms Brangorre, Brangoires, and so forth, of the *Vulgate Lancelot* are supplanted in Malory (and doubtless were already supplanted in his source) by Brandegorys.[29] Apparently someone assumed, on the analogy of such forms as Ban de Gomeret and Bran de Lis, that the second half of Brangorre's name was a place name, and so was moved to supply a *de.* A similar mistake would account for the *de* of Baudemaguz.

What of the remaining element *-maguz?* The most tempting suggestion (and I believe the right one) was put forward by Dr. Brugger [30]—that it is a corruption of the name of King Mangounz, described in *Le Lai du Cor* as "brave and courtly." We know that the compounding of two separate names into one was possible to the romancers, for Pseudo-Wauchier introduces us to a King Brangemuer, who was the son of Guingamuer and the fay Brangepart; "For this reason his name was divided in two." [31] Moreover, there is the name Guingambresil, which we shall see in our investigation of *Le Conte del Graal* is a portmanteau word, made up of Guingamor and Bercilak.[32] In this instance the names have been telescoped because, as I shall show, two stories have been combined in which Guingamor and Bercilak respectively played the part of host to Gauvain and connived at an amorous affair between that hero and the beautiful lady of the castle. Thus we see that it was possible for French romancers to combine the names of persons to whom tradition assigned somewhat similar roles. We have already seen, moreover, that the name of Mabonagrain in *Erec* is a compound of the names of two brother enchanters, called in *Le Bel Inconnu* Mabon and Evrain, in *Libeaus Desconus* Maboun and Irain.[33] This combining of two brothers into a single personage and the linking of their names to form a single name is a phenomenon which has already been recognized by M. Lot, Philipot, and Bruce.[34] It is of

[28] Cf. *supra,* n. 3.
[29] Malory, *op. cit.,* ed. H. O. Sommer, II, 156. Another instance of the insertion of *de* between the two elements of a name is Laquins de Lampadaiz in *Meraugis de Portlesguez* (ed. M. Friedwagner), vs. 2040, ms. V; vs. 4578, ms. T. Cf. *Romania,* LIV (1928), 517 f.
[30] *Zts. f. franz. Sprache u. Lit.,* XXVIII (1905), "Abhandlungen," 12 f.
[31] C. Potvin, *Perceval le Gallois,* IV, vss. 21857–71. Cf. Newstead, pp. 122–27.
[32] Cf. Chap. LXXII.   [33] Cf. *supra,* p. 178.
[34] *Romania,* XXIV (1895), 321 f.; XXV (1896), 258 ff. Bruce, *Evolution of Arthurian Romance,* I, 109, n. 16.

marked interest to us in connection with the names Baudemaguz and Branmague. Was there any similarity, any fraternal kinship between the Arthurian descendants of Bran on the one hand and King Mangounz on the other? There was, and that of a very striking nature.

1. The same adventure is localized at the courts of Amangon, Brangorre, and Bron.

According to *Meraugis de Portlesguez*,[35] the hero was brought by a dwarf to a meadow, where King Amangon was sitting before his tent. Here, according to custom, every year barons sent their daughters, and the knight who proved himself best in jousting won the right to select one of the damsels for himself and to choose husbands for the others. Meraugis proved victor over the knight who had won the contest the previous year, and thus won the right to demand an appropriately diminutive bride for the dwarf who had escorted him to Amangon's court. Urged to choose wives for the other knights, Meraugis excused himself because he had not time, requested Amangon to make a selection, and departed.

In the *Vulgate Lancelot* [36] a squire brought Bohort to a meadow, where King Brangorre was about to hold a tourney on the anniversary of his coronation. The knight who proved himself best was entitled to wed the King's daughter and to choose husbands for twelve other damsels. Bohort was pronounced victor in the tourney. A pavilion was pitched for the King, and another for Bohort and the twelve next best knights. Bohort took his seat in a chair of gold and turned red with shame. Urged to choose wives for himself and the twelve champions, Bohort excused himself on the ground that he was engaged in a quest, and asked King Brangorre to make the selection. Wives were then chosen for the twelve champions. Bohort by means of enchantment begat on King Brangorre's daughter a son Helain or Alain, of whom much is told in the quest of the Holy Grail.

In *L'Estoire del Saint Graal*,[37] Bron and Josephe with their company, arriving at a high hill, took their seats at the table of the Holy Grail, modeled on that at which Christ sat at the last supper with his twelve apostles. One seat remained vacant, for it could be occupied only by one who was "more valiant (*preudons*) than others." The next day Moys, who was declared to be "a valiant man of right good life," took the seat, and at once flaming hands cast fire upon him so that he began to burn. After the meal Bron begged Josephe to advise him about the marriage of his twelve sons. Eleven announced their desire to marry; but the twelfth, Alain, vowed virginity, and was promised the guardianship of the Grail after Josephe's death.

Despite the singular variations between these three stories, especially the absence of any chivalric features in the *Estoire* and the introduction of pious themes, the similarity can be recognized.[38] The basic tradition told

[35] Ed. Friedwagner, vss. 2220–403.   [36] Sommer, IV, 258 f., 262–67.

[37] *Ibid.*, I, 246–49. On the relation of this episode to the *Metrical Joseph* of Boron and to the Brangorre episode cf. Newstead, pp. 51–55.

[38] There are also resemblances to the tourney at Noauz in the *Charrette* (cf. Chap. XLII), to the tourney held by Tibaut in the *Conte del Graal* (cf. Chap. LXXIV), to the tourney between Baudemagus and the King of Norgales (Sommer, *op. cit.*, V, 97–102), and to the tournament at Winchester (*ibid.*, VI, 204–13).

how a knight of Arthur's fellowship came to a tourney held by King Bran or King Amangon and proved himself superior to all the other partici- pants. A table was set for him and twelve other knights who had distin- guished themselves. He took a seat of special peril and honor and turned a fiery red. The King informed him that by custom he was entitled to choose wives for himself and the twelve knights from among the damsels at the tourney. He refused the privilege, begged the King to make the choice for the other knights, and departed. It seems clear that Brangorre, whose name is given the form Brangor in the *Vulgate Merlin* and is easily resolved into Bran plus the Welsh noun *gawr,* meaning giant,[39] duplicates the role of Amangon.

2. In *Le Chevalier as Deus Espees,*[40] King Amangon is said to rule the land "whence no one returns," and this links him to several descendants of the Welsh Bran. As we have seen above, very similar phrases are applied to the kingdom of Baudemaguz, to the castle of Brandigan, and the castle of Brandus des Illes. Of the castle of Corbenic in *L'Estoire del Saint Graal,*[41] where dwelt the Maimed King, recognized by several scholars as the Welsh Bran,[42] it is said that "many a knight came there who wished to abide, but without fail no one abode there who was not found dead in the morning." Thus Amangon and the Arthurian descendants of Bran are represented as rulers over what seems to be the same land.

3. If it be thought that these equations of Amangon with Brangorre, Brandus des Illes, Baudemaguz, the Maimed King, and so forth, are due not to a traditional similarity but to the mere whims or mistakes of the romancers, we should observe that the Fisher King in *Perlesvaus* had a brother who for a time occupied his land and castle; we know from the *Didot Perceval* that the Fisher King's name was Bron,[43] and we have the following reasons to believe that his brother's name was Amangon or Mangon. This brother,[44] the King of Chastel Mortel, was the most cruel and fierce man alive, had slain many of the knights and damsels of the Roine des Puceles, and every week came to an island below her castle to do her all the damage he could. Her knights and maidens stood silent and motionless, "without other house wherein to drink or eat." Perlesvaus engaged the King of Chastel Mortel in combat and put him to flight. Now a persecuter of maidens appears in at least five stories, each time under a name which resembles Mangon. In Manessier's continuation of *Le Conte del Graal*[45] a king named Magon, Margon, or Margun men- aced a noble maiden. Gauvain came to her castle, espoused her cause,

---

[39] Though Bran is never called a giant in the Welsh texts, he was of enormous size. Note the names Gwrnach Gawr, Ogurvan Gawr, etc. Newstead, *op. cit.,* p. 54, n. 26.
[40] *Chevalier aux Deux Epées,* ed. W. Foerster (1877), vss. 12121 f.   [41] Sommer, I, 289.
[42] Listed *infra,* p. 386.   [43] *Didot-Perceval,* ed. W. Roach, p. 150.
[44] *Perlesvaus,* ed. Nitze and others, I, 176–80.
[45] Potvin, *Perceval le Gallois,* V, vss. 38114–38455.

defeated Margon, who had threatened to tear out her breasts if he could capture her, and sent him a prisoner to Arthur. In the *Vulgate Lancelot* [46] Hector came to the castle of Mangars or Marigant, who had been wont to dishonor every day a maiden of the town. Hector fought and killed Mangars, and released the lady, whom Mangars had violated, from a cave where she had spent four years. Note the subterranean abode. In the *Elucidation* [47] we find the most primitive form of the tale. King Amangon or Magon violated one of the *puceles* who issued from the wells to provide food and drink for the wayfarers, and took her golden cup away from her. As a result the land became unfruitful and the maidens retired to their underground abodes. Arthur's knights set out to avenge their wrongs; Gauwain was the first to overcome one of the ravishers of the well-maidens, and sent him to Arthur's court. In certain manuscripts of Pseudo-Wauchier's continuation of the *Conte del Graal* there is the remarkable parallel of the Pucelle au Cor d'Ivoire.[48] She was a damsel of great beauty, met by Gauvain in "the Adventurous Glade," twenty leagues from any hostel. She invited him to dine with her, blew her ivory horn, and at once a hundred youths and maidens appeared, set up tables, and produced a repast. But a knight rode up, seized the horn, and was off again. Gauvain pursued, slew the knight, and returned with the horn, to the maiden's great joy. We learn that the felon knight was named Marcarot, and that the horn possessed such virtue that whoever had it would never suffer hunger or thirst.[49] Another variant of the same tradition appears in the *Vulgate Merlin,*[50] where we read that Gavain with other knights of the Round Table came upon the Queen of Garlot beside a very beautiful spring. She swooned in the arms of some Saxons who were abducting her, and made great dole. Gavain demanded her release, but Margon, Margoun, or Marganor, the cupbearer, leader of the Saxons, refused. Gavain attacked, slew all the Saxons except Margon, who escaped, and rescued the Queen.

Though a superficial reading might lead one to conclude that these five stories displayed such differences that any basic similarity might be purely accidental, yet certain facts militate against this conclusion. It is hardly fortuitous that in the *Elucidation* the ravisher of the well-maiden and the stealer of her cup is called King Amangon; that the abductor of a lady, discovered lamenting beside a spring, was a cupbearer named Margon; that the stealer of the horn of plenty from a faery maiden was

[46] Sommer, IV, 350–54. For name forms cf. Index volume s.v. *Marigart.*
[47] Ed. A. W. Thompson (1931), vss. 29–134. Thompson has a useful discussion of the episode and of Amangon on pp. 37–50. A remarkable parallel is furnished by modern Welsh folklore. M. Trevelyan, *Folklore and Folk-Stories of Wales,* pp. 19 f.
[48] *Romanische Forschungen,* XLV (1931), 92. Bibl. Nat. fr. 12577, f. 64*v*–66*v.*
[49] F. 66*v.* "Que ia li homs quil [sic] lait o soi Naura ne fain ne froit ne soi, Ja ni ert en si estrange leu."   [50] Sommer, II, 393.

called Marcarot; that in *Le Lai du Cor* it is King Mangounz who sent to Arthur's court a testing horn, made by a fay. There is curiously converging evidence not only as to the name of this persecutor of maidens but also as to the identity of the maidens. The horn of King Mangounz, made by a fay and sent to Arthur's court, possessed exactly the property of the horn sent by Morgain la Fée to Arthur's court.[51] The Queen of Garlot, abducted by the cupbearer Margon, and found swooning beside a spring, was, according to the *Huth Merlin* and the English *Prose Merlin*,[52] Morgain la Fée. The well-maiden ravished by Amangon surely belongs to the same faery family as the *amie* of Guingamor and the sister of the Petit Chevalier, both of whom are discovered sitting beside springs and both of whom are identifiable with Morgain.[53] The Pucelle au Cor d'Ivoire also belongs to the same family as the well-maiden since she provides Gauvain with food and drink in a remote region and is robbed of her vessel; and she suggests identification with Morgain since she presents Gauvain at parting with a ring which enables him to overcome any five men—a favorite gift, as we know,[54] of the faery queen.

Surely behind all these stories of Mangon, Margon, Marcarot, Mangars, and so forth, persecuters and ravishers of maidens, there was a common tradition, and surely it is the same tradition which presents us in *Perlesvaus* with the King of Chastel Mortel as the persecuter of the Roine des Puceles. His name, therefore, was Mangon; the name of his brother, the Fisher King, would be Bran. If we combine the names of the two brothers, as, scholars agree, was done in the case of Mabonagrain, we have Branmangon—the very combination which by hypothesis was corrupted into Baudemaguz.

Of course it is disconcerting, not to say shocking, to find the noble Fisher King and the hospitable and generous Baudemaguz thus bound up with so repulsive a villain as Mangon appears in these tales of ravished maidens. But the supernatural and even the natural personages of Arthurian romance have, as every scholar knows, a chameleon's variability.[55] The very same Mangon who behaves so outrageously in the episodes we have summarized is called "brave and courtly" in *Le Lai du Cor,* and appears in *Meraugis* seated with his queen in domestic felicity, a regal figure of unchallenged honor. In fact, there is no sharper contrast between the various roles of Mangon then between the Fisher King Bron and his alter

[51] Cf. *supra*, p. 97.   [52] L. A. Paton, *Fairy Mythology*, p. 143.
[53] Cf. *supra*, pp. 95 f., 145.
[54] Cf. *supra*, pp. 123 f. It is also worth noting that the lady whom Hector delivered from a cave where she had been kept four years by her ravisher Mangars or Marigant was named, according to one ms. of the *Vulgate Lancelot*, Orgale—a form which suggests that once more we have the common corruption of Morgain by the omission of the first letter. Cf. *Mod. Lang. Notes*, XXVI, 68; *Romanic Review*, III (1912), 190; *Speculum*, XX (1945), 185.
[55] A. B. Hopkins, *Influence of Wace*, pp. 82–92, 100–102. Paton, *op. cit.*, pp. 13–48.

ego, Brandus des Illes.[56] In the figure of Baudemaguz it is only the nobler aspects of Bran and Mangon which have been blended.

4. The conclusion at which we have arrived on the basis of the Arthurian evidence is partly corroborated by the Welsh. For Bran, the original of the Fisher King, is thrice coupled with his brother Manawydan. In *Branwen* Bran and Manawydan sit together on the rock of Harlech; they sit together at a banquet at Aberffraw; [57] in the Book of Taliesin the bard declares that he sang before the sons of Llyr (Bran and Manawydan) at Ebyr Henvelen.[58] This close association of the two brothers would explain the confusion of their identities, their playing the same roles in Arthurian story and the ultimate combination of their names, according to hypothesis, in Branmague and Baudemaguz. The Book of Taliesin also informs us that Manawyd knew the island fortress of Caer Siddi, where neither plague nor old age harmed the dwellers.[59] This passage proves that Manawydan had his abode in that island castle of bliss of which his brother Bran must have been conceived as the lord. It is also the traditional castle whence no man returned. Thus Manawydan, we may infer, would be ruler of the land "whence no one returns," and thus Welsh tradition would support this description of the territory of Amangon. As for the transition from Manawydan to Mangon, it may be accounted for by the tendency to replace the outlandish sound of the Welsh name by the word *mangon,* which is in French both a common noun and a proper name.[60] The addition of initial *a* in Amangon is a recognized phenomenon in the French romances; [61] I find for instance in Manuscript B.N. fr. 95, f. 239, the following examples; Amerangis, Agornain, Alait Hardi, Acalogrenant, Akehedin.

Only one serious objection to the derivation of Mangon and -*maguz* from Manawydan occurs to me, and that is the lack of stronger analogies between the Welsh and the French figures. It must be conceded that the mabinogi of *Manawydan* finds no echo in what the romances tell us about Mangon, Amangon, Mangars, and Magon. But the objection, though strong, is not insuperable. No one who has read in this book thus far with a receptive mind can help realizing how large a body of Welsh tradition is forever lost to us. There must have been tales of Manawydan

[56] Newstead, pp. 146–50.   [57] Loth, *op. cit.,* I, 121, 124.
[58] *Cymmrodor,* XXVIII (1918), 197. *PMLA,* LVI (1941), 902, 904. Cf. also *Revue celt.,* XLIX (1932), 259.   [59] *PMLA,* LVI, 902.
[60] Guillaume le Clerc, *Fergus,* ed. E. Martin, p. xxii. Godefroy, *Lexique français.* There may also have been an influence from the name of the Saracen king, Amalgon, Amargon, Amaugon, Maargon, Magon, Margon, Mahugon, who is mentioned 15 times in the *Chanson d'Aspremont,* ed. L. Brandin (Paris, 1924), II, 191. But since we find in the same *chanson* names such as Graalent, Cador, Orcanie, Lampal, and Tintagor, which seem to be borrowed from the *Matière de Bretagne,* the influence may have worked the other way.
[61] *Zts. f. franz. Sprache u. Lit.,* XXVIII, "Abhandlungen," 13, n. 21. *Elucidation,* ed. Thompson, p. 47, n. 32. Bruce, *op. cit.,* II, 131n.

unrecorded in the mabinogion. The positive evidence assembled above for the derivation of Mangon from Manawydan outweighs the negative evidence against it. Baudemaguz must therefore represent a fusion of the personalities and the names of Bran and Manawydan. Chrétien's use of this form of the name evidently standardized it so that, with the exception of Branmague and its variants, the older forms, revealing more exactly the original components, disappeared. Thus disguised, the elements, Bran and Mangon, failed to be recognized by scholars. The absence of the more distinctive attributes of the Fisher King in Chrétien's portrayal of Baudemaguz, the connection with Meleagant, who nowhere appears in the Grail legend proper, the contrast between Baudemaguz' character and that of Mangon—these facts naturally encouraged skepticism. But it should certainly be apparent by now that the descendants of the Welsh Bran are cast in many roles besides that of the infirm Fisher King and are not always fed by the Grail, and that Mangon is a Jekyll as well as a Hyde. Nothing, therefore, stands in the way of accepting the ample evidence for the double derivation of Baudemaguz from Bran and Manawydan.

Chapter XLI

THE BLOODSTAINED BED AND THE MISLEADING OATH

VERSES 4586–5006

When Lancelot had become reconciled to the Queen, she bade him come to the barred window of her chamber at night. He did so, and, yearning to achieve his desire, he bent the bars and entered the chamber, though not without cutting his fingers. The wounded Keu was, strange to say, sleeping in the same room, but this did not prevent the lovers from the satisfaction of their desires. At dawn Lancelot departed through the window. When later Meleagant entered, he discovered the bloodstained bedding and accused Guenievre of admitting the wounded Keu to her bed. Though she and Keu denied the accusation, the evidence was against them. Lancelot thereupon undertook to defend the Queen's innocence by judicial combat. Meleagant swore on holy relics that Keu had lain with the Queen, and Lancelot swore that Keu had not. The third fight between Lancelot and Meleagant then began, but was interrupted by Baudemaguz.

SEVERAL SCHOLARS, including Professor Cross and M. Cohen,[1] have recognized that this whole episode is a borrowing from the Tristan legend, whether by Chrétien or by the author of his source. The latter alternative seems to me the more likely, since Chrétien's personal attitude toward adultery was, so far as one can judge, disapproving,[2] and he was hardly the man to introduce a brazenly cynical episode, such as this, into his narrative. Nevertheless, one cannot overlook the fact that Chrétien was thoroughly familiar with the most famous of medieval love stories. There is good evidence that before 1137 the Welsh conteur Bleheris had recited his enthralling tales at the court of Poitou, and two troubadours who had been connected with that court refer in the fifties to Tristan as a great lover.[3] Chrétien himself, of course, tells us that he had written "del roi Marc et d'Iseut la blonde," mentions Tristan in his *Philomena,* and makes several references to the legend in *Erec* and *Cliges.*[4] In fact, the latter poem is a sort of critique and correction of the morality of the Tristan legend.[5] At any rate, whoever it was who incorporated the Tristan matter in the *Charrette,* he would seem to have followed a version like that employed by Thomas, for, among the extant versions, only Thomas and his derivatives combined the themes of the bloodstained bed and the deceptive oath. Here is a résumé of the episode as Bédier reconstructed it from the derivatives of Thomas.[6]

King Mark resolved to test Tristan and his wife. All three, as well as the treacherous dwarf and Bringvain, were to sleep in the same bedchamber. When at Mark's request Tristan had put out the candles, the dwarf sprinkled the floor with flour. Bringvain noticed this and informed Tristan of the trap. At midnight Mark announced that he would go to matins, attended by the dwarf. Tristan saw an opportunity to lie with the Queen, and, to avoid leaving footprints on the floor, he leaped across to her bed. The effort opened his wounds, and he bled all night. When he had had his will, he leaped back to his own couch. When the King returned, there were no telltale footprints, but the beds of both Isolt and Tristan were stained with blood. At a council summoned in London Isolt demanded the trial by red-hot iron to prove her innocence. The trial was arranged to take place at Carlion. Isolt contrived that on her way to the ordeal, Tristan should

[1] T. P. Cross and W. A. Nitze, *Lancelot and Guenevere,* p. 16, n. 1. G. Cohen, *Chrétien de Troyes et son œuvre,* p. 260.

[2] Cf. *Cliges,* vss. 3145–63, where Fenice condemns Iseut because the latter grants the use of her body to two men. Cf. also *Chevalier de la Charrette,* vss. 21–29, where Chrétien places the entire responsibility for "matiere et san" on his patroness, Countess Marie.

[3] *Romanic Review,* XXXII (1941), 16–19. *Neophilologus,* XV (1929), 30–34. *Romania,* LIII (1927), 82–92. *Revue des langues romanes,* LXV (1927–28), 238 f.

[4] *Cliges,* vs. 5. *Ovide Moralisé,* ed. C. De Boer (Amsterdam, 1915), I, 340. *Erec,* vss. 424, 1248, 1713, 2076, 4946. *Cliges,* vss. 2076, 2790, 3147, 3151, 5260 f., 5312 f.

[5] J. D. Bruce, *Evolution of Arthurian Romance,* I, 116–18.

[6] Thomas, *Tristan,* ed. J. Bédier, I, 203–11. The version of this episode given by Gottfried von Strassburg inspired the mural paintings at the Castle of Runkelstein. Cf. R. S. and L. H. Loomis, *Arthurian Legends in Medieval Art,* p. 50; figs. 73–75.

meet her, well disguised, carry her from her boat to the shore, and there fall over her. Thus she was able to take the deceptive oath that she had never lain with any man save her husband and the stranger, passed successfully the test of the red-hot iron, and convinced everyone that she was guiltless.

This crude narrative of successful cuckoldry and triumphant deceit provoked Gottfried von Strassburg, when he retold it, to append his celebrated ironic comment, thus translated by Bédier:

"Ainsi fut manifesté et attesté à tout le monde que le très glorieux Christ se plie comme la manche d'un bliaut; il se plie et se dispose, comme chacun désire, aussi exactement et aussi parfaitement comme on le veut. Il est prêt, au gré de chacun, soit à la verité, soit à la fraude. Le jeu est-il sérieux, est-il plaisant, le Christ est comme on veut l'avoir." [7]

There can be little doubt that some such unedifying account as that of Thomas inspired the equally immoral incidents of the bloodstained beds and the misleading oath in *Le Chevalier de la Charrette*. But it may well be doubted whether Thomas himself was the source. There is no such close correspondence as would prove indebtedness, and several scholars believe that Thomas wrote after Chrétien's time.[8]

For the ultimate origin of the elements thus linked by Thomas and Chrétien, we cannot turn to the Celtic West but rather to a mass of widely circulated tales of trickery and intrigue. The presence of Keu in the Queen's bedchamber, as depicted by Chrétien, and the even more crowded sleeping arrangements described by Thomas reflect a social milieu very different from that of a twelfth-century royal castle.[9] This is clear proof that the situation was derived from a tale of humble life, where the members of a household would be imagined as sharing a common bedroom. Gertrude Schoepperle showed that both the bloodstained bed and the flour-sprinkled floor belong to variants of the Master Thief cycle of stories.[10] According to certain versions, the thief cuts himself on blades set about the treasure; in others he leaves his footprints on the flour; in both types of story he evades detection by a counter-ruse. These motifs have been combined, adapted to the circumstances of a lover stealing a night's enjoyment of his mistress, and otherwise modified. As a counter-ruse a new element is introduced, the ambiguous or deceptive oath.[11] This motif is probably derived from one of those many Oriental tales of designing women which came into the West in the twelfth century,[12] for example, in the *Disciplina clericalis* of Petrus Alfonsi (*ca.* 1110) and the Seven Sages

[7] Thomas, *Tristan*, I, 212. Gottfried, *Tristan*, ed. F. Ranke (Berlin, 1930), vss. 15733–44.
[8] *Romania*, LIII, 101, n. 2; LV (1929), 1–16, especially p. 13.
[9] G. Schoepperle, *Tristan and Isolt*, I, 216–18.   [10] *Ibid.*, I, 213–22.
[11] *Ibid.*, I, 224–26. For bibliography cf. Stith Thompson, *Motif-Index of Folk-Literature* (1934), IV, 414.
[12] K. Voretzsch, *Introduction to the Study of Old French Literature*, pp. 370 f., 374–77. G. H. McKnight, *Middle English Humorous Tales in Verse* (Boston, 1913), pp. xxii–xxviii.

cycle. Gertrude Schoepperle pointed out striking analogues in the *Cuka-saptati* and the *Pantschatantra* to Iseut's employment of the misleading oath.[13]

Chrétien's account of Lancelot's assignation and the vindication by combat of the Queen's innocence has, like so many other episodes, a long and complicated history behind it. But that history varies greatly from the typical evolution of his other narrative patterns. Both in origin and moral tone the episode belongs to the fabliau type, not to the romantic, though often clandestine, amours which recur throughout the *Matière de Bretagne*.

Chapter XLII

THE TOURNEY OF NOAUZ

VERSES 5077–5110, 5187–6077

A mounted dwarf bearing a scourge induced Lancelot with deceitful words to follow him. Lancelot was captured and placed in the custody of Meleagant's seneschal. Gauvain organized a search for him. The unmarried damsels of Logres arranged a tourney that they might select husbands among the knights who distinguished themselves. The place was Noauz, and Guenievre consented to be present. When news of this reached Lancelot, he persuaded the seneschal's wife to lend him a marvelously good horse and her husband's vermeil arms, and she permitted him to attend the tourney on condition that he would return and grant her his love. He arrived at Noauz incognito. Guenievre and many ladies were gathered in a magnificent loge to witness the sport. When Lancelot entered the fray, he proved himself the equal of twenty other knights. The Queen recognized her lover and sent a damsel to him with the command that he should fight "au noauz"—as badly as possible. He obeyed and the rest of the day played the coward. The next morning Guenievre again commanded him through her messenger to fight his worst. When he meekly agreed to do so, she countermanded the order and bade him do his best. Thereafter he carried all before him, and the watching damsels were unanimous in wishing the knight with the vermeil shield for a husband. But at the end of the day he disappeared in accordance with his oath to the seneschal's wife, and the disappointed maidens adjourned the tourney and declared that they would marry no man at all that year.

THE IMPRISONMENT of Lancelot and his participation in the tourney at Noauz may be analyzed as a combination of two stories which have already been examined separately in this study. The first of

[13] Schoepperle, *op. cit.*, I, 225 f.

these traditional patterns, barely recognizable in Chrétien's narrative of Erec's humiliating encounter with the dwarf, his entertainment by Enide, his wooing, her provision of arms for his fight with Yder, emerged more clearly as we compared the Pluris adventure in *Lanzelet*.[1] The same pattern, moreover, may be plainly detected (though the dwarf is absent) in *Historia Meriadoci, Il Bel Gherardino,* and *Peredur*.[2] The recurrent features of the plot are: (1) The hero meets a mounted dwarf with a scourge. (2) He is placed in the custody of an amorous lady. (3) He gives her but slight encouragement or none. (4) She permits him to attend a tournament on condition that he return. (5) She gives him a marvelous horse and her husband's red arms. (6) He appears incognito at the tourney and rouses curiosity as to his identity. (7) He vanquishes the lady's husband. (8) Gauvain organizes a search for the hero. All of these features except 7 are found in Chrétien's story of the tourney at Noauz.

The second pattern is most distinctly represented in the tale of Bohort at King Brangorre's tourney, which we had occasion to notice in connection with the study of King Baudemaguz' name and nature. For purposes of comparison with the tourney of Noauz, the following features are significant.[3] (1) King Brangorre holds an anniversary festival. (2) The unwedded damsels of his land are to be assigned husbands among the knights who distinguish themselves. (3) Bohort on his arrival hesitates to take part. (4) The King's daughter spurs him to action by a mocking remark. (5) He proves himself the best knight. (6) The princess falls in love with him. (7) To her profound chagrin he will have none of her.

That this plot has influenced the tourney of Noauz is manifest: it also was arranged to secure, from among the participants, husbands for highborn maidens, and it was evidently an annual affair since the disappointed maidens vowed to remain unwedded for a year. In the behavior of Bohort we see the meager hints of situations which in the *Charrette* are most ingeniously and significantly expanded in accordance with the doctrine of a lover's abject submission to his lady's whim. Bohort's initial delay, which called forth the princess' taunt, and her responsibility for his later prowess offer a parallel to Lancelot's playing first the coward and then the matchless champion at the behest of Guenievre. And instead of one infatuated princess, left forlorn by the hero's indifference, Chrétien has given us a whole assemblage of lovesick and disappointed damsels.

Although Chrétien made the most of the opportunity afforded him by the combined plots to display Lancelot as the paragon of lovers, proof against the blandishments of any but the Queen, ready to submit to blows

---

[1] Cf. *supra*, pp. 79–81.
[2] *Speculum*, XX (1945), 186–88. Loth, *Mabinogion*, 2nd ed., II, 111–14.
[3] Sommer, *Vulgate Version*, IV, 258 f., 262–67.

and ignominy at her slightest whim, he certainly did not invent the separate plots or make the combination. In fact, the same combination occurs in a highly elaborated form in the Dame de Malehot episode in the *Vulgate Lancelot,* and, though possibly influenced by the tourney of Noauz, the episode was demonstrably based on a common source. Let me summarize.[4]

Lancelot, being attacked by overwhelming numbers in the city of Malehot, yields himself to the Dame de Malehot, who places him in a jail of transparent stone, so that he can both see and be seen. He hears of a great war between Arthur and King Galehos, and persuades his fair jailer to provide him with a horse and a red shield on condition that he return. Guenievre and many ladies are gathered in a *loge* to watch the conflict. Lancelot appears on the field incognito, and sinks into a revery, provoking the contempt of the menials and heralds. Finally aroused, he performs great feats of arms against the forces of Galehos. Lancelot returns to his prison, and the Dame de Malehot, hearing that a knight in red arms has vanquished all, offers him her love, but in vain. The disappearance of the red knight prompts Gauvain to organize a party to seek him. Galehos arranges a truce for a year. When the war is renewed, Lancelot, now clad in black arms provided by the Dame de Malehot, arrives on the scene, where Guenievre and her ladies are again assembled to witness the fray. Again Lancelot takes no part at first, but is recognized by Gauvain as the red knight of the earlier battle. The lovelorn Dame de Malehot, who is present, induces the other ladies, with the exception of Guenievre, to send a messenger to Lancelot, beseeching him to fight for their love. He gallantly responds and displays a measure of his might against a troop of a hundred knights. When the Queen herself sends him a request to fight for her love, he performs prodigies of valor, to the grief of the King of the Hundred Knights. Galehos, smitten with admiration for the unknown, brings him at the end of the day's conflict to his own tent, and in the presence of the King of the Hundred Knights pledges his friendship to Lancelot and promises to yield to Arthur. The next day Lancelot dons Galehos' armor, Galehos surrenders, becomes reconciled to Arthur, and sleeps in his tent.

A careful scrutiny of this narrative reveals that, though disguised as a series of battles between the hosts of Arthur and Galehos, the successive clashes before a grandstand of sentimental ladies are based on the account of a tournament. One can detect, moreover, characteristic features of the enamored jaileress plot (2, 3, 4, 5, 6, 8 above) and of the marriage tourney plot (3, 4, 5, 6)—the same two plots which were combined in Chrétien's tale of the passage of arms at Noauz. But though Chrétien's precedent may well be responsible for the introduction of Guenievre and her message to Lancelot, the differences between his treatment of the combined plots and that of the author of the *Vulgate Lancelot* lead us to postulate a common composite source for both authors. And further examination of the Dame de Malehot episode strengthens this postulate.

The Dame de Malehot, it should be observed, kept Lancelot in a

[4] *Ibid.,* III, 209-15, 223-51. Trans. L. A. Paton, *Sir Lancelot of the Lake,* pp. 155-92.

strangely transparent chamber.[5] The name Malehot looks like the oblique case of Malehoes, a variant reading of Maheloas.[6] Malehoes, therefore, must have been, like Maheloas, "sire de l'Isle de Voirre." All authorities agree that Malehoes or Maheloas was identical with Meleagant, and it was Meleagant who placed Lancelot in the custody of his seneschal's wife. May we not, therefore, suspect some relation between Lancelot in the transparent prison of the amorous Dame de Malehot and Lancelot placed in charge of an amorous lady by Meleagant, who was prince of the Isle of Glass? May we not suspect that Malehot is not the name of a city but the name of the Dame de Malehot's husband, Malehos alias Meleagant?

This suspicion is strengthened by an examination of Galehos, who betrays in his turn a singular resemblance to Meleagant. Meleagant makes his first appearance presenting a haughty challenge to Arthur at Camalot; Galehos likewise first appears in the *Vulgate Lancelot* as sending a haughty challenge to Arthur at Camaalot.[7] Both are lords of lands approached only by two perilous bridges.[8] Both conduct Guenievre to these islands.[9] Galehos is Lancelot's chief opponent in the Dame de Malehot episode; Meleagant is his chief opponent in the *Charrette*. On the last day of the war with Galehos Lancelot appears clad in his opponent's arms;[10] at the tourney of Noauz Lancelot appears in the arms of the husband of his fair custodian. The parallel between the two stories would become quite clear if we recognized that they both reposed on a common ultimate source, that both Galehos and Meleagant go back to Malehos or Melwas, lord of the "Isle de Voirre," and that the Dame de Malehot and the wife of Meleagant's seneschal both go back to the "dame" of Malehoes, that is, the wife of Melwas. It also becomes plain that in the original story this lady gave Lancelot her husband's arms and marvelous horse with treacherous intent in order that he might bring about her husband's death. This motivation is expressed in the parallel story of the Soldan's wife in *Il Bel Gherardino*.[11] It has been suppressed, of course, in the *Charrette,* as well as the fight with Meleagant which it implied. After all, the poem could not well accommodate more than four such combats without becoming unduly monotonous.

To this hypothesis of the original identity of Galehos with Malehoes-Meleagant both the name and the role of Galehos offer serious opposition.

[5] Sommer, III, 210. "En chascune quareure de la iaiole auoit .ij. fenestres de voire si cleres que tout chil qui estoient dedens pooient veoir tous chels qui entroient en la sale." Cf. p. 213. "si le tenoit en .j. gaiole qui est de piere. & si est si cleire la piere que il veoit tous chels defors. & chil de defors veoient li."

[6] *Erec,* ed. W. Foerster, vs. 1946. Ms. V gives Malehoes; ms. A, Mahalos.

[7] Sommer, III, 201 f.   [8] *Ibid.,* 269 f. Cf. *ibid.,* IV, 41.   [9] *Ibid.,* IV, 72.

[10] *Ibid.,* III, 248. This is evidently a distorted form of the tradition found in J. D. Bruce, *Historia Meriadoci,* pp. 69, 72.

[11] E. Levi, *Fiore di leggende, Scrittori d'Italia* (Bari, 1914), pp. 23–27. Cf. *Giornale storico della letteratura italiana,* Supplemento No. 16 (1914), p. 34.

Why the change from initial *M* to *G?* How can the chivalrous friend of Lancelot be equated with his unchivalrous enemy? That such transformations of names and characters are possible, no one can deny, and the evidence presented above seems to make it clear that these changes did take place in the case of Galehos. And I believe that the reason can be discovered. Either by some misunderstanding or by deliberate intent, the author of the *Vulgate Lancelot* confused Malehos, Lancelot's foe, with Galoain (Gauvain), Lancelot's devoted friend. If Galehos' name is what Lewis Carroll would call a portmanteau word,[12] his character is what we might call a portmanteau character. He has, we have noted, many of the characteristics of Malehoes-Meleagant, and becomes the *ami* of the Dame de Malehot; but from the time when he is carried away by admiration for Lancelot's prowess, all is subordinated to the theme of his friendship with his former enemy, and this theme seems to have been inspired by the friendship between Lancelot and Gauvain.

The *Charrette* itself contains many instances of the mutual devotion of Lancelot and Gauvain. When the one is lost, the other searches for him. It is Gauvain, near the end of the romance, who takes up Meleagant's challenge rather than permit Lancelot's honor to suffer by default. The account of the beginnings of that friendship in *Lanzelet* [13] is most significant since it seems to echo again and again the Dame de Malehot episode and the beginnings of the friendship of Lancelot and Galehos, and yet it cannot, because of its date (*ca.* 1200), be derived from the *Vulgate Lancelot*. There must have been a common French source.

Lanzelet, being attacked by overwhelming numbers, yields himself to a beautiful lady, Ade, who, though fascinated by his looks, places him in a dungeon. She bathes him and feeds him well, and gives him arms for a combat, which takes place three days later with a giant, two lions, and her uncle Linier.[14] Lanzelet slays them all and becomes the *ami* of Ade. The fame of his exploits reaches

[12] *Through the Looking Glass,* Chap. 6.

[13] P. Piper, *Höfische Epik,* II, 175–81. The relationship to the *Vulgate Lancelot* has been discussed by P. Märtens in *Romanische Studien* (Bonn), V (1880), 693–95. Much the same formula was employed by the author of the German romance *Tandareis. Cf. Zts. f. Deutsches Altertum,* XXIX (1897), 155–64. Remarkable evidence for the relationship between the Dame de Malehot story and the Ade episode is contained in the story of the Empress of Christinobyl in *Peredur* (Loth, *Mabinogion,* 2d ed., II, 100–103; *Mabinogion,* trans. T. P. Ellis, J. Lloyd, Oxford, 1929, II, 120–23, 182–86). Corresponding to the Dame de Malehot episode are Peredur's devotion to the Empress, who is present at the tourney, his love trance, interrupted by a rude blow from a miller, his return to his lodgings after each day's fighting, his victory over all on the third day, the hundred knights sent against him. Corresponding to the Ade episode are the three days' tournament, the hundred knights sent against Peredur, his despatching the vanquished knights to his lady-love, the appeal of an emissary in the name of his beloved, the slaying of the three adversaries. Such a triangular relationship between the Welsh, the Swiss, and the French romances can only mean that they drew on a common French tradition.

[14] This is pretty obviously an intrusive element, perhaps derived from the visit of Cuchulainn to Curoi's fortress. Cf. *PMLA,* XLVIII (1933), 1005, 1013–18.

Arthur's court, which he has not yet visited. Ginover desires to see him. Walwein is selected to find him and bring him to Arthur. Walwein meets the youth and Ade, and, recognizing him, lays aside spear, helm, and shield as a sign of peaceful intent and issues Arthur's invitation. Lanzelet, despite all Walwein's persuasions, proudly refuses, and there is a fight. A youth approaches and bids them desist in the name of the best women alive, and promises them their fill of blows at a tourney where Arthur is to be present. The prospect is tempting, and Walwein offers to accompany Lanzelet and Ade to the tourney. Lanzelet refuses the offer, and parts from Walwein, after swearing friendship. He returns to Ade's castle, but as the time of the tourney draws near, grows impatient. Ade gives him two steeds besides his own, many squires, and ample funds. She accompanies him to the assembly. The first day, appearing in green arms, Lanzelet performs great feats, and is recognized by Walwein, who tries in vain to encounter him. The next day in white arms, he empties saddles, and joins the company of Count Ritschart with his hundred knights. The third day in red arms Lanzelet wins the praises of all and is again recognized by Walwein. In the evening he goes to the tent of the Count with the hundred knights, and there Arthur and Walwein find him. Lanzelet receives Walwein with great joy. Though Arthur invites Lanzelet to the royal quarters, Lanzelet prefers to bring Walwein to his own inn and shows him every courtesy. The friendship between Lanzelet and Walwein remains one of the prominent themes of the romance.

Anyone familiar with the Dame de Malehot episode will hear echoes in almost every line of this summary. The motifs are shuffled about differently, but they are discernible. The larger themes of the enamored jaileress and the three days' tourney are handled more simply and sensibly than in the *Vulgate Lancelot*. Very important is the fact that the Swiss author is much concerned with the first acquaintance and the growing affection between Lanzelet and Walwein, and that in striking ways he reminds us of the story of Lancelot and Galehos. Both stories tell of an effort to bring a formidable and famous warrior to Arthur's presence, of the mutual admiration and growing friendship between the warrior and Arthur's emissary, of an assembly in which Lancelot or Lanzelet in arms of different colors carries all before him, of the final success of the effort to bring about the meeting with Arthur, and of the subsequent devotion of the two friends. The resemblance is sufficiently patent to establish an indebtedness to a common source. The author of the *Vulgate Lancelot* has put everyone off the scent by compounding a new character, Galehos, out of Walwein or Galoain and Malehos, by assigning the part of Walwein to Lancelot and that of Lanzelet to Galehos, and by leaving to Walwein under his own name Gauvain a portion of his original role [15]—his quest for Lancelot and his recognition of the disguised Lancelot at the tourney.

To return to the Dame de Malehot and her counterpart, the wife of

[15] He seems also to have left to Malehos-Meleagant a portion of his role, for the King of the Hundred Knights, Lancelot's chief opponent, is called Malaguin. Sommer, III, 236, 337, n. 2.

Meleagant's seneschal, their role as enamored jaileress of Lancelot and their gift of horse and arms disclose the secret of their origin; they are patterned after Morgain. Their original relationship to Malehos and Meleagant respectively seems also to have been a matter of tradition, for we find it reflected in two stories. In the *Charrette* itself, as we shall presently discover, Meleagant's sister also plays the part of Morgain in releasing Lancelot from prison and supplying him with a marvelous horse for his combat with her brother. In *Le Conte del Graal,* as we shall see in due course,[16] Chrétien introduces a novel and charming variation on the theme, and the part of the love-smitten Morgain, much altered, is assigned to the foster-sister of Meliant. If Welsh literature fails to connect Morgain's prototype, Modron, in any way with Melwas, we need not be disconcerted. Sooner or later, Melvas, king of the "aestiva regio," with his fortress in the "insula vitrea," was bound to be brought into relationship with the Queen of Meydelant, whose castle crowned a crystal mountain on an island where flowers bloomed throughout the year as if it were mid-May.

What of the three days' tournament motif which underlies the tourney of Noauz and the wars of Arthur and Galehos? [17] Was it a floating folktale motif of indeterminate origin which was adopted by the romancers as one of their favorite incidents? Carter's argument to this effect cannot be regarded as convincing until it has been shown that the nineteenth-century folktales which contain the incident are not merely debased and contaminated survivals of the romances. The descent of romance materials into the fiction of the lower classes can be observed in several English ballads,[18] and likewise, the plots of the aristocratic Breton lais, transmitted through the popular *cantari,* turn up as Italian folktales in recent times.[19] This process of the popularization of medieval romance offers a satisfactory explanation of the recurrence in modern folklore of the three days' tournament. Since the motif in its earliest forms is inextricably tangled with Celtic matter, it seems likely to be itself of Celtic origin. Three recurrent features of the tournament theme seem definitely associated with Morgain: the gift of a wonderful horse by an amorous jaileress; the hero's incognito; the change of colors. Morgain's gift of a steed to her protégé or lover, we know, is a stereotyped feature. The Queen of Meydelant did not permit Lanzelet to know his own name, and his early

[16] Cf. Chap. LXXIV.
[17] On Three Days' Tournament cf. Carter in *Haverford Essays* (Haverford, Pa., 1909), pp. 246 ff.; J. L. Weston, *Three Days' Tournament* (London, 1902); *Englische Studien*, XVII (1892), 60–64, 345–52; L. A. Hibbard, *Mediaeval Romance in England*, pp. 55, 152, 225 f., 229; Stith Thompson, *Motif-Index of Folk-Literature*, V, 215; *Deutsche Forschungen*, XXVII (1934), 52 ff.
[18] For example, *Thomas Rhymer, Hind Horn, Marriage of Sir Gawain, Boy and the Mantle.*
[19] *Giornale storico della letteratura italiana,* Suppl. No. 16, pp. 46 ff. Marie de France, *Lais,* ed. Warnke, 3d ed. (1925), p. cxxxix.

adventures he performed incognito. As for the change of colors, it was Ade who provided the green, white, and red arms for Lanzelet; it was the Soldan's wife who provided exactly the same colors for Gherardino;[20] while in Malory's Book of Gareth it was Dame Lyones who gave her lover a magic ring which enabled him to change the color of his equipment at a tourney;[21] and all three of these ladies had their prototype in Morgain.[22] Since these features of the tournament pattern belong to the faery queen, it is a legitimate, though not a certain, inference that the pattern as a whole first took shape about the figure of Morgain's original, Modron, except that the tournament, of course, in the early Welsh stage of the tradition must have been a more primitive kind of conflict.

Chapter XLIII

MELEAGANT'S SISTER

VERSES 2793–2955, 6395–6728, 6890–6903

As Lancelot, on his way to the Sword Bridge, had forced an insolent knight to beg for mercy, a maiden rode up on a mule which moved more rapidly at an ambling gait than a horse could gallop. She begged Lancelot for the knight's head and so placed him in a dilemma between the claims of pity and generosity. Lancelot managed to satisfy his scruples by renewing the fight under a handicap, again won, and presented the damsel with her gory boon. She left him, promising to recompense him at some later date for his service. Long after, when he had been imprisoned in a tower on an island near Goirre, the damsel, who turns out to be Meleagant's sister, learned that Lancelot was missing and set out on her mule to find him. After a month's search, she discovered him, half starved, in the tower, released him, and, setting him before her on the mule, brought him to her "bel repeire." Here she nursed him back to health. When he desired to set out for his rendezvous with Meleagant at Arthur's court, he addressed her as "douce amie deboneire," and asked her "par amors" to let him go; she called him "biaus douz amis chiers," and provided him with the best steed that ever was.

WHEN MELEAGANT'S sister makes her first entrance, Chrétien at once gives a clue to her nature by his description of her mule: "In truth, no horse ever moved so fast at a full gallop that the mule did not outspeed it at an amble." It is evident that the animal belongs

[20] E. Levi, *Fiore di leggende*, p. 24.
[21] Malory, *Morte d'Arthur*, ed. H. O. Sommer, Bk. VII, chaps. 28–31.
[22] Cf. *supra*, pp. 80 f., 86, 101 f., and *Speculum*, XX, 187.

to the same unearthly breed as the palfrey of Enide's cousin, the white palfreys of the faery cavalcade in *Le Lai du Trot,* and the white steed of the fay Riannon, all of which, we remember, were distinguished by preternatural celerity and a deceptive smoothness of motion.[1] There is even a verbal similarity between Chrétien's description of the mule and the statement in the *Lai* that the palfreys of the fays "moved far more fleetly than one would gallop on the tallest Spanish horse." We have a right to suspect that Meleagant's sister belongs to the Celtic faery world.

We can be more specific. We were able to show that Enide's cousin, whose palfrey was as swift as a bird in flight and yet glided as smoothly as a boat, derived some of her characteristics from Niniane, the Lady of the Lake. It is interesting, therefore, to observe that the *Huth Merlin* twice introduces Niniane in a manner which reminds us of Meleagant's sister. On the first occasion a damsel, identified as the Lady of the Lake,[2] appears at Arthur's court on horseback and demands either the head of another damsel there present or the head of Balaain, whom she accuses of having killed her brother.[3] On the second occasion a damsel whose name is later revealed as Niviene, "la damoisiele dou lac," [4] came galloping past Arthur's hall on a palfrey "with as great haste as she could achieve." [5] Thus the *Huth Merlin* ascribes to Niniane two distinctive traits which Chrétien ascribes to Meleagant's sister—her rapid riding and her demand for the head of a knight. We seem to be warranted, therefore, in discerning the figure of Niniane behind a nameless damsel in the same romance whose role offers a close parallel to that of Meleagant's sister.[6]

Tor has battered a knight into helplessness when a damsel rides up, in great haste, and begs Tor for his opponent's head. When Tor demurs, she accuses the knight of having killed her brother. Finally Tor yields to her entreaty and strikes off the head. The damsel gleefully picks up the gory object, and promises Tor a guerdon for his civility when opportunity offers. He asks for shelter so that his wounds may be staunched, and accompanies the damsel to her home and finds there a most hospitable reception.

There are obvious reminders here of Niniane as she appears earlier in the *Huth Merlin;* there is a stronger and fuller parallel to the role of Meleagant's sister in the *Charrette.* Altogether the evidence justifies the equation of the two women.

But on her second entrance into the story Meleagant's sister seems to take rather after Morgain. She releases Lancelot from prison, cares for

---

[1] Cf. Chap. XIV.
[2] The *Huth Merlin* (ed. Paris and Ulrich, I, 218) identifies her as the damsel who gave Arthur the sword at the lake, and Malory (ed. H. O. Sommer, I, 80), who is following a missing portion of the *Merlin,* calls her the Lady of the Lake. In *Perlesvaus* (ed. Nitze and others, I, 40 f.) there is a damsel who demands the head of a knight from King Arthur.
[3] *Huth Merlin,* I, 218 f.   [4] *Ibid.,* II, 136 f.   [5] *Ibid.,* II, 77.   [6] *Ibid.,* II, 110–13.

him tenderly, addresses him in terms of extreme affection, supplies him with a marvelous horse, and sends him forth to the final and decisive duel with Meleagant. This is evidently the same basic story as those of the wife of Meleagant's seneschal and the Dame de Malehot. We have just seen that the original of these amorous ladies was Morgain, and Morgain's renowned therapeutic skill may well account for the rapid improvement which their counterpart, Meleagant's sister, wrought in Lancelot's health after his sufferings in the tower. The tower itself, erected by Meleagant's orders on an island near Goirre, seems to represent the same tradition as Maheloas' Isle of Glass and the transparent jail, with its windows of glass, where the Dame de Malehot kept Lancelot. The enmity which Meleagant's sister feels for her brother, which leads her to release Lancelot and equip him for the final combat, perhaps reflects the tradition of hostility between the amorous jaileress and her husband, dimly discernible in certain stories of this type, and sharply emphasized in *Il Bel Gherardino*, where the Soldan's wife equips her lover for the three days' tourney in order that he may rid her of her spouse. Godefroy de Lagny, who is responsible for this episode in which Meleagant's sister makes her second appearance, seems to have followed a Morgain tradition, just as Chrétien, in his account of her first appearance, followed a tradition of Niniane. This is but another instance of the way in which the descendants of Modron and Riannon tended to merge into each other.

Chapter XLIV

LANCELOT'S LAST COMBAT WITH MELEAGANT

VERSES 6729–7119

After leaving Meleagant's sister, Lancelot made his way rapidly to Arthur's court, the year having elapsed since Meleagant had challenged him to a duel there. Meanwhile Gauvain prepared to keep the pledge which he had made, out of friendship for Lancelot, to take his place in the duel with Meleagant. But just as the duel was about to begin, Lancelot arrived on the scene, and in spite of Gauvain's willingness to go through with the combat, Lancelot insisted on paying off his score with Meleagant in person. So Gauvain removed his armor and Lancelot put it on. Arthur gave orders that everyone should go down (a val) to a glade near by, and the whole company adjourned to where a sycamore stood beside a spring in the midst of the glade, bordered by herbage which was green at all seasons of the year. A stream flowed down (a val) *from the spring into a valley between two woods. Lancelot and Meleagant charged at each other, and at the second encounter both were hurled from their saddles. The masterless steeds attacked each other; one kicked, the other bit.*[1] *Finally Lancelot cut off his opponent's arm and then his head. Everyone was jubilant.*

FOUR TIMES in the course of *Le Chevalier de la Charrette* does Lancelot fight with Meleagant—once in the forest, twice at Baudemaguz' castle, once near Arthur's court. Four times the struggle involves the abducted Guenievre; three times it ends without complete victory. Twice we are assured that Guenievre was not ravished by her abductor, since Baudemaguz gave her protection.[2] Finally, in accordance with an arrangement made after the third duel, Meleagant goes to Arthur's court and summons Lancelot, who is absent, to meet him there at the end of a year in a decisive battle for the Queen.[3] Why these repeated, indecisive combats involving the possession or the honor of Guenievre? Why is Baudemaguz so effective in protecting her chastity, when he seems in other ways to have little control over his son? What of the one year interval between Meleagant's challenge and the final fight?

The answer to these mysteries is happily supplied by the passage from *Kulhwch and Olwen,* already quoted in the discussion of Meleagant.[4] The virgin bride of Gwythyr was stolen by Gwynn ab Nudd; her husband went in pursuit. Arthur intervened between the rivals and decreed that "the maid was to remain in her father's house inviolate by both sides, and Gwynn and Gwythyr were to fight every Mayday till the Day of Judgment, and he who won the victory on the Day of Judgment would take the maid."

This Welsh tale, it has been shown, offers a marked parallel to Caradoc's account of Melvas' abduction of Guennuvar, and consequently is related to the main theme of the *Charrette*. It is therefore no accident that we recognize several features of the *Kulhwch* episode in the French romance, that Baudemaguz effectively guards the chastity of Guenievre against Meleagant, that the combats for her possession are twice broken off without a decision, and that a year elapses between Meleagant's formal challenge and the last battle.

Certain features of this last battle—Gauvain's undertaking from motives of friendship to fight in Lancelot's place after the lapse of a year, Lancelot's assuming Gauvain's armor, the assemblage of courtiers to witness the fight, the localization near a stream, and the death of Meleagant—seem to be indebted to another Welsh legend. Let us recall the first epi-

---

[1] On this motif cf. Chap. LIII.   [2] Vss. 3378–80, 4068–75.   [3] Vss. 3895–3916, 6167–6220.
[4] See Chap. XXXI. Loth, *Mabinogion,* 2d ed., I, 331 f.

sode in *Pwyll*,[5] which had such a prodigious influence on Arthurian romance.[6] Pwyll, from motives of friendship, undertook to fight in Arawn's stead with Havgan after the lapse of a year. He assumed Arawn's shape, encountered Havgan at a ford in the presence of an assemblage of nobles, and slew him. The parallelism is surely impressive.

Our consideration of this episode in *Pwyll* in connection with Erec's fight with the robbers made it apparent that we were dealing with a seasonal myth, the conflict of Winter and Summer.[7] Arawn, clad in gray wool, attended by his pack of baying hounds, was revealed as the Wild Huntsman of European folklore, the personification of winter and its howling storms.[8] His enemy, Havgan, whose name means "Summer White," represents the softer season. The influence of this early Welsh tradition on the details of the last combat between Lancelot and Meleagant leads us to inquire whether something of its mythical significance has not filtered through. It seems obvious that Havgan, "Summer White," King of Annwn, corresponds to Caradoc of Lancarvan's Melvas, king of the Summer Region, and to Chrétien's Maheloas, lord of the isle where there was neither lightning nor tempest and it was neither too hot nor too wintry; consequently Havgan is the counterpart of Meleagant. A trace of Meleagant's connection with the land of summer is found in the scene of his fight with Lancelot, a glade where the herbage was ever fresh at all seasons and where an ancient, spreading sycamore overshadowed a spring.[9] Though ostensibly this romantic setting is a short distance from Arthur's court, it is evidently transposed from the Summer Country. The sycamore and the ever-green vegetation remind us of the scene of Erec's fight with Mabonagrain, the garden where all summer and all winter there were flowers and ripe fruit, and where a sycamore shaded the couch of Enide's cousin.[10] An even closer parallel is furnished by Ulrich von Zatzikhoven, who places Lanzelet's combat with Iweret in a wood which was green both summer and winter, bearing fruit and flowers throughout the year, and where a linden tree overshadowed a spring.[11] It is clear that the setting of Meleagant's last combat was a bit of landscape from his own land of eternal summer.

[5] Loth, *op. cit.*, I, 84–89.
[6] See Chaps. XVII, XVIII, XXXVI, LXXII, and *Journ. of Eng. and Germ. Phil.*, XLII (1943), 170–78; *Mod. Phil.*, XLIII (1945), 63–71.   [7] See Chap. XVIII.
[8] E. B. Tylor, *Primitive Culture*, 6th ed. (London, 1920), I, 362. "The peasant who keeps up in fireside talk the memory of the Wild Huntsman, Wodejäger, the Grand Veneur of Fontainebleau, Herne the Hunter of Windsor Forest, has almost lost the significance of this grand old storm myth. . . . As of old, the Heaven-God drives the clouds before him in raging tempest across the sky, while, safe within the cottage walls, the tale-teller unwittingly describes in personal legendary shape this same Wild Hunt of the Storm."
[9] Vss. 6993–7014. Possibly in the fact that Arthur and his court went "a val" and "furent tost jus avalé" there is a faint trace of their going to Avalon. On association of Avalon with *avaler* cf. A. Nutt, *Studies on the Legend of the Holy Grail* (London, 1888), p. 78.
[10] *Erec*, vss. 5746 f., 5882.   [11] P. Piper, *Höfische Epik*, II, 182, 184.

The similarity in setting between Lancelot's final duel with Meleagant and Lanzelet's fight with Iweret is not the only sign of an intimate connection between the two narratives; there are others. Meleagant's sister, we know, played the part of Morgain la Fée in releasing Lancelot from prison and giving him a marvelous horse to take him to his encounter with Meleagant. So too, the Queen of Meydelant, who was Morgain, gave Lanzelet a spirited mount to take him to his encounter with Iweret.[12] Moreover, Meleagant fought for possession of Guenievre, who, on the authority of Malory, went Maying in the woods and fields with her attendants and gathered herbs, mosses, and flowers, and who, according to William Owen, was accustomed to go out on May morning with her attendants to gather birch for garlands.[13] Likewise, the prize of Lanzelet's victory over Iweret was the lovely Iblis, who was accustomed to go out every day with her attendants into a valley to pluck flowers and weave garlands.[14] May we not infer that Guenievre and Iblis have inherited the role of a May Queen, for whom in the folk-customs of the Isle of Man the forces of Winter and Summer used to contend in ritual battle? And when Ulrich tells us that wherever Iblis culled a flower another sprang up in its place, is this not a hint of her floral nature? [15]

The evidence of seasonal myth implicit in the abduction of Guenievre and the successive clashes of Lancelot and Meleagant is well concealed, but it is there, and is corroborated by a study of the Irish and Welsh sources and the Arthurian analogues. Meleagant wins Guenievre by combat in a wood on the May festival of Ascension Day; he is prince of a land whence no one returns; twice his duels with Lancelot are interrupted without a decision; a year elapses between his challenge and the final conflict; that conflict takes place in a glade where the herbage is fresh at all seasons. By themselves these features would prove little. Examined in the light of Celtic sources and cognate romances they prove that Gaston Paris was right in pronouncing the *Charrette* a romance evolved out of seasonal myth. Though Lancelot displays no characteristics of the winter spirit but was rather, in origin, a solar figure,[16] yet it is clear from a comparison of the *Charrette* with Caradoc's story of Melvas that Lancelot has displaced Arthur as the opponent of Meleagant, and Arthur, from at least the end of the twelfth century and doubtless earlier, was identified with the leader of the Wild Hunt,[17] the genius of storm and winter. The restoration of Arthur to his original part in the repeated encounters with Meleagant would restore the primitive opposition between

---

[12] *Ibid.*, II, 172.   [13] Cf. Chap. XXXI.   [14] Piper, *op. cit.*, II, 184.
[15] Cf. Loth, *Mabinogion*, 2d ed., I, 295. "Quatre trèfles blancs naissaient sous ses pas partout où elle allait: c'est pourquoi on l'avait appelée Olwen (trace blanche)."
[16] R. S. Loomis, *Celtic Myth*, pp. 90–94.
[17] *Romanic Review*, III (1912), 191; XII (1921), 286. P. Sébillot, *Folk-lore de France*, I, 167–69, 241.

the forces of winter and summer. Moreover, though it seems strange that Meleagant should be treated with such hostility and that the poem should conclude with his death, yet this is precisely the attitude of the author of *Pwyll* toward Havgan, "Summer White," Meleagant's counterpart, and the mabinogi likewise terminates the warfare of the seasons with the death of summer. What the explanation for this unsympathetic and seemingly unnatural treatment may be, one can only guess. One may still rest secure in the conviction that the basic theme of the *Charrette* was the annual struggle of the Kings of Winter and Summer for the possession of a vegetation goddess.

BOOK IV.   Yvain

Chapter XLV

YVAIN, SON OF URIEN

Yvain, son of Urien, is one of the few personages in Arthurian romance, besides Arthur and Tristan, who actually lived—Owain ap Uryen.[1] His father was a historic king of Rheged, a district of uncertain location somewhere in northern England or southern Scotland.[2] Together with other British kinglets Urien fought triumphantly against the sons of Ida, kings of Bernicia, in the latter half of the sixth century, but was slain, according to Nennius, during an expedition against Deodric, whose regnal dates are given in an eighth-century genealogy of Northumbrian kings as 582–589.[3] Owain continued the struggle after his father's death. Both Urien and his son won such glory by their martial exploits that their memory was preserved in panegyrics composed by the Welsh bards, particularly those attributed to Taliesin and Llywarch Hen.

Of the historic earthly career of Owain and Urien nothing is preserved in the Arthurian cycle, and it was, of course, a gross chronological blunder to make them contemporaries of Arthur. They were evidently names to be conjured with, however, and the Welsh *cyvarwyddon* and Breton *conteurs* created new legends about them, and we have already met Urien disguised as King Eurain of the "Joie de la Cort" adventure. An early and most significant development represented Owain as the son of Urien by the mythical Modron, daughter of Avallach. Modron's name, we know, was a regular phonetic development from that of Matrona, worshiped from Cisalpine Gaul to the mouth of the Rhine, as many inscriptions and images attest.[4] Her divine son Mabon was worshiped in pagan times as Apollo Maponos at Hexham, Ainstable, and Ribchester.[5] The tradition that Modron mated with the mortal Urien was probably inspired by the belief, of which we have ample evidence in Irish literature, that every

[1] On Owain and Uryen cf. J. Loth, *Mabinogion*, 2d ed., II, 1n. This should be corrected by the studies of Morris-Jones in *Cymmrodor*, XXVIII (1918), 64–71, 151–99, and of Ifor Williams in *Proceedings of the Brit. Acad.*, XVIII (1932), 270 ff.
[2] *Cymmrodor*, XXVIII, 64–71. *Proc. Brit. Acad.*, XVIII, 292. W. J. Watson, *History of Celtic Place-Names of Scotland* (1926), p. 156.
[3] F. Lot, *Nennius et l'Historia Brittonum*, I, 73–75, 202, 224. *Antiquity*, XVI (1942), 247.
[4] *Speculum*, XX (1945), 200 f. *Germanic Review*, XIX (1944), 81–142. For description and reproductions cf. E. Esperandieu, *Recueil général des bas-reliefs, statues et bustes de la Gaule romaine* (Paris, 1907–38), VIII, nos. 6356, 6358, 6401, 6412, 6559, 6560. On cult of Matronae and Matres cf. *Archaeologia Aeliana*, XV (1892), 314–36; Hastings, *Encyclopaedia of Religion and Ethics*, IV, 406–11; *Jahrbücher des Vereins von Alterthumsfreunden im Rheinlande*, LXXXIII (1887), 1–200; A. Maury, *Croyances et légendes du moyen âge*, pp. 10–17.
[5] Cf. *supra*, pp. 46, 165.

king mated with a goddess, and that his sovranty even depended on the union.[6]

The most explicit evidence for this tradition is a Welsh triad which names among the three blessed births of the Isle of Britain "Owain son of Urien and Morvudd, his sister, who were at the same time in the womb of Modron, daughter of Avallach." [7] A short Welsh tale of the sixteenth century, which has an early Irish analogue in the mating of the Dagda with the Morrigan, relates the circumstances under which Urien begat Owain and Morvudd.[8]

Uryen of Rheged came to a ford at Llanferres in Denbighshire, found there a lone woman washing, and had his will of her. She declared that she was the daughter of the King of Annwn (the abode of the gods), foretold the birth of a child, and when Urien returned after a year, presented him with twins, Owain and Morfydd.

This tale and this triad are immensely important for several reasons.

1. The tale explains why we frequently meet in the French romances an Yvain l'Aoutre, "the Bastard," [9] for, though he is differentiated from Yvain fils d'Urien, he is obviously the son whom Urien begat out of wedlock on the daughter of the King of Annwn.

2. The anonymous daughter of the King of Annwn is certainly Modron. Modron, since she is daughter of Avallach and mother of Owain by Urien, is identical with Morgain la Fée, daughter of Avalloc or King Avallo and mother of Yvain by Urien.[10]

3. This equation explains the mystery of Owain's ravens, to which there is reference in *Owain* and a number of Welsh poems.[11] In that strange phantasmagoria, *The Dream of Rhonabwy*, the ravens play a considerable part.[12] Arthur and Owain were engaged in a game of chess,[13] when a battle began near by between the youths of Arthur's household and Owain's ravens. At first the youths had the best of it, slaying and wounding the

---

[6] R. S. Loomis, *Celtic Myth*, pp. 296–300; *Zts. f. celt. Phil.*, XIX (1933), 352 f.; *Eriu*, XIV (1943), 14–28. Prof. O'Rahilly seems to be mistaken in asserting that Eriu was a sun-goddess (*Eriu*, XIV, 14–27). She was the bride of the sun-god Lug (J. Rhys, *Lectures on the Origin and Growth of Religion as Illustrated by Celtic Heathendom*, 2d ed., pp. 414–18), but was herself a goddess of the earth and vegetation. Cf. D'Arbois de Jubainville, *Cours de littérature celtique*, VI (Paris, 1899), 165: "Un caractère commun aux dieux homériques et aux dieux celtiques c'est l'anthropomorphisme . . . ils peuvent avoir et ils ont des rapports sexuels avec les simples mortels; un homme peut être fils d'un dieu et d'une femme, d'une déesse et d'un homme." This pagan concept descended into Arthurian romance, e.g. Potvin, *Perceval le Gallois*, III, vss. 21859 f.: "Morteus estoit envers le père, Mais non pas, sire, envers la mère." [7] Loth, *Mabinogion*, 2d ed., II, 283 f.
[8] *Aberystwyth Studies*, IV (1922), 105. *Mod. Phil.*, XLIII (1945), 67.
[9] *Erec*, vs. 1708. *Conte del Graal*, vss. 8157–59. H. O. Sommer, *Vulgate Version*, II, 165.
[10] Cf. *supra*, p. 91.
[11] Loth, *op. cit.*, I, 370n. *Mabinogion*, trans. C. Guest, Everyman ed., pp. 349 f., 357 f., 382.
[12] Loth, *op. cit.*, I, 366–71.
[13] For interpretation of the chess game cf. *Arkiv för nordisk Filologi*, VI (1934), 218–42.

birds, but when Owain ordered his standard to be lifted, the ravens rose into the air and attacked the youths; "they tore the heads of some and the eyes of others." They continued to destroy the youths until Owain ordered his standard to be lowered. Windisch had an inkling that these ravens had some connection with the crow (*badb*) into which the Irish goddess Morrigan and her sisters were wont to transform themselves,[14] and the Morrigan, as Miss Paton and Zenker showed,[15] is in striking ways a Goidelic counterpart of Morgain. Turning to the *Didot Perceval,* we find Morgain and her sisters taking part in a combat at a ford in the form of black birds.[16] Perceval is fighting with a certain Urbain, guardian of the ford, when he is suddenly attacked by a flock of birds, "blacker than anything he had ever seen. They flew at the opening of his helm (*parmi le hiaume*) to tear the eyes out of his head." The battle went against Perceval, but he cut down one of the birds. "As it fell, it turned into a dead woman, and she was of the loveliest form that he had ever seen." The other birds carried her away, and Perceval learned that she was the sister of Urbain's mistress and was now safe and well in Avalon. The whole episode of Perceval at the ford is full of reminders of the mabinogion,[17] and there can be no doubt that this is an authentic Welsh tradition of Morgain and her sisters, the fays of Avalon, concerning whom Geoffrey of Monmouth and Hartmann von Aue assure us that they could fly through the air on wings.[18] Urbain, the defender of the ford, was probably Urien, whose name, we know, was corrupted into Urain and Eurain.[19] Just as Urbain's mistress, Morgain, and her companions came to his aid in the form of black birds, so beyond doubt the ravens who fought on behalf of Owain in *The Dream of Rhonabwy* were his mother Modron and his aunts. It is amusing to observe that, according to Lady Guest,[20] three ravens form the heraldic charge of the House of Dynevor, which claims descent from Urien and his son Owain.

4. In the lai of *Desiré,*[21] the hero, his unnamed mistress of the spring, and the two beautiful children, a boy and a girl, with whom she presents him, are recognizable as counterparts of Urien, Modron (the fay of the ford), and their two children, Owain and Morfydd. The story is an elaborated form of the tabu theme so constantly attached to Morgain in her anonymous roles.[22] And Morgain was Modron.

Whereas the *Didot Perceval* is highly significant as showing that Urien's affair with Modron left its impress on a French romance of the thirteenth

14 E. Windisch, *Das keltische Brittannien bis zu Kaiser Arthur,* p. 77n.

15 Paton, *Fairy Mythology,* pp. 148–66. *Zts. f. franz. Sprache u. Lit.,* XLVIII (1925–26), 82–92.

16 *Didot-Perceval,* ed. W. Roach, pp. 200–202.   17 *Mod. Phil.,* XLIII, 65–71.

18 *Vita Merlini,* vss. 922 f. *Erek,* ed. M. Haupt, vss. 5177 f., 5185 f.

19 Cf. *supra,* pp. 176 f.

20 *Mabinogion,* trans. C. Guest, Everyman ed., p. 358.

21 *Lays of Desiré, Graelent, and Melion,* ed. E. M. Grimes, pp. 52–75. F. Michel, *Lais inédits des XIIᵉ et XIIIᵉ siècles* (Paris, 1826), pp. 5 ff.   22 *Speculum,* XX, 191–96.

century, the lai of *Desiré* is most important for the study of *Yvain* since it shows that Urien's affair with Modron was localized not only in Wales but in Lothian. For we are told that Desiré met his faery love near a fountain described in terms somewhat similar to those applied to the fountain in *Yvain,* and this fountain was in the Blanche Lande not far from Calatir,[23] a district which scholars have succeeded in identifying with Calder,[24] just west of Edinburgh and therefore within the confines of Lothian. This localization was no accident. The Scots author of a life of St. Kentigern, writing between 1147 and 1164, declared that Ewen, son of King Urien, celebrated by the *histriones* (that is, *conteurs*), wooed the stepdaughter of Leudonus, King of Leudonia (Lothian), surprised her beside a brook where she was wont to wash, ravished her, and begat on her the future Saint Kentigern.[25] This is apparently an ecclesiastical version of Urien's rape of Modron beside a ford—a version transferred to his son, and conformed to the not unusual practice of making secular heroes the progenitors of saints.[26]

This interpretation of *Desiré* and the *Life of Kentigern* is fully confirmed by *Yvain.* Ahlström and Arthur Brown have drawn attention to the detailed parallelism between Desiré's winning, losing, and then rewinning the fay of the fountain and Yvain's winning, losing, and then rewinning Laudine,[27] a parallelism which will be examined more minutely in our consideration of the heroine. Ahlström also emphasized the point that the original title of the Welsh *Owain* was *The Countess of the Fountain.* As the *Life of Kentigern* transfers the amour from Urien to his son, so does Chrétien. As the *Life* makes Ewen's beloved the daughter of the King of Leudonia (Lothian), so Chrétien makes Yvain's beloved the daughter of Duke Laudonez.[28] Though a fuller discussion of these matters must be reserved for a later point, enough has been said, I believe, to show that the love story of Yvain and Laudine was drawn from the same general body of tradition which is variously reflected in *Desiré* and the *Life of Kentigern,* the same, moreover, which we have often observed persistently centers tales of Morgain about Edinburgh. Though this body of tradition was made up of elements from old Irish and Welsh sagas, there can be little doubt that it was largely put together and localized in Lothian by Breton *conteurs* visiting the region after the Norman Conquest.

[23] *Lays of Desiré*, pp. 48, 52 f., 58.
[24] A. O. Anderson, *Early Sources of Scottish History* (Edinburgh, 1922), I, 234.
[25] *Lives of St. Ninian and St. Kentigern*, ed. A. P. Forbes (Edinburgh, 1874), pp. 245–47. Cf. *infra*, p. 302 and H. M. and N. K. Chadwick, *Growth of Literature*, I, 237.
[26] *Vitae Sanctorum Britanniae*, ed. A. W. Wade-Evans (Cardiff, 1944), pp. 320–23. In this twelfth-century text not only is Kyndeyrn (Kentigern) the son of Owein mab Uryen, but also ten saints are listed as descendants of Cuneda, Yestin as the son of Gereint mab Erbin, Peblic as the son of Maxen Wledic, and Dyfnauc as the great-grandson of Caradauc Vreichvras.
[27] *Mélanges de philologie romane dédiés à Carl Wahlund*, pp. 297, 299. *Studies and Notes in Philology and Literature*, VIII, 128 f., 140 f.   [28] Vss. 2152 f.

The story of the loves of Yvain and Laudine, localized in southern Scotland, seems to have passed through the hands of a Breton careless of geography. For Chrétien, to the bewilderment of his readers, says not a word of Yvain's crossing the Channel on his way from Carduel to the Forest of Broceliande. Apparently, to the mind of this Breton redactor, a spring in the Blanche Lande suggested the famous spring in the Forest of Broceliande, and without any regard for the resultant confusion he transferred the romance of Yvain and the Countess of the Fountain to his native Brittany, retaining, however, the telltale fact that his heroine was the daughter of Duke Laudonez.

As for Yvain's name, it too betrays the influence of the Breton *conteurs*. For it is the Breton name Ivan, recorded as early as the eleventh century,[29] which supplies the intermediate form between Welsh Owein and French Yvain. The contagion of Gauvain probably standardized the second syllable as a diphthong.

To recapitulate, the love story of Yvain goes back to the ancient legend of his father's amour with the water-fay Modron;[30] from Wales the tradition passed like the rest of the *Matière de Bretagne* to Brittany; it was then brought back and localized in southern Scotland with many other legends of Morgain la Fée; transmitted once more through Breton hands and attracting the local tradition of the fountain of Berenton, it reached the author of Y, the common source of *Yvain* and *Owain*. It was he, probably, who added a number of preliminary and later adventures from the common stock of Arthurian fiction—adventures which had no early connection with Yvain, but which could be told indifferently of any knight of the Round Table. It is with a sequence of these originally alien incidents that Chrétien's poem begins.

Chapter XLVI

CALOGRENANT'S HUMILIATION AND ITS SEQUEL

VERSES 1–872

When Arthur was holding a Whitsun feast at Carduel, he retired after the banquet to his chamber with the Queen, and fell asleep. Several knights, including Keu and Yvain, were sitting outside the chamber door, listening to a story of misadventure which Calogrenant had begun. Guenievre over-

[29] H. Morice, *Mémoires pour servir de preuves à l'histoire ecclésiastique et civile de Bretagne* (Paris, 1742–46), I, 457, 469. Here we find the Latinized forms Ivani and Ivanus.
[30] Similarly the *Beowulf* poet credited to Sigemund the dragon exploit which was later ascribed to his son Sigurd or Sigfrit. Cf. *Beowulf*, ed. F. Klaeber (1936), p. 160.

heard Calogrenant and stealthily came out of her chamber and joined the circle. As Calogrenant leaped courteously to his feet, Keu sneered at him, and an exchange of insults followed. Guenievre bade Calogrenant resume his narrative, which ran as follows. Seven years before, he had ridden through the forest of Broceliande, had met with some adventures, had been attacked at a storm-making spring by a tall knight, who overthrew him, led away his horse, and left him to make his ignominious way back on foot. When Calogrenant's story was ended, Arthur emerged from his chamber and heard the tale of misadventure repeated by the Queen. He then swore that he would find his way to the spring, reaching it by the eve of St. John, and spend the night there. Yvain, however, determined to anticipate the King and avenge the shame of his cousin Calogrenant himself. He slipped away secretly, armed himself, and after meeting experiences similar to those of Calogrenant, came to the spring and fatally wounded the tall knight. Arthur, too, observing his vow, came to the fountain on the eve of St. John.

THE OPENING SCENE in *Yvain* and its sequel evidently make use of a story pattern found, with considerable modifications, in *Perlesvaus* and in Pseudo-Wauchier's continuation of *Le Conte del Graal.*

According to *Perlesvaus,*[1] Arthur has gone to sleep in his chamber at Cardoil, when a young squire, Cahus, Chaus, or Keux,[2] son of Yvain l'Avotre, lying in a hall near by, dreams of a disastrous adventure. He finds a chapel in a glade of the forest, surrounded by a cemetery. Within the chapel a dead knight lies on a bier in the midst of four golden candlesticks. Cahus seizes one and rides away. A black giant meets him and deals him a mortal blow. Waking from his dream, Cahus calls for a priest and, when Arthur and the Queen come from their chamber, tells them his dream before he dies. Arthur himself sets out, equipped with the shield and spear of Yvain, Cahus' father (with the intent, it would seem, of avenging the young squire). He comes to a chapel where the body of a hermit is lying, and hears fiends and angels disputing over the dying man's soul. At another chapel he witnesses the miracle of St. Gregory, and is counseled by a holy hermit. Finally he encounters a Black Knight with a flaming spear, who challenges him because he has received the golden candlestick from Cahus. (One surmises that this is the same black giant who attacked Cahus.) Arthur slays the Black Knight.

Pseudo-Wauchier gives two versions of the same fundamental plot. The first runs as follows.[3]

[1] *Perlesvaus,* ed. Nitze and others, I, 26–40. For comment on this episode cf. *ibid.,* II, 105–20.
[2] Keux is the form given in the 1516 and 1523 Black Letter editions of *Perlesvaus.* Cf. *ibid.,* I, 412 and 12. Though the author of the romance did not apparently recognize this young squire as the notoriously unlucky Keu, the later editor of the text did. That he was right is proved by the parallels from Pseudo-Wauchier.
[3] Potvin, *Perceval le Gallois,* III, 239 ff. Trans. J. L. Weston, *Sir Gawain and the Lady of Lys* (London, 1907), pp. 16–48. For discussions of this story cf. Newstead, *Bran the Blessed,* pp. 70–85, and P. J. Kettrick, *Relation of Golagros and Gawane to the Old French Perceval* (Washington, D.C., 1931), pp. 34 ff.

Arthur and his knights are resting beside a spring. Keu sets out to forage, comes to a tower, finds there at first no living soul, but in the hall discovers a dwarf, roasting a peacock on a spit. When the dwarf refuses to give up the bird, Keu knocks him against a column. A tall knight enters, strikes Keu violently to the earth, and the seneschal returns humiliated to Arthur. Gauvain sets out on the same errand, and obtains hospitable entertainment for Arthur and his knights at the same tower where Keu had been shamed. Next there is brief mention of a perilous garden of sepulchres and the hermits who dwell there. Finally, in an enchanted castle Keu discovers the tall knight Bran de Lis, and Gauvain engages in combat with him.

The second version by Pseudo-Wauchier is this.[4]

Keu is sent by the Queen to bring to her tent a knight who is riding by. Keu is promptly unhorsed by the stranger and returns on foot to report his failure to the Queen. Gauvain sets out in turn, and by courtesy persuades the stranger to return with him. But as they ride together, the stranger knight is transfixed by the javelin of an invisible foe. Gauvain takes his arms and follows his quest. He comes by night to a chapel, where he sees a black hand come in through a window and extinguish a taper in a golden candlestick and hears a hideous voice. Next he arrives at a mysterious hall, the folk vanish, and he sees a body lying on a bier, surrounded by four golden candlesticks.

It is apparent that these three narratives present variations on one basic plot, and that this plot, though differing on important points, furnished to *Yvain* the following elements: (1) The King is sleeping in his chamber. (2) A knight, usually Keu, goes on a perilous adventure, and returns discomfited. (3) He tells his story before Arthur and the Queen. (4) Arthur, or one of his knights, undertakes the adventure with success. It is also apparent that Calogrenant, who plays the traditional role of Keu, is really Cai-lo-grenant, "Kay the Grumbler." Kay's churlish disposition is already familiar to us, and the very verb *grenir* is applied to him by Raoul de Houdenc.[5] The fact that Calogrenant appears quarreling with Keu is merely an illustration of the doubling of characters not uncommon in Arthurian romance, so that more than once we find a figure fighting himself under a variant name.[6] The unhappy outcome of Calogrenant's combat at the storm-making spring likewise shows his identity with Keu, for we are already aware of Keu's inveterate habit of getting the worst of any encounter. It is interesting to note that, whereas Chrétien represents Yvain as setting out to avenge the shame done to his cousin Calogrenant,[7] the

[4] Potvin, *op. cit.,* III, 352–65. Trans. J. L. Weston, *Sir Gawain at the Grail Castle* (London, 1903), pp. 4–19.

[5] Raoul de Houdenc, *Vengeance Raguidel,* ed. Friedwagner, vss. 4637 f. The Welsh author of *Owain,* meeting the totally unfamiliar name Calogrenant in Y, substituted Cynon, son of Clydno, the name of a renowned warrior in Welsh tradition. Cf. Loth, *Mabinogion,* 2d ed., II, 2, n. 1; *Cymmrodor,* XXXII (1922), 15.

[6] *PMLA,* LIV (1939), 667 f. Cf. also the fight between Gawein and Gasozein in *Diu Krone,* vss. 11854–12139. We saw in Chap. XIX that Gasozein not only plays the part of Walwanius but also owes his name to a corruption of Galoain.

[7] Vss. 581–89.

author of *Perlesvaus* tells us that Arthur assumed Yvain's arms when he set out for the chapel where Cahus had been mortally wounded.

But though there is much in common between the adventures of Calogrenant in *Yvain* and those of Keu in *Perlesvaus* and in Pseudo-Wauchier's tales, there are many differences. The most important will be dealt with in later sections, but here it is possible to point out three elements in Chrétien's narrative which derive from the traditional theme of the Combat at the Ford, which we considered in connection with Erec's fight with the robbers.[8] It will be remembered that in *Le Lai de l'Espine,* which contains the most eerie and purely Celtic form of this theme preserved in French, the hero sets out on the eve of St. John to watch at the Perilous Ford throughout the night, and that great importance is attached to the hero's seizing and keeping his opponent's steed. The latter feature becomes one of the distinctive elements in the many versions of the Ford Combat. From this plot, therefore, are probably derived Calogrenant's loss of his steed to the victorious knight at the storm-making spring,[9] and Arthur's announcement that he intends to arrive there on the vigil of St. John and abide through the night.[10]

Further influence of the Ford Combat tradition on *Yvain* becomes apparent when we examine the Scottish romance of *Eger and Grime*. Though this is a fifteenth-century work, the nature of its correspondences with *Le Lai de l'Espine* and the first episode in *Pwyll* proves the authenticity of the material; [11] it is no haphazard collection of borrowings from French and English romances. The story opens with the return of an adventurous knight, Eger, sore wounded as the result of his combat at a ford with Sir Gray-Steel, an eldritch knight.[12] Eger related his misfortunes to his sworn brother, Grime, in the secrecy of his chamber. But a damsel, Winliane or Winglayne, overheard the sorry tale.

> The bour wherein the Lady was
> Was from the hall a little space. . . .
> A scarlet mantle hath she tane
> And to the chamber is she gane,
> She heard them with a privie din,
> She stood right still, and stood within,
> Under the wall she stood so still
> Heard the manner that it was ill.[13]

[8] Chap. XVIII.   [9] Vs. 544.
[10] Vss. 661–70. Cf. *supra,* p. 94, n. 47, on St. John's Eve.
[11] *Eger and Grime* parallels *L'Espine* in that the hero, having heard of a perilous adventure at a ford, encounters there an unearthly champion in red arms. *Eger and Grime* parallels *Pwyll* in that a knight is defeated at a perilous ford, and his sworn friend, who closely resembles him in feature, goes to the neighborhood of the ford, is hospitably entertained by a fair lady, and slays his friend's unearthly antagonist.
[12] *Eger and Grime,* ed. J. R. Caldwell, pp. 182–207.
[13] *Ibid.,* p. 209.

Compare this situation with that in *Yvain,* and note the lines: "Outside the chamber door were Dodinel and Sagremor . . . and with them Calogrenant, a right seemly knight, who had begun to tell a tale, not of his honor but of his shame. While he was relating his story and the Queen was overhearing it, she rose from beside the King and stealthily approached the group." [14]

Professor Hibbard pointed out the marked similarity between the plot of *Eger and Grime* and that of *Yvain,* and showed the possibility that the Scottish author knew the English *Ywain and Gawain,*[15] but it is not possible that he drew upon this poem either for his main plot or for the detail of Winliane's eavesdropping. The main plot is too clearly related to *Le Lai de l'Espine* and the first episode in *Pwyll* as regards its characteristic features to be based on any version of *Yvain.* Nor can the correspondence between Winliane's overhearing the tale of Eger's disastrous adventure at the ford and Guenievre's overhearing the tale of Calogrenant's disastrous adventure at the spring be explained by direct borrowing. For it is highly unlikely that the Scottish poet knew that at an early stage in Continental Arthurian tradition there was some confusion between the names Guenievre and Winlogee, Guenloie, and Guendoloena.[16] It must have been at this stage that one version of the eavesdropping lady attached itself to Guenievre and another version to Winliane.

We may conclude, then, that the Ford Combat tradition supplied *Yvain* with three features: (1) Guenievre overhears, from a chamber near by, the beginning of Calogrenant's tale of misadventure. (2) The victorious knight of the spring seizes Calogrenant's steed and obliges him to start back on foot. (3) Arthur vows to spend the night of St. John's vigil at the spring.

---

[14] Vss. 53–64.   [15] L. A. Hibbard, *Mediaeval Romance in England,* pp. 314 f.
[16] *Medieval Studies in Memory of G. Schoepperle Loomis,* p. 222. T. P. Cross and W. A. Nitze, *Lancelot and Guenevere,* p. 23: "It can hardly be doubted that Winlogee and Guenevere are parallel figures." It is interesting to note that though Guendoloena, Arthur's queen in *De Ortu Walwanii,* does not *over*hear the tale of a defeat at a ford, thus differing from Winliane, she does *hear* from Arthur his false account of his overthrow at a ford. There is certainly a remote connection between the *De Ortu* and *Eger and Grime.* On the form Guendoloena cf. *Annales de Bretagne,* XV (1899–1900), 533 f.

Chapter XLVII

THE HOSPITABLE HOST AND THE
STORM-KNIGHT

VERSES 175–2155

As we know, Calogrenant told how he had set out seven years before in search of adventure, had passed through the forest of Broceliande, and had come late in the day to a fortress. Its owner, a vavasor, invited him in. A fair, slim maiden disarmed him and robed him in a mantle. The two being left alone, she entertained her guest so charmingly in a walled meadow that he was annoyed when the Hospitable Host interrupted them to announce supper. Nevertheless Calogrenant enjoyed the meal because of his fair vis-à-vis, and he was comfortably lodged that night. The next day he met a Giant Herdsman, and was directed to a fountain near a chapel. He summoned the guardian of the spring and straightway there was a violent storm of lightning and hail. A tall knight rode up with a great noise, accused Calogrenant of injuring his domain, and hurled him to earth. Humiliated, Calogrenant returned. When, long after, Yvain heard this story, he set out to try the adventure, spent a night with the Hospitable Host and his daughter, met the Herdsman, arrived at the spring, and endured the storm. The tall knight, burning with anger like a live coal, attacked him, but received a mortal wound and fled to his castle. Thither Yvain followed him, saw him lying dead on his bier, and was smitten with love for his beautiful widow. Through the helpful agency of the maiden Lunete, within a few days Yvain was united in marriage to the wife of the Storm-Knight. The latter's name was Esclados li Ros.

THE HISTORY of the episodes in which the Hospitable Host and the Storm-Knight figure may best be studied by setting side by side the corresponding elements in the Welsh *Owain*, the Middle English *Gawain and the Green Knight*, and the Irish saga of *Bricriu's Feast*.[1] The first of these texts, of course, parallels closely Chrétien's version, but supplies significant variants. It may be summarized thus.[2]

Kynon [a name substituted by the Welsh author for the baffling Calogrenant] sets out to try whether he is superior to all other knights, and at evening comes to a large and shining castle. A yellow-haired man in the prime of life, clad in yellow, invites him in. The women of the castle, more beautiful than Gwenhwy-

[1] I have already discussed these in *Celtic Myth*, pp. 68–71. Cf. also *PMLA*, XLVII (1932), 317–25.
[2] Loth, *Mabinogion*, 2d ed., II, 5–17.

var, attend to his wants. The "Yellow Man," [3] learning the purpose of Kynon's quest, directs him to an adventure which will test his superiority. After meeting a giant herdsman, Kynon goes on to a fountain in the forest and summons its guardian. There is a peal of thunder and a shower of hail. A knight all in black on a black horse rides up, accuses Kynon of injuring his dominions, and hurls him to the earth. Humiliated, Kynon returns to his court. Long after, Owain sets out, spends the night in the castle of the "Yellow Man," sees the beauteous maidens, and is directed by the "Yellow Man" to the fountain. There he hears the thunder, endures the hailstorm, is attacked by the black knight, and deals him a mortal wound.

Chrétien's version, it will be noted, differs in two points significant for our inquiry. Instead of the many damsels, more lovely than Gwenhwyvar, who attend on Kynon, there is but one damsel, who is left alone with Calogrenant, and entertains him so gaily that he is annoyed when his host summons him to supper.[4] The second difference is that Chrétien mentions a chapel near the perilous spring.[5] Now let us turn to the corresponding story in *Gawain and the Green Knight.*[6]

Gawain sets out from Arthur's court to find the Green Chapel and its perilous adventure. He comes to a castle that shimmers and shines through the trees. A man of advanced age, with a bright beard and a face as fierce as fire, welcomes him. A lady more lovely than Wenore (Guenievre) sits beside Gawain at table, and they had great comfort in each other's company. For three days the host leaves them together. Finally, having learned the goal of Gawain's quest, he sends him with a guide to the Green Chapel. There Gawain finds a tumbling stream, hears a grinding roar, and promptly a knight in green appears.[7] Gawain undergoes the Beheading Test, and learns that his host with the fiery face and the shimmering castle is identical with the Green Knight.

It has long been established that *Gawain and the Green Knight* owes much to the Irish saga, *Bricriu's Feast,* and Miss Buchanan showed that the elements just summarized have their principal source in the second version of the Beheading Test incident in that saga, which she called the Yellow and Terror version.[8] .

[3] Loth's translation of *melyn* (yellow) as "blond" is not obligatory, since the man was clad in yellow as well as having yellow hair.
[4] Vss. 225–55. In vs. 566 the damsel is identified as the Host's daughter.
[5] Vss. 393 f., 412.
[6] *Gawain and the Green Knight*, ed. J. R. R. Tolkien and E. V. Gordon, vss. 691–2357. For analysis of Celtic elements in the poem cf. *PMLA*, XLVII, 315–38; *Journ. of Eng. and Germ. Phil.*, XLII (1943), 149–84. For other discussions of the material cf. G. L. Kittredge, *Study of Gawain and the Green Knight; Mod. Phil.*, XIII (1915), 433–62, 689–730; XXXIII (1936), 351–66.
[7] The reason for the green color of the knight must be the ambiguity of the Irish and Welsh word *glas*, which may mean either gray or green. Cf. *PMLA*, XLVII, 327, 330; *Journ. of Eng. and Germ. Phil.*, XLII, 180.
[8] *PMLA*, XLVII, 315–38. *Feast of Bricriu*, ed. G. Henderson, pp. 97–101. French translation in D'Arbois de Jubainville, *L'Epopée celtique en Irlande*, pp, 132–35.

Three warriors of Ulster, disputing which of them was the mightiest, set out from the royal court, to be judged by Yellow son of White. They come to his house beside a ford. They tell their errand, and Yellow sends them on with a guide to Terror son of Great Fear, a wizard who changes his shape. They arrive at a loch, where Terror proposes to them the Beheading Test. Conall and Loigaire shirk the test, but Cuchulainn carries it through, the detail of the three blows matching closely the account in *Gawain and the Green Knight*.

We have, then, in *Owain, Gawain and the Green Knight,* and *Bricriu's Feast* something like a common pattern: One or more warriors set out from a royal court (*GGK, BF*) to determine who is the mightiest warrior (*O, BF*). They come to a shining castle of a hospitable host (*O, GGK*), who is called "the Yellow Man" or Yellow (*O, BF*), and tell him their errand (*O, GGK, BF*). There are one or more women who surpass Guenievre in beauty (*O, GGK*). The host sends them with a guide (*GGK, BF*) to a spring, stream, or loch (*O, GGK, BF*). There is a roaring sound (*O, GGK*). A shapeshifter appears to carry out the Beheading Test (*GGK, BF*). One or two warriors fail to meet the test (*O, BF*). The hero is successful (*O, GGK, BF*).

Since Yvain's adventures with the Hospitable Host and with the Storm-Knight parallel those of Owain, and on two points—the charming tête-à-tête during the Host's absence, and the chapel at the perilous rendezvous—come closer than the Welsh version to *Gawain and the Green Knight*, there can be little doubt that they are derived in part from the common source of all three narratives, the Yellow and Terror episode in *Bricriu's Feast*.

Some of the discrepancies between *Owain* and the Yellow and Terror episode are accounted for by another story of the testing of the Ulster heroes, also narrated in *Bricriu's Feast*.[9] The three rivals are sent to Curoi mac Dairi for trial; they set out singly; on a plain each is overtaken by a black mist or cloud; Curoi appears in a dark gray mantle (*arit odar*); he charges that his lands have been damaged; two of the rivals are ignominiously defeated; Cuchulainn is triumphant. This version of the testing of the Ulster heroes seems also to have influenced *Owain,* since here are precedents for the separate journeys of Kynon and Owain, for the premonitory storm, for the black garb of the knight, for the knight's charge of damage done to his possessions. Altogether the two Irish accounts of the testing of the rival warriors contain ten features which reappear in *Owain;* and this correspondence, taken together with the analogies which the Irish and the Welsh tales both present to *Gawain and the Green Knight,* makes an impressive case for the dependence of *Owain* on *Bricriu's Feast* for much in the adventures with the Hospitable Host and the Storm-Knight. And a similar dependence must also be maintained for the *Yvain* version of the same adventures.

[9] Ed. Henderson, pp. 42-51. D'Arbois, pp. 104-8.

Yvain, moreover, as has been already noted, tells how Calogrenant after his reception by the Hospitable Host was left alone by all the household except the Host's lovely daughter. She entertained him so charmingly that he was disappointed when his Host returned to summon him to supper. But the repast was entirely to his liking since the maiden was seated before him. There is nothing like this in the Yellow and Terror episode, but there is a marked correspondence with still a third version of the testing of the Ulster heroes in *Bricriu's Feast.*[10] It is significant that in this version when the three warriors arrived at Curoi's fortress, Curoi was absent, but his wife Blathnat waited on them, providing refreshing drinks and excellent beds, and "it liked them well." Thus it would seem that Calogrenant's sojourn with the Hospitable Host combines two Irish accounts of the testing of the Ulster warriors, the Welsh *Owain* retaining clear traces of the stay at the house of Yellow, while Chrétien retains a trace of Blathnat's hospitality in the fortress of Curoi.[11]

Gawain and the Green Knight makes it possible to draw interesting conclusions regarding the nature of the Hospitable Host and the Storm-Knight in *Yvain* and *Owain,* conclusions which are verified by the Irish sources. Bercilak, who corresponds to the Storm-Knight, enters Arthur's hall with a noise, and his glance is like lightning.[12] When he appears at the rendezvous with Gawain, there is a premonitory harsh roar;[13] his grim tool, the ax, is in many mythologies a lightning symbol.[14] He declares that he is identical with the Hospitable Host, who, we remember, dwelt in a shining castle and had a bright beard and a face as fierce as fire. The very phrase, "felle face as the fyre," is applied in *The Wars of Alexander* to the sun-god.[15] It would seem that Bercilak is a dual personality, at one time suggesting the roar of the storm and the flash of lightning, at another the radiance of the sun. If this be so, we can understand why the double role of Bercilak as solar Host and Storm-Knight should be filled in *Owain* by the Yellow Man with his lustrous castle and by the black knight, whose arrival is preluded by a peal of thunder and a violent storm.

This mythic interpretation is neatly confirmed by the Irish evidence. The yellow Host and the black Storm-Knight of *Owain* correspond, as we have seen, to Yellow son of White and Terror son of Great Fear in one of the tales in *Bricriu's Feast.* Since the Ulster heroes in this tale are sent to Yellow to be tested and Terror actually carries out the test, there is a hint of the

---

[10] Ed. Henderson, pp. 100–103. D'Arbois, pp. 135 f. Henderson was mistaken in translating "dia reir" as "according to his (Curoi's) wish," since the phrase means "at their service." Cf. E. Windisch, *Irische Texte mit Wörterbuch* (Leipzig, 1880), p. 739, s.v. *riar.*

[11] The Irish story of Blathnat's hospitality during Curoi's absence was contaminated by the Welsh legend of the hospitality of Arawn's wife during her husband's absence, and the result may be seen in *Gawain and the Green Knight,* the Guingambresil episode, and in *Fergus,* pp. 41–55. Cf. Chap. LXXII.   [12] Vss. 132, 199.

[13] Vss. 2199–2204.   [14] Loomis, *Celtic Myth,* p. 50.

[15] *Gawain and the Green Knight,* ed. Tolkien and Gordon, p. 96, note on vs. 847.

identity of Yellow and Terror, which is corroborated by the identity of the corresponding figures in *Gawain and the Green Knight,* namely, the Hospitable Host and the Green Knight. We perceive now why Yellow and Terror have taken the place of Curoi in the Beheading Test, for these names are appropriate titles of the sun and the storm, and it has been shown in an earlier chapter that Curoi offered ample credentials of his dual nature, his split personality. As the bringer of light to the household but not burning, as traveler to the uttermost parts of the earth, as dweller in the sky, which revolves during his absence on a nocturnal journey to the east, he is the sun. As the man in the dark gray mantle, whose approach is heralded by a black mist, and who deals mighty blows with an ax, he is the incarnation of the storm.

There is some curious additional evidence that Curoi is the remote prototype of the Storm-Knight in *Yvain.* The latter Chrétien calls Esclados li Ros (vs. 1970), and describes him as follows: "The knight came blazing more than a live coal, with as much noise as if he were chasing a rutting stag" (vss. 812–14). As for the name, we may note that in Arthurian nomenclature the syllable *es* was sometimes arbitrarily prefixed to proper names, as in Escalibor [16] and Escavalon.[17] If we subtract the *es* from Esclados, the remaining element suggests the name of a king hostile to Arthur in the *Vulgate Lancelot,* Claudas de la Terre Deserte.[18] His portrait distinctly recalls that of Curoi. "The tale tells that he was fully nine feet in height, measured in the feet of that time. His face was black and coarse, his eyebrows matted, and his eyes large and black and wide apart. He had a short, hideous nose and a red beard." [19] We read, moreover, that he loved to wield an ax in battle more than any other man.[20] Compare the description of Curoi in "The Champion's Covenant." "A huge, ugly churl. It seemed that there was not a warrior among the Ulstermen who was half his height. . . . In his right hand was an ax." [21] Moreover, when we compare Curoi as he has developed into the Green Knight and the Hospitable Host in *Gawain and the Green Knight,* we discover further remarkable resemblances to Claudas and Esclados. Like Claudas, the Green Knight is gigantic, wields a great ax, is king of a desert land (Hautdesert),[22] and,

16 On prefix Es- cf. *Zts. f. franz. Sprache u. Lit.,* XII (1890), "Abhandlungen," 236; XXVII (1904), "Abhandlungen," 103.   17 *Romanic Review,* XXIX (1938), 176 f.
18 How these names and Karadas, Cardoil, and Carado came to be applied to the Arthurian descendants of Curoi, I am unable to say, but I suspect contamination in the Welsh stage with Caradoc. Cf. *PMLA,* XLV (1930), 428 f.; XLVIII (1933), 1002–9, 1013–15, 1031–33.
19 Sommer, *Vulgate Version,* III, 26.   20 *Ibid.,* p. 61.
21 D'Arbois de Jubainville, *L'Epopée Celtique,* pp. 143 f. Cross and Slover, *Ancient Irish Tales,* p. 277.
22 *Gawain and the Green Knight,* ed. Tolkien and Gordon, vs. 2445. The note on p. 115 of this edition to the effect that Hautdesert means "high hermitage" and refers to the Green Chapel is contradicted by the fact that the chapel lies in a valley (vss. 2145–47). That the Green Knight was a king is shown by the ms. reading of vs. 992, where the editors have mistakenly substituted "lord." On Claudas de la Deserte cf. *PMLA,* XLV, 441.

as the Hospitable Host, he displays a reddish-brown beard. The Green Knight's approach, like that of Esclados, is preceded by a loud noise.[23] As the Hospitable Host, he has a face as fierce as fire and a reddish beard, and thus reveals some likeness to Esclados, whose epithet, "li Ros," suggests that he has red hair,[24] and who, metaphorically at least, blazed like a live coal. These correspondences between Esclados, Claudas, the Green Knight, and Curoi are too marked to be merely fortuitous. Added to the other evidence, they seem to establish the derivation of Esclados from Curoi.

Another link between Esclados and Curoi is provided by *La Mule sans Frein* of Paien de Maisieres (early thirteenth century). Brown, Zenker, Orlowski, and Kittredge have pointed out [25] that this poem retains a primitive feature to which Chrétien (and the author of Y before him) has given a realistic turn. As Yvain pursued Esclados through the gateway of his palace, the portcullis dropped on Yvain's horse, cutting it in two and slicing off Yvain's spurs. Paien represents Gauvain as arriving before a whirling castle, spurring his mule through the gateway as it passed, and coming through intact, though the mule lost its tail.[26] If we admit the parallel with *Yvain*, as did the eminent scholars named above, then there can be no doubt that the later poem has preserved the earlier form. Now this revolving castle is surely derived from Curoi's fortress as described in *Bricriu's Feast*. Both are said to revolve as rapidly as a millstone.[27] Within the castle Gauvain met a huge *vilain*, bearing a *jusarme*, who carried out the Beheading Test, just as Cuchulainn carried out the Beheading Test with Curoi, disguised as a gigantic herdsman with an ax.[28] Thus we are led to the conclusion that Esclados' castle preserves, in the dropping portcullis, a curiously modernized relic of Curoi's fortress.

There is a final suggestion that Esclados is derived from Curoi. Brown long since observed [29] that the famous story of Curoi's death and the union of his widow or mistress with his slayer may well have furnished the basis for the speedy wedding of Laudine with her husband's slayer. In that case,

---

[23] Vss. 2199–2204.   [24] *PMLA*, LI (1936), 9–12.

[25] *Studies and Notes in Philology and Literature*, VIII, 80. *PMLA*, XX (1905), 693. *Beihefte zur Zts. f. rom. Phil.*, LXX, 26. Paien de Maisieres, *La Damoisele à la Mule*, ed. B. Orlowski, pp. 74 f., 89. Kittredge, *Study of Gawain and the Green Knight*, pp. 42–47, 244 f.

[26] Paien de Maisieres, *op. cit.*, vss. 440–70.

[27] *Ibid.*, vs. 440 f.: "Li chastiaus si fort tornoioit con muele de molin qui muet." Cross and Slover, *Ancient Irish Tales*, p. 273: "The fort revolved as swiftly as a mill-stone." Orlowski and Brown seem to be mistaken in following Rhys's interpretation of Caer Siddi in *The Spoils of Annwn* as a revolving castle with an active door (Paien de Maisieres, *op. cit.*, pp. 79 f.; *Studies and Notes in Philology and Literature*, VIII, 77, n. 1; 79. J. Rhys, *Studies in the Arthurian Legend*, p. 301). Caer Siddi does not mean "revolving castle" (*PMLA*, LVI, 901–3), and *ynys pybyrdor*, which means literally "isle of the strong door," seems not to refer to any motion of the island or the fortress, but rather parallels the description of the island castle of maidens in *Lanzelet*: "albeit there was a gate, it was of hardest adamant." L. A. Paton, *Lancelot of the Lake*, p. 7.

[28] Paien, *op. cit.*, vss. 504–633. Cross and Slover, *op. cit.*, pp. 277–80.

[29] *Studies and Notes*, VIII, 51, 56.

Laudine's dilemma as to whether she should take Yvain for her husband was not due to Chrétien's imitation of Jocaste's dilemma in *Le Roman de Thèbes,* though Foerster may have been right in suspecting some influence from this quarter.[30] Though, as we shall presently see, Yvain's relations with Lunete and Laudine are based on quite different Celtic sources from those which furnished his adventures up to his being trapped in the gateway, it is quite possible that the theme of Laudine's precipitate acceptance of her husband's slayer is a survival of Blathnat's return to Cuchulainn as soon as he had killed Curoi. At least, there is no parallel, so far as I know, in any other likely Celtic source for *Yvain.*

Of course, one may feel hesitant about subscribing to the view that these various Irish traditions about Curoi's testing of the Ulster warriors and his final death at the hands of Cuchulainn were somehow brought together to form the adventures of Calogrenant and Yvain. Yet there should be no doubt that these very traditions were among the most powerful influences on Arthurian romance; there can be no doubt that *La Mule sans Frein* combines the picture of Curoi as lord of a whirling fortress, which we get from one episode in *Bricriu's Feast,* with the picture of Curoi as the churl who carries out the Beheading Test, which we get from another episode in *Bricriu's Feast.* Miss Buchanan demonstrated that *Gawain and the Green Knight* was largely a composite of the stories of Cuchulainn and Curoi which we find separately in Irish saga.[31] There is nothing, therefore, incredible in the hypothesis that the first part of *Yvain* is a similar composite, an attempt to carry out the obligations of the old Irish *fili:* "He is no *fili* who does not synchronize and harmonize all the stories." [32]

To sum up, then. The following elements in the Cuchulainn-Curoi group of stories seem to be represented in Chrétien's poem: (1) The successive testings of two or more warriors who set out from a royal court. (2) The host who directs the warriors to the abode of the testing giant. (3) The woman in the host's fortress who entertains the warriors during the host's absence. (4) The storm which precedes the approach of the giant.[33] (5) The giant's complaint of the damage done to his lands. (6) The humiliating defeat of the first warrior and the victory of the hero.

---

[30] W. Foerster, *Kristian von Troyes, Wörterbuch,* pp. 107–09. Kristian von Troyes, *Yvain,* ed. Foerster and Hilka (Halle, 1926), pp. xx, xxx, xxxvi. Cf. *Beihefte zur Zts. f. rom. Phil.,* LXX, 202 f.

[31] *PMLA,* XLVII (1932), 315–338. Miss Buchanan was probably mistaken in assuming that the combination was made by Irish *filid* as early as the ninth century. It seems more likely that the Cuchulainn-Curoi complex was recognized as a homogeneous group of stories even after they had been transmitted to the Welsh and the Bretons. There would then be a continuous tendency to unify them.

[32] E. O'Curry, *Lectures on the Manuscript Materials of Ancient Irish History* (Dublin, 1861), p. 583.

[33] The dark cloud which preludes the approach of the Storm-Giant in the Irish saga was very naturally transformed into a terrific storm when the scene was laid at the famous fountain of Berenton, as we shall see in Chap. XLIX.

(7) The giant's revolving fortress. (8) The death of the giant and the precipitate uniting of his widow with his slayer.

Chapter XLVIII

THE GIANT HERDSMAN

VERSES 278–366

After leaving the Hospitable Host, Calogrenant came to a clearing filled with savage bulls. In the midst of them, sitting on the stump of a tree, was a huge churl, who looked like a Moor. He was clad in hides and leaned on a club. He leaped up on seeing the knight, and the following dialogue ensued. "Art thou a creature of good or not?" "I am a man." "What sort of man art thou?" "Such as thou seest; I am never any other." "What dost thou here?" "I stand and guard these beasts throughout the forest." The incredulous Calogrenant asked how the churl guarded and controlled such wild creatures, and was told that they were kept in terror of their master by the force with which he caught them by the horns and subdued them. No other person could go among them without being killed. When Calogrenant disclosed that he was in search of adventures to prove his hardihood, the Giant Herdsman directed him to the storm-making spring near by.

OUR INVESTIGATION of the Hospitable Host and the Storm Giant has shed some light on their origin and nature. What of that other mysterious figure, the Giant Herdsman? Arthur Brown long since urged that the Hospitable Host and the Herdsman were "originally appearances of the same Otherworld being," [1] and Kittredge likewise pointed out that the Herdsman tempts comparison with the gigantic *vilain* in *La Mule sans Frein,* [2] who, as the master of a revolving fortress and as the uncouth administrator of the Beheading Test, is modeled on Curoi. The evidence bears out these suggestions and proves that we have in the Giant Herdsman another form of the same Protean character.

Chrétien describes the monster thus: "a churl who resembled a Moor, exceedingly huge and hideous . . . with a large club in his hand." He is clad in hides and is encircled by ferocious bulls. The churl in *La Mule sans Frein* is manifestly the same personage. "He was taller than St. Marcel, and on his shoulder he carried a big, broad *jusarme* [long-handled ax]. . . .

[1] *Studies and Notes in Philology and Literature*, VIII, 114. I can see no reason for Brown's supposition that the Herdsman or the Host was a creature or servant of the fay.
[2] Kittredge, *Study of Gawain and the Green Knight*, p. 256.

He was like a Moor of Mauretania." [3] He has under his control lions and fire-breathing serpents, which have slain many adventurous knights. But he is also Gauvain's hospitable host in a turning castle, is decapitated by him, and comes to life again. These facts not only suggest the identity of the churl in *La Mule sans Frein* with Curoi [4] but also equate him with the giant host of Gawain in *The Carl of Carlisle*,[5] who controls ferocious animals, including a bull, a bear, and a lion, which have slain many adventurous knights, and who is decapitated and comes to life again. It is plain, then, that Curoi turns up in these romances not only in his familiar roles as ugly gigantic churl, hospitable host, and administrator of the Beheading Test, but also, significantly, as the master of wild animals. The term *bachlach* applied to him in *Bricriu's Feast* held more than its general sense of rustic, boor, *vilain,* and denoted specifically a herdsman.[6]

The Welsh portrayals of the Giant Herdsman confirm in a roundabout way the identification with Curoi. In *Owain* [7] Kynon espies the black giant in a clearing of the forest, sitting on a mound; a heavy iron club in his hand; he has but one eye and one foot; he is surrounded by a thousand beasts, including serpents and lions; he is called *coydwr,* "wood man." [8] In *Kulhwch* [9] the hero and his companions come upon a vast flock of sheep, watched by a herdsman, clad in a hide, sitting on a mound. A huge fire-breathing mastiff guards the flock so that no one passes by without injury. The dialogue which takes place between Kulhwch's company and the Herdsman, though obscure, bears some resemblance to that in *Yvain.* There are the same questions and answers as to identity of the Herdsman and as to his herd. In both texts the Herdsman inquires the hero's errand and warns him. Calogrenant is told: "If you can depart [from the spring] without great harm and distress, you will be more lucky than any knight has ever been." [10] Kulhwch is told: "No one has ever come to make this request who has returned alive." [11] The Herdsman brings Kulhwch and his companions to his home, and they are welcomed by his wife, whose powerful embrace implies that she is a giantess like her husband.

[3] *La Damoisele à la Mule,* ed. B. Orlowski, vss. 510–891. This *vilain* is surely related to the *vilains* who loose ferocious lions against the hero in two versions of the Perilous Bed theme. Chrétien de Troyes, *Conte del Graal,* vss. 7851–70. Wolfram von Eschenbach, *Parzival,* section 571. For illustrations of this scene cf. R. S. and L. H. Loomis, *Arthurian Legends in Medieval Art,* figs. 136, 137, 143, 265, 382; R. S. Loomis, *Celtic Myth,* p. 173.

[4] It will be remembered that in *Bricriu's Feast* Curoi arranges for Cuchulainn's hospitable entertainment in his revolving fortress, and in another episode is decapitated by Cuchulainn and comes to life again. T. P. Cross, C. H. Slover, *Ancient Irish Tales,* pp. 273, 279. *Feast of Bricriu,* ed. Henderson, pp. 101–3, 125.

[5] F. Madden, *Sir Gawayne,* pp. 263 f., 269 f. Cf. Kittredge, *op. cit.,* pp. 87 f.; *PMLA,* XLVII (1932), 331–36.

[6] E. Windisch, *Irische Texte mit Wörterbuch,* p. 382.

[7] *Mabinogion,* trans. T. P. Ellis, J. Lloyd, II, 34 f.

[8] This is the reading of the White Book of Rhydderch, the better text. J. G. Evans, *White Book Mabinogion,* col. 228. "Achoydwr ar y koet hwnnw yw."

[9] Loth, *Mabinogion,* 2d ed., I, 289–92.   [10] Vss. 404–7.   [11] Loth, *op. cit.,* I, 291.

There is a mysterious figure in the ninth-century Irish saga, *The Destruction of Da Derga's Hostel*,[12] who on the one hand reminds us of the two herdsmen of the Welsh texts, and on the other suggests that he is Curoi himself under one of the aliases which the Irish delighted to apply to their gods and supernatural beings.[13] He is called *Fer Caille*, "Man of the Wood," the exact equivalent of the Welsh *coydwr*. He has one eye and one foot, and carries an iron pole. He is black-haired. He is accompanied by an equally monstrous female. All these features connect him with the herdsmen in *Owain* and *Kulhwch*. The *Fer Caille* also reminds one of Curoi. Both are described as *maeldub*, "black-headed"; both are called *bachlach*, "herdsman"; both carry a pole or club; both have a predilection for taking their stand beside a fire.[14]

The *Fer Caille* thus reveals a kinship with the gigantic herdsman Curoi and the Giant Herdsmen in *Owain* and *Kulhwch;* while the latter in turn reveal their identity with the *vilain* of the *Mule sans Frein* and with the Carl of Carlisle, both of whom play the part of Curoi. The dovetailing evidence, then, tends to prove that all these herdsmen were one and the same, and that the cryptic name, *Fer Caille*, belongs to the riddling nomenclature of which we have examples in the *Wooing of Emer*,[15] and, like the names Yellow son of White and Terror son of Great Fear, hides the identity of Curoi. Brown was therefore right in his conclusion that the Herdsman and the Hospitable Host of *Yvain* were two forms of one Otherworld being.

What are we to make of the fact that the *Fer Caille* had one foot and one eye, and the *coydwr* of *Owain* likewise? Though suppressed by Chrétien, these were evidently traditional features of the Giant Herdsman. One finds that Lug in the mythological text, *The Second Battle of Moytura*,[16] went round the men of Ireland on one foot and with one eye, and that Cuchulainn, his son, according to an early text, was wont when angry to withdraw one of his eyes into his head and to thrust out the other so that it was as great as a caldron, and the women of Ulster who became infatuated with him became one-eyed in imitation of this eccentricity.[17] The

---

[12] Cross and Slover, *Ancient Irish Tales*, pp. 102 f. *Revue celt.*, XXII (1901), 41–43, 56, 309.
[13] Westropp in *Proceedings of the Royal Irish Academy*, XXXIV, C, p. 54, says: "The Celtic mythology suffered from a plague of alias-names which obscure the identity of the various gods." E. MacNeill, *Celtic Ireland* (Dublin, 1921), p. 57: "We have seen, too, that in some cases the name of the god is disguised in mythical synonyms." T. P. Cross in *Mod. Phil.*, XII, 605, n. 3: "Heathen gods frequently have many names."
[14] *Togail Bruidne Da Derga*, ed. E. Knott (Dublin, 1936), p. 11, ll. 345, 352; p. 40, ll. 1350 f.; p. 80, n. 367. *Revue celt.*, XXII (1901), 42. *Feast of Bricriu*, ed. Henderson, p. 46, ll. 5–7; p. 116, l. 8; p. 118, l. 1.
[15] R. Thurneysen, *Irische Helden- u. Königsage*, pp. 384–86.
[16] *Revue celt.*, XII (1891), 99. D'Arbois de Jubainville, *L'Epopée celtique*, p. 436.
[17] D'Arbois, *op. cit.*, p. 177. Cross and Slover, *op. cit.*, p. 178. Cf. *Revue celt.*, XXVIII (1907), 132–36; XLV (1928), 334 f. Roscher in *Ausführliches Lexikon*, I, col. 1997, A. B. Cook in *Zeus* (Cambridge, 1914–40), I, 312–17, Grimm in *Teutonic Mythology*, trans. Stallybrass,

one foot I cannot interpret, but the one eye which characterized Cuchulainn in his distortion and which distinguished Lug at the Battle of Moytura may be one of the solar traits of these notoriously solar personages.[18] Though Curoi is never said to be one-eyed, yet since he mimics the behavior of the sun in other ways, as has been pointed out, one can understand why this grotesque deformity should attach to his hypostases—the *Fer Caille* and the Giant Herdsman in *Owain*. Moreover, when Curoi turns up as the Hospitable Host in *Gawain and the Green Knight,* his face is fierce as fire,[19] and when he appears as the Carl of Carlisle, he has two great eyes burning as fire.[20] These descriptive details suggest that there was a strange brilliance in Curoi's eyes or eye. If it seem odd that the sun should be incarnated as the keeper of a herd of savage animals in a woodland glade, one may remember that Helios had his great herds of cattle, that Apollo tended the flocks of Admetus, and, above all, that the Cyclops, a herdsman with one round eye, is held by eminent classical mythologists to be a solar figure.[21] No certainty is attainable, but there is a probability, fortified by these parallels from Greek myth, that the one-eyed Giant Herdsman in *Owain* corresponds to Curoi, the incarnate sun, lord of beasts, tame and wild.

At some fairly early stage in the development of Welsh tradition, when the mythical antecedents of the Yellow Man and the Giant Herdsman were recognized and their original identity was known, the Herdsman was introduced into the originally Irish plot of the visit of the Ulster heroes to Yellow and Terror. This would be in accordance with the practice, certainly familiar to story-tellers both Irish and Welsh, of introducing the same shape-shifting personage in various guises into the same story. It is found in *Peredur,*[22] which survives in a form of the late twelfth or early thirteenth century. It is found in *The Lay of the Great Fool,*[23] known in Ireland since the seventeenth century. It is characteristic of modern Irish folktales, as Dr. Hyde attests:

"The reader familiar with Irish story-telling will understand at once that all this machinery of the hounds, the hunting, and the ferule was put in motion by a mysterious being, by a god in fact. . . . It is he who appears as the messenger with the hounds, and an untrue tale about the Queen of Pride. It is he again who, having by means of his hounds placed Murough in a dilemma, takes service with

---

II, 702 f., and Prof. T. O'Rahilly in *Early Irish History and Mythology* (Dublin, 1946), pp. 58 f., adduce evidence that the sun is sometimes conceived as a creature with one eye.
[18] R. S. Loomis, *Celtic Myth,* pp. 46 f.
[19] *Sir Gawain and the Green Knight,* ed. J. R. R. Tolkien, E. V. Gordon, vs. 847. See note on p. 96: "Similarly in *Wars of Alexander* 4922 the sun-god is said to have 'fell face as the fire.' "
[20] F. Madden, *Sir Gawayne,* p. 262, vs. 181.   [21] A. B. Cook, *Zeus,* I, 312-17, 409-12.
[22] Loth, *Mabinogion,* 2d ed., II, 118.
[23] A. Nutt, *Studies on the Legend of the Holy Grail* (London, 1887), pp. 160 f. *Mod. Phil.,* XLII, 197-211.

him as his gillie; and it is he who finally entices him down to Tir na n-Og, and makes use of him to set free the country." [24]

Though the plot of *The Lad of the Ferule* resembles in no way that of *Owain,* it seems fairly clear that the same principle was employed, and is responsible for the successive appearances of Curoi, first as the Yellow Man of the shining castle, second as the one-eyed Giant Herdsman, and third as the Storm Giant.

It is interesting to observe that in the *Vulgate Merlin,* the *Huth Merlin* (both prose redactions of Robert de Boron's *Merlin*), and *Le Livre d'Artus* Merlin appears as an ugly man, watching over beasts in a forest, and a somewhat similar picture of him is given in Geoffrey of Monmouth's *Vita Merlini.*[25] It would seem as if Curoi, the celebrated shape-shifter of Irish saga, was equated by the Welsh and Bretons with their own shape-shifting Merlin.

Chapter XLIX

THE FOUNTAIN

VERSES 370–477, 800–810

The Giant Herdsman informed Calogrenant that near by there was a spring whence he would not return without pain. The spring bubbled up under a very beautiful and tall pine, which did not shed its needles in winter. An iron basin hung from the tree, and beside it was a block of stone and on the other side stood a small but very fair chapel. If one should pour water from the spring on the stone, a terrific storm of wind, thunder, and lightning would arise, and one could escape only with great hardship. Calogrenant, undismayed, followed the Herdsman's directions, came to the tree and spring, found a basin of gold (not iron), and the block of emerald, supported by four rubies, redder than the rising sun. He poured the water from the spring on the stone, and the heavens broke loose. Presently the air cleared, and a flock of birds settled so thickly on the tree that not a leaf was to be seen, and began to sing a joyous song in harmony. There followed Calogrenant's unhappy encounter with Esclados, and his crestfallen return. When Yvain later reached the same spot to wreak vengeance for his cousin, he found all as before and followed the same procedure, but with a happier outcome.

[24] *Lad of the Ferule,* ed. D. Hyde (London, 1899), pp. vii–x.
[25] H. O. Sommer, *Vulgate Version,* II, 38, 40; VII, 124–26. *Huth Merlin,* ed. G. Paris, J. Ulrich, I, 65 f. *Vita Merlini* vss. 75–80, 138–44, 451–63. Cf. R. S. Loomis, *op. cit.,* pp. 128–36.

W E HAVE SEEN that ancient Irish tradition provided *Yvain* with the basic theme of several warriors who arrive at a body of water and are tested successively by a storm-giant. At some indeterminate time this theme was Arthurianized and the Irish loch was replaced by a spring.[1] Also at some indeterminate time but probably in the first half of the twelfth century this new setting for the combats prompted the addition of a number of features associated with springs.

The wonder voyages of Irish literature, as Arthur Brown made clear,[2] were responsible for the overhanging tree and the chorus of birds. According to the *Navigatio Sancti Brendani*,[3] a tenth-century text, the voyagers landed on an island called the Paradise of Birds. They found there a spring, and above it a tree of marvelous spread, completely covered with birds, which on holy days sang as if with one voice the canonical hours. These birds correspond to those in *Yvain,* which after the storm gathered on the pine so thickly that not a leaf was to be seen, and sang their "servise" so harmoniously. There is a verbal identity between the Latin, "ut folia et rami ejus vix viderentur," and the French, "Qu'il ne paroit branche ne fuelle."[4] Ultimately this concept may be traced back to the saga tradition found in the seventh-century *Voyage of Bran,* for there we read:

> An ancient tree there is with blossoms,
> On which birds call the canonical hours.
> 'Tis in harmony it is their wont
> To call together every hour.[5]

The details borrowed from the pious Brendan legend either were suggested by, or themselves suggested, the addition of certain features derived from some description of a fountain in the land of Lothian, haunted by fays. The lai of *Desiré* [6] relates that a hero of Scottish birth was riding in the Blanche Lande near Calatir, now identified as the district of Calder just west of Edinburgh.[7] He saw the trees white with bloom and listened with

---

[1] As early as 1884 MacBain discovered a very full and detailed parallel to the combat at the fountain in the Irish tale, *The Slothful Gillie* (*In Gilla Decair*), and Brown argued strongly that this tale represented a much older Irish saga which was the source of this incident in *Yvain.* (*Studies and Notes in Philology and Literature,* VIII, 104–18.) But though some relationship must exist between the Irish tale and Chrétien's episode, the evidence points rather to a French *conte* as the common source. For one thing, nothing is heard of *The Slothful Gillie* before 1630, and there are good reasons for suspecting that Arthurian romance was by this time infiltrating Irish popular fiction. Cf. *Mod. Phil.,* XLII (1945), 197–209. Moreover, Zenker, after a very searching examination of the problem, came to the conclusion that *The Slothful Gillie* and the German *Wolfdietrich* incorporate an account of the combat at the spring which is independent of Chrétien's. *Beihefte zur Zts. f. romanische Philologie,* LXX, 41–83. With this opinion I am forced to agree.

[2] *Studies and Notes,* VIII, 86 f.

[3] For bibliography of Brendan cf. J. F. Kenney, *Sources for the Early History of Ireland,* I, 406–17; Benedeit, *Voyage of St. Brendan,* ed. E. G. R. Waters (Oxford, 1928).

[4] *Studies and Notes,* VIII, 87.   [5] Cross and Slover, *Ancient Irish Tales,* p. 589.

[6] *Lays of Desiré, Graelent, and Melion,* ed. E. M. Grimes, pp. 51–55.

[7] A. O. Anderson, *Early Sources of Scottish History,* I, 234.

delight to the song of birds. He came to a chapel and then to a fountain, welling up under a great tree. Beside it sat a maiden with two gold basins in her hands, obviously a water-fay, who encouraged the hero to make love to her beautiful mistress. The hero's union with the at first reluctant mistress, their separation owing to her displeasure, and their final reunion bear so marked a resemblance to Yvain's affair with Laudine, the countess of the Fountain, that there can be no doubt of a relationship.[8] Let us observe how easily the description of the spring in Lothian might call to mind the spring beneath the tree in the Brendan legend, or how easily the reverse process might occur. In either case it seems clear that to the Lothian tradition of the faery fountain *Yvain* owes, if not the overhanging tree, at least the golden basin and the chapel.[9]

It was surely at a comparatively late date—perhaps the first half of the twelfth century—that the adventures of the Arthurian knights leading up to the combats at the fountain were attached to the independent legend of the fountain-fay of Lothian, for this legend would hardly have developed until some time after the Norman Conquest and the infiltration of Breton *conteurs* into Scotland. Probably as a result of this combination Arthur's court was designedly placed at Carduel (Carlisle) in order to serve as a natural starting point for the journey which was to lead Yvain to the spring near the district of Calder, between ninety and a hundred miles away. That this was deliberately done is suggested by the fact that Yvain proposes to reach the forest where the spring lies by the third day, "jusqu'a tierz jor" (vs. 696); and one might well cover ninety miles in three days' riding.[10] Moreover, Guillaume le Clerc, who was careful of his geography and knew southern Scotland well, has Fergus set out from Carduel likewise, on the series of adventures which begins with his meeting and ends with his marrying "la Dame de Lodien."[11]

Apparently this composite story fell into the hands of a Breton unfamiliar with Carduel and Lothian. At any rate, Chrétien mistakenly places Carduel in Wales,[12] and, to the bewilderment of his attentive readers, brings Calo-

---

[8] Cf. Chap. LI.

[9] That the chapel is an alien and intrusive element seems indicated by the fact that it is absurdly represented as Lunete's prison in *Yvain*, vss. 3563 ff.

[10] Vss. 1821–30 corroborate this, for Lunete calculates that it would take five days for a swift messenger to reach Arthur's court at Carduel and return with Yvain to Laudine's castle.

[11] *Fergus*, ed. E. Martin, pp. 20, 41. Fergus meets Galiene at Lidel on p. 42, and on p. 180 we learn that she was "dame de Lodien." On p. 186 Arthur promises Fergus the realm of Lodiien if he will marry her. The story of Fergus and the Dame de Lodien offers several very striking parallels to the story of Gareth and Dame Lyones in Malory, Bk. VII. Cf. *supra*, pp. 115 f.

[12] I am unable to discover that anyone who really knew Wales ever thought it stretched as far north as Carlisle. Foerster's notion (*Löwenritter*, Halle, 1887, p. 274) that Gales was used in the sense of all the land inhabited by the Cymri seems unjustified by facts, and implies an antiquarian knowledge on the part of Chrétien's sources most unlikely in men of the twelfth century. Gaimar (vs. 4117) distinguishes the Waleis from the Cumbreis.

grenant and Yvain to a famous spring in the Breton Forest of Broceliande on horseback, without any mention of a Channel crossing. For a Breton who had traveled little or not at all in northern Britain it would be natural to suppose that Carduel, like other places beginning with *Car-,* such as Carlion, Caruent, Caradigan, was in Wales. To a Breton a spring in the Blanche Lande where strange adventures took place would suggest the marvelous fountain of Berenton in the Forest of Broceliande. He would be likely to transfer the scene of the combats to his native country without regard for the confusion produced in his geography. He would have no realization, any more than the modern reader, that his heroine was the heiress of Lothian and that it would be incongruous to find her mistress of a castle in Brittany. Some late Breton redactor, then, is in all probability to be blamed for the inconsistent localizations of *Yvain.*

The marvels of the Forest of Broceliande were widely known in the twelfth century, thanks doubtless to the Breton *conteurs.* Wace testified in his *Roman de Rou* (1160–74) that in his day the Bretons told many tales of the region and that it was customary to see fays there and many other marvels, "if the Bretons tell us the truth. . . . But churls have made it all a desert. I went there seeking wonders; I saw the forest, I saw the land; wonders I sought but I found none. A fool I returned, a fool I went." [13] The authors of *Le Tornoiement Anticrist, Claris et Laris,* and *Brun de la Montaigne* were likewise familiar with these legends.[14] As for the storm-making spring, Giraldus Cambrensis doubtless had it in mind in the following passage: "There is a spring in Armoric Britain. . . . If you take up water from it in the horn of a wild ox and pour it on a stone near by, however clear the weather and unlikely to rain, you will not escape an immediate downpour." [15] Wace included also among the wonders of Broceliande this fountain.

"In one part the spring of Berenton wells up near a block of stone. Hunters were wont to go to Berenton when the weather was very hot, to pour the water from their horns and to wet the top of the stone, for thus they were wont to bring on rain. Thus it was wont to rain in the forest and round about, but I do not know for what cause." [16]

It is now possible to determine with some assurance whence came the various elements in the description of the fountain. The combats with the Storm Knight belonged to an entirely independent tradition going back

[13] Wace, *Roman de Rou,* ed. H. Andresen (Heilbronn, 1879), II, 283 f., vss. 6395 f., 6409–18.
[14] *Beihefte zur Zts. f. rom. Phil.,* LXX, 134–37.
[15] Giraldus Cambrensis, *Opera,* V, ed. J. F. Dimock (London, 1867), pp. 89 f. On this and other storm-making springs cf. G. L. Hamilton in *Romanic Review,* II (1911), 355 ff.; W. Foerster, *Kristian von Troyes, Wörterbuch,* pp. 99–105; F. Bellamy, *La Forêt de Bréchéliant* (Rennes, 1896), II, 274 ff.; *Beihefte zur Zts. f. rom. Phil.,* LXX, 129–42; Guest, *Mabinogion,* Everyman ed., p. 390.
[16] Wace, *Roman de Rou,* vss. 6399–408.

to the testing of the Ulster warriors by Curoi in his role as a storm giant. The spring, the large overhanging tree, the golden cup, and the chapel near by were contributed by the Lothian legend, probably created by Breton *conteurs,* for these features are all found in the Breton lai of *Desiré.* The birds which covered the tree so thickly that not a leaf could be seen and which chanted their service in harmony seem to have been added from the Irish story of the Paradise of Birds, perhaps as found in the *Navigatio Sancti Brendani.* Finally, the localization in the Forest of Broceliande, the *perron,* the pouring of the water, and the ensuing storm obviously reflect the picturesque traditions of the Fontaine de Berenton.

Readers of the late Professor Lowes' stimulating book, *The Road to Xanadu,* will recall his theory of the "atomes crochus," the hooked atoms which cause the association of images, and his application to the poetry of Coleridge. They may recall in particular the demonstration that the marvelous fountain of *Kubla Khan* is a composite of images and phrases met in the travel books of Bartram and of Bruce.[17] Two furiously eruptive springs in Florida, a similarly outbursting source of the Nile, their meandering aftercourses—these merged in the poet's mind and emerged as a seething fountain and a sacred river in the palace grounds of Kubla Khan. The fountain scenes in *Yvain* are the result of a similar coalescence of images, though it did not happen in the brain of one man and it did not produce poetry as magical. Still we have seen that a loch in Ulster, a spring in one of St. Brendan's isles, a fay-haunted fountain in Lothian, and the storm-making spring of Berenton in Brittany have blended into one. Indeed, it is highly probable that it was the motif of the spring which suggested the union of Calogrenant's and Yvain's adventures culminating at the spring with the independent tradition of Yvain's love for the Countess of the Fountain—the two main elements in the romance.

Chapter L

LUNETE

VERSES 961–2036, 2395–2442

When Yvain found himself trapped in the gateway of Esclados' castle, a lovely damsel, Lunete, entered from an adjoining chamber and assured him of her friendly aid. For she recognized him as the result of an earlier meeting, when she had been sent by her mistress to Arthur's court. There she had not conducted herself wisely or courteously, and no knight would speak a word to her. Yvain alone had honored and served her, and she was

17 J. L. Lowes, *Road to Xanadu* (Boston, 1927), pp. 367-72.

now eager to pay the debt of gratitude. She placed on his finger a ring
which rendered him invisible, and when the knights of Esclados entered
to avenge their lord, they failed to discover Yvain. After Esclados' death
Lunete persuaded his widow Laudine to accept Yvain as her husband.
When Arthur and his knights came to the castle of the newly wedded
Yvain and were graciously entertained, Gauvain fell in love with Lunete
and offered her his faithful service, which she accepted. This relationship
(of which we hear nothing more later) is referred to as the acquaintance
between the sun and the moon, Gauvain being the sun and Lunete the
moon.

WITH THE ENTRANCE of Lunete into the gateway where Yvain was entrapped an entirely new and elaborate story pattern is introduced. We have finished with the web of traditions derived from Curoi's testing the rival warriors of Ulster, though there is some overlapping in Yvain's later encounters at the storm-making spring. The new design is a love story. Traces there may be of Blathnat's reunion with her old lover Cuchulainn after he has slain Curoi, but in the main the story of Yvain and Laudine is an intricately interlaced pattern formed of the Lothian legend of the wooing, winning, and losing of a fountain-fay, and the Irish saga of Cuchulainn's winning and losing the sea-goddess Fand and his subsequent madness. In the latter tradition Lunete has her prototype in the figure of Liban.

But before we concern ourselves with the relation of Lunete to the Irish saga, let us see whether anything can be made of her name. It is significant that Chrétien makes it the occasion for comparing her to the moon, just as he compares Gauvain to the sun.[1] In Gauvain's case we know that the analogy was not a mere complimentary metaphor, since there is ample testimony in Arthurian romance that he possessed solar traits.[2] Is it possible that Lunete had similarly a lunar nature? She was doubtless a fay, since French and German texts call her Felinete,[3] just as Morgain la Fée is called Feimurgan. And in the latter instance we have been able to trace her origin in the Welsh Modron, descendant of the Celtic goddess Matrona. We are therefore warranted in looking for a Welsh mythological figure who by name or nature suggests the moon. There is Aranrot, whose name means "Silver Wheel."[4] The Celts sometimes conceived of the sun as a golden wheel, as Gaidoz demonstrated.[5] Perhaps, therefore,

---

[1] Vss. 2395–2414.   [2] *Mort Artu*, ed. J. D. Bruce, pp. 287 f. *Romania*, LIV (1928), 520.
[3] Warnatsch, *Der Mantel* (Breslau, 1883), p. 75. Gerard d'Amiens, *Escanor*, ed. H. Michelant, vs. 20130.
[4] On Aranrot cf. W. J. Gruffydd, *Math Vab Mathonwy*, pp. 19–27, 187–89. I cannot agree with Gruffydd that Aranrot is really a place name derived from Argentoratum. Cf. also Ifor Williams, *Pedeir Keinc y Mabinogi*, pp. 269 f.
[5] H. Gaidoz, *Etudes de mythologie gauloise, Le Dieu gaulois du soleil* (Paris, 1886), p. 9. On the sun as wheel cf. *Etudes celtiques*, III (1938), 58; E. Windisch, *Das keltische Brittanien*

since there is ample evidence of moon worship among the Celts,[6] Aranrot was a moon-goddess. Though nothing told of her in *The Four Branches of the Mabinogi* or elsewhere supports this view, it is entirely possible that some recognition of her mythical nature should descend to Lunete, since we have seen, time and again, that mythical traits of other personages in Irish and Welsh saga are preserved in Arthurian romance. It is even demonstrable that Blathnat turns up in *Artus de la Petite Bretagne* as Florence, who we are told exactly resembled the faery queen Proserpine; [7] and Blathnat's Welsh descendant, Blodeuwedd, seems to be equated with Diane in the *Huth Merlin,* for very similar stories are told of both.[8] If we grant that the *Matière de Bretagne,* in several instances and in various ways, retains mythical meanings, obscured or obliterated in the Celtic texts, there is no difficulty in supposing that the naming of Lunete and Chrétien's likening her to the moon reveal the original nature of her divinity.

It is, perhaps, no more than an odd coincidence, but there are points of resemblance between the history of Aranrot [9] and an affair of Gauvain's, whom Chrétien represents as the lover of Lunete. Aranrot bore a son to her brother Gwydion. Gwydion, after giving the child to a wet nurse and rearing him till the age of four, brought him to his mother. She exclaimed: "Man, what design has seized thee to shame me thus, and to pursue and maintain my dishonor so long a time?" When informed that the boy as yet had no name, she swore that he would never receive one except from herself. By means of a stratagem Gwydion succeeded in getting her to name the lad Llew, which means in Welsh "Lion." Now, according to Pseudo-Wauchier,[10] Gauvain begat a natural son on a damsel. The child was stolen from his mother and found by another damsel. When he met his father at a ford, we are told that "the boy was named Lion," and three other times he is called Lionel. When asked by Gauvain, however, what his name was, Lion replied: "I know, truly, that all the folk of the castle called and named me 'the nephew of his uncle,' and the lord caused all to speak of me thus. Often my mother told me that she dared not name my father in the castle because of the great injury which he had done to my family." Thus there is no complete parallel between the tales of Llew

---

bis zu Kaiser Arthur, pp. 77, 79, 87, 200 f.; J. Grimm, *Teutonic Mythology,* trans. Stallybrass, II, 620, 701; *Journ. of Eng. and Germ. Phil.,* XLII (1943), 168 f.

[6] This possibility was suggested by Lessmann in *Mitra,* I, 161, n. 4. On Celtic moon-worship cf. M. O'Donnell, *Life of Columcille,* ed. A. O'Kelleher, G. Schoepperle (Chicago, 1918), p. 357; J. A. MacCulloch, *Religion of the Ancient Celts,* pp. 172-78.

[7] R. S. Loomis, *Celtic Myth,* pp. 172-75, 303 f.

[8] Compare Loth, *Mabinogion,* 2d ed., I, 200-5, with *Huth Merlin,* ed. Paris and Ulrich, II, 145-48. On relation of Blodeuwedd to Blathnat cf. Gruffydd, *op. cit.,* pp. 265-70.

[9] Gruffydd, *op. cit.,* pp. 19-23, 60. Loth, *op. cit.,* I, 192-95.

[10] On this story cf. J. L. Weston, *Legend of Perceval,* I, 241-45; *PMLA,* XLV (1930), 432-38. I was mistaken in following Miss Weston as to the reading "le fis son oncle," instead of "le neveu son oncle." Prof. Roach, who has been most generous in answering my queries, informs me that no ms. reads "fis."

and Lion, but it is curious that both were the children of shame, both were in a sense nameless, and that one is the offspring of Aranrot, "Silver Wheel," and the other of Gauvain, the lover of Lunete.

Though it seems likely, therefore, that Lunete in *Yvain* owes her name to a lunar Aranrot, she owes little else. Some elements in her story, as Brown long since pointed out,[11] can be traced back to the Irish goddess Liban, who appears in *The Sickbed of Cuchulainn,* a saga which was already shaped by the ninth century and of which a conflated form exists in the Book of the Dun Cow (*ca.* 1100).[12] The relationship can be perceived only by comparing in turn the salient features of Chrétien's story of Lunete and Laudine, of Malory's story of Lynet and Lyones, and of the Irish saga. For Malory's Lynet is clearly the counterpart of Lunete on the one hand and of the Irish Liban on the other. First, let me summarize Chrétien.

Lunete was sent by Laudine to Arthur's court on an errand, there displayed scant courtesy, but was honored and aided by Yvain. After Yvain arrives at Laudine's castle and overcomes Esclados, Lunete brings about his marriage with her mistress. When Yvain departs after his honeymoon, Laudine gives him a ring which will preserve him from loss of blood. Rebuked by Laudine's messenger for breach of faith, Yvain goes mad with grief, and roams through wild regions, sleeping in the open. He is restored to his senses by an ointment ministered by a maiden. Finally he is reconciled to his wife.

Next let me summarize Malory's book,[13] which has already lighted for us several dark corners in Arthurian romance.

Lynet comes to Arthur's court, asks for a champion to aid her sister Lyones, is most scornful of young Gareth, who undertakes the mission, but with dwindling contempt and growing admiration she accompanies him to a castle beside the faery isle of Avylyon, where her sister dwells. On the way he overcomes several hostile warriors, and before the castle of Lyones he vanquishes the most formidable of them all. Lyones, however, will not admit him to her presence, and he rides off, making great dole. He sleeps in the open. Many times he plunges into deep mires, "for he knewe not the wey, but took the gaynest waye in that woodenes [madness] that many tymes he was lyke to perysshe." Later Lynet heals him of a wound by means of an ointment. Still later, Lyones gives Gareth a ring which would save him from loss of blood. Finally the two are wedded.

Malory's story presents certain marked similarities to Chrétien's. Not only the fact that Lunete had been sent on an errand to Arthur's court, had been discourteous, but had received nothing but honor and service from Yvain, not only her active part in bringing together Yvain and Lau-

[11] *Studies and Notes in Philology and Literature,* VIII, 34–45.
[12] *Serglige Con Culainn,* ed. M. Dillon (Columbus, Ohio, 1941), p. viii.
[13] Malory, *Morte d'Arthur,* ed. H. O. Sommer, I, 215–70.

dine, but also Yvain's sorrow, his madness, his wanderings in wild regions, his sleeping in the open, his healing by means of an ointment, and Laudine's gift to him of a ring which would protect him from loss of blood—all these prove that Chrétien's story of Lunete and Laudine rests on the same foundation as does Malory's narrative of Lynet and Lyones.[14]

This common foundation was itself ultimately based on *The Sickbed of Cuchulainn,* as the following summary of the essentials will show.[15]

The faery woman Liban comes to Cuchulainn in a dream, laughs at him, and strikes him. A year later she comes to him in a very changed mood, and summons him to combat with three champions in order to win possession of her sister Fand. Though refusing at first, he goes at last, accompanied by Liban, to the beautiful island where her sister dwells. He slays the hostile warriors and enjoys the love of Fand for a month. Finally, he deserts her and she returns to her husband Manannan. Cuchulainn then wanders on the mountains in a frenzy, without food and drink, sleeping every night in the open. Finally, he is restored to his senses.

It will be seen that the plots of Malory's Book of Gareth and the *Sickbed* are roughly the same, the latter portions strikingly similar. Liban corresponds to Lynet, Fand to Lyones, and Cuchulainn to Gareth. Liban is therefore the ultimate original of Chrétien's Lunete.

If further confirmation of this hypothesis is needed, let us note four facts: (1) In two curiously ecclesiasticized forms of Irish myth there appears a mermaid Liban. (2) Despite the differences between her story and that of Liban, the sister-in-law of the sea-god Manannan, the identity of the two sea-fays of the same name was recognized by Rhys and Zenker.[16] (3) Liban, the mermaid, appears riding in a chariot drawn by stags. (4) A counterpart of Lynet in Arthurian romance is accompanied by a chariot drawn by stags. In short, a unique motif is attached to Liban; the same unique motif is attached to a counterpart of Lynet. Let me expand these points more fully.

1. In *The Colloquy of the Ancients* (1142-1167) [17] a mermaid named Liban appears swimming in the sea and then riding on a wave near the base of the Mourne Mountains. She proclaims herself the daughter of Eochaid mac Eoghan and says that she has been in the water for a hun-

---

[14] It is an odd fact that Malory (ed. Sommer, I, 267, 270) twice calls Lynet the "damoysel saveage," and that Chrétien in his allusion (vs. 1620) to "la Dameisele Sauvage" seems to preserve a blurred memory of this appelation.

[15] D'Arbois de Jubainville, *L'Epopée celtique en Irlande,* pp. 178–215. *Serglige Con Culainn,* ed. M. Dillon, pp. 31–48. A. H. Leahy, *Heroic Romances of Ireland* (London, 1905), I, 59–85. For comparison between Malory and the *Sickbed* cf. *Beihefte zur Zts. f. rom. Phil.,* LXX, 307–15.

[16] J. Rhys, *Lectures on the Origin and Growth of Religion as Illustrated by Celtic Heathendom,* 2d ed. (London, 1892), p. 463. *Beihefte zur Zts. f. rom. Phil.,* LXX, 14–16.

[17] S. H. O'Grady, *Silva Gadelica* (London, 1892), II, 184 f.

dred years. From *The Death of Eochaid mac Maireda*,[18] contained in the Book of the Dun Cow (*ca.* 1100), we learn that Eochaid's daughter, Liban, ranged the sea for three hundred years and had a sun-house beneath Lough Neagh. She was caught in a net in Larne Water, was conveyed to Tech Dabheoc, where she was baptized, and died in the odor of sanctity. "In that place wonders and miracles are wrought through her." One could hardly ask for a clearer illustration of the transformation of pagan worship into a Christian cult, a phenomenon for which, of course, there are numerous parallels throughout Europe.[19]

2. That all three Libans were supernatural creatures goes without saying. Liban in the *Sickbed* appeared in the shape of a bird and dived into a pool;[20] Liban in the *Colloquy* transformed herself into a salmon. Both the water-nymphs were daughters of a Eochaid, and Eochaid Ollathair, "the All-Father," was one of the names of the Dagda,[21] chief of the Irish gods. Liban in the *Sickbed* was the sister of Oengus and daughter of Aed Abrat.[22] This apparently reflects the same tradition, for Oengus was the son of the Dagda, and Aed Abaid was a name of the Dagda.[23] All three Libans, then, seem to be daughters of the great god of wizardry of the Tuatha De Danann. They were one and the same.

3. Liban, in *The Death of Eochaid,* was driven in a chariot drawn by two stags.[24] This ride of the mermaid Liban in a chariot drawn by stags is, I believe, unique in Irish literature.

4. It is therefore significant that the same motif turns up in a unique

---

[18] O'Grady, *op.cit.*, II, 266–69. Rhys in *Celtic Folklore, Welsh and Manx*, I, 367–95, presents a number of Irish and Welsh parallels to the story of Liban as the guardian of a well or spring. Cf. also J. A. MacCulloch, *Religion of the Ancient Celts*, p. 192.

[19] P. Saintyves, *Les Saints successeurs des dieux* (Paris, 1907). For the amazing survival of pagan cults and ceremonies in Christian Ireland, the Isle of Man, and Wales cf. D. Hyde, *Legends of Saints and Sinners* (Dublin, n.d.), pp. 2, 5; MacCulloch, *op. cit.*, pp. 79 f.; W. Y. E. Wentz, *Fairy Faith in Celtic Countries* (Oxford, 1911), p. 118; Rhys, *Celtic Folklore*, I, 15 f., 312 f.; Rhys, *Lectures on Origin and Growth*, pp. 422, 423, n. 1.

[20] That the two birds linked by a golden chain which Cuchulainn wounded were Liban and Fand is suggested by the fact that the goddess Dechtire and her maidens appeared in a very similar manner as birds linked by chains of silver. Thurneysen, *Irische Helden- und Königsage*, pp. 268–72. Though Dillon (*Serglige Con Culainn*, p. 30) translates "Lotair foa lind" (*ibid.*, p. 2) as "They went out over the pool," there seems to be no reason for rejecting the usual meaning of *fo*, "under." Cf. *Feast of Bricriu*, ed. G. Henderson, p. 98, where "Luid iarom fon loch," certainly means, "He then went under the lake." Cf. also *Speculum*, XVII (1942), p. 382, l. 66.

[21] E. MacNeill, *Celtic Ireland* (1921), pp. 33 f. R. S. Loomis, *Celtic Myth*, p. 123. MacCulloch, *op. cit.*, pp. 77–79. That Eochaid mac Eoghan and Eochaid mac Maireda were mythological figures is evident from the nature of their daughters, and that they represent variations on Eochaid, the Dagda, is suggested by MacNeill's statement (*op. cit.*, p. 61): "I take it that, no matter how often each name occurs, it is the name of the same mythological ancestor, e.g., that Eochu Cenn Mairc (the horse-headed), Eochu Cenn Reithi (the ram-headed), Eochu Mumo (of Munster), etc., are all one and the same Eochu of Irish mythology."

[22] D'Arbois, *op. cit.*, pp. 180–82. *Serglige Con Culainn*, ed. Dillon, pp. 31 f.

[23] Leahy, *op. cit.*, I, 7. MacCulloch, *op. cit.*, pp. 78, 81–83. *Medieval Studies in Memory of G. Schoepperle Loomis*, p. 404.   [24] O'Grady, *Silva Gadelica*, II, 269.

passage in Arthurian romance and in connection with a counterpart of Lynet. Let us turn to *Perlesvaus*.[25]

During a high feast at Arthur's court a damsel rides into the hall on a mule. She is accompanied by a chariot drawn by three stags and is called "la Damoisele du Char." She complains of Arthur's conduct. After her departure she meets with Gavain and persuades him to escort her. Gavain overcomes a knight called the Black Hermit, lord of a land where the trees are "black as if burned with fire, and the earth beneath scorched and black, without verdure." Before parting from Gavain the Damoisele du Char directs him on his way. In due time Gavain arrives before the castle of a widow lady and her daughter, who are besieged by Kahot the Red and the Lord of the Fens. The daughter implores Gavain to deliver them, and he conquers their enemies and restores their lands.

The author of *Perlesvaus* dealt very freely with his materials, and the Damoisele du Char is one of his most complex figures. She is certainly modeled in part after the Grail Messenger and the Grail Bearer of Arthurian tradition, and at the same time she is allegorized as Fortune and the Church.[26] In spite of these complications it is still possible to perceive a likeness to Lynet in the damsel of the stag-drawn chariot.[27]

During a high feast at Arthur's court Lynet enters the hall. (Elsewhere she is said to ride a mule.)[28] Arthur refuses her the service of any of his knights but Beaumayns, and she departs in wrath. Beaumayns insists on acting as her escort. He overcomes the Black Knight of the Black Laundes and takes his arms from him. In the course of time Beaumayns arrives before the castle of Dame Lyones, who is besieged by the Red Knight of the Red Laundes, and at her request overcomes him.

The parallel between Lynet and the Damoisele du Char is not as complete and exact as one could wish, but one can hardly deny that it is there.

Whence came the stag-drawn chariot? Such a vehicle is never found in association with the Grail Messenger or any other wandering maiden of Arthurian romance, and, to be sure, it is never found in company with Lynet or Lunete. But its only other occurrence outside *Perlesvaus* and its Welsh translation, so far as I can discover, is in *The Death of Eochaid Mac Maireda,* where it serves as the vehicle of Liban, the prototype of Lynet. If this be coincidence, it is a very extraordinary coincidence indeed.

Though there is some reason to suppose that the fay Lunete of Chrétien's

[25] *Perlesvaus*, ed. Nitze, I, 48–59, 66–72.
[26] *Revue celt.*, XLVII (1930), 59–62. *Perlesvaus*, ed. Nitze, II, 130 f., 227–29. The damsel of the chariot has a double in *Perlesvaus* itself—another damsel who carries a head about (*ibid.*, pp. 213 f.). Her story is also influenced by the adventure of Montesclaire. Cf. J. L. Weston, *Legend of Perceval*, I (London, 1906), 6, 224 f., noting particularly the vault (*croute*) which opens automatically at the approach of the best knight, devised by Joseph of Arimathea at his death, and comparing it with the sepulchre of one "qui Nostre Seignor eda a desclofichier de la croiz," and which opened automatically at the approach of the best knight (*Perlesvaus*, I, 66, 228 f.).
[27] Malory, *Morte d'Arthur*, ed. Sommer, I, 215–22, 237–41.   [28] *Ibid.*, I, 267.

poem is descended from Aranrot and a great deal of reason to suppose that she is descended from Liban, these Welsh and Irish goddesses have bequeathed to her little but her name, her identification with the moon, her journey to Arthur's court, her rude behavior there, and her bringing Yvain to Laudine.

The ring of invisibility which Lunete presents to Yvain belongs, of course, among the most ancient properties of fairy lore and magic. Foerster referred to the ring of Gyges.[29] Wilmotte pointed out that Benoît in *Le Roman de Troie* (vss. 1690–93) represents Medea as giving such a ring to Jason.[30] It should be noted that in verses 1216 to 1228 Benoît describes Medea's necromantic powers in much the same terms as Geoffrey of Monmouth describes the magic arts of Morgen and her sisters.[31] Lunete's possession of a ring such as Medea's therefore adds to the cumulative evidence that she was akin to the fays.[32] How powerful and tenacious was this association between fays and the ring of invisibility is proved by the form of conjuration printed by Reginald Scot in *The Discoverie of Witchcraft* as late as 1584.[33]

"I conjure you three sisters of fairies, Milia, Achilia, Sibylia,[34] by the father, by the sonne, and by the Holie-ghost, and by their vertues and powers. . . . I charge you that you doo appeare before me visiblie, in forme and shape of faire women, in white vestures, and to bring with you to me, the ring of invisibilitie, by the which I may go invisible at mine owne will and pleasure, and that in all houres and minuts: in nomine patris, et filii, et spiritus sancti, Amen."

[29] W. Foerster, *Kristian von Troyes, Wörterbuch* (Halle, 1914), p. 122 *.
[30] M. Wilmotte, *Evolution du roman français aux environs de 1150, Acad. Roy. de Belgique, Bull. de la cl. des lettres* (1903), p. 24.
[31] Geoffrey of Monmouth, *Vita Merlini*, ed. J. J. Parry, vss. 916–25.
[32] *Le Livre d'Artus* has some interesting matter on Lunete, representing her as the cousin of Niniane, from whom she learned enchantment, and as the beloved of Brehus sans Pitié, for whose sake she established the storm-making spring of Breceliande. Zenker discusses this section in his *Ivainstudien*, pp. 243–47, but its traditional authority is questionable.
[33] Ed. M. Summers (New York, 1930), p. 236. Bk. XV, chap. 10. Two descriptions, one in Latin, one in French, of seals representing a mermaid attribute to them, when set in rings, the power of rendering the wearer invisible. T. Wright, *Essays on Archaeological Subjects* (London, 1861), I, 298, 303.
[34] On the Sibyl as a fay cf. L. A. Paton, *Fairy Mythology*, p. 52, n. 2; P. S. Barto, *Tannhaüser and the Mountain of Venus* (New York, 1916), pp. 11 f., 18, 37, 47–57.

Chapter LI

LAUDINE

VERSES 1144–3005, 6717–6813

Yvain, protected from observation by Lunete's magic ring, witnessed the lamentations of Laudine over the corpse of her husband. Her beauty captivated him and he indulged in a long soliloquy. Lunete discovered his infatuation and at once set herself to making a match between him and her mistress. So cleverly did she work that Yvain and Laudine were married. Shortly after Arthur and his knights came to the storm-making spring and were entertained sumptuously by Yvain and his bride for a week. On their departure Yvain begged permission of Laudine to accompany them, and she consented only on condition that he would return to her before the lapse of a year. She placed on his finger a ring which would protect him from imprisonment and loss of blood so long as he remained loyal to her. But Yvain, absorbed in tournaments, forgot his promise, and it was over a year later that a maiden messenger, sent by his forsaken wife, came to the court at Chester, bitterly rebuked him for his treachery, and snatched the ring from his finger. He was overcome with remorse, went mad, and wandered for some time in the wilderness. Restored to his senses by a magic ointment, he entered on a series of gallant exploits. Finally Lunete persuaded Laudine to receive her repentant husband back into her good graces.

LAUDINE is probably one of the most complex characters in Arthurian romance. We have already observed that in the precipitancy with which she marries the slayer of her husband there is possibly a faint vestige of Blathnat's relationship to Cuchulainn, the slayer of Curoi. Probably Hilka and Foerster were right in maintaining that Chrétien elaborated the psychological possibilities of the situation by transferring to Laudine the qualms and the scruples of Jocaste, who also married the slayer of her husband.[1] Laudine's relation to Lunete, as well as the love-madness of Yvain, reflect the relation of Fand to Liban and the love-madness of Cuchulainn.

A close scrutiny of the one passage where Chrétien names his heroine shows that still a fourth personage has been blended with Blathnat, Jocaste, and Fand. It is very odd that while Lunete is frequently mentioned by

[1] W. Foerster, *Kristian von Troyes, Wörterbuch*, pp. 107–9. Kristian von Troyes, *Yvain*, ed. W. Foerster and A. Hilka (Halle, 1926), pp. xx, xxx, xxxvi. Zenker has shown that the Laudine episode, though possibly influenced by, was not derived from, *Thèbes*, and Guyer disputes the debt of Chrétien to *Thèbes*. Cf. *Zts. f. franz. Sprache u. Lit.*, XLI (1913), 140–48; *Mod. Phil.*, XXVI (1929), 273–76.

name, her mistress is always referred to simply as "la dame" except in one place, and here the manuscripts offer different readings. Foerster's text may be translated as follows: "In the presence of all her barons the lady (*la dame*) gives herself to my lord Yvain. From the hand of her chaplain he has taken Laudine of Landuc, the lady (*la dame*) who was daughter of Duke Laudunet, about whom a lai is sung." [2] The first point to be noted is that only one manuscript out of the nine which contain this passage (ms. F) gives the form Laudine; one (ms. V) gives Laudune; seven, including the two base manuscripts PH and the Annonay fragment, give merely "la dame." This last would make sense and would accord with Chrétien's practice elsewhere in *Yvain*. One is thus led to suspect the reading "Laudine." On the other hand, Chrétien, doubtless familiar with the rhetorical principle, "the repetition of the same word detracts from the excellence of a line of verse," would hardly have repeated "la dame" thrice in four lines; [3] and the two German versions and the English version of the poem give Laudine, Laudamya, and Alundyne, thus supporting Foerster's reading as against "la dame." But whether Chrétien called his heroine Laudine or not, it is certain that she was of Landuc or Lauduc, and was the daughter of Duke Laudunet, Laudinet, Laudonez, or Landonnez.

One is reminded of that King Leudonus of Leudonia mentioned in Chapter XLV, whose stepdaughter was beloved by Ewen son of Urien, just as Duke Laudonez' daughter was beloved by Yvain son of Urien. We read in a Scottish *Life of Saint Kentigern,* written between 1147 and 1164, the statement:

"King Leudonus, from whom the province in northern Britain which he ruled took the name of Leudonia, had a stepdaughter who was called Thaney. . . . Her lover was a most attractive youth, namely Ewen, the son of Erwegenda, descended from the most noble lineage of the Britons. . . . In the historical narratives of the minstrels (*in gestis histrionum*) [4] he is called Ewen son of King Ulien [*read* Urien]." [5]

[2] Vss. 2148–53.

[3] Ms. Bib. Nat. fr. 12603, of which Foerster declared, "Einigemal hat S allein einen lesbaren Text, der aber dann wohl emendirt, aber nicht ursprünglich ist" (*Löwenritter,* ed. 1887, p. xii), substitutes for "la dame" or "Laudine" the name Gloris. It would seem as if the ingenious scribe recognized the similarity between Chrétien's heroine and Florie, whose story as related in Wirnt von Gravenberg's *Wigalois* curiously parallels that of Laudine after her marriage to Yvain. Both Yvain and Gawein desire to leave their newly wedded wives in order to return to Arthur's court at Carduel (Karidol); both ask permission of their wives, which is granted on condition that they return within a given time; both leave their wives sorrowful; Gloris gives Yvain a protective ring, whereas Gawein leaves a protective girdle with Florie; both heroes break their promises to return. The Austrian poet seems to have preserved one of the many French traditions about Gawain's love Florie. Cf. *supra,* pp. 82–84. The scribe of ms. S, apparently familiar with this tradition, though the lady's name had been corrupted into Gloris, arbitrarily substituted it for Chrétien's "la dame" or "Laudine."

[4] "Histrionum" is certainly the reading of the ms. Cf. *Romania,* XXII (1893), 506; J. Ritson, *Ancient English Metrical Romances* (London, 1802), III, 226.

[5] *Lives of St. Ninian and St. Kentigern,* ed. A. P. Forbes, p. 245. On this passage cf. *Mod. Phil.,* XXXVIII (1941), 284 f.; *Beihefte zur Zts. f. rom. Phil.,* LXX (1921), 186, n. 2. It is

To be sure, the name of Ewen's beloved does not correspond to that of Yvain's bride, nor does anything in her story offer a direct parallel. Manifestly, two Ewens—Ewen, the son of Erwegenda and father of St. Kentigern, and Ewen, the son of Urien and hero of romance—have been compounded into one character.[6] Nevertheless, it can hardly be accidental that an author antedating Chrétien's *Yvain* knew an Ewen, identified with Ewen son of Urien, celebrated by the *conteurs*,[7] and made him the lover of the daughter of King Leudonus, whereas Chrétien made Yvain son of Urien the lover and husband of the daughter of Duke Laudonez, and at the conclusion of his romance declared, "Onques plus *conter* n'an oi." Since Leudonia is certainly the district of Lothian, and since other forms are Laudonia and Lodonesia,[8] it seems as if both authors have preserved a *conteur* tradition that Yvain's bride was the daughter of the King or Duke of Lothian.

This interpretation is buttressed by Malory's Book of Gareth. For there we have found that the counterpart of Lunete is Lynet, and therefore the counterpart of Laudine is Dame Lyones, as Malory repeatedly calls her. First, observe the title "Dame," which recalls Chrétien's habitual reference to Laudine as "la dame." Next, note that Lyones is not properly a personal name at all, but elsewhere is applied by Malory to a region, Tristram's native land, French Loenois.[9] And Loenois, as Dr. Brugger has established and as all authorities agree, is precisely Lothian.[10] It is clear as day that Dame Lyones goes back to a French "la Dame de Loenois," and this title represents exactly the same tradition which made the counterpart of Dame Lyones the daughter and presumably the heiress of Duke Laudonez. The name of Laudine herself rests, as we have observed, on very slender support from the manuscripts. But since both the English and German adapters of *Yvain* used other manuscripts which had some such form as Laudine, and since the literature of scholarship has confirmed its use, there is no advantage in discarding the familiar name of Yvain's bride. If authentic, it forms one of the most significant threads of evidence connecting Laudine with Lothian, a land which in one Middle English poem is actually called Laudyan.[11] In any case, her father's name, Laudunet or Laudonez, certainly represents a corruption of Lodonesia, and she herself was Lady of Lothian.

---

the likely source of the genealogy of Kyndeyrn (Kentigern) in *Vitae Sanctorum Britanniae*, ed. Wade-Evans, p. 320.
[6] Both Brugger and Zenker (cf. *supra*, n. 5) recognize this confusion of the two Ewens.
[7] For the equivalence of *histriones* and *conteurs* cf. the passage from Peter of Blois, quoted in *Romania*, XV, 547, from Migne, *Pat. Lat.*, CCVII, col. 1088.
[8] *Mod. Phil.*, XXII (1924), 186–89.   [9] *Morte d'Arthur*, ed. H. O. Sommer, I, 272, 275, etc.
[10] *Mod. Phil.*, XXII, 159 ff. Bruce, *Evolution of Arthurian Romance*, I, 179 f. G. Schoepperle, *Tristan and Isolt*, II, 273. Thomas, *Tristan*, ed. Bédier, II (1905), 109. *Comptes rendus de l'Acad. des Inscriptions*, 1924, p. 128. *Neophilologus*, XV (1929), 24. J. Kelemina, *Geschichte der Tristansage* (Vienna, 1923), p. 197.
[11] F. Madden, *Syr Gawayne*, p. 188, vs. 41.

Though, to be sure, Laudine's history fails to match that of Lyonés as to the name of her lover and many other points, there are agreements. Both heroines, as we have observed, inherited their relationship to Lunete–Lynet from that of Fand to Liban. Both have likewise derived from *The Sickbed of Cuchulainn* the tradition that they rebuffed their lovers, who consequently wandered through wild regions in a fit of madness. These correspondences between Laudine and Lyonés are due to their common inheritance from Fand.

Other correspondences are due to the fact that both have inherited much from Morgain, who, we saw on an earlier page,[12] was the chief prototype of Lyonés and was well established in tradition as queen of Lothian. Morgain, we remember, in her various impersonations was always giving her lover a magic ring.[13] Naturally, therefore, we learn that Lyonés lent Gareth a ring which prevented the loss of blood,[14] and Laudine gave Yvain a ring which protected him from imprisonment and loss of blood so long as he remained true to her.[15] This condition on which Laudine's ring exercised its potency directs attention to a very significant parallel, noted by Ahlström and Arthur Brown, in the lai of *Desiré*,[16] the faery heroine of which we have already had occasion to recognize as one of the many forms of Morgain.[17]

Desiré, traveling through the Blanche Lande, beside Calatir (a district included in Lothian [18]), espied a maiden sitting near a fountain, "which rose under a great tree; two golden basins she held in her hand." She led him to her beautiful mistress, seated before a couch near by, and promised him her aid. Though the mistress fled swiftly at Desiré's approach, she was won over by his plea and granted him her love. She gave him a ring, with the warning that if he were false

[12] Cf. *supra*, pp. 112–16, 181.   [13] Cf. *supra*, pp. 123 f.   [14] *Morte d'Arthur*, I, 257.

[15] Vss. 2600–2610. There may be a reminiscence of Morgain's castle in the fact that Laudine's *sale* in which Yvain was trapped had walls painted "de buen oevre et de colors chieres," and the corresponding passage in *Owain* reads: "il n'y avait pas un clou qui ne fût peint de riche couleur, pas un panneau qui ne fût décoré de diverses figures dorées." (On the significance of these passages for the relationship of *Yvain* to *Owain* cf. A. C. L. Brown in *Romanic Review*, III, 146–50.) We have three independent testimonies to the splendid mural paintings which adorned Morgain's castle. Cf. R. S. and L. H. Loomis, *Arthurian Legends in Medieval Art*, pp. 16 f., 24 f.

[16] *Lays of Desiré, Graelent, and Melion*, ed. E. M. Grimes, pp. 52–75. *Mélanges de philologie romane dédiés à Carl Wahlund* (Macon, 1896), pp. 297, 299. *Studies and Notes in Philology and Literature*, VIII, 128 f. The name Desiré is apparently developed from the participle, which is applied to Lancelot, Galaad, and Artus de la Petite Bretagne. The Dame du Lac says to Lancelot: "Mais ore vous en ales. boins & biaus jentiex & gratiex, desires de toutes gens. . . ." The aged man who introduces Galaad at Arthur's court says: "Rois Artus, je t'ameign le Chevalier Desirré." A varlet greets Artus de la Petite Bretagne during his adventures at the Porte Noire with the words: "Sire, vous soies le tres bien venu en la terre de Soreleis comme le plus desiré chevalier qui oncques sainsist espee." Cf. Sommer, *Vulgate Version*, III, 123, ll. 39–41; *Queste del S. Graal*, ed. A. Pauphilet, p. 7, ll. 25 f.; *Artus de la Petite Bretagne*, ms. in New York Public Library, fol. 57r.

[17] Cf. Chap. XLV.

[18] A. O. Anderson, *Early Sources of Scottish History*, I, 234.

to her, he would lose both ring and herself forever. For some time he enjoyed her secretly, and she bore him a boy and a girl. But one day he confessed his amour to a hermit; the ring disappeared from his finger, and his lady no longer kept tryst. He was filled with sorrow. At the end of a year the fay restored him to favor, and later still she came to the court of the King of Scotland in Calatir, riding a white mule, a sparrow-hawk on her fist, bringing her two children with her. The King of Scotland knighted her son in the presence of the kings of Moray and Lothian, and married her daughter. Then Desiré departed with his faery mistress, never to return.

On the one hand, Desiré's love reveals her kinship to Laudine in the details of her story: the fountain beneath the tree, and the gold basins; the handmaid who brings the hero to the fay as a lover; the overcoming of the fay's scruples; the conditional gift of the ring; the hero's breach of faith and loss of the ring; the fay's anger and the hero's misery; the final reconciliation. Moreover, Desiré's love was met near Calatir, and therefore in Lothian, while Laudine was daughter of the Duke of Lothian. All these similarities point to the essential oneness of Laudine and Desiré's mistress. On the other hand, there is much to show that Desiré's mistress was Morgain. First, there is the link with Lothian. Secondly, there is the gift of a ring. Thirdly, the plot of the lai, as Professor Grimes has shown,[19] bears an unmistakable likeness to that of *Lanval,* and Lanval's faery mistress is identified as Morgain because her home is in the isle of Avalon. Fourthly, it is most significant that, as has already been remarked,[20] Desiré's love bore him a son and a lovely daughter, just as Modron, the original of Morgain, bore a son and a lovely daughter to Urien, who had ravished her beside a ford. As the counterpart of Dame Lyones and Desiré's *amie,* Laudine betrays her descent from Morgain, Queen of Lothian, fay of Avalon, and nymph of a spring.

Though Morgain's connection with Lothian has already been treated sufficiently in this book, and though her earlier association with the Isle of Avalon is familiar to everyone, her naiad nature has not been recognized, especially her role as a fountain-nymph. Etienne de Rouen (1167–69) refers to "Morganis, nympha perennis."[21] The mistress of Guingamor, who we know on Chrétien's authority was Morgain, is depicted in the lai bathing in a spring.[22] Likewise, Wauchier, as we saw many pages back,[23] represents the sister of the Petit Chevalier, sitting beside a spring, and her role in the shield adventure is similar to that of Morgain in the *Prose Tristan.* We saw in our consideration of Amangon [24] that the well-maiden whom he violated was identical with the Queen of Garlot,[25] whom Gauvain

[19] *Lays of Desiré,* pp. 12–25.   [20] Cf. Chap. XLV.
[21] E. K. Chambers, *Arthur of Britain,* p. 265.
[22] *Erec,* vss. 1954–58. Marie de France, *Lais,* ed. Warnke (1925), p. 247, vss. 422–33.
[23] *Supra,* pp. 95–97.   [24] *Supra,* pp. 246 f.
[25] Garlot may be a corruption of Escalot by aphaeresis. Cf. Cotoatre from Escotoatre, *merilun* from *esmerillon* (*Zts. f. rom. Phil.,* LIV, 753–55; *Speculum,* XVIII, 72). Escalot is probably

rescued from her abductor Margon near a spring; and the *Huth Merlin* tells us that the Queen of Garlot was Morgain. The most sensational account of Morgain as a fountain-nymph is supplied by the Provençal romance of *Jaufré* (1222–32).[26]

Jaufré, a knight of Arthur's court, was attracted by the cries of a lady to a spring. As he leaned over it in the attempt to rescue her handmaid, the lady pushed him in and sprang after him. Arrived in the fairest land in the world, Jaufré undertook to fight the lady's oppressor, a monster knight with a head bigger than that of an ox, a throat bigger than that of a leopard, and the neck of a horse.[27] When Jaufré had vanquished him and extracted a promise to reform, he returned to the upper world through the spring, accompanied by the lady and a great retinue. Some time later Jaufré happened to pass near the spring, and was startled to behold the same lady rising from it on her palfrey, together with hundreds of knights and dames. She ordered a tent to be set up, so vast that it extended for half a league, though it could be contained in a single cart. A banquet of every viand which one could imagine was provided by her for Jaufré and his company. When at long last Jaufré became curious to know her name, she replied merely, "I am the fay of Gibel."

This is sufficient, however, to establish the identity of the fay of the spring, for *Le Chevalier du Papegau* and *Floriant et Florete* concur in calling Morgain "la fée de Montgibel," that is, Mount Etna, one of the many sites of her fabulous palace.[28]

That the author of *Jaufré* was not merely exercising his fancy is proved by his use of a motif connected by Ulrich von Zatzikhoven with the Queen of Meydelant, namely, her giving the hero a tent which could be compressed into a small space.[29] The conception of a subaqueous land of faerye has already been noted in connection with Chrétien's Water Bridge,[30] and was familiar not only in ancient Irish saga but also in modern Celtic folklore.

---

itself a corruption of Alclut, the Welsh name for the great fortress of Dumbarton on the Clyde (F. Lot, *Etude sur le Lancelot en prose*, p. 143, n. 16; *Mort Artu*, ed. J. D. Bruce, p. 269). In view of the persistent association of Morgain with Scotland and the fact that Urien was a historic chief of Rheged, probably in Southern Scotland, it would be natural to connect Urien and Morgain with Dumbarton. In *Vulgate Merlin* (Sommer, *Vulgate Version*, II, 390) "la cité de Garlot" is described as "la maistre forterece" of Morgain's husband.

[26] *Jaufré*, ed. H. Breuer, *Gesellschaft f. rom. Lit.*, XLVI, vss. 8378–9288, 10346–10676. The fact that Jaufré was son of Dovon equates him with Giflet son of Do (or Doon or Deon), whose name at least goes back to Gilvaethwy son of Don in the mabinogi of *Math*. Cf. W. J. Gruffydd, *Math Vab Mathonwy*, p. 204.

[27] This monster was probably the Chapalu, though the author calls him (vs. 8763) Felons d'Albarua. Cf. Jean d'Outremeuse, *Myreur des Histors*, IV, 47 ff.; Le Roux de Lincy, *Livre des Légendes*, pp. 248–55; J. Runeberg, *Etudes sur la Geste Rainouart* (Helsingfors, 1905), pp. 165 ff.; *Beiträge z. romanischen Philologie, Festgabe f. G. Gröber* (Halle, 1899), pp. 191–93.

[28] L. A. Paton, *Fairy Mythology*, p. 250. *Chevalier du Papegau*, ed. Heuckenkamp (Halle, 1896), p. 11. For other connections with Sicily cf. *supra*, p. 97, n. 65.

[29] L. A. Paton, *Sir Lancelot of the Lake*, pp. 7, 12. Cf. *supra*, p. 66.

[30] Cf. Chap. XXXIII.

Bretons in the last century told tales of a land at the bottom of a well.[31] A Welsh nonagenarian told Dr. Wentz about the year 1910: "A special sort of *Tylwyth Teg* [fairies] used to come out of lakes and dance, and their fine looks enticed young men to follow them back into the lakes, and there marry one of them. . . . This sort of *Tylwyth Teg* were as big as ordinary people; and they were often seen riding out of the lakes and back again on horses." [32] This Welshman lived at Pont Rhydfendigaid in north Cardiganshire, and a few miles away at Ponterwyd Sir John Rhys heard as a child (say about 1845) some peasants hinting at weird, uncanny associations with the name Morgan.[33] The striking point is that Rhys was able to show that Morgan was a water-sprite of indeterminate gender who carried off naughty boys into the lake of Glasfryn in Carnarvonshire.[34] If we combine the evidence gathered by Dr. Wentz and Rhys in these neighboring communities, we have a tradition of fays who rose from lakes, seated on horses, and who lured young men down to their watery homes, and one of them was named Morgan—a legend strangely similar to that in *Jaufré*. If it seems a far cry from western Wales to the court of Aragon, where *Jaufré* was written, it should be noted that modern Breton folklore partially fills the gap with a common legend of a sea-nymph who resembles the Welsh lake ladies in bearing the masculine name Morgan and in drawing young men down to her home beneath the waves.[35] That such similar behavior should be ascribed to the Morgans of Welsh and Breton folklore and to the fay of Gibel of the Provencal romance seems hardly due to chance in view of the other proofs of the Welsh provenance of Morgain la Fée, of the wide dissemination of her legend, and of her aquatic origins.[36]

Two radical modifications were made in the Lothian legend, evidently before it reached the author of Y, since the same modifications appear in the story of Dame Lyones, which was certainly not derived from Y. First, all traces of the Lady of Lothian as a water-nymph were removed, except for the telltale title, "the Countess of the Fountain," which survived in *Owain*, though rejected by Chrétien. Secondly, all suggestions of the illicit relations between the hero and the Lady of Lothian were discreetly ex-

[31] F. M. Luzel, *Contes populaires de Basse-Bretagne*, I, 267 f.
[32] W. Y. E. Wentz, *Fairy Faith in Celtic Countries*, (New York, 1911), p. 148.
[33] J. Rhys, *Celtic Folklore*, I, 372 f. As Miss Paton first maintained (*Fairy Mythology*, pp. 148–66), Morgain shows a striking likeness to the Irish goddess, the Morrigan. I have tried to demonstrate this point more fully and to show that the Morgan of western Wales owed his or her name to a natural substitution for Morrigan and that the Irish tradition was naturally blended with the native Welsh traditions of Modron. Cf. *Speculum*, XX (1945), 183–200.   [34] Rhys, *Celtic Folklore*, I, 372–75.
[35] Wentz, *op. cit.*, pp. 200 f. P. Sébillot, *Folklore de France*, II, 36. F. J. Snell, *King Arthur's Country*, pp. 263–65.
[36] Froissart, in his Arthurian romance of *Meliador*, tells how Saigremor, riding on the back of a stag, plunged into a lake and arrived at a land of nymphs. *Meliador*, ed. Longnon (Paris, 1895), vss. 28362–831.

punged. Laudine may have had scruples about uniting herself with the slayer of her husband, but once she had made up her mind, she had her decision ratified by her council and was wedded to Yvain with the sanction of the Church. It is evident that Laudine's nature and character had been subjected to rationalizing and purifying influences before Chrétien undertook to relate her history. None of the mythological attributes of the ancient goddess Modron which still remain in the story of Desiré's faery mistress was allowed to remain and smirch the reputation of Yvain's bride. But the story of the fay's ire at her lover's breach of faith, the loss of the ring, and the final reconciliation was retained, and the interval of disfavor was adroitly used by the author of Y for the insertion of a number of incidents which lengthened the romance and added to the renown of the hero. *Yvain* has been properly recognized as the best constructed of Chrétien's romances, and the credit for this architectonic feat should go to the author of Y.

It is appropriate at this point to review our investigation of the poem and, disregarding the minor influences and confusing intricacies, to concentrate on the main structure. *Yvain* is a combination of two major elements which we will call A and B. A is itself a composite of various Irish stories dealing with Curoi's testing of the Ulster warriors and with Cuchulainn's slaying of Curoi. It ends with the victory of Yvain at the spring and the dropping of the portcullis behind the mortally wounded Esclados. B begins with the appearance of Lunete. It also is a composite, made up of the Irish story of Cuchulainn, Liban, and Fand, and the Lothian tradition of Yvain and the fountain-fay. Apparently Yvain's combat at the fountain formed the link between plots A and B, serving as a climax to A and as a preface to B. There is, moreover, some overlapping of the two plots since we have noted that Laudine's wedding the slayer of her husband may possibly reflect Blathnat's reunion with Cuchulainn, and since the motif of the fountain combat is repeated in the course of plot B.

In order to effect the dovetailing of the two plots, a considerable portion of B had to be sacrificed. We know that B had once contained an introductory series of adventures in which Lunete went to Arthur's court, seeking a champion for her mistress, treated Yvain (or Gauvain) with contempt, but was courteously accompanied by him back to Laudine's castle. This was, of course, inconsistent with A and was dropped. But the combiner left a brief reference to it and cleverly used Lunete's gratitude for Yvain's courtesy to motivate her zealous activities in his behalf. The author of Y, who was responsible for most of the final adjustments in plot, as well as for much of the psychological interest displayed in *Yvain* and *Owain,* must have been a literary craftsman of no mean order.

Chapter LII

THE HERMIT AND THE LADY OF NOIROISON

VERSES 2827–3340

When Yvain, crazed with remorse, wandered mad through the wilderness, he came upon a hermit's dwelling, very low and small, and the hermit provided him with food for some time. One day a lady and her two damsels found Yvain lying asleep in the forest, and one of them recognized him. The lady returned to her castle, gave one of the damsels an ointment which Morgue la Sage had given her, and the damsel went back to Yvain and, rubbing the ointment on his forehead and body, restored him to sanity. Yvain was brought to the castle, bathed and tended, and supplied with arms and a horse, handsome, big, and strong. When the lady's enemy, Count Alier, came to burn and pillage her domain, Yvain sallied forth and brought him back a prisoner. The lady wished to retain Yvain as her husband or lover, but he departed and left her very angry. The lady's title was "la dame de Noiroison."

WE HAVE SEEN that in so far as the story of Laudine followed the pattern of the Lothian legend as found in *Desiré* it called for Yvain's breach of faith with Laudine, the consequent loss of the ring she had given him, a long estrangement between the lovers, and their final reconciliation. So far as the story of Laudine followed the pattern of *The Sickbed of Cuchulainn* it called for the separation of Yvain from Laudine, his wandering like a madman on the mountains and sleeping out each night, and the eventual return of his senses. These two patterns combined to form the framework of the latter portion of Chrétien's poem. Since the author of Y (or perhaps some predecessor) planned to fill the interval of estrangement between Yvain and Laudine with incidents exhibiting the hero's prowess, he first had to bring about his cure from madness.

For this purpose he found an appropriate narrative pattern lying ready to his hand, the one which we discovered in our consideration of Guivret, the Little King, and his sisters.[1] By putting together evidence from various sources we saw what the elements in this formula must have been. There was a certain "rois de la basse gent," a king of the short folk, whose name was Pelles; he dwelt as a hermit in the forest; his house had a low

[1] Cf. Chap. XX.

door; he sheltered the hero in sickness. He had a female cousin or daughter who was very wise, and who recognized the mad hero as he lay asleep and had him conveyed to her castle for healing. The evidence of *Erec, Perlesvaus, Didot Perceval,* and the *Vulgate Lancelot* proved the existence of this traditional formula of the dwarf king and his kinswoman, and showed that the prototype of the latter was Morgain.

Do we not detect this same tradition in Chrétien's account of the healing of Yvain? Here is a hermit who dwells in the forest in a house, "mout basse et mout petite." He ministers to the hero's needs in sickness. Here, too, is a lady who recognizes the mad hero as he lies asleep; who has an ointment prepared by Morgue la Sage with which she brings about the hero's cure; and who has him brought to her castle.[2]

If any further proof were needed that Chrétien's narrative rests upon this tradition, it is only necessary to observe the other links between the Lady of Noiroison and Morgain. Again and again we have found Morgain or her counterparts, not only curing a hero, but also providing him with arms and a marvelous horse.[3] This latter feature, which occurs in *Yvain,* is particularly stressed in *Owain.*[4] When Owain asked the handmaid of his hostess whether her mistress could furnish a horse and arms, she replied: "Yes, the best in the world." And the hostess herself, having made Owain a gift of a perfect black steed and weapons, affirmed: "He has surely never had in his possession their equals." We shall see in our study of Perceval's beloved, Blancheflor, that another formula persistently attached to Morgain was her deliverance by a hero from siege and his abrupt abandonment of her, though she would fain have kept him as lover or husband.

Two other bits of evidence tend to confirm this relationship of the Dame de Noiroison to Morgain. The Welsh *Owain* (Red Book of Hergest) has the lady discover the madman as she is walking by the side of a lake,[5] and we have just seen that Morgain was a water-nymph. The title, Dame de Noiroison,[6] otherwise so meaningless, loses some of its mystery when we remember that in the *Didot Perceval* the fay of Avalon and her sisters were able to transform themselves into black birds, and that Morgain's Irish prototype, the Morrigan, was in the habit of turning into a crow.[7] For if Morgain was able to take the shape of a *noir oisel,* one may well

---

[2] This pattern has evidently influenced a modern Breton folktale, in which the hero, suffering from a tremor of the limbs, meets two hermits in succession, and then comes on a princess sitting by a fountain, who makes an unguent of herbs, rubs it over his body, and thus cures him. F. M. Luzel, *Contes populaires de la Basse-Bretagne,* I, 179–84.

[3] Cf. *supra,* pp. 144 f., 253–62. Also *Speculum,* XX (1945), 183–91.

[4] Loth, *Mabinogion,* 2d ed., II, 36 f.   [5] *Ibid.,* II, 34.

[6] Foerster and Reid in their editions of *Yvain* give the reading Noroison (vs. 3287). Ms. G, however, gives "noiroison," and two others read "uoir reson." There is reason therefore to believe that the first syllable of the name as Chrétien wrote it was "noir," not "nor."

[7] Cf. *supra,* pp. 270–72.

entertain the suspicion that her counterpart owed to this fact her curious title of "la dame de Noiroison."

Just as we have been able to trace the essentials of the story of Yvain and Laudine to that branch of the Morgain tradition which took shape in Lothian, so it seems clear that this episode is derived from those other branches which associate the healing fay with a hermit and which represent her as an amorous chatelaine whose matrimonial expectations the hero disappoints.

Chapter LIII

THE GRATEFUL LION

VERSES 3341–6727

After leaving the Dame de Noiroison, Yvain was passing through a wood when he heard a roar and saw a serpent holding a lion by the tail and scorching its rump with flame. Yvain cleft the serpent in two and released the noble beast, which stood on its hind feet, bowed, then knelt and did homage to its rescuer. As the knight proceeded on his way, the lion accompanied him, brought him a deer for food, and when he slept that night, kept vigilant watch. On his arrival at the storm-making spring, Yvain, swooning with grief, fell on his sword, and the lion, thinking him dead, picked up the weapon and tried to commit suicide, but the opportune recovery of its master saved it from this fate. Near by was the chapel, and here Yvain found Lunete imprisoned and promised to fight on her behalf on the morrow against her accusers, Laudine's seneschal and his two brothers. In the meantime, seeking harborage, Yvain came to a castle where he spent the night, and early the next morning, with the help of his lion, killed a giant. He then hurried back toward the chapel and found a throng gathered to witness the burning of Lunete. When he announced himself as her champion, the false seneschal protested against any interference by the lion, and at Yvain's command the animal meekly withdrew. The battle began, Yvain against the seneschal and his brothers, and it would have gone hardly with the hero if his lion had not sprung into the fray, torn the seneschal's hauberk, and laid bare his entrails. Thus Yvain was the victor, and the three accusers of Lunete were burned at the pyre prepared for her. Some time after, the Knight of the Lion came to the Castle of Evil Adventure, where custom obliged him to fight two champions, armed with round shields and bastons cornus. These antagonists demanded that the lion be shut up during the combat, and its master complied. When Yvain was hard pressed, the animal scratched its way

*out of confinement and again brought succor and victory. Left behind
at a certain house where Yvain had taken shelter before his incognito
fight with Gauvain, the lion again made its appearance after the heroes
had recognized each other, traveled on with Yvain to the storm-making
spring, and was present at his final reconciliation with Laudine.*

THE STORY of Yvain and his lion must have made a great appeal to
Chrétien and his readers, furnishing amusement by the semihuman
antics of the beast, stimulating admiration by its noble example of
gratitude, loyalty, and courage. Here was a theme nicely adapted to the
medieval sense of humor and sense of honor. At the great courtly festival
held at Hem-Monacu in 1278 Robert II, count of Artois, played the part
of the Chevalier au Lion and apparently was accompanied by some
thirteenth-century Snug the Joiner in a lion's skin, who furnished farcical
entertainment.[1] The author of *Gui de Warewic* filched the episode from
Yvain,[2] and an English illuminator, who filled the lower margins of the
Smithfield Decretals with miscellaneous scenes, depicted with zest the beast
sitting on its haunches and holding up its paws in gratitude to Gui.[3]

Whence came this series of adventures in which the lion plays almost
the title role? The most satisfactory treatments of the problem are those
of Chotzen and Professor Brodeur.[4] Though their theories might seem
irreconcilable at first glance, they are, I believe, capable of harmonization,
and, taken together, provide a fairly complete explanation of Chrétien's
treatment of the grateful lion.

It has, of course, been long recognized that there was some remote
connection with the story of Androcles. Professor Brodeur traced the
evolution of the theme from that source to a western European type which

[1] *Histoire des ducs de Normandie,* ed. F. Michel (Paris, 1840), pp. 222–83. *Mediaeval
Studies in Memory of A. Kingsley Porter* (Cambridge, Mass., 1939), I, 92–95.
[2] *Gui de Warewic,* ed. A. Ewert (Paris, 1932), I, vss. 4125–4368.
[3] British Museum, Royal 10. E. iv., fol. 80*v*–83*v*. The Museum catalogue of Royal mss.
wrongly identifies these scenes as illustrations of *Yvain.* Another proof of the popularity of this
tale is found in the unpublished *Ci Nous Dit,* which moralized a number of famous themes.
In ms. Bib. Nat., fr. 429, fol. 48*v*, occurs this passage: "Ci nous dist comment un chevalier tua
une serpent qui se combatoit a un lion et dues yleuc le lion usa toute sa vie de servir le chevalier
si comme bon chien son maistre si grant gre le savoit de ce quil lavoit delivre dun serpent et
lapelloit on le chevalier au lion. Si poons entendre grandement de nous tuit amer notre
segneur qui nous a fait tant de bien que nous nen savons le nombre quant le lion qui est une
beste mue vot user toute sa vie en servir le chevalier pource quil lavoit delivre du serpent."
On *Ci Nous Dit* cf. *Histoire littéraire de la France,* XXXVI, 237; R. S. and L. H. Loomis,
Arthurian Legends in Medieval Art, p. 28. Other examples of the popularity of the story are
cited by Dr. Krappe in *Mod. Lang. Quarterly,* IV (1943), 276 f.
[4] *PMLA,* XXXIX (1924), 485–524. *Neophilologus,* XVIII (1933), 131–36. Cf. also A. H.
Krappe, in *Mod. Lang. Quarterly,* IV, 274–78. Unsatisfactory treatments of the subject are in
Studies and Notes in Phil. and Lit., VIII (1903), 129–31; *Zts. f. franz. Sprache u. Lit.,* XXXI,
157 ff.; *Mélusine,* V, cols. 217 ff., 241 ff.; F. Settegast, *Antike Elemente im altfranzösische
Merowingerzyklus* (Leipzig, 1907); *PMLA,* XX (1905), 673–706.

appeared in the *Epistles* of Petrus Damianus before 1072.[5] Here, for the first time, the lion is rescued from the coils of a dragon and out of gratitude supplies his deliverers with game. There is a much more complete parallel to *Yvain* in Neckam's *De Naturis Rerum* composed near the end of the twelfth century.[6]

A certain noble and valiant knight hears a lion groaning in a recess near the road. A serpent has coiled itself about the animal's neck. The knight hastens to the rescue with drawn sword, slays the reptile, and releases the lion. The grateful beast wags its tail, licks its new master's hand, and, like a dog, now runs ahead, now joyfully returns to him. When the knight lies down to sleep, the lion keeps guard at his feet, and when he is engaged in battle, lends him aid, often saving him from death. It follows him everywhere and fills all spectators with wonder. The knight, however, sneaks off when his faithful companion is asleep and takes ship for his native land. The lion, on waking, tries to swim out to the vessel and is drowned.

A similar tale is told of the Crusader, Golfier de Lastours, by Jaufré de Vigeois in 1184, and is often repeated in later chronicles.[7] Jaufré adds the detail: "In hunting as well as in war the lion provided him abundantly with game and overthrew the adversary of his master by his swift rush."

Professor Brodeur demonstrated that Neckam and Jaufré both derived the story from a French chivalric development of the Petrus Damianus version, and that this French tale furnished *Yvain* indirectly with the following elements: the rescue of the lion from the serpent by a knight, the lion's gratitude, the supply of game, the watch by night, the effective aid in battle. Two details present in Neckam and presumably derived from the French tale are not found in *Yvain* but do appear in *Owain*: the knight finds the noble animal in a recess, and after its release it gambols about him like a hound.[8] It is most unlikely that the Welsh author turned to Neckam to supplement the information he obtained from his source, and yet he did not find these details in *Yvain*. Professor Brodeur rightly considers these facts as strong evidence that *Yvain* and *Owain* are based on a common immediate source, the romance which we call Y.

There are certain elements which must have been in that common source and yet correspond to nothing in the grateful-lion tradition as represented by Petrus, Neckam, or Jaufré. It will be remembered that according to Chrétien the noble beast thrice intervenes in combats on behalf of his master and brings him victory.[9] In *Owain* he intervenes twice.[10]

[5] *PMLA*, XXXIX, 499. *Romanische Forschungen*, XXIX (1910), 317. *Beihefte zur Zts. f. rom. Phil.*, LXX (1921), 156.

[6] *PMLA*, XXXIX, 495 f. Alexander Neckam, *De Naturis Rerum*, ed. T. Wright (London, 1863), pp. 229 f.

[7] *PMLA*, XXXIX, 494. *Beihefte zur Zts. f. rom. Phil.*, LXX, 157–59.

[8] *PMLA*, XXXIX, 498. Loth, *Mabinogion*, 2d ed., II, 38.

[9] Vss. 4164–4247; 4449–4565; 5512–5693.   [10] Loth, *op. cit.*, pp. 41–43.

The French poem tells how successively the seneschal and the two "diables" protest against the participation of the lion, and how Yvain twice takes measures (ineffectual, to be sure) to prevent the beast from coming to his aid. The Welsh tale likewise introduces twice the protest of the adversaries of Owain against the participation of the lion as giving him an unfair advantage, and Owain's sportsmanlike response. Moreover, according to *Yvain,* the lion tears away the seneschal's side. "It pulls downward so strongly that it tears away the flesh of his shoulder as well as his side. Whatever it seizes, it pulls away, so that the entrails are exposed." [11] In *Owain* the same detail is reported of the fight with the giant. The animal "struck such a blow with its paw on the tall man's shoulder that it passed down to the joining of his hips, and his entrails could be seen falling out of him." [12]

Chotzen has shown [13] that these three elements—the protest, the hero's sportsmanlike response, the wound which exposes the entrails—which certainly did not come into *Yvain* and *Owain* from the tradition represented by Petrus, Neckam, and Jaufré de Vigeois, are found together in what must have been, even as early as the eighth century, a famous Irish story, the vengeance which Conall took for his foster brother Cuchulainn on Lugaid son of Curoi.[14]

In the duel Conall obtained an initial advantage by wounding Lugaid. Lugaid protested: " 'I would that you would act toward me with the fairness which behoves a warrior.' 'What is the matter?' 'You ought,' Lugaid replied, 'to use only one hand against me.' " Conall agreed and had one hand bound to his side. The fight continued. "Conall the Victorious, seeing that he could not overcome his adversary, cast a glance at his horse, 'Red Dewy.' This horse had a dog's head and used it to kill men in battles and duels. The horse approached Lugaid and tore away his flank, from which the entrails burst forth. . . . 'This is not, O Conall the Victorious, the fair play which behoves a warrior.' Conall answered: 'I have given my promise but I have not given that of beasts and animals which lack reason.' " Thereupon Conall cut off Lugaid's head.

Here, then, are the three elements so emphasized in the battles waged by Yvain or Owain with the aid of his lion—the protest of the adversary against an unfair advantage, the hero's magnanimous effort to eliminate that advantage, the wound inflicted by the helpful animal, exposing the adversary's bowels. Of course, a dog-headed horse is not a lion; but would not the story of a monstrous horse which came to the aid of his master in a prolonged conflict recall to the mind of a twelfth-century Frenchman the familiar story of the grateful lion, and suggest the substitution of a lion

[11] Vss. 4527–32. A. Kitze, *Das Ross in den altfr. Artus- und Abenteuer-Romanen* (Marburg, 1888), p. 45.   [12] Loth, *op. cit.,* 41 f.   [13] *Neophilologus,* XVIII, 134 f.
[14] D'Arbois de Jubainville, *L'Epopée celtique en Irlande,* pp. 351–53. Thurneysen, *Irische Helden- und Königsage,* p. 555. On date cf. *ibid.,* p. 548.

for the hybrid creature? Would not a fusion of the two traditions be natural?

The influence on *Yvain* of the story of Conall's horse is rendered more likely by the fact that the Irish motif of steeds participating in battle beside or on behalf of their masters has left its imprint, surely though inconspicuously, on the *Matière de Bretagne*. In *Bricriu's Feast* Loegaire, Conall, and Cuchulainn and their horses successively fight against Ercol and his horse. Ercol's horse kills those of Loegaire and Conall but is in turn killed by the Gray of Macha.[15] In an earlier passage of the saga which relates the vengeance of Conall on Lugaid with the aid of his horse, we read that after Cuchulainn's downfall the Gray arrived on the scene. "He wished to protect Cuchulainn so long as the soul of the hero was in him. . . . He made three terrible charges around his master; with his teeth he killed fifty men and thirty with each of his hoofs." [16] This Irish motif seems to be reflected in romances known to be of Celtic derivation. When Lancelot and Meleagant have hurled each other from their saddles in their last fight, "their steeds run at large and wander hither and yon; one kicks, the other bites, for each wishes to kill the other." [17] In a German embroidery depicting scenes from the Tristan legend,[18] which Gertrude Schoepperle proved to contain many Irish elements,[19] the hero appears fighting on foot with Morholt, while his white charger, rearing on its hind legs, bites and kicks Morholt's steed. In the English *Sir Launfal*,[20] based on a Breton lai, the hero during a tournament alighted from his white horse and was attacked by a troop of Welsh knights, but "through him and his steed's blows many a knight was borne to ground." The Scottish romance of *Eger and Grime*,[21] shown by Professor Hibbard to be related to *Yvain* and influenced by Celtic tradition,[22] tells how Grime during his combat with Gray-Steel dismounted from his horse, and while he fought on foot with the giant, "the steeds together have they run, fighting as they first begun." The *enfances* of Maugis d'Aigremont follow the Arthurian pattern in the most palpable fashion, and here again when the hero and his antagonist are thrown to earth, the steed Baiart "grate et fronce et henist," attacks the other horse and kills it.[23] Though these

[15] D'Arbois, *op. cit.*, p. 128. Thurneysen, *op. cit.*, p. 465.

[16] D'Arbois, *op. cit.*, p. 347. Thurneysen, *op. cit.*, p. 554.

[17] Chrétien de Troyes, *Karrenritter*, ed. W. Foerster, vss. 7061–64.

[18] R. S. and L. H. Loomis, *Arthurian Legends in Medieval Art*, Fig. 79.

[19] G. Schoepperle, *Tristan and Isolt*, II, 267 ff. Cf. also *Beiblatt zur Anglia*, XV, 16–21; *Romania*, LIII (1927), 92–95; *Romanische Forschungen*, XLV (1931), 95 ff.

[20] W. H. French, C. B. Hale, *Middle English Metrical Romances*, pp. 361 f., vss. 475–86.

[21] *Eger and Grime*, ed. J. R. Caldwell, p. 283, vss. 1629 f.

[22] L. A. Hibbard, *Mediaeval Romance in England*, pp. 314–16.

[23] *Maugis d'Aigremont*, ed. F. Castets (Montpellier, 1893), p. 51. Note that Baiart also retains the Celtic feature of mourning at separation from his master. Cf. *ibid.*, p. 314, and E. M. Grimes, *Lais of Desiré, Graelent, and Melion*, p. 101, French and Hale, *op. cit.*, p. 379, and D'Arbois de Jubainville, *op. cit.*, p. 333. Cf. also F. Bangert, *Die Tiere im altfr. Epos*

five examples of belligerent horses do not parallel exactly Yvain's fighting lion, they do show the persistence in medieval romance of the Irish tradition of the faithful animal, aiding his master in combat, and they corroborate Dr. Chotzen's thesis that the same Irish tradition influenced Chrétien's skillful narrative of the grateful lion.

Why did this blend of Irish and French tradition attach itself to Yvain rather than to any other? Two possible causes have been suggested. In native Welsh literature, we may recall, Owain son of Urien was well known for his flock of ravens which fought with the men of Arthur.[24] Another plausible suggestion is that of Dr. Brugger.[25] We have already seen that Yvain was connected by the *conteurs* with the daughter of the King of Lothian.[26] Brugger also points out that Gaimar (*ca.* 1150) represented Yvain himself as King of Mureif (Moray in Scotland) and Loeneis.[27] Chrétien in his *Erec* mentions an Yvain de Loenel,[28] while in Wauchier's continuation of the *Conte del Graal* and the Vulgate romances we come across an Yvain de Lyonel, Leonel, or Lionel.[29] Finally, in certain manuscripts of the *Vulgate Lancelot* the name has become Y(w)ains del Lyonel,[30] which would mean Yvain of the Little Lion, and the form with the article is regularly used by the author of *Rigomer*.[31] Unfortunately for this hypothesis, which would explain the association of Yvain with a lion by the corruption of "de Loeneis" into "del Lyonel," the latter form is first recorded in a passage composed at least thirty years after Chrétien's poem and in manuscripts copied later still. In fact, one of the manuscripts containing the passage (Royal 19. B. vii) gives instead of Lyonel the original form Loonois.[32] One cannot avoid the suspicion that the late recordings of "Yvain del Lyonel" were suggested to the scribes by the story of the grateful lion as made familiar by Chrétien. Neither Owain's ravens nor the corruption of Loeneis explains satisfactorily Yvain's association with a helpful lion. It may have been a purely arbitrary choice of some *conteur* which linked the theme to Yvain rather than to any other knight of the Arthurian cycle.

In sum, the French chivalric tradition represented by Jaufré de Vigeois and Neckam supplied *Yvain* with these motifs: (1) A knight hears the outcry of a lion and rescues him from a serpent. (2) The grateful beast displays its gratitude, fetches him game, stands guard over him by night,

---

(Marburg, 1885), p. 79. According to *Aiol et Mirabel,* ed. W. Foerster (Heilbronn, 1876–82), vss. 925–38, the horse of Arthur had the reputation of attacking all strangers who approached him. There is a stallion fight in *Grettissaga,* Chap. 29, but the circumstances are entirely different from those in the Irish and romance examples.

[24] Loth, *Mabinogion,* 2d ed., I, 366–71, especially p. 370n. A connection between the helpful lion of Yvain and Owain's ravens was suggested by E. Windisch in *Das keltische Brittannien bis zu Kaiser Arthur,* p. 223.   [25] *Mod. Phil.,* XXXVIII (1941), 267–87.   [26] Cf. Chap. LI.
[27] *Mod. Phil.,* XXXVIII, 286.   [28] Vs. 1707.   [29] *Mod. Phil.,* XXXVIII, 272 f.
[30] Sommer, *Vulgate Version,* III, 275.   [31] *Mod. Phil.,* XXXVIII, 272.
[32] Sommer, *op. cit.,* III, 275, n. 2.

and attacks his enemies when he is engaged in battle. The Irish tradition of the faithful horse supplied three motifs: (1) The hero's enemies remonstrate against the animal's participation. (2) The hero magnanimously accepts their protest. (3) The beast intervenes and tears open their bowls.

Chapter LIV

THE RESCUE OF LUNETE FROM THE PYRE

VERSES 4313–4575

Yvain, hurrying to save Lunete from her unjust punishment for treachery to her mistress, arrived with his lion in the nick of time. The damsel had been brought out, clad only in her shift, had made her last confession, and was kneeling beside a pyre, surrounded by a throng. Yvain announced himself as her defender, undertook the combat with her three accusers, and through the help of his lion forced them to acknowledge defeat. They were burned on the pyre intended for Lunete.

THE SECOND of the battles which Yvain wins with the aid of his lion brings about the deliverance of Lunete from the pyre. Of the three fights it approximates most closely, as we have seen, the Irish story of Conall's vengeance on Lugaid with the aid of his dog-headed horse. Is there any possibility that the condemnation of Lunete to the pyre and her rescue involves another Irish motif?

Professor Reinhard has examined most fully and most critically the Celtic evidence for the practice of burning as a punishment for crime, and finds comparatively little.[1] And none of the Irish or Welsh instances cited by him presents a dramatic situation at all resembling that in *Yvain*.[2] The theme of the rescue of a woman from death by fire cannot have a Celtic provenance.

Yet punishment of a woman by burning her alive seems to have entered Arthurian romance by the middle of the twelfth century at latest and continued long to have a vogue.[3] According to Eilhart and Béroul,

[1] *Speculum*, XVI (1941), 186–209. This article supersedes the discussion in *Revue celt.*, XXX (1909), 277–79, and G. Schoepperle, *Tristan and Isolt*, II, 464 f.
[2] A legendary example of a woman condemned to death by fire for illicit intercourse is found in the *Book of Llan Dav*, ed. J. G. Evans, J. Rhys (Oxford, 1893), p. 79. Cf. also Baring-Gould and Fisher, *Lives of the British Saints*, III, 363.
[3] Examples in European fiction of punishment by burning alive have been collected not only in the *Speculum* article just cited, but also in *Studien zur englischen Philologie*, L (1913),

King Mark commanded Iseut to be burned, and, according to the Norse *Tristramssaga,* based on Thomas's poem, Mark declared his intention to commit her to the flames.[4] Since the concurrence of these three romances indicates that the motif was present in the common tradition, and since that tradition was fully formed by 1150 at latest,[5] .we seem to have an early date for the appearance of the motif in the *Matière de Bretagne.* Death by fire is the punishment announced (though never carried out) for Merlin's mother in the *Vulgate Merlin* and the *Huth Merlin;*[6] it was therefore in the common source, Robert de Boron's poem. The *Prose Tristan* asserts the origin of the custom in a judgment pronounced by a certain Queen of Leonoys.[7] Condemnation of a woman to the stake is followed by her rescue twice in the *Vulgate Lancelot,* once (the famous case of Guenievre) in *La Mort Artu,* once in Manessier's continuation of *Le Conte del Graal,* and once in *Claris and Laris.*[8]

But this combination of the threatened death by fire with the opportune intervention of the hero was no monopoly of the Arthurian romancers but occurs also in *Orson de Beauvais, Bueve de Hantone, Doon de Maience, Le Chevalier au Cygne, Le Roman de la Violette, Tristan de Nanteuil, Valentin und Namelos, Seghelijn van Jerusalem, Loher und Maller, La Gran Conquista de Ultramar, The Earl of Toulouse,* and the ballad of *Sir Aldingar.*[9] The timely rescue of a woman from the stake, then, seems to have been a *lieu commun* of medieval fiction, and though it appears first in *Yvain,* there is no reason to suppose that it was a Celtic theme. Rather, as Bruce and M. Gustave Cohen have suggested,[10] it is the reflection in literature of a barbaric law to the effect that a woman who accused another person or who was accused should be burned if her champion was worsted in a wager of battle. In the *Assises de Jérusalem* one finds:

"If a woman makes a charge, and her surety or her champion is defeated, she shall be burned. . . . If a charge is brought against a woman for any crime, if she has a husband and he wishes to defend her, he can defend her with his body.

180–89; P. Rajna, *Fonti dell'Orlando Furioso,* 2d ed., pp. 154 ff.; F. J. Child, *English and Scottish Popular Ballads,* II, 113; B. Matulka, *Novels of Juan de Flores and Their European Diffusion* (New York, 1931), 55–69; A. Dickson, *Valentine and Orson,* pp. 38, 44, 70–78; *Beihefte zur Zts. f. rom. Phil.,* XIX (1909), 116; *Mort Artu,* ed. J. D. Bruce, pp. 282 f.
[4] G. Schoepperle, *op. cit.,* I, 30. Béroul, *Tristan,* vss. 867–83. *Tristramssaga,* ed. E. Kölbing (Heilbronn, 1878), Chap. 67.
[5] Thomas, *Tristan,* ed. J. Bédier, II, 186. *Romanic Review,* XXXII (1941), 16–19.
[6] Sommer, *Vulgate Version,* II, 14–17. *Huth Merlin,* ed. Paris and Ulrich, I, 22–29.
[7] Rajna, *op. cit.,* p. 154. E. Löseth, *Tristan en Prose,* p. 14.
[8] Sommer, *op. cit.,* IV, 275–81; V, 162 f.; VI, 279–82. *Mort Artu,* ed. J. Frappier, pp. 97–100. Potvin, *Perceval le Gallois,* V, vss. 37758–37884. *Claris et Laris,* ed. J. Alton (Tübingen, 1884), vss. 9664–9769.
[9] For references cf. *supra,* n. 3.
[10] J. D. Bruce, *Evolution of Arthurian Romance,* I, 437, n. 201. *Annales de l'Univ. de Paris,* VIII (1933), 516–19.

If he does not wish to defend her, she may be defended by some other champion. . . . If her champion is defeated, she shall be burned." [11]

The editor Beugnot remarks apropos of this passage: "Les Assises conservèrent donc une punition barbare qui n'avait jamais été admise dans la plus grande partie de l'Europe. Nous doutons que ces deux peines aient été rigoureusement appliquées, même dans le royaume de Jérusalem." [12] But an incident reported by Froissart [13] concerning the wife of Sir Jean de Carouges proves that even as late as 1387 a woman was liable to go to the stake if her champion suffered defeat. It is probably, then, this French custom and the sympathy it evoked which gave rise to the numerous examples in European fiction of the rescue at the stake.

Chapter LV

THE DISINHERITED SISTER

VERSES 4703–5106

On the death of the Sire de la Noire Espine, the elder of his two daughters seized all his estates and refused any share to her sister. The younger then declared her intent to find a champion of her claim at Arthur's court, but was forestalled by the elder, who procured the services of Gauvain. Accordingly, when the younger damsel arrived, she found no worthy defender of her cause, but Arthur granted her forty days to find one. News of Yvain's victory over the giant prompted her to seek the Knight of the Lion. On her quest she fell ill. Another damsel took up the search, succeeded in overtaking Yvain, and secured his aid for the disinherited damsel.

THE THEME of the disinherited sister is absent from *Owain* and is probably to be credited to Chrétien. In fact, it is possible to guess the mental processes which led him to introduce it. He seems to have felt that the series of combats in which Yvain engaged after his cure from madness required a climax, a combat more terrific and with a worthier opponent than any he had encountered. The poet therefore suppressed the fight of his hero with Gauvain (Gwalchmai) which occurs in the middle of *Owain* [1] and presumably occurred at the same point also in Y, and reserved this for a final great scene. But how was he to bring about this duel between the friends? He turned to a version of the disinherited-sister theme which he found in a form akin to that preserved

[11] *Assises de Jérusalem*, ed. Beugnot (Paris, 1841), I, 175 f.   [12] *Ibid.*, I, 175, note a.
[13] Froissart, *Oeuvres*, ed. Kervyn de Lettenhove (Brussels, 1871), XII, 37.
[1] Loth, *Mabinogion*, 2d ed., II, 30–32.

in *Diu Krone*.[2] The relationship is proved by the fact that Chrétien calls the father of the sisters "li sire de la noire espine," while Heinrich calls him Laniure [3]—a corruption due in part to the need for a rime with *torriure* and *aventiure*. It was apparently an established tradition that one of the sisters should obtain Gauvain for her champion to oppose to her sister's champion. By introducing this extraneous motif into the plot of Y Chrétien was able to bring about the incognito duel between Yvain and Gauvain. The motif, so far as I can discover, had no Celtic original.

Chapter LVI

THE CASTLE OF EVIL ADVENTURE

VERSES 5107–5809

Accompanied by his lion and the damsel who had enlisted him in the cause of the disinherited sister, Yvain entered the Castle of Evil Adventure, and the inhabitants repeatedly cried out that an unhappy fate awaited him. Undeterred, he passed through the gate of the main tower and found an enclosure where three hundred miserable maidens in tattered clothing were confined, engaged in embroidery. He inquired of the porter who these damsels were who were weaving silk and gold brocade. The porter refused to answer, but one of the women told the following story. Long ago, the King of the Isle des Puceles had come to this same castle, held by two half-diabolic brothers. In order to save his life, the King had promised to send to these devils, so long as they lived, a yearly tribute of thirty maidens. The number of these unfortunates had increased, and all were kept toiling long hours at a wage of four pence a day, though their product was worth twenty sous a week (a 900% profit!). Many excellent knights had lost their lives in the vain effort to free the maidens from their sweatshop existence. Yvain and his companion passed through the hall, where they found no one, but in a garden they spied a nobleman and his wife, reclining and listening to their lovely daughter as she read a roman. These three rose at once to greet the strangers and bestowed on them every attention. But the next morning the host informed Yvain that before he could depart he must fight with his two servants (the devils

[2] Heinrich von dem Türlin, *Krone*, ed. Scholl, vss. 7660–9128. On the relation of Heinrich's story of the rival sisters and Chrétien's cf. Paien de Maisieres, *La Damoisele à la Mule*, ed. B. Orlowski (Paris, 1911), pp. 46–63; *Beihefte zur Zts. f. rom. Phil.*, LXX (1921), pp. 292–301.

[3] Chrétien, *Yvain*, vs. 4705. *Krone*, vss. 8864, 8924. It is significant that Laniure was defeated by Gawein at a ford (*ibid.*, vss. 8853–8925) and that in the *Didot-Perceval* (ed. W. Roach, pp. 195 f.) the son of "le roine de le Noire Espine" was defeated by Perceval at a ford. Cf. *Mod. Phil.*, XLIII (1945), 65, n. 10.

already mentioned). They appeared as chanpions, *their heads and lower legs bare, equipped with round shields and* bastons cornus, *and were well skilled in fencing. But Yvain with his lion's aid killed one and forced the other to yield. Though pressed to take the nobleman's daughter in marriage, he departed, released the wretched embroidery-workers, and received their blessing.*

THIS EPISODE was evidently suggested to Chrétien by a similar tale of the deliverance of many captive widows from the castle of a single evil knight. Such a tale was included in Y, since it is found in *Owain* as an awkward appendage and in Malory's Book of Gareth.[1] Chrétien, however, substituted a different, more elaborate story, for his captive ladies are not widows and there are two evil oppressors instead of one. Chrétien, moreover, makes much of a characteristic feature of this second formula, the employment of the captive ladies in silk-weaving. This tale which Chrétien substituted for the tale of the captive widows in Y appears in four variants—one in Pseudo-Wauchier's portion of *Le Conte del Graal,* the second in Malory's Book VI, the third and fourth in the *Vulgate Lancelot.* Pseudo-Wauchier's version is one which we have already met in other connections and found to be highly composite, so that only in part does it parallel Chrétien's Evil Adventure.[2]

Carahes (there are several variants of the name) enters a splendid castle, and, passing through the chambers, finds them empty of inhabitants. He descends into a *vergier,* where he sees a tall knight, the lord of the castle, reclining, tended by a dwarf and a damsel. The lord orders Carahes removed, and a tiny knight comes on the scene and in an ensuing joust overthrows the intruder. He declares that he has a custom of forcing all those whom he conquers to become weavers and to work at gold-embroidered silk, but he permits Carahes to depart on condition that he return a year later to renew the combat. As Carahes passes through the formerly vacant castle, he sees many people, including eighty or a hundred maidens, making purses and girdles, and all taunt him with his defeat. At the appointed time Carahes returns to the *vergier,* and kills both the tiny knight and the lord of the castle.

Though Pseudo-Wauchier's tale is composed of different strands of tradition, which account for the many divergences from Chrétien's Evil Adventure, yet there are five undeniable points of similarity: (1) the passage of the hero through an empty room and out into a *vergier;* (2) the reclining lord of the castle, attended by a damsel; (3) the captive ladies engaged in silk work; (4) the scornful shouts of the inmates of the castle; (5) the defeat of two formidable oppressors.

[1] Loth, *Mabinogion,* 2d ed., II, 43–45. Cf. *Beihefte zur Zts. f. rom. Phil.,* LXX, 302–07; Malory, *Morte d'Arthur,* ed. H. O. Sommer, I, 265 f.
[2] Potvin *Perceval le Gallois,* IV, 33–53. For previous treatments of this episode cf. *supra,* pp. 80, 213.

A closer parallel to Chrétien is provided in Malory's Book VI.[3]

Lancelot, riding over a bridge, is attacked by a churlish porter with a club, and cleaves his head in return. The people whom Lancelot meets in a village beyond cry out that he has done an evil deed. He enters a castle, alights, and makes for a green court; many folk from doors and windows around call him ill fated. Two giants, all armed save their heads, attack him with clubs and are speedily killed. In the hall Lancelot is greeted by threescore gentlewomen, who have been prisoners for seven years, working at all manner of silk works for their meat. Many knights have been slain by the two giants. Lancelot gives the ladies their freedom and restores the castle, which is Tyntygayl, to its rightful owner.

The *Vulgate Lancelot* tells substantially the same story of the churlish porter, the two giants, the grateful ladies, and the castle of Tinaguel.[4] Curiously enough, Sommer's manuscripts say nothing of the silk works, but add certain features which confirm the relation to Chrétien. The lord of Tinaguel had surrendered the castle to the giants as a reward for their liberating him from prison, and the description of the giants is more detailed. "They were armed in the guise of *campions* who are about to fence, for their heads were bare and uncovered, and they carried good, strong shields and wore good hauberks."

Still another form of the same basic tale occurs in the *Vulgate Lancelot*.[5]

Galeschin is led by a damsel to a castle where there is a perilous adventure. Both are well harbored for the night. The next morning after mass Galeschin is brought to a vault, where he finds four *sergans,* a father and three sons, fencing. "They have *bastons cornus,* of which the horns are of steel, trenchant and sharp, and they have round shields of boiled leather." Galeschin defeats all, and then rides on to a castle named Pintagoel,[6] where he is welcomed as deliverer and which he restores to its lord. In time past this lord had been delivered from prison by the *grant vilain,* father of the three fencers, and had been obliged to send him a child from every household.

Yvain's experiences at the castle of Evil Adventure are certainly related to these three stories from Malory and the *Vulgate Lancelot;* but how? as the source or as a cognate? We have already observed that when the author of the *Vulgate Lancelot* draws on Chrétien, as he does on the *Charrette,* he leaves no doubt of his indebtedness. Furthermore, he shows no trace of certain outstanding features of Chrétien's narrative of the Evil Adventure—the reading party, the lovely maiden, the helpful lion. It is fair to conclude, then, that Chrétien, Malory, and the *Lancelot* all drew ultimately on a lost *conte,* which contained the following elements: (1) the hero's arrival at a perilous castle, accompanied by a damsel; (2) the surly porter; (3) the warning inmates; (4) the captive ladies sent as a tribute to the castle and condemned to earn their food by "silk works"; (5) the

---

[3] Malory, *Morte d'Arthur,* ed. Sommer, I, 198 f.   [4] Sommer, *Vulgate Version,* V, 212–14.
[5] *Ibid.,* IV, 105–7.   [6] *Ibid.,* IV, 109, n. 2.

two churls with uncovered heads, equipped like "champions" with "bastons cornus" and round shields; (6) the hero's victory and the deliverance of the ladies. The common source of the two versions in the *Lancelot* probably contained also certain motifs absent from *Yvain:* (1) the obligation placed on the lord of the castle by his release from prison by the *vilains;* (2) the restoration of the castle to him by the hero; (3) the name of the castle, Tintagel.

Chrétien seems to have combined this formula of the deliverance of the captive silk-workers with certain features of the humiliation of Gaheries in the *vergier* and introduced the faithful lion; perhaps he is responsible also for certain modifications in the direction of realism. As Professor Hall has shown,[7] the description of the three hundred captive ladies, working under intolerable conditions at wretched wages, was influenced by the actual employment of Christian slave girls in the silk factories of the Moslem world, for though it was customary for highborn women of the Middle Ages to occupy themselves in embroidery and needlework,[8] nothing that contemporary documents tell us of this amateur industry or of the weaving shops of Western Europe corresponds to the large-scale silk operations conducted in the castle of Evil Adventure. A reflection of customs more likely to have come under Chrétien's own eye is the charming scene where the lord of the castle and his wife listen to a romance read by their daughter, for we know from various sources that reading in the vernacular was an accomplishment in which noble ladies seem to have surpassed their menfolk.[9]

The most remarkable reflection of contemporary usage is one which hitherto, so far as I am aware, has been overlooked by even the most distinguished Romance scholars. Apparently, as the two passages from the *Vulgate Lancelot* show, the *conte* which Chrétien followed pictured the hero's opponents as "champions, qui doivent escremir," with bodies protected but heads bare, equipped with round shields and "bastons cornus." Chrétien himself retains these features. The opponents of Yvain are referred to as "li dui chanpion"; [10] each is armed from shoulder to knee, but his head and lower legs are bare; each has a "baston cornu de corneillier," and a round shield, strong and light "por escremir." [11] No editor has commented on the special technical sense of *chanpion.* Foerster in his *Wörterbuch* (1914) translates *cornu* by the ambiguous word *gehörnt* and the mistaken word *gekrümmt,* "crooked." Breuer's revised *Wörterbuch* (1933) translates by the ambiguous word *zackig,* which may mean "pointed, jagged, or pronged." Mr. Reid in his edition of *Yvain* (1942) mistakenly translates "jagged." Now *champion* is a technical term for

[7] *Mod. Lang. Notes,* LVI (1941), 418–22.
[8] *Beihefte zur Zts. f. rom. Phil.,* XVI (1908), 35–45.
[9] *Ibid.,* p. 58. *Archiv f. Kulturgeschichte,* XXVI (1936), 140 ff. *Floriant et Florete,* ed. F. Michel (Edinburgh, 1873), pp. xlix f.   [10] Vs. 5575.   [11] Vss. 5514–25.

a participant in a judicial duel, and in Ducange under the word *cam-piones* are grouped many extracts not only describing the conditions under which such duels were held but also specifying the equipment of the combatants.[12] Let me quote some illuminating passages, the first being from the *Coutumier de Normandie* (1194–1223).

"On the day which is fixed for the battle, the *champions* must present themselves for judgment before midday is past, all accoutered in their leather tunics or in their coats, with their shields and their *bastons cornus,* and armed as may be necessary with cloth, leather, wool, and padding." [13]

From the thirteenth century we have the *Assises de Jérusalem*.

"Persons of all ranks, except knights, whatever the quarrel may be, must fight on foot in robes or in red coats, . . . and they must be shaved in a circle round the head, and have hempen cloth and *bastons de champions*." [14]

The *Coutumier d'Amiens* of the same century has similar provisions.

"They should come to the court protected by clothing of leather, tow, felt, and linen, with their legs guarded and covered by splints of whalebone or wood, and with shields made of leather, wood, and sinews, and their *bastons* also." [15]

From late in the thirteenth century comes the Norman-French compilation which goes under the name of Britton.

"Then they fight, armed without iron and long armor, with heads uncovered and bare hands, on foot, with two *bastons cornuz* of the same length, and each of them with a four-cornered shield, without other weapon with which one could injure the other." [16]

No argument is needed to prove that Chrétien's portrayal of the two *chanpions,* like those in the *Vulgate Lancelot,* is based on the judicial practices of Christendom from Acre to England.

England, moreover, supplies several pictorial illustrations of these champions: a twelfth-century mural painting,[17] a tile from Chertsey Abbey (*ca.* 1270),[18] a sketch from an assize roll of Henry III's reign,[19] a minia-

---

[12] Ducange, *Glossarium,* ed. L. Favre (1937), II, 62, 64. On the subject of these champions and their equipment cf. A. Coulin, *Gerichtliche Zweikampf* (Berlin, 1906), pp. 107 f.; *Zts. f. rom. Phil.,* IX (1885), 6, 69 f.; *Essential Portions of Nicholas Upton's De Studio Militari,* trans. J. Blount, ed. F. P. Barnard (Oxford, 1931), pp. 22, 59–61; G. G. Coulton, *Life in the Middle Ages* (Cambridge, New York, 1931), III, 11–14, 87–91; *Speculum,* XI (1936), 238–58; *Leeds Studies in English,* V (1936), 68–70. For bibliography cf. G. E. Levi, *Duello giudiziario, enciclopedia e bibliografia* (Florence, 1932), pp. 132–44. The fight between Renard and Roonel, the hound, is described as such a duel. Cf. *Roman de Renard,* ed. E. Martin (Strasbourg, 1882), I, 101.   [13] Ducange, II, 62.
[14] *Ibid. Assises de Jérusalem,* ed. Beugnot (Paris, 1841), I, 178.   [15] Ducange, II, 64.
[16] Britton, ed. F. M. Nichols (Oxford, 1865), p. 107.
[17] E. W. Tristram, *English Medieval Wall Painting,* I (1944), Pl. 67.
[18] Coulton, *op. cit.,* III, 12. *University of Illinois, Studies in Lang. and Lit.* (Urbana, 1916), pp. 328 f.
[19] J. R. Green, *Short History of the English People,* ill. ed. (London, 1892), I, 372.

ture in a manuscript of Beaumanoir's *Coutumes de Beauvaisis*,[20] the brass of Bishop Wyvil (1375) at Salisbury cathedral,[21] and two stained-glass panels (*ca.* 1410) at York Minster.[22] These differ from Chrétien's description in that the shields depicted are not round, but they show plainly the heads shaved in a circle above the ears, the light tunics reaching to the knees, and the "bastons cornus," which are evidently straight staves, sometimes strengthened by sinews (*ners*) wound about them, and tipped with *cornes,* that is, projecting horns.[23] The Chertsey tile, moreover, represents the combatants as carrying their light shields high to protect their heads; thus it combines with a line in *Gaydon,* "Son escu lieve à loi de champion,"[24] to confirm the reading of verse 5524 adopted by Hilka and followed by Mr. Reid: "Escuz reonz sor lor chies tindrent."[25]

Neither Chrétien nor the *conte* on which he drew for this episode seems to have followed strictly the regulations governing the trial by combat, except for these details of equipment. Since the regulations were devised with the purpose of ensuring equality between the two sides, a knight with all the advantages of full armor and a sword would not have been permitted to engage with a feebly equipped champion,[26] nor would the intervention of the lion have been tolerated.[27] On the other hand, it would have been contrary to custom for two champions to fight on one side. It is only in the description of their equipment that Chrétien conforms to the provisions of a wager of battle.

In this whole episode there are two elements only which can be traced back with any probability to a Celtic source. One, the helpful lion, has already been treated. The other is the forced annual tribute of maidens. The analogous tribute of boys which Morhaut, according to the Tristan legend, collected from Cornwall has been proved by Deutschbein to be founded on the legend preserved in *The Wooing of Emer*—the rescue of the daughter of Ruad, king of the Isles, from the Fomorian tax gatherers.[28] Gertrude Schoepperle pointed out that the Fomorians "levied upon Ireland an annual tribute of two thirds of the sons and daughters of the

[20] *Zts. f. rom. Phil.,* IX, 69, n. 4.   [21] Coulton, *op. cit.,* III, opp. p. 89.
[22] *Leeds Studies in English,* V, opp. p. 68.
[23] Sometimes, apparently, as the passage from the *Vulgate Lancelot* (Sommer, *Vulgate Version,* IV, 105) quoted above shows, the "cornes" were of steel, but usually this was forbidden. Cf. *Coutumier de Normandie* (Ducange, II, 62); "Es escus ne és bastons ne és armeures des jambes ne doit avoir fors fust ou cuir, ou ce qui est par devant dit."
[24] *Gaydon,* ed. F. Guessard and S. Luce (Paris, 1862), vs. 2929.
[25] *Yvain,* ed. W. Foerster and A. Hilka (Halle, 1926). *Yvain,* ed. T. B. W. Reid (Manchester, 1942). This is the reading of ms. H. Cf. *Löwenritter,* ed. Foerster (Halle, 1887), p. 222.
[26] Cf. the case cited in Philippe de Beaumanoir, *Coutumes de Beauvaisis,* ed. A. Salmon (Paris, 1900), II, 427 f., where a squire who presented himself for combat with full arms on horseback to fight a subject simply equipped with *cote,* shield, and *baston* was required either to fight in his shirt, without any weapon, or not at all.
[27] Interference of any sort was banned. Cf. *ibid.,* II, 433.
[28] *Beiblatt zur Anglia,* XV (1904), 16–21. For passage in *Wooing of Emer,* cf. R. Thurneysen, *Irische Helden- und Königsage,* pp. 392 f.

inhabitants." [29] Since Celtic origin can be predicated with something like certainty of the tribute motif in the Tristan romances, it is highly probable that the annual tribute exacted from the King of the Isle des Puceles found its way into *Yvain* from some ultimate Irish source.

Chapter LVII

YVAIN'S DUEL WITH GAUVAIN

VERSES 5810–6454

The damsel who had secured the aid of Yvain guided him to the house where she had left the disinherited sister, and all three proceeded toward Arthur's court, where the claims of the two sisters were to be decided by a judicial combat. On the last day assigned for the decision the elder sister produced her champion, Gauvain, who was so armed that no one knew him. At the last moment the younger sister appeared with Yvain, who was also unrecognizable. She demanded her rights, and when they were arrogantly refused by her sister, the trial by combat began. The two unknown champions were so evenly matched that they fought till night began to fall and then drew apart to recover. They disclosed their names, and then each insisted that he was beaten and that the honor of victory belonged to the other. Arthur intervened and decided the quarrel on its merits, awarding to the younger sister her rightful inheritance.

THE INCOGNITO duel between Yvain and Gauvain, which we have seen that Chrétien transferred from its original position in Y for artistic reasons, is one of the favorite themes not only of Arthurian romance but also of universal fiction. Potter made a classic study of the many versions in which the participants are father and son.[1] Five, at least, are found in Arthurian romance: Gauvain fights Lionel; Loth, Gauvain; Lancelot, Galaad; Nuc, Yder; and Hoel, Kahedin.[2] The same type also occurs in the Breton lais of *Milun* and *Doon* and the English lai of *Degaré*.[3] The lais and the Nuc–Yder version show a marked sameness, for all con-

[29] G. Schoepperle, *Tristan and Isolt*, II, 333.

[1] M. A. Potter, *Sohrab and Rustem* (London, 1902). Cf. bibliography in Stith Thompson, *Motif-Index*, V, 100, N. 731.2; and in Marie de France, *Lais*, éd. Warnke, 3d ed., pp. clx–clxii.

[2] Potter, *op. cit.*, pp. 48, 51, 57, 96. Potvin, *Perceval le Gallois*, IV, 16–18. (On name of Gauvain's son cf. J. L. Weston, *Legend of Perceval*, I, 244 f., and *PMLA*, XLIII [1928], 433.) Sommer, *Vulgate Version*, II, 317 f.; VI, 40. *Yderroman*, ed. H. Gelzer, vss. 4594–825. E. Löseth, *Tristan en Prose*, pp. 81 f.

[3] Potter, *op. cit.*, pp. 46–48, 51 f. Marie de France, *op. cit.*, pp. clvi–clx, 152–71. *Romania*, VIII (1879), 61–64. W. H. French, C. B. Hale, *Middle English Metrical Romances*, pp. 288–320.

tain the motif of recognition by means of a token which the father has left with the boy's mother or aunt; in all but *Degaré* the token is a ring. According to both *Doon* and *Degaré*, the father on parting from his mistress foretells the birth of a son and leaves the token with instructions that, when the boy is grown, he is to be given the token and to seek his father. In *Degaré* the father announces himself as a faery knight. These elements —the supernatural father, his prophecy and instructions, the ring, the recognition—indicate that the lais and the incident in *Yder* are based in part on an Irish tradition found in *The Second Battle of Moytura,* a saga of the ninth century.[4]

Eri,[5] a woman of the Tuatha De, was approached by a golden-haired, splendidly accoutered man. They cohabited, and when the stranger was about to leave her, he gave her a ring to be bestowed only on one whom it would fit. He announced himself as Elotha, king of the Fomorians. "Of our meeting thou shalt bear a son, and no name shall be given him save Eochaid Bres." Eri brought forth the boy, and after a week he had a fortnight's growth, and at the end of seven years he had reached the growth of fourteen years. Later, when he asked his mother whence he derived his blood, she placed the ring on his finger and it fitted. She brought him to the land of the Fomorians, and there Bres was about to engage in swordplay when his father recognized the ring, and asked who he was. Eri answered and told the King that Bres was his son.

That this story in some form or other has influenced the Breton lais will, I trust, be granted.

Another version of the father-and-son combat, preserved in *The Tragic Death of Connla,* also seems to have affected the *Matière de Bretagne*. This saga may have taken shape as early as the eighth century, and its subject remained popular in Ireland and Gaelic Scotland down into the nineteenth; it was adapted by Macpherson as "Carthon," and inserted in his *Ossian.*[6] A summary of the oldest form follows.[7]

Cuchulainn, during his stay on the Continent, lay with the Princess Aife, sister of the woman-warrior Scathach, and herself "the hardest woman-warrior in the world." Before returning to Ireland, he left with the pregnant Aife a ring for his son. When it fitted the boy, he was to seek his father, but he was under a tabu (*geis*) not to reveal his identity to any man. After seven years, during which the boy Connla had been given expert training in arms by Scathach, he set out for the Court of Ulster. As he approached, he provoked the wonder of King Concho-

[4] D'Arbois de Jubainville, *L'Epopée celtique en Irlande,* pp. 406–08, 415–17. T. P. Cross, C. N. Slover, *Ancient Irish Tales,* pp. 29 f., 34.
[5] On the identity of Eri cf. *Eriu,* XIV (1943), 14–28; R. S. Loomis, *Celtic Myth,* pp. 220–22, 296–99; *Folklore,* XXXI, 120 f. O'Rahilly is surely mistaken in taking Eriu for a sun-goddess. It was her consort Lug who was the sun, and the bride of the sun is the earth. Cf. J. G. Frazer, *Magic Art* (1911), II, 98 f.
[6] D'Arbois de Jubainville, *op. cit.,* pp. 54–61. Thurneysen, *Irische Helden- und Königsage,* pp. 403–12.
[7] D'Arbois, *op. cit.,* pp. 52–54. Cross, Slover, *op. cit.,* pp. 172–75.

bar and his warriors by his feats. One of them went to meet him, extolled the glory of the court, and urged him to come to the King. But Connla refused to reveal his name, and defeated all the champions sent against him until he met his death in the struggle with his father.

This form of the father-and-son combat, combined with the motif of precocious growth from the story of Elotha and Bres,[8] filtered down through the Brythonic peoples and the French into German literature, for it is plainly recognizable in Wirnt von Gravenberg's *Wigalois*.[9]

Gawein, after six months of wedded life with Florie, left her pregnant and returned to Arthur's court, entrusting to her a magic girdle. He failed to keep his promise to return. His son Wigalois was born, and grew more in one year than another child in two. He had twelve years of expert training in arms and accomplishments under the supervision of a certain queen (*ein richiu künigin*). Twenty years after his father's departure, Wigalois set out to find him and received from his mother the magic girdle which his father had instructed her to give him. A youth of Arthur's court met him, praised the prowess of the Table Round, and urged him to join them. When Wigalois arrived at the court, he roused the wonder of all by sitting on a perilous seat. He refused to tell his father's name, but was courteously received and placed under the charge of Gawein. There was no combat between them.

Despite the absence of the combat motif, the combined pattern of the stories of Bres and Connla is easily perceived in the story of Wigalois. And the incognito combat between Gawain and his son, which is missing in *Wigalois,* does occur in *Le Conte del Graal* and in a very late prose text, *L'Histoire de Giglan, Filz de Messire Gauvain*.[10] As in the lais, these combats end happily in mutual recognition. We may rightly conclude, therefore, that the two Irish stories of Bres and Connla descended into the Breton lais and Arthurian romance and supplied the following details: the supernatural father; the temporary union; the father's departure to his own land, after prophesying the birth of a son and leaving a ring for him; the son's precocious growth; his training by a woman not his mother; his meeting with his father at a royal court; his refusal to tell his name; the combat; and the recognition.

Arthurian romance offers many examples of incognito duels between brothers and between friends,[11] and one is tempted to assume that these are variations on the father-and-son combat. But specific evidence for this assumption is lacking, so far as I am aware, and accordingly one cannot claim Celtic origin for these themes with any certainty. But a plausible

[8] Cf. precocious growth of Gwri or Pryderi in *Pwyll*. Loth, *Mabinogion*, 2d ed., I, 110 f.
[9] Wirnt von Gravenberc, *Wigalois*, ed. J. M. N. Kapteyn (Bonn, 1926), pp. 47–69, vss. 1053–596.
[10] Potter, *op. cit.*, pp. 48 f. *Histoire littéraire de la France*, XXX, 197 f. *Romania*, XV (1886), 23.
[11] Potter, *op. cit.*, pp. 207–09. F. Lot, *Étude sur le Lancelot en Prose*, p. 264.

case for Irish influence on some of the versions of the incognito duel between friends may be offered. It is worth noting that the battle between Yvain and Gauvain is the earliest occurrence of this theme in Arthurian romance, and, being found likewise in *Owain*,[12] must have occurred in Chrétien's source Y. Now both the Welsh and the French versions stress the magnanimity of the two friends, each knight insisting repeatedly that he is "outrez et recreanz sanz faille," and that the other is the victor. In one version of the combat between friends this point of chivalric generosity is carried even further; one of the combatants agrees to pretend that he is actually vanquished in order to oblige the other. This version is in *Meraugis de Portlesguez*.[13]

Meraugis, in quest of Gauvain, came to the Cité sans Nom, and was welcomed by a procession of ladies. He learned that an island near by was owned by a lady and defended by a knight. If Meraugis should overcome the knight, he would win possession of the isle and the lady. Meraugis crossed over and engaged the unknown defender of the isle, but after midday the latter's strength increased, and the battle came to a standstill. The unknown then revealed himself as Gauvain, and Meraugis agreed to allow himself to be thoroughly beaten and apparently left for dead, in order to deceive the lady. The plan was carried out.

The story which Raoul de Houdenc incorporated in his *Meraugis* must have been based on a familiar formula. One discovers many distinctive details repeated in the *Huth Merlin* as part of Balaain's fatal meeting with his brother Balaan.[14] One recognizes another version in the tale of Gauvain's duel with the Riche Soudoier as told by Wauchier de Denain.[15]

Gauvain in the course of a hunt met successively with a very tall knight, seated beneath a tree, and with his ladylove, who rode a swift, white palfrey. Later he saw a great company of folk issuing from a city to welcome the tall knight and his *amie* from the forest, and the city was illuminated and a great feast was held in their honor. Two days later Gauvain went to encounter with the unknown knight outside Chastel Orguelleus, and engaged in a long struggle. Gauvain's strength waxed after noon and he overpowered his antagonist. But when the latter disclosed that his *amie* would die if she knew of his defeat, Gauvain agreed to surrender and yield himself captive to the lady. The plan was carried out, and the two knights became fast friends.

It is evident that Wauchier and Raoul present us with two variants of the same basic story; both authors connect the story with Gauvain and both dwell on his solar attribute of waxing strength. Friedwagner noted other Celtic elements in Raoul's version of the episode,[16] and Wauchier's

[12] Loth, *Mabinogion*, 2d ed., II, 30–32.

[13] Raoul de Houdenc, *Meraugis de Portlesguez*, vss. 2739–3276.

[14] *Huth Merlin*, ed. G. Paris, J. Ulrich, II, 44–56. Abridged in Malory, *Morte d'Arthur*, Bk. II, chaps. 17, 18.

[15] Potvin, *Perceval le Gallois*, III, 320–41. Adaptation by J. L. Weston, *Sir Gawain and the Lady of Lys*, pp. 78–95. [16] Raoul de Houdenc, *op. cit.*, p. lxxi.

description of the lady riding past Gauvain on her swift white palfrey without speaking a word recalls the similar behavior of Riannon in *Pwyll*.[17] One is prompted to ask: is there any Celtic analogue for the essential element in the two stories, the willingness of one warrior, engaged in combat with another, to yield himself magnanimously in order to deceive a lady? There is such a situation in the famous Irish prose epic, *The Cattle Raid of Cooley*.[18]

Fergus mac Roich was urged by his mistress, Queen Medb,[19] to fight with Cuchulainn, the champion of Ulster. Fergus objected at first to encountering his own pupil, but yielded at last to Medb's entreaties. Fergus went to the ford where Cuchulainn stood, but, instead of attacking him, besought the youth, because of the nurture he had given him, to flee before him in sight of the men of Erin. Cuchulainn agreed to do so. Thus Fergus, in order to satisfy his mistress, persuaded Cuchulainn to assume the role of a vanquished warrior.

This incident in the Irish saga of the eighth century bears a notable resemblance to the incident related by Wauchier. Fergus' relation to Medb is much like that of the Riche Soudoier to his lady; Cuchulainn's behavior is like that of his Arthurian descendant, Gauvain, in responding to an appeal to his magnanimity and accepting apparent defeat. Raoul's version of the theme, though transferring the part of Gauvain to Meraugis, is nevertheless formed on the same pattern, and shows that it could be combined with the formula of the incognito duel between friends. Thus it seems possible that the emphasis which the author of Y placed on the magnanimity of Yvain and Gauvain and on the eagerness of both friends to admit defeat at the hands of the other was suggested by the highly dramatic and even more exaggerated example of magnanimity displayed in the common source of Raoul and Wauchier. And that source, in turn, may go back ultimately to an episode in *The Cattle Raid of Cooley*.

To summarize briefly a somewhat complicated argument:

1. The incognito duel between father and son, as it appears in the lais and Arthurian romance, has been strongly influenced by, if not wholly derived from, Irish sagas.

2. It is a plausible, though far from certain, inference that the numerous incognito combats between brothers and friends in the *Matière de Bretagne* have drawn somewhat also from Irish tradition.

3. The incognito duel between friends, as narrated in *Meraugis,* represents an Arthurian tradition, found also in Wauchier's continuation of *Le Conte del Graal,* and to be derived in all likelihood from the battle of Fergus and Cuchulainn in the *Cattle Raid*.

[17] Loth, *Mabinogion,* 2d ed., I, 93–96.
[18] J. Dunn, *Ancient Irish Epic Tale, Tain Bo Cualnge* (London, 1914), pp. 205–8. E. Hull, *Cuchullin Saga in Irish Literature* (London, 1898), pp. 180–82.
[19] On Medb and her many lovers or husbands cf. *Zts. f. celt. Phil.,* XIX (1933), 352 f.

4. When we find that the same principle of chivalric generosity which characterizes the action of the hero in *Meraugis* is also emphasized in a somewhat similar way by Chrétien and the author of *Owain* in their versions of the incognito combat between friends, there is a possibility, even a probability, that they are dimly reflecting the battle of Fergus and Cuchulainn.

BOOK V.   Le Conte del Graal

Chapter LVIII

PERCEVAL'S ENFANCES

VERSES 69–1698, 6238–6438

Perceval's father was wounded and shortly thereafter died. His widow reared the infant son secretly in the Waste Forest. Perceval as a boy amused himself by casting javelins both high and low. He did not know his name, for he was always called "biaus filz," "biaus frere," or "biaus sire." Learning of Arthur's court, he announced to his mother his intention of going thither and received her reluctant consent. He rode away, equipped with a javelin. He came to the King's court, but left without making himself known. Later he arrived at the castle of a gentleman, who instructed the ignorant youth in the ways of chivalry and bestowed on him the order of knighthood. Perceval visited the Grail castle, home of his maternal uncle, the Fisher King's father. After many adventures and five years of wandering he came to a desert, and there found a hermit. To him Perceval told his experiences, and learned that he too was a maternal uncle.

LIKE THE OTHER traditional romances of Chrétien, *Le Conte del Graal* is a gallimaufry of originally independent stories and motifs. In *Erec* and *Yvain* there was no basic story into which the minor elements were fitted, merely a skillful concatenation of the separate elements. *Le Chevalier de la Charrette*, however, differed in that scholars have recognized a basic story, a framework, the abduction of Guenievre and her rescue. To this framework the many minor episodes and motifs were attached. The same is true of a good portion of *Le Conte del Graal*. For scholars have detected that the *enfances* of Perceval parallel in striking ways the youthful history of two of the most renowned of Irish heroes. Nutt, Zimmer, Windisch, Professor Mary Williams, and Dr. Los have called attention to the influence of the *macgnimrada* (boyhood exploits) of Cuchulainn.[1] Zimmer declared: "Die Aehnlichkeit mit Percevals Jugendgeschichte springt in die Augen." The influence of the *macgnimartha* of Finn has been pointed out by Nutt, Pace, Brown, Professor Griffith, and Dr. Los.[2] The two Irish traditions, which bore some resemblance to each

[1] *Folklore Record*, IV (1881), 27–31. *Göttingische Gelehrte Anzeigen*, 1890, p. 519. E. Windisch, *Das keltische Brittannien bis zu Kaiser Arthur*, pp. 136 f. M. R. Williams, *Essai sur la composition de Peredur*, pp. 116 f. F. C. J. Los, *Das Keltentum in Wolframs Parzival* (Amsterdam, 1927), pp. 84–102.

[2] *Folklore Record*, IV, 7–21. A. Nutt, *Studies on the Legend of the Holy Grail* (London, 1888), pp. 158 f. *PMLA*, XXXII (1917), 598–604. R. H. Griffith, *Sir Perceval of Galles* (Chicago, 1911). *Mod. Phil.*, XVIII (1920), 211–21. Los, *op. cit.*, pp. 84–101.

other, were evidently intertwined to furnish a framework for the *enfances* of Perceval. In order to distinguish clearly the influence of the Cuchulainn and the Finn legends on *Le Conte del Graal,* I propose to take them up separately.

The *Macgnimrada Conculainn* presents a sufficiently striking parallel to Chrétien's story to call forth Zimmer's remark just quoted, but there is a much more detailed parallel to the Welsh *Peredur.* We have found that again and again the Welsh versions of Chrétien's *Erec* and *Yvain* have preserved authentic features of tradition which Chrétien discarded, and we are therefore justified in treating *Peredur* as preserving, at least in some respects, a more authentic tradition than Chrétien does. Let us see what the Welsh author tells us of Peredur's upbringing and early adventures.[3]

Peredur was brought up in the wilderness by his mother. As a boy he amused himself by casting sticks ahead of him (*daflu blaen ysgyrion*).[4] By his extraordinary swiftness of foot he drove two hinds of the forest into his mother's goat pen. Hearing of Arthur's court, he announced to his mother his intention of going thither, and received her reluctant consent. He set out with a handful of darts. After his experiences at Arthur's court, he left and came to the castle of a maternal uncle. There he witnessed a combat with staves between two youths, sons of his uncle, and then taking a staff he defeated the better fencer of the two. His uncle, prophesying that he would be the greatest swordsman in the island, offered to teach him the use of arms and to make him a knight. (We are to infer that, as in Chrétien's poem, this offer was carried out.) Peredur then proceeded to the castle of another maternal uncle, and there demonstrated his prowess by thrice cleaving an iron pillar and thrice breaking his sword. This uncle proclaimed that Peredur was now the best swordsman in the kingdom.

Loth and Professor Mary Williams have perceived that the Welsh author confused the two uncles of Peredur.[5] It is not surprising, then, to find that these experiences of Peredur at the castles of two maternal uncles are found combined in the Irish counterpart and probable source, and are localized at Emain Macha, the fortress of Cuchulainn's maternal uncle. Let us examine the *Macgnimrada Conculainn,* included in the famous *Cattle Raid of Cooley.*[6]

Cuchulainn was brought up by his mother Dechtire in the plain of Muirthemne. Hearing of the court of Conchobar, king of Ulster, he announced to his mother his intention of going thither and obtained her reluctant consent. En route he amused himself by casting his javelin ahead of him and catching it before it touched the ground. He came to the court of the king, his maternal uncle. There he found the boys of the court, headed by his uncle's son, "hurling" and practicing martial exercises. They attacked him with hurlies (resembling hockey

---

[3] Loth, *Mabinogion,* 2d ed., II, 47–64. *Mabinogion,* tr. T. P. Ellis, J. Lloyd, II, 72–87, 138–55.
[4] *Romanische Forschungen,* XL (1927), 291.
[5] Loth, *op. cit.,* II, 60, n. 2. M. R. Williams, *op. cit.,* p. 54. The Welsh author has confused both uncles with the Fisher King.
[6] T. P. Cross and C. H. Slover, *Ancient Irish Tales,* pp. 137–50.

sticks), but he laid them all low. Later his uncle conferred arms on Cuchulainn. The boy demonstrated his prowess by breaking seventeen sets of spears and swords. Cathbad, the druid, prophesied that he would surpass in renown all the youths of Ireland. On another occasion Cuchulainn by his extraordinary swiftness of foot captured two stags.

Can there be any doubt that this story from the *Cattle Raid,* which Thurneysen would trace back to an original of the first half of the eighth century, furnished the outline for the *enfances* of Peredur, including the visits of the youthful hero to his maternal uncles? The Welsh author has transposed the capture of the deer, reduced the number of youths encountered by the hero and of the swords broken by him, and confused the maternal uncles with the Grail King. Otherwise he parallels the famous Irish narrative to an extraordinary degree. Chrétien or his immediate source eliminated many of the most significant parallels in his account of Perceval's youth, but he preserved the following features of the Irish original: The hero is brought up by his mother, hears of a royal court, announces to her his intention of going thither, obtains her reluctant consent, departs equipped with a javelin, arrives at the fortress of a *prodon,* and receives arms from him. Thanks to the cognate (though corrupt) version supplied by *Peredur,* we can feel assured of the descent of Perceval's *enfances* from the boyhood deeds of Cuchulainn.

But Chrétien's narrative shows also the influence of the *Macgnimartha Finn.* Besides the mythological cycle and the pseudo-historic Ulster cycle, a third cycle, that of Finn mac Cumaill,[7] sprang up in the Dark Ages in the modern county of Leinster and spread throughout Ireland and into the Scottish islands and highlands, supplanting eventually in popular favor the more ancient, aristocratic traditions, and eventually through Macpherson's Ossianic fabrications rousing the interest of all cultivated Europe. The Finn cycle, though never attaining great favor with the *filid* (the Irish professional reciters of tales),[8] nevertheless left an impression on Welsh literature and Arthurian romance. The list of Arthur's warriors in *Kulhwch* mentions Scilti Yscawntroet, "Lightfoot," and Scilti must be a corruption of Cailte, the famous runner of the Fianna.[9] The elopement of Finn's wife Grainne with Diarmaid stamped its outlines on the late Welsh *Ystoria Trystan* and left vestiges, as Gertrude Schoepperle demonstrated, on the earliest French forms of the Tristan romance.[10]

[7] On Finn cycle, cf. *Duanaire Finn,* ed. Eoin Mac Neill, Irish Texts Soc., Vol. 7 (London, 1908), pp. xxiv–lix; K. Meyer, *Fianaigecht,* Royal Irish Acad., Todd Lecture Ser., XVI (Dublin, 1910), pp. v–xxxi; R. D. Scott, *The Thumb of Knowledge in Legends of Finn, Sigurd, and Taliesin* (New York, 1930); T. F. O'Rahilly, *Early Irish History and Mythology* (Dublin, 1946), pp. 271–81. [8] *Duanaire Finn,* ed. MacNeill, p. xxxiv.
[9] C. O'Rahilly, *Ireland and Wales,* p. 115, n. 3. J. G. Campbell, *The Fians* (London, 1891), pp. 64, 172 f.
[10] *Romania,* LIII (1927), 92–94. Thomas of Britain, *Romance of Tristram and Ysolt,* tr. R. S. Loomis, rev. ed. (1931), pp. xiii–xviii. G. Schoepperle, *Tristan and Isolt,* II, 391–446.

The tradition of Finn's thumb of knowledge has been shown by Professor Robert Scott to reappear in the late Welsh *Tale of Taliesin*.[11] The *enfances* of Finn bear certain marked resemblances to those of Cuchulainn, and very naturally made likewise a contribution to the *enfances* of Perceval. Here is a summary of the significant points in *The Youthful Exploits of Finn,* composed in the twelfth century.[12]

Finn's father, Cumall, was slain in battle. His widow gave birth to a son; and his sister Bodball, together with another woman warrior, reared the child secretly in the forest. The boy grew up to be a skillful hunter and was so swift of foot that he outran and captured two bucks. His weapon was a casting spear. He got the nickname "Finn," meaning "fair." He took service with the King of Bantry without making himself known. He departed on a series of adventures. He visited two uncles, Crimall and Fiacal mac Conchinn. To the first of these, an old man in a desert wood, he told his story from beginning to end.

The influence of this story on Chrétien is apparent in the following features: Perceval's father was wounded in battle and later died; the orphan was brought up by a woman secretly in a forest; his weapon was a casting spear; he knew only that he was called "biaus filz," "biaus frere," or "biaus sire"; he demanded knighthood of King Arthur, but departed without making himself known; he visited two uncles—the Fisher King's father and the hermit; to the latter, who dwelt in a *desert,* he told his story. As we shall see later,[13] another motif from the Finn saga, the hero's obligation to avenge his father's death, is dimly reflected in *Le Conte del Graal* and more clearly in *Sir Percyvelle* and the *Prose Tristan.* Very important elements in the *enfances* of Perceval, therefore, were contributed by the *enfances* of Cuchulainn and Finn.

To return to Cuchulainn, one characteristic barely touched on in the *Macgnimrada* seems to have undergone a very significant elaboration in the romances of Perceval—his ignorance. When Cuchulainn had received arms from King Conchobar, he went forth in Conchobar's chariot, driven by Iubar.[14] After performing several prodigious feats of strength, he was returning to Emain Macha when he saw a herd of deer. "The boy sought to know what were those numerous and restless cattle. Iubar explained that they were not cattle, but a herd of wild deer that kept in the dark glens of Sliab Fuait." Unable to overtake the deer in the chariot, Cuchulainn dismounted and by sheer running captured two large stags, and made them fast to the chariot. Continuing on his way, he perceived a flock of swans. "The boy asked were they pet birds or wild, and learned that they were wild swans which used to congregate from rocks and islands

[11] Scott, *op. cit.,* pp. 118–72.
[12] For Irish text cf. *Revue celt.,* V (1881–83), 195–204. For English trans. cf. Cross and Slover, *op. cit.,* pp. 360–69; *Eriu,* I (1904), 180–90. For more modern versions cf. *Mod. Phil.,* XVIII (1921), 664, n. 5.   [13] See Chap. LXIX.
[14] Cross and Slover, *Ancient Irish Tales,* p. 150.

of the sea." Cuchulainn then brought down twenty-four swans with his sling, retrieved them, and secured them to the chariot.[15] On his approaching Emain Macha, the woman messenger Leborcham exclaimed with wonder: "Beautiful white birds he has which in the chariot bear him company, and wild unbroken stags tethered to the same." That this tradition of Cuchulainn's boyish ignorance survived in the legend of Perceval is shown most directly and clearly by the parallel episode in *Peredur*.

"One day Peredur espied his mother's flock of goats and two hinds near the goats. The boy wondered greatly that they were without horns, whereas all the others had them, and he thought that they must have been lost a long time and so had lost their horns. There was at the end of the forest a house for the goats, and by strength and agility he drove the hinds as well as the goats into it. Then he returned home to his mother. 'My mother,' said he, 'I have seen near by a strange thing: two of thy goats have become wild and have lost their horns because they have run wild a long time in the wood. . . .' Then everyone rose and came to look; when they saw the hinds, they were much astonished." [16]

Two points emerge from the consideration of this parallel: (1) Peredur's naive ignorance is an inheritance from the Cuchulainn tradition. (2) It receives greater emphasis and is given a humorous twist. This emphasis on Peredur's ignorance and its ludicrous results is something new; Cuchulainn's naive questions about the deer and the birds supplied the hint, but hardly more, and as for Finn, he was no simpleton but a lad of astounding precocity.[17] It is probable, however, that Finn's upbringing by women lent itself to this interpretation of Perceval's character, and that the widespread medieval theme of the *Dümmling* hero stimulated this development not only in the case of Perceval, but also of Lanzelet and Guiglain.[18] This concept of Perceval as a comic character must have achieved success well before Chrétien's day, for it brought about the invention and modification of several scenes to illustrate the boy's naiveté. In fact, a new Arthurian figure, Dodin or Dodinel le Sauvage, mentioned in *Erec*, came into being as a result of this development. Dr. Brugger has made it clear that the name of this figure is simply a double epithet, "Little Fool, the Wild," appropriate to a simpleton of the Perceval type.[19] The *Vulgate Merlin*

[15] The slaying of the swans seems to have survived in Wolfram's *Parzival*. Cf. *Parzival*, 118, 6–10; M. F. Richey, *Story of Parzival and the Graal*, p. 32.
[16] *Mabinogion*, tr. Ellis and Lloyd, II, 73. Loth (*op. cit.*, II, 48 f.) makes the mistake of translating *ewiged* as "chevreaux."   [17] Cross and Slover, *op. cit.*, pp. 364 f.
[18] Wolfram von Eschenbach, *Parzival*, tr. W. Hertz, 7th ed. (1927), pp. 443 f. A. Dickson, *Valentine and Orson*, pp. 128 f.
[19] *Medieval Studies in Memory of G. Schoepperle Loomis*, pp. 166–70. It is worth noting that Dodines in *Lanzelet* dwells among the wild moors during the summer, but in winter is a member of Arthur's court. Cf. P. W. Joyce, *Old Celtic Romances* (1920), p. 223: "They [the Fena] divided the year into two parts. During the first half, namely, from Beltane to Samin, they hunted each day with their dogs; and during the second half, namely from Samin to Beltane, they lived in the mansions and the betas of Erin; so that there was not a

informs us that Dodynel was so called "because he wanted nothing but to shoot boars, stags, and bucks in these great and savage forests," that he was the son of King Belinant, and that he went as a young squire to Arthur's court to be knighted.[20] This information enables us to equate Dodynel with Perceval, whom common tradition represents as uncouth and ignorant, save in hunting "the hinds and harts"; [21] who in the Vulgate cycle, the *Huth Merlin,* and the *Prose Tristan* is the son of King Pellinor; and who, by all accounts, went to Arthur's court to be knighted. Though Perceval as a comic figure was certainly evolved before Chrétien's time and amusing scenes had been concocted by earlier narrators for the display of his naiveté, yet nowhere does Chrétien's own genius assert itself more happily than in the lifelike and charming portrayal of the blundering boy.

This concept of Perceval as an uncouth lad had an extraordinary fortune. It was copied in the Italian *cantare* of *Carduino.*[22] Its moral implications were developed by Wolfram von Eschenbach in his *Parzival.* "Der reine Thor, durch Mitleid wissend," is the central theme of Wagner's lofty drama of the Grail. By some accident, the French prose version of Chrétien's poem, printed in 1530, seems to have reached Ireland and stimulated the composition, sometime in the seventeenth century, of the tale of the Great Fool.[23] Spreading through oral channels, this tale became one of the favorites told over the peat fires in the cottages of Ireland and the Hebrides. Thus in the nineteenth century the Perceval legend, curiously transformed, cast its spell over the sophisticated Wagnerite at Bayreuth and the lowly "shepherd of the Hebrid-Isles, plac'd far amid the melancholy main."

---

chief . . . in the whole country that had not nine of the Fena quartered on him during the winter half of the year." Note also that Dodines is characterized as "mit den breiten handen." Malory's Gareth (*Morte d'Arthur,* Bk. VII, chap. 1) is described on his first appearance as "the largest handed that ever man sawe." Dodines' horse, which "berührte kaum den Boden, in dem andre Rosse einsanken," is matched by Kulhwch's steed. "Pas un brin d'herbe ne pliait sous lui, si léger était le trot du coursier, qui le portait à la cour d'Arthur." Loth, *Mabinogion,* 2d ed., I, 251. For speculations on Dodinel cf. *Romania,* XLIII (1914), 96 ff.; *Zts. f. franz. Sprache u. Lit.,* XLIV, "Abhandlungen," 169.

[20] H. O. Sommer, *Vulgate Version,* II, 171, 174, 253 f.

[21] Chrétien, *Conte del Graal,* ed. Hilka, vss. 273 f.

[22] W. H. Schofield, *Studies on the Libeaus Desconus,* pp. 183–94.

[23] *Zts. f. celt. Phil.,* XVII (1928), 1–30. It is quite certain that Nutt, Griffith, and others who have assumed that the Great Fool tale and lay represented an old Celtic tradition which influenced the Perceval legend have put the cart before the horse. Cf. *Mod. Phil.,* XLII (1945), 197–211.

Chapter LIX
PERCEVAL'S WELSH PROTOTYPE

THAT THE *enfances* of Cuchulainn and Finn were intertwined to provide a framework for the birth, upbringing, and early adventures of Perceval, has been pointed out by several scholars, and seems well established. But the Irish traditions must have reached the French through Wales, and doubtless were attached to one or more youthful heroes of the Welsh in the course of transmission. Can we detect in extant Welsh literature these intermediate figures between Cuchulainn and Finn on the one hand and Perceval on the other? To what Welsh personages were the *macgnimrada* of Cuchulainn and the *macgnimartha* of Finn likely to be attracted?

Professor Gruffydd has shown that Pryderi was the hero of *The Four Branches of the Mabinogi,* and *mabinogi* is the Welsh equivalent of *macgnimrada.*[1] If we examine the story of Pryderi's birth and boyhood, however, we find nothing except the simultaneous colt birth which corresponds to the story of Cuchulainn,[2] and nothing whatever which corresponds to the story of Finn. Though this lack of parallelism might seem to disqualify Pryderi as the intermediate figure between the Irish heroes and Perceval, one fact removes the obstacle to this hypothesis. In an earlier chapter it was shown that in the account of Pryderi's birth and early boyhood, he bore another name, Gwri, and that Gwri was the prototype of Gawain.[3] The change of name really signals a substitution of character; for some reason unknown the author of the mabinogi grafted the story of Pryderi's youth and manhood on the stock of Gwri's birth and infancy. We have, therefore, no true *enfances* of Pryderi, and we should not be put off by the lack of any sign of influence from the *enfances* of Cuchulainn and Finn. It is still possible that if an authentic, not a contaminated, legend of Pryderi had survived, we should find there a story of his birth and early career which showed as clearly as *Peredur* the debt to the sagas of Cuchulainn and Finn. There is no solid objection to Pryderi as the inheritor of those Irish *enfances,* and as the transmitter of them to Perceval.

And when we turn to the French romances it becomes evident that

[1] W. J. Gruffydd, *Math Vab Mathonwy,* pp. 324–27. C. O'Rahilly, *Ireland and Wales,* p. 103. On Pryderi cf. Loth, *Mabinogion,* 2d ed., I, 114; Ifor Williams, *Pedeir Keinc y Mabinogi* (Cardiff, 1930), pp. 157 f.
[2] J. Rhys, *Lectures on the Origin and Growth of Religion,* 2d ed., pp. 501–3. *Folklore,* XXVII, 49.
[3] Cf. *supra,* pp. 149–51. Anwyl in *Zts. f. celt Phil.,* III (1901), 126, remarks: "The identification of Pryderi with Gwri . . . may have been an afterthought."

Pryderi did pass on some of the most striking and individual elements of his legend to Perceval; he presents the strongest claim to be considered Perceval's Welsh prototype. The evidence is not to be found in Chrétien but in two French prose texts. If we compare certain incidents in *Manawydan,* one of the *Four Branches,* with incidents in the *Didot Perceval* and in *Perlesvaus,* the similarities almost stand out from the page. Pryderi,[4] after a royal feast at the chief palace (*llys*) of Narberth, went out with his wife, mother, and stepfather and seated himself on a perilous mound. "And as they sat thus, there was a roar, and so great was the noise, there came a shower of mist so that not one of them saw the other, and after the mist, behold every place became clear. When they looked in the direction where they had seen flocks, cattle, and dwellings before, they saw nothing, nor house nor animal nor smoke nor fire nor man nor dwelling except the palace of the court empty and desolate and deserted, without man or beast in it." When, months later, Llwyt removed the enchantment from Dyved, he said to Manawydan: "'Look around thee on the country, and thou shalt behold all the dwellings and habitations as they were at their best.' . . . Manawydan saw the whole country inhabited and full of habitations, wealth, and dwellings."

Let us turn to the *Didot Perceval.*[5] The young hero wished to sit in the Siege Perilous of the Round Table during the Feast of Pentecost, and though Arthur warned him of possible calamity, he did so. "As soon as he was seated, the stone split beneath him and roared so dreadfully that it seemed to all those who were there that the world would sink into the abyss. From the roar which the earth uttered there issued so great a darkness that they could not see each other for the space of more than a league." A mysterious voice then proclaimed: "This Perceval has displayed the greatest audacity that ever man has shown, and for this cause he will fall into the greatest suffering in the world, he and all those of the Table Round." Not until a knight shall ask concerning the Grail at the castle of the Fisher King "will the enchantments end which have bespelled this day the land of Britain." The correspondence between the fateful acts of Pryderi and Perceval and between their consequences is fairly obvious.

In the various French romances different causes are assigned for the desolating enchantments of Britain, and somewhat different accounts are given as to their nature.[6] But in Gerbert de Montreuil's continuation of *Le Conte del Graal* the ending of the enchantment through Perceval's asking the question is described in terms neatly contrasting with those employed in *Manawydan* to describe its beginning. Speaking of Perceval, Gerbert writes: "He saw a plain and right fair fields and fair tillage. In

[4] Loth, *op. cit.,* I, 154 f., 170 f. C. Guest, *Mabinogion,* ed. A. Nutt, pp. 45, 57.
[5] *Didot-Perceval,* ed. W. Roach, pp. 149 f. J. L. Weston, *Legend of Perceval,* II, 20 f.
[6] *Perlesvaus,* ed. Nitze and others, II, 244 f. *Speculum,* VIII, 422–28. Cf. *infra* pp. 389–91.

one direction were the farms, vineyards, river-meads, and many kinds of dwellings, filled with people and supplied with great wealth. Perceval marveled greatly: 'I behold a wonder which should astonish me. Last evening when I came into this land, I saw it waste and desolate; now I see it covered with every good thing.' " [7] The motifs of the Siege Perilous and the Waste Land are as clearly connected with Perceval in the French romances as they are with Pryderi in *Manawydan*.

There is another remarkable parallel between Pryderi and Perceval. Pryderi entered a magic castle. "He saw, as it were about the middle of the floor of the castle a fountain enclosed with marble, and on the edge of the fountain a golden bowl, fastened to four chains, resting on a slab of marble, and the chains ascending to the sky, and he could see no end to them." [8] He there became a prisoner. Likewise in *Perlesvaus* the hero enters a magic castle. "He looks . . . and sees the fairest fountain and the clearest that anyone could imagine, and it was all surrounded by rich golden pillars, and it seemed that the gravel bottom was of precious stones." Soon after, "he looks up and sees a golden chain descending, adorned with very sweet precious stones, and in the midst was a crown of gold. The chain descended with great precision, and was held by nothing but the will of our Lord." [9] Perlesvaus is warned that when he becomes king of a plenteous isle near by, he must see that it is "well supplied," or he will be placed in an isle lacking in all good things; and from a later passage we learn that his punishment would take the form of being chained to a rock, [10] This threatened punishment is never carried out, evidently because Perlesvaus never permitted the plenteous land of which he became king to lack good provisions. But observe: Pryderi had done precisely that; he had brought desolation on his rich land of Dyved. Before that catastrophe he, his mother, and his stepfather made a tour of the country; "they had never seen a land with more inhabitants, better hunting grounds, and more abundant in honey and fish." [11] As a consequence of their sitting on the perilous mound, however, the realm became desolate. Ultimately Pryderi found himself a prisoner, attached by his hands to a bowl and chains and by his feet to a stone.[12] What had been prophesied for Perlesvaus was fulfilled for Pryderi.

There is therefore an elaborate correspondence between the legend of Pryderi in *Manawydan* and that of Perceval in the *Didot Perceval* and in

[7] Gerbert de Montreuil, *Continuation de Perceval,* ed. M. Williams (Paris, 1922), I, vss. 312–24.
[8] Loth, *op. cit.,* I, 160. I. Williams, *Pedeir Keinc,* p. 56.
[9] *Perlesvaus,* ed. Nitze, I, ll. 9551–9634.   [10] *Ibid.,* ll. 9774–9809.
[11] Loth, *op, cit.,* I, 154. Guest, *op. cit.,* pp. 44 f.
[12] Loth, *op. cit.,* I, 160. Pryderi's hands stuck to the bowl, and the bowl was attached to the chain. This feature seems to combine the literal chaining of a captive, which we find in *Perlesvaus,* with the motif of sticking to an object in a faery palace, common in modern Welsh folklore. Cf. W. Sikes, *British Goblins,* pp. 163, 361, 366 f.

Perlesvaus. Both legends contain the royal feast, the siege perilous, the roar, the darkness, the waste land. Both contain the enchanted castle, the richly adorned fountain, the chain descending from the sky and attached to an object of gold. Both contain the motif of the ruler who brings poverty on his prosperous land and is subsequently held prisoner by a chain, his feet on a rock. Surely there is a reason for these correspondences and for the prominence of Perceval in the Grail romances, if his original was Pryderi, the hero of the *Four Branches*.

Nevertheless, an embarrassing afterthought intrudes. The parallels are not continuous; the legends diverge widely. Though the enchantments of Dyved are brought to an end in the mabinogi, the method employed by Manawydan for achieving this result is utterly different from that employed by Perceval to lift the enchantments of Britain. How is one to explain this and other major discrepancies between the legends of Pryderi and Perceval?

Professor Gruffydd has demonstrated in his study of the mabinogi of *Math Vab Mathonwy* that the author of the *Four Branches* was addicted to combining originally separate themes.[13] We have seen that in *Pwyll* he tacked on to the story of Gwri's birth and boyhood the tale of Pryderi's youth and manhood. His tale of the disenchanting of Dyved by Manawydan was shaped to accord with Llwyt's vengeance on Pryderi and Riannon for the trick which Pryderi's father and Riannon had played on Llwyt's friend Gwawl. This strangely rustic narrative—where Manawydan becomes a successful farmer, the ladies of Llwyt's court, in the form of mice, destroy his harvest, and Riannon is held prisoner by asses' collars round her neck—may have had some traditional backing; but surely it was not the only Welsh legend of the disenchanting of a land, for in *Lludd and Llevelys* three other methods of ridding Britain of enchantments are described.[14] Since the stories of the Waste Land, its causes, and its restoration, presented such a variety, no wonder that the rustic version selected by the author of *Manawydan* did not commend itself to the Breton *conteurs,* entertainers of the French aristocracy. In view of these facts, it is not surprising that the parallel between the careers of Pryderi and Perceval is limited to the elements listed above. These are sufficient to indicate that Pryderi was a Welsh prototype of Perceval.

Other facts suggest that Perceval inherited certain features of his legend from one of the seven sons of Eliffer, the historic warrior Peredur, a chieftain of North Britain, who according to the *Annales Cambriae* died about A.D. 580.[15] It is probably this Peredur who is referred to in the Black Book of Carmarthen (*ca.* 1175). "The tomb of Mor, the magnificent, stead-

---

[13] Gruffydd, *op. cit.*   [14] Loth, *op. cit.,* I, 231 ff. Guest, *op. cit.,* pp. 92 ff.
[15] Loth, *op. cit.,* II, 47, n. 1. Geoffrey of Monmouth, *Vita Merlini,* ed. J. J. Parry (Urbana, Ill., 1925), pp. 18, 31–35. E. Windisch, *Das keltische Brittannien,* p. 171.

fast lord, the son of Peredur, the supreme physician (*penwetic*)."[16] Gwenogvryn Evans and Professor Mary Williams suppose that the epithet of Peredur has reference to the renown of Perceval as healer of the Maimed King,[17] and they may well be right. Jessie Weston, moreover, pointed out that, according to the Dutch poem *Morien,* some books declared that Perceval was the father of a black youth, Morien, begotten in the land of the Moors.[18] It is very likely that, as M. Lot proposed,[19] this notion originated in the Welsh belief that Peredur was the father of Mor, the personal name being mistaken by the French for the proper noun *Mor,* meaning "Moor." This same story, according to Jessie Weston, was transferred from Perceval to his father and highly elaborated, so that Wolfram's hero Parzival came to have a pied half-brother, begotten by Gahmuret on a Moorish queen. Furthermore, it is hardly a coincidence that a Welsh triad gives the historic Peredur a sister named Keindrech, whereas *Perlesvaus* declares that "the good knight [Perlesvaus] had a sister named Dandrane."[20] It is also a curious fact that by the twelfth century both the historic Peredur and Perceval were attached to a particular district, Gwynedd, that is northwestern Wales. Geoffrey of Monmouth in the *Vita Merlini* calls Peredur "dux Venedotorum," that is, "lord of the men of Gwynedd."[21] The boy Perceval, according to manuscript H of Chrétien's poem, meeting five knights of Arthur's court near his mother's home, pointed out to them a high wood surrounding a mountain, and said that there were the mountain-passes of Scaudone, "li destroit de Scaudone."[22] The significance of this lies in the fact that, as I shall show in my comments on Scaudone in the list of proper names at the end of this book, "de Scaudone" must represent a corruption of "de Snaudone," and that a manuscript of about 1200 glosses the Latin Guinodocia (Gwynedd) by Snaudune, an Anglo-Norman form of modern Snowdon.[23] Moreover, the so-called Rochat *Perceval* attributes to the hero the statement that he was born at Sinadon—another corruption of Snaudon.[24] In the next chapter it will be seen how strong are the links between Perceval's father and Gwynedd.

These hints of a connection between the historic Peredur and Perceval, especially the fact that Peredur was the father of Mor and Perceval was reputed to be the father of a Moor (O. F. *Mor*), render it probable that Peredur bequeathed a portion of his story to Chrétien's hero. This conclusion in turn suggests two things: (1) Pryderi was confounded with

[16] M. R. Williams, *Essai sur la composition de Peredur,* p. 47.
[17] *Ibid.,* J. G. Evans, *White Book Mabinogion,* p. xvi.
[18] Weston, *Legend of Perceval,* I, 125 f.   [19] *Romania,* XXIV (1895), 336 f.
[20] Loth, *op. cit.,* II, 284. *Perlesvaus,* ed. Nitze, I, l. 41.   [21] Vs. 26.
[22] *Conte del Graal,* ed. Hilka, vss. 295–98. Hilka misread the *u* of Scaudone as *n.*
[23] *Vitae Sanctorum Britanniae,* ed. A. W. Wade-Evans (Cardiff, 1944), pp. 232, 246.
[24] A. Rochat, *Ueber einen bisher unbekannten Percheval li Galois* (Zürich, 1855), p. 91.

Peredur because of similarity in name.[25] (2) The latter name, transmitted to France, was metamorphosed into Perceval on the analogy of French names such as Percehaie ("Pierce-Hedge"), which occurs as early as *Domesday Book* (1086).[26] At any rate, when a lost French romance of Perceval fell into the hands of a Welshman late in the twelfth or early in the thirteenth century,[27] he reinstated Peredur as the titular hero of his redaction. Knowing Peredur as one of the seven sons of a chieftain of the North, he rejected the early French tradition which consistently made Perceval one of two or three sons of a noble or king of Wales,[28] and returned to the native tradition that Peredur was one of the seven sons of an earl of the North. Desiring a name for this earl, he created, in a manner characteristic of Geoffrey of Monmouth,[29] an eponymous figure from the Welsh name of York, that is, Evrawc. Thus the romance of *Peredur* opens: "Earl Evrawc possessed the earldom of the North. He had seven sons. . . . His seventh son was called Peredur." [30]

The assembled evidence, then, seems to support the following account of the growth of the Perceval legend. The semimythical Pryderi, prince of South Wales, was the hero of a saga, including the Siege Perilous, the Waste Land, and the Castle of the Chain, as well as some features of the Irish Cuchulainn and Finn *enfances*. Through similarity of names, Pryderi's saga was blended with the more or less historic tradition of Peredur, prince of North Britain. The blended saga, now attached to Peredur, passed on to the Breton *conteurs* and emerged in French literature as the romances of Perceval. An offshoot of the French tradition, carried back to Wales, was restored by the Welsh author to the historic hero and was entitled *Peredur*.

[25] Cf. the substitution of the common Welsh name Madawc for the mythical Mabon in a triad. Loth, *op. cit.*, II, 267, 318.

[26] J. D. Bruce, *Evolution of Arthurian Romance*, I, 251, n. 35. Wolfram von Eschenbach, *Parzival*, tr. W. Hertz, ed. 7 (1927), p. 491.

[27] On date of *Peredur* cf. M. R. Williams, *Essai*, p. 28: "On peut signaler enfin des fautes du copiste de Peniarth 4, qui démontrent qu'il avait sous les yeux un manuscrit antérieur au XIIIe siècle." Cf., however, *Zts. f. celt. Phil.*, VIII (1910), 188.

[28] In the *Prose Tristan*, however, Perceval is one of the five sons of Pellinor.

[29] Geoffrey of Monmouth, *Historia Regum Britanniae*, ed. A. Griscom, pp. 258 f. E. Faral, *Légende arthurienne*, II, 97; III, 97. Geoffrey's introduction of Peredur map Eridur among the vassals who attended Arthur's coronation does not represent an early inclusion of Peredur among Arthur's knights, since Geoffrey merely stole the name from a Welsh genealogy. Cf. *ibid.*, II, 276.   [30] Loth, *op. cit.*, II, 47 f.

Chapter LX

PERCEVAL'S FATHER

VERSES 412–88

Perceval's widowed mother informed the youth, after his meeting with Arthur's knights, that his father had been the most renowned warrior in all the islands of the sea. He had been wounded through the legs so that he was crippled in body. His lands and treasures had been ruined, and he had fallen into great poverty. He had taken refuge in his manor in a waste forest, being transported thither in a litter. At the time his son Perceval had been only a little over two years old, but he had had two elder brothers. These had grown up to be knighted, one by the King of Escavalon, and the younger by King Ban de Gomeret. Both had been slain after their return to their parents, and their father had died of grief.

THERE CAN BE no doubt that Pryderi was celebrated as a youthful hero by the *cyvarwyddon* of medieval Wales, and the arguments adduced in the last chapter mark him out as the chief prototype of Perceval. Since the Welsh evidence on this point was found in *The Four Branches of the Mabinogi,* we naturally turn to the same source to discover the prototype of Perceval's father. But this is no easy task. In the first place, the *Four Branches* provide no genuine story of Pryderi's birth, only a version of the birth of Gwri, arbitrarily identified with Pryderi; and thus the most obvious method of discovering the true begetter of Pryderi and the original of Perceval's father fails us. Secondly, in Chrétien's poem Perceval's father is anonymous and the other texts assign him such a wide variety of names, some of them (such as Evrawc) merely arbitrary choices, that the prospect of detecting his Welsh prototype through identity or similarity of names seems hopeless.

Certainly there was great confusion as to the name and identity of the man by the second half of the twelfth century. But there is also such insistence in the so-called *Bliocadran Prologue,* prefixed to *Le Conte del Graal,* and in Wolfram's *Parzival* on the connection of Perceval's father with Wales (no one but Perceval himself is more explicitly connected with that land) that one is justified in scrutinizing the evidence closely. Professor Newstead has pointed out a path, with many signposts, which leads us surely to Bran the Blessed,[1] that conspicuous personage in Welsh song and story and the original of numerous prominent persons in Arthurian romance.[2] Though Professor Newstead's argument is much fuller

---

[1] *Romanic Review,* XXXVI (1945), 3–31.   [2] See Chaps. XXV, XL.

and more conclusive, I trust that the points which follow will suffice to prove that Bran was the chief prototype of Perceval's father.

According to the prologue to *Le Conte del Graal,* the hero's father was Bliocadran; [3] according to Wolfram, he was named Gahmuret. Though at first glance there might seem to be no correspondence here, scholars have recognized that the latter name is simply the last element in the name occurring in *Erec* as Ban or Braus de Gomeret [4] and probably representing an original Bran de Gomeret. Bliocadran, too, should be a grotesque deformation of Bran, and we should be prepared to find correspondences between Bliocadran, Bran de Gomeret, and Gahmuret. That is precisely what we do find.

First, let us observe the marked parallelism between the histories of Bliocadran and Gahmuret. To quote Miss Weston:

"In both versions the devotion of the father to warlike exercises is insisted upon. In both he is overcome with grief at the death in tourney of a brother or brothers, which death leaves him the sole surviving member of his family. In both he is summoned from home, shortly before the birth of his first child, to attend a tourney; in both he is there slain, and buried away from home with great honours. In both versions an old man plays an important role at the moment of breaking the news to the widow. . . . The details of the lady's subsequent flight, and the ultimate loss of her lands, in the German poem, are entirely in agreement with the version of the French fragment." [5]

Let me add some additional resemblances. Bliocadran's wife is referred to as "his wife of sorrowful heart"; [6] Gahmuret's wife is called Herzeloide, [7] which seems to be a deliberate or accidental substitute for *Herzeleide,* "heart-sorrow." [8] Bliocadran is a knight of Wales, he participates in a tournament held by the King of Wales, and his widow retires to a castle on the sea of Wales; [9] Gahmuret marries the Queen of Wales and North Wales (Norgals), [10] and consequently becomes king of these regions.

The importance of this last fact, that Gahmuret is King of North Wales, becomes apparent when we compare him with Bran de Gomeret. For not only does Wolfram insist on the youthfulness of the troop which accom-

---

[3] *Conte del Graal,* ed. Hilka, p. 431.

[4] *Erec* (Halle, 1890), vs. 1975. Braus, Professor Misrahi informs me, is the reading of ms. E.

[5] J. L. Weston, *Legend of Perceval,* I, 72.

[6] *Conte del Graal,* ed. Hilka, p. 434, vs. 153. Note that we have the same tradition in the *Vulgate Lancelot,* where King Ban's widow is called "la roine as grans dolors." Sommer, *Vulgate Version,* III, 15.

[7] Wolfram von Eschenbach, *Parzival,* ed. K. Lachmann, 5th ed. (Berlin, 1891), 84, 9, reading of ms. G; 84, 13, Hertzeloide, reading of ms. d.

[8] Herzeloide comes closer to Herzeleide than to Herselot, which Bruce (*Evolution of Arthurian Romance,* I, 314, n.) and Hertz (*Parzival,* 7th ed., p. 478) accept as the original. Furthermore, it coincides with the tradition represented in the *Bliocadran Prolog* by "cuer dolent" and in the *Vulgate Lancelot* by "grans dolors." Miss Weston, evidently realizing the force of this tradition, calls Parzival's mother Herzeleide.

[9] *Conte del Graal,* ed. Hilka, pp. 430, 433, 450.　　　　[10] *Parzival,* 103, 6-9.

panied Gahmuret on his wars,[11] merely *Knappen* and *Kint,* thus parallel-ing Chrétien's statement [12] that Bran de Gomeret was attended at the wedding of Erec only by "young pages," but also the name Gomeret itself was shown by M. Lot to be a corruption of Goinnet, Welsh Gwynedd, that is, North Wales.[13] Gomeret represents a natural misreading of Goiñet, the *in* being mistaken for *m,* and the stroke over the *n,* representing a second *n,* being mistaken for the sign for *er.* How natural this error would be is proved by Potvin's misreading of Gom*er*ec in a later passage of the Montpellier manuscript as Goinnec.[14] This error of Potvin's was generously pointed out to me by Professor Roach, who wrote: "The scribe of M [Montpellier] does not make much distinction between his *n* over-stroke and his *er* overstroke, and this is what led Potvin astray." The very same lack of distinction led earlier scribes to misread Goiñet as Gomeret. Lot, then, correctly identified Goinnet as a French form for Gwynedd, North Wales.[15] Wolfram in taking the corrupt place name Gahmuret for a personal name was not alone, for in *L'Atre Périlleux* Gomeret or Gou-meret appears as a knight.[16] Thus we are led to conclude not only that Gahmuret and Bran de Gomeret were identical, but also that Gahmuret as King of Norgals and Bran as King of Gomeret derive from an ultimate common source which represented Bran as King of Gwynedd.

This ultimate source must have been Welsh tradition; for in the mabinogi of *Branwen* the chief figure is Bran, who held his royal court first at Harlech in North Wales and then at Aberffraw in Anglesea, chief seat of the kings of Gwynedd.[17] And despite the obvious elaboration of Gahmuret's story both by Wolfram himself and his immediate source,[18]

---

[11] *Ibid.,* 8, 2–5; 18, 17–19, 6; 61, 6–62, 9; 105, 1–3.   [12] *Erec,* vss. 1976–78.

[13] *Romania,* XXIV (1895), 335. Lot was entirely mistaken, however, in supposing that Gomeret and Benoic have the same derivation. For the latter is obviously a ms. misreading of Benoit, and Bran was regularly called in the mabinogi "Bran the Blessed." Cf. *Romania, LIV* (1928), 518 f. The substitution of *de* for *le,* illustrated in the transformation of Bran le Benoit into Ban de Benoic, may also be observed in the name Girard de Roussillon (instead of "le roussillon"), in Boleyn de Grace (instead of Boleyn la Grasse), and in Rinaldo de Zamberlan (instead of Renaud le Chambellan). Çf. Prof. Misrahi's article in *PMLA,* LI (1936), 8–12; *The Book of Margery Kempe,* ed. W. Butler-Bowdon (London, 1936), p. 103n.; Philippe de Novare, *Mémoires,* ed. C. Kohler (Paris, 1913), pp. 124, 160.

[14] C. Potvin, *Perceval le Gallois,* III, 88, vs. 8. This error, with other misreadings, was re-peated by Miss Weston, *Legend of Perceval,* I, 299, and by Dr. Brugger, in *Medieval Studies in Memory of G. Schoepperle Loomis,* p. 148.

[15] Cf. *Fouke Fitz Warin,* ed. L. Brandin, p. 1, where Owain Gwynedd (i.e. of Gwynedd) is called Yweyn Goynez, and F. Lot, *Nennius et l'Historia Brittonum,* I, 149, 179, which gives the forms Gue(r)net and Guined.

[16] *L'Atre Périlleux,* ed. B. Woledge, vss. 5477, 5918, 6243. Wolfram again mistakes a place name for a personal name in *Parzival,* 56, 19, when he calls Morgain la Fée Terdelaschoye.

[17] Loth, *Mabinogion,* 2d ed., I, 121, 124; II, 368.

[18] That Wolfram must have had a source other than Chrétien for the first two books of *Parzival* is demonstrated not only by the correspondences with the *Bliocadran Prolog* and his evident knowledge concerning Bran de Gomeret, but also by the interest displayed in the

and despite the confusions and distortions which characterize the mabinogi, curious similarities between Gahmuret and Bran glimmer through. Gahmuret's retinue, we remember, as well as Bran de Gomeret's, was composed of youths. Bran's followers banqueted on the isle of Grassholm for eighty years yet none of them grew older,[19] and we are justified in assuming that this feast corresponded to that instituted by the Irish sea-god, Manannan mac Lir, the partakers of which were free ever after from decay and old age.[20] Gahmuret went on an expedition to a foreign land and fought on behalf of a persecuted queen; [21] so did Bran.[22] Gahmuret gave gifts as lavishly as if the trees bore gold; [23] Bran gave gifts lavishly, including a plate of gold.[24] Gahmuret possessed a magnificent pavilion in which he entertained his future bride, the Queen of Norgals.[25] Bran entertained a royal suitor for his sister in a tent at Aberffraw, the capital of Gwynedd.[26] Finally, when Gahmuret was battling in a foreign land, his helm was softened by a dash of goat's blood,[27] and he was fatally wounded in the head by a spear; before dying he entrusted this spear to his followers; his helm was placed above his tomb in far-off Bagdad.[28] Bran, while battling in a foreign land, was wounded by a poisoned spear; before dying, he entrusted his head to his followers, and it was buried in far-off London.[29] Of course, these similarities are by no means exact; one could hardly expect them to be, considering the very different channels through which the traditions of Gahmuret and of Bran have flowed. But they are sufficiently numerous and unusual so that, taken in conjunction with the plain evidence pointing to Bran of Gwynedd as the original of Bran de Gomeret, they seem decisive.

Chrétien's account of the father of Perceval, meager though it is, and his narrative of Perceval's birth and upbringing display in turn a sufficient likeness to the corresponding narratives of Wolfram and the *Bliocadran Prologue* to render it probable that Chrétien's ultimate source also was the Welsh legend of Bran. It is perhaps a further sign of a common tradition

---

Anjou connection of Gahmuret, an interest hardly attributable to Wolfram himself. Cf. Wolfram von Eschenbach, *Parzival*, mod. W. Hertz, 7th ed., pp. 418 f.; ed. E. Martin, *Germanistische Handbibliothek*, IX, 2 (Halle, 1903), pp. xl–xlvi; E. Wechssler, *Sage vom Heiligen Graal* (Halle, 1898), pp. 164–77; M. Wilmotte, *Le Poème du Graal* (Paris, 1930), pp. 15–24.

[19] Loth, *op. cit.*, I, 148. Cf. *Perlesvaus*, ed. Nitze, I, ll. 940–47, 2414–17, 9557 f.
[20] P. Joyce, *Old Celtic Romances* (1920), p. 457.   [21] *Parzival*, Bk. I.
[22] Loth, *op. cit.*, I, 134–44.   [23] *Parzival*, 53, 15–19.   [24] Loth, *op. cit.*, I, 127–29.
[25] *Parzival*, 52, 17–26; 61, 8–15; 62, 17–24; 81, 15–85, 4.
[26] Loth, *op. cit.*, I, 124. For the connection of Bran with tents cf. *supra*, pp. 241 f.
[27] *Parzival*, mod. Hertz, 7th ed., p. 481.   [28] *Parzival*, 105, 11–108, 1.
[29] Loth, *op. cit.*, I, 144–49. On Bran's head in Welsh and Arthurian romance cf. *ibid.*, I, 120, n. 2; II, 239–42; C. Guest, *Mabinogion*, Everyman ed., p. 292; H. Newstead, *Bran the Blessed in Arthurian Romance*, pp. 19, 70–85; *Rev. celt.*, XLVII (1930), 39–62. On analogous traditions cf. *Folklore Record*, V (1882), 14; Faral, *Légende arthurienne*, I, 126; II, 224–26; III, 33, 182, 299.

that, while Wolfram remarks in the most casual way, without explanation, "Wasted was his [Gahmuret's] land," [30] Chrétien says that when Perceval's father was wounded, "His great lands, his great treasures . . . all were destroyed." There are also correspondences worth noting between Chrétien's account of Perceval's father and the Welsh tradition of Bran. Chrétien asserts that no knight was so feared as was Perceval's father "in all the islands of the sea"; Bran was king of the Island of the Mighty.[31] Chrétien says that Perceval's father was wounded by a javelin "through the legs" or "through the thighs," and Bran was wounded by a spear in the foot.[32] Chrétien, as we have just seen, tells how the wounding of Perceval's father was followed by the desolation of his land. After the wounding and death of Bran, his sister laments that two islands have been laid waste, namely, Britain and Ireland.[33] The verb is *diffeithwyt,* "have been laid waste," and later there is reference to the *diffeithwch,* "desert, wilderness," of Ireland.[34] It is surely significant that the adjective *diffeith* is applied in *Manawydan* to the waste land of Dyved,[35] the counterpart of the waste land described by Gerbert de Montreuil. Therefore this famous motif of the waste land was attached not only to Gahmuret and Perceval's father but also to Bran, and in the two latter instances it follows upon, and is presumably a consequence of, the maiming motif.

All the evidence concerning Perceval's father, assembled from Wolfram, the *Bliocadran Prologue,* and Chrétien's poem, points consistently to a Welsh legend of Bran, differing materially, though not wholly, from that in the mabinogi, as the ultimate source.

Before we can feel entirely secure in this conclusion, however, we must consider certain objections.

1. Chrétien distinguishes Perceval's father from Ban de Gomeret, the king who bestowed arms on Perceval's elder brother. But we have long since recognized the appearance of doublets, triplets, and even quadruplets as one of the characteristic features of any long Arthurian romance, and need not wonder at this duplication of Bran de Gomeret.

2. There are two important rival traditions as to the name of Perceval's father. Several of the prose romances agree that it was Pellinor; [36] *La Queste del Saint Graal* in one passage gives either Pellean or Pellehen; [37] the *Vulgate Merlin,* as we have seen,[38] gives to the father of Perceval's alter ego, Dodinel, "Little Simpleton," the name of Belinant. These are

[30] *Parzival*, 53, 15. [31] Loth, *op. cit.*, I, 123 f. [32] *Ibid.*, I, 144.

[33] *Ibid.*, I, 146. On wasting of, or warring on, two kingdoms cf. *Queste del S. Graal,* ed. A. Pauphilet, p. 204; Wolfram, *Parzival,* 128, 3–7; 141, 7.

[34] I. Williams, *Pedeir Keinc y Mabinogi,* pp. 45, 48. [35] *Ibid.*, p. 52.

[36] *Mod. Phil.*, XVI (1918), 341–43. Bruce gives in this article (*ibid.*, XVI, 113–28, 337–50) all the facts about the occurrence of Pelles, Pellinor, and Pellean in the romances, but his interpretation of them seems to me quite mistaken.

[37] *Ibid.*, XVI, 346. *Queste,* ed. Pauphilet, p. 201. [38] *Supra,* pp. 339 f.

evidently forms based on Welsh Beli, sometimes called Beli Mawr.[39] But though Pryderi, through his mother's marriage with Manawydan, became a remote relative of Beli's,[40] there is nothing to be discovered in Welsh tradition which would show Beli to be the authentic counterpart of Perceval's father, whereas there is a good deal of evidence to identify him with Perceval's uncle, Pelles.[41] There is also an important branch of Grail romance which assigns the part of Perceval's father to Alain le Gros.[42] This name, as everyone agrees, was derived from, or affected by, the common Breton name Alan,[43] but no historic Alan presents the slightest likeness to Alain le Gros. The latter name is therefore an *ignis fatuus*.

3. If the hypothesis that Perceval and his father correspond to Pryderi and Bran is sound, one would expect to find some hint of this paternal relationship in the Welsh texts, but the *Four Branches* mention Pryderi merely as a follower of Bran,[44] whereas a son and heir of Bran appears, called Caradawc.[45] In answer to this objection it is necessary to emphasize once more the drastic liberties which the author of the *Four Branches* took with his traditional material. We have seen that he identified Pryderi with Gwri[46] and thus deprived us of the story of Pryderi's birth and upbringing. The same capricious step necessarily made Pryderi son of the mysterious Pwyll, Head of Annwn, not of Bran, the Noble Head. The author therefore could not make Pryderi son of Bran, no matter what orthodox tradition may have asserted. As for his introduction of Caradawc as the heir of Bran, one may surmise that the author was seized by an impulse to give his narrative a pseudo-historic coloring, introduced a certain Caradawc, king of Gwynedd (the very district with which Bran was associated), who was according to the *Annales Cambriae* slain in battle with the Saxons in 798,[47] and so created a son for Bran. In so mixing euhemerized mythology with pseudo-history he was but anticipating the notorious Geof-

---

[39] Cf. *supra*, p. 143, and Loth, *op. cit.*, II, 388, s.v. *Beli Mawr*. On Beli cf. also J. Rhys and J. B. Jones, *Welsh People* (1909), p. 41; *PMLA*, LVI (1941), 920.

[40] Loth, *op. cit.*, I, 121 f., 147, 152 f. Cf. Rhys and Jones, *Welsh People*, p. 39.

[41] See Chap. XX.

[42] *Perlesvaus*, ed. Nitze, I, 410; II, 195 f. *Didot Perceval*, ed. Roach, pp. 33 f., 321.

[43] R. Heinzel, *Ueber die altfranzösischen Gralromane, Denkschriften*, Vienna Academy, phil.-hist. Kl., XL (1891), 122. Bruce, *Evolution of Arthurian Romance*, I, 235n. *Perlesvaus*, II, 196. *Morf Festschrift* (Halle, 1905), pp. 78 f., 88–94. *Zts. f. franz. Sprache u. Lit.*, XLIX (1927), 227 f. Though agreeing that the Breton name affected Alain le Gros, I believe that the real origin of the latter is to be sought in the name given in *Perlesvaus* to one of the hero's uncles—Gosgalains, Gos Gavians, Gorgalians, etc. (*Perlesvaus*, I, 414). A hypothetical Gors Galains would explain the forms in *Perlesvaus*. Some other author or scribe might guess that it stood for Gros Galains and substitute Galains li Gros, and the historical Alan Mor, Alain li Granz, would suggest transformation from Galains to Alain. The hypothetical Gors Galains would go back to the hypothetical Gwri Gwallt-a(d)vwyn. All these, of course, are conjectures, and they do not explain how Alain le Gros came to be Perceval's father instead of his alter ego, as Gwri was Pryderi's alias. Still I know of no other adequate explanation of Alain's appearance as the son of Bron (Hebron) in Boron's *Metrical Joseph* and the *Didot Perceval*.

[44] Loth, *Mabinogion*, 2d ed., I, 144. [45] *Ibid.*, I, 136, 147. [46] Cf. *supra*, pp. 73 f.

[47] Loth, *op. cit.*, II, 378. Cf. J. E. Lloyd, *History of Wales*, 3d ed., I, 90, 237.

frey of Monmouth and the composers of *Lludd and Llevelys* and *The Dream of Maxen.*[48] Possibly he had already been anticipated by others; for the Welsh triads contain a number of statements about Caradawc son of Bran which do not seem to be based on *Branwen.*[49] At any rate, this Caradawc is an impostor; if anything is certain, it is that no historic Caradawc was sired by the old sea-god, Bran son of Llyr.

4. The most formidable objection to Bran as the prototype of Perceval's father will be produced by those who have already recognized Bran, correctly as we shall see, as the prototype of the Fisher King. For though the Fisher King is Perceval's cousin in Chrétien, his uncle in *Perlesvaus* and Wolfram, and his grandfather in the *Didot Perceval,* and though he resembles Perceval's father in being wounded through the thighs and in the wasting of his land,[50] yet it is impossible to reconcile his role and chronological position with that of Perceval's father. The latter, we know died before or shortly after the birth of his son. All the Fisher Kings on the contrary lived on for years after Perceval's birth, were visited in their castles by that hero when he was of age to bear arms, and, according to some versions, expired only after a second visit years later. These stereotyped legends of Perceval's father and of the Fisher King cannot be harmonized if the two persons were identical. Does this fact preclude the hypothesis that both legends had a common origin in the stories of Bran? Needless to say, inconsistencies abound in the *Matière de Bretagne,* and this particular inconsistency, though serious, need not baffle us completely. In fact, it calls attention to the existence of two separate traditions concerning Pryderi and Bran which we must postulate if we are to unravel the tangled skein of Perceval's history in *Le Conte del Graal.* Long since, Nutt divined with great acumen the presence in the Grail romances of two distinct themes—the Feud or Vengeance Quest and the Unspelling Quest,[51] and it has been one of the great misfortunes of Arthurian scholarship that his analysis, though faulty in detail, has not been followed. Nutt says of these two originally distinct themes: "At an early stage of their development these stories, crystallising round the same hero, would have a tendency to influence each other, to become confused." [52] We have already learned that the *enfances* of Finn influenced the *enfances* of Perceval, and Finn was the avenger of his father's death.[53] Here, then, was the origin of the Vengeance Quest.[54] Localized in Wales, attached to Pryderi, the tradition of Finn's revenge for his slain father evolved at last into Perceval's slaying the Lord

[48] On Geoffrey's methods cf. R. H. Fletcher, *Arthurian Material in the Chronicles,* pp. 49–108; H. Newstead, *op. cit.,* pp. 163–67; *Romanic Rev.,* XXXVI, 15–20. On *Dream of Maxen,* cf. *Speculum,* XXII (1947), 523–26.   [49] Loth, *op. cit.,* I, 135, n. 1; II, 305–9, 314.
[50] Chrétien, *Conte del Graal,* vss. 3509–20, 4679.
[51] A. Nutt, *Studies on the Legend of the Holy Grail,* pp. 180–83. A. Nutt, *Legends of the Holy Grail* (London, 1902), pp. 50–54.   [52] Nutt, *Legends of the Holy Grail,* p. 52.
[53] Nutt, *Studies on the Legend,* p. 189. *Mod. Phil.,* XVIII (1920), 216, 219. J. G. Campbell, *The Fians,* pp. 16, 26 f.   [54] Cf. Chap. LXIX.

of the Red Tower, the murderer of his uncle Boon Desert; [55] Perlesvaus' slaying the Red Knight of the Deep Forest, the murderer of the son of his uncle Brun; [56] Sir Percyvelle's slaying the Red Knight, the murderer of his father; [57] Peredur's vengeance for the killing of his cousin and the laming of his uncle.[58] On the other hand, there was the Unspelling Quest. This, too, was affected, as we shall see in due course, by Irish tales, but the main theme, the Waste Land and its disenchantment, seems to have been indigenous to Wales. Bran was the Maimed King of the Waste Land, and Pryderi his deliverer. This Unspelling Quest became the central theme of the glamorous and mystifying legend of the Grail. The commingling of these two distinct patterns, both attached to Pryderi and Bran, will be traced in detail when we consider Perceval's visit to the Fisher King's castle. It was responsible for the bewildering confusion we shall find there. It was also responsible for the duplication of the figure of Bran, who appears both as Perceval's father and as his cousin, the Fisher King. For there was a radical inconsistency between the roles assigned to Bran by the Vengeance Quest and the Unspelling Quest. Bran could not be both the dead father required by the vengeance theme and the wounded but living kinsman required by the unspelling theme. Accordingly, two characters had to be made out of one. Chrétien represents Perceval's father as wounded in the thighs and tells of the consequent desolation of his lands—motifs derived from the Unspelling Quest. But the Vengeance theme required that he should die, and so we learn of his death while Perceval was still an infant. Later Perceval met his cousin, the Fisher King, and he too was wounded in the thighs and as a result of Perceval's failure to ask the unspelling question his lands also were ruined. But in accordance with the demands of the Unspelling Quest he lived on, not only to welcome Perceval on his first visit but also, presumably, to be healed by him on a second visit. By this device of creating two personages out of one the inheritors of the Bran legends were able to reconcile the conflicting données of the Vengeance and the Unspelling Quests. Thus Bran appears in Chrétien's poem both as Perceval's father and Perceval's cousin, the Fisher King. There was no need, however, to duplicate the figure of the youthful hero. Thus Perceval, as the representative of Pryderi, appears in the French romances charged with the double function of avenging a kinsman's death and of delivering the land from a spell by the healing of another kinsman. And thus we shall find him in our study of his adventures at the Grail castle.

None of the arguments against the derivation of Perceval's father from Bran is conclusive; all the difficulties may be surmounted. The positive evi-

[55] Potvin, *Perceval le Gallois*, V, 159–63; VI, 122–29.
[56] *Perlesvaus*, ed. Nitze, I, ll. 8681–8848.
[57] W. H. French, C. B. Hale, *Middle English Metrical Romances*, pp. 551–54.
[58] Loth, *Mabinogion*, 2d ed., II, 119 f.

dence in favor of this hypothesis is so strong that, when supplemented by the equally cogent evidence presented by Professor Newstead, it should be admitted among the certainties attained in Arthurian scholarship. It is easy to understand how the name Bran became first Braus, or Ban, de Gomeret and then Gahmuret. And though the development of the form Bliocadran remains one of the mysteries of the Arthurian onomasticon,[59] there can be little doubt that it too originated in Bran.

Chapter LXI

THE DAMSEL OF THE TENT AND THE PROUD KNIGHT OF THE GLADE

VERSES 635–833, 3691–3995

Perceval's first adventure after leaving his mother's manoir was to come upon a magnificent tent, surmounted by a golden eagle, pitched beside a spring. Mistaking it for a church, he entered to perform his devotions. A damsel, sleeping within, was alarmed and warned the youth to flee. But he, in obedience to his mother's instructions, kissed her twenty times and snatched a ring from her hand. Then he helped himself to wine and a pasty. Soon after his departure the damsel's lover arrived, saw signs of a visitor, and refused to believe that she had not entertained a rival in his absence. He declared that her horse should not be fed nor should she change her dress, but she must follow him till he could avenge himself on his supposed rival. Some time later Perceval met the same damsel, pale and clad in a ragged gown, mounted on a bony and trembling nag. She recognized him, reproached him, and warned him to flee. Her lover, the Proud Knight of the Glade, now rode up in a fury, and when Perceval admitted that he had been the cause of his suspicions, a combat followed. Perceval had the upper hand; his adversary promised to make amends to his innocent mistress and betook himself to Arthur's court.

THESE TWO INCIDENTS have no counterpart in the *enfances* of Cuchulainn and Finn or in the history of Pryderi as it is preserved to us. They are among the many episodes derived from the general fund of the *Matière de Bretagne* which might be attached to any hero, and are here fitted into the framework of Perceval's youthful career. We have already in our study of *Erec* [1] found them attached to Guerehes, and have seen that they provided an explanation of Erec's harsh treatment of Enide.

---

[59] For surmises (mistaken in my opinion) as to this name cf. Bruce, *Evolution of Arthurian Romance*, II, 90, n. 10, and *Medieval Studies in Memory of G. Schoepperle Loomis*, pp. 148–74.   [1] See Chap. XVII.

There is no need to recapitulate the evidence for a common tradition and for its derivation from a tale about Morgain. But let me point out once more that Perceval's damsel of the tent beside a spring is the water-fay Morgain, whom we meet in similar surroundings in the lai of *Sir Launfal;* that her jealous *ami*, the Proud Knight of the Glade, returning from the hunt, had his original in the haughty huntsman of the glade, Arawn, in *Pwyll*. The form of the story found in the *Vulgate Lancelot* supports the hints in *Erec* and *Geraint* that the husband had grounds for his jealous suspicion, for Guerehes actually lay with the damsel of the tent. But, as in *Erec* Enide's character has been saved from the suspicion of infidelity by the total suppression of any such compromising incident, so in *Le Conte del Graal* Perceval's innocence has been preserved by representing his not altogether chaste behavior with the damsel of the tent as the ingenuous vivacity of an untaught youngster. What had once been an erotic escapade has been transformed with great skill into a charming comedy of an innocent abroad. Here Chrétien writes in his happiest, most natural vein.

Chapter LXII

THE RED KNIGHT

VERSES 859–1000, 1064–1119

When Perceval approached King Arthur's castle, he met a knight issuing from it, clad in arms "totes vermoilles," and carrying a golden cup. The Red Knight asked Perceval to deliver a message to the King that he surrender his lands or send someone out to meet the Red Knight in battle. On entering Arthur's hall, Perceval learned that the Red Knight had seized the King's own cup and spilled its contents over the Queen. Perceval himself rode out, determined to secure the Red Knight's arms for himself, found him awaiting battle, and, flinging a javelin through his eye, killed him.

ONE OF THE COMMONEST conventions of the *conteurs* demanded that the hero should fight and vanquish a Red Knight, and we have already met with several instances.[1] The form in which we find this convention in *Le Conte del Graal* seems to be a condensed and modified version of the first adventure of Gauvain in *L'Atre Périlleux*.[2]

A knight Escanor, whose shield we learn later was "of a vermeil color," [3] rides up to Arthur's table during a feast, seizes the damsel who bears the royal cup, challenges the King to send someone after him, and rides off toward a wood to

[1] Cf. *supra*, pp. 165, 175, 203, 282.　　　[2] Ed. B. Woledge, vss. 122–374, 2070–2462.
[3] *Ibid.*, vss. 1516 f.

await a battle. Gauvain, after some delay, pursues, and a few days later catches up with the Red Knight and kills him.

It seems pretty clear that Chrétien's account of the Red Knight's dashing the wine from the King's cup over Guenievre, riding off with the golden vessel, and sending back a challenge to Arthur, is ultimately based on the same *conte* as that which furnished the Red Knight episode to *L'Atre Périlleux.*[4]

This episode in turn, as we saw in an earlier chapter,[5] reveals by a number of details not reproduced in the summary above that it is descended from Curoi's abduction of Blathnat with her caldron. It is particularly significant that Escanor, like other Red Knights, possesses the solar trait of decreasing in strength after *none.*[6] And it is no accident, therefore, that his counterpart in *Le Conte del Graal* should wear "arms all vermeil." [7]

In our subsequent examination of Perceval's Vengeance Quest we shall find that the Finn saga also contributed elements to the combat with the Red Knight as found in *Sir Percyvelle, Perlesvaus,* and Wolfram's *Parzival,* but Chrétien's account summarized above shows nothing of this second influence.

Chapter LXIII

PERCEVAL'S ARRIVAL AT ARTHUR'S COURT

VERSES 900–1033

The young Perceval set out for Arthur's court, and rode on horseback into the hall, where the King and his knights were seated at table. When the youth demanded to be made a knight, Arthur consented to do so. Keu, however, mocked the youth and was promptly rebuked by Arthur.

THIS INCIDENT, though ultimately sprung from Finn's going incognito to take service with the King of Bantry,[1] is one of the clearest examples of Welsh influence. For in *Kulhwch,* composed a decade or two before or after 1100, the young hero sets out for Arthur's court; Kei on hearing of his arrival displays his grudging nature and is promptly rebuked by Arthur; the youth rides on horseback into the hall, where the King and his

---

[4] This had already been perceived by Prof. O'Rahilly, who wrote (*Eriu,* XIV, 1943, 17): "In the Welsh 'Peredur' we are told of a knight who entered Arthur's hall and forcibly carried off Gwenhwyfar's golden goblet; originally this signified the carrying off of Gwenhwyfar herself."

[5] Cf. *supra,* pp. 203 f.   [6] *L'Atre Périlleux,* vss. 1620–24. [7] *Conte del Graal,* vss. 871 f.
[1] Cf. *supra,* p. 338.

warriors are at meat, and asks a boon, which Arthur grants.[2] All these features, though in a somewhat different order, are found in our romance.

Chapter LXIV

THE LAUGHING MAIDEN

VERSES 1033–66, 1192–1279

When Keu had told Perceval in mockery to win the arms of the Red Knight, the youth observed a fair maiden, attendant on the Queen,[1] who laughed and declared loudly that in the whole world there never had been or would be a better knight than Perceval. She had not laughed for more than six years. Keu in anger knocked her down, and kicked into the fireplace a fool who had been wont to say: "This maiden will not laugh until she sees the man who will achieve the supremacy in knighthood." After Perceval had overcome the Red Knight, he sent a message by Yonet to the maiden that he would avenge the blow Keu had dealt her. On the delivery of the message, the fool leapt up joyfully and prophesied that within forty days Keu would pay with a broken arm for the kick and the buffet.

THE INCIDENT of the maiden who laughs after a silence of six years and announces that the youthful hero, despite his uncouth behavior, is destined for great things seems to be a variant on a formula which we find in the widespread legend of Robert the Devil and its English counterpart, the romance of *Sir Gowther*.[2] Breul showed that the legend, though the earliest extant form is of the thirteenth century, must have been current earlier still,[3] and there are reasons for believing that it originated as a Breton lai, cast into an unusually pious mold. The author of *Sir Gowther* declares explicitly that his source was "a lai of Breyten."[4] Miss Ravenel proved a marked correspondence with the lai of *Tydorel*.[5] Crane pointed out that the motif of the Child Vowed to the Devil occurred in the Irish *Voyage of the Sons of O'Corra* at least a century before the earliest version of Robert the Devil.[6] Several other motifs beloved by the Arthurian romancers occur: the hero's precocious growth,[7] the three days' tourney in

---

[2] Loth, *Mabinogion*, 2d ed., I, 251–260, 285 f.

[1] Vs. 1247. It is possible that Wolfram von Eschenbach, in calling the dumb maiden "frou Cunneware," is giving a mistaken rendering of "la pucele la reine," the handmaid of Guenievre, whose name occurs (though not in *Parzival*) in forms not unlike Cunneware. For instance, certain mss. of Geoffrey of Monmouth's *Historia* give Guanuara, Guenhuara, Guenhuuara; cf. *Historia Regum Britanniae*, ed. A. Griscom (New York, 1929), p. 652.

[2] L. A. Hibbard, *Mediaeval Romance in England*, pp. 49–57.

[3] *Sir Gowther*, ed. K. Breul (Oppeln, 1886), pp. 51 f.   [4] *Ibid.*, p. 136, vss. 28–30.

[5] *PMLA*, XX (1905), 152–77.   [6] *Romanic Review*, V (1914), 55–67.

[7] P. Piper, *Höfische Epik*, II, 212. Sommer, *Vulgate Version*, III, 33.

arms of various colors,[8] the false claimant,[9] the recognition of the hero by a wound.[10] There is therefore an antecedent probability that any romantic feature in the legend of Robert the Devil belonged to the stock in trade of the Breton *conteurs,* and the motif of the long silent maiden is one of these. Let me translate from a condensed Latin version of the legend furnished by Etienne de Bourbon about 1250.

"Tonsured like a fool by the hermit, Robert went to a royal city; pursued by boys, he went up to the king's palace, fought with the dogs and snatched away from their teeth the things which were tossed to them. . . . He would not lie down except with the dogs under the stairs, where he spent the night in weeping and prayer. The king, however, had pity on him and would not let him be molested. When barbarians made war on the king, ravaging the realm, and Robert out of compassion was praying for him, an angel of the Lord appeared to him, telling him to follow and receive arms sent him by God, and to go to the aid of his lord, and after winning the victory, to return the arms to the place where he had received them. The angel led him to a spring in the royal estate, and there clad him in white arms with a red cross and mounted him on a white horse. Robert, hastening to join the army, dashed among the enemy, put them to flight, and destroyed them. When he had won the victory, he returned and left the arms and the horse where he had received them, as the angel had directed. The only daughter of the king, who was dumb, had espied this from the window of her chamber. When the king returned and asked his men who the knight in white arms was, who had performed such feats and could not be found, his dumb daughter pointed out the fool, whom the king reproved. When the enemy returned with a greater army, Robert, counseled by the angel, did as before, rescued the king and his army, and vanquished all the foe. When the king saw this, he ordered his knights to seize him, if they could not bring him otherwise, so that he might exalt and honor him. One of the knights, unable to capture Robert as he wished, thrust a lance into his leg, wounded him, and the blade of the lance remained in the wound. Robert removed his armor at the spring, took out and cast away the blade, and applied new wine to the wound. The daughter of the king, on seeing this, ran and brought away the blade. When the king announced that if that knight who had gained the victory would come, he would give him his daughter in marriage and make him heir to the kingdom, the seneschal wounded his own leg and brought the blade of a lance; and the knight who had wounded Robert, though he well perceived the deception, did not dare to say that the blade was not his. When the maiden was about to be wedded to the seneschal, and she was refusing so far as she could with signs, rejecting the seneschal and pointing to the fool, and her father was flogging and constraining her, the Lord opened her mouth and she told her father what she had seen and brought the blade, which the knight recognized and fixed to his lance."[11]

[8] Cf. Chap. XLII.
[9] G. Schoepperle, *Tristan and Isolt,* I, 205. J. L. Weston, *Legend of Lancelot,* pp. 31–35. The source of the motif in the Tristram romances seems to be the story of Drust, the Pictish king. Cf. Thomas of Britain, *Romance of Tristram and Ysolt,* trans. R. S. Loomis, rev. ed. (1931), p. xii; *Beiblatt zur Anglia,* XV (1904), 16–21.
[10] This also is derived from the story of Drust.   [11] *Sir Gowther,* ed. Breul, p. 209.

It is obvious that we have here in Etienne's story a pious adaptation of romantic materials such as we have in the tale of Patient Griselda,[12] the birth and upbringing of Gawain,[13] and *Amis and Amile*. It is also obvious that several of these romantic elements, though reshuffled and altered, appear in Chrétien's incident of the laughing maiden: to wit, the handsome but mannerless hero arriving at a king's court incognito, the maiden who divines his worth and breaks her silence to proclaim it, the malicious seneschal. Though ultimately the motif of the laughing maiden may have originated in a folktale of a suitor who won a dumb princess by making her laugh,[14] its immediate source seems to have been the repertoire of the Breton *conteurs*.

Chapter LXV

GORNEMANT DE GOHORT

VERSES 1312–1698

After leaving Arthur's castle, Perceval arrived before another castle, consisting of a great central tower and four lesser towers at the corners. A gentleman in a robe of ermine and two youths were lingering at the drawbridge. The gentleman, though wondering at Perceval's uncouth management of horse and arms, granted his request for hospitality, and promptly instructed him in the practices of chivalry. Three times the host mounted Perceval's horse and gave an object lesson, and Perceval showed great precocity in imitation. At the close of the lesson, Perceval was informed that his host was called Gornemant de Gohort. Though invited to stay a year, he declared that he must return home to learn news of his mother. The next day Gornemant knighted the youth, gave him good advice, adjuring him not to be too talkative, and blessed him on his departure.

I T HAS ALREADY been shown that Perceval's *enfances* had their chief source in the boyhood deeds of Cuchulainn and Finn, and that the knighting of Perceval by Gornemant was in all probability derived from the conferring of arms on Cuchulainn by his maternal uncle, Conchobar, since Gornemant's role in *Peredur* is taken by Peredur's maternal uncle. It is possible that the training which Perceval receives at Gornemant's castle was ultimately inspired by the training which Cuchulainn receives from

---

[12] Chaucer, *Works,* ed. F. N. Robinson (Boston, 1933), p. 814.
[13] R. S. Loomis, *Celtic Myth,* pp. 330–39.
[14] Antti Aarne, *Types of the Folktale,* trans. Stith Thompson, Folklore Fellows Communications No. 74 (Helsinki, 1928), p. 97.

the druid Cathbad at Conchobar's court,[1] though this, of course, cannot be proved.

Certain it is, however, that a formula concerning the training of a young hero by a hospitable knight was current. Gaston Paris[2] long since noted the similarity between the Gornemant episode and one in *Lanzelet*.[3]

Shortly after leaving hs foster-mother's island castle, Lanzelet met a young knight on horseback, Johfrit de Liez, who was astonished at the lad's clumsy management of his spirited steed. Johfrit taught him how to hold his bridle, invited him to his castle, and rode ahead to prepare the ladies for the boy's arrival. There Lanzelet was courteously received and seated next to his hostess. Afterwards an exhibition of horsemanship and jousting was put on for his benefit, followed by a dance with garlanded damsels. In three days the youth became an accomplished knight and courtier.

The initiation of Lanzelet into the ways of chivalry goes back apparently to the same tradition as that of Perceval, but it offers no clue to remoter origins.

The name Gornemant de Gohort presents a rough approximation to that of the Welsh giant Gwrnach Gawr, but the story of Kulhwch's visit to Gwrnach's fortress bears no resemblance to Chrétien's episode.[4] The name Gornemant de Gohort is mentioned perfunctorily in *Erec* as that of one of Arthur's greatest knights,[5] and Gornemant himself reappears in Gerbert's continuation of *Le Conte del Graal*.[6] Here, as a venerable man, wounded in battle, who lies on a couch beside a fire in the hall of his castle, hospitably entertains Perceval, and is ultimately cured of his wounds by the hero, he has apparently taken over some of the characteristics of the Fisher King.[7] But this fact does not help us with the interpretation of Chrétien's Gornemant, for only in the muddled *Peredur* is the venerable fisherman portrayed as the instructor of the Grail hero in the ways of

[1] Cross and Slover, *Ancient Irish Tales*, p. 142. It is well worth noting by way of corroboration that *Peredur* contains an alternative account of the hero's training in arms (Loth, *Mabinogion*, 2d ed., II, 75 f.) which attributes it to the sorceresses of Kaer Loyw, and this account certainly, as Zimmer, Rhys, and Prof. Mary Williams have observed, has been influenced by an episode in the legend of Cuchulainn. Cf. *Göttingische gelehrte Anzeigen*, 1890, p. 519; J. Rhys, *Studies in the Arthurian Legend*, pp. 81 f.; M. R. Williams, *Essai sur la composition de Peredur*, pp. 117 f.
[2] *Romania*, X (1881), 473. The resemblance has also been noted by Philipot and A. C. L. Brown; cf. *Romania*, XXVI (1897), 290 f., *Mod. Phil.*, XVII (1919), 369 n. 4.
[3] P. Piper, *Höfische Epik*, II, 173.   [4] Loth, *Mabinogion*, 2d ed., I, 317-21.
[5] Vs. 1695. The mss. offer many variants of the name. Other appearances of Gornemant are listed in *Le Conte del Graal*, ed. Hilka, p. 650.
[6] Gerbert de Montreuil, *Continuation de Perceval*, ed. Mary Williams, I, vss. 4869-6187.
[7] The fact that the author of *Peredur* also confused the figure corresponding to Gornemant with the Grail King, representing him as lame and as watching his attendants fishing, and also assigned to him sons, suggests a common source for this confusion. It is unlikely that the Welsh author derived these points from Gerbert, since he handles them so differently, and since his date seems to be earlier. Gerbert's introduction into this episode of the witch with her reviving balsam is also paralleled in *Peredur*. Cf. M. R. Williams, *op. cit.*, pp. 109-12; R. H. Griffith, *Sir Perceval of Galles*, pp. 50-55.

knighthood and courtesy. Gornemant's name and his function remain something of a riddle.

One detail in the description of his castle may possibly reflect a Celtic tradition of the Otherworld fortress: "At four points in the wall . . . there were four low towers." [8] It is at least a curious fact that three descriptions of Otherworld castles in Arthurian romance mention the same number of towers. In the *Historia Meriadoci* the island stronghold of Gundebaldus, king of the land whence no man returns, is thus described: "From four sides four little castles protect the island." [9] In *Sone de Nansai* the island castle where the Grail and the Fisher King's body are kept is thus described: "Outside on the wall there are four towers. . . . In the midst of the four was a large one which surpassed all." [10] Another island castle in the same poem is identified as that of Meleagant, and this "had four halls (*palais*) erected at the four corners of the walls." [11] In *Perlesvaus* the island castle of the ageless elders formed a quadrangle, for we read of the four ends (*chies*) of the walls." [12] Of course, one must grant that Chrétien and the other romancers were familiar with quadrangular castles, with or without a central *donjon* or keep. Enlart wrote: "La plupart des châteaux réguliers forment un tracé très répandu chez les Byzantins dès les premiers siècles de notre ère: c'est un rectangle avec tours aux angles, mais dans les châteaux de ce plan l'une des tours est souvent un donjon de diamètre bien supérieur aux autres tours, comme à Dourdan (1229)." [13] Thus Chrétien may have based his description of Gornemant's castle on observation. But the fact remains that other romancers quite independently refer to the four towers or the four corners of certain Otherworld strongholds. Now in the Welsh poem, *The Spoils of Annwn*, attributed by Professor Ifor Williams to a period well before the Norman Conquest, perhaps as early as 900,[14] the abode of the gods is referred to as *Kaer Pedryvan*, "the Four-Cornered Fortress." [15] A strong and cumulative body of evidence proves that this Welsh four-cornered abode of the gods determined the quadrangular shape of the island castles in *Sone, Historia Meriadoci*, and *Perlesvaus*.[16] Conceiva-

---

[8] Vss. 1335–37.   [9] J. D. Bruce, *Historia Meriadoci*, p. 44.
[10] *Sone von Nausay*, ed. M. Goldschmidt (Tübingen, 1899), vss. 4381–84.
[11] *Ibid.*, vss. 17165 f.   [12] *Perlesvaus*, ed. Nitze and others, I, l. 9547, variant of ms. Br (P).
[13] C. Enlart, *Manuel d'archéologie française*, deuxième partie, tome II, *Architecture militaire et navale*, 2d ed. (Paris, 1932), pp. 585 f. Cf. H. Schumacher, *Befestigungswesen in der altfranzösischen Literatur*, pp. 39 f.   [14] *PMLA*, LVI (1941), 887.   [15] *Ibid.*, pp. 889 f.
[16] *Ibid.*, pp. 933–35. In this discussion I made the error of translating *crestiaus* (vss. 4380, 17160) as crystals. As the context proves, this word is simply the plural of *crestel*, *cretel*, meaning battlement. Cf. H. Schumacher, *op. cit.*, p. 43. I still suspect, however, that the lines, "Li mur dessur la roce sont, Qui batillié as crestiaus sont," are a misinterpretation of the tradition found in Ulrich von Zatzikhoven's *Lanzelet*, vss. 209–11, describing the island fortress of maidens: "der berc was ein cristalle, sinewel als ein balle, dar ûf stuont diu burc vast." If this is correct, then both descriptions would go back to the Welsh Kaer Wydyr (Fortress of Glass) approached by sea, and to Nennius' *turris vitrea* on an island. *PMLA*, LVI, 891, 925 f.

bly, though far from certainly, the concept influenced also the description of Gornemant's castle.

Chapter LXVI

BLANCHEFLOR

VERSES 1699-2973

Leaving the castle of Gornemant, Perceval rode on and was admitted to the somewhat ruinous and almost deserted castle of Belrepeire. When he reached the hall, attendants took charge of his horse, and two aged gentlemen and a maiden welcomed him. Her name was Blancheflor; she wore a mantle furred with ermine. Never before or since has God created her equal for beauty; and her people remarked that she was a fitting mate for the handsome Perceval. She told the stranger youth that she was the niece of his late host, Gornemant. After a meager souper, Perceval was escorted to his chamber and slept. But the maiden, after tossing restlessly on her bed, donned a mantle over her shift and knelt by the bedside of Perceval, weeping. He awoke and learned from her lips that her men had been slain and her castle besieged for a year by the army of a rejected suitor, Clamadeu. She had taken this bold course, we learn, to win Perceval as her champion in battle. Perceval comforted her, kissed her, and drew her into bed with him. That night they slept together mouth to mouth, but it would appear that she remained a virgin.[1] The next morning the hero vanquished Anguingeron, the seneschal of Clamadeu, and charged him to yield himself to King Arthur. Later in the same day he destroyed a troop of Clamadeu's knights. The next day he sallied forth to single combat with Clamadeu, and forced him also to surrender himself at Arthur's court. While Clamadeu and

---

[1] Chrétien calls Blancheflor *pucele* after the night in Perceval's bed (vss. 2071, 2080, 2600, 2607, 2911). The word does not seem to be decisive, however, and various constructions have been put on Chrétien's text. The 1530 paraphrase, though it refers to Blancheflor throughout the episode as *pucelle,* nevertheless implies sexual union: "sans cesser de prendre leur soulas" (*Conte del Graal,* ed. Hilka, p. 529). Bruce (*Evolution,* I, 226, n. 6) was of the same opinion. But certain continuators of Chrétien thought of Blancheflor as still a virgin. A ms. of Wauchier, B.N. fr. 12576 (J. L. Weston, *Legend of Perceval,* I, 105, n. 1) represents her relations with Perceval on his second visit as innocent. So does Gerbert in his account of Perceval's last visit (ed. Mary Williams, I), vs. 6561: "du sorplus n'i ot il point;" vss. 6594 f.: "Pucele i coucha voirement, Ensement pucele en leva." *Peredur,* which furnishes a cognate version of the first visit to Belrepeire (Loth, *Mabinogion,* 2d ed., II, 71), represents the chatelaine as chastely retiring to her own bed after Peredur has promised his aid. Wolfram (*Parzival,* 193, 2–193, 14) emphatically asserts the innocence of the pair. Since Gerbert and Wolfram both knew Chrétien's poem and interpreted it in the same way, I believe Bruce was wrong and Wechssler and Wilmotte were right (Wechssler, *Sage vom Heiligen Gral,* p. 63; Wilmotte, *Roman du Gral,* p. 115) in supposing that Chrétien intended to depict his hero as refraining from coitus. Cf. W. Hertz, *Parzival,* 7th ed., pp. 501 f.

Anguingeron departed and brought tidings of Perceval's exploits to the King, the hero remained at Belrepeire with his enamored hostess. But remembering his mother, whom he had left in a swoon at her castle gate, he left the grieving Blancheflor with a promise to return shortly.

THE INVETERATE READER of Arthurian romance does not need to be informed that the deliverance of the castle of Belrepeire and its mistress from the attacks of a formidable and hated suitor follows a banal pattern. We have already had occasion to examine two examples of the pattern;[2] Yvain's rescue of the Lady of Noiroison from Count Alier and Gareth's rescue of Dame Lyones from the Red Knight of the Red Laundes; and we reached the conclusion that both the Lady of Noiroison and Dame Lyones had inherited their roles, in the main, from Morgain la Fée. A scrutiny of the evidence regarding Blancheflor leads to the same conclusion.

1. The generally acknowledged counterpart of Blancheflor in the English *Sir Percyvelle* is Lufamour, queen of Maydenlande;[3] and the Queen of Meydelant in *Lanzelet*, the hero's foster mother, we were able to identify as Morgain.[4] In a later discussion of Chrétien's Roche de Sanguin,[5] inhabited by five hundred maidens and ladies, we shall discover that one of its two queens was Morcades, whose name represents a corruption of Morgain. In fact, there is abundant testimony to Morgain's being the mistress of a land or castle of women. Of course, Chrétien in his description of Blancheflor's household has retained nothing of this except the fact that there are but a few men, and they very feeble, to defend her against her foes. It is Blancheflor's counterpart in *Sir Percyvelle* who, as queen of Maydenlande, suggests her identity with Morgain.

2. Blancheflor's counterpart in *Peredur* confirms this inference, for in a roundabout way she too may be identified with Morgain. She does not seek the hero's bedchamber and offer herself to him of her own accord but does so at the command of her foster-brothers. This situation corresponds in remarkable detail to Malory's story of Gareth's reception by Dame Lyones and her brother in the castle of Avylyon. Let us examine the parallel, taking first the Welsh narrative of Peredur's arrival at the besieged castle of Blancheflor's counterpart.

"The maiden welcomed Peredur, put her arms around his neck, and sat down by her side. . . . Thereupon they went to eat. Peredur noticed that the maiden wished to give him more of the food and drink than to the others. . . . When it was time, a chamber was prepared for Peredur, and he went to sleep. 'Hark, sister,' said the youths [the maiden's foster brothers], . . . 'to what we counsel thee.' 'What is that?' said she. 'It is to go to the chamber above and offer thy-

[2] Cf. *supra*, pp. 296, 304, 309–11.
[3] W. H. French and C. B. Hale, *Middle English Metrical Romances*, pp. 562, 567, 583, 586.
[4] Cf. *supra*, pp. 88 f.   [5] See Chap. LXXVIII.

self to the youth in the way it may please him, either as a wife or as a mistress.'
. . . Fearful, the maiden, shedding tears, went straight to the chamber." [6]

According to Chrétien, Blancheflor was wearing a mantle, and after declaring her errand was easily persuaded to enter Perceval's bed; and he kissed her.

Compare Malory's account of Gareth's reception at Dame Lyones's castle after he has delivered her from siege by the Red Knight of the Red Laundes.

"And thenne came forth Dame Lyones . . . and there she made hym [Gareth] passyng good chere. . . . And forth toward nyghte they yede unto souper, and syre Gareth myghte not ete, for his love was soo hote that he wist not where he was. Alle these lokes aspyed syr Gryngamor [Lyones' brother], and thenne at after souper he callid his syster Dame Lyones unto a chamber and sayd: 'Fair syster, I have wel aspyed your countenaunce betwixe you and this knyght. And I wil, syster, that ye wete he is a ful noble knyght, and yf ye can make hym to abyde here, I wil do hym all the pleasyr that I can . . .' 'Fayre broder,' said Dame Lyones, '. . . I am moost beholdyng to hym of ony erthely man, for he hath had grete labour for my love and passid many a daungerous passage. . . .' At after souper was made clene avoydaunce, that every lord and lady shold goo unto his rest . . . and so there were ordeyned grete couches & theron fether beddes, & there leyde hym doune to slepe, & within a whyle cam Dame Lyones, wrapped in a mantel furred with ermyne, & leid her doun besydes Syr Gareth. And there with alle he beganne to kysse her." [7]

The parallel between Blancheflor's reception of Perceval and her visit to his bed, as told by Chrétien and the Welsh author, and Lyones' reception of Gareth and her visit to his bed, as told by Malory, is so close as to warrant the belief that both narratives repose on the same base. The differences are easily accounted for. Malory, doubtless following his immediate source, awkwardly transposed the visit to the besieged castle until after Gareth has raised the siege, and consequently the motivation of Lyones is different from that of Blancheflor in visiting the hero's bed, and so too the hero's experiences during the night are radically changed. Nevertheless, the essential resemblance in the two situations, as sketched above, remains. Since Dame Lyones derived her story in large measure from Morgain, we have an added reason for equating Blancheflor with the famous queen of the isle of maidens.

3. A third reason for suspecting that Blancheflor was originally the Lady of Lothian, Morgain, is found in Guillaume le Clerc's romance of *Fergus,* composed in the first quarter of the thirteenth century. Here the heroine, Galiene, is again and again identified as "la dame de Lodien." [8] Again and

<hr/>

[6] Loth, *op. cit.,* II, 68 f.   [7] Malory, *Morte d'Arthur,* ed. H. O. Sommer, I, 246 f.
[8] Guillaume le Clerc, *Fergus,* ed. E. Martin, pp. 119 f., 180, 186. For the name Galiene cf. *Miscellany of Studies in Romance Languages and Literatures in Honour of L. E. Kastner,* p. 94, n. 2.

again her story parallels that of Dame Lyones,[9] though the sequence of events is different. The hero, Fergus, is, like Gareth, a youth who comes to Arthur's court and is knighted by the King and ridiculed by Ke. He rides away to the castle where "la dame de Lodien" is staying with her uncle, and is welcomed. During supper she falls violently in love with her guest. Clad only in a shift and mantle, she goes to his bedside by night with amorous intent. Later, when she is besieged in her castle of Roxburgh (Roceborc) in Lothian, Fergus delivers her, having been summoned to the task by her maiden messenger. Arthur, at Cardoil, receives the submission of knights whom Fergus has vanquished, and becomes alarmed at his long absence. He is persuaded to proclaim a tournament at Jedburgh (Gedeorde) as a means of attracting the youth. The ruse is successful, and before a great assembly of Arthur's court Fergus, incognito, displays his prowess. Finally, the Lady of Lothian arrives and asks the King to bestow her on the victor. After consulting the wishes of Fergus, who is more than willing, Arthur approves the marriage, and the nuptials are celebrated at a great festival.

Patently, the stories of the winning of Dame Lyones and of "la dame de Lodien" are variations on the same basic pattern, just as the story of Laudine, daughter of the Duke of Lothian represents still another. Guillaume le Clerc must have known some form of this *conte* of the Lady of Lothian. Being familiar with southern and eastern Scotland and being interested in the descendants of a historic Fergus, chief of Galloway, as Professor Schlauch and Dr. Brugger have amply proved,[10] Guillaume cannily gave a local habitation and a name to the vague and impossible geography of his source. For his incidents, then, Guillaume was following established tradition, and this is significant for the Blancheflor episode because Chrétien's account of Blancheflor's nocturnal visit to Perceval's bed finds a parallel not only in the story of Dame Lyones, but also in that of "la dame de Lodien." Though the latter retains nothing of the supernatural, her prototype must be the same as that of Dame Lyones—Morgain. And thus we are led once more to the conclusion that Blancheflor's story is modeled on the well-known theme of Morgain's amorous overtures to her guests.

4. A fourth argument in favor of Blancheflor's derivation from Morgain lies in the fact that Perceval left her a virgin. Chrétien repeatedly refers to her as "pucele," even after she had spent the night in the youth's embrace; and Wolfram, *Peredur,* Wauchier, and Gerbert de Montreuil are clear as to the restrained relations between the pair, at least on the first night.[11] Now this looks like an adaptation to Perceval's established character as an innocent abroad of the recurrent motif that Morgain's lustful advances

[9] Cf. *supra,* pp. 115 f.   [10] *Miscellany of Studies,* pp. 94–107; *PMLA,* XLIV, 360–76.
[11] Cf. *supra,* p. 363, n. 1.

were met with coldness. Hector of Troy, Tristan, Alisandre l'Orphelin, all spurned her; Lancelot almost made a habit of it.[12] Particularly significant for us is Lancelot's chaste behavior in the castle of the amorous hostess as related in the *Charrette,* for though she is not named, our study of the incident revealed that she is modeled after Morgain.[13] The interruption of Lancelot's assignation by men armed with axes, we saw, paralleled the interruption of Gareth's assignation with Lyones by a knight armed with a gysarme, and the interruption of Gauvain's love-making with the King of Cavalon's sister by *vilains* equipped with axes and *jusarmes;* and both Lyones and the King of Cavalon's sister are identifiable as Morgain. Moreover, Lancelot's turning his back on the amorous chatelaine resembled strikingly Pwyll's chaste behavior in the bed of Arawn's wife; and we have often had occasion to remark that Arawn's wife was Modron, Morgain's welsh prototype. In fact, there seems little reason to doubt that the eleventh-century mabinogi of *Pwyll* contains the root of the whole tradition that Morgain's overtures toward her handsome guests were met by coldness.

Few phenomena in the shaping of romance, one may add, are more interesting and significant than the adaptation of this fixed formula to the character and the circumstances of the particular guest. Pwyll's conduct is motivated by his oath of friendship to Arawn, Lancelot's by his fidelity to Guenievre, Alisandre's by repugnance for Morgain's ugliness. In the famous temptation scenes in *Gawain and the Green Knight,* which several years ago I showed were based on Pwyll's behavior with Arawn's wife,[14] Gawain is motivated by knightly honor and Christian virtue. In each instance there has been a realistic effort to fit the stereotyped action to the established character of the actor, and to provide the most plausible motive. It therefore seems most probable that Perceval's failure to take full advantage of his *bonne fortune* was to be explained, as indeed Wolfram explains it,[15] by his most prominent characteristic at this stage in his development, namely, boyish ignorance. When the Grail legend acquired a sacred character, drastic changes of course had to be made, and Perceval, as the successful seeker and ultimate guardian of the Grail, underwent a thorough metamorphosis. Gerbert de Montreuil has him leave Blancheflor a virgin even after their marriage, and both in *Perlesvaus* and *La Queste del Saint Graal* he is a maiden knight, another Galaad. His motivation is now Christian asceticism. We may thus regard Perceval's failure to consummate his union with Blancheflor as a heritage from the powerful tradition that Modron and Morgain were treated with coldness by their princely guests, for this interpretation accords with the ample evidence that Morgain was the immediate prototype of Blancheflor.

[12] *Speculum*, XX (1945), pp. 183–86.   [13] Chap. XXXVI.
[14] *Journ. of Eng. and Germ. Phil.*, XLII (1943), 170–78.   [15] *Parzival*, 193, 8–193, 14.

5. This hypothesis derives further support from the fact that Perceval, after delivering Blancheflor from siege by an unwelcome suitor and after receiving her offer of marriage and of lordship over her dominions, abandons her. "He leaves his lovely *amie* very angry and very sorrowful." This desertion and Perceval's subsequent conduct toward Blancheflor are utterly unworthy of a gallant gentleman, a chivalric hero,[16] and yet, strangely enough, Chrétien neglects every opportunity to reproach him for it. Evidently this is one of those many cases where the inexplicable can be explained by tradition, and the tradition was one attached to Morgain. In fact, Perceval's rescue of Blancheflor from Clamadeu corresponds closely, as we have noted, to Yvain's rescue of the Lady of Noiroison from Alier; Yvain, too, after receiving the lady's offer of herself and her lands, rejected them and left her very angry. And the Lady of Noiroison, we know, was modeled after Morgain.[17]

Altogether, then, five lines of evidence lead to the conclusion that Morgain was the chief prototype of Blancheflor.

But in the course of our investigations we have seen that the formula of the deliverance of a besieged chatelaine from the assaults of an unwelcome suitor was affected by other legends than those of Morgain. Gareth's deliverance of Dame Lyones from the Red Knight of the Red Laundes, for instance, was in considerable part derived from the Irish *Sickbed of Cuchulainn;* and though Lyones inherited much from Morgain, she also inherited much from Fand.[18] In fact, if it were possible to recover the Morgain legend in an early stage of its development, we should probably see obvious borrowings from the Irish saga. Still clearly discernible in the story of Lyones, they can also be detected in the Blancheflor episode.

Let us note certain significant parallels between the *Sickbed*[19] on the one hand and the Perceval and Peredur romances on the other.

[16] Weston, *Legend of Perceval*, I, 106. "For cool cynicism it must be admitted that the immaculate Perceval could give points to the much maligned Gawain; it would require the ready wit and sharp tongue of an Orgueilleuse de Logres to deal effectively with so evasive a lover."

[17] In many ways the Blancheflor episode corresponds to Guinglain's affair with the Pucele as Blances Mains in Renaud de Beaujeu's *Le Bel Inconnu* (ed. G. P. Williams, 1929), vss. 1874–2484. Both narratives contain the hero's arrival at a castle, his deliverance of the chatelaine from a hated suitor, her desire to reward the hero with her hand and her domains, her nocturnal visit to the hero's bedchamber, her retirement without satisfying the hero's desires, his desertion of her. Twice we are told that this damsel was skilled in magic arts (vss. 1933–35, 4932–47); once she is depicted as the mistress of a faery cavalcade, with sparrow hawk on fist (vss. 3936–94). She resembles Lanzelet's foster mother, the Queen of Meydelant, in several respects: her abode in the Ile d'Or, "qui siet sor mer" (vs. 3935), her watching over his destiny, and her revealing to him his name (vss. 4961–5008). Since we know that the Queen of Meydelant was Morgain, everything points to Morgain as the original of the Pucele as Blances Mains. On this lady cf. Schofield, *Studies on the Libeaus Desconus*, pp. 36–41, 54 f., 197–99; L. A. Paton, *Fairy Mythology*, pp. 172–76.   [18] Cf. *supra*, pp. 296 f.

[19] D'Arbois de Jubainville, *L'Epopée celtique en Irlande*, pp. 181–208. *Serglige Con Culainn*, ed. M. Dillon, pp. 32, 40–46.

Fand's brother-in-law, Labraid, sent a message to Cuchulainn, offering him Fand as his mistress if he would fight against Labraid's three enemies. "He [Labraid] will give the woman to thee for one day's fighting with him against Senach Siabortha and Eochaid Iuil and Eogan Inbir." After some delays, Cuchulainn was told to hasten, for the battle was to be fought that very day. He arrived at Labraid's isle and was warmly welcomed, especially by Fand. He first slew Eochaid, then Senach, then Eogan. Fand sang a chant in his praise and spent the night with him. But though Cuchulainn stayed with her for a month, he left her then forever.

Compare this with what we find in the Peredur–Perceval story. (1) The foster-brothers of the beautiful chatelaine urged her to offer herself to Peredur as wife or mistress, and she did so in order to secure him as their defender. (2) Perceval was welcomed by the chatelaine and spent several nights with her. (3) Peredur overcame successively three enemies of the chatelaine.[20] (4) Perceval left the chatelaine.

Though the correspondences are not many and not very precise, they must be regarded seriously because of the other evidence connecting the Irish saga with the Arthurian formula of the deliverance of a besieged chatelaine. It is most probable, then, that the story of Fand blended with that of Modron to produce the Blancheflor episode. Moreover, it is easy to perceive why the blend took place since there is a fundamental similarity between the story of Fand in the *Sickbed* and the story of Arawn's wife, Modron, in *Pwyll*.[21] In both narratives a supernatural personage (Labraid, Arawn) sought the aid of a mortal (Cuchulainn, Pwyll[22]) in combat against his foes. As Labraid offered Cuchulainn his sister-in-law Fand, so Arawn said to Pwyll: "I will give thee to sleep with thee each night the most beautiful woman whom thou hast ever seen." Both Cuchulainn and Pwyll accepted the invitation, went to the beautiful Otherworld palace, were welcomed by the beautiful and amorous hostess, and shared her bed. Both Cuchulainn and Pwyll overcame the foes of their supernatural hosts. In view of these similarities, is it any wonder that the two stories tended to coalesce, and that we find traces of both in Malory's romance of Lyones and in Chrétien's account of Blancheflor?

There is reason to suspect that another famous Irish saga has left a slight trace on the Blancheflor episode. Lancelot's nocturnal assignation with

---

[20] Loth, *Mabinogion*, 2d ed., II, 71–73.

[21] *Ibid.*, I, 84–89. The similarity was observed by Rhys in *Lectures on the Origin and Growth of Religion*, 2d ed., pp. 337–42.

[22] There is some reason to suppose that Cuchulainn and Pwyll were originally immortals. On Cuchulainn cf. R. S. Loomis, *Celtic Myth*, pp. 47–49. Pwyll may well have enjoyed the title Chief of Annwn (Loth, *op. cit.*, I, 92), not, as the mabinogi asserts, because of his temporary reign over that land, but because he was really a divine person. However this may be, both Cuchulainn and Pwyll are thought of in these tales as mortals. On Pwyll's fighting on behalf of Arawn and assuming his shape, cf. Gruffydd in *Transactions of the Hon. Soc. of Cymmrodorion*, 1912–13, pp. 72–80.

the amorous chatelaine in the *Charrette,* we remember,[23] was interrupted by men armed with axes; Gareth's nocturnal assignation with Lyones was interrupted by a knight with a gysarme; Gauvain's love-making with the King of Cavalon's sister was interrupted by *vilains* equipped with axes and *jusarmes.* Our study of this motif in connection with the first example revealed that it represented the fusion of the Morgain tradition with the Irish complex of traditions centering about Cuchulainn, Curoi, and Blathnat. As I pointed out, it seems most probable that when Cuchulainn visited Curoi's revolving fortress and was attacked by Curoi by night, the hospitality of Cuchulainn's hostess and former mistress, Blathnat, had extended considerably beyond the provision of refreshing drinks and good beds. Zimmer and Miss Buchanan had both inferred the existence of a love scene between Cuchulainn and Blathnat which had been expunged by the author of *Bricriu's Feast.*[24]

This inference is corroborated by three medieval romances. Be it remembered that the name Blathnat means "Little Flower," [25] and that every night while Cuchulainn was entertained by Blathnat, the fortress revolved.[26] In *Le Livre d'Artus,*[27] the damsel Floree, enamored of her guest Gauvain, came attired only in a chemise and *surcot* and knelt, like Blancheflor, at her beloved's bedside at night. She warned him against certain enemies of his, and Gauvain's response to her seductive behavior was, like Perceval's, to embrace and kiss her, though, unlike Perceval, he did not stop at that point. The romance of *Artus de la Petite Bretagne,* we have also observed,[28] contains a long episode undeniably based on Cuchulainn's visit to Curoi's fortress; and here Queen Florence, mistress of a turning castle, provided for the entertainment of the hero, and her exact double, the fay Proserpine, appeared at his bedside by night. It would seem that the author substituted Proserpine for Florence to avoid compromising his heroine's virtue, and that in an earlier version Florence herself, like Floree and Blancheflor, shared the hero's couch. A cognate Arthurian story, incorporated in the German *Wolfdietrich,*[29] presents us with a beautiful enchantress who likewise visited the hero's chamber by night and vainly endeavored to seduce him. She too discloses her kinship with Blathnat by dwelling in a revolving fortress. Though the Blancheflor episode retains no telltale feature, such as the interruption by men with axes or the revolving castle, it is more than possible that the heroine was given her floral name because of her kinship to Blathnat, Floree, and Florence.[30]

[23] Cf. Chap. XXXVI.

[24] *Sitzungsberichte der Königlichen Preussischen Akademie der Wissenschaften,* phil.-hist. Kl., IX (1911), 174. *PMLA,* XLVII (1932), 315–38.

[25] Thurneysen, *Irische Helden- und Königsage,* p. 436.   [26] *Ibid.,* p. 458, n. 3.

[27] Sommer, *Vulgate Version,* VII, 108–10.   [28] Cf. *supra,* pp. 206 f.

[29] A. Amelung, O. Jänicke, *Deutsches Heldenbuch* (Berlin, 1871), III, 154–57. *PMLA,* XLVIII (1933), 1010 f.

[30] The name Blancheflor was doubtless already familiar in literature. Cf. J. Reinhold, *Floire et*

Thus the same keys which unlock the problem of Lyones' complex personality and role, unlock those of Blancheflor. Morgain certainly, Fand very probably, and Blathnat less probably were the ancestresses of the lady of Belrepeire.[31]

Chapter LXVII

THE ADVENTURE OF THE GRAIL

THE ADVENTURES at the Grail Castle exercised a potent fascination over the minds of our ancestors. Chrétien in giving a title to his poem ignored the other romantic and thrilling incidents in his nine thousand lines and called it simply "li Contes del Graal." His continuators returned again and again to the theme, multiplying the scenes at the Grail castle. Wolfram von Eschenbach and Heinrich von dem Türlin added their accounts of the mysterious vessel. It became the subject of pious fiction on a grandiose scale, culminating in *Perlesvaus,* the *Vulgate Estoire* and *Queste.* There must have been an immense curiosity on the subject to inspire a literature so prolific.

The literature of the Grail amazes us not only by its bulk but also by its inconsistency. No Grail romancer agrees with any other and each not infrequently contradicts himself. We have a variety of heroes—Perceval, Gauvain, Bohort, Galaad; a variety of names for the maimed or languishing keeper of the Grail—Bron, Anfortas, Pellinor, even Joseph of Arimathea. The Grail itself is variously conceived, and in *Perlesvaus* is said to assume five different forms. Various causes are alleged for the desolation of the land. Besides the numerous visits to the castle where the Grail is specifically mentioned and the Maimed King is easily identified, there are, as we have seen, other episodes in which we have merely an anonymous tall knight, lying wounded on a bed and fed by a maiden from a hanap, or

---

Blancheflor (Paris, 1906), pp. 9-11; Thomas, *Tristan,* ed. J. Bédier, II, 124; R. K. Bowman, *Connections of the Geste des Lorrains with Other French Epics and Mediaeval Genres* (New York, 1940), p. 159. The name of Blancheflor's hated suitor, Clamadeu (vs. 2005, ms. C, Clamados), as I tried to show in *PMLA,* XLVIII, 1031-33, may be derived also from the Blathnat tradition. As Dr. Brugger suggested in *Zts. f. franz. Sprache u. Lit.,* XLIX (1927), 453, n. 1, the form seems to be due to folk etymology.

[31] A further hint that Blancheflor derived elements in her story from Morgain lies in the fact that, according to the *Enfances Gauvain,* Arthur's sister and Gauvain's mother, named Morcades (who, of course, is Morgain), retired with a *pucele* to a castle called Bel Repaire. Cf. J. D. Bruce, *Historia Meriadoci and De Ortu Walwanii,* p. xlv; *Romania,* XXXIX (1910), 25, vs. 254. Another curious link between Blancheflor and Morgain lies in the fact that one ms. of the *Conte del Graal* gives the reading Belissant in vs. 2912 (cf. Hilka's edition) instead of Blancheflor, whereas the Middle English *Arthour and Merlin* calls Lot's wife and Gawain's mother Belisant instead of Morcades or Morgause. Cf. L. A. Paton, *Fairy Mythology,* p. 138.

in which a sick king awaits the coming of a knight to heal him. There is no one authentic Grail legend but a multitude of Grail legends, each a medley of incoherent motifs.

The bewildering diversity and inconsistency of the tradition have perplexed modern scholars and have led to the most diverse and irreconcilable answers to the riddle of its origin and meaning. Germanic, Persian, Egyptian sources have been proposed. Miss Weston found a clue in the cult of Adonis, Burdach in the relics and ritual of the Byzantine church. Even those who have contended for Celtic origin have offered the most incompatible arguments and some of the feeblest evidence. There is much in my own *Celtic Myth and Arthurian Romance* on the subject of the Grail which I would recant.

Nevertheless, an unbiased examination should lead to two basic inferences about this mysterious legend. (1) A tradition which, from its first appearance in literature to the last, forms an integral part of the Arthurian cycle has a strong claim to be Celtic. (2) A tradition which on its first appearance in Chrétien's *Conte del Graal* violates the most elementary proprieties of Christian ethics and ritual could not have originated in a pious fabrication. Perceval came from his amorous, if not immoral, affair with Blancheflor directly to the Grail castle; he saw a beautiful damsel pass repeatedly through the hall from one chamber to another, bearing a jewel-decked vessel; obedient to Gornemant's warning against talkativeness, he failed to ask the question, "Whom does one serve with the Grail?"; for this reason the Fisher King remained unhealed of his wound and great calamity lay in store for Perceval and others. Does this sound like a work of pious edification? Would a holy relic or even a common paten or ciborium have been placed in charge of a lovely damsel, not of a priest or a sacristan? What conceivable moral lesson is conveyed by the failure of Perceval to meet the question test? What meaning has the question itself? No wonder the Church has never recognized the Grail romances as authentic and has displayed a shrewd suspicion of their unorthodox background. We have every right to assume that the clues to these mysteries lie in the same body of Irish and Welsh myth and hero tale which has provided answers to the other riddles of Arthurian romance.

As we study the experiences of Perceval at the Grail castle and their sequel, many features will reveal at once their connections with Celtic literature and will offer little difficulty in interpretation. Even the most perplexing problems will yield up their secret, if we keep in mind the basic analysis of the Grail legend offered by Nutt, which has already proved useful in explaining the duplication of Bran as Perceval's father and the Fisher King. We have here a fusion of two themes, the Feud or Vengeance Quest and the Unspelling Quest. When the hero is presented with a broken sword or gazes on the body or the severed head of a kinsman, these are reminders of his duty to avenge that kinsman's death. When he sees the king of a Waste Land lying wounded between the thighs, when he sees the Grail pass before him and hesitates to ask the momentous question, he is failing to heal his royal kinsman and disenchant his land. A certain resemblance between these situations brought about their fusion, not once but many times and in various ways. Accordingly one finds traces of both these formulae in all the visits to the Grail castle, and only by keeping them distinct can we begin to understand Chrétien's narrative of the events within the castle of the "riche roi Pescheor." Other subsidiary motifs from Celtic tradition have been absorbed into this narrative, but these two themes have furnished the basic patterns.

For reasons already set forth the Feud Quest is not represented in the story of Pryderi as it survives in the *Four Branches*. Certain elements in the Unspelling Quest may be recognized in *Branwen* and *Manawydan*— the wounding of King Bran in the foot, the subsequent wasting of two lands, the enchantment of Dyved and its disenchantment; but the treatment of these themes by the Welsh author diverges so widely from that in the French romances that it is no wonder that scholarly opinion has remained unconvinced of the relationship. Nevertheless, the case for Pryderi as the prototype of Perceval is so strong, and the original identity of King Bran and the Fisher King, accepted by Heinrich, Martin, Nutt, Rhys, Brown, Anwyl, Professor Nitze, and Miss Kempe, has been so powerfully supported by Professor Newstead that one can only conclude that the Unspelling Quest must once have been told of Pryderi and Bran in a form resembling that in the less pious Grail romances. And this conclusion is corroborated by the number of subsidiary features we are about to consider which can be traced back to Wales. Furthermore, what is not available in the scanty remains of Welsh can be discovered in Irish saga and folktale. Ireland is the ultimate source of the vengeance theme and of several prominent and perplexing elements in the visit to the Grail Castle, such as the question test. To reach Chrétien they must have followed the usual route through Wales. The Grail legend is a Celtic heritage.

Let us first consider the Unspelling Quest.

Chapter LXVIII
THE UNSPELLING QUEST

VERSES 2974-3592, 4652-83

After deserting Blancheflor, Perceval came to a river. He asked two men in a boat, one of whom was fishing, where he could find harborage. The fisherman invited Perceval to his own house, which he said would be visible from the top of a rock near by. Perceval rode as directed to the summit, but, seeing nothing, cursed the fisherman as a deceiver. Hardly had he done so when he descried below a castle fairer than any this side of Beirut. He entered the gate, was attended by youths, and led into a spacious square hall. In the midst a grizzled man in purple and sable robes lay on a couch. Before him was a fireplace, and four brass pillars supported the hood. Four hundred men could be seated around it. The noble host invited Perceval to sit beside him and presented him with a sword. A youth emerged from a chamber, grasping a lance, from the point of which a drop of blood flowed down. He was followed by two youths carrying golden candelabra, and by a beautiful damsel, holding a graal in her hands. It radiated a brilliant light and was encrusted with many precious stones. The Grail Bearer was followed by a damsel with a silver tailleor (carving platter). The little procession passed before Perceval and his host and out of the hall into another chamber. Restrained by Gornemant's counsel not to be too talkative, Perceval was silent and dared not ask whom one served with the Grail. A luxurious repast was served in the hall, and at each course the Grail was brought in, but still Perceval refrained from asking whom one served with it. After the meal, spices and wine followed. The host was then carried out by servants to his chamber, and Perceval was made comfortable for the night in the hall. In the morning he saw no one, and no one answered to his call. Finding his horse saddled and hoping to find someone outside the castle who could tell him about the lance and the Grail, he rode out over the drawbridge. As he did so, the bridge rose into the air and only by a powerful spring did his horse clear the moat and land on the further bank. He came on a damsel sitting under a tree beside the headless body of her lover. From her Perceval learned that his host of the night before was called the rich King Fisherman, and that he had been maimed in battle by a javelin-thrust between the thighs. Unable to hunt, he took his diversion in fishing. When the damsel discovered that Perceval had not asked about the strange procession, she reproached him bitterly, for, if he had in-

quired, the Fisher King would have regained the use of his limbs and great good would have come of it. Some time later, the Loathly Damsel appeared at Arthur's court and likewise reproached Perceval for his silence at the Fisher King's castle; if he had inquired concerning the lance and Grail, the King would have been healed; as it was, knights would be slain and lands ruined.

IN DISENTANGLING the complicated snarl of threads which constitutes the adventures of Perceval at the Grail Castle, it may clarify matters to take the Irish threads first, and then the Welsh.

To anyone familiar with the interior arrangements of a French castle of the Romanesque period as revealed by archaeology, the Fisher King's hall must seem strange. Instead of being seated at a long table on a dais at the end of the hall, the Fisher King lies on a couch before a fireplace in the middle of the hall. Four brass columns support the hood (*cheminal*).[1] Four hundred men could be accommodated around the fire. All this is quite unlike anything Chrétien would have seen in twelfth-century France. But Professor Nitze has pointed out that these features are strongly reminiscent of the banquet hall in the royal palace of Connaught at Cruachan, of which we have two descriptions, one in *Bricriu's Feast* and the other in *The Cattle Raid of Fraech*.[2] It is important to note that the ancient Irish, when at their meals, were accustomed to sit on couches (*imdada*). Both texts agree that the royal couch of Ailill and Medb was in the center of the hall, and that there were seven rows of couches between the fire and the wall all around; from which one infers that the fire likewise was in the middle. The Fraech version says that "four pillars of copper were over the bed of Ailill and Medb." The other version adds: "Such was the spaciousness of the house that it had room for the hosts of valiant heroes of the whole province in the suite of Conchobar." Thus Chrétien's description of the Fisher King's hall corresponds in four respects to the royal hall of Cruachan: a central fireplace; a royal couch before it; four pillars of brass; and space for a large company. It seems probable that the descriptive formula which we find in Irish sagas as early as the eighth century would not have been greatly altered in passing through Wales, where we may assume similar architecture and custom to prevail. Once crystallized, the formula would be transmitted to the Breton *conteurs* and so to Chrétien.

The circumstances of Perceval's visit to the Grail castle bear a sugges-

[1] A *cheminal* seems to be the hood of a fireplace, supported by small columns and, in the twelfth century, normally set against the wall. Cf. *Mediaeval England*, ed. H. W. C. Davis (Oxford, 1924), Fig. 349; Enlart, *Manuel d'archéologie française*, 2d ed., *Archit. civ.*, pp. 147-53.

[2] *Studies in Honor of A. M. Elliott* (Baltimore, 1911), I, 19-51. *Etudes celtiques*, II (1937), 3. *Feast of Bricriu*, ed. G. Henderson, pp. 69, 71. Henderson mistranslates *imda* as "apartment," when it means "couch." Cf. *Elliott Studies*, I, 35.

tive likeness to those of King Conn's visit to the dwelling of the god Lug, as narrated in *The Prophetic Ecstasy of the Phantom* (earlier than 1056).[3]

Lug mac Ethnen appeared as a horseman at Tara and called Conn to his abode. When Conn arrived in response to the invitation, he found his host already arrived before him, seated on a throne. A crowned damsel, the Sovranty of Erin (Ireland), gave Conn huge portions of meat, and then asked of Lug, "To whom shall this cup be given?" "Pour it," said Lug, "for Conn." The damsel served Conn, and then, repeating the question, she was instructed by the prophetic phantom, Lug, to fill it for each of Conn's royal descendants, who are named in succession. Finally the house and Lug vanished and Conn was left with the cup and other vessels.

This narrative belongs to a type known as *echtra,* relating the visit of a mortal to the palace of a god. The ending is strikingly similar to the ending of one example of the type, *The Adventures of Cormac in the Land of Promise,* for Cormac, Conn's grandson, after a visit to the palace of Manannan, found himself on the green at Tara with a testing cup given him by the god. Evidently the formula of the *echtra* was adapted to different purposes, to furnish a prophetic list of kings or to explain the origin of a testing cup.

Now two examples of the *echtra, The Adventures of Cormac* and *The Adventures of Art Son of Conn,* have been shown to contain marked parallels to versions of the visit to the Grail Castle.[4] And it is therefore highly significant that, though *The Prophetic Ecstasy of the Phantom* is utterly dissimilar from Chrétien's account of Perceval's visit to the Grail Castle in its purpose and outcome, there are some obvious parallels and some demonstrable connections. Both contain the supernatural host who invites the hero to his abode and mysteriously arrives before him, the maiden who repeatedly serves with her vessel, and the disappearance of the host. The repeated question of the maiden must awake an echo in the mind of every reader of the Grail romances. For the form of the question asked by the Sovranty of Erin, "To whom shall this cup be given?" comes close to that question which Perceval failed to ask, "Whom does one serve with the Grail?" [5] It is most important to note that whereas Perceval's question has no conceivable relation to the healing of the Fisher King and the res-

---

[3] For bibliography, summary, and partial translation cf. A. C. L. Brown, *Origin of the Grail Legend,* pp. 218–20. Brown's translation is not too accurate; *con-gart* means "called," not "took," *scal* means "phantom, supernatural being," not "shadow." The form of the question given above is translated from ms. Harley 5280 (*Zts. f. celt. Phil.,* III, 460): "cia da tiberthar an airdeoch sa?" On this saga cf. H. M. and N. K. Chadwick, *Growth of Literature,* I, 455 f., 462 f.

[4] *Romanische Forschungen,* XLV (1931), 71–94. *Speculum,* VIII, 423 f.

[5] Vss. 3292 f.: "Et li vaslez ne demanda/ Del graal cui l'an an servoit." Vss. 4659 ff.: " 'Et del graal que tu veis/ Ne demandas ne n'anqueis/ Quel riche home l'an an servoit.' " Cf. *Didot-Perceval,* ed. W. Roach, p. 151: "quant il avra demandé que on en fait et cui on en sert de cel Graal."

toration of his land, as Chrétien would have us suppose that it did, the question asked by the Sovranty and answered by Lug does have meaning and sense. The natural inference is that the Irish text preserves the question in its original context, and that in the French Grail romances the question has been placed in an alien setting, so that the question which the Sovranty did repeatedly ask became the question which Perceval failed to ask. Hence arose much of the mystification concerning the Grail and much vain speculation on the part of modern scholars.

This inference is strengthened by the fact that the Sovranty of Erin appears in several Irish tales as a hideous hag, later transformed into a glorious beauty, and so in *Peredur* and *Perlesvaus* does the Grail Bearer appear in both lovely and loathly forms.[6] In fact, the description of the Sovranty of Erin in the eleventh-century *Adventures of the Sons of Eochaid Mugmedon* startles us with its resemblance to the portrait in *Peredur* of the black maiden, one of the forms assumed by the bearer of the *dysgl*, or Grail. The Welsh text may be thus translated: "Her face and her two hands were blacker than the blackest iron dipped in pitch; . . . one eye was mottled gray and glittering, and the other black as jet; . . . her teeth were long and yellow. . . . Her thighs were broad and bony, and below all was thin, except her feet and knees which were plump."[7] Compare this with the Irish description of the Sovranty of Erin: "Thus was the hag: every joint and limb of her, from the top of her head to the earth, was as black as coal. . . . The green branch of an oak in bearing would be severed by the sickle of green teeth that lay in her head and reached to her ears. Dark smoky eyes she had. . . . Her ankles were thick, her shoulder blades were broad, her knees were big."[8] This confrontation should suffice to prove that the Grail Bearer inherited certain roles from the Sovranty of Erin: her appearance to the hero in beauteous aspect in the palace of a hospitable host, her function of serving with a precious vessel, and her transformation into a hideous hag.

It is not hard to discern the essential nature of the Sovranty of Erin. She is the bride of Lug, and annually their wedding was celebrated at the feast and the games of the Lugnasad about the first of August at Teltown. Rhys quoted from a manuscript belonging to the Royal Irish Academy a ref-

[6] Loth, *Mabinogion*, 2d ed., II, 119 f. The youth declares that he is identical with the black maiden at Arthur's court and with one of the maidens who appeared with the head in a platter (*dyscyl = graal*). Cf. *ibid.*, pp. 65, 103 f. *Perlesvaus*, ed. W. A. Nitze and T. A. Jenkins, I, ll. 600 f., 647–49, 1404–11. Though *Perlesvaus* does not record that the bearer of the Grail in the Fisher King's castle was beautiful, yet that is the prevailing tradition. Her appearance as a reproachful messenger at Arthur's court identifies her with the Loathly Damsel of Chrétien, as does the fact that she "n'estoit pas molt bele de vis," and was bald.

[7] Loth, *Mabinogion*, 2d ed., II, 103 f.

[8] T. P. Cross and C. H. Slover, *Ancient Irish Tales*, pp. 510 f. *Revue celt.*, XXIV, 197. On the stories of the transformation of the Sovranty of Erin cf. H. Maynadier, *The Wife of Bath's Tale* (London, 1901); R. S. Loomis, *Celtic Myth*, pp. 298–300; *Eriu*, XIV (1943), 14–21; *Revue celt.*, I, 48 f.

erence to a place called Taillne, which must be a corrupt form of Taillten (Teltown): "It is here that Lug Scimaig proceeded to make a great feast for Lug mac Ethlenn for his entertainment after the battle of Mag Tured; for this was his wedding of the kingship, since the Tuatha De Danann made the aforesaid Lug king after the death of Nuada." [9] Rhys assembled some evidence to show that this feast must be the Lugnasad, and that the original meaning of *nasad* was marriage. Since Lug is quite generally regarded as a sun-god,[10] and since Mac Greine, "the son of the sun," was married to the goddess Eriu,[11] a personification of Ireland itself, it is a natural inference that the Lugnasad celebrated the mating of the sun-god with the land of Ireland.

This would explain why we have several versions of the transformation of the Sovranty of Erin from a creature of preternatural ugliness to one of glorious beauty through union with one of the destined kings of Ireland —kings who partook of the solar nature of their divine ancestors.[12] For there are suggestions in these stories that the Sovranty in her hideous form was the bleak, wintry land of Ireland, which was transformed by the sun into flowery loveliness. Before her metamorphosis, "a rugged, hilly, thick block head was upon her, like a furzy mountain;"[13] and "as it were a flash(?) from a mountainside in the month of March . . . even so blazed her bitter eyes."[14] After her union with the prince, the radiance of her face seemed like "the sun rising in the month of May," "her fragrance was likened unto an odorous herb garden,"[15] "blooming her countenance in hue as the crimson lichen of Leinster crags . . . her locks were like Bregon's buttercups; a mantle about her, matchless, green."[16] Here is ample justification for the view that Eriu was the green land of Ireland in mythological form. To quote Professor O'Rahilly: "The idea that Ireland is a goddess, and is wedded to the king of the country, is of hoary antiquity; yet it has preserved its vitality down, one might almost say, to our own day. It has its roots in the time when men regarded the material earth as a Mother, and when the ruler of the land was inaugurated with a ceremony which professed to espouse him to this divine mother, with the intent that his reign might be prosperous and that the earth might produce her fruits in abundance."[17]

When gods and their stories were no longer tolerated as such, Lug was obliged, as in *The Prophetic Ecstasy*,[18] to declare himself a son of Adam,

---

[9] J. Rhys, *Lectures on the Origin and Growth of Religion*, pp. 414 f.
[10] *Ibid.*, pp. 396 f.; R. S. Loomis, *op. cit.*, p. 46. J. A. MacCulloch, *Religion of the Ancient Celts*, pp. 89, 91. *Revue archéologique*, ser. 5, XXXIII (1931), 105. E. Hull, *Text Book of Irish Literature* (London, 1910), I, 14.
[11] *Lebor Gabala Erenn*, ed. R. A. S. Macalister, IV (1941), 195.   [12] Cf. *supra*, n. 8.
[13] *Miscellany of the Celtic Soc.*, 1849, 69–75. *Metrical Dinnshenchas*, ed. E. Gwynn, IV, 135 f.
[14] *Eriu*, IV (1910), 103.   [15] *Irische Texte*, III, ii, 319–23.   [16] *Eriu*, IV, 105.
[17] *Eriu*, XIV, 21.
[18] R. S. Loomis, *Celtic Myth*, p. 221. E. O'Curry, *Lectures on the Manuscript Materials* (Dublin, 1861), p. 388.

a mere mortal, and his divine bride was allegorized into an abstraction, the Kingship of Ireland. Yet, as Professor O'Rahilly has pointed out,[19] she remained for centuries a very living abstraction, and Yeats immortalized her as Cathleen ni Houlihan. In Arthurian romance, though Eriu emerges as the Grail Bearer, the Loathly Damsel, and the Transformed Hag, there is no hint of the earth-goddess. Only by a lucky guess did Glennie in 1869 propose that the legend of *The Marriage of Sir Gawayne* belonged to the class of sun myths.[20]

The identification of the Grail Bearer with the Sovranty of Erin, Lug's bride, serves to confirm the relationship between Perceval's visit to the Grail castle and Conn's visit to the palace of Lug. The identification of the bleeding spear with Lug's spear leaves little room for doubt. The clue to this identity is to be found not in Chrétien, but in the first continuation of his poem, where we find the lance, not carried in procession, but fixed upright in a silver vessel in the hall of the Grail castle.[21] Gauvain "saw, resting in a stand(?), a lance which bled copiously into a silver cup; it was upright in that vessel, and it was surrounded with blood." In two Irish sagas, as Arthur Brown noted,[22] we find descriptions of the Luin of Celtchar, a fiery spear, which was plunged at intervals into a caldron filled with blood. The Ulster warrior Dubtach Chafer-Tongue is represented in *The Intoxication of the Ulstermen* as carrying it *on loan*. "The quick deedful Luin of Celtchar is in his hand, on loan, and a cauldron of crimson blood is before it, for it would burn its handle, or the man that is bearing it, unless it was bathed in the cauldron of noxious blood." [23] Elsewhere we are told that the Luin was discovered at the battle of Moytura,[24] and we know that a similar spear was procured by the sons of Turenn for the god Lug, to be used at the battle of Moytura.[25] These were the circumstances as related in *The Fate of the Children of Turenn.*[26]

[19] *Eriu*, XIV, 17–21.   [20] *Merlin*, ed. H. B. Wheatley, E.E.T.S., Part III (1869), p. xc.
[21] C. Potvin, *Perceval le Gallois*, IV (Mons, 1868), p. 1.   [22] *PMLA*, XXV (1910), 22.
[23] *Ibid.*, Crosss and Slover, *Ancient Irish Tales*, p. 230.
[24] *PMLA*, XXV, 18. Cross and Slover, *op. cit.*, p. 120.
[25] Cross and Slover, *op. cit.*, pp. 62–64.
[26] *Ibid.*, pp. 60–63, 70 f. Quotation from version in P. W. Joyce, *Old Celtic Romances* (1920), p. 74. In *Bealoideas*, I (1927), 20, Prof. Macalister maintained that the name of Pisear and the description of the spear were derived from the Grail romances, Pisear being a corruption of "Pecheoir." This suggestion is rendered plausible by the fact that mss. containing the name Pisear are no earlier than 1734 (cf. Joyce, p. xi), and that in the short twelfth-century version of the same story (*Zts. f. celt. Phil.*, XII, 243 f.) the owner of the spear is called Assal and the spear itself is not described as plunged deep in a caldron. On the other hand, there are only two passages in the romances in which the bleeding spear is described as standing fixed over a vessel, and in neither is there a single mention of "le roi Pescheor." Moreover, though mss. of the *Conte del Graal* were fairly common and the prose rendering printed in 1530 may have reached Ireland, the narrative of Pseudo-Wauchier in which the spear is described (cf. *supra*, n. 21) bears no resemblance to the story of Brian and the spear of Pisear. If the latter story was inspired by any Arthurian romance, it was by the very similar story of Balaain in the *Huth Merlin* (which gives the king's name as Pellehans), or by Malory's version of Balaain's story (which gives the king's name as Pellam). Neither Pellehans nor Pellam is very close to Pisear or Pezar. Furthermore, we should have to assume that

The three sons of Turenn were compelled by Lug to fetch for him, among other talismans, the spear of Pisear. They came to King Pisear's palace and Brian demanded the famous weapon. When attacked by the king, Brian killed him and put the courtiers to flight. Then he went with his brothers "to the room where the spear was kept; and they found it with its head down deep in a caldron of water, which hissed and bubbled round it. Brian, seizing it boldly in his hand, drew it forth," and departed. The weapon was delivered to Lug to be used in the Battle of Moytura.

There is a close analogy between this episode and that told of the spear of King Pellehan in the *Huth Merlin* and its derivatives—Malory's Book of Balin and the Spanish *Demanda del Sancto Grial*.[27]

Balaain came to the castle of King Pellehan, was attacked by the king, and when his sword was broken, fled weaponless through the palace. He entered a rich chamber and saw a silver table; "and on the table in the very middle, there was a basin of silver and gold, and in this basin there stood a lance, the point below and the handle above. Whoever looked long at the lance would wonder how it was kept straight, for it was not supported either in one place or another." Balaain seized the lance, drove it through Pellehan's thighs, and then restored it to its place. Only by Merlin's aid was he able to depart.

---

the composer of the later version of *The Fate of the Children of Turenn,* knowing that the old plot required the quest for a formidable spear, found in the medieval French text of the *Huth Merlin* (which I suspect very few Irishmen of the eighteenth century found it easy to read), or in Malory, the story of Balaain's striking down King Pellehan, substituted this for whatever tradition he may have had about the spear of Assal, substituted the caldron for the basin, and added the bubbling and hissing of the liquid in which the spear was immersed—features suggested by the native Irish tradition of the blazing Luin of Celtchar. Now such a complicated explanation of the spear of Pisear is possible though not very probable. It seems far simpler and more natural to suppose that the author of the later *Fate of the Children of Turenn* knew that the three brothers were compelled by Lug to fetch for him the fiery spear he was to use at the Battle of Moytura, namely, the Luin of Celtchar, and therefore described it as the Luin was described, its blazing head plunged in a caldron. This supposition is confirmed by the old text, *The Second Battle of Moytura,* which asserts that Lug, the Dagda, and Ogma went to the "three gods of Danu," who prepared seven years for the battle and made weapons for it. Cf. Cross and Slover, *op. cit.,* p. 38; D'Arbois de Jubainville, *L'Epopée celtique en Irlande,* p. 424. Now the three gods of Danu are no other than the three brothers who, according to the *Fate of the Children of Turenn,* were compelled to fetch for Lug the blazing spear of Pisear to use at the Battle of Moytura. Cf. *Irische Texte,* III, i, 58; G. Keating, *History of Ireland,* I, ed. D. Comyn (London, 1902), p. 215; T. F. O'Rahilly, *Early Irish History and Mythology,* pp. 308–17. Even in the tenth century, then, to which *The Second Battle of Moytura* goes back, there was a tradition that Lug obtained weapons from the three sons of Turenn for use in the conflict, and one of them must have been his famous blazing spear. Finally, any influence from Arthurian romance on Irish sagas is rare, whereas the converse is fairly common. In fact, *The Fate of the Children of Turenn* seems to have contributed not only to the episode of King Pellehan's spear in the *Huth Merlin,* but also to the voyages of Galaad, Perceval, and Bohort in the *Queste del St. Graal.* Cf. *Speculum,* VIII, 422 f. Altogether there is a much stronger case for the derivation of the Bleeding Lance of the Grail romances from the spear of Pisear than for the converse relationship.

[27] Thanks to Prof. Vinaver, I have been able to fill out the defective text of the *Huth Merlin,* II, 26–28, from the complete text furnished by the newly discovered Cambridge University ms. Cf. also *PMLA,* XXV, 46 f.

Malory and the Spanish text associate King Pellehan's spear with the Grail,[28] and in fact the sequel to the adventure is found in *La Queste del Saint Graal*,[29] where we read that Galaad comes to the castle of Corbenic, sees the Holy Grail on the silver table, is fed, together with his companions, by Christ himself, and heals the wounded legs of the Maimed King with blood from the lance.

Since the spear which wounded Pellehan is surely the spear of the Grail Castle, and since the narrative setting so closely resembles that of the spear of Pisear, which was delivered to Lug, it seems reasonable to find the origin of the bleeding spear in the spear of Lug. And this is as it should be, since Perceval's visit to the Grail Castle was modeled in part on Conn's visit to the palace of Lug.

The spear of Pisear, used by Lug at the battle of Moytura, and the Luin of Celtchar, found in the battle of the gods at Moytura, are linked not only by this circumstance and their standing, point downward, in a caldron, but also by the fact that their fiery nature is shared with the spear of Lug, of which we read: "When battle was near . . . it roared and struggled against its thongs; fire flashed from it; and once slipped from its leash, it tore through and through the ranks of the enemy." [30] Perhaps it is not irrelevant to recall that Lug was a solar divinity, and that many solar divinities were credited with wielding lightning weapons.[31] The original of the Bleeding Lance of the Grail Castle would seem to have its mythical origin in the flashing, roaring weapon of a sky-god.

Two objections might be raised against this derivation: the Irish spears blaze; they are not described as borne in procession through a palace hall; thus in two respects they do not resemble Chrétien's bleeding lance. However, the Ulster hero Celtchar, who owned the Luin long after Lug's day, met his death in this manner: he raised the Luin aloft, a blood drop ran down, passed through his body, and so killed him. This may show that even in the Irish stage the transformation from blazing to bleeding spear had begun; at any rate, it shows that such a metamorphosis was possible. The introduction of the bleeding lance into the Grail procession seems due to a natural but mistaken attraction. For though we learn later that the reason for the Grail Bearer's passing through the hall was to serve the Fisher King's father and so to play a useful, rational part, no meaning can be discovered in the passage of the youth with the bleeding lance. He evidently has no real business passing back and forth, back and forth, through the hall. It is not Chrétien but his continuator and the author of

[28] The *Demanda* must be wrong, however, in implying the identity of the golden basin with the Grail.
[29] *Queste del St. Graal*, ed. A. Pauphilet, pp. 266–72. H. O. Sommer, *Vulgate Version*, VI, 187–91. [30] C. Squire, *Mythology of the British Islands*, p. 62.
[31] R. S. Loomis, *Celtic Myth*, pp. 45 f. Prof. O'Rahilly comes to the same conclusion in *Early Irish History and Mythology*, pp. 65 f., 309–16.

the *Huth Merlin* who have preserved the lance in its proper setting, fixed perpendicularly above a vessel, much as we find the Luin, the spear of Lug, in the Irish sagas.

Ireland, moreover, and Ireland alone, supplies an adequate answer to one of the most baffling problems of the Grail legend, the question test. Already we have observed that the wording of the question, so pointless in the romances, seems to have been suggested by the very natural query of the Sovranty of Erin, "To whom shall this cup be given?" But the strange employment of the question as a test for the hero to pass and as a means toward the healing of the Fisher King and the restoration of his land is unknown to *The Prophetic Ecstasy of the Phantom*. I have made inquiry of folklorists of such wide bibliographical range as Dr. Krappe and Mr. Duilearga, and they knew of no instance of this motif outside the Grail romances. Professor Stith Thompson cites no other examples in his *Motif-Index*. Of course, there are examples galore of the opposite situation, where the hero is expected to answer a question or solve a riddle, but that is a different matter. Much as one hesitates to use a modern folktale to answer a twelfth-century problem, one should not forget that the modern Welsh tradition of the *ceffyl-dwr* corresponds to the story of the supernatural horse in *Le Lai de l'Espine,* and that Dr. Krappe has found in modern tales of the peasantry of Ireland remarkable parallels to an episode in *Le Bel Inconnu* and to the lai of *Tydorel*.[32] Nor can one escape the fact that the unique analogue to the question test is a tale reported by the Rev. Caesar Otway in 1841 from County Mayo. The use of this tale is further justified by the unlikelihood that this extreme western district of Ireland had heard echoes of the Grail legend, and by the fact that the *Märchen,* apart from the test, shows not the slightest trace of Arthurian influence. Otway's book contains other tales, all equally clear of French contamination; indeed, the story of Donald Doolwee and his Delilah is manifestly descended from the eighth-century tradition of Curoi and the treacherous Blathnat.[33] One cannot prove an equal antiquity for the question motif, but the odds are strongly against foreign or literary origin. Otway's version of the question test is, in substance, as follows.[34]

There lies off the coast of Erris an enchanted isle, crowned with a lofty castle, which is visible once every seven years. Within it are warriors sleeping, waiting

[32] *Romania,* LVIII (1932), 426–30. *Mod. Lang. Rev.,* XXIV (1929), 200–204.

[33] Compare Otway's tale (*Sketches in Erris and Tyrawley* [Dublin, 1841], pp. 39–41) with the story of Curoi, Cuchulainn and Blathnat, one of the most ancient and famous of Irish sagas. Other survivals of this saga tradition are the tales of the Hung-Up Naked Man (cf. Loomis, *op. cit.,* pp. 18–21; *Eriu,* VII, 202) and the Hebridean lay recorded by Henderson (*Miscellany Presented to Kuno Meyer* [Halle, 1912], pp. 26–33). The same betrayal story appears in the *Four Branches of the Mabinogi* (W. J. Gruffydd, *Math Vab Mathonwy,* pp. 29–33, 260–66). It even filtered into the *cantare* of Gismirante (E. Levi, *Fiore di leggende* [Bari, 1914], pp. 182–98). The 8th-century *Echtra Nerai* survives in modern folktales (*Essays and Studies Presented to E. MacNeill,* ed. J. Ryan [Dublin, 1940], pp. 222–34).

[34] C. Otway, *op. cit.,* pp. 251–54. For other tales of this enchanted island cf. *ibid.,* pp. 80, 104 f.

to be waked by the sound of a great bell. The king of this land has sometimes been seen on the mainland as a small, royally dressed man of pleasant presence. "It is supposed that if *rightly* asked, this hide-and-go-seek potentate will tell the questioner where he can find untold heaps of gold, but the querist must be very particular, for if he ask as he should do, the wealth will be obtained by the one [the querist], and the enchantment will be removed by the other; but if not, the king vanishes never to return, amidst wild laughter resounding from the ocean wave, at the folly of him who might have wealth, but had not the wit to win it." A certain drunken Watty O'Kelly invoked the presence of the king, and a dialogue ensued which ended as follows: "Wat—. 'Is it any harm to ask you who you are?' King—'None in life; I'm King of the three Kingdoms behind. And each of these three times larger than Ireland. And that's your share of them, Watty O'Kelly.'"

Otway implies that Watty asked the wrong question, the king vanished, and the spell remained over the enchanted castle.

Here, then, in Ireland, and in Ireland alone, do we find a question test, and here it is with a setting of characters and circumstances not unlike those which we meet with, over and over again, in the Grail legend: a land which lies under enchantment; a castle which, though usually invisible, becomes visible at times to human eyes; the king of the land who appears in friendly fashion to a mortal; the man who through his stupidity fails to ask the right question and is dismissed with mockery and who might, by asking the question, have removed the enchantment and won great wealth.

It is not perhaps irrelevant to the problem of the faery king's identity that Westropp reported in 1918 that on this very Mayo coast Manannan mac Lir, the ancient sea-god, remained in half-secret belief a being of great and dangerous power.[35] For, as we shall presently see, it is Bran vab Llyr, also a sea-god, who is the Welsh prototype of the Fisher King.

The one outstanding difference between the Mayo folk belief and the Grail story is that in the latter the scene of the question test is not outside but within the enchanted castle. Even this discrepancy vanishes in a group of kindred tales from Munster, in which the drunken peasant finds himself in a magnificent palace of the fairies.[36] He spontaneously adds a missing line to their song, they are delighted, and offer him whatever he desires. A crabbed fellow, who tries to imitate his success, adds the wrong words, which are greeted with screaming and laughter; the lights go out, and he is found at daybreak more dead than alive. These tales are apparently the Munster counterparts of the Mayo tale of Watty O'Kelly. They are equally innocent of contamination by French literature. If we combine the interior setting of the Munster version with the question test from

[35] *Proceedings of the Royal Irish Academy,* XXXIV, C, 151.
[36] P. Kennedy, *Legendary Fictions of the Irish Celts,* pp. 99–104. W. B. Yeats, *Irish Fairy and Folk Tales,* (New York, Modern Library), pp. 43–48.

Mayo, we have the essentials of the question test of the Grail romances.

Ireland, it seems, provides a unique parallel in modern folklore to the central theme of the medieval legend. The parallel can hardly be attributed to the influence of that legend. Unless we are faced with an amazing coincidence, we must conclude that the modern fairy tales are the humble and degraded survivors of a once-romantic saga concerned with the testing of a hero in the *sidh* of a god—a saga which by some freak of circumstance has not been preserved in any ancient text. Possibly it was a variation on the adventure of King Cormac in the palace of Manannan,[37] which, though not found in any manuscript earlier than the fourteenth century, is cited as early as the tenth. Manannan's fortress suddenly appears to the hero out of a mist; the hero is hospitably entertained and waited upon by invisible agency; his noble host produces a golden cup, which tests truth and falsehood; the next morning the hero finds himself lying on the green of Tara. One cannot but be struck by the resemblance between the adventures of Cormac and Pseudo-Wauchier's account of Gauvain's experiences at the Grail Castle, where the Grail itself is moved by invisible agency and where Gauvain wakes in the morning to find himself lying on the edge of a cliff.[38] Since several ancient sagas were told in variant forms, it is surely possible that there existed variants of *The Adventures of Cormac* which embodied the question test. No one can say, of course, what the original question was which the hero was supposed to ask. But since the basic situation was a visit to the palace of a god, the analogy with the visit of Conn to the palace of Lug led, perhaps in some Welsh or Breton stage in the development of the tradition, to the introduction of the quite inappropriate query asked by the Sovranty of Erin, "To whom shall this cup be given?"

There are unfortunately gaps in the evidence regarding the question test, but one may at any rate ask the skeptic: What other hypothesis but that of Celtic origin has the support of antecedent probability? What other hypothesis accords with so many facts?

Perceval's humiliating departure from the Fisher King's castle and particularly the rising drawbridge which forces his charger to make a sudden leap to the further bank also argue for Irish origin. Miss Dunn pointed out [39] that, in *The Wooing of Emer,* Cuchulainn, in the attempt to reach the fortress of the woman warrior Scathach on an island, tries thrice to cross a marvelous bridge.[40] When he steps on one end, the other rises and throws him on his back. After the third attempt, he leaps on the middle and so reaches the fortress. Already in our discussion of the Sword Bridge,

---

[37] Cross and Slover, *Ancient Irish Tales,* pp. 503–7. On connection with Grail romances cf. *Romanische Forschungen,* XLV (1931), 71 ff.

[38] C. Potvin, *Perceval le Gallois,* III, 367 f.; IV, 6.

[39] *Mod. Lang. Notes,* XXXIII (1918), 399 ff.

[40] For translation cf. Cross and Slover, *op. cit.,* p. 165.

we observed that (1) it led to the castle of Baudemaguz, who, as a figure descended from the Welsh Bran, is a cognate of the Fisher King; (2) in *Perlesvaus* the Fisher King's castle was approached by three bridges, one of which "lifted itself by engine behind" Gauvain as he passed over; (3) the prototypes of the bridges in *Perlesvaus* and the *Charrette* are found in a late form of *The Wooing of Emer,* namely, *The Instruction of Cuchulainn*. These facts fortify Miss Dunn's conclusion that some form of the *Wooing* was the source of the rising bridge.

Nevertheless, Chrétien's placing of this hazard at the exit instead of the entrance to an Otherworld fortress requires an explanation, and this was provided by Dr. Krappe.[41] He called attention to a common motif in folktales of a visit to the fairies' abode: the hero barely escapes when the door closes on his departing steps. Krappe was not able to cite any Celtic instance of this motif, nor am I. But whatever the provenance, the motif evidently influenced Chrétien's use of the drawbridge.

It seems highly probable, therefore, that Ireland contributed the following elements to the Unspelling Quest in Chrétien: the interior arrangements of the Fisher King's hall, the King's invitation to Perceval, his arrival before Perceval, the Grail Bearer, the Bleeding Spear, the question test and its wording, and the rising drawbridge. Separately or in combination they must have passed into Wales, and become entangled with native Welsh traditions. Let us now attempt to disentangle these Welsh strands.

The sudden appearance of the Fisher King's castle where a moment before Perceval had been unable to see anything, though it has Irish analogues, finds a closer parallel in *The Four Branches of the Mabinogi*.[42] Pryderi and Manawydan chased a white boar "until they saw a great lofty castle, apparently newly built, where they had never seen stone or sign of work. . . . They were amazed to see the castle in the place where they had never seen construction before. From the top of the mound they gazed. . . ." Compare the verses in our poem: "When he was on top of the hill, he gazed long before him and saw nothing save sky and earth. . . . Then he espied before him in a vale the top of a tower appearing." [43] It is pertinent to note that Pryderi discovered within the magic fort the splendid fountain and the mysteriously suspended chain attached to a golden object which we have already discussed [44] and which are paralleled in the magic castle of the ageless elders visited by Perlesvaus. The similarity between the mabinogi and *Le Conte del Graal* is not, therefore, wholly fortuitous.

The most significant Welsh contributions to the Grail legend were the replacing of the Irish gods who played host to Conn and Cormac by the hospitable Bran the Blessed, a euhemerized sea-god; the replacing of the

[41] A. H. Krappe, *Balor with the Evil Eye* (New York, 1927), pp. 106–13.
[42] Loth, *Mabinogion*, 2d ed., I, 159 f.   [43] Vss. 3037–51.   [44] Cf. *supra,* p. 343.

golden cup of the Sovranty of Erin by a rather deep platter of plenty, the Grail; the introduction of the Waste Land motif.

Bran the Blessed, the central figure of the mabinogi of *Branwen,* has been recognized as the prototype of the Fisher King by a long line of scholars—Heinrich, Nutt, Martin, Rhys, Anwyl, Brown, Miss Kempe, and Professor Nitze.[45] In our studies of Baudemaguz and of Perceval's father some of the evidence for this derivation has been produced,[46] and Professor Newstead in her *Bran the Blessed in Arthurian Romance* made out an elaborate and closely argued case. Let us review some of the most direct and palpable correspondences between Bran and the Fisher King.

(1) In the *Didot Perceval* the Fisher King is called Bron.

(2) In *L'Estoire del Saint Graal* Bron is the ancestor of a line of holy guardians of the Grail.[47] A Welsh triad declares that Bran son of Llyr was the ancestor of one of the three holy lineages of Britain.[48]

(3) In Boron's *Joseph* Bron was instructed to set out with his followers to the west.[49] The followers of Bran, in the company of his head, journeyed to Gwales, the westernmost isle of Wales.[50]

(4) According to Chrétien, the Fisher King was wounded during a battle through the thighs or through the legs with a javelin.[51] Bran was wounded in the foot with a lance during a battle.[52]

(5) According to Chrétien (and other romancers) the Fisher King held sumptuous banquets. Bran was noted for his hospitality, and we read again and again of his feasts.

(6) In *Perlesvaus* Gawain was present at a feast in the Fisher King's splendid castle, in company with twelve knights,[53] "aged and gray-haired, and they did not seem to be so old as they were; for each was a hundred years old or more, and yet none seemed to be forty." [54] Bran's followers, including Perceval's counterpart Pryderi, passed eighty years in a great hall in the midst of abundance and joy; "none of them perceived that another was older by that time than when they came there." [55]

Add to these six points of resemblance the many other less direct but still cogent evidences for a connection between the Fisher King and King

[45] G. A. Heinrich, *Le Parcival de Wolfram von Eschenbach et la légende du Saint Graal* (Paris, 1855), p. 59. A. Nutt, *Studies on the Legend of the Holy Grail,* pp. 306 ff. E. Martin, *Zur Gralsage* (Strassburg, 1880), p. 37. J. Rhys, *Studies in the Arthurian Legend,* pp. 306–11. Hastings, *Encyclopaedia of Religion and Ethics,* II, 5. D. Kempe, *Legend of the Holy Grail, Its Sources, Character and Development,* E.E.T.S.E.S., XCV (London, 1905), pp. xviii–xxv.   [46] Cf. *supra,* pp. 240–44, 347–54.

[47] The pedigree is Bron, Josue, Aminadap, Catheloys, Manaal, Lambor, Pelleham, Pelles. Cf. Sommer, *Vulgate Version,* I, 251, 286–90.   [48] Loth, *Mabinogion,* 2d ed., II, 280.

[49] Robert de Boron, *Roman de l'Estoire dou Graal,* ed. W. A. Nitze (Paris, 1927), vss. 3289–416.   [50] Loth, *op. cit.,* I, 144 ff. Cf. *PMLA,* LVI (1941), 903–5.

[51] Vss. 3509–13.   [52] Loth, *op. cit.,* I, 144.

[53] *Perlesvaus,* ed. Nitze and Jenkins, I, l. 2414. Though the Oxford ms., followed in the text, gives "xxii," the editors assert (Vol. II, 21) that P is the most reliable ms., and this and the Brussels ms. read "xii."   [54] *Ibid.,* ll. 2415–17.   [55] Loth, *op. cit.,* I, 148.

Bran, and can there be any doubt of their original identity? To be sure, the author of *Branwen* has been distracted by a strange tale of Bran's severed head which affected the story of Gahmuret's death in *Parzival* [56] and influenced accounts of heads in platters in *Peredur* and in Bercheur's *Reductorium Morale*.[57] But that Bran himself, not his head, presided over the feasts in the isle of Gwales is proved by the fact that in one of the poems attributed to Taliesin the bard speaks of himself as singing "before the sons of Llyr [Bran and Manawydan] at Ebyr Henvelen," [58] whereas, according to *Branwen,* Taliesin and Manawydan were included in the company who were forbidden to look out towards Aber Henvelen. The confusion caused by the narrative of Bran's decapitation and the burial of his head at London has obscured his relationship to the Fisher King, but there should be no doubt that from the Welsh Bran legend Chrétien ultimately derived the wounding of the Fisher King by a javelin in battle, his hospitality, and the sumptuous service of food and drink in his castle.

The fact that Bran's followers spent eighty years in the lonely isle of Gwales "in the midst of abundance and joy" suggests that there was some miraculous source of supply. In *Kulhwch and Olwen* there are mentioned together three vessels which might qualify: [59] the cup of Llwyr, which contains *penllad,* that is, "supreme drink"; the *mwys* (dish?) [60] of Gwyddneu: "should the whole world assemble . . . each would find food therein according to his desire"; the drinking horn of Gwlgawt. Loth has pointed out that two of these vessels reappear in the list of the Thirteen Treasures of the Isle of Britain: the *mwys* and the horn.[61] The latter is thus described: "The Horn of Bran Galed from the North; the drink and the food that one asked one received in it when one desired." [62] Closely akin is another object found in the list: "The Platter (*Dysgl*) of the illustrious-born [?] Rhydderch the Scholar; whatever food one wished thereon was instantly obtained." [63] These two vessels acquire great significance when it is realized that the first is the possession of Bran, and that the second has strong claims to being the direct original of the Grail.

First, the very word *dysgl* (in the earlier form *dyscyl*) is that employed in *Peredur* to designate the vessel which the damsels bore through the hall of the Lame King, and concerning which the hero failed to ask the unspelling question.[64] Thurneysen and Windisch recognized the word as

---

[56] Cf. *supra,* pp. 349–51.
[57] *Revue celt.,* XLVII (1930), 39–60. H. Newstead, *Bran the Blessed in Arthurian Romance,* pp. 70–80. Cf. *supra,* p. 223.
[58] *PMLA,* LVI (1941), 904 f. *Cymmrodor,* XXVIII, 197.   [59] Loth, *op. cit.,* I, 305 f.
[60] On the meaning of *mwys* cf. J. Rhys, *Studies in the Arthurian Legend,* p. 313.
[61] Loth, *op. cit.,* I, 305, n. 2; 306, n. 1. On the Thirteen Treasures cf. *PMLA,* LVI, 910–13.
[62] *Romanische Forschungen,* XLV, 71.   [63] *Ibid.,* p. 70.
[64] J. G. Evans, *White Book Mabinogion,* col. 130, 166. Col. 613, following another ms., gives *dysgyl.*

the equivalent of *graal*.[65] Secondly, Helinandus defined the word *graal* some fifty years after Chrétien used it as "a wide and somewhat deep dish (*scutella*)";[66] whereas Giraldus Cambrensis says that the Welsh ate from "wide and capacious dishes (*scutellis*)."[67] In the *Vulgate Estoire* the French derivative of *scutella, escuele,* is regularly employed for the sacred vessel, and in one line of *Le Conte del Graal,* the word *platiaus* (platter) is found as a manuscript variant for *graaus*.[68] Thirdly, the Grail possesses precisely the virtue ascribed in the list of Thirteen Treasures to the *Dysgl* of Rhydderch. According to Manessier, after the grail has passed, "then all the tables were provided with delectable viands and so nobly filled that no man could name a food which he could not find there."[69] In *L'Estoire del Saint Graal* we read that the vessel brought to the holy in life "all the good viands which heart of man could conceive."[70] *La Queste del Saint Graal* says that as the vessel passed before the tables, "they were instantly filled at each seat with such food as each desired."[71] In both form and function, then, the *Dysgl* of Rhydderch corresponds to the Grail. That it has been transferred from Bran to the historic Rhydderch, King of Strathclyde in the sixth century, is of course due to the euhemeristic process which Arthur Brown observed in Irish literature: "The sagas bear witness that these talismans of the gods had been transferred to the historical or supposedly historical heroes: Cuchulinn, Cormac, Crimthann, Finn, and the like."[72] The Grail, therefore, had its closest prototype in a Welsh platter of plenty, the vessel of the euhemerized god, Bran the Blessed.[73] Evidently the feeding vessel superseded the drinking vessel which the Sovranty of Erin filled for Conn.

[65] *Zts. f. celt. Phil.*, VIII (1910), 187. Windisch, *Das keltische Brittannien bis zu Kaiser Arthur*, pp. 195, 279.
[66] Migne, *Patrologia Latina*, CCXII, col. 814. *Mod. Phil.*, XIII (1916), 681.
[67] Giraldus Cambrensis, *Opera*, ed. Dimock, VI (London, 1868), 183.
[68] In the passage in Pseudo-Wauchier where ms. B. N. 12577, f. 115*v*, gives *greaus*, and ms. Edinburgh, f. 107*r*, gives *graaus*, ms. Montpellier 249, f. 118*v*, gives *platiaus*. Cf. Potvin, *Perceval le Gallois*, III, 254, n. 2.
[69] Potvin, *op. cit.*, VI, 151.   [70] Sommer, *op. cit.*, I, 250.
[71] *Ibid.*, VI, 13. *Queste*, ed. Pauphilet, p. 15.   [72] *Mod. Phil.*, XXII (1924), 113.
[73] Four vessels surviving to our time have been claimed as the Holy Grail. There is the green glass dish, the Sacro Catino, in the cathedral of Genoa, first mentioned by William of Tyre late in the twelfth century and reputed to be the dish of the Last Supper. Cf. Bruce, *Evolution of Arthurian Romance*, I, 360–62; P. Paris, *Guillaume de Tyr et ses continuateurs* (Paris, 1879), I, 273n. There is the holy chalice of dark red agate on a pedestal, which was deposited in the sacristy of the cathedral of Valencia in 1437 and has been venerated as that in which Christ consecrated His blood. Cf. J. S. y Sivera, *El Santo Caliz de la Cena (Santo Grial) Venerado en Valencia* (Valencia, 1914). There is the so-called Antioch Chalice, which Eisen seriously identified with the actual cup of the Last Supper. Cf. G. Eisen, *Great Chalice of Antioch* (New York, 1923); *Syria*, I (1921), 81 ff. Finally there is the Nanteos bowl, of which J. Ceredig Davies, *Folklore of West and Mid-Wales* (Aberystwyth, 1911), pp. 293–97, wrote as follows: "At Nanteos House near Aberystwyth is the fragment of a wooden bowl, originally about 5 in. high, called the Phiol, which is supposed to have healing virtues. No ancient records refer to it, but modern genteel tradition asserts that it was once the sacred possession of a monastery and that it was the cup used by Christ at the Last Supper."

The *tailleor,* which immediately follows the Grail, is probably a mere doublet, since the word, meaning a carving dish, is practically a synonym of *graal.* Chrétien's narrative represents a conflation of two accounts in one of which the damsel bore a *graal,* in the other a *tailleor.* The superfluity of the second maiden is indicated by the fact that the Loathly Damsel, when she rebukes Perceval for his silence regarding the Bleeding Lance and the Grail, makes no mention of the *tailleor.*

To the Welsh the Grail legend owes also the pervasive theme of the Waste Land. Chrétien merely hints at this very significant feature and its connection with the Fisher King's wound. Perceval is told that if he had asked the magic question, he would have helped the Maimed King, for the latter would have altogether recovered the use of his limbs and would have ruled his lands, and great good would have ensued.[74] Again, the Loathly Damsel tells Perceval that, because of his failure, "ladies will lose their husbands, lands will be ruined, maidens, who will be left orphans, will be disconsolate, and many a knight will die." [75] Other texts confirm this connection between the health of the Fisher King and the well-being of his domains and bring out, as Chrétien does not, the sympathetic relation of his wound to the Waste Land. According to the *Didot Perceval* and Wolfram's poem, asking the fateful question cures the king; [76] in Pseudo-Wauchier's and Gerbert's continuations of *Le Conte del Graal* it restores the fertility of the land.[77] *Sone de Nansai* attributes the wasting of the land of Lorgres to the wounding of the Fisher King; the *Queste* attributes the wasting of two kingdoms (one being evidently Logres) to the killing of the Maimed King's father, Labran. These last two texts furnish most significant details. According to *Sone,*[78] when the Fisher King was wounded by God "in the reins and below," the land of Lorgres (England) fell under an enchantment. "Neither peas nor wheat were sown, no child was born to man, nor maiden had husband, nor tree bore leaf, nor meadow turned green; neither bird nor beast had young, so sore was the king maimed." A closely related tradition is preserved in the *Queste.*

" 'It is true,' said the damsel [Perceval's sister], 'that this ship arrived in the realm of Logres. At that time there was mortal war between King Labran [at least three manuscripts give this form of the name],[79] who was father of that king who is called the Maimed King, and King Urlain, who had been a Saracen all the days of his life. . . . One day, it chanced that King Labran and King Urlain had assembled their hosts on the seashore where this ship had arrived. . . . When King Urlain saw King Labran, he raised his sword and smote him on the

---

[74] Vss. 3582–92.   [75] Vss. 4678–82.

[76] *Didot-Perceval,* ed. Roach, p. 239. Wolfram, *Parzival,* 795, 28–796, 6.

[77] Potvin, *op. cit.,* IV, 7. Gerbert de Montreuil, *Continuation,* ed. M. Williams, I, 2, 11–13. For another account of the Waste Land cf. *Elucidation,* ed. A. W. Thompson (New York, 1931), pp. 86–89, 98; Potvin, II, 4, 14.

[78] *Sone de Nausai,* ed. M. Goldschmidt, vss. 4777 f., 4846–53.

[79] Sommer, *Vulgate Version,* VI, 146, n. 10, 13; p. 147, n. 2.

helm so hard that he clove him and his horse down to the ground. . . . This happened in the realm of Logres. . . . Thus there followed so great a pestilence and so great destruction in two realms that never since have the lands yielded their crops to the husbandmen. For never since has wheat grown there or other grain, nor the trees borne fruit, nor have fish been found in the water save a few. Therefore is the land of the two realms called the Waste Land because it was made waste by this dolorous stroke.' " [80]

Though this passage makes Labran the father of the Maimed King and not the Maimed King himself, and though it represents the wound as fatal, it has preserved in the form of his name a strong hint of his identity with Bran and the tradition of his wounding in battle, as well as the manifestly primitive feature of a sympathetic relation between the vigor of the king and the productivity of his land.

The belief in this sympathetic relation is, of course, widespread.[81] For the clearest Celtic evidence we must turn back for a moment to Ireland. We read of the great king of Ulster, Conchobar (who, like Bran, may have been a euhemerized god since he and his sister Dechtire are both explicitly referred to as divinities),[82] as follows:

"He never pronounced judgment, since it was not permitted to him to do so, in order that he might not deliver a false judgment; so that his crops might not be the worse thereof. . . . He was never suffered to encounter danger, in order to guard the king's son. In battles and contests, champions and veterans of war and heroes of valor were ever in front of him, so that he should not be imperilled." [83]

Eleanor Hull remarks of this passage: "The importance of the life and well-being of a king to his posterity and people has never been more clearly expressed. His loss or injury would bring corresponding troubles upon his family and realm." [84] The precautions adopted by the Ulstermen for the protection of King Conchobar did not prevent a warrior of Connaught from driving a hard ball into his head. Thereupon he, like the Fisher King, was not permitted to ride a horse or to run, for the people said that the blemish was a small thing for them compared with his death.[85] Moreover, the Irish associated the prosperity of the land with the marital function of their kings, and this belief too seems to be reflected in the Grail romances. According to *The Adventures of Art*,[86] while King Conn was wedded to his loving and affectionate wife Ethne, "there was nothing lacking to the men of Ireland . . . for indeed they used to reap the corn three times in the year." But when, after her death, he mated with the adulteress Becuma from the Land of Promise,

[80] *Ibid.*, 146 f.　　　[81] J. G. Frazer, *Dying God* (London, 1911), pp. 21, 27.

[82] J. Rhys, *Lectures on the Origin and Growth of Religion*, p. 144.

[83] E. Hull, *Folklore of the British Isles*, pp. 276 f.

[84] *Ibid.*, p. 277. For other Celtic evidence of this kind cf. R. S. Loomis, *Celtic Myth*, p. 185. n. 36.　　　　　　[85] Hull, *op. cit.*, p. 278.

[86] T. P. Cross and C. N. Slover, *Ancient Irish Tales*, p. 491.

"there was neither corn nor milk in Ireland during that time." [87] According to *Sone,* the Fisher King was wounded and his land became sterile because he wedded a Saracen princess.[88]

Welsh literature does not provide us with as clear evidence on the sympathetic relation between king and kingdom, but it does provide several accounts of mysterious enchantments which desolate Britain or its provinces, and for which varying causes are assigned. We have already observed in Chapter LIX that Pryderi's sitting on the Gorsedd of Narberth produced a roar and brought about the desolation of Dyved, and that this incident had its obvious counterpart in the Siege Perilous adventure of the *Didot Perceval* and the consequent enchantments of Britain. *Lludd and Llevelys* describes three plagues which fell on the Isle of Britain. The second of these was caused by a roar and involved the following consequences: "the men lost their color and their strength, and the women the infants in their wombs. . . . Animals, trees, the earth, the waters, all remained sterile." [89] The roar links this calamity to the enchantments of Britain in the *Didot Perceval,* which were introduced with a "brait." [90] The barrenness of men and Nature presents a strong likeness to the enchantments of Lorgres as described in the lines quoted above from *Sone.*

Bran's wounding and death also, as was pointed out in the discussion of Perceval's father,[91] were followed by the desolation of two kingdoms, Britain and Ireland. His sister Branwen lamented that for her sake two fair islands had been laid waste. The verb is *diffeithwyt,* and later there is reference to the *diffeithwch,* "desert, wilderness," of Ireland. It is important to note that the adjective *diffeith,* "waste," is applied to the land of Dyved after Pryderi had sat on the Gorsedd of Narberth. Though the causal relation between Bran's wounding and the Waste Land motif is not explicit in the mabinogi, yet one can hardly doubt, in view of the cumulative evidence, that an earlier and more authentic Welsh tradition made it as plain as the effect of the Fisher King's wound in *Sone* and of King Labran's deathblow in the *Queste* on the reproductive forces of Logres.

The title, "li rois Peschierre," seems to be the result of an ingenious attempt to reconcile the fact that the King was maimed with the fact that, as a former marine deity, he was wont to appear in a boat.[92] To be sure, there is no record of Bran's being seen in a boat, but his Irish counterpart, the sea-god Manannan mac Lir, is at least thrice described as riding on a

---

[87] *Ibid.,* p. 493.   [88] *Sone,* vss. 4757–4856.   [89] Loth, *Mabinogion,* 2d ed., I, 234.
[90] *Didot-Perceval,* ed. Roach, pp. 149 f. For other examples of the motif of the *brait* cf. *Huth Merlin,* ed. G. Paris and J. Ulrich, I, lxxiii, lxxxvi; Sommer, *op. cit.,* VII, 170, 311 f.; Ulrich von Zatzikhoven, *Lanzelet,* ed. K. A. Hahn (Frankfurt, 1845), vss. 7062 ff.
[91] Cf. *supra,* p. 351.
[92] The explanations of the title in Robert's *Metrical Joseph* and the *Estoire del S. Graal* are doubtless likewise inventions of some pious author, who wrote the common source of both romances. Newstead, *Bran the Blessed in Arthurian Romance,* pp. 38–40.

horse or in a chariot over his domain,[93] and Manannan's *currach,* the Wave-Sweeper, plays an important part in *The Fate of the Children of Turenn.*[94] Bran vab Llyr might well, therefore, have been imagined as a venerable figure in a boat. When his character as a marine deity faded, some reason had to be invented for his appearance on the waters, and what more rational hypothesis than that, because of his malady, he could not hunt or hawk? "He had himself placed in a boat and went fishing with a hook."[95] The transfer of his fishing grounds from sea to river was probably caused, in part by the general tendency of Arthurian romance, noted by Philipot and M. Lot,[96] to adapt adventures to the conditions of knight errantry and to reduce to a minimum maritime elements from the Irish voyages, and in part by the localization of Bran's enchanted abode, not only in elysian isles, but also at Dinas Bran on the borders of "Logres," high above the River Dee.[97] At any rate, since Chrétien mentions Arthur as holding court at "Dinasdaron an Gales" in this very poem (vs. 2753), it is almost certain that the place had achieved a reputation among the *conteurs* and poets of France.[98] It is possible even at this day to match Perceval's approach to the Fisher King's castle by following the banks of "the wizard stream" down the romantic Vale of Llangollen, and to approach the ruins of Castell Dinas Bran, situated, not "an un val" to be sure, but high on a green hill, with a wide and lovely prospect over the realms of Gales and Logres.

This very Chastiel Bran on the borders of Wales, the romance of *Fouke Fitz Warin* informs us, was called "la Vele Marche," and had been rebuilt by a King Bran.[99] The same tradition is represented in the *Vulgate Lancelot,*[100] which testifies that King Brangorre [101] held court at "le Chastel de la Marche." *Fouke* also describes a nocturnal combat in the ruins of this castle [102] which strongly reminds one of the nocturnal combats of Gauvain and Bohort in the castle of Corbenic, where dwelt the Maimed King.[103] In our study of the *Joie de la Cort* episode we discovered

---

[93] *Studies and Notes in Philology and Literature,* VIII (1903), 96. Cross and Slover, *op. cit.,* pp. 196, 591.　　[94] Cross and Slover, *op. cit.,* pp. 64 f.　　[95] *Conte del Graal,* vss. 3518 f.

[96] *Romania,* XXIV (1895), 331; XXV (1896), 267. Cf. also *ibid.,* LIX (1933), 557–64.

[97] Newstead, *op. cit.,* pp. 23, 54 f., 95–106, 195. For other mythological associations of this region cf. *supra,* p. 184.

[98] By a curious freak of chance Benoît de Ste. Maure arbitrarily attached this name Dinas d'Aron to one of the bastard sons of Priam. Cf. *Roman de Troie,* ed. L. Constans (Paris, 1912), VI, 245; *Speculum,* XX (1945), 184 f.

[99] *Fouke Fitz Warin,* ed. L. Brandin pp. 3 f.

[100] Sommer, *Vulgate Version,* IV, 259. On this episode cf. *supra,* pp. 241 f., 245.

[101] What is evidently the same name appears in the *Vulgate Merlin* (Sommer, *op. cit.,* II, 400, l. 6) as Brangor, and is presumably a compound of Bran and Gawr, the latter being a mutated form of *Kawr,* "giant," frequent as an epithet. Cf. Newstead, *op. cit.,* p. 54, n. 26.

[102] *Fouke,* pp. 4–7. On Arthurian connections cf. Newstead, pp. 97–106; *Miscellany of Studies in Romance Languages and Literatures in Honour of L. E. Kastner,* pp. 342–50.

[103] Sommer, *op. cit.,* IV, 343–47; V, 298–303. On other elements which entered into the nocturnal adventures of Gauvain and Bohort at Corbenic cf. *supra,* pp. 204–10.

that the castle of Corbenic took its name from the Horn of Bran, "le Cor Beneit," and the Maimed King was, of course, Bran himself. Since Dinas Bran was a traditional abode of Bran the Blessed, and a prototype of the Grail Castle, its site beside the River Dee may well have affected the story of Perceval's meeting with the Fisher King.

Welsh traditions, therefore, particularly those connected with King Bran, are represented, though dimly, in Chrétien's narrative of Perceval's visit to the Fisher King. The venerable personage in the boat, the ride along the river bank, the suddenly appearing tower where none had been visible a moment before, the lavish hospitality, the *graal* and its food-providing function, the account of the king's wounding in battle with a javelin, the Waste Land motif—all these features are a heritage from the legends of Wales.

One feature of Chrétien's story finds its closest analogue in a twelfth-century Breton tale. Jessie Weston rightly asserted that Chrétien's description of the Fisher King as "wounded with a javelin between the two thighs" was a euphemism for emasculation.[104] This interpretation is confirmed by the passage in *Sone* which represents the wounding of the Fisher King "in the reins and below" as inducing the sterility of men, plants, trees, birds and beasts. It is also confirmed by Wolfram, who says explicitly that Anfortas, the Fisher King, was wounded at a joust with a poisoned spear in the genitals.[105] Now Walter Map in his *De Nugis Curialium* [106] reports that in the parish where a certain Alan, King of Brittany, was castrated, it came about that "no animals even today can bring forth young, but, when ripe for bearing, they go outside of the parish to deliver the offspring." This is plainly a somewhat rationalized and limited form of the superstition that the sterilization of the ruler extended itself to all forms of life in his kingdom. It is, of course, possible that this heathenish belief was present in the Welsh legend of Bran, and was expurgated by the author of *Branwen*. But, as far as I am aware, the only Celtic testimony to its existence is Map's tale of Alan, King of Brittany.

Thus by assembling these many scattered analogues from Irish, Welsh, and Breton tradition we are able to match most of the elements in the Unspelling Quest as furnished by Chrétien de Troyes. The remaining elements in Chrétien's story of the visit to the Grail Castle and its sequel are due, as has been forecast, to contamination by the Feud or Vengeance Quest. To these we shall now turn our attention.

[104] J. L. Weston, *From Ritual to Romance* (Cambridge, 1920), p. 20. I cannot subscribe, however, to Miss Weston's theory that the procession in the Grail Castle represents the ritual of a fertility cult. [105] *Parzival,* 479, 8–12.
[106] Distinctio IV, Chap. 15. Trans. F. Tupper and M. B. Ogle (London, 1924), p. 242.

Chapter LXIX

THE VENGEANCE QUEST

VERSES 3130–3997

As soon as Perceval had been welcomed by the Fisher King, a squire brought in a magnificent sword, sent by the King's niece. It had been destined for Perceval and he accepted it, though warned that it would break in a certain peril. After his silent observation of the damsels with the graal *and the* tailleor *as they passed repeatedly through the hall, he retired for the night to his chamber. Leaving the castle the next morning under strange circumstances, he came upon a damsel sitting under a tree, weeping over the headless body of her lover. She revealed herself to Perceval as his cousin, and rebuked him violently for his silence at the Grail Castle. Perceval undertook to fight the knight who had slain her lover that morning and to force him to admit defeat, but she warned him that the sword he was wearing would fly in pieces when he came to combat, and told him that a certain smith at the lake above Cotoatre could alone restore it. Perceval departed, and presently met the Damsel of the Tent and her lover, the Proud Knight of the Glade, who had slain another knight that very day [1] and was therefore, presumably, the very man whom Perceval was seeking. The Proud Knight was forced to admit defeat and beg for mercy, which Perceval granted on condition that he would recognize his lady's innocence and surrender himself at Arthur's court. Perceval uttered not a word in reference to the death of his cousin's lover at the hands of the Proud Knight.*

THOUGH Chrétien continued his poem for over 5,000 lines he never reverted to the treacherous sword or the female cousin or the vengeance motif. As with the Unspelling Quest, we are left with a number of loose threads. Not only does the prophecy regarding the sword remain unfulfilled though Perceval engages in many dangerous battles, but the Proud Knight, as the wanton slayer of the *ami* of Perceval's cousin, gets off far too easily with a promise to surrender at Arthur's court; Perceval even forgets to reproach him for the crime. The explanation of this fatuous dénouement lies doubtless in the fact that the story of the Lady of the Tent and the Proud Knight had originally nothing to do with the story of Perceval's meeting with the damsel under the tree and his obligation to avenge her dead lover. Our study of the former story [2] revealed no complication with a blood feud. The two quarrels were orig-

---

[1] Vs. 3827.   [2] Cf. *supra*, pp. 122–27.

inally distinct, the one originating in jealous misunderstanding, the other in a murder. Naturally the outcome suitable for the one was not suited to the other. Chrétien, or more probably his source, telescoped the two quarrels in Perceval's combat with the Proud Knight, satisfactorily terminated the one quarrel with the vindication of the lady's innocence, but blandly disregarded the requirements of the blood feud.

It is interesting to observe that the author of *Peredur,* who, if he did not know Chrétien, at least followed a similar version of these adventures, realized the unsatisfactory outcome of the blood feud, and with some intelligence endeavored to improve matters by making two Proud Knights of the Glade to satisfy the requirements of the two situations. The first of the two knights is forced by Peredur to make amends—of a sort—by marrying the widow of the dead man.[3] The second, like his counterpart in Chrétien's poem, is compelled to admit his wife's innocence.[4] Here is a solution of the difficulty, artificial to be sure, but still a solution.

Wolfram, however, who surely had Chrétien for one, though not his only, source for these events, leaves things in as unsatisfactory a state as Chrétien did. Three times Parzival comes upon his cousin, Sigune; each time she is found with the body of her lover.[5] On the first occasion she tells Parzival explicitly that Orilus de Lalander (Chrétien's Proud Knight of the Glade) is the slayer not only of her lover but also of the boy's uncle, and the boy vows vengeance. On the second occasion, which corresponds to the meeting narrated by Chrétien, Sigune seems to be interested only in Parzival's adventure at the Grail Castle and in the treacherous sword. Parzival rides away without a word as to revenge on Orilus. Presently he comes upon the unfortunate damsel of the tent and her jealous husband Orilus, overcomes him, compels him to acknowledge her innocence and proceed to Arthur's court. Not a word of Orilus' crime in killing Sigune's lover; not a word of Parzival's obligation to mete out justice to the culprit. At the third meeting between Parzival and Sigune, though Orilus' crime is mentioned, the obligation to punish him is again forgotten. Parzival visits no retribution on the slayer of both his uncle and his cousin's lover.

We are forced to turn elsewhere if we are to discover a version of Perceval's meeting with the damsel under the tree which has a sequel in a real Vengeance Quest. Professor Nitze recognized such a version in *Perlesvaus.*[6] Twice Arthur sees the maiden sitting under a tree; as in Chrétien, she knows much of Perlesvaus' youth.[7] When later she comes upon Perlesvaus himself, instead of supporting the body of a headless knight as in Chrétien, she carries the head of a knight in a rich vessel of ivory.[8] It is the head of

---

[3] Loth, *Mabinogion,* 2d ed., II, 65–67.   [4] *Ibid.,* pp. 73 f.
[5] *Parzival,* 138, 9–142, 5; 249, 11–255, 29; 435, 1–442, 26.
[6] *Perlesvaus,* ed. W. A. Nitze and others, II, 213 f.   [7] *Ibid.,* I, ll. 266–81, 443–536.
[8] *Ibid.,* I, ll. 8678–8710.

Perlesvaus' cousin, the son of his uncle Brun Brandalis. At the damsel's instigation, Perlesvaus eventually avenges his kinsman's death on the slayer, "li Rous Chevaliers de la Parfonde Forest." He later rescues the damsel herself from a friend or vassal of the Rous Chevalier.[9] Though Professor Nitze maintained that the story is based merely on Chrétien, this can hardly be. Nothing is said of the damsel's kinship to the hero or of the sword, and there are several marked divergences. On the other hand, there is a noteworthy agreement with another vendetta in *Peredur,* in that the hero is destined to avenge his male cousin whose head is borne in a vessel by a maiden;[10] and also an agreement with several forms of the Vengeance Quest, to be examined presently, which depict Perceval's foes as Red Knights. It seems clear that *Perlesvaus* tells the story of the damsel under the tree in a form independent of Chrétien, a form, moreover, which instead of the crude attempts of Wolfram and *Peredur* to link the theme of retribution to the Proud Knight episode, furnishes a traditional conclusion in the killing of a Red Knight.

The first important inference to be drawn from all this is that there existed anterior to *Le Conte del Graal* and *Perlesvaus* a traditional tale that Perceval met in a wood a weeping damsel under a tree, cherishing the head or the body of Perceval's newly slain kinsman, and that she roused Perceval to the duty of revenge. We have isolated, then, in what we may call the formula of the weeping damsel the first element in the Vengeance Quest.

Let us now give our attention to the second persistent feature—Perceval's feud with one or more Red Knights, generally identified as the slayers of his kinsman and the objects of his vengeance.

Manessier seems to have been cognizant of this feature in his ingenious and successful attempt to knit together the loose strands of the Unspelling and the Vengeance Quests. Wauchier de Denain had related Perceval's second arrival at the Fisher King's castle and his partial success in rewelding the pieces of a broken sword.[11] Manessier continued as follows:[12]

Perceval sat down to a sumptuous feast and saw passing before him two damsels, one bearing the Grail and the other a *tailleor.* The first, he learned, was the Fisher King's daughter, the other the King's niece, the daughter of Boon or Gron "roi du desert."[13] This second king, whose name, we may infer, was originally Bron, had been killed treacherously by Partinal, "sire de la Rouge Tour," with a sword which broke in pieces with the fatal blow. Bron's body had been sent to the Fisher King's Castle, and his daughter had brought also the broken brand,

9 *Ibid.,* I, ll. 8825–8864, 8985–9036.   10 Loth, *op. cit.,* II, 119 f.
11 C. Potvin, *Perceval le Gallois,* V, 139–49.   12 *Ibid.,* V, 150 f., 159–64; VI, 35–37, 122–31.
13 Prof. Roach generously communicated to me the readings of the mss. for this name. Where Potvin, vs. 35172, gives "Goot Delsert," Montpellier gives "boon de sert," and Bib. Nat., fr. 1453 gives "boon desert." Where Potvin, vs. 35429, gives "Goon," Montpellier gives "Gron." Potvin's vs. 45279 is given by Montpellier as "la fille au bon roi du desert," and Bib. Nat., fr. 1453 gives "la fille au roy du desert."

informing her uncle that the knight who could repair it would avenge her father's death. It was while handling the fragments that the Fisher King had maimed himself "through the legs," and he could not be cured until he too was avenged on the "sire de la Rouge Tour." Perceval undertook the task. After many adventures he came to the abode of a smith, who completely restored the weapon. He rode on, killed the "sire de la Rouge Tour," and returned triumphant to the Grail Castle. On hearing of his approach, the Fisher King leaped to his feet, miraculously cured of his wound.

No text of the Grail cycle combines so neatly the two traditions—the Unspelling and the Vengeance quests—as does this. Here we have the two counterparts of the Welsh Bran—the Fisher King, alias Bron, and his brother whose name we infer must also have been Bron. One is the Maimed King, who is to be healed; the other is the Slain King, who is to be avenged. The daughter of the one bears the *graal,* the daughter of the other bears the *tailleor.* Like their fathers, they are doublets of the same personage. The Unspelling Quest is responsible for the wounding and healing of the Fisher King and for the title of his brother, "roi du desert." The Vengeance Quest is worked out with great clarity. The mysterious broken sword has a coherent history; we learn how it came to be shattered, how it was partially, then fully repaired, and how finally it served as the instrument of Perceval's vengeance for his slain kinsman. We may well doubt, however, that Manessier's felicitous reconciliation of the two traditions, whether he found it ready to his hand or worked it out himself, is in accord with the oldest traditions of the Vengeance Quest. Certainly he omitted the meeting of Perceval with the weeping damsel in the forest. Certainly he ignored the tradition which made Bron Perceval's father. But he retained in the title of Bron's slayer, "sire de la Rouge Tour," a trace of the tradition which made a Red Knight the slayer of Perceval's kinsman and the object of his revenge.

In *Perlesvaus* we have an extraordinary proliferation of Red Knights, enemies of the hero.[14] Like Chrétien's Perceval, Perlesvaus killed at the outset of his career a Vermeil Chevalier, more imposingly styled "le Chevalier au Vermel Escu de la Forest des Onbres." [15] As a consequence, the Red Knight's son sought reprisal,[16] and his brother Cahot le Roux, "who was a big knight and a red," and the Sire des Mares also took up the feud against Perlesvaus.[17] They made war on his mother, seized her castles and slew one of her men. The hero drowned the Sire des Mares in a tub of blood, and mortally wounded Cahot le Roux.[18] We have already seen that in *Perlesvaus* the formula of the damsel under the tree terminates with the killing of "li Rous Chevaliers de la Parfonde Forest." Finally, we learn that the hero's father and his uncle Alibran had been murdered by "li Rous Jaianz." [19] Seemingly, the author of this romance inherited an

[14] Cf. *Perlesvaus,* ed. Nitze, II, 167 f. [15] *Ibid.,* I, ll. 488–97, 3042 f. [16] *Ibid.,* I, ll. 978–90. [17] *Ibid.,* I, ll. 1065–1180, 3201. [18] *Ibid.,* I, ll. 3197–3233, 5245–5402. [19] *Ibid.,* I, ll. 9836–38.

elaborate tradition of a feud between the hero's family and a clan of red men.

It is significant that this red group in *Perlesvaus* included: (1) the Red Knight of the hero's first encounter; (2) the slayer of his father and his uncle Alibran de la Gaste Cité; (3) the slayer of his cousin, son of his uncle Brun Brandalis; (4) two lords who made war on his mother and invaded his patrimony. It is significant because these figures have their counterparts in romances which were not influenced by *Perlesvaus*. In *Peredur* the hero not only killed the Red Knight of his first encounter [20] but also avenged the death of his male cousin; [21] in Manessier Perceval avenged the death of his uncle Bron, "roi du desert," on the Sire de la Rouge Tour; in *Sir Percyvelle* the Red Knight whom the hero slew in his first encounter is identified with the slayer of his father and the enemy of his uncle and cousins.[22] It is significant that in Wolfram's poem we have traces of the same feud, for he presents us with two brothers, Orilus and Lähelin, who, like Cahot le Roux and the Sire des Mares in *Perlesvaus,* invaded the hero's patrimony and killed one of his knights.[23] Orilus, we have seen, had killed also Parzival's uncle and his liegeman, the lover of Sigune. Lähelin robbed Parzival of two kingdoms and made war on his people. Neither of these brothers hostile to Parzival is explicitly said to be a Red Knight, but there is convincing evidence that Wolfram knew and suppressed a tradition that Lähelin was the Red Knight of Parzival's first combat.[24] Before leaving his mother, the youth vowed vengeance on Lähelin, promising to wound him with his javelin. On meeting the Red Knight, he remarked, "Maybe thou art Lähelin," [25] and killed him with his javelin. This evidently is the fulfillment of his promise. Moreover, when long after, riding in the Red Knight's armor and being known as "der Rote Ritter," Parzival came upon his hermit uncle, who asked if he were Lähelin, he replied: "Sir, I am not Lähelin. If ever I robbed the dead, it was when I had no wisdom." [26] All this makes no sense unless Lähelin had worn red armor. It implies, too, that the dead man whom Parzival had despoiled was in fact Lähelin, although Wolfram gives him another name for reasons which will be apparent later. This suggestion that the Red Knight whom Parzival killed in his first fight and whose arms he assumed was the enemy of his family is confirmed by the parallel in *Sir Percyvelle*. For in the English poem the hero encountered and slew the Red Knight, who was, like Lähelin, the foe of his family; he stripped the body and donned the red arms; when he met his uncle, he

[20] The Welsh text does not mention the color of the knight's arms, but we can safely assume that they were red.   [21] Loth, *Mabinogion*, 2d ed., II, 119 f.
[22] W. H. French and C. B. Hale, *Middle English Metrical Romances*, pp. 553–61.
[23] *Parzival*, 128, 3–128, 12; 140, 26–141, 10.
[24] This point has already been made by C. Strucks, *Der junge Parzival*, p. 46; by A. C. L. Brown in *Mod. Phil.*, XVI (1919), 556–58. Cf. E. Wechssler, *Sage vom heiligen Gral*, p. 170.
[25] Wolfram, *Parzival*, 154, 25.   [26] *Ibid.*, 474, 1; 475, 4–6.

was mistaken for the Red Knight, just as Parzival was mistaken by his uncle for Lähelin.[27] Is it not obvious that Wolfram, by calling this Red Knight Ither von Gaheviez instead of Lähelin, clumsily covered up a tradition that represented him as involved in a feud with the hero and his family and as the proper object of the hero's vengeance—a tradition shared with *Sir Percyvelle?*

Thus the feud between Perceval and his family on the one hand and one or more Red Knights on the other appears obscurely in Manessier and Wolfram, clearly in *Sir Percyvelle,* and most elaborately in *Perlesvaus.* Like Perceval's meeting with the weeping damsel under the tree, it could not have been developed from the indications of Chrétien. It constitutes the second traditional element in the Vengeance Quest.

A third feature which must possess a considerable antiquity is the tradition which makes the starting point of the feud the slaying, not of Perceval's uncle or cousin, but of his father. It is, above all, his father's death which the youthful hero is bound to avenge.

There are hints of this in several romances. We remember that in *Perlesvaus* the hero's father, as well as his uncle, Alibran de la Gaste Cité, was murdered by "li Rous Jaians." In our study of Perceval's father we saw that his chief Welsh prototype was Bran, and it is noteworthy that according to Manessier the uncle whose death Perceval avenged was named Boon or Gron, indicating an original Bron. Perceval's father in Chrétien's and Wolfram's poems was lord of a waste land, and Manessier's Bron was "roi du desert." The prevailing uncertainty as to Perceval's relationship to the Arthurian counterparts of Bran may have caused the attachment to his uncle of traditions which properly belonged to his father.

And in *Sir Percyvelle,* the *Prose Tristan,* and the Perceval-like romance of *Carduino,* it is in fact the hero's father who is killed and whose death is to be avenged; [28] and even Wolfram shows the influence of this tradition. According to the English poem, Percyvelle unwittingly met and killed with his dart the Red Knight who had murdered his father in a tournament and who for fifteen years had terrorized his uncle and cousins. We are expressly told that the Red Knight was afraid that when the nephews of his victim grew up they would kill him.[29] It is apparently the same basic tradition (though with interesting differences) which emerges in the *Prose Tristan.*[30] The sons of Loth—Gauvain, Gaheriet,

[27] French and Hale, *op. cit.,* pp. 553–57, 559 f.
[28] For discussion of the vengeance motif in these romances cf. W. H. Schofield, *Studies on the Libeaus Desconus,* pp. 183–94; A. Mennung, *Der Bel Inconnu des Renaut de Beaujeu in seinem Verhältnis zum Lybeaus Desconus, Carduino, und Wigalois* (Halle, 1890), pp. 38–43; Strucks, *op. cit.,* pp. 43–48.
[29] French and Hale, *op. cit.,* p. 561.
[30] E. Löseth, *Le Roman en prose de Tristan* (*Bibl. Ec. Hautes Et.,* LXXXII, Paris, 1890), pp. 167–69, 234–38, 241 f.

Mordret, and Agravain—were involved in a feud with the sons of Pellinor, since Gauvain had killed Pellinor. Fearing retaliation, Gauvain also put to death Pellinor's older sons, Lamorat and Driant. When Perceval, the youngest son of Pellinor, came to Arthur's court, the fears of Loth's sons were reawakened. "Gaheriet observed to Gauvain that the young knight might well avenge Pellinor, Lamorat, and Driant." So far we seem to have a variation on the death of Perceval's father and two elder brothers in Chrétien and on the slayer's fear of reprisal in *Sir Percyvelle*. The *Tristan* (cyclic version) goes on to say that the young Perceval, wholly ignorant of this blood feud, departs from Arthur's court. To translate from Löseth's summary:

"Perceval, guided by a damsel, arrives in the Forest Perilous, near an island where his sister, desiring to avenge the death of Pellinor and her brothers on Gauvain, has had two towers erected. She herself dwells in one of them, after placing in the other ten knights of her kindred who were bound to joust with all passing knights. The vanquished are compelled to remain and fight with those who pass by. Perceval comes there and combats victoriously with Gaheriet [who apparently is one of the vanquished knights]; on the advice of Perceval, who does not suspect that his sister is in the island, both [Perceval and Gaheriet] flee from the castle." [31]

Not long after, Gauvain too comes to the island of Perceval's sister and persuades Hector to join in attacking the defenders of the castle, Perceval's kinsmen. The defenders are slaughtered, and Perceval's sister heaps reproaches on Gauvain. Gauvain and Hector depart together. Later we read of a victory won by Perceval over Mordret and Gauvain, but Perceval again neglects the opportunity to settle scores with his father's slayer. Such is the lame conclusion of the great feud between Perceval and the sons of Loth!

The sheer fatuity of the redactors of the *Prose Tristan* could not be better illustrated than by their treatment of this vendetta, which receives such emphasis and yet leads to nothing. Perceval gets the best of Gaheriet, Gauvain, and Mordret, but the dramatic possibilities of the situation are altogether missed. His sister's efforts to trap these same hereditary foes are equally futile. Though such bungling on the part of the authors is not to be pardoned, one can understand the cause. They spared the lives of Loth's sons because, though the feud tradition demanded their deaths, other traditions required their presence later in the story. So Perceval was allowed to defeat but not to kill them.

The probability that this incomplete vendetta was borrowed from a lost source was recognized by Löseth.[32] The probability becomes a certainty when we turn to the cognate form in *Carduino*,[33] the Italian poem of about

[31] *Ibid.*, p. 213, 215 f., 244.   [32] *Ibid.*, p. 213, n. 3.
[33] *I Cantari di Carduino*, ed. P. Rajna (Bologna, 1873). Summarized in E. G. Gardner, *Arthurian Legend in Italian Literature* (London, 1930), pp. 252–58; Schofield, *op. cit.*,

1375 which several scholars have recognized as an independent version of the *enfances* of Perceval.[34] Carduino's obligation to avenge his father's death is not left hanging in the air; one of Loth's sons is killed, the others, contrite, ask pardon and are forgiven. Let us then examine the evidence which shows that the feud story in *Carduino* is cognate with those in the *Prose Tristan* and *Sir Percyvelle*. As in *Sir Percyvelle,* the hero's father lives at Arthur's court and is greatly beloved by the King. As in the *Tristan,* the hero's father is the victim of a plot by Gauvain (Calvano), Mordret (Mordarette), and Gaheriet (Agueriesse). As in *Sir Percyvelle,* the hero is an only son; he becomes possessed of one or two darts picked up in the forest, and his mother instructs him in their use. As in the *Tristan,* the hero unwittingly encounters Gaheriet in combat and vanquishes him. As in *Sir Percevelle,* the hero unwittingly kills his father's murderer with a dart. Since the author of *Carduino* could not have read *Sir Percyvelle,* nor could the English poet have read Italian, we must postulate a lost French *conte* to explain their resemblances.

Though, of course, the author of *Carduino* might have known the *Prose Tristan,* yet the Italian's far neater handling of the vengeance theme suggests a common source for their common features; and this suggestion is confirmed by a curious blunder on the Italian's part. Carduino's father is called Dondinello, and Dr. Brugger has proved beyond any doubt that the name was originally an epithet meaning "Little Fool," and that it properly belonged to the son, not the father.[35] Now the account of Dodinel provided by the *Vulgate Merlin* not only resembles in a general way the *enfances* of Perceval, but also, as I showed in Chapter LVIII, indicates that the name was really a sobriquet for Perceval.[36] Therefore, the author of *Carduino* must have borrowed the feud story, not from *Sir Percyvelle* or the *Tristan,* in which the epithet is not applied to Perceval, but more or less directly from a *conte* in which Perceval was nicknamed Dodinel. Thus we can be sure that behind *Sir Percyvelle,* the *Prose Tristan,* and *Carduino* was an established tradition that the vendetta in the Perceval legend was occasioned by the slaying of the hero's father.

It is a puzzling but highly significant fact that, whereas in the branch of this tradition represented by *Sir Percyvelle* the slayer of the hero's father was the unchivalrous figure of the Red Knight, in the other branch represented by the *Tristan* and *Carduino* those responsible for the murder included the patterns of chivalry, Gauvain and Gaheriet. In due course, we shall consider why these brothers, usually so noble, came to be cast in roles so out of character. Now let us merely observe that both the *Tristan*

pp. 5–53. Schofield was wrong in arguing (pp. 184–90) that *Carduino* was based on the *Tristan.*

[34] J. L. Weston, *Legend of Perceval* (London, 1906), I, 83 f. Mennung, *op. cit.,* p. 43. *Medieval Studies in Memory of G. Schoepperle Loomis,* p. 164. Strucks, *op. cit.,* p. 64.

[35] *Medieval Studies in Memory of G. Schoepperle Loomis,* pp. 168–71.

[36] Cf. *supra,* pp. 339–40.

and *Carduino* seem to equate Gaheriet in particular with Chrétien's Red Knight, for in both texts Gaheriet is the first knight whom the boy hero encounters, and in the second text he is killed by the boy's dart. This equation explains why Wolfram discarded the name Lähelin for the Red Knight of Parzival's first encounter and substituted Ither von Gaheviez or, in two places, simply Gaheviez.[37] For Gaheviez is manifestly a corruption of the recorded nominative form Gaheriez;[38] and Wolfram gave the Red Knight not only the name but also the character of Gaheriet.[39] Gaheviez was Arthur's cousin,[40] Gaheriet was his nephew. Gaheviez was "the flower of chivalrous breeding, the delight of women's eyes," and his death caused many a knight and lady of Arthur's court to weep, whereas Gaheriet was "fair and brave and almost the best of all the brothers,"[41] his death was mourned by old and young, and Arthur declared: "Here lies dead Gaheriet, the most valiant knight of all our kindred."[42] Certainly, then, Wolfram was following the revolutionary tradition which identified the Red Knight with Gaheriet, the tradition reflected in the *Tristan* and *Carduino,* the tradition which represented Gaheriet and his brothers as the murderers of Perceval's father, and a tradition which, since Wolfram wrote about 1210, probably goes back to the twelfth century. Wolfram therefore indirectly supports the evidence of *Sir Percyvelle,* the *Tristan,* and *Carduino,* that one of the fixed elements in the Vengeance Quest was Perceval's unwitting killing of his father's slayer.

To summarize the results of our investigation up to this point, we are certain that some sort of vendetta must have been early associated with Perceval, for it turns up in almost every version of his legend, sometimes in more than one form in the same text. We have isolated three recurrent elements in this tradition. The first, the weeping damsel formula found in Chrétien, Wolfram, *Peredur,* and most completely in *Perlesvaus,* represents the hero as coming upon a mourning damsel under a tree, who is cherishing the head or the body of Perceval's newly slain kinsman; she incites the hero to revenge, and he later slays the murderer. The second, the Red Knight formula supplied by Manessier, Wolfram, *Sir Percyvelle,* and above all by *Perlesvaus,* represents the hero as involved in a blood feud with one or more Red Knights, who were not only the slayers of his kinsmen but also the invaders of his patrimony and the enemies of his

---

[37] *Parzival,* 246, 4; 744, 10. On the origin of the name Ither von Gaheviez cf. *Neophilologus,* V (1920), 115-21.   [38] Chrétien, *Erec,* vs. 1725.

[39] Miss Richey in *Mod. Lang. Rev.,* XXVI (1931), 315-29, has well remarked: "In Ither we see an imperfect attempt to combine the Red Knight of Crestien's *Perceval* with another character, one who is the flower of chivalrous breeding and the delight of women's eyes." She did not perceive, as did Strucks, p. 61, that the second character was Gaheriet rather than Ider.   [40] *Parzival,* 145, 11. "Artuses basen sun . . . Ez was Ither von Gaheviez."

[41] H. O. Sommer, *Vulgate Version,* I, 280. Paulin Paris in *Romania,* IV, 141, wrote: "Dans *l'Artus,* dans le *Lancelot,* et dans le *Tristan,* Gaheriet est le plus loyal, le plus preux et le plus sage des quatre fils du roi Loth."   [42] Sommer, *op. cit.,* VI, 286 f.

surviving family. The third, the father-vengeance formula directly represented in *Sir Percyvelle,* the *Prose Tristan, Carduino,* and indirectly attested by Wolfram, attributes the origin of the feud to the treacherous slaying of the boy hero's father.

Readers who have followed the argument through the maze of evidence have doubtless noted that in no romance do all three of these patterns occur in a single coordinated plot. Manessier, to be sure, has a coherent plot and does reflect dimly each of the three patterns—the damsel in charge of a dead body, instigating revenge; the lord of the Red Tower as the slayer of Perceval's kinsman; the possibility suggested by the kinsman's name, Bron, "roi du desert," that he might once have been Perceval's father rather than his uncle. But Manessier achieved coherence only by drastic alterations and omissions, and in *Perlesvaus* the hero's quarrels with various Red Knights are imperfectly correlated. And though Chrétien exhibits the first pattern of the weeping damsel clearly, he fails to connect it with the death of Perceval's father or the slaying of the Red Knight. No one reading the first 4,000 lines of *Le Conte del Graal* would suspect that these incidents were parts of a unified whole, an originally coherent tradition of Perceval's revenge for the death of his father. Were not, then, the three patterns distinct in origin, and were not such partial integrations as we find in *Sir Percyvelle* and Manessier purely artificial and late? The answer to this fundamental question must be sought in the Celtic sources.

There are, to be sure, no traces of the vendetta in the surviving Welsh tales of Pryderi and Bran, where one would expect to find them, since Pryderi was the original of Perceval and Bran was the original of Perceval's father. Nevertheless, we know that the *Four Branches of the Mabinogi* supply anything but a complete picture of the Pryderi–Bran tradition; the Unspelling Quest takes an utterly different form, and the influence of the Finn saga on the *enfances* of Pryderi, which we must presuppose to account for its influence on the *enfances* of Perceval, does not appear at all. Therefore, the absence of the vendetta from the *Four Branches* does not mean that it did not form a part, and an important part, of the lost Pryderi legend.

When we turn to what has already been proved to be an ultimate and important source of the Perceval legend, the Finn saga, we perceive, as Nutt, somewhat hazily, and Arthur Brown, more clearly, have already done,[43] that here is not only an elaborate story of a blood feud, but also a story which weaves into one pattern the three formulae which we have isolated in the Perceval Vengeance Quest. Let us review the story of Finn as we find it in the *Macgnimartha,* supplying a conclusion from other documents.[44]

[43] A. Nutt, *Studies on the Legend of the Holy Grail,* p. 159. *Mod. Phil.,* XVIII (1920), 211–19.
[44] Cross and Slover, *Ancient Irish Tales,* pp. 360–65, 359. *Eriu,* I (1904), 180–90. K. Meyer, *Fianaigecht,* p. 71. Nutt, *op. cit.,* pp. 158, 189. Prof. MacNeill rightly stresses the importance

At the battle of Cnucha, Finn's father, Cumall, was first wounded by the Gray of Luachar, and was killed by Aed (Fire), son of Daire the Red, alias Morna. Aed himself was wounded in the eye so that he was known thereafter as Goll, "the One-Eyed." Many of Cumall's people fell, and because of this battle a hereditary feud arose between the sons of Daire the Red (alias Morna) and the posthumous son of Cumall. For fear of the sons of Daire the Red, Finn was reared secretly by two women in a forest. He grew up to be a skillful hunter and was so nimble of foot that he outran and captured two bucks. His weapon was a casting spear. He got the nickname Finn, meaning "Fair." He took service with the King of Bantry without making himself known, but the King remarked of him that if Cumall had left a son, this would be he. Finn went to seek his father's brother, Crimall, in Connaught. He heard the wail of a woman, and found her alone, weeping for the death of her son at the hands of a terrible warrior. Finn went in pursuit of the warrior and slew him. "He who had fallen there was the Gray of Luachar, who had dealt the first wound to Cumall at the battle of Cnucha. Thereupon Finn went into Connacht, and found Crimall [his uncle] as an old man in a desert wood there . . . and told him his story from beginning to end." This is all that the *Macgnimartha* tells of the blood feud, but another ancient text tells of a temporary peace made between Finn and the Clan Morna on the payment of a fine by the latter. But the old quarrel broke out again, and a text copied in 1419 mentions the death of Goll at the hands of Finn and the great slaughter wrought by the hero among the Clan Morna, the descendants of Daire the Red. The late folktales also agree that Finn fulfilled his destiny by avenging his father's death on his father's slayer.

If we piece together the Vengeance Quest from the various Perceval texts,[45] we find an extraordinary resemblance.

Perceval's father was killed in battle or tourney by a Red Knight, and his kinsmen also fell at the hands of the Red Knight or his clan. Thus a hereditary feud arose between the Red Knight and Perceval, a posthumous son. For fear that the boy would likewise lose his life, his mother reared him secretly in a forest. He grew up to be a skillful hunter and was so nimble of foot that he rounded up two hinds. His weapon was a casting spear. He was called always "fair son," or "fair brother," or "fair sire." He went to King Arthur's court, demanded knighthood, and though he failed to make himself known, the King detected a resemblance between the boy and his father. Perceval, after leaving the castle of an uncle, came upon a damsel alone, weeping for the death of her lover at the hands of a terrible knight. Perceval went in quest of the slayer. He met a Red Knight, slew him, and thus unwittingly avenged his father's death. He also slew other members of the hostile clan of Red Knights who had invaded his patrimony. He came upon his uncle, a hermit in a desert wood, and told him his story.

Despite dislocations and alterations, the vendetta theme of the Finn saga is the manifest source of the Vengeance Quest in the Perceval legend.

of the vendetta in the Finn cycle in *Duanaire Finn*, Part I (London, 1908), pp. xlvi–xlviii: "In the Macgnimartha the inexpiable feud arises out of the killing of Cumhall in battle by the Luagni and the House of Morna. Whence it was the destiny of Cumhall's unborn son to follow the game of vengeance to the end." [45] Chrétien, *Peredur, Sir Percyvelle, Perlesvaus*.

Here are the originals of the first and third formulae of the Vengeance Quest—the lone woman, weeping for a newly slain youth and calling for revenge, the hero's requiting his father's death upon his father's slayer. The second formula, the feud between the hero and one or more Red Knights, was probably inspired by the feud between Finn and the sons of Daire the Red, particularly Goll, whose real name was Aed, "Fire." [46] There might be some doubt as to this derivation, since the Irish texts lay no stress on the redness of Finn's hereditary enemies. But the Perceval romances are so insistent on the red arms or the red coloring of Perceval's foes that this feature must have come down from an old tradition. And if we assume that it was derived from the sons of Daire the Red, the chief of whom was named "Fire," we should have a neat explanation for two of the most perplexing and troublesome facts in the Vengeance Quest. For the Red Knights of this Quest, presumably derived from the Finn saga, have been mistakenly equated by the *conteurs* with those other Red Knights whom we have met in Arthurian romance and whose Celtic antecedents we have found to be quite different.

The first instance of this mistaken blending is the Red Knight whom Perceval killed in his first encounter as narrated in Chrétien's and Wolfram's poems, in *Perlesvaus* and *Sir Percyvelle*.[47] The combined evidence of these texts, as we have just seen, shows that this Red Knight and his clan are the Arthurian representatives of the sons of Daire the Red. Yet it was also shown, in our first discussion of Perceval's combat with the Red Knight,[48] that the latter had inherited his role from Curoi, and that the color of his arms was a solar feature. The apparent contradiction can, of course, be easily resolved. Again and again we have found that Arthurian characters represent a blending of two or more traditional figures. Such were Eurain, Mabonagrain's mistress, Galehot, and Laudine. Perceval himself inherited his legend from both Finn and Cuchulainn.[49] It would be most natural that if the sons of Daire the Red, the hereditary foes of Finn, are represented in Arthurian romance by the Red Knights, hereditary foes of Perceval, they would be confused with the representatives of Cuchulainn's mortal enemy, the solar Curoi. Just such a fusion of traditional figures must have occurred in the episode of the Red Knight as recounted by Chrétien and in *Sir Percyvelle*.

The same hypothesis offers a solution to a second baffling feature in the Vengeance Quest. Why, in the tradition represented by the *Prose Tristan* and *Carduino,* do Gauvain and Gaheriet take the places of the Red Knights as the hereditary foes of Perceval and as the slayers of his father and kinsmen? Why does Wolfram likewise assign the odious role of the Red Knight to the noble Gaheviez? How could such slanderous

---

[46] T. F. O'Rahilly, in *Early Irish History and Mythology*, p. 278, says Goll is the sun-deity.
[47] *Parzival,* 154, 11–155, 18. *Perlesvaus,* ed. Nitze, I, ll. 488–97. French and Hale, *op. cit.,* pp. 553 f.   [48] See Chap. LXII.   [49] See Chap. LVIII.

libels on these paragons of knighthood have been accepted by the romancers and their readers? As a matter of fact, they were not wholly accepted. The authors of the *Tristan* assign the major guilt to Gauvain and exempt Gaheriet from responsibility for the murder of Pellinor and his elder sons.[50] The author of *Carduino* does not exculpate Gaheriet (Agueriesse) but pardons his repentant brothers. Wolfram insists on the noble nature of Gaheviez,[51] despite his outrageous conduct at Arthur's court. These are clearly partial concessions to the prevailing concept of Gauvain and Gaheriet as embodiments of knightly valor and honor; but they are only partial concessions. The fact remains that these three romancers replaced the treacherous and murderous Red Knights of the Vengeance Quest by Gauvain or Gaheriet or both. Why did they introduce so revolutionary, so unwelcome an innovation? There must have been a reason, and I can think of none so adequate as this same confusion of Red Knights— the Arthurian counterparts of the sons of Daire the Red and the counterparts of the solar Curoi and Cuchulainn.

It remains to inquire whether Gauvain and Gaheriet were ever assigned red arms. The most direct testimony regarding Gauvain comes from *Gawain and the Green Knight* and *De Ortu Walwanii*. The English poet described Gawain's horse trappings as red and his shield as gules, painted with a golden pentangle.[52] In the Latin romance Walwanius, the Boy without a Name, donned a crimson surcoat on the day he was knighted by an emperor, and was known thereafter as the Knight of the Surcoat,[53] just as Perceval, ignorant of his name, acquired red arms on the day when he came to Arthur's court to be knighted, and was henceforth known as "le chevalier vermoil." There is indirect evidence to the same effect. In *Yvain,* we remember, Gauvain is referred to as the sun, and elsewhere is credited with the trait of waxing and waning in strength in sympathy with the rising and setting of the sun,[54] a trait which in three romances is attached to a knight with red arms.[55] Gauvain is likely to have acquired these solar attributes from Cuchulainn, his prototype in many episodes. As for Gaheriet, there exists, I believe, no authority of any consequence as to the color of his arms, but it has been shown already that he is the alter ego of Gauvain,[56] descended from the same Gwri or Gware of the Golden Hair and inheriting a number of the same traditions. It is likely, therefore, that both Gauvain and Gaheriet were once known as Red

---

[50] Löseth, *Tristan en prose*, pp. 167 f. Note that in a certain ms. there is proof that one reader rebelled against the libel on Gauvain. Cf. *ibid.* pp. 224 f.: "Dans 772, le nom de Gauvain, presque partout où ce chevalier joue un rôle peu honorable, a été gratté par une main postérieure et remplacé le plus souvent par celui d'Agravain."

[51] *Parzival*, 159, 20–161, 2.   [52] *Gawain and the Green Knight*, vss. 601–3.

[53] *Historia Meriadoci and De Ortu Walwanii*, ed. J. D. Bruce, pp. 59 f. ". . . tunicam sibi paraverat purpuream." Though Bruce on p. lxxii translates *purpuream* as "purple," it is well known that the word often designates a deep crimson.

[54] *Mort Artu*, ed. J. D. Bruce, pp. 287 f. J. L. Weston, *Legend of Gawain*, pp. 12 f. *PMLA*, XLIII (1928), 391.   [55] Cf. *supra*, p. 165.   [56] Cf. *supra*, pp. 150 f.

Knights.[57] And in this probability we have an explanation for the repellent role which both play in *Carduino,* which Gauvain plays in the *Prose Tristan,* and which Gaheviez plays in *Parzival.*

The hypothesis set forth above as to the confusion between the Arthurian counterparts of the sons of Daire the Red and the counterparts of the solar heroes, Curoi and Cuchulainn, is almost demonstrable in the case of the Red Knight in *Sir Percyvelle;* it also offers a solution to one of the most mystifying features of the Vengeance Quest as we find it in the *Prose Tristan, Carduino,* and *Parzival.* Until a better solution is offered, the hypothesis deserves to be granted a tentative validity.

There remains one feature of the Vengeance Quest which seems to have no parallel in the ancient Finn saga—the sword.[58] There are in the Round Table romances countless swords with different histories and presumably of different origins. For some of them Celtic provenance seems to be proved. Already we have had occasion to connect the sword which Peredur thrice broke and twice mended at the castle of his second maternal uncle with the spears and swords which Cuchulainn broke at the court of his maternal uncle.[59] The derivation of the famous brand Calibor, better known as Excalibur, from the sword Caledvwlch in the Mabinogion, and ultimately from the sword variously called Caladcolg or Caladbolg in the Irish sagas, is accepted by all scholars.[60] The sword which Gauvain procured from Gurgalain in *Perlesvaus* seems to bear some relation to the sword which Kulhwch won from Gwrnach Gawr, and also to the sword of Rhydderch, numbered among the Thirteen Treasures of Britain.[61] The brands with which alone Carado of the Dolorous Tower and

[57] The reason why they do not appear as such in the extant romances is probably the fear on the part of the authors that there would be confusion with the malevolent Red Knights who had inherited their roles either from the sons of Daire the Red or from Curoi. Nevertheless, three knights whose names appear to be deformations or substitutes for Gauvain bear red arms: Galaad, who is a sanctified Gauvain (cf. R. S. Loomis, *Celtic Myth,* pp. 155, 216 f., 250–52); Balaan, whose role approximates that of Gauvain in *Meraugis* (cf. *ibid.,* p. 251, n. 10); and Gasozein, whose role has been shown above (p. 135) to correspond to that of Walwanius in *De Ortu Walwanii,* and who carried a red spear and wore red hose (Heinrich von dem Türlin, *Krone,* vss. 3420, 3709 f.). Gasozein, however, inherited his role also from Havgan, "Summer White," and therefore wore a white shirt. Cf. *Journ. of Eng. and Germ. Phil.,* XLII (1943), 170–74.

[58] For the sword of the Grail romances cf. Nitze in *PMLA,* XXIV (1909), 406–10; Weston, *Legend of Perceval,* I, 132–52; R. S. Loomis, *Celtic Myth,* 244–48. Nutt, in his *Studies on the Legend of the Holy Grail,* p. 189, cited a unique example of the sword of vengeance from a modern Gaelic folktale of Finn, and offered it as a cognate tradition with that found in Manessier. But the similarity is probably due to coincidence. The folktale account of the testing of the sword by shaking is probably derived from Cuchulainn's similar feat in the *Macgnimrada Conchulainn* (Cross and Slover, *Ancient Irish Tales,* p. 143).

[59] Cf. *supra,* pp. 336 f.

[60] *Göttingische gelehrte Anzeigen,* 1890, pp. 516 f. Weston, *Legend of Gawain,* pp. 16 f. Bruce, *Evolution of Arthurian Romance,* I, 87 f. Loth, *Mabinogion,* 2d ed., I, 258, n. 2. *Zts. f. celt. Phil.,* XII (1918), 281–83.

[61] *PMLA,* XLIII, 392 f. *Perlesvaus,* ed. Nitze, II, 246–50. *Speculum,* VIII (1933), 430. *Romanische Forschungen,* XLV (1931), 68–70.

Milocrates could be killed can certainly be traced back to the sword with which alone Curoi could be slain.[62] Only the first of these weapons of Arthurian legend, since Peredur was twice able to rejoin the pieces in the castle of his uncle, suggests that it has been affected by the sword of the Vengeance Quest, and it is the latter with which we are here concerned.

Before we attempt the arduous task of determining its nebulous history and origin, let us review the evidence. What, first of all, does Chrétien tell us? [63] There was an inscription on the blade, telling where it was forged. It would break only in a certain peril which the maker alone knew, and he would die before he made such another. The damsel under the tree warned Perceval that the weapon would fly in pieces in battle, and that the smith, Trebuchet, who made it and who dwelt "at the lake which is above or below Cotoatre," could alone reforge and retemper it. An important fact has been established by Mr. Alexander Bell: Cotoatre is a corruption of Scottewatre, meaning the Firth of Forth.[64] Thus in the contemporary *Chronicles of the Picts and Scots* we read of "that best water which in Scots is called Froch [read Forth], in British Werid, in French Scottewatre, that is, the Water of the Scots." That this Anglo-French word became known to the French romancers is shown by its occurrence in *Escanor:* "son of the King of Escossuatre." [65] Chrétien was certainly following a text which localized the home of the smith near the Firth of Forth, perhaps for no other reason than that the region was remote and mysterious.[66]

Chrétien does not expressly associate the sword with the vengeance theme. But the Pseudo-Wauchier continuation introduces the motif.[67] Gauwain saw in the hall of the Grail Castle a rich bier and on it the half of a sword. Later the Grail King entered bearing the other half, and, addressing the body on the bier, cried out: "How great an injury lies here, whereby all the land languishes! God grant that thou be avenged and thereby the land be restored to peace!" The king then placed both halves of the sword in Gauwain's hands and bade him re-join them, but they failed to unite. When Gauwain asked concerning the weapon, he was told: "The realm of Logres and all the country were destroyed by the blow dealt by this sword." After this tantalizing disclosure, he fell asleep and we learn no more of the fatal stroke or the vengeance due to the body on the bier.

[62] *Journ. of Eng. and Germ. Phil.*, XLII, 156–58.   [63] Vss. 3131–84, 3654–87.

[64] *Zts. f. rom. Phil.*, LIV (1934), 753–55.

[65] Gerard d'Amiens, *Escanor*, ed. H. Michelant (Tübingen, 1886), vs. 4203. Cf. Wace, *Brut*, ed. I. Arnold, I, vs. 1307.

[66] Cf. "les porz de Galvoie" and "la cité d'Orcanie" (*Conte del Graal*, ed. Hilka, vss. 8648, 9101) and "En Escoce a une contrée Qui Calatir est apelée (*Lays of Desiré, Graelent, and Melion*, ed. E. M. Grimes, p. 48).   [67] Potvin, *Perceval le Gallois*, III, 364 f.; IV, 1–6.

At the end of Wauchier's continuation these threads are picked up and Manessier weaves them into his narrative.[68] Perceval, returning after many years to the Grail Castle, succeeded in uniting the fragments except for a slight crack. He learned that the blade had broken when Partinal slew Boon or Gron, "roi du desert." The king's body and the fragments had been brought by Perceval's female cousin to the Grail Castle. Perceval vowed to avenge his uncle's death, took the brand, and set forth. He came by chance to the forge, where the smith Tribuet completely restored the faulty weapon. With it Perceval finally beheaded Partinal.

Gerbert, starting like Manessier with the partial mending of the sword by Perceval, gives a quite different sequel.[69] Perceval, in an access of impatience, broke the sword in two by striking at the door of the Earthly Paradise. He rode on and came to a castle standing above a river, and was welcomed with joy by all, including a lovely damsel named Escolasse. The castle was named Cothoatre. Near by was a smithy, where the aged Trebuchet had forged three swords, one of them destined to break in a sore peril. He alone could repair it, but would live only a short time thereafter. After a night's sleep, Perceval killed with an ax two *serpens* (dragons) [70] which blocked the way to the smithy. Trebuchet received the pieces of the blade from Perceval, forged them together, and restored the weapon whole, with the assurance that Perceval was the best knight in the world. Perceval parted from Escolasse and the castle of Cotoatre, and as he rode away, heard bells tolling for the passing of Trebuchet's soul. After years of wandering he returned for a third visit to the Grail Castle, was, strangely enough, presented with a broken sword again, and himself pieced it together successfully. Gerbert, it will be seen, fulfills in the visit to Cotoatre the forecast of Chrétien, and like Chrétien fails to associate the sword with the Vengeance Quest. It seems probable that both were drawing from a common source, for Gerbert could not have realized that Cotoatre had any connection with Escotoatre, and yet he names the lady of the castle Escolasse, which can hardly be anything else but a corruption of Escotaise, a woman of Escoche, the country lying beyond Escotoatre.[71] Both Chrétien and Gerbert, therefore, were following at one or more removes a text which localized the smith's home near the Firth of Forth.

[68] Cf. *supra*, n. 11, 12.

[69] Gerbert de Montreuil, *Continuation*, ed. M. Williams, I, vss. 168–909. Potvin, *op. cit.*, VI, 164–69.

[70] Possibly these *serpens* may have been suggested through some association of the sword with Calibor, for in *The Dream of Rhonabwy* the sword of Arthur (Caledvwlch) is thus described (Loth, *Mabinogion*, I, 363): "l'épée d'Arthur sur laquelle étaient gravés deux serpents d'or. Lorsqu'on tirait l'épée du fourreau, on voyait comme deux langues de feu sortir de la bouche des serpents." Cf. Nitze in *PMLA*, XXIV, 410; R. S. Loomis, *Celtic Myth*, p. 246.

[71] On the meaning of Escoche cf. *Mod. Lang. Rev.*, XX (1925), 160; *Mod. Phil.*, XXVI (1928), 7 f. The *l* of Escolasse probably represents a misreading of the *t* of Escotaise.

A very strange mosaic of the traditions connected with the sword is contained in *La Queste del Saint Graal*.[72]

Galaad rode through the forest of Celibe with Perceval's sister and was entertained by her in her castle overnight. The next day the two joined Perceval and Bohort, entered a ship, and were borne away from the realm of Logres. Arriving at a desert isle, they discovered another magnificent ship and in it a sword, partly drawn from the sheath. The hilt was made of two beasts, one a serpent of Calidoine, the other a fish of the Euphrates.[73] On the blade an inscription warned that only he who best deserved to draw it should make the attempt; otherwise death or maiming would ensue. Perceval's sister then revealed that this was the sword with which King Urlain had killed King Labran,[74] with the result that two realms had become sterile and were called the Waste Land. Urlain himself fell dead in accordance with the inscription. Another inscription on the sheath read: "He who shall prize me more will find more to blame in me in his great need than he could believe." This prognostic also had been fulfilled. Forty years after Christ's Passion, Nascien caught up this sword to defend himself against a giant but, brandishing, broke it. When Nascien met his brother-in-law, King Mordrain, he told the story of the sword and showed the pieces. Mordrain placed them together and they united. But unfortunately Nascien was smitten in the shoulder by a sword for his presumption in drawing this sword. A similar fate befell the Maimed King, Pellinor, who, finding the weapon in the ship, drew it, only to be smitten with a lance through the thighs; and he would not be healed till Galaad came to him. After a long discourse on the other wonders of the ship, Perceval's sister changed the hempen girdle of the sword for new ones made of her own hair, and declared that it was called "the Sword of the Strange Girdle." [75] Bohort and Perceval declared that the sword should belong to Galaad, for by its means the remaining perilous adventures of Logres would be accomplished. The damsel girded the sword on Galaad. The four then departed in their own ship, and after a night's sail they landed near the castle of Cartelois in the march of Escoce.[76] There the three companions destroyed ten wicked knights and their followers. Galaad had twinges of conscience, saying: "It is not for us to take vengeance." [77] But when the companions were brought before the good Count Ernol, the former lord of the castle, he laid his head on Galaad's breast and said: "The High Lord sends thee word that thou hast this day so avenged Him on His enemies that the company of heaven rejoiced thereof." [78] He urged Galaad to speed to the succor of the Maimed King, and then his soul left his body. Not long after, when the three companions arrived at the Castle of Corbenic, each in turn tried to mend another brand—the broken sword with which Joseph of Arimathea had been smitten through the thigh—and Galaad was successful.[79]

[72] H. O. Sommer, *Vulgate Version*, VI, 144–50.   [73] Cf. Loomis, *Celtic Myth*, pp. 246 f.
[74] Cf. *supra*, pp. 389 f.   [75] Sommer, *op. cit.*, VI, 162.
[76] *Ibid.*, p. 163. Probably Cartelois "en la marche d'Escoce" is to be identified with modern Caithness, Wace's Cateneis. Cf. *Brut*, ed. I. Arnold, I, vss. 2618–20; F. Lot, *Etude sur le Lancelot*, p. 143, n. 13; Chrétien de Troyes, *Karrenritter*, ed. W. Foerster, p. clxxxi.
[77] Sommer, *op. cit.*, VI, 164. On the significance of this scruple cf. A. Pauphilet, *Etudes sur la Queste del S. Graal* (Paris, 1921), pp. 34 f.
[78] Sommer, *op. cit.*, VI, 166.   [79] *Ibid.*, VI, 187 f.

After the vision of the Grail and the service of the communion by Christ himself, Galaad healed the Maimed King, and the three companions departed, came to the ship in which they had found the strange sword, and sailed away to the land of Sarras.

This account of the two swords, their breaking, and their mending, is of course a composite. Just how much of it was inspired by *Le Conte del Graal* it is impossible to tell, but it would seem very little.[80] We have seen in the previous chapter how much more primitive is the account of the Dolorous Stroke and its effect on the two lands than anything of the sort to be met elsewhere. The vengeance motif is treated in so different a fashion from the form in Manessier that one hardly recognizes its presence. The constant association of the Sword of the Strange Girdle with a mysterious ship is something unknown to the poets of *Le Conte del Graal*.[81] Perhaps most curious of all is the fact that though the author of the *Queste* knows nothing about the smith of Cotoatre or about Escolasse, he too seems to feel a connection between the sword and Scotland. A part of the hilt is formed of a serpent of Calidoine, which must be the Roman name for Scotland, Caledonia, preserved by the Welsh as Celyddon and occurring in Geoffrey of Monmouth's *Vita Merlini* as Calidon. Again, when Galaad has received the sword, he proceeds at once to the march of Scotland, and there executes vengeance on the wicked knights. Possibly the fact that three romancers connect the sword in different ways with Scotland may be due to coincidence, but it does not seem likely.

From all this discussion of the sword of the Grail Castle in *Le Conte del Graal* and the Sword of the Strange Girdle in *La Queste del Saint Graal* it becomes plain that we are dealing with a highly complicated tradition. Many of the recurrent features seem to be traceable to no extant Celtic source. So far as I am aware, there is no Welsh or Irish smith who forges a sword destined to break in an hour of peril, who alone can reunite the fragments, and who dies after completing the task. No magic sword enters into the Welsh versions of the Waste Land theme as a cause of the disaster. Though the voyages of Perceval, Bohort, and Galaad suggest derivation from the voyages of the three sons of Turenn in Manannan's coracle,[82] there is nothing in the Irish saga corresponding to the

[80] Cf. F. Lot, *op. cit.*, p. 191; Bruce, *Evolution*, I, 419–25; A. Pauphilet, *op. cit.*, pp. 152–54.
[81] There is probably a connection with Pseudo-Wauchier's story of the arrival of the body of Brangemuer, who was king of an island where no mortal man dwelt, at Arthur's court. The body is pierced by a broken weapon, and Gaheriet is obliged to use the blade in avenging the dead king. Cf. H. Newstead, *Bran the Blessed in Arthurian Romance*, pp. 121–25. Though agreeing with Prof. Newstead that there was much confusion as to Bran's horn (*cors*), I do not believe that in this instance the body of Brangemuer was anything else than the body of the slain Bran, as we find it also in Pseudo-Wauchier's description of Gauvain at the Grail Castle and in Manessier's version of the bringing of King Bron's body to the Grail Castle. Note the persistence of the vengeance motif. Cf. the same pattern in *Vengeance Raguidel* and *Vulgate Lancelot* (summarized in Bruce, *Evolution*, II, 209–14, 327).
[82] *Speculum*, VIII, 423 f. Cross and Slover, *op. cit.*, pp. 64 f.

Sword of the Strange Girdle. But there is one recurrent pattern which does seem traceable to Ireland.

In *Peredur,* Pseudo-Wauchier, Wauchier, Gerbert, and the *Queste* we find one or more of the Grail heroes coming to the Grail Castle and being requested by the host to unite the fragments of a broken sword. Sometimes they succeed in the task, though Peredur's success is partial, Gauwain fails in Pseudo-Wauchier, and Bohort and Perceval fail in the *Queste.* The weapon, when restored, is destined to perform an act of vengeance. According to Pseudo-Wauchier, the fragments are directly connected with the death of a king whose body lies in the Grail Castle, and whose land is waste; and it is implied that if Gauwain had been able to piece together the weapon, he would have used it to avenge the king's death, and thus have brought joy to the land. What is implied in Pseudo-Wauchier is explicit in Manessier. Perceval, having reunited the pieces of the sword which killed Bron, "roi du desert," whose body lies in the Grail Castle, eventually uses the weapon to behead the slayer, Partinal. Well-established features of the sword tradition, then, are these: One or more knights come to an Otherworld dwelling and are welcomed. The host asks the hero to repair a broken sword. The hero accomplishes the task, receives the sword, and departs on a mission of vengeance for which many folk will be grateful.

Professor Pennington has pointed out an analogous pattern in *The Colloquy of the Ancients,*[83] an Irish compilation which can be dated 1142–1167.[84] The principal character in the tale is Cailte, one of the *Fiana* and the nephew of Finn.

Cailte and a companion came by chance on a faery palace [85] in Connaught and were invited to enter. The host, Fergus Fairhair, son of the great god Dagda, asked Cailte to repair a broken sword which the Tuath De Danann (the chief Irish gods) had refused to mend. Cailte spent a day in completing the task, and also mended a spear and a javelin. Fergus revealed that each of these weapons was fated to slay one of the enemies of the Tuath De Danann. Cailte announced that it was his destiny to do some deed for which the men of Ireland and Scotland (Alba) and the Tuath De Danann would be thankful. After three days Cailte and two companions proceeded on their way with the mended weapons, came to another faery palace and were entertained by a troop of beautiful women. The enemies of the Tuath De landed to attack the palace, and in the ensuing battle Cailte slew the King of Norway with the mended spear, and his two companions employed the sword and the javelin to accomplish their destined ends.

[83] *Mod. Lang. Notes,* XLIII (1928), 534–36. For trans. cf. W. Stokes, E. Windisch, *Irische Texte,* Ser. IV, Heft 1 (Leipzig, 1900), 254–58; S. H. O'Grady, *Silva Gadelica* (London, 1892), II, 247–49.

[84] R. Thurneysen, *Irische Helden- und Königsage,* p. 45. *Eriu,* X (1926), 74.

[85] The Irish word, which Stokes translates "elfmound," is *sidh.* Within these mounds were the palaces of the gods. Cf. *PMLA,* LVI (1941), 892; Thurneysen, *op. cit.,* pp. 62 f.; E. MacNeill, *Duanaire Finn,* Part I, pp. 144 f.

Needless to say, the resemblances between this tale and the tradition of the sword of vengeance in the French romances are by no means compelling, and the differences are many. Yet there is a fundamental sameness. One or more warriors come to an Otherworld dwelling and are welcomed. The host asks the hero to repair a broken sword. The hero accomplishes the task, his companion receives the mended sword, and they depart on a mission for which the mended weapons are essential and for which many folk will be grateful. Such differences as exist may well be due to the lateness of the Irish text,[86] which cannot of course be the direct ancestor of the Arthurian tradition, and to the adjustments necessitated by fusion with the Finn vendetta and other additions. And fusion with the Finn vendetta would be likely since both tales belong to the same cycle, both are partially localized in Connaught, and both deal with a struggle between two hostile tribes or clans. The hypothesis of such a fusion would explain why the breaking and the mending of a sword are so persistently attached to the Feud Quest of the Grail romances.

Proceeding on this hypothesis, let us see what happened. In Wales, as we know, the Finn complex must have become attached to Pryderi, and consequently Pryderi became the avenger of his father or uncle Bran, just as Finn was the avenger of his father Cumall. In some versions of the death of Bran it would seem that the poisoned spear, which was the fatal weapon in Welsh tradition, was replaced by the broken sword of the Irish tradition, for while the poisoned spear is retained in Wolfram's account of Gahmuret's death,[87] the broken sword which Gauwain attempted to repair in the Grail Castle and which Perceval did repair was not only the instrument of Bron's death according to Manessier, but also the instrument of retribution upon his slayer. Association of the sword with the death of Bran would inevitably bring in the Waste Land motif;[88] and thus we find the broken sword, the death of King Bron, the Waste Land, and the obligation to revenge, all combined in Pseudo-Wauchier's and Manessier's versions of the visit to the Grail Castle; while the Sword of the Strange Girdle, the death of Labran, and the Waste Land motif in its most primitive form are linked together in the *Queste*. Other originally extraneous traditions were in course of time absorbed into the Feud Quest. At a late stage an inconsistent legend which attributed the mending of the sword, not to the hero at the Grail Castle, but to an uncanny smith who lived near Escotoatre, intruded itself, and added to the confusion.

Much of this history of the sword is hypothetical, but the hypothesis has some foundation in facts, and harmonizes with conclusions already reached concerning the Perceval legend and the Vengeance Quest. If it be

[86] Though antedating Chrétien's *Conte del Graal*, the *Colloquy* is comparatively late in the development of the Finn cycle as is shown by the prominence of St. Patrick and the viking influence.   [87] Cf. *supra*, p. 350.   [88] Cf. *supra*, pp. 389–91.

accepted, it will, I believe, offer at least a plausible explanation of the sword in Chrétien's poem. The presentation of the brand to Perceval by the Fisher King is a blurred reminiscence of the more common account in which Perceval is presented with the fragments by the Grail King and is asked to unite them. Its ultimate origin would then go back to a story like Cailte's mending the sword of Fergus. The special interest which the damsel under the tree takes in the sword is the result of the linking of the Finn vendetta—where her prototype appears—with the same Irish tale of the mending of a sword. The relationship has, of course, been obscured by the intrusion of the smith of Cotoatre, instead of the hero, as the mender. If we had only Chrétien's text to go by, this explanation would be flimsy enough. It is the evidence of the other texts which gives it some solidity. Is there any other hypothesis which accounts for so much?

To sum up, the Feud Quest in the Perceval romances followed in its broad outline and in many details the vendetta between Finn and the sons of Daire the Red. It developed several branches; elements became separated from each other, so that the formulas of the weeping damsel, the Red Knight feud, and the father-vengeance appear often as unrelated incidents. Extraneous tales were absorbed, such as the mending of the broken sword at the Otherworld palace. In the Welsh stage, Pryderi took over the role of Finn as the avenger of his father's death on the Clan Morna, the sons of Daire the Red. Strange misunderstandings as to the identity of the Red Knights took place. The French romances, Wolfram's *Parzival, Sir Percyvelle,* and *Carduino* give us the confused result, Chrétien one of the most confused of all.

Chapter LXX

THE BLOOD DROPS ON THE SNOW

VERSES 4160–4210

Snow had fallen overnight. Perceval, approaching the site of Arthur's camp, saw a falcon attacking a flock of wild geese. One of the geese was wounded and left three drops of blood on the snow. Perceval at the sight of the red on white was reminded of the coloring of Blancheflor's face, and fell into a deep love trance.

As FAR BACK as 1884 Zimmer demonstrated that this episode was akin to a scene in a tragic Irish saga of the eighth century, *The Exile of the Sons of Usnech*.[1] The beautiful maiden Deirdre observed a

[1] H. Zimmer, *Keltische Studien* (Berlin, 1884), II, 201 ff. Cf. also A. Nutt, *Studies on the Legend of the Holy Grail*, pp. 137 f.; M. R. Williams, *Essai sur la composition de Peredur*, pp.

raven drinking the blood of a calf on the snow. She said to her attendant: "That man only will I love who hath the three colors that I see yonder— his hair as black as the raven, his cheeks red like blood, and his body as white as the snow." [2] Her attendant replied that such a man was Naisi, and Deirdre declared that she would never enjoy health until she saw him.

First, be it noted that Perceval's love trance took place some days after Pentecost,[3] and therefore this snow scene is on the face of it an independent, extraneous theme. Secondly, *Peredur,* which we know often preserves more accurately the original tradition, adds a significant detail: the hawk, after killing the wild fowl, had flown away, and a raven had alighted on the dead bird. "Peredur stopped, and seeing the blackness of the raven, the whiteness of the snow, and the redness of the blood, he thought of the hair of the woman he loved best, as black as jet, of her skin as white as snow, of her cheeks as red as the blood on the snow." [4] Here evidently the Irish motif has been retained in its integrity. Chrétien or his source eliminated the raven and the reference to the black hair of Perceval's lady for the very good reason that no French poet would libel his heroine by comparing her tresses to a crow's plumage.[5] In fact, Chrétien asserted that one would have thought Blancheflor's locks were all of gold.[6] Whether he found in his source two colors or, as in *Peredur,* three, the origin of this motif and of the consequent love trance was surely Irish.

Chapter LXXI

THE LOATHLY DAMSEL

VERSES 4603–4746

Perceval returned with the royal court to Carlion, and on the third day there came before the King a loathly damsel on a mule. "If the book tells the truth," her tresses, neck, and hands were black; she had rat's eyes, a nose like that of a monkey or a cat, yellow teeth, a goat's beard, a hump

57 f.; R. Zenker, *Zur Mabinogionfrage,* p. 4, n.; Loth, *Mabinogion,* 2d ed., II, 76, n. 3; E. Windisch, *Das keltische Brittannien bis zu Kaiser Arthur,* pp. 133 f. On date of *Exile* cf. Thurneysen, *Irische Helden- und Königsage,* p. 323.
[2] H. D'Arbois de Jubainville, *L'Epopée celtique en Irlande,* p. 225. English trans. Cross and Slover, *Ancient Irish Tales,* p. 242. German summary Thurneysen, *op. cit.,* p. 324. On survival of this motif in modern Gaelic folktales cf. D. MacInnes, *Folk and Hero Tales from Argyllshire, Waifs and Strays of Celtic Tradition* (London, 1890), pp. 431–35.
[3] Cf. vs. 2785.   [4] Loth, *Mabinogion,* 2d ed., II, 76.
[5] H. Maynadier, *Wife of Bath's Tale* (London, 1901), p. 197. O. Voigt, *Das Ideal der Schönheit und Hässlichkeit in den Altfranz. Chansons de Geste* (1891), pp. 34 ff. J. Houdoy, *La Beauté des femmes dans la littérature et dans l'art du XIIe au XVIe siècle* (Paris, 1876), pp. 35–41. R. Renier, *Il Tipo estetico della donna nel medioevo* (Ancona, 1885), p. 16 and *passim.*   [6] Vss. 1810–14.

*on both chest and back, and crooked legs. She cursed Perceval for his
failure to ask the question concerning the Lance and the Grail, for as a result lands had been ruined, ladies had lost their husbands, and maidens
had been orphaned. She told also of the adventure of Chastel Orguelleus,
and of the supreme adventure of Montescleire—the deliverance of a
maiden from siege and the winning of the Sword of the Strange Girdle.
Gauvain undertook to rescue the maiden of Montescleire, and Perceval
to return to the Grail Castle and remedy his omission. Fifty other knights
swore likewise to set out in search of perilous adventure.*

ONE THING is certain about the Loathly Damsel: she is a dual personality. It has already been pointed out that one of her prototypes
was Eriu, the goddess of Ireland,[1] and that the other was the
water-goddess Liban.[2] The one divinity accounts for her hideous appearance; the other for her bitter tongue and for her enlisting Gauvain for the
deliverance of the maiden of Montescleire. Without repeating all the
evidence, the essential points may be recalled.

What is the connection with Eriu? Both *Peredur* and *Perlesvaus* identify the Loathly Damsel with the Grail Bearer. In this respect these texts
reproduce the Irish tradition of the Sovranty of Erin, who appears in *The
Prophetic Ecstasy of the Phantom* as a crowned maiden, the prototype of
the Grail Bearer,[3] and in a number of other tales as a hideously deformed
hag. Moreover, the description in *Peredur* of the Loathly Damsel at
Arthur's court tallies in feature after feature with the description of the
Sovranty of Erin in *The Adventures of the Sons of Eochaid Mugmedon*.
Thus the descent of the Loathly Damsel from the Sovranty of Erin is
assured. Behind the allegorical figure of the Sovranty stands the goddess
Eriu, Ireland personified; and the story of her transformation from a
repulsive monster into a marvel of beauty is the story of Ireland transformed by the caresses of the sun from wintry bleakness to the floral
splendor of spring.

There is nothing, however, in the Irish legends of the Sovranty to
account for: (1) the arrival of the Loathly Damsel at Arthur's court, accompanied, in *Perlesvaus,* by a stag-drawn chariot; (2) her harsh treatment of the hero; (3) her proposing the rescue of the maiden of Montescleire. Precisely these three features in the conduct of the Loathly Damsel
serve to reveal her descent from the Irish Liban. For Liban came to the
court of Ulster, whipped Cuchulainn and laughed at him in scorn, came
again to summon him to the aid of her sister against her foes, and on
another occasion rode in a stag-drawn chariot.

[1] Cf. *supra,* pp. 375–79.   [2] Cf. *supra,* pp. 298 f.
[3] This is true of the romances in which the prototype of the Grail King is the Welsh Bran. In
the Vulgate cycle, where Pelles and Pellehan have become lords of the Grail castle, the Grail
Bearer has evidently been remodeled on the figure of Morgain, as was pointed out in Chap. XX.

Chrétien's figure of the Loathly Damsel is a blend of the two Irish goddesses, Eriu and Liban.

Chrétien himself never reached in his narrative either the adventure of Chastel Orguelleus or that of Montescleire, but they are found in the continuations of *Le Conte del Graal,* and some brief remarks about them may be found on earlier pages of this book.[4]

Chapter LXXII

THE GUINGAMBRESIL EPISODE

VERSES 4747–4813, 5703–6215

Just as the knights of the Round Table were recovering from the astonishing visit of the Loathly Damsel, there entered Guingambresil. He greeted King Arthur, but charged Gauvain with slaying his lord (the King of Cavalon) without previously defying him. Agravain offered to defend his brother from the charge, but Gauvain took up the gage himself and pledged his word to defend his honor before the new King of Cavalon forty days later. Guingambresil departed, and Gauvain in turn, amid the lamentations of the courtiers and ladies, set out to keep his rendezvous. After the affair at the castle of Tintaguel, Gauvain met a hunting party, under the lead of a tall and handsome youth, who turned out to be the new King of Cavalon. He obviously did not recognize Gauvain as the slayer of his father, for he at once insisted on sending the stranger to his castle, accompanied by a messenger to his sister with the charge that she should love and cherish his unknown guest till his return from the chase. The maiden was more than ready to comply with the King's request, seated Gauvain beside her, and presently they were kissing and making great joy. They were attacked by the townsfolk and by certain vilains armed with axes and jusarmes (long-handled axes). Gauvain and the lady defended themselves, oddly enough, by hurling large chess pieces. Guingambresil arrived on the scene, and the King of Cavalon shortly afterwards. They dispersed the rabble, and Gauvain swore to return after a year for a fight with Guingambresil.

THE KEY to unlock the riddle of this episode lies in the name Guingambresil. It suggests a composite origin, like Brangemuer, which Pseudo-Wauchier tells us was made up from the names Brangepart and Guingamuer. Guingambresil seems to resolve itself into *Guingam-* and *-bresil.* We have already noted [1] that Chrétien mentions in *Erec* a Guigamor, lord of Avalon, who was the original of Malory's Gryngamor, lord

[4] Cf. *supra,* p. 299, n. 26; p. 329.   [1] Cf. *supra,* p. 86.

of a castle in the isle of Avylyon, host of Beaumayns,[2] and brother of the amorous Lyones. In the element -*bresil* we may recognize, in metathesized and apocopated form, the name of Bercilak,[3] host of Gawain and husband of an amorous lady. Is it possible that in the Guingambresil episode we find telescoped the adventures of Beaumayns and those of Gawain in the castles of Gryngamor and Bercilak and their seductive ladies?

That is precisely what we do find. In Malory's story of Beaumayns and in *Gawain and the Green Knight* are comprised nearly all the features of Chrétien's narrative. First let us look at Malory.[4]

Beaumayns was warmly welcomed at the castle in the isle of Avylyon and was recommended by his host Gryngamor to his sister's favor; both were inflamed with passion, and were about to consummate their union in the hall one night when they were interrupted by a knight with a gysarme. This corresponds fairly well to Chrétien: Gauvain was welcomed to the King of Cavalon's castle; he was recommended by the King to his sister's favor; both were inflamed with passion and were making great love in the hall when they were interrupted by men with *jusarmes*.

Now let us turn to *Gawain and the Green Knight*.[5] A stranger knight, Bercilak, came bursting into Arthur's hall, issued a challenge, and arranged a rendezvous with Gawain for a different place and a later date; Gawain set out amid the lamentations of the courtiers, was welcomed at the castle of his challenger, and was tempted by his beautiful hostess during her husband's absence on the chase. I think it will be granted that this likewise offers a marked correspondence to Chrétien:[6] A stranger knight, Guingambresil, came bursting into Arthur's hall, issued a challenge to Gauvain, and arranged a rendezvous for a different place and a later date. Gauvain set out amid the lamentations of the courtiers, was welcomed at the castle of his challenger, and was involved in an amorous affair with his hostess during her brother's absence on the chase.

Can there be any manner of doubt that the Guingambresil episode was compounded from the sources of Beaumayns' adventure at the castle of Gryngamor and of Gawain's adventure at the castle of Bercilak?

[2] On the name Beaumayns cf. *PMLA*, LIV (1939), 656–68. There are seven parallels between the adventures of Beaumayns and those of Gauvain(s). Initial *g* and *b* were sometimes confused. Beaumayns is of course grammatically impossible as a French rendering of "Fair Hands." It seems certain that Beaumayns is an Anglo-Norman's crude attempt to etymologize the name Gauvain(s), which he misread as Bauuains. This conclusion harmonizes with the fact that Gauvain itself originated as a descriptive epithet, derived from Welsh Gwallt-A(d)vwyn.

[3] *Sir Gawayn and the Green Knight*, ed. J. R. R. Tolkien, E. V. Gordon, vs. 2445.

[4] Bk. VII, chaps. 20–23. Ed. Sommer, I, 244–50.

[5] Ed. Tolkien and Gordon, vss. 130–1869. An excellent translation is that of T. H. Banks (New York, 1929).

[6] Even more detailed is the likeness between *Gawain and the Green Knight* and Wolfram's version of the Guingambresil episode, *Parzival*, 319, 20–325, 16; 399, 1–432, 30. Cf. *PMLA*, LIV, 1026 f.

It is, perhaps, a little puzzling that the composite name Guingambresil is not attached to the huntsman host, the King of Cavalon, who combines the roles of Gryngamor and Bercilak. In all likelihood the name was once attached both to the challenging knight and the huntsman host, just as the name Bercilak in the English poem belongs both to the challenging knight and the huntsman host. The English poet makes it quite plain, moreover, that Bercilak was a shape-shifter. But the *conte* which Chrétien followed had effaced this essential point, with the result that two characters were made out of this shape-shifter—one bearing the name Guingambresil and assuming the role of the challenger; the other becoming the anonymous King of Cavalon and playing the part of the huntsman host.

Just as it is possible to analyze the Guingambresil episode as a compound of the Gryngamor and Bercilak stories, so it is possible to analyze these stories into their component elements. We have already succeeded in tracing several sources for Malory's account of Beaumayns' adventures at the castle of Gryngamor.[7] (1) Gryngamor himself, his castle in the isle of Avylyon, and his sister, the amorous Lyones, doubtless represent the Breton tradition, mentioned in *Erec,* of Guigamor, lord of Avalon and lover of the amorous Morgain la Fée. (2) Gryngamor's recommending Beaumayns to his sister's love probably derives, as we saw, from *The Sickbed of Cuchulainn,* where Labraid, prince of an Otherworld isle, promised the hero the embraces of his sister-in-law Fand. (3) The interruption of Beaumayns' nocturnal assignation with Lyones by a man with a gysarme and a replaceable head surely goes back to two stories in *Bricriu's Feast:* [8] according to one, Curoi attacked Cuchulainn by night while he was being entertained by his mistress Blathnat; according to the other, Curoi, in the guise of a churl with an ax, submitted to decapitation by Cuchulainn, replaced his head, and walked away. It is significant that though, on the whole, Malory preserved the Breton traditions of Guingamor and Morgain and the Irish traditions of Cuchulainn, Curoi, and Blathnat more faithfully than Chrétien, Chrétien retained in the Guingambresil episode two features omitted by Malory. One is the very odd employment of chessmen as missiles by Gauvain's hostess. Since that hostess was modeled in part on Morgain, it is not irrelevant that Morgain was the owner of a magic chessboard and may have been the original of the water-fay of the chessboard castle in Wauchier.[9] The other feature is Chrétien's assertion that the men who attacked Gauvain with axes and *jusarmes* were a mere rabble, some of them *vilains.* Now we know that Curoi when he attacked Cuchulainn in his fortress was called a *bachlach,*[10] that is, a herdsman or churl, and his counterpart in Arthurian romance is twice

[7] Cf. *supra,* pp. 180 f., 229–32, 296 f., 364 f., 368 f.
[8] *Feast of Bricriu,* ed. G. Henderson, pp. 101–29.
[9] Cf. *supra,* p. 232, n. 21. Potvin, *Perceval le Gallois,* IV, 333–37. R. Briffault, *The Mothers* (New York, 1927), III, 458, n. 3.   [10] *Feast of Bricriu,* p. 108, l. 11.

described as a *vilain* with an ax or *jusarme*.[11] Beyond doubt, then, the Guingambresil episode derived much of its material ultimately from the same Irish and Breton sources as Malory's story of Beaumayns' stay at the castle of Gryngamor.

The second immediate source of the Guingambresil episode, the adventures of Gawain with Bercilak and Bercilak's wife can also be analyzed. The name Bercilak itself is a corruption of the common noun *bachlach*, as applied to Bercilak's original, Curoi.[12] Bercilak's challenge to Gawain at Arthur's court is based, as everyone knows, on Curoi's challenge to Cuchulainn at the court of Ulster. The lamentation of the courtiers on Gawain's departure to his rendezvous with Bercilak [13] is matched by the anxiety of the men of Ulster when the hour approached for Cuchulainn to keep his rendezvous with the *bachlach;* "it had been fitting had they sung his dirge; they felt sure that his life would last only till the *bachlach* came." [14] The absence of Gawain's host on the chase while his wife vainly sought to seduce Gawain may be paralleled in the mabinogi by the absence of Arawn, the huntsman, while his wife vainly offered connubial favors to Pwyll.[15] The one-year interval between Gawain's meetings with Bercilak seems to reflect the tradition of an anniversary combat between Pwyll and Havgan.[16] Moreover, Chrétien has retained an original feature which is missing from *Gawain and the Green Knight*. Gauvain meets the huntsman King of Cavalon outside his castle, and proceeds with his sanction to make love to the lady of the castle in the huntsman's absence. This situation is clearly foreshadowed in the Welsh account of Pwyll's meeting with the huntsman king of Annwn in the glade and proceeding with his sanction to his palace and sharing the bed of his wife.[17] The same Welsh and Irish legends which underlie *Gawain and the Green Knight* form the basis of the Guingambresil episode.

As far back as 1883 Martha Carey Thomas, later famous as president of Bryn Mawr College, discerned the affinity of this episode with *Gawain and the Green Knight*,[18] though she, like many a later scholar, labored under the delusion that Chrétien was the source of the Arthurian romances. Succeeding years, however, have not only proved the falsity of this simple notion, but have also illuminated one after another the complex relationships of the Guingambresil episode to the English poem, to the Irish sagas, and to the Morgain–Guingamor legend.[19] Now it is possible to claim that the whole cryptic record has been deciphered.

[11] Paien de Maisières, *Damoisele à la Mule*, ed. B. Orlowski, vss. 504–633. *Hunbaut*, ed. Stuerzinger and Breuer (Dresden, 1914), vss. 1464–79.
[12] *Manly Anniversary Studies in Language and Literature* (Chicago, 1923), pp. 12–16. R. S. Loomis, *Celtic Myth*, pp. 59 f. [13] Vss. 672–86. [14] *Feast of Bricriu*, p. 127.
[15] Loth, *Mabinogion*, 2d ed., I, 84–88. [16] *Ibid.*, pp. 86, 88. [17] Loth, *op. cit.*, I, 84–88.
[18] M. C. Thomas, *Sir Gawayne and the Green Knight* (Zürich, 1883).
[19] See especially *PMLA*, XLVIII (1933), 1000–1027; *Journ. of Eng. and Germ. Phil.*, XLII, 170–83.

Chapter LXXIII

ESCALIBOR

VERSES 5899–5904

When Gauvain and the King of Cavalon's sister realized that they were about to be attacked by the townsmen, she armed the knight and he girded on Escalibor, "the best sword that ever was, for it cut iron like wood." Gauvain took his stand at the door of the damsel's chamber and dealt the first person to attack him such a blow with the sword that the others feared to advance.

T HERE ARE TWO very odd facts about this introduction of the most famous blade of Arthurian romance. Though Chrétien may well have derived the name Escalibor from some manuscript of Wace's *Brut,* yet without comment or explanation he transfers it from the possession of Arthur to that of Gauvain. Moreover, though Gauvain had been and was to be involved in many fierce combats with such redoubtable foes as Meliant de Lis, Greoreas' nephew, the lion of the Castle of Ladies, and the guardian of the passages of Galvoie, yet the only occasion on which his sword is named, and that somewhat casually, is when he faces a mere rabble of burghers and *vilains*. To attribute such ineptitudes to Chrétien's free invention is a serious charge against his intelligence and artistry. Is it not fair to attribute these flaws rather to the inconsistencies of tradition and the casual art of the *conteurs?*

In fact, there is ample evidence of two traditions as to the possessor of Escalibor. In Pseudo-Wauchier's continuation [1] Arthur girds his good sword Escalliborc [2] on Gauvain in preparation for the combat with the Riche Soudoier. The *Vulgate Merlin,* however, represents Arthur as giving his sword to his nephew when the latter was first made knight, [3] and throughout the rest of that book Gauvain remains the possessor. In the *Vulgate Lancelot* Gauvain lends this sword to Lancelot for his battle in defence of Guenievre against the three barons of Carmelide. [4] *La Mort Artu* has Gauvain employ the weapon against Lancelot in their great duel

---

[1] Potvin, *Perceval le Gallois,* III, vs. 16337. J. L. Weston, *Sir Gawain and the Lady of Lys* (London, 1907), p. 87.

[2] The form with final *c* is found elsewhere; in Wace's *Brut,* ed. Le Roux de Lincy, vss. 10323, 13291, 13330; *Didot-Perceval,* ed. W. Roach, ll. 2028, 2051. Zimmer remarks (*Zts. f. franz. Sprache u. Lit.,* XIII [1890], "Abhandlungen," 236): "Von diesen Formen steht am durch irische und kymrische Lautform gesicherten keltischen Ausgangsform am nächsten Calibourc (Caliborc), worin *c* die Gutturalspirans, welsch-bretonisch *ch,* widergibt." Cf. *infra*. On Gawain's sword cf. F. Madden, *Syr Gawayne,* pp. 343 f.

[3] H. O. Sommer, *Vulgate Version,* II, 253.   [4] *Ibid.,* IV, 61.

outside the city of Gaunes,[5] but it is once more in the hands of Arthur in his last battle with Modred and, as everyone knows, it is the famous sword which Lucan or Bedivere, received from the wounded Arthur and cast into the lake.[6] In fact, the earliest and the most widely current tradition knows it as the sword of Arthur. Geoffrey of Monmouth has the well-known passage concerning Arthur's arms:

"Arthur himself, donning a hauberk worthy of so great a king, set on his head a helmet of gold, graven with the semblance of a dragon. On his shoulders, moreover, a shield that was named Pridwen, wherein the image of Holy Mary, Mother of God, was painted, often called her to his memory. Girded also with Caliburnus, the best of swords, fashioned in the isle of Avallon, he graced his right hand with a lance, which was called by the name Ron." [7]

The *Huth Merlin* also regards Escalibor as the possession of Arthur and tells the romantic tale, well known to readers of Malory, of how it came into his hands.[8] When Arthur needs a sword Merlin tells him that there is but one good sword in the land and that is in a lake where fays have their dwelling. Both the King and the mage ride to the lake and see an arm clothed in white samite, rising from the water and holding a sword. Presently a damsel rides rapidly towards them, and at Merlin's bidding dismounts and walks with dry feet over the water. She takes the sword, the arm vanishes, and the damsel brings the coveted weapon back to Arthur. Merlin informs the King that, though the sword is good, the sheath is even better, for no one who wears it can receive a mortal wound. Later in the same romance the damsel who had given Arthur the sword tells him that its name is Escalibor.[9]

As to the properties of the magic brand, the *Vulgate Merlin* repeatedly says that it blazed. When Arthur drew it from the scabbard, it "cast as great a light as if two torches had been kindled there." [10] Again we read that it blazed like a torch, and that Rion was frightened by its flashing.[11]

---

[5] Sommer, *Vulgate Version*, VI, 338. *Mort Artu*, ed. J. Frappier, p. 170.

[6] *Ibid., op. cit.*, VII, 379 f. *Mort Artu*, ed. Frappier, pp. 223 f. Malory, *Morte d'Arthur*, Bk. XXI, chap. 5. *Le Morte Arthur*, ed. S. B. Hemingway (Boston, 1912), vss. 3446–93. On this magnificent incident cf. G. Schoepperle in *Vassar Mediaeval Studies*, ed. C. F. Fiske (New Haven, 1923), pp. 10–12; *Mort Artu*, ed. J. D. Bruce, p. 297.

[7] Geoffrey of Monmouth, *Historia Regum Britanniae*, ed. A. Griscom, p. 438. E. Faral, *Légende arthurienne*, III, 233. In *Kulhwch* (Loth, *Mabinogion*, 2d ed., I, 259, 328) Arthur's lance Rongomyant and his ship Prytwenn are mentioned. Benedict of Peterborough in his *Gesta Regis Ricardi*, ed. W. Stubbs, II, 159, tells us that Richard Coeur de Lion gave to King Tancred of Sicily in 1191 "gladium optimum Arcturi, nobilis quondam regis Britonum, quem Britones vocaverunt Caliburnum." In the alliterative *Morte Arthure* (ed. E. Björkman, vss. 4193, 4202) we hear of another sword of Arthur's (besides Caliburne), which he had left in the keeping of Waynor (Guenevere) and which was wielded by Mordred in the last battle. It is called Clarent(e), is the crown of swords, and is as bright as silver. Evidently Clarent in its name and its brightness preserves the tradition that Arthur's was a blazing weapon. Geoffrey's form Caliburnus must have been influenced by the Latin word *chalybs* (steel).

[8] *Huth Merlin*, ed. G. Paris, J. Ulrich, I, 195 ff. Malory, *op. cit.*, Bk. I, chap. 25.

[9] *Huth Merlin*, I, 219.   [10] Sommer, *op. cit.*, II, 94.   [11] *Ibid.*, II, 230.

When Escalibor had passed into the hands of Gauvain, it again cast a great light.[12] The most awesome account is given of its behavior during a battle with the Saxons. When Gauvain charged into the fray,

"he held Escalibor in his hand . . . and he came through the midst of the ranks roaring like thunder. . . . He was so heated when it drew toward the hour of *none* that nothing endured against him, and it seemed verily, when he raised the sword on high to strike and it descended, that it was lightning, so violent was the blow, for the sword made a noise as of thunder." [13]

Here we find attributed to Gauvain his familiar solar trait of increasing in strength till the hour of *none,* and to Escalibor the properties of lightning and thunder. If this combination of mythical attributes is accidental,[14] it is a remarkable accident.

The origin of the name Calibor or Caliborc has long been known, and forms one of the most impressive arguments for the infiltration of Welsh and even Irish names into Arthurian romance. In *Kulhwch* Arthur mentions his sword Caledvwlch among his prized belongings, and his warrior, Llenlleawc the Irishman, brandishes it in the fight to win the caldron of Diwrnach.[15] The name resolves itself into *calet,* "hard," and *bwlch,* "notch." [16] Just what sense the Welsh attached to the word is of no great consequence, however, since it is plainly an attempt to approximate the Irish word Caladbolg, as we shall soon see. The distinguishing property of this sword of Arthur's is much like that of Escalibor in the *Vulgate Merlin,* for it is thus described in *The Dream of Rhonabwy:* "He [Kadwr, Earl of Cornwall] arose, with the sword of Arthur in his hand, and there was the figure of two serpents of gold on the sword. When the sword was drawn from the sheath, they saw as it were two flames of fire issuing from the mouths of the serpents. It was not easy for anyone to look at it because of the terror." [17] This Kadwr enjoyed the privilege of arming Arthur on the day of battle.[18]

The Welsh evidence, then, makes it clear that Caledvwlch was the name of Arthur's sword, that it flamed when drawn from the sheath,[19]

---

[12] *Ibid.,* II, 317.   [13] *Ibid.,* II, 367.

[14] On the combination of the attributes of sun and storm god in Celtic mythology cf. R. S. Loomis, *Celtic Myth,* pp. 45–50.

[15] Loth, *Mabinogion,* 2d ed., I, 258 f., 335. J. G. Evans, *White Book Mabinogion,* cols. 459, 498.

[16] *Zts. f. celt. Phil.,* XII (1918), 282. Loth, *op. cit.,* I, 258, n. 2.   [17] Loth, *op. cit.,* I, 363.

[18] As Cador, Duke of Cornwall, this figure is prominent in Geoffrey's *Historia* (ed. Griscom, pp. 434–82; Faral, *op. cit.,* III, 229–64), and his son Constantinus succeeded Arthur as King (Griscom, p. 501; Faral, III, 278).

[19] Welsh tradition knows another such weapon, Dyrnwyn, the sword of Rhydderch Hael, a famous King of Dumbarton, first mentioned in Adamnan's *Life of St. Columba.* This sword is listed among the Thirteen Treasures of the Isle of Britain in a ms. of about 1460 (Nat. Lib. of Wales, ms. Peniarth 51, pp. 169 f.), and is described more fully in later mss. Lady Guest (*Mabinogion,* Everyman ed., p. 328) translates from one of them as follows: "Dyrnwyn the sword of Rhydderch Hael; if any man drew it except himself, it burst into a flame from the

and that it was borne at times by Kadwr, at times by Llenlleawc. The Welsh name became in Geoffrey's book Caliburnus, and in Wace Calibour, Caliborne, and so forth. A peculiar tendency to attach the prefix *es-* to names (as for instance Escalvaire from Calvaire,[20] Escavalon from Cavalon, Estor from Tor [21]) led to the form Escalibor or Escaliborc. The author of the *Vulgate Merlin,* employing the device characteristic of the Vulgate cycle of concocting spurious etymologies, asserts boldly: "It is a Hebrew name which means in French 'cuts iron, steel, and wood.' " [22]

Caledvwlch in turn, as Zimmer discovered,[23] goes back to a famous sword of the Ulster cycle. According to *The Cattle Raid of Cooley* in the Book of the Dun Cow,[24] the exiled Fergus mac Roich, when called on to take part in the battle against the Ulstermen, demands his sword. King Ailill sends for it and presents it to Fergus, who greets it as "Caladcolc" and as the possession of Leite's son, another Fergus.[25] With this blade, Fergus mac Roich enters the fray, slaughters his foes, encounters King Conchobar of Ulster, and cuts off the tops of three hills. In the Book of Leinster version [26] we have much the same story, except that the sword is called Caladbolg, and is said to come from the faery palaces and to become as long as a rainbow when it is brandished.[27] In another saga, *The Cattle Raid of Flidais,*[28] Fergus mac Roich is robbed of his sword during an assignation with Queen Medb and a wooden one is substituted; only in the

cross to the point, and all who asked it received it; but because of this property all shunned it: and therefore was he called Rhydderch Hael (the Generous)." On Rhydderch and his sword cf. *Romanische Forschungen,* XLV (1931), 68 f.; *PMLA,* LVI (1941), 911–13; *Vita Merlini,* ed. J. J. Parry, pp. 18 f.; and *supra,* p. 407, n. 61.

[20] *Zts. f. franz. Sprache u. Lit.,* XII (1890), "Abhandlungen," 236; XXVII (1904), "Abhandlungen," 103. *Mod. Phil.,* X (1913), 449 f.

[21] In *Erec,* vs. 1528, where the proper reading is probably that given by Foerster, "Et Torz li fiz au roi Ares," certain mss. give Estor(s), Esturz, probably by assimilation to the common noun *estor, estur,* "battle, fray." A similar phenomenon may be detected in the development of the name of King Bohors in the Vulgate cycle which seems to be derived from "le rei Gohors" (Biket, *Lai du Cor,* ed. H. Dörner, Strassburg, 1907, vs. 421), first through the common error of misreading initial *b* for *g* and secondly under the influence of *bohors,* "a kind of tourney." On Hector cf. *Histoire littéraire de la France,* XXXI, 168.

[22] Sommer, *op. cit.,* II, 94. Probably the author was influenced in his etymology, as Geoffrey was in his form, by the Latin *chalybs* (steel). Malory, Bk. II, ch. 3, also gives the meaning "cut stele." M. Faral, *op. cit.,* II, 266, proposed that Caliburnus was merely "quelque étrange adaptation du latin *chalybs.*"

[23] *Göttingische gelehrte Anzeigen,* 1890, 516 f. *Zts. f. franz. Sprache u. Lit.,* XII (1890), "Abhandlungen," 235–37. The latest and perhaps the best discussion is in T. O'Rahilly, *Early Irish History and Mythology,* pp. 67–71.

[24] R. Thurneysen, *Die Irische Helden- u. Königsage,* pp. 212–14.

[25] *Ibid.,* p. 212, n. 3 (upper). Thurneysen says: "Der Verfasser scheint Fergus mac Le(i)te mit den sonst von ihm unterschiedenen Fergus mac Roich zu vermengen."

[26] *Ibid.,* pp. 212–14 (below).

[27] *Ibid.,* p. 214 (below). *Göttingische Gel. Anz.,* 1890, p. 517. The Irish words *a sidib* mean literally "from the faery mounds." The gods, the Tuatha De Danann, were supposed to have their palaces within these ancient tumuli. Cf. Thurneysen, *op. cit.,* p. 62.

[28] Thurneysen, *op. cit.,* p. 344.

midst of a battle does Fergus discover that Caladcolg is missing. *The Death of Fergus Mac Leite* [29] tells how this other Fergus met an enormous lake-monster in a deadly struggle, and though he hacked it in pieces with his sword Caladcolg, he was himself mortally wounded. With his dying breath he implored the Ulstermen to give his sword to one who would be worthy of it, whose name would be Fergus mac Roich. And to the poet Aed he chanted: "By you be this sword treasured, that none other take it from you; my share of the matter for all time shall be this: that men shall rehearse the story of the sword." The two Irish names for the sword, Caladcolg and Caladbolg, mean, respectively, "Hard Sword" and "Hard Sheath," the first being doubtless the earlier.[30] It is a curious possibility that not only the name but also two Irish traditions descended into Arthurian romance. The treacherous substitution of a wooden sword for Caladcolg and Fergus' discovery of the trick in the midst of his fight remind one of the episode in the *Huth Merlin*,[31] where Morgain sends a counterfeit Escalibor to Arthur, and Arthur discovers the trick in the midst of his fight with Accalon. Likewise Fergus mac Leite's dying speech, as he lies wounded beside a lake, expressing concern lest his sword fall into the hands of any but Fergus mac Roich, strangely recalls Arthur's speech as he lies wounded beside a lake.

" 'Ah, Escalibor . . . now wilt thou lose thy master! Where wilt thou find a man by whom thou wilt be as well employed as by me, if thou come not into the hands of Lancelot? Ah, Lancelot, the worthiest man of the world and the best knight, may it now please Jesu Christ that you may hold it and that I may know it! Certes, my soul would thereby be more at ease for ever.' " [32]

Neither of these parallels between the history of Caladcolc and that of Escalibor proves a genetic connection, even though the influence of *The Death of Fergus Mac Leite* on Arthurian romance seems assured.[33] Yet the names are certainly connected, as scholars agree. And the prophecy of Fergus that for all time men shall rehearse the story of the sword has been in a strange way fulfilled. For Excalibur has been famed throughout the Western world for eight hundred years. *The Sword in the Stone,* by T. H. White, was selected by the Book-of-the-Month Club as recently as 1939.

[29] *Ibid.*, p. 546. T. P. Cross and C. N. Slover, *Ancient Irish Tales*, pp. 486 f.
[30] *Zts. f. celt. Phil.*, XII, 281.   [31] *Huth Merlin*, II, 199–207.
[32] *Mort Artu,* ed. Frappier, p. 223. Possibly, too, this adieu to Escalibor may owe something, as Dr. Marjorie Fox (*La Mort le Roi Artus*, Paris, 1933, pp. 117 f.) and M. Frappier (*Etude sur la Mort le Roi Artu*, Paris, 1936, p. 201) believe, to Roland's famous apostrophe to Durendal. The *Prose Tristan* was doubtless inspired by the *Mort Artu* to put into Tristan's mouth a farewell to his sword. Cf. Paulin Paris, *Manuscrits François* (Paris, 1836), I, 205 f.
[33] Cf. Chap. XIX.

Chapter LXXIV

GAUVAIN AT THE TOURNEY OF TINTAGEL

VERSES 4816–5655

Gauvain, riding to his rendezvous with Guingambresil, learned from a squire that a tourney was about to be held before the castle of Tintagel. The lord of the castle, Tiebaut, had brought up as his foster son Meliant de Lis, who in order to win the love of Tiebaut's elder daughter had arranged a tourney between his forces and those of Tiebaut. Gauvain, accompanied by seven squires and seven horses, and bringing two shields, proceeded to the neighborhood of Tintagel. Here beneath the walls he dismounted and hung the two shields on an oak. The tourney began; Meliant de Lis and his party carried all before them. The daughters of Tiebaut and other ladies watched the fray from the loges. All admired the prowess of Meliant, and viewed with scorn Gauvain, who took no part in the sport lest he should be prevented from keeping his day with Guingambresil. Only Tiebaut's younger daughter, "the Maid of the Little Sleeves," questioned Meliant's superiority and stood up for Gauvain. At the end of the day, when the tourney was broken off, Gauvain entered the castle and obtained harborage with an aged vavasor, Garin. That evening the Maid of the Little Sleeves went to Garin's home, clasped the knees of Gauvain, and besought him to enter the tourney the next day as her knight, and thus justify her praise of him and humiliate her sister. Gauvain yielded to her entreaty, and accepted a sleeve of red samite which she brought him the next morning. This he wore when the tourney recommenced, and he speedily bore Meliant to the ground and sent his steed to the Maid of the Little Sleeves as a gift. Before noon Gauvain was the acknowledged victor, and revealed to Tiebaut his name. The Maid rendered him five hundred thanks, and he promised to serve her whenever she called upon him. Though urged to stay, he departed on his journey.

THE READER who has followed the "Arturi regis ambages pulcerrimae" through the preceding pages will recognize here certain familiar narrative patterns: (1) the rival sisters; (2) the hospitable vavasor and the charming damsel who gives the hero a favor to wear in a trial of arms; (3) the hero's apparent cowardice and his later triumph. The first pattern, already met in *Yvain*, provides the two rival sisters, each enlisting a knight to champion her cause.[1] The second element, though dimly rec-

[1] Cf. Chap. LV.

ognizable in the entertainment of Erec by the hospitable vavasor and his lovely daughter Enide,[2] is more clearly illustrated in the Maid of Escalot episode in *La Mort Artu*.[3] There we read that the hero, Lancelot, came incognito to a joust or tourney; he lodged with a vavasor; the vavasor's lovely daughter gave Lancelot her sleeve to wear and besought him to perform feats of arms for her sake; he undertook to do so and emerged the victor in the tournament. The third pattern is exemplified by the tourney of Noauz in the *Charrette* and by the Dame de Malehot episode in the *Vulgate Lancelot*. In these two cognate tales, as we saw,[4] the hero found favor with the wife of Meleagant's seneschal or with the Dame de Malehot, attended a tourney with equipment supplied by her, performed so poorly at first that he was mocked, but later, to the surprise of all, excelled all the other participants. Our previous examination of the first and third of these patterns made it plain that they were not original with Chrétien, but formed a part of the *conteurs'* stock in trade; and the second pattern is treated so differently by the author of *La Mort Artu* and by Chrétien that it is hardly conceivable that one version is directly derived from the other.

There are other signs that the third pattern as found in the Tourney of Tintagel was not borrowed from Chrétien's use of it in the Tourney of Noauz or from the Dame de Malehot episode. We learned from these two latter versions that Lancelot's chief opponent in combat had *originally* been Meleagant and Malehot respectively, and that both these names represented developments from Welsh Melwas. It is, therefore, no mere chance that Gauvain's chief opponent at the Tourney of Tintagel was called Meliant, another derivative from Melwas.[5] And the identification of Meliant with Meleagant would clarify other relationships in our story. Meliant's foster father, the generous and hospitable Tiebaut, would be the counterpart of Meleagant's father, the generous and hospitable Baudemaguz. And since it was proved that the first syllable of Baudemaguz' name represented a corruption of Bran,[6] so the *-bau-* of Tiebaut seems to represent a similar corruption. Chrétien, or the author of his source, stumbling on the name Baut[7] of Tintagel, substituted the alliterating French name Tiebaut. Moreover, in support of this hypothesis, there are points of

---

[2] Cf. *supra*, pp. 81–83.

[3] Sommer, *Vulgate Version*, VI, 207-13. *Mort Artu*, ed. J. Frappier, pp. 8–14.

[4] Cf. *supra*, pp. 253–55.

[5] That Meliant is merely a variant of Meleagant is proved by the fact that we find in the *Vulgate Lancelot*, where one ms. has Meliagant de Cardoil, another has Milianz li Sires de Carduel (Sommer, *op. cit.*, *Index of Names and Places*, p. 62), and by the fact that Heinrich von dem Türlin called the abductor of Ginover Milianz (J. L. Weston, *Legend of Gawain*, p. 80n.   [6] Cf. *supra*, pp. 240–44.

[7] That Baut is a possible corruption of Bran is shown by Ulrich von Zatzikhoven's form, Pant von Genewis, cognate with Ban de Benoic, both being corruptions of Bran le Benoit. H. Newstead, *Bran the Blessed in Arthurian Romance*, pp. 155–57. The *t* of Pant is surely a mistaken back-formation from a nominative Pans or Panz.

resemblance between Gauvain's innocent affair with Meliant's foster sister and Lancelot's apparently innocent affair with Meleagant's sister in Godefroy de Lagny's conclusion of the *Charrette*.[8] In both cases the maiden falls in love with the hero and provides him with a horse or a token, he pledges his service to her at all times, goes forth to fight with her brother Meleagant or her foster brother Meliant, and vanquishes him. Even though there are so many discrepancies between the two stories as to show that the relationship is not close, there must have been a common basis in a traditional affair between Lancelot or Gauvain and the sister of his foe Meleagant or Meliant.

A neat confirmation of this belief is furnished by an episode in the *Vulgate Lancelot*.[9]

After suffering from a severe illness and being cured by a lovelorn maiden, and after being released from prison by another maiden, who provides him with horse and arms, Lancelot sets out to take part in a tourney between the King of Norgales and King Bandemagus.[10] He learns from some squires that the tourney is being held in a meadow near by. Taking shelter for the night at a nunnery, he finds there Meleagant's sister, who had freed him from the dolorous prison—not, however, the maiden just mentioned. She notes the signs of his late illness, but asks him to take her father's side in the tourney. Obtaining his consent, she summons, from a castle near by, her father Bandemagus, who is overjoyed to see Lancelot and to obtain his help. The next day Meleagant's sister proceeds to the tourneying field and takes her place in the *loges* with the other ladies, among them the daughter of the King of Norgales, Gauvain's former *amie*. Lancelot comes on the field, disguised in white arms, and for a time delays entering the fray while the foes of King Bandemagus carry all before them. A dispute arises between the two princesses, one boasting the prowess of the knights of the King of Norgales, the other predicting that they will suffer overwhelming defeat. At last, Lancelot charges into the ranks and at once the fortunes of war are reversed and the knights of Norgales flee. To avoid recognition Lancelot rides off into the forest.

Three things are remarkable about this story. First, it contains certain elements of the story of Lancelot and Meleagant's sister as told by Godefroy de Lagny: Lancelot's sickness and imprisonment and release (with a suggestion that it was Meleagant's sister who released him) and the provision of a horse. Secondly, it contains certain elements of Gauvain's affair with the Maid of the Little Sleeves, Meliant's foster sister: the meeting with the squires and the news of the tourney; the maiden who asks the hero to take her father's side; the quarrel of the maidens watching the tourney; the hero's delay in taking part; his victorious participation. Thirdly, though

---

[8] Ed. Foerster, vss. 6678–728, 6896–903.
[9] Sommer, *Vulgate Version*, V, 72–84, 93–95, 97–102.
[10] On this form cf. *ibid.*, p. 95, n. 3. "The scribe writes . . . mostly Bandemagus. I have uniformly adopted the spelling 'Baudemagus.' "

the story parallels Gauvain's romance with Meliant's foster sister, the names have undergone precisely that substitution which one would expect if our hypothesis were true. Instead of Tiebaut as the father of the heroine we have Bandemagus; instead of aiding the forces of Tiebaut at the heroine's request, the hero espouses the cause of Bandemagus. Instead of Meliant's foster sister as heroine we have Meleagant's sister. It is most unlikely that the author of the *Vulgate Lancelot,* if he were combining features from Godefroy's *Charrette* and Chrétien's *Conte del Graal,* would have adapted his nomenclature to a hypothesis to be worked out seven centuries later. Surely, it is far easier to suppose that this episode represents pretty faithfully (except for the absence of Meleagant, who had already been killed off [11]) the common source of the Tourney of Tintagel and Lancelot's affair with Meleagant's sister.

In the common source we should expect to find the hero released from prison and brought back to health by a damsel; supplied by her with a horse; coming incognito to a tourney held by the damsel's father, King Bran; at first holding back and inviting the scorn of the beholders but stoutly defended by his ladylove; being prompted by her to display his prowess; overthrowing her brother, Meliant or Meleagant, and winning the tournament. Reflections of this story, let us remind ourselves, are to be found not only in the Tourney of Tintagel, the Tourney of King Bandemagus, the Tourney of Noauz, and the Dame de Malehot episode, but also in the tourney held by King Brangorre, which we examined in our study of the Tourney of Noauz.[12] Bohort came incognito to the castle of King Brangorre in the midst of a tourney, delayed entering the fray, was the subject of scornful remarks, was prompted by the King's daughter to fight on her father's side, and won the tournament. Here is one more support for the thesis that the tradition of King Bran's tournament gave rise to, or influenced, the many stories we have mentioned, including the Tourney of Tintagel.

The prototypes of the principal figures in the idyl of the Maid of the Little Sleeves can now be identified. Her father, Tiebaut, goes back to Bran; her foster brother, Meliant, to Melwas. She herself—playing as she does the role of Meleagant's sister, Bandemagus' daughter—must be, like her, one of the numerous hypostases of Morgain la Fée.[13] It is not, of course, to be maintained that such a basic tale as we have sketched above was actually told, in the Welsh stage, of Bran, Melwas, and Modron. Something like it *may* have been recited by the *cyvarwyddon,* without those adaptations to French manners and sentiment and without those special complications, such as the Rival Sisters, which we find in Chrétien's poem. On the other hand, the whole basic plot of King Bran's tourney may have been an invention of the Breton *conteurs.* Certain it is that nowhere in

[11] *Ibid.,* IV, 225.   [12] *Ibid.,* pp. 262–64. Cf. Chap. XLII.   [13] Cf. *supra,* pp. 260–62.

Chrétien's work has a stock formula assumed such a thoroughly coherent and shapely form, nowhere is there less of the banal and the preposterous, nowhere are the characters more vital than in the household of Tiebaut of Tintagel. The incident of "the Maid of the Little Sleeves" is one of the happiest, if not the happiest of the poet's retellings of an old story.

Chapter LXXV

THE VISIT TO THE HERMIT UNCLE

VERSES 6217–6513

Perceval wandered for five years without entering a church or confessing to a priest, but triumphing over sixty knights and sending them to Arthur's court. One day he was riding, fully armed, through a desert when he met a party of penitents. One of them rebuked him for riding thus on Good Friday, and directed him to the chapel of a holy hermit. Perceval followed a path through the wood and found the hermit, a priest, and a clerk about to celebrate mass. The hermit bade him confess his sins, and Perceval told how he had forgotten God, how he had neglected to ask at the castle of the Fisher King concerning the Bleeding Lance and the Grail. When he revealed his name, the hermit told him that the cause of his failure was his unfeeling desertion of his mother. The hermit went on to reveal that he himself was Perceval's maternal uncle, that it was the Fisher King's father who was served with the Grail, and that this holy man had been unable to leave his chamber for fifteen years and had been kept alive by a mass wafer which one brought him in the Grail. "So holy a thing is the Grail and so spiritual that he needs no more to preserve his life than the wafer which comes in the Grail." The hermit then gave his nephew religious instructions and kept him with him, fasting, through Easter Day.

IT HAS ALREADY been pointed out [1] that the Finn saga was one of the most important sources of the Perceval legend, and that young Finn visited an uncle, Crimall, an old man in a desert wood, and told him his story from beginning to end. This purely secular Irish tradition offers the only plausible source for Perceval's visit to his uncle. It is interesting to speculate on the reasons for the religious tone which Chrétien gives it. For this is the first hint we have that Perceval's experiences have any sacred implications. The earlier episodes in his history, including the strange adventures at the Fisher King's castle, reveal no pious feeling or intent on the part of the author. Though Perceval's mother preaches him a lesson on the rudiments of the faith, it leads up only to the comic blunders

[1] See Chap. LVIII.

of mistaking the five knights for God and his angels, and of entering a tent under the impression that it was a church. The hero's affair with Blancheflor was indecorous, to say the least, yet the poet omits the obvious opportunity to condemn or to moralize. The Grail itself on its first appearance cannot have been regarded as a holy thing since it is carried by a damsel from one castle chamber to another. Not until we come to the Good Friday episode do we get a suggestion of what was to become the prevailing concept of the Grail and its quest; and even then the profane atmosphere returns as soon as the episode is over and prevails throughout the rest of the poem. How did such a wholly secular incident as the visit of Finn to his uncle in a desert wood evolve into the one thoroughly sanctified episode in Chrétien's *Conte del Graal?*

Rash though it may seem to interpret a process on which we have no direct evidence, yet one may hazard a guess. The original Irish story was rather pointless; Finn merely discovers his uncle in the wood, tells him his adventure with the man who had slain Cumall, and then bids him farewell! Such a tale would provoke speculation when it was adopted into the Perceval legend. Why should the hero's uncle be living solitary in a desert wood unless he were a hermit? If so, what more natural than that the hero should reveal his identity and relate his adventures in the course of a long confession? Why such a long confession unless he had neglected that duty? What more appropriate day for such a confession than Good Friday? In some such way, we may conjecture, this scene, which indirectly inspired Wagner to one of his most magical passages, came into existence.

We can be more confident in tracing the sanctification of another profane, even pagan, feature, the presence of the Host in the Grail. In our analysis of the "Joie de la Cort" episode [2] we discovered that, according to *La Queste del Saint Graal,* Galaad and his companions were fed in the castle of Corbenic, where dwelt the Maimed King; their food was the body of the Savior, contained in the Holy Grail. We saw also that the same romance tells how Perceval came to an abbey and saw there a wounded king, Mordrain, who for hundreds of years had been kept alive only by "li cors Jhesucrist." We saw that these and a number of other mysterious facts are all to be explained by the fact that the euhemerized sea-god, Bran, the original of the Maimed King, possessed a drinking horn which furnished whatever drink and food a man desired. The castle of Corbenic took its name from this horn, Cor Beneit being corrupted into Corbenic.[3]

[2] See Chap. XXV.

[3] Though I know of no ms. of the *Estoire del Saint Graal* or the *Queste* which gives other than Corbenic or Corbenyc, the author of the Dutch *Lancelot* (cf. J. L. Weston, *Legend of Lancelot,* p. 159), who gives Cambenoyc, Cambenoyt, Cabenoyt, must have translated from a ms. which gave the second element in the word correctly. Cf. the testing horn in the *Livre de Caradoc:* (Montpellier ms.) "Cest cor qui Beneïz a non;" (Edinburgh ms.) "Ce cor qui Beneoiz a non."

The *cors* which fed the wounded Mordrain represents the mistaking of *cors,* meaning horn, for *cors,* meaning body. The pagan horn of plenty thus became the miraculous Host. Being coupled with the platter of plenty, the Grail, the horn became "the Host which comes in the Grail."

There are some embarrassing facts, however, in connection with Perceval's uncle which must be faced. In our earlier study of Guivret [4] we noted that the author of *Perlesvaus* calls the hero's hermit uncle Pelles, "rois de la Basse Gent," and it was argued that the original of this Pelles was the Welsh dwarf king Beli. Evidence since accumulated confirmed this argument.[5] If this derivation of Perceval's hermit uncle from the Welsh Beli is correct—and the case could hardly be stronger—must not the derivation from Finn's uncle Crimall be abandoned? Or is it possible that the two traditions have been combined: the Irish tradition which represented the hero's uncle as an old man in a desert, and the Welsh tradition which represented the hero's uncle as the dwarf king, Beli?

The second hypothesis relieves us from our embarrassment; it neatly accords with the whole complex of facts. Perceval must have inherited from the Finn story an aged uncle who lived in a wood and who was therefore taken to be a hermit. Perceval must also have inherited from the lost Pryderi tradition a royal kinsman, named Pelles or one of its variations, who is usually his uncle and the brother of the Grail King. The Vulgate cycle, significantly, knows only the latter tradition, for Pelles is no hermit but is the king who dwells in the castle of Corbenic with the Maimed King, his father.[6] Chrétien reflects both traditions: though Perceval's uncle corresponds to Crimall, the old man in the desert wood, he is also the brother of the infirm king of the Grail Castle, thus corresponding to Beli, the brother of Bran. The same hybrid tradition confronts us in *Perlesvaus,* the *Didot Perceval,* and in Wauchier's and Gerbert's continuations of *Le Conte del Graal;* the Crimall and the Beli parts can still be distinguished in the role and relationships of the Hermit Uncle.

There is still another puzzle: who was the Fisher King's father? I believe that Bruce was right in regarding him as simply a double of the Fisher King,[7] though I am far from subscribing to his interpretation of this double as the Holy Ghost! Bruce pointed out that many accounts of the visit to the Grail Castle make no mention of this mysterious personage; [8] and in some it is obviously the King himself who is fed by the Grail.

If this be so, what, then, led to the duplication of the Fisher King in Chrétien's poem? I believe that two forces were operative, one traditional,

---

[4] See Chap. XX.   [5] *Supra,* pp. 309 f. Cf. *PMLA,* LVI (1941), 917–24.
[6] Sommer, *Vulgate Version,* V, 296, 303; VI, 187–91. Only in one passage of the *Queste* (*ibid.,* VI, 150) certain mss. describe Pelles as wounded by a mysterious lance, but mss. M and R are free from this inconsistency, giving the name Pellinor.
[7] J. D. Bruce, *Evolution,* I, 261 f. Cf. J. L. Weston, *From Ritual to Romance,* p. 115.
[8] Bruce, *op. cit.,* I, 262, n. 51.

the other rational. As we have just had occasion to observe, the *Vulgate Lancelot* and the *Queste* know of two kings dwelling in the castle of Corbenic, Pelles and his father, the Maimed King. Pelles, in accordance with all we know of his cognates, the dwarfs of Arthurian romance, is properly represented as sound of wind and limb,[9] and therefore cannot be equated with Chrétien's infirm king, fed by the Grail. Nevertheless, there was apparently a tradition of two royal personages in the Grail Castle, and so a precedent of a sort for Chrétien. Moreover, there was a good reason for providing this additional figure. For Perceval was supposed to ask an all-important and presumably intelligent question: "Whom does one serve with the Grail?" What sense could there be in such a question if he saw with his own eyes the Fisher King served by the Grail Bearer? The happenings in the hall of the Grail Castle might be bewildering and mysterious, but they must not be completely fatuous, as they would be if Perceval had to undergo years of humiliation and suffering merely for failing to ask a nonsensical question. To give some semblance of rationality to this basic motif was the problem. The second king provided the solution. Deliberately Chrétien, or his source, suppressed all mention of the Grail Bearer's serving food in the Fisher King's hall, though nearly every other version of the incident speaks of the Grail's provision of food to those who sat in the King's presence and to the King himself. Deliberately, too, the Grail Bearer is made to pass through the hall and into a chamber whither Perceval's gaze cannot follow her. Thus the famous question test acquires a certain reasonableness, and the answer to the question was provided by doubling the Fisher King, and making the second infirm figure the invisible occupant of the chamber.

Chapter LXXVI

GREOREAS AND THE HIDEOUS SQUIRE

VERSES 6519–6656, 6904–7144, 7285–7363

Gauvain came on a wounded knight, Greoreas, tended by a mourning damsel. Greoreas warned Gauvain against proceeding further, but Gauvain insisted on pursuing his way. On returning from an adventure which bore no relation to Greoreas' warning, Gauvain plucked an herb, bound it on Greoreas' wounds with the aid of the damsel, and thus restored his

---

[9] In the *Prose Tristan*, however (ed. Löseth, pp. 278 ff., 397), Pelles is the Maimed King. An enormous amount of confusion accumulated on the subject, since we find Pellinor and Pellean, whose names are derived from Beli Mawr and Belin(?), and who were doubtless originally identical with Pelles, are Maimed Kings. Bruce's collection of facts regarding Pelles, Pellinor, and Pellean (*Mod. Phil.*, XVI [1918], 113–38, 337–50) is very valuable, though I totally disagree with his interpretation of them.

strength. A shaggy and deformed squire, mounted on a wretched nag, then
appeared, and for his insolence was knocked by Gauvain out of his saddle.
Greoreas recognized Gauvain as one who had accused him of rape, and
maliciously rode away on Gauvain's horse, leaving him to mount the squire's
nag. As Gauvain approached the Castle of Ladies, he was overtaken by a
knight mounted on his own steed, who had been sent by Greoreas to bring
back his head. Gauvain, in spite of his feeble animal, succeeded in hurling
his antagonist to the earth.

Hilka, without realizing it, gave the best clue to the elucidation of this episode when in his note on the description of the monstrous squire he cited the conventional portraits of malevolent dwarfs.[1] For if we substitute a dwarf for the squire, we cannot but be reminded of a story of Pseudo-Wauchier's to which we have thrice referred and which certainly incorporated one of the most influential formulae of Arthurian romance.[2] Let me summarize it once more.[3]

Carahes found in a garden a wounded knight tended by a maiden. A mounted dwarf appeared on the scene, displayed great insolence, and hurled Carahes to the ground. As Carahes departed from the scene, he was jeered and pelted by the inhabitants of the castle. Some time later, having extracted a spearhead from the body of a dead knight, Carahes returned with it to the scene of his humiliation, and killed both the dwarf and the wounded knight.

The *Vulgate Lancelot* gives a somewhat different *mélange* of the same ingredients.[4]

A knight named Sarras was met outside a castle by an insolent dwarf, and was promptly overthrown by a knight named Belias, who led away his destrier. Sarras was obliged to mount the nag of his own squire, and as he departed was jeered and pelted by the spectators from the castle. Lancelot then challenged Belias and mortally wounded him, as well as his more formidable brother Bridan.[5] As Lancelot left the castle, a squire informed him that on a previous occasion, Gauvain had overthrown Belias but had himself been unhorsed by Bridan.

It is a curious fact that immediately after this adventure [6] Lancelot met a "Knight of the Litter," who had been seeking him. Some time before,[7] Lancelot had been lying asleep in a forest and had been waked by the passing of a knight in a litter borne by two palfreys. The knight was wounded in the thigh, but refused to allow Lancelot to withdraw the arrow and heal him. At the second meeting with Lancelot, however, he begged him to perform this service, and Lancelot did so. Now it is evidently

---

[1] *Conte del Graal*, ed. Hilka, p. 749, n. on vs. 6986.
[2] Cf. *supra*, pp. 80, 213, 321, and *Revue celt.*, XLVII (1930), 39–62; *PMLA*, LVI (1941), 921–24; *Speculum*, XVI (1941), 34–50.   [3] Potvin, *Perceval le Gallois*, IV, vss. 21236–724.
[4] Sommer, *Vulgate Version*, V, 251–54, 263–68. On this tale cf. *PMLA*, LVI, 922 f.
[5] For this form of the name cf. Sommer, *op. cit.*, V, 268, n. 2.
[6] *Ibid.*, V, 268 f.   [7] *Ibid.*, V, 224–26.

this same "Knight of the Litter" who turns up again in *La Queste del Saint Graal*.[8]

Lancelot was lying half asleep in a forest when he saw a knight approaching in a litter borne by two palfreys and suffering great anguish. The Grail mysteriously drew near, healed the sick knight of the litter, and departed. A squire belonging to the knight appeared and spoke scornfully of Lancelot. The knight then mounted Lancelot's steed and rode away with the squire. Two days later this same knight attacked Lancelot without provocation and was hurled from his saddle.

Despite the shuffling of elements, the same pattern seems to underlie the four stories. Again and again we meet a wounded knight, an attendant maiden, an insolent dwarf or squire who comes on the scene. Again and again the hero heals the wounded knight, fights with the dwarf, loses his steed, and is obliged to proceed on his way humiliated. Particularly noticeable is the fact that, according to Chrétien, Greoreas, though healed by Gauvain of his wound, cherishes enmity towards him, rides off with his horse, and sends a knight on the same horse to attack him; whereas according to the *Lancelot* the hero heals the knight of the litter, and according to the *Queste* the knight of the litter cherishes enmity towards the hero, rides off with his horse, and later attacks him. By this time we have learned to recognize in these wounded knights who seek relief at the hands of the hero the descendants of the Welsh Bran;[9] we have also learned that the combative dwarfs of Arthurian romance are descendants of the Welsh Beli.[10] Bran and Beli appear as brothers in the Welsh redactions of Geoffrey of Monmouth.[11] They also appear as brothers in the dwarf Bilis and his gigantic brother Brien or Brihan of Chrétien's *Erec*. They are doubtless the brothers Belias and Bridan of the story summarized above, even though Belias has ceased to be a dwarf and is merely announced by a dwarf, presumably because it would not do for a knight like Sarras to be discomfited by a mere midget.[12] This dwarf and Bridan have their counterparts in the hideous squire and Greoreas of Chrétien's narrative. The Welsh personage Bran was therefore the prototype of Greoreas,[13] and his brother Beli was the prototype of the hideous squire.

It is, of course, disconcerting to realize that so infamous a character as

[8] *Ibid.*, VI, 42–44. *Queste del S. Graal*, ed. Pauphilet, pp. 58–61.
[9] Cf. *supra*, pp. 242 f.   [10] See Chap. XX.
[11] Geoffrey of Monmonth, *Historia Regum Britanniae*, ed. Griscom, p. 276.
[12] Note how in *Erec*, vss. 5003–5, Chrétien was at pains to explain that his hero was weak from wounds when he was unhorsed by the dwarf Guivret. Note also that whereas, in the *Vulgate Lancelot* episode summarized above, Belias unhorsed Sarras and led away his destrier, forcing him to mount the nag of his squire—evidently the original version—Chrétien represents Gauvain as overthrowing the hideous squire and yet losing his steed and being forced to mount the squire's nag. The change was evidently prompted by the desire to save Gauvain's reputation for prowess. Cf. also *supra*, p. 213.
[13] I am at a loss to explain this name.

Greoreas is, in a sense, the Maimed King, and the monstrous and insolent squire is, in a sense, the gracious King Pelles. Nevertheless, the cumulative proof is strong, and it is not hard to understand such a pejorative development for these two august figures. In Chrétien's source, as in Pseudo-Wauchier, the *Lancelot,* and the *Queste,* they were presented as hostile to the hero, and for this concept of the Arthurian counterparts of Bran and Beli there was traditional warrant, just as there was for the contrary attitude on their part. Professor Newstead has shown [14] that we must recognize Bran not only in the hospitable and courteous figures of the Fisher King, Baudemaguz, and the King of Brandigan, but also in the malignant Brandus des Illes and the hostile Bran de Lis. As for the dwarf Beli, it is well to remember that the dwarf Guivret was at first challenging and aggressive toward Erec, but later became his sworn friend and extended to him every aid and hospitality.[15] Here the change of attitude was rationally explained. But when the ingenuity of the *conteurs* was unequal to accounting for such diverse roles for the same person, it was natural that they should divide the characters and separate the roles, as we have frequently noted in the case of Morgain and her various counterparts. Bran and Beli in their friendly, benevolent parts would tend to become more and more honorable or saintly; in their insolent, aggressive, or sinister parts they would become increasingly abhorrent. By some such process of dichotomy Greoreas and the hideous squire evolved from the same originals as the Fisher King and his brother Pelles.

The sequel to the Greoreas story, contained in certain manuscripts of the continuation of Chrétien's poem, supplements in most revealing fashion what we have been able to gather as to the genesis of the adventure. To quote Jessie Weston's summary of this sequel:

"Gawain continues his road till he comes to a house, the door of which stands invitingly open. He enters, and it closes swiftly upon him. There is no one to be seen, but in the hall a table stands ready spread. Gawain sits down to meat when an armed knight enters and challenges him. They fight, and Gawain is victorious. A maiden now appears, and prays the life of the vanquished; 'tis her fault, the 'custom' was established for love of her. She is the maiden outraged by Greoreas, and has persuaded her lover to leave the door of the 'manoir' open to all comers and to challenge any knight who may enter, in hope that Greoreas may be among them, and may receive his deserts. Gawain tells her he has already been well punished, at which she is rejoiced." [16]

This sequel reminds one of another highly dramatic story found at a later point in Pseudo-Wauchier's continuation.[17]

[14] Newstead, *Bran the Blessed in Arthurian Romance,* pp. 70–85, 146–50.
[15] See Chap. XX.   [16] J. L. Weston, *Legend of Perceval,* I, 220 f.
[17] Potvin, *Perceval le Gallois,* III, vss. 16719–18184. Trans. in Weston, *Sir Gawain and the Lady of Lys,* pp. 27–58.

Gauvain comes to a castle, the doors of which stand invitingly open. There is no one to be seen, but in the hall a table stands ready spread. Gauvain rides back and fetches Arthur and his men. As they sit down to meat, a half-armed knight, Bran de Lis, enters and challenges Gauvain. They fight, and at last Gauvain is victorious. Meanwhile a maiden has entered, and holding up her child, asks him to intercede with Gauvain, his father, in behalf of Bran de Lis, her brother. She is in fact the maiden outraged by Gauvain five years before. Arthur intervenes and reconciles the combatants.

One might be inclined to dismiss this story of Gauvain's adventure at the castle of Bran de Lis as a mere refurbishing, though a highly artistic one, of the Greoreas sequel. But there are objections. For one thing, the Greoreas sequel occurs in but three manuscripts,[18] the Bran de Lis story in all; and for another, Professor Newstead has shown that the latter represents an authentic tradition with several cognates.[19] Therefore, the Greoreas sequel is not the source of the Bran de Lis adventure. Miss Newstead's demonstration compels us to believe that the knight whom Gauvain vanquished in the mysterious castle was not nameless, as in the Greoreas sequel, but was called Bran, and that this Bran had a legitimate quarrel with Gauvain, who had violated his sister.[20] It therefore follows that Chrétien and his unknown continuator departed from this original tradition by introducing Bran first, as we have seen, under the name Greoreas and then as a nameless knight, and by making him, not Gauvain, the ravisher of a maiden. Thus our interpretation of Greoreas as the Maimed King, originally derived from the Welsh Bran, but deliberately debased in character because of his opposition to the hero Gauvain, is again confirmed. And it is easy to see that the same motive, together with the desire to save the character of Gauvain from a blot on his chivalry, was responsible for transferring to Greoreas the crime of rape.

To recapitulate, Gauvain's meeting with Greoreas and the hideous squire reveals itself as a variation on the stock formula of the meeting with the Maimed King and his dwarf brother; the sequel in the empty castle reveals itself as a variation on the formula of Gauvain's visit to the castle of Bran de Lis. The linking of these two incidents in the common source of Chrétien and his continuator was doubtless due to the fact that Gauvain and Bran were originally the chief personages in both. The study of the analogues enables us to see how drastically the original patterns could be reshaped, and what were some of the motives at work in such reshaping.

[18] Weston, *Legend of Perceval*, I, 13.   [19] Newstead, *op. cit.,* pp. 70–85.
[20] Miss Weston, in *Sir Gawain and the Lady of Lys*, p. x, remarked that this is "a survival of a very early, pre-chivalric stage of tradition."

Chapter LXXVII

L'ORGUELLEUSE DE LOGRES

verses 6657–6903, 7145–7370, 7432–68, 8286–8648, 8829–9002

After his first meeting with Greoreas, Gauvain entered a walled town and discovered in a garden a damsel under a tree. She consented to accompany him if he would fetch her palfrey from an orchard near by. In spite of the warnings of a crowd of folk and a tall knight sitting under a tree, Gauvain met with no misfortune and brought the animal, whose head was half black, half white, back to the scornful damsel. She heaped insults on him and forbade him to touch her with his dirty hands, yet she agreed to ride after him until he met disaster. After his experience with the ungrateful Greoreas and his hideous squire, Gauvain rode on followed by the damsel, who mocked him for his feeble mount and its shabby furnishings. He rebuked her with courtesy. As they reached a river, she warned him of the approach of Greoreas' nephew and counseled flight, but Gauvain staunchly refused to flee and promptly unhorsed his pursuer. When he looked about for the damsel, she had vanished. The ferryman who took him across the river to the Castle of Ladies informed him that she had caused many a knight to lose his head at that passage. After enduring the perils of the castle that night, Gauvain espied the next morning the dangerous damsel riding with a knight on the opposite bank of the river. He issued forth, was ferried across, and easily overcame this knight, who was guarding the ferries of Galloway (les porz de Galvoie). Still the scornful damsel treated Gauvain with contempt and, leading him to a tree, dared him to cross the Perilous Ford beside it. He succeeded in doing so and met on the far side the knight Guiromelant with his bird hounds, evidently engaged in falconry. Guiromelant revealed that he had once loved the mocking damsel, who was called "l'Orguelleuse de Logres," but she had not reciprocated his feeling and had attached herself to the knight whom Gauvain had just defeated. Guiromelant also disclosed that he hated Gauvain with a mortal hatred, but was at the same time the accepted suitor of Gauvain's sister, who dwelt in the Castle of Ladies. There also dwelt Gauvain's mother, whom evidently Gauvain had not recognized, for he declared that she had been dead for at least twenty years. When Gauvain in turn revealed his identity, Guiromelant arranged to settle the quarrel between them in a duel to be held a week later before the Castle of Ladies, and to which Gauvain's vassals were to be summoned as spectators. Leaving Guiromelant, Gauvain returned across the ford to Orguelleuse,

*who at last admitted his prowess and begged his pardon. Together they
were ferried over to the Castle of Ladies and received a jubilant welcome.
Orguelleuse is not mentioned again. Gauvain sent to Orcanie to summon
King Arthur and his court to attend the coming duel.*

IN THE CONTINUATION of Chrétien's poem we read at length of the assembling of the courts of Arthur and Guiromelant near the Perilous
Ford below the Castle of Ladies.[1] All these knights and the ladies of
the castle, including Gauvain's mother Morcades,[2] were present at the
great duel. Gauvain gained the upper hand of Guiromelant before King
Arthur intervened.

There is no need to emphasize the fact that the story of Orguelleuse is
among the most disconnected in Chrétien's work. There are obvious in-
terpolations, whole incidents in which she plays no part. Gauvain's return
to Greoreas, the punishment of the ugly squire, and the ingratitude of
Greoreas, constitute, as we have observed, a separate episode. Gauvain's
entertainment by the ferryman and his experiences in the Castle of Ladies,
we shall see later, form another irrelevant element. Likewise, there is much
in the story of Guiromelant which belongs to a different tradition. In fact,
it is easy to see that those episodes, which merely mention Orguelleuse and
her evil ways, but which do not introduce her as a participant, serve to in-
terrupt and confuse the story of Gauvain and his vinegar-tongued companion.

If we scrutinize those passages where the lady plays an important part,
and attempt to find their traditional basis, we shall at first be disappointed.
At least, it is difficult to find a convincing parallel or source for Gauvain's
first meeting with the lady and her sending him to fetch her palfrey. The
animal itself, with its parti-colored head, reminds one of the palfrey which
Guivret presented to Enide, so far as its markings are concerned. But
neither in *Erec* nor elsewhere does a damsel dispatch a knight on such
a mission. The motif of folk prognosticating disaster for the adventurous
hero is, of course, a stock feature and has already been noted in the episodes
of the "Joie de la Cort" and of Evil Adventure. But beyond this one motif
the correspondence does not go.

Once the extraneous elements and this one baffling feature of Gauvain's
mission to fetch the palfrey have been set aside, however, it becomes plain
that the story of Orguelleuse is patterned on the tradition of the Damoisele
Maudisante, which we find in *Le Bel Inconnu, Libeaus Desconus, Wigalois,
Le Chevalier de la Cote Maltaillié,* and most clearly in Malory's Book of
Beaumayns. This pattern must have existed early since it powerfully in-
fluenced, as we have seen,[3] the common source of Chrétien's *Erec* and
Geraint. Apparently, then, by 1150 at latest, there existed a "grand conte"

---

[1] Potvin, *Perceval le Gallois,* III, 57–68.
[2] J. L. Weston, *Legend of Perceval,* I, 193.   [3] See Chap. X.

about the hero whose name or sobriquet assumed the various forms of Guerec, Garet, Gauvain, or Beaumayns, relating his journey in the company of a contemptuous damsel, his triumphs over sundry knights, including at least one combat at a ford, his winning the respect of the damsel, and his final deliverance of her sister or mistress from a hated suitor. This frame story won favor with the *conteurs,* partly because of the piquant relationship between the damsel and her escort, and partly because it permitted the inclusion of any number of thrilling rencontres on the road and nocturnal adventures in mysterious castles. Perhaps the clumsiest employment of this narrative framework is to be found in *Le Conte del Graal,* though, of course, Chrétien cannot be held accountable. The best version and perhaps the closest to the archetype is that which Malory took from a lost Anglo-French romance and made into his Book of Beaumayns.

The parallels between Chrétien's handling of the tradition and Malory's are striking.[4]

1. One hero is named Gauvain(s), the other is nicknamed Beaumayns. The latter preserves the tradition that it originated as a sobriquet, the Welsh Gwallt-a(d)vwyn, but the initial *G* of Gauvains was misread as *B,* and the whole word has been grotesquely tortured into Beaumayns, probably by some illiterate Anglo-Norman, who was trying to make the epithet yield a meaning.[5] That the name Gauvain was derived from this same Gwallt-a(d)vwyn through the form Galvagin has been shown earlier.[6] The two heroes were therefore identical in origin.

2. Both Gauvain(s) and Beaumayns rode in company with a contemptuous damsel and replied courteously to her insults.

3. Both Gauvain(s) and Beaumayns were warned by the damsel of the approach of a hostile knight and were urged to flee; yet both rejected her counsel and proved superior in the fight.[7]

4. Both Gauvain(s) and Beaumayns were victorious over this adversary at a river passage.[8]

5. Both Gauvain(s) and Beaumayns had a mother, Morcades or Morgause, whom they had not seen for fifteen or more years.[9]

6. Both Gauvain(s) and Beaumayns were connected with Orkney. The former undertook to send to his land for all his host,[10] and in accordance with this undertaking sent to Orcanie. The latter hero is repeatedly referred to as Gareth of Orkeney.

7. Both Gauvain(s) and Beaumayns received the apologies of the scornful damsel, and granted her forgiveness.[11]

---

[4] Malory, *Morte d'Arthur,* Bk. VII.   [5] *PMLA,* LIV (1939), 656–68.   [6] See Chap. XVIII.
[7] *Conte del Graal,* ed. Hilka, vss. 7273–359. Malory, Bk. VII, chap. 6.
[8] Cf. *supra,* pp. 128–31.
[9] *Conte del Graal,* vss. 8755 f. Malory, ed. H. O. Sommer, Bk. VII, chap. 26; other editions, chap. 25.   [10] *Conte del Graal,* vss. 8886 f.
[11] *Ibid.,* vss. 8917–67. Malory, Bk. VII, chap. 11.

If we add the evidence of the continuator of Chrétien's poem, usually referred to as Pseudo-Wauchier, we discover two other parallels between Gauvain(s) and Beaumayns.

8. Both engaged in a duel before a castle with a knight who was at once a suitor of a lady who dwelt within and an enemy of Gauvain.[12]

9. Both performed feats of arms before the same castle in the presence of a great assembly, including Arthur, Guenievre, and Morcades or Morgause.[13]

Despite all shuffling and contamination, Chrétien's story of Gauvain's adventures with Orguelleuse shows clear marks of having been derived mainly from the same *grand conte* on which Malory ultimately drew for his story of Beaumayns' adventures with Lynet. Lynet, therefore, was the immediate prototype of Orguelleuse. And Lynet herself had her origin in the Irish goddess Liban, as we saw in our consideration of Chrétien's Lunete.[14] It was Liban who came to Cuchulainn in a vision, laughed at him, beat him, and yet finally served as his guide to the faery isle where they were welcomed by her sister Fand and where he overcame three enemies. It was therefore Liban who bequeathed her somewhat inconsistent role to Orguelleuse, for Orguelleuse treated Gauvain with contumely and yet served as his guide to the faery castle beyond a river, where they were finally welcomed by his sister and beside which he fought with three opponents—Greoreas' nephew, the guardian of the "porz de Galvoie," and Guiromelant.

Though, like Lynet, Orguelleuse inherited her role as the Damoisele Maudisante mainly from Liban, yet, like Lynet, she played a part in adventures which bear no likeness to those of the Irish goddess. The Damoisele Maudisante was usually present when the hero overcame one or more antagonists at a river crossing,[15] and it was shown in Chapter XVIII that this incident was based on the Welsh tale of Pwyll's meeting with the huntsman Arawn and the subsequent combat at a ford. It will appear on a later page that Gauvain's meeting with the falconer Guiromelant and the subsequent combat near the Perilous Ford (narrated by Pseudo-Wauchier) have been colored by this same Welsh tradition. In fact, the adventures of Gauvain from the time he sallies forth from the Castle of Ladies to the end of his duel with Guiromelant represent a conflation of several forms of this most famous and influential episode. When, therefore, we learn that Orguelleuse had once been the mistress of the falconer-knight Guiromelant, and later of the guardian of the "porz de Galvoie," it seems likely (though by no means certain) that she inherited these relationships from Modron,

[12] Weston, *Legend of Perceval*, I, 11 f. Malory, Bk. VII, chaps. 16, 17.
[13] Potvin, *op. cit.*, III, 59–78. Malory, ed. Sommer, Bk. VII, chaps. 28–31; other editions, chaps. 27–30.   [14] See Chap. L.
[15] Malory, Bk. VII, chap. 6. *Libeaus Desconus*, ed. M. Kaluza, vss. 277–408. Renaud de Beaujeu, *Le Bel Inconnu*, ed. G. P. Williams (1929), vss. 317–485.

the wife of Arawn, who was both a huntsman and a combatant at a ford. And it is at least possible that, while Orguelleuse is descended from the Irish Liban, with a slight admixture of the Welsh Modron, so the three antagonists whom Gauvain encountered beside the Castle of Ladies (Greoreas' nephew, the defender of the "porz de Galvoie," and Guiromelant) are descended from the three antagonists of Cuchulainn in Fand's faery isle (Eochaid Iuil, Senach Siabortha, and Eogan Inbir), though also inheriting certain characteristics from a closer ancestor, the Welsh Arawn.

Liban surely, Modron possibly, contributed to the making of Orguelleuse. In the following chapter it will appear probable that still another Celtic fay bequeathed a small detail to her story. No wonder Orguelleuse seems erratic! Though she offers the defense that she has been driven mad by the murder of her first lover,[16] the reader will, I hope, find a more adequate excuse in her mingled and mythological ancestry.

Chapter LXXVIII

GAUVAIN AT THE CASTLE OF LADIES

VERSES 7224–8371

Riding silently with Orguelleuse, Gauvain came to a deep and broad river, beyond which stood a magnificent castle. Five hundred richly gowned dames and damsels gazed down from the windows. The mocking damsel entered a boat, and when Gauvain after his fight with Greoreas' nephew looked around, she had disappeared; "he knew not what had become of her." A boatman came across the water, bringing greetings from the ladies. He ferried Gauvain over the river and entertained him lavishly at his house. The next morning Gauvain learned that the Castle of Ladies contained a perilous hall where no coward or perjurer could tarry for an hour. The boatman conducted his guest to the castle, and at the entrance there was sitting a man with a silver leg banded with gold and jewels, who was carving with a knife a stick of ashwood. Gauvain learned that this mysterious personage was very rich. He entered the splendid palace. In the midst of the floor was a bed of gold, mounted on wheels, with bells suspended below. Above the bed, around the hall were glass panes through which all those who entered the hall could be observed, and there were five hundred windows. Failing to dissuade Gauvain from attempting the adventure, the ferryman left. The knight sat on the Perilous Bed, all armed. At once the bed cords cried out, the bells rang, the windows flew open, and with a crashing sound arrows and bolts shot in at Gauvain, from whom or what

[16] Conte del Graal, ed. Hilka, vss. 8927–59.

he could not perceive. Presently the windows closed, and he drew out the missiles from his shield and flesh. Then a churl in a hide opened a door, and a lion sprang out and brought the hero to his knees; but he recovered and sliced off the lion's paws and head. Then the ferryman returned with glad countenance, proclaiming the end of the enchantments, and youths knelt to Gauvain as their awaited deliverer. Lovely maidens greeted him as their lord and proclaimed him "the best of all valiant men." Together with the ferryman he ascended a tower to survey the landscape round, and was displeased to learn that as lord of the castle he could not leave. He conversed with the queen, and was served at a banquet with "whatsoever he desired." The next day when he asked leave of the queen to depart, she forbade it. But at last she consented on condition that he would return, and he left the castle in a boat.

O NE ELEMENT in this narrative is easily recognizable as the adventure of the Perilous Bed, already treated in our study of *Le Chevalier de la Charrette*.[1] The origin of the formula was discovered in the Irish saga of *Bricriu's Feast*,[2] where Cuchulainn is described as sitting alone in the seat of watch in Curoi's revolving fortress, enduring a shower of missile weapons, being attacked by a churl (*bachlach*) and monsters, and finally, after his victory, being acclaimed as the nonpareil of Ulster's warriors. We saw that Chrétien in narrating Lancelot's adventure in the Perilous Bed had retained three Irish features: there is a hospitable hostess; there are three beds, suggesting that originally there had been three knights to occupy them; the testing takes place by night. We saw also that a far more elaborate version of the Perilous Bed theme in *Artus de la Petite Bretagne* retained twelve features of the Irish story, removing all doubt as to the derivation of this recurring pattern in the *Matière de Bretagne*.

A comparison of the Irish saga with Gauvain's adventure of the Perilous Bed reveals six fairly obvious parallels: (1) Gauvain was left alone in the castle hall by his host; likewise, Cuchulainn's host, Curoi, had departed before Cuchulainn arrived at his fortress. (2) Gauvain took his seat alone on the Perilous Bed; likewise, Cuchulainn took his seat alone. (3) Gauvain was assailed by a shower of missiles; likewise, Cuchulainn was assailed by a shower of stakes. (4) A churl loosed a lion at Gauvain; Cuchulainn was attacked successively by a huge monster and by a giant whom he addressed as a churl (*bachlach*). (5) Gauvain's host returned; Cuchulainn's host returned. (6) Gauvain was acclaimed as "the best of all valiant men"; Cuchulainn was awarded "the sovranty of valor over all the Gael." There are in Chrétien's narrative two other reflections of this same Irish tradition. (1) The churl who loosed the lion at Gauvain as he sat on the Perilous Bed

---

[1] Cf. Chap. XXX.
[2] T. P. Cross and C. N. Slover, *Ancient Irish Tales*, pp. 272–76. *Feast of Bricriu*, ed. G. Henderson, pp. 101–15.

was wearing a hide; scholars have recognized [3] that the gigantic churl who attacked Cuchulainn as he sat on the seat of watch was Curoi; and Curoi, we know, appeared on another occasion in the guise of a churl clad in a hide.[4] (2) The Perilous Bed was, for no expressed reason, equipped with wheels; in Wolfram's parallel account it rolled around; [5] in *Artus de la Petite Bretagne* the enchanted castle itself revolved, carrying the bed round with it; the Irish saga tells us that Curoi's fortress revolved by night during its master's absence on an eastern journey.[6] The wheels on the Perilous Bed, therefore, are the fossilized remains of the old mythological conception of the sky as a dome which could be seen to revolve by night during the absence of the sun on its journey to the east, just as we perceived that the flaming lance which descended on Lancelot as he lay on the Perilous Bed is a prosaic survival of the fiery levin. Few things in the study of Arthurian romance are more astonishing than the way in which the various versions of the Perilous Bed adventure supplement each other to prove their common derivation from the testing of Cuchulainn in Curoi's fortress, and to corroborate their origin in myth.

A second Irish pattern was detected long since by Jessie Weston.[7] It occurs in *The Voyage of Bran,* usually assigned, like *Bricriu's Feast,* to the eighth century, and recognized universally as a potent influence on the medieval literature of the marvelous voyage. Let me summarize the significant portions.[8]

A faery woman appeared in Bran's fortress and summoned him in a song to the Land of Women. Then suddenly she departed "while they knew not whither she went." Bran thereupon set out across the sea and met Manannan, the sea-god, coming over the waters, who announced that it was not far to the Land of Women. As Bran and his men drew near to this land, they saw the queen of the women. She brought Bran to her large house with many beds, and there he was feasted. "No savor was wanting to them." After many years Bran sought to leave, and the queen told him he would rue it. Nevertheless he departed, with the warning that he should not set foot on shore, and rowed away in his boat over the sea.

Although, in the process of amalgamation with the visit to Curoi's fortress, this tale of the sojourn in the Land of Women has undergone some modifications, it still shows a marked correspondence to Gauvain's experiences at the Castle of Ladies. Here is the maiden messenger who, like Orguelleuse, suddenly disappeared so that Bran knew not whither she went. Here is the noble figure who came across the water and announced

---

[3] Cf. *supra,* p. 207, n. 8.   [4] *Feast of Bricriu,* pp. 117, 129.
[5] There is a remarkable parallel in modern Irish folklore—a revolving couch on wheels in an Otherworld palace. J. Curtin, *Myths and Folklore of Ireland* (Boston, 1890), p. 106. I suspect here the influence of Arthurian romance. For proof of such influence on Irish folktales cf. *Mod. Phil.,* XLII (1945), 197–211.
[6] *Feast of Bricriu,* pp. 101, 103.   [7] J. L. Weston, *Legend of Gawain,* pp. 36–38.
[8] Cross and Slover, *op. cit.,* pp. 588–95. A. Nutt and K. Meyer, *Voyage of Bran* (London, 1895), I, 4–32.

that the Land of Women was near. Here is the queen who entertained the hero. Here is the feast which provided all that one desired. Here is the motif of the hero's desire to leave and the queen's reluctance to let him go. Here is the hero's departure across the waters in a boat. There could be no neater illustration of Philipot's acute remarks of fifty years ago:

"Les romans de la Table Ronde nous offrent à chaque pas de ces châteaux mystérieux, protégés par de hautes murailles, entourés par une eau profonde, abritant des coutumes étranges. C'étaient primitivement des îles lointaines, accessibles aux seuls navigateurs. . . . Les voyages des héros de romans dans les pays féeriques nous apparaissent comme des odyssées ou des *imrama*, qui se seraient adaptés aux necessités de la chevalerie errante et où l'élément maritime serait réduit à son minimum." [9]

And by the same process, the ancient sea-god Manannan, whom Bishop Cormac called a *navigator* and who possessed a magic coracle, the Wave-Sweeper,[10] has become a river boatman. He has also merged his personality and his role with those of Curoi, and thus the mystery of the ferryman's wealth and of the strange freedom with which he comes and goes in the castle of royal and noble ladies is solved. As Manannan he is a rich and lavish host;[11] as Curoi he naturally comes and goes in his own fortress.

Another mysterious figure is the strangely uncommunicative man whom Gauvain and the ferryman encountered at the entrance to the palace.

"They proceed until at the foot of the steps which were before the palace they find, sitting alone on a bundle of rushes (*de gles*), a man with a silver leg (*un eschacier . . . qui avoit eschace d'arjant*); the leg was well inlaid with gold, and was banded here and there with gold and precious stones. The man with the artificial leg (*eschaciers*) did not have idle hands, for he held a little knife and was busy carving a rod of ashwood." [12]

Though we learn that this *eschacier* was silent as Gauvain passed him and was rich with great revenues, we never learn why he was sitting there, and he plays no part in the action. He certainly needs explaining.

A somewhat similar personage, similarly occupied, appears in the Welsh tale *The Dream of Maxen*,[13] which Loth assigned to the second half of the twelfth century.[14] The emperor of Rome, Maxen, dreamed that he entered a magnificent castle, the fairest ever seen, at the mouth of a river, and found himself in a hall decked with precious jewels. Two youths were playing chess; their chessboard was of silver. "At the foot of one of the pillars a man with white hair was seated on an ivory throne with the

[9] *Romania*, XXV (1896), 267. Cf. Nutt, *Studies on the Legend of the Holy Grail*, pp. 190 f. For other illustrations of the Irish *imrama* in the *Conte del Graal* cf. *Romania*, LIX (1933), 557–62.

[10] *Cormac's Glossary*, ed. W. Stokes (Calcutta, 1868), p. 114. P. W. Joyce, *Old Celtic Romances* (Dublin, London, 1920), p. 61.   [11] Cross and Slover, *op. cit.*, pp. 504–7.

[12] Vss. 7648–59.   [13] Loth, *Mabinogion*, 2d ed., I, 215–22.

[14] *Ibid.*, I, 30. On the history of the *Dream* cf. *Speculum*, XXII (1947), 523–26.

image of two eagles of red gold on it. . . . He had in front of him a golden chessboard with its chessmen." He was holding a rod of gold and steel files or saws, and was carving chessmen out of the rod. Inspired by this dream, Maxen sent messengers, and they discovered at last the castle at the mouth of the River Seint, near the present site of Carnarvon. The venerable lord of the castle, Eudav, was carving chessmen as in the dream. Maxen himself went, arrived at the castle, and saw the same lord sitting in the hall, still carving chessmen.

This situation presents a tantalizing resemblance to that described by Chrétien: the river and the castle beside it, so rich that never had eyes of living man seen its equal; the man of great wealth, seated before or within the hall; his carving a rod with a steel instrument. And everything begins to clear up if one realizes that Chrétien or his source has mistaken the words *eschaquier* and *eschac,* meaning chessboard and chessman, for *eschacier* and *eschace,* meaning respectively a man with an artificial leg and the leg itself. How easily the error might occur is shown by the fact that three manuscripts of the poem actually give, instead of *eschacier,* forms (*eschaquier, eskiekier, eschequier*) which mean chessboard, and one manuscript gives, instead of *eschace, eskies,* that is, chessmen.[15] It was surely not the rich man's leg, but a chessboard which was of silver, like that on which the youths were playing in the Welsh story. Further corroboration is found in the *Didot Perceval* (Modena ms) and in *Perlesvaus.* According to the former text, Perceval entered an empty palace (though later, as in Chrétien's Castle of Ladies, maidens and youths appear) and spied in the hall "a chessboard (*eskekier*) of fine silver." [16] According to the corresponding portion of *Perlesvaus,* Gauvain entered a very fair, rich hall, "and found in the midst a very rich and high couch, and at the foot of this couch there was a chessboard (*eschequier*), very fair and rich, with a golden margin, full of precious stones." [17] Nothing could be much plainer than that the wealthy man's silver leg, banded with gold and encrusted with jewels, is a blundering substitution for a silver chessboard, with a border of gold, set with precious stones; and that the man himself, instead of idly whittling at a wooden rod, was engaged in carving chessmen from a rod of gold. Even the puzzling bundle of rushes (*trossel de gles*) on which he sat is palpably a substitution for a *trosne aornee d'egles,* such as that which Eudav occupied.

Strong support for this conclusion will be presented in the next chapter, where it will be seen that Maxen's wooing of Eudav's daughter, the princess Elen, parallels in striking ways Guiromelant's wooing of the princess Clarianz of the Castle of Ladies. Thus two of the most curious and unusual

---

[15] Variant readings of vss. 7651 f.

[16] *Didot-Perceval,* ed. W. Roach, p. 167. *PMLA,* L (1935), 30.

[17] *Perlesvaus,* ed. W. A. Nitze, I, 115. *PMLA,* L, 30. On magic chessboard in Arthurian and Welsh literature cf. *PMLA,* L, 27, n. 11; *Romanische Forschungen,* XLV (1931), 69, n. 2.

elements in the story which Chrétien tells of Gauvain's experiences at or near this castle are best understood as borrowings from some form of *The Dream of Maxen*. Now I have shown elsewhere [18] that the *Dream,* as it stands in the manuscripts, has certainly been influenced by the *Dingestow Brut,* itself a redaction of Geoffrey of Monmouth's *Historia,* and therefore must have been composed about 1150 or even later. If, as is possible, it was *The Dream of Maxen* which came to the knowledge of some *conteur* sojourning in Wales and furnished him with the narrative elements which found their way into Count Philippe's book and so into *Le Conte del Graal,* then we would have an extraordinary example of the influence of a comparatively late literary composition in Welsh upon French romance, as distinct from the influence of early Welsh oral tradition. But it is also possible, and much more probable, that the author of the *Dream* was simply adapting to the historical framework supplied by the *Brut* an earlier oral tradition of a dream princess Elen, discovered by her royal lover in a splendid Otherworld palace, together with her venerable father, who was occupied in carving chessmen. This hypothesis is favored by the fact that there is no trace in Chrétien's poem of the historical framework which the author of the *Dream* took over from the *Brut*.[19]

In any case we have been able to discern thus far in our examination of Gauvain's adventures at the Castle of Ladies the blurred outlines of three Celtic patterns: (1) the nocturnal testing of Cuchulainn in Curoi's fortress; (2) the voyage of Bran son of Febal to the Land of Women; (3) the figure of Eudav carving chessmen in the hall of a splendid palace.

Chapter LXXIX

THE FORD PERILOUS AND GUIROMELANT

VERSES 8286–9234

Looking out from a window of the Castle of Ladies, Gauvain spied the scornful damsel who had led him thither, riding in a meadow beyond the river, accompanied by a knight who guarded the water crossing of Galloway (les porz de Galvoie). *Issuing from the castle, Gauvain was ferried over the river and with no great difficulty defeated the damsel's knight and delivered him over to the ferryman. The damsel, still contemptu-*

---

[18] Cf. *supra,* n. 14.

[19] Though in the next chapter I show that the name Clarianz is due to scribal corruption of Elaine, and ultimately goes back to Welsh Elen, yet it does not necessarily follow that it is therefore derived from the *Dream of Maxen*. It is quite possible that Elen was the name of the dream-maiden in an earlier version of the story, and if so, this fact would account for her identification with Elen, daughter of Eudav, of the *Dingestow Brut*.

*ous of Gauvain's prowess, dared him to go to a certain tree, there to cross
a deep river, and pluck flowers for her on the other side. He who could
pass the Ford Perilous would win all the glory of the world. Gauvain
leaped his horse into the middle of the current and reached the farther
bank. There he met a knight out hawking with a sparrow hawk and bird
hounds. The falconer-knight complimented Gauvain on being the first
to cross the Ford Perilous, and the two pledged faith to tell each other the
truth. Gauvain learned that the falconer was named Guiromelant, the
scornful damsel was called Orguelleuse de Logres, the Castle of Ladies was
La Roche de Sanguin, so styled because cloth of sanguine color was dyed
there! The ladies of the castle included Gauvain's grandmother Yguerne,
his mother (called Morcades by Pseudo-Wauchier[1]), and his supremely
beautiful sister, Clarianz. Guiromelant avowed his love for Clarianz and
begged Gauvain to convey a ring and a message to her. Strange to say,
however, he nursed a mortal hatred against Gauvain, and when the latter
revealed his identity, a duel was arranged for a week later at that very
place. To it the two foes were to bring as spectators the lords and ladies
of their respective lands. Gauvain parted amicably from the falconer
and leaped his horse back successfully over the ford. The scornful Orguelleuse then approached him, and since she begged forgiveness for her
behavior, the two were reconciled and were ferried back to the Roche de
Sanguin. No more is said of Orguelleuse. Gauvain, still incognito, was
welcomed by the maidens of the castle, dancing hand in hand, and by the
two queens. He gave Guiromelant's ring and message to Clarianz, and
received the odd information that she had never seen her lover, nor he
her. Secretly Gauvain dispatched a messenger to King Arthur, who was
holding court at Orcanie, to announce the coming duel and request his
attendance.*

HERE Chrétien's remarkable narrative stops. The continuation tells
of the joy of Arthur on learning that his nephew was alive, of
Clarianz' grief when she discovered that it was her brother who
was engaged to battle with her suitor Guiromelant, of the arrival of the
trains of Arthur and Guiromelant at the tree near the Ford Perilous, of
the long combat between Gauvain and Guiromelant, of its termination
through the efforts of Clarianz, and of her marriage to her lover.[2]

Hilka was provoked, particularly by the affair of Guiromelant with
Gauvain's sister, to some vigorous language on the artistry of *Le Conte
del Graal*. "Unerklärt bleiben die merkwürdigen Rollen der Mutter Artus'
und jener Gauvains im märchenhaften Schloss, auch der Schwester Gauvains Clarissant, von der er sonst ebensowenig, wie von den beiden Damen

---

[1] J. L. Weston, *Legend of Perceval*, I, 193.
[2] *Ibid.*, I, 12. On variations of mss. for this continuation cf. *ibid.*, 192–210.

ehrwürdigen Alters vernommen hat." [3] Hilka also remarked on the "phantastischen Märchenstil" which represents "Guiromelant gleichzeitig als Gauvains Todfeind und Clarissants Liebhaber, der er auch nach erfolgter Erkennung seinen Ring zusendet," and which represents Guiromelant and Clarissant as lovers "ohne je einander gesehen zu haben." This "Märchenstil," this unbridled fantasy, Hilka attributed to the fact that *Le Conte del Graal* was "ein unfertiges Werk," thereby implying that Chrétien's first inspirations, the unstudied products of his imagination, took the form of wildly improbable and incoherent narratives, into which he painstakingly introduced reason and order. Such an unreasonable explanation of the "phantastischen Märchenstil" as originating in Chrétien's own mind need not be taken seriously, and we may pass directly to the analysis of the traditional matter which Chrétien found so crudely blended in Count Philippe's book.

As we might suspect from the emphasis on the Ford Perilous and the tree beside it, both in Chrétien's work and in the continuation, one of the patterns which went into this composite narrative was that of the combat at the Ford of the Thorn, of which we had a blurred version in *Erec* and of which there are nine other examples in the Arthurian cycle and two in kindred romances.[4] Our study revealed ample evidence that the Ford Perilous adventure was based on the Welsh tradition of the annual combat at a ford, represented in the first episode in *Pwyll*. Let us recall the story.[5]

Pwyll, Prince of Dyved (southwestern Wales), met Arawn, king of Annwn, as a solitary huntsman accompanied by his hounds. Arawn had a grievance against Pwyll for driving the hounds off the quarry, but nevertheless the two exchanged pledges of friendship. It develops that Arawn had fought unsuccessfully against his enemy Havgan, and Pwyll, from motives of friendship, agreed to fight Havgan a year later at a ford in Arawn's stead. Then Arawn sent Pwyll to his splendid palace near by, and Pwyll, whose identity was unknown, was welcomed by Arawn's beautiful wife. At the time determined he went attended by all his court to the ford, met Havgan, also attended by his nobles, and vanquished him.

It is astonishing to realize how, despite Chrétien's reducing the number of principal male actors in this affair from three to two, the outlines of the Welsh story are discernible in the meeting of Gauvain with Guiromelant and the subsequent events. Like Arawn, Guiromelant is met in the guise of a solitary sportsman with hounds; like Arawn, though he has a grievance against the hero, he pledges his faith to him and is most courteous; like Arawn, he is attached by ties of love or marriage to a beautiful lady in a palace near by and sends the hero to her; like Arawn, he arranges

[3] *Conte del Graal*, ed. A. Hilka, p. xxxvii. [4] Cf. Chap. XVIII.
[5] Loth, *Mabinogion*, 2d ed., I, 84–89.

for a combat after a stated interval near a ford. Like Pwyll and Havgan, Gauvain and Guiromelant come to the combat attended by all the nobles of their lands. Be it noted that whereas Guiromelant for the most part plays the role of Arawn, he takes that of Arawn's mortal foe Havgan as the hero's opponent at the ford. It is this assignment to Guiromelant of two such incompatible roles which is responsible for the strange mingling of friendliness and enmity toward Gauvain, which provoked the scorn of Hilka.

Some significance should be attached to the fact that the combat at the ford both in the mabinogi and in *Le Conte del Graal* seems to have taken place at or near a border stream. It was at Glyn Cuch that Pwyll met Arawn, and probably at a ford of the River Cuch that Pwyll fought Havgan. Now the Cuch formed the boundary between Pembrokeshire and Carmarthenshire. Gauvain had just met and overcome the guardian of the water crossing of Galloway when he met Guiromelant, and certain manuscripts of the continuation imply that the Ford Perilous was itself the passage.[6] Both the Welsh and the French texts, then, suggest that the ford was a border barrier, and for this view we shall presently find strong corroboration.

It is in Wolfram's *Parzival* that we discover corroboration both for the Welsh origin of the Combat at the Ford and for the supposition that it was localized at a river boundary. It has not escaped the attentive reader's notice that the emphasis placed by the mabinogi on the fact that Pwyll undertook to substitute for Arawn in the ford combat out of motives of friendship has no counterpart in *Le Conte del Graal*. But Wolfram introduces precisely this missing element.[7]

Gawan, rising early to freshen himself for the fight with Gramoflanz (Guiromelant), sallied forth to the bank of the River Sabins, where lay the Ford Perilous, and spied a knight all in red. Each mistook the other for Gramoflanz, and engaged in combat. Only when some squires came on the scene did the Red Knight learn that his antagonist was his friend Gawan, and fling away his sword. The stranger was Parzival. When Gramoflanz arrived for the prearranged duel with Gawan, he found his enemy already too exhausted to fight, and postponed the encounter. Parzival repeatedly sought to take Gawan's place in the duel, and in spite of Gawan's refusal, went out at dawn next day and fought Gramoflanz in his friend's stead. When the combat was interrupted by the coming of Gawan, it

---

[6] Weston, *op. cit.*, I, 188. Compare the verses, "Passez a les porz de Gauvoie que nus fors il sol ne passast que son cors destruit ne lassast," with vss. 8508–10 of the *Conte del Graal:* "cil qui del Gué Perilleus porroit passer l'eve parfonde qu'il avroit tot le pris del monde." Note also the evidence that Guiromelant was a doublet of the guardian of the *porz;* at any rate, in Renaut de Beaujeu's *Bel Inconnu* we find a character who combines features of both: like the guardian of the *porz* he is called "l'Orguillous" (vs. 1486), and is vanquished by the hero in the presence of a scornful damsel; like Guiromelant, he is a sportsman, accompanied by hounds, returns to his castle, arms himself, and fights with the hero. A close scrutiny of Renaut's poem, vss. 321–485, 1276–1492, reveals dependence on the first episode in *Pwyll*.   [7] *Parzival*, 678, 15–729, 25.

was Gramoflanz' turn to fail his pledge as a result of the wounds inflicted by Parzival. The much-arranged combat was again put off and finally abandoned through the intervention of Arthur.

Is it conceivable that Wolfram, by sheer chance, should have created a situation corresponding to that in the mabinogi: the defeat of a knight and his replacement by his friend in a prearranged combat beside a ford? The German poet must have found somewhere this feature of the old Welsh plot—a feature which is even more clearly preserved in the romance of *Eger and Grime* [8]—and used it skillfully as a means of reintroducing Parzival into his story. Or perhaps it was the enigmatic Kyot who had the requisite skill. At any rate, here is another confirmation of the Welsh Ford Combat formula as the basis of the adventures of Gauvain and Guiromelant.

Wolfram must have good authority also for the name which he gives to the river of the Ford Perilous, since it harmonizes with much other evidence and provides a clue to many still puzzling features of the whole complex of events clustered about the Castle of Ladies. He tells us: "The water was called Sabins." [9] Martin and Miss Richey have suggested that this river was the Severn,[10] though without adducing proof. We have already noted some signs that the river at which the combat took place was a border barrier, and if we turn to the *Descriptio Cambriae* of Giraldus Cambrensis we read of the noble river of Sabrina: "This water, very long ago, formed the march between Cambria and Loegria, that is, between Wales and England." [11] This tradition was known also to Geoffrey of Monmouth and Froissart.[12] Is it possible that Wolfram got the name Sabins from some lost source preserving the old tradition? Is it possible that Chrétien, who called the Castle of Ladies "la Roche de Sanguin" and gave the preposterous explanation that the name was due to the many cloths, dyed blood-red and green, which were bought and sold there, was

---

[8] French and Hale, *Middle English Metrical Romances*, pp. 672–706. Miss Mabel Van Duzee is engaged on a doctoral dissertation dealing with this romance.

[9] *Parzival*, 604, 1. It is noteworthy that Wolfram gives the name Rosche Sabbins, not (as one would expect from Chrétien's Roche de Sanguin) to the Castle of Ladies, but to Gramoflanz' own castle (*Parzival*, 610, 26; 677, 3; 693, 13); and he represents Gramoflanz as inviting Gawan to cross the Sabins by way of his own castle because there was no other bridge. This may well preserve the original Welsh tradition that Arawn, after arranging the combat at the ford, sent Pwyll to his own palace. It is curious to note that, though Arawn did not send Pwyll with a ring to his wife, yet in a story which Prof. Gruffydd proved to have had a considerable influence on this episode (*Transactions Hon. Soc. Cymmrodorion*, 1912–13, pp. 72–80) Manannan sent King Fiachna with a ring to his wife. K. Meyer and A. Nutt, *Voyage of Bran*, I, 72. It is possible that in Guiromelant's sending Gauvain with a ring to his lady-love there is a survival of this Irish motif.

[10] Wolfram, *Parzival und Titurel*, ed. E. Martin (Halle, 1903), II, 429. M. F. Richey, *Story of Parzival and the Graal*, p. 158.

[11] Giraldus Cambrensis, *Opera*, VI, ed. J. F. Dimock, Rolls Ser., p. 171.

[12] Geoffrey of Monmouth, *Historia*, ed. A. Griscom, pp. 253, 324. Froissart, *Oeuvres*, ed. Kervyn de Lettenhove, XVI (Brussels, 1872), p. 19.

dependent on a corrupt form of the same tradition? Is it possible that Chrétien's implication that the river-crossing below the Castle of Ladies constituted "les porz de Galvoie" was simply another instance of the Scotticizing influence on the topography of *Le Conte del Graal* which we had occasion to note in the case of Cotoatre? Should the river form the boundary, not of Galvoie (which was not bounded by a river), but of Gales, which was known to have as its ancient frontier the Severn? In short, does Chrétien's story of the Roche de Sanguin, a Castle of Ladies, situated on a river which formed the boundary of Galvoie, distortedly reflect the old tradition of the Severn as the boundary of Gales?

To these venturesome queries the answer is furnished by a number of tales which demonstrate the existence of a strong Arthurian tradition that there was a Castle of Ladies on the Severn, and that the Severn was a boundary which no knight could pass save at his peril. Before turning to these tales, let me recall some important details regarding Gauvain's journey to the Castle of Ladies.[13] Greoreas warned Gauvain that he must go no further, for he had reached "the bourn of Galloway. No knight can ever pass there who càn return. . . . Therefore I counsel you rather to depart than to descend this hill." Gauvain answered: "To turn back thus would be base. I did not come in order to turn back." Though Gauvain has some strange experiences after this and undergoes some severe trials of his mettle, none of them seem to have any connection with the boundary of Galloway until, 1,800 lines later, Greoreas' direful prognostic is fulfilled by Gauvain's encounter with the guardian of "les porz de Galvoie."[14] It seems clear that Greoreas' warning against descending the hill and passing the bourn of Galloway should lead directly on to the combat with the guardian of the river passage below the Castle of Ladies. At any rate, this connection of the descent of the hill, the warning, and the Castle of Ladies beside a river is what we find in the well-known adventure of Galaad in *La Queste del Saint Graal*.[15]

Galaad, looking down from a mountain, saw in the valley below a castle and a rapid water which was called Saverne. As he approached the castle, an aged man informed him that it was the Castle of Maidens, and advised him to turn back lest he come to shame. Galaad refused: "It would be much against my will to return." He then met seven maidens, richly mounted, who warned: "Sir knight, you have passed the boundaries!" Proceeding, however he was attacked by seven knights and at midday put them all to flight. A white-haired priest then brought Galaad the keys of the castle; he entered and was welcomed by many maidens with great joy. The vassals were summoned by the blast of a horn, and they treated him as their lord.

Clearly this adventure parallels in certain points those of Gauvain en route to and at the Castle of Ladies: the descent of the hill; the warning about

---

13 *Conte del Graal*, ed. Hilka, vss. 6602–17.   14 *Ibid.*, vs. 8385.
15 *Queste del Saint Graal*, ed. A. Pauphilet, pp. 46–51. Sommer, *Vulgate Version*, VI, 34–37.

passing the borders; the hero's insistence on proceeding; the river with a castle of maidens beside it; the joyous reception by the maidens. And presumably it is the ancient tradition of the Severn as a border stream which is here recognized, even though not a word is said of Galaad's crossing it.

This point comes out far more strongly in the *Vulgate Lancelot*. Here one learns that Logres was separated from the land of Sorelois by a river which (according to Sommer's transcript from ms B.M. Add. 10293) is first called Assurne but in later passages "the water of Sauverne." [16] It could be crossed only by two narrow bridges, each defended by a knight and ten yeomen, who served for a year. [17]

Gauvain came to the hermit who dwelt on the Round Mountain and was informed by him of "the evil passage of the road which crosses over the water of Sauverne." He reached the river at the Pont Norgalois, at the far end of which was a castle. He vanquished the guardian knight and the yeomen, and one of the latter presented him with the keys of the castle. His name was inscribed on a stone table, together with the names of others who had succeeded in passing the river. The next day when he assumed the defense of the bridge, he was challenged by his good friend Hector, and they fought without recognizing each other till noon. When they paused to rest, recognition followed.

Here, as in the Galaad adventure, we have the hill, the descent to the Severn, the guarded passage, and the delivery of the keys of the castle. The Castle of Maidens has disappeared, and its place has been taken by the motif of the two passages to the land of Goirre, which we have studied elsewhere. [18] It is significant that the Severn is represented as the boundary between Logres and Sorelois, whereas Giraldus stated that it was the ancient boundary between Loegria and Kambria. Since the French author was correct as to Logres, was he wholly wrong as to Sorelois? Though he wrote that Sorelois lay between Gales and "les estranges illes," [19] and therefore differentiated it from Wales, his following statement that it was enclosed by the Severn on the side of Logres and on all other sides by the sea would apply (though not exactly) to South Wales. South Wales was called Sugales by the French, [20] and this was corrupted, under the influence of Norgales (North Wales), into Sorgales. [21] Sorgales, in turn, may have become in the hands of a French scribe Sorelois. In fact, the defender of the passage over the Severn whom Gauvain defeated was named Belinans, and

[16] Sommer, *op. cit.*, III, 269, ll. 29, 32; p. 308, l. 7; p. 361, n. 1; p. 395, l. 23.
[17] *Ibid.*, III, 395–97.
[18] See Chaps. XXXIII, XXXIV.
[19] Sommer, *op. cit.*, III, 269. For speculations on Sorelois cf. F. Lot, *Etude sur le Lancelot en Prose*, p. 145, n. 3.
[20] Sommer, IV, 39, l. 35. Marie de France uses Suhtwales (*Lais*, ed. Warnke, 1925, pp. 153, 181). Cf. *Romania*, XXV (1896), 32n.
[21] For Sorgales and confusion with Norgales cf. Sommer, *Vulgate Version, Index of Names and Places*, p. 77, n. 3.

LE CONTE DEL GRAAL

elsewhere Belinans is styled King of Sorgales.[22] There is a fair presumption, then, that underneath the confused concept of the Severn and its passages in the *Vulgate Lancelot* there lay a correct conception of it as the old border between Logres and Sugales.[23]

The *Huth Merlin* provides still another version of the same basic tradition, though the Severn is not named.[24]

Balaain (whose name represents a corruption of some early form of Gauvain, such as Galaain)[25] approached a beautiful castle, girdled partly by the sea and partly by "a water . . . strong and swift." A grizzled vavasor met him and said: "Sir knight, you have passed the boundaries; there is no more chance of returning." Balaain replied: "Yet will I go forward." He heard the loud blast of a horn, and then more than a hundred damsels issued forth from the castle, dancing, singing, and making the greatest joy. He was then told that he must joust with the knight of an isle near by. After changing his shield for a newer one, he entered a boat and was rowed across by mariners to the island. Unrecognized because of his shield, he fought with his brother Balaan till both were fatally wounded. Only then did they discover their relationship. The lady of the tower on the island dwelt there with seven knights. Balaan had vanquished the previous defender of the island, and had been obliged to assume his office and his lady. Merlin appeared on the scene after the death of the brothers and inscribed their names on a slab of stone. He also established a narrow bridge across the river where knights could prove their hardihood.

It is easy to see that though this author did not know, or did not choose to name, the river, he was acquainted with traditions almost identical with those which Wolfram attached to the Sabins, and the authors of the *Lancelot* and the *Queste* to the Severn. With Wolfram he has in common the castle of ladies beyond a river, the joyous reception of the hero by the ladies, the ferrying of the hero over a river from the castle of ladies to fight with the keeper of a passage. With the *Lancelot* the *Huth Merlin* has in common the defense of a passage, where the victor must assume the duty of his predecessor; the incognito combat; the names inscribed on the stone; and the narrow bridge. With the *Queste* the *Merlin* has in common the castle of ladies beside "a swift water," the warning against passing the boundaries, the hero's reply, the blast of the horn, the seven knights, and the combat. Needless to say, then, there was a complex of traditions centering round a Castle of Ladies on the Severn, and it supplied many of the significant features of Chrétien's narrative from the point where Gau-

22 Sommer, *op. cit.*, III, 397; II, 171.

23 The Leyden and Harlech mss. of Geoffrey's *Historia* state that Gloucester, standing on the Severn, was on the border between Loegria (England) and Demetia (Dyved, here used in broader meaning of South Wales). E. Faral, *Légende arthurienne*, III, 140 (variant for Kambriae). Geoffrey, *Historia*, ed. Griscom, p. 324.

24 *Huth Merlin*, ed. Paris and Ulrich (S.A.T.F.), II, 44–59.

25 Cf. *supra*, pp. 134 f. and R. S. Loomis, *Celtic Myth*, 250–52. On substitution of B for G cf. *PMLA*, LIV (1939), 659.

vain was warned by Greoreas against passing the bourn of Galloway to the point where he returned with Orguelleuse de Logres to the Roche de Sanguin, and was greeted by the dancing and singing maidens. Our earlier guess that Galvoie was a mistake for Gales or perhaps a deliberate effort to Scotticize the topography, and that Sanguin was deformation of Sabin or Sabrin, seems to have been a good one.

What inspired this tradition of a Castle of Ladies on the Severn? Turn to Geoffrey of Monmouth's *Historia*,[26] and read how the emperor Claudius caused to be built a city, Kerglou, "that is Gloucestria"; "to the present day it is situated on the confines of Kambria [27] and Loegria on the banks of the Sabrina." Geoffrey offered two etymologies for Kaerglou, one representing an old Welsh tradition since it occurs in Nennius.[28] This text asserted that one Glovus "built on the bank of the River Sabrina a great city, which is called in the British language Cair Glovi, but in Saxon Gloecester." Since it is well known that the real derivation of Gloucester is from the Roman Glevum, the eponymous Glovus is, of course, a mere figment of the Celtic fancy. What is significant is that from an early time Gloucester was called Kaer Gloyw, which by regular laws of lenation became Kaer Loyw. Thus in *Kulhwch* (*ca.* 1100), Kaer Loyw, the prison of Mabon son of Modron, lies on a salmon river, doubtless the Severn.[29] It is even more significant that *gloyw* is an adjective meaning "shining, transparent," and this too would be lenated into *loyw* after the feminine noun *kaer*.[30] Thus Kaer Loyw could be interpreted as the Shining or Transparent Fortress.

Here we have the key to the mystery of the Castle of Maidens on the Severn. In the earliest Arthurian poem in the Welsh language, which may go back as far as the year 900,[31] Arthur and his warriors are described as attacking Kaer Wydyr, "the Fortress of Glass." [32] There dwelt nine maidens, who tended a caldron of prophetic inspiration.[33] In *Peredur* we read of the nine sorceresses of Kaer Loyw, the chief of whom possessed the gift of prophecy.[34] They play strangely diverse roles, on the one hand being warlike Amazons, whom Peredur finally slew, and on the other bringing the youth to their palace, teaching him chivalry and the use of weapons, and giving him on his departure a choice of horse and arms. Ulrich's *Lanzelet* [35] tells us how the young hero was brought up in a shining castle of ever-joyful maidens, on a mountain of crystal. There he was taught courtesy and the use of arms, and on his departure he was given

[26] Ed. A. Griscom, p. 324.

[27] The Harlech and Leyden mss. substitute *Demetie*. Cf. *supra*, n. 23.

[28] The first etymology Geoffrey took from William of Malmesbury's *Gesta Pontificum* (Faral, *op. cit.*, II, 160). The second is found in Nennius (*ibid.*, III, 35 f. *Antiquity*, XII, 1938, p. 52).   [29] Loth, *op. cit.*, I, 326–28. Cf. *supra*, p. 89, n. 21; p. 177.

[30] J. Strachan, *Introduction to Early Welsh* (Manchester, 1909), p. 11.

[31] *PMLA*, LVI (1941), 887.   [32] *Ibid.*, p. 891.   [33] *Ibid.*, pp. 890, 907.

[34] Loth, *op. cit.*, II, 75 f.   [35] L. A. Paton, *Sir Lancelot of the Lake*, pp. 7 f.

a horse, armor, and weapons. All the maidens were in love with him, and the mistress of the land sought to keep him with her. The *Vulgate Lancelot* [36] represents the hero as held captive by the Dame de Malehot in a prison so transparent that he could see all those without and they could see him. The Dame fell in love with him and sought to keep him with her, but when he departed, she provided him with an excellent horse and a red shield. When he emerged from the town, he came to a ford beside which Arthur and the ladies of his court were gathered to witness a battle. The knight with the red shield so sorely handled the enemies of Arthur that they arranged a truce for a year.

Now we have in our previous studies discovered ample reasons for equating these ladies who dwelt in transparent fortresses with Morgain and her sister fays, and there is no need to repeat the evidence. [37] Kaer Loyw, Gloucester, [38] became identified with the mythical Fortress of Glass through one of those mistaken etymologies which brought about the identification of Glastonbury with the *insula vitrea* or "Isle de Voirre" where Melvas–Meleagant had his abode, and which found in Somersetshire the mythical land of summer, *aestiva regio,* over which the same Melvas reigned. [39] Thus through a mistaken interpretation of Kaer Loyw as "Transparent Fortress" the Castle of Ladies came to be localized on the Severn. Thus Gauvain's mother Morcades, whom long since we recognized as Morgain, [40] is one of the two queens in the Roche de Sanguin. Thus Chrétien was led to stress the hundreds of windows of the Roche de Sanguin and to declare that the palace was equipped with "glass panes (*verrieres*) so clear that whoever took heed could see through the glass (*voirre*) all who entered the palace." [41] Thus Wolfram came to describe the same hall as floored with glass, and added to the castle an observation tower, set with windows of precious stones, and equipped with a magic pillar in which one could see all that went on in the country for miles around. [42] Thus the old tradition, preserved in *Pwyll,* of the mythical combat at the ford near the faery palace of Modron came to be interpreted as the defense of the Severn as the border between Logres and Gales or Sor-

---

[36] Sommer, *op. cit.,* III, 210–15. See Chap. XLII.   [37] Cf. *supra,* pp. 89, 255 f.

[38] The *Vulgate Lancelot* relates a somewhat commonplace tale of Bohort's rescuing a maiden who was about to be thrown, naked save for her shift, into a river, and escorting her to her castle of Glocedon. As they approached, "si voient issir dames & damoiseles a grant plente dont les unes dansoient et lez autres karoloient & baloient et gieuent de divers jus. Si estoient toutes vestues trop richement." Sommer, *op. cit.,* IV, 271–73. This seems to equate Gloucester with the Castle of Ladies on the Severn, and there may be a reminiscence of the Sabrina legend of which Geoffrey of Monmouth has preserved a form (*Historia,* ed. Griscom, pp. 256 f.).   [39] See Chap. XXXII.   [40] Cf. *supra,* pp. 53, 114, 191.

[41] *Conte del Graal,* ed. Hilka, vss. 7243–45, 7720–23. Cf. also the continuation (Potvin, *Perceval le Gallois,* III, 63) which tells how Yguerne displayed the arms of 500 newly made knights around Chastel Merveilleus: "Lor armes qui sont mervelloses, Plaines de pières présiouses, A fait portendre par lor estres Et environ par lor fenestres, Si que les pières de viertu Donent en l'ost le roi Artu Une tel clarté, ce vos di, Com s'il fust à plain midi; Esbahi sont por le clarté, Si quident estre enfantomé."   [42] *Parzival,* 566, 13 f.; 589, 1–590, 14.

gales, and hence the ominous warnings to the hero against passing the bourn.

There is nothing, therefore, in the speculations of Jessie Weston and Arthur Brown on the Castle of Ladies as the abode of the dead.[43] Even if Chrétien's references to the borders of Galvoie reflected an old *donnée* (and we have seen good reason to doubt it), Miss Weston was quite correct in saying: "I am not aware that there is, apart from our text, any evidence in favour of Galloway being regarded as the Other-World." Four manuscripts of Chrétien's poem which add to the word Galvoie, "a right savage land, and there dwells a malicious folk," [44] offer an adequate explanation of the dread which the name of the region inspired. For Professor Schlauch has called attention to the bad repute of the Galwegians,[45] and Ailred of Rievaulx puts in the mouth of Walter Espec before the Battle of the Standard (1138) the following: "Children tossed into the air and caught on the points of lances afforded a delectable sight to the Galwegians. . . . By chance many children were found in the same house. A Galwegian took his stand, and snatching up one after another by both feet, dashed their heads against a post." [46] One does not need to seek any further than this in order to understand why one would be reluctant to pass "la bosne de Galvoie." Even if Chrétien's name for the Castle of Ladies, Roche de Sanguin, were correct (and we may feel sure that it is a corruption), it is a very far cry from this Rock of Crimson Cloth to the Irish "red-cornered rock" of Donn,[47] which has no legends attached to it in any way resembling those connected with the Chastel Merveilleus. If Gauvain sent to Orcanie for the nobles and ladies who were to represent as spectators his side in the quarrel with Guiromelant, it was not because Orcanie had any suggestion of the classical Orcus,[48] but simply because the old Welsh formula prescribed that the combatants be attended by the nobles of their lands (Guiromelant bade Gauvain, "Thou shalt send to thy land for all thy host" [49]); and Gauvain's land, which he inherited from his father Loth, was, according to one tradition, Orcanie.[50] If Gauvain believed his mother to be dead,[51] it is probably because either Chrétien or his source, forced to invent some explanation for the strange inability of Gauvain and his kinswomen to recognize each other, naturally concluded that they must have been separated for many years, and hence Gauvain must have thought them dead. Moreover, our previous investigations have shown us that the Celtic Land of Women and the Arthurian Fortress

---

[43] Weston, *Legend of Perceval*, I, 191 f. A. C. L. Brown, *Origin of the Grail Legend*, p. 142, n. 57; p. 143, n. 58, 59; pp. 195, 198.

[44] *Conte del Graal*, ed. Hilka, p. 294, reading of mss. PSU.   [45] *PMLA*, XLIV (1929), 371.

[46] *Chronicles of the Reigns of Stephen, Henry II, and Richard I*, ed. R. Howlett (London, 1886), III, 187 f.

[47] Brown, *op. cit.*, p. 168.   [48] *Ibid.*, pp. 109, 142, n. 57.

[49] *Conte del Graal*, ed. Hilka, vss. 8886 f.   [50] Cf. *supra*, p. 72.

[51] *Conte del Graal*, vss. 8753–56.

of Glass or Castle of Ladies were not inhabited by the dead but by the ever-living ones, the fays. The Chastel de Limors in *Erec* preserves the only clear trace in Chrétien's poems of the realm of Death, and that, we have seen, was probably a Breton addition to the *Matière de Bretagne*.

There remains the mystery of Clarianz' name and the strange fact that her lover had never seen her, nor she him. Let us look first at her name. Richter noted that the name Clarine in *Lanzelet* replaced the name Elaine in the *Vulgate Lancelot* as that of the hero's mother, and remarked: "Wer weiss, wie Namen in den Handschriften entstellt, verunstaltet, verändert werden, wird nicht zweifeln können, dass aus der Elaine die Clarine geworden ist." [52] Now the same explanation applies to Chrétien's Clarianz, for as Gauvain's sister she has her counterpart in the Elainne of the *Didot Perceval*.[53] There are two reasons, then, for suspecting that the name Clarianz is a distorted form of Elaine; and there is still another.

Both Clarianz and Clarine are described as beautiful,[54] and so too are the Elaines. In fact, Elainne, the beloved of the red knight, Perceval, was "the most beautiful damsel who lived in her time," [55] and one is inclined to identify her with "Elaine without Peer, the wife of Persides the Red," who is mentioned in the *Vulgate Merlin* as one of the two most lovely women of Britain, surpassing even Guenievre.[56] There is also an Elene in *Libeaus Desconus,* of whom we read that there was neither countess nor queen who might be her peer in seemliness.[57] Though cast in quite different roles, all these ladies share a reputation for beauty, three of them for supreme beauty. Is it possible that there was a single prototype for these peerless Elaines, as well as for Clarine and Clarianz? It would be rash to risk such a generalization, but for two of them a common Welsh original can be claimed in the Elen of *The Dream of Maxen*.

We saw in the last chapter that *The Dream of Maxen* offers in the venerable Eudav a model for the mysterious *eschacier* of the Castle of Ladies. I have tried to show in *Speculum,* Volume XXII (1947), 523–29, that Eudav's daughter, Elen, offers a partial prototype of the Elene of *Libeaus Desconus*.[58] It is hardly an accident, therefore, that this Welsh Elen presents a remarkable similarity to the princess Clarianz of the Castle of Ladies.[59] Elen dwelt in a castle above a river, with a hall glittering with gold and jewels. She was so fair that it was not easier to look on her than on the sun in its splendor. A huntsman emperor, who had never seen her except in a dream and whom she had never seen, dispatched messengers

---

[52] *Deutsche Forschungen,* XXVII (1934), 50.   [53] *Didot Perceval,* ed. Roach, p. 145.
[54] *Conte del Graal,* ed. Hilka, vss. 7899–908, 8269 f., 8760 f., 9053–56. Ulrich von Zatzikhoven, *Lanzelet,* ed. K. A. Hahn (Frankfurt, 1845), vs. 72.   [55] Cf. n. 53.
[56] *Mod. Phil.,* XVI (1918), 338.   [57] *Libeaus Desconus,* ed. Kaluza, vss. 121–26.
[58] As a maiden guide with a sharp tongue Elene belongs to the category of the "Damoiseles Maudisantes," like Lynet and Orguelleuse, and is therefore in part derived from Liban.
[59] Loth, *Mabinogion,* 2d ed., I, 211–22. On the motif of falling in love with a dream-maiden cf. *PMLA,* XXIX (1914), 527 f.

to woo her. She gave them a favorable reception. She was united in marriage to her suitor. Compare this Elen with Clarianz, whose name is presumably due to a scribal distortion of Elaine. Clarianz dwelt in a castle above a river, with a *palais* decked with gold and jewels. She was the most beautiful of five hundred ladies. A falconer, lord of a great territory, who had never seen her and whom she had never seen, sent Gauvain to her with a love message She received it favorably. She was united in marriage to her suitor. *The Dream of Maxen,* therefore, provides an explanation, not only of the venerable *eschacier* of the Castle of Ladies, but also of the name, beauty, dwelling, and curious love affair of the Princess Clarianz. It explains also the otherwise unaccountable divergences of Chrétien from the pattern of Pwyll's meeting with and relationship to Arawn's wife.

Even a cursory reading of Gauvain's adventures in and about the Castle of Ladies would suggest that they were something of a patchwork quilt, and our study has amply confirmed the guess. In the preceding chapter we recognized the outlines of two Irish and one Welsh tradition: (1) Cuchulainn's nocturnal testing in Curoi's revolving fortress; (2) the voyage of Bran son of Febal to the Land of Women; (3) the figure of Eudav carving chessmen in the hall of a castle above a river. We have now recognized three additional Welsh patterns: (1) the story of Pwyll, Arawn, and Havgan and the annual combat at the ford; (2) the fortress of glass on the Severn, the abode of Morgain and her sister fays; (3) the princess Elen in her splendid castle above a river, and her wooing by a huntsman who had never seen her and whom she had never seen.

Nothing in all Arthurian literature reveals more clearly its conglomerate nature than the last thousand lines which we owe to Chrétien de Troyes. It is fortunate that we can determine the elements which went into them with such clarity that almost every feature can be adequately accounted for.

BOOK VI.   Conclusions

Chapter LXXX

CHRETIEN DE TROYES AND HIS MATIERE

HAVING COMPLETED an analysis of the traditional elements in Chrétien's four romances, we are now in a position to answer with greater fullness and assurance than has hitherto been possible certain major questions concerning his art and the development of the *Matière de Bretagne*.

1. What were Chrétien's immediate sources? They seem to have been four long narratives in French prose, set down in manuscripts, based on the tales of the Breton *conteurs* and centered round famous knights of the Round Table. The incoherences and irrationalities which mar Chrétien's poems, particularly *Le Chevalier de la Charrette* and *Le Conte del Graal,* were for the most part already present in these sources. Chrétien must therefore be absolved of responsibility for many of the blemishes which must be laid at his door if he was the freely working creator of his plots. The fact that the source-narratives contained elaborate descriptions of tournaments and consistently exploited problems of sentiment and chivalric conduct suggests that they did not long antedate their redaction by Chrétien. One may assume that it was their modernity which commended them to the taste of the Countess Marie, Count Philippe, and of the poet himself in the two instances where he presumably made his own choice.

It is highly significant that these two romances, *Erec* and *Yvain,* which were not undertaken, so far as we know, at the dictate of any patron, are precisely those which display few faults of construction and, except for the adventures of the storm-making spring and the "Joie de la Cort," show a strong tendency toward realism. Their sources, moreover, attained some circulation since they were known to the South Welsh author or authors of *Geraint* and *Owain;* evidently others besides Chrétien appreciated their merits. It may well be that X and Y were the work of a single author, since both employ the same general scheme: the wooing and winning of a bride by the hero, marriage, estrangement, forgiveness, and reconciliation. Besides this parallelism in plot, there is a neat antithesis in the moral. Erec, after his marriage, becomes the uxorious slacker and forgets the obligations of chivalry, with unhappy results. Yvain, after his marriage, forgets his wife in the excitements of the tourney, likewise with unhappy results. Both plots seem to have originated in the same mind, a mind not insensitive to the attractions of the marvelous, but more than ordinarily conscious of the need for rationality and realism. It is a very different mind from that which conceived the inchoate plots of the *Charrette* and *Le Conte del Graal,* and it reveals the French genius for clarity and reason applied to the "nugae Britonum." If we may predicate unity of authorship for X and Y, we can better understand how both romances found their way into the hands of Chrétien and the author of *Geraint* and *Owain;* they would naturally be included in the same volume, and we should not have to ascribe to mere chance the existence of redactions in both French and Welsh. That their author, a man of such unusual powers, should remain anonymous is no wonder, considering the many great unknowns who have left to posterity such masterpieces as *La Chanson de Roland, Aucassin and Nicolete,* and *La Queste del Saint Graal.* Neither is it surprising that no manuscript of his work has come down to us, since no twelfth-century manuscript of Chrétien or Marie de France's lais has been preserved.

2. How did Chrétien handle his sources? It is manifest that he made such additions as reveal the sophistication of a well-read cleric: the introductory proverbs of *Erec* and *Le Conte del Graal,* prescribed by poetic manuals; a few names from Wace's *Brut;* presumably the references to Durandart, Ospiniaus, Fernagu, and Ysoré from the *chansons de geste;* references to Piramus, Helaine, Lavine, and Eneas; the mistaken invocation of Macrobius as authority for the description of Erec's mantle; probably the classical names Thoas and Pilades in the *Charrette;* the comparison of Erec with Absalon, Salemon, Alixandre, and Cesar. These are minutiae. More significant are long passages of soliloquy or dialectic, prominent in the *Charrette* and *Yvain,* which seem to have been suggested to Chrétien by his reading in Ovid or the recent classical romances, and which reflect the contemporary interest in problems of love and friendship. As for the strictly narrative materials, Chrétien on the whole followed his sources with some fidelity. This is attested for *Erec* and *Yvain* by the correspondence with *Geraint* and *Owain;* it is indicated for the *Charrette* and *Le Conte del Graal* by their meandering and sometimes mystifying plots, which we cannot ascribe to Chrétien's invention, by the presence of many demonstrably traditional elements, and by the express testimony of the poet himself that he was using material supplied by his patrons. Nevertheless, it is clear that he exercised some freedom in his treatment of these sources. For example, he omitted the references to the color yellow which must have occurred in the description of the costume of the Hospitable Host in Y; he reduced Enide's father from a count to a vavasor; he obscured the cause of Erec's anger at Enide when he removed the traditional motive of jealousy which we find in *Geraint.* Other minor changes have been noted in the course of our discussion. More important examples of Chrétien's independence are his conclusions to *Erec* and *Yvain.* The coronation of Erec and Enide at Nantes seems to have been devised as a grand climax. The duel of Yvain with his friend Gauvain

was transposed to the end of the poem with the same artistic purpose, and the traditional theme of the quarreling sisters was introduced in order to bring about this supreme demonstration of Yvain's prowess and magnanimity. The evidence shows that the episode at the Castle of Evil Adventure was a deliberate substitution for a similar but more banal story of the deliverance of captive ladies. But apart from certain minor changes and these major innovations, Chrétien was content to follow the adventures of Erec and Yvain much as he found them in his sources. The stories were apparently of his own choosing and would satisfy a fairly high standard of rationality, realism, and morals. In retelling them he achieved his most consistently happy effects.

How did the poet treat the two narratives which were not of his choosing but which were furnished by the Countess Marie and Count Philippe? Few critics, if any, will doubt that in composing the *Charrette* he took great liberties with his *matière,* though there will be differences of opinion as to just how far he went. Seemingly, he allowed many of the glaring crudities of his original to stand, thus provoking the caustic comments of modern scholars. Many of the episodes which contain these flaws had their origin, as we have observed, in the *conteur* tradition. But it is obvious that Chrétien did carry out a drastic process of re-interpretation at the behest of his patroness, adding probably the incident of the finding of Guenievre's comb, heightening her role as the imperious lady, and dwelling on the pangs and ecstasies of her lover and slave, Lancelot. But whether the Champenois poet was the first to assign this role to Lancelot, whether he interpolated many new scenes to illustrate the new *san,* whether he borrowed the incidents of the bloodstained bed and the misleading oath from the Tristan legend, whether, as Professor Nitze believes,[1] he employed the rhetorical principle of *expolitio* to pad out his *matière*—these are questions to which it seems hazardous to give a categorical answer. For the *Charrette* we lack a close cognate romance such as we have for *Erec* and *Yvain,* and we have no secure basis for distinguishing the original narrative from Chrétien's additions and alterations. My own impression is that his originality did not extend thus far, and that Lancelot was already familiar to the poet's immediate circle (though not, perhaps, outside it) as the lover of Guenievre and was already the hero of the somewhat inconsequent and sometimes irrelevant series of adventures which constituted the *matière.* Some of them, in fact, as Webster pointed out,[2] are to be detected in remotely cognate forms in the *Lanzelet,* and one of them, the affair of Lancelot with Meleagant's sister, related by Godefroi de Lagny, suggests that in Chrétien's *matière,* as in the *Lanzelet,* the hero was not a perfect exemplar of fidelity. If these inferences regarding the

[1] T. P. Cross and W. A. Nitze, *Lancelot and Guenevere,* pp. 69–78.
[2] *Harvard Studies and Notes in Philology and Literature,* XVI (1934), 203–28.

source of the *Charrette* are correct, then the poet's task was not the revolutionary one of creating a hitherto unheard of liaison between Lancelot and the Queen, but was limited in the main to developing a relationship already established, bringing it into conformity with the doctrines of *amour courtois,* and touching up the given scenes and situations in order to illustrate the behavior of an ideal lover as conceived by Marie de Champagne. Even though thus limited, Chrétien's remodeling of the Lancelot story would constitute the most significant and drastic operation he performed on his *données.* Precisely because of this remodeling the *Charrette* is an important document for the cult of sublimated adultery, but as literature it is artificial and at times absurd. It is to the author's credit that he disclaimed all responsibility for either *matière* or *san.*

Le Conte del Graal was also a command performance. Again we lack a *close* cognate romance which would furnish a simple criterion for determining the extent of Chrétien's departures from his source. But again we find numerous examples of crude narrative art, and our investigations have revealed everywhere the marks of traditional origin. These facts indicate a close reliance on Count Philippe's book, and there is nothing in the poet's own testimony or in the internal evidence of the poem to prove that Chrétien was doing much more than turning the *conte* which his patron provided into graceful rimed couplets. Recent claims that he was modifying his material to reflect the interest of his patron in the Byzantine mass or the life history of the leper King of Jerusalem, Baldwin IV, are to me quite unconvincing.[3] Nor can I believe, as some have maintained, that because Chrétien's last poem contains a short passage (some 300 out of 9,200 lines) relating the visit of Perceval to his Hermit Uncle, describing the *graal* as a receptacle for a magical mass wafer, and setting forth some rudimentary lessons in the Christian faith, the poet turned over a new leaf in his old age and consecrated his declining years to a work of piety. The last 2,800 lines of the poem, as well as the flagrantly unsanctified atmosphere of the Grail scene itself, should suffice to condemn such a theory. If, as I believe, Chrétien was a man of high intelligence, literary genius, and a more than elementary knowledge of religious matters, he could not have been satisfied with the inadequate motivation, the rambling plot, the strange moral emphasis, and the fantastically uncanonical representation of the Grail as a receptacle for the Host which we discover in his romance; far less could he have invented them. We know that the choice of a source was made for him; he seems to have followed it through thick and thin, happy when he dealt with the humorous escapades of his simpleton hero or with the romance of the Maid of Little Sleeves, but somewhat embarrassed by the Blancheflor affair, puzzled by the procession of *graal* and lance, probably even more puz-

[3] *PMLA,* LVIII (1943), 597–620. *Speculum,* XXI (1946), 302–11.

zled by the casual explanation of the Hermit, finally pursuing with re-signed bewilderment the erratic itinerary of Gauvain and his capricious guide, Orguelleuse de Logres. Nowhere in all this can I discover any sign of marked independence, of addition or alteration. Just as in the *Charrette* Chrétien did just what he said he did, so we can believe him when he professed to do no more with Count Philippe's book than to turn it into rime. The style, of course, is his own, and probably he added life to the dialogue in his best dramatic scenes. Taking all four romances into con-sideration, one may say of him that, in spite of handicaps imposed by some of his materials and by the doctrinaire Marie, he deserves to be called the most accomplished (as he may have been the first) of the French poets who worked with the stuff of Arthurian romance.

3. How much of this stuff was derived from the Celts? *Cliges,* as I believe almost everyone would agree, is an artificial composite of Chrétien's own making, with a few traditional Arthurian characters and with some reminiscences of the treachery of Modred and the three days' tourna-ment. But a very considerable portion of the other four poems is of Celtic origin. For one thing, most of the personal names are Celtic; many of them are Welsh, as modified by the Bretons; some are Breton; a few can be traced back through Wales to Ireland. As for the narrative patterns, *Erec* is largely compounded of Welsh legends about the fays Modron and Riannon, Modron's son Mabon, the dwarf-king Beli and his brother Bran. The framework of the *Charrette* is the Welsh story of the abduction of Gwenhwyvar by Melwas, embellished by features from the abduction of Creiddylat by Gwynn and by subsidiary incidents from the saga of Cuchulainn and the legend of Modron. *Yvain* combines in the first part several versions of the testing of the warriors of Ulster by Curoi with the Breton tradition of Barenton; in the second part it blends the plot of *The Sickbed of Cuchulainn* with legends of Modron as a water-fay. *Le Conte del Graal* is a highly complex pattern, to which the *enfances* of Cuchu-lainn, the story of Finn's birth, his vengeance, and his meeting with his uncle, the account of Conn's visit to the palace of Lug and the Sovranty of Erin, Welsh traditions of the wounded King Bran and his brother Beli, of a Castle of Ladies on the Severn, and of meetings and combats with the proud huntsman Arawn, have all contributed. Besides these Celtic contributions of primary importance, there are, as we have observed, minor features and incidents which are paralleled in the extant Irish and Welsh literature of the Middle Ages. In spite of the great gaps in our knowledge about Bran, Beli, Pryderi, Gwri, Llwch, Modron, and Riannon, it is sur-prising how much can be pieced together from the scraps of information we possess, and how neatly these patterns conform, despite rationaliza-tion and confusion, to those present in Chrétien's work. Evidently there was a great ferment in the Welsh imagination during the Dark Ages

which blended into one great seething mass the hereditary lore of the Goidelic and Brythonic peoples. And what the *cyvarwyddon* recited in Wales they passed on to the Breton *conteurs* before the year 1000, and doubtless later as well. These tales, gradually adapted to French tastes, given a new localization in Anglo-Norman Britain after the Conquest, receiving new authority from the quasi-historical productions of Geoffrey of Monmouth and Wace, were the great sensation of the twelfth century and enjoyed great favor wherever French was understood. Linked into more or less coherent long narratives and written down in prose, they furnished Chrétien with his *matière*.

What causes have prevented the general recognition of Celtic elements in Arthurian romance? It would seem that, on the Celtic side, Irish scholars have restricted their interest to the literature in their own native tongue, and that Welsh scholars have been discouraged by the largely speculative efforts of Rhys in his *Studies in the Arthurian Legend* to establish a Cymric foundation for the *Matière de Bretagne*. As for students of Old French literature, it would seem that the powerful influence of Foerster, Bédier, M. Lot, and M. Faral has blinded most of them to the possibility of a traditional basis for the Arthurian cycle. Even among the champions of Celtic origins, such as the late Arthur Brown, there seems to have been little comprehension of the mode and the channels of transmission and a tendency to ignore the vital role of the Welsh and the significance of the *Four Branches of the Mabinogi*. So that, while in the United States at least, thanks to the efforts of Kittredge, Gertrude Schoepperle, Professor Tom Peete Cross, and Professor William A. Nitze, there has been an increasing realization of the Irish contribution to the cycle, there is only Professor Newstead's book on *Bran the Blessed in Arthurian Romance* to suggest the importance of the Welsh elements.

One major cause, perhaps, for the widespread skepticism regarding the Celtic origin of the *Matière de Bretagne* is the common failure to take into account those changes and distortions which inevitably occur in the course of traditional development, especially in the transmission from one race and language to other races and languages. I have discussed these phenomena already in Chapter V, and will not recur to the matter, except to point out how misreading has led to the distortion of names and other features in Chrétien's poems.

As for *Erec,* Lalut, the home of Enide, possibly owes its name to a garbled form of "le lac," and thus an interesting hint of her faery ancestry may be here concealed. The episode of the "Joie de la Cort," we have seen, had originally nothing to do with a court but with a Welsh cornucopia; the whole sense of the adventure has been obscured by a confusion between *li cors* (horn) and *la cors* (court). *La Charrette* supplies us with a mysterious water-girdled land of Goirre, which scholars have sought to localize, not suspecting that it owes its existence to misreading the initial of *voirre* in the phrase "isle de voirre," which translates Welsh *ynys wydrin*. No one penetrated the disguise of Calogrenant in *Yvain* until I pointed out that he was simply Keu in his characteristic role of the churlish grumbler, Cai-lo-Grenant. In the same poem there is the Dame de Noiroison, and one may legitimately suspect that she owes her title to a capacity for transforming herself into a "noir oisel," like her counterpart Morgain and her ancestress the Morrigan.

Le Conte del Graal offers the most impressive examples of this phenomenon. In the Castle of Ladies a solitary venerable personage with a silver leg (*eschacier*) sits on a bundle of rushes (*trossel de gles*), carving a rod of ashwood. We have seen that Chrétien or the author of his source must have misread a description in French corresponding to that of the venerable Eudav in *The Dream of Maxen*. Eudav sits in the hall of a splendid fortress on a throne (O.F. *trosne*) adorned with figures of eagles (O.F. *d'egles*), carving chessmen out of a golden rod, with a chessboard (O.F. *eschaquier*) before him. The most startling and momentous of all the confusions is that which mistook the magic drinking horn (O.F. *li cors*) of the Blessed Bran for the blessed body (O.F. *li cors beneiz*) of Christ. This blunder colored the whole history of the Grail legend, and is responsible for Chrétien's representing the Fisher King's father as miraculously fed with the mass wafer, that is, the *corpus Christi,* brought to him in the Grail. Only when one has come to expect and to recognize such tortuous relationships as these can one estimate fully the influence of Celtic tradition on Arthurian romance.

4. How much of this compound of Irish and Welsh material was mythical in origin? It is to be hoped that our efforts to elucidate the complex relationships of Chrétien to his remoter sources not only enable us to perceive how and why he wrote as he did, but also enrich the poetic suggestion; for the latent poetry of Arthurian romance is due in large measure to its inheritance from mythology. We hear not only the plain melody of Chrétien's narrative, but also the haunting undertones contributed by generations of older story-tellers, recalling faintly the fantasies of Celtic paganism. To change the metaphor, we perceive, built into the twelfth-century façade, the crumbling sculptures of a heathen temple and the memorials of "battles long ago." Our study, like other similar studies, uncovers a world of forgotten history and magical associations. The names (though not the stories) of Arthur, Urien, and Yvain commemorate the heroic resistance of the Britons to the Germanic invaders. The name of Mabonagrain and his vermeil arms remind us that the Britons once worshiped an Apollo Maponos, while Lancelot and his predilection for red arms lead us back through a series of links to the Irish deity Lug Lonnbemnech, who had a red color on him from sunset to morning. The

nocturnal adventures of Gauvain on the Perilous Bed with its motionless wheels are the crude survivals of the testing of Cuchulainn in a revolving sky-palace by the storm-giant Curoi. The Loathly Damsel is the descendant of Eriu, the personification of Ireland, in its bleak, wintry aspect. The abduction of Guenievre and the repeatedly interrupted and postponed combats of Lancelot with Meleagant go back to a Welsh Persephone myth and the annual battles of the kings of Summer and Winter for the possession of the Earth-Maiden. The three sportsmen—the Proud Knight of the Glade, the King of Cavalon, and Guiromelant—are the descendants of the leader of the Wild Hunt, Arawn, whom Pwyll provoked to haughty remonstrance in a glade near Glyn Cuch. The Welsh dwarf king Beli is recognizable in the dwarf kings, Bilis and Guivret, and appears, strangely transmogrified, as Perceval's Hermit Uncle and as the hideous squire of Greoreas. The euhemerized sea-god Bran adopts many disguises and aliases, turning up as Ban or Brauz de Gomeret with his blithe and youthful retinue, as the tall king Brien, as the King of Brandigan, as Baudemaguz, as Perceval's father, as the Fisher King, and as Greoreas. The disasters which overtook the realms of Perceval's father and the Fisher King after they were wounded between the thighs reflect a wide-spread heathen belief in the sympathetic relation between the fertility of the land and the generative powers of its ruler.

The mighty and many-sided goddess Modron, who was worshiped for centuries in Gaul and Britain under the name of Matrona and whose stately seated image in triplicate is carved on countless votive tablets, is perhaps the most pervasive influence on Arthurian romance. Having attracted to herself in her long career the greatest variety of legends, she could assume the most diverse aspects and could play the most inconsistent roles. Having borrowed from the Irish lamia, the Morrigan, something of her name and story, she was destined to appear most patently as Morgain la Fée. But there are few female figures in Chrètien's work (except Guenievre, Iseut, Lunete, and the Loathly Damsel) who have not taken over some characteristic attributes or activities from Modron. It is likely that in the uxorious indolence which overcame Erec we see Morgain's power to hold her lovers in enchanted idleness. The garden of Mabonagrain's mistress, with its healing herbs and its fruit, is reminiscent of Morgain's Isle of Apples. The chatelaine who tried to seduce Lancelot, the amorous wife of Meleagant's seneschal who presented him with a horse and arms, Meleagant's sister who healed him and also presented him with a horse—all play characteristic parts of the faery queen. Laudine, Countess of the Fountain, may be traced through the fountain fay of Lothian back to Modron. The Lady of Noiroison and Blancheflor, both delivered from siege and then deserted by their champions, inherit this role ultimately from Fand but immediately from Morgain. In the Castle of Ladies Gauvain's mother Morcades plays the part of Morgain as mistress of a Castle of Maidens. The elfin glamour and the tantalizing mysteries of the Round Table cycle are the bright afterglow of Celtic paganism. Permit me to quote again the memorable dictum of Ker:

"Whether in the Teutonic countries, which in one of their corners preserved a record of old mythology, or in the Celtic, which allowed mythology, though never forgotten, to fall into a kind of neglect and to lose its original meaning, the value of mythology is equally recognizable, and it is equally clear that mythology is nothing more than romance. Everything in the poets that is most enthralling through the mere charm of wonder, from the land of the Golden Fleece to that of the Holy Grail, is more or less nearly related to mythology." [4]

It is hoped that our investigation has not only made possible a more accurate view of Chrétien's literary art, his place in the evolution of Arthurian romance, and his debt to antecedent Celtic saga, but that it has also brought out in new ways the amazing vitality and persistence of those pagan traditions which he inherited. Those traditions have come down through the ages not only in the literary compositions of Chrétien and later Arthurian romancers, in the Breton lais and Italian *cantari*, in *chansons de geste* which have borrowed heavily from Arthurian romance (such as *Floovant, Maugis d'Aigremont*, and *Huon de Bordeaux*), in masterworks of the Renaissance such as the *Orlando Furioso* and the *Faerie Queene*, and in the poems of Tennyson and Wagner's *Parsifal*, but also in the humbler forms of folktale and folk-custom. For the lands which produced the Irish sagas, the *mabinogion*, and the Breton *contes* and lais, which were the forerunners of the Round Table romances, preserved until a hundred years or so ago certain related beliefs and fictions. In Ireland a whitethorn growing alone on the banks of streams was considered to be the haunt of the fairies [5]—a belief which is echoed clearly in *Le Lai de l'Espine* and less clearly in the adventure beside the ford of Noirespine in *Diu Krone*.[6] At Tober-Kilna-Greine in County Cork a nymph was said to live in a well [7]—a version of the widespread and ancient association of fays with springs which turns up in the lais of *Desiré* and *Guingamor*, in *Jaufré*, and in the title given in *Owain* to Laudine, "the Countess of the Fountain." The peasantry of County Clare celebrated an annual sacrifice of bulls and rams to the sun [8]—a vestige of that heliolatry which is perpetuated in certain familiar Arthurian motifs.[9] County Mayo preserved in the story of Watty O'Kelly and the fairy king the unique parallel to the question test of the Grail legend. In

[4] W. P. Ker, *Dark Ages*, p. 47.
[5] W. G. Wood-Martin, *Traces of the Elder Faiths of Ireland*, II, 156.
[6] *Mod. Phil.*, XLIII (1945), 65, n. 10.
[7] E. Hull, *Folklore of the British Isles*, p. 68. Lady Wilde, *Ancient Legends, Mystic Charms, and Superstitions of Ireland* (Boston, 1888), p. 242.   [8] R. S. Loomis, *Celtic Myth*, p. 42.
[9] *Ibid.*, pp. 39-51.

various parts of Ireland the old saga of Blathnat's betrayal of Curoi survived in the form of folktales, just as it survived in Arthurian tradition.[10]

The same is even more true of Brythonic lands. Place names preserve the memory of Aranrot, Mabon, and Bran.[11] In South Wales every May Day the King of Winter and the King of Summer played out their ritual contest for supremacy—a custom which has its narrative counterpart in the repeated fights of Lancelot and Meleagant. Every first Sunday in August the neighboring peasantry used to flock to Llyn y Fan Fach to see the lake-maiden who married a farm lad, bore him sons, and taught them the lore of herbs; and the lake-maiden seems to be descended from the same water-goddess as Morgain la Fée.[12] Off the coast of Cardiganshire there lay an invisible island of virtuous dwarfs, presumably akin to Chrétien's noble dwarfs, Guivret, Bilis, and Gleodalen.[13] Belief in the Wild Huntsman who appeared with his hounds, particularly between Christmas and Twelfth Night, was still strong,[14]—a belief also reflected by the sportsman host of *Gawain and the Green Knight* [15] and dimly by the three sportsmen of *Le Conte del Graal,* mentioned above. Oddly enough, the Bran legend, so potent in its influence on Arthurian romance, seems to have died out on its home ground almost completely. Only some fragmentary traditions about a treasure beneath Dinas Bran and about fairy men to be seen in the neighborhood still clung to the site of the Fisher King's castle.[16]

In Brittany the spring of Berenton was still credited with magic properties, and religious processions, headed by priests of the neighboring parishes, went there to pray for rain.[17] A number of folktales about females variously named Morgan, Morganes, Mari Morgan, or Margot la Fée were current and attest the passage of the legends of the faery queen through Brittany.[18] And there were many stories about the personified sun, who was also Death, and who wedded a mortal maiden and took her away to his shining palace—stories which offer the best clue to the interpretation of Erec's and Enide's adventure at the castle of Limors.

Surely our sense of the poetry of Arthurian romance must be intensified when we realize its kinship to the living faiths and traditions of the Celtic peoples only a century ago.

It is to be hoped, moreover, that our sense of the nearness and vitality of

[10] *Journ. of Eng. and Germ. Phil.,* XLII, 156–58. *Eriu,* VII, 202. C. Otway, *Sketches in Erris and Tyrawley,* pp. 39–41. Loomis, *Celtic Myth,* pp. 18–20.

[11] W. J. Gruffydd, *Math Vab Mathonwy,* p. 179, n. 41. J. Rhys, *Celtic Folklore,* I, 207–9. *Celtic Review,* IV (1907), 248. *Aberystwyth Studies,* VIII (1926), 71n.

[12] Rhys, *Celtic Folklore,* I, 2–12, 15 f. E. S. Hartland, *Science of Fairy Tales,* p. 330. *Speculum,* XX, 195 f.   [13] Rhys, *Celtic Folklore,* I, 158–60, 166–69. *PMLA,* LVI, 917–24.

[14] M. Trevelyan, *Folklore and Folk-stories of Wales,* p. 53. Unfortunately Miss Trevelyan cannot always be trusted. She borrowed bits verbatim from Stallybrass' translation of Grimm's *Mythologie.*   [15] *Journ. of Eng. and Germ. Phil.,* XLII, 170–74.

[16] Rhys, *op. cit.,* I, 148, 238. *Miscellany of Studies in Honour of L. E. Kastner,* p. 349. W. Sikes, *British Goblins,* pp. 79–81.   [17] F. Bellamy, *Forêt de Bréchéliant,* II, 282.

[18] *Speculum,* XX, 198 f. L. A. Paton, *Fairy Mythology,* p. 101n., p. 164, n. 2, p. 251, n. 2.

the *Matière de Bretagne* may be enhanced by the realization that many of the towns and castles, rivers and islands which were known to the twelfth-century *conteurs* and were for them the scenes of marvel and chivalric adventure can be identified and visited today. If our examination of Arthurian geography has been conducted with the requisite caution, we need not fear that we will be wandering in a maze of false conjectures. We need not rely on the amusing guesses of a Froissart, a Malory,[19] or a Leland, or on the ingenious but often erroneous hypotheses of modern scholars. Tristan's Lyones was not a lost sunken region between Land's End and the Scilly Isles; Astolat was not Guildford, nor Sinadon Stirling, nor Camelot Cadbury Castle. To be sure, some of the places famed in Arthurian romance never had an existence except on parchment, Goirre being a corruption of the common noun *voirre,* and Benoic of the adjective *benoit*. But there is an authentic geography of the Arthurian cycle, the geography created chiefly by the men who in the twelfth century created the romances we know. It consists of the lands and sites which the *conteurs* had in mind and which some of them must have visited when they laid their scenes in Destregales or Logres, at Caradigan, Carlion, Caruent, or Cardoil, Sinadon or Tintagel, Daneborc or Dinasdaron, at the Castle of Maidens in Lothian or the Castle of Maidens beside the Severn, or in the vale of Avalon. All of these places existed for the *conteurs,* not in an imaginary world, but in the Isle of Britain; many of them have since been correctly identified—Destregales and Logres with South Wales and England, Carlion and Tintagel with Caerleon on Usk and Tintagel on the Cornish Sea, Caradigan and Cardoil with Cardigan and Carlisle, both Danebroc and the Castle of Maidens in Lothian with Edinburgh, and the vale of Avalon with Glastonbury.

But it has not been fully recognized how the fallen remains of Roman architecture in particular stirred the imaginations of the Breton *conteurs,* as well as of other story-tellers. Bédier declared of the *chansons de geste*: "les abris préferés de nos légendes furent les ruines romaines," [20] and cited a number of scenes laid in or near amphitheatres, aqueducts, and arches. Professor Gruffydd notes a similar phenomenon in Welsh saga:

". . . the old caers of the Romans were to the Britons, in whose mind these legends grew, the symbols of a great past in which they had no part, and . . . it was the wistful memory of ancient greatness which made them connect their Arthur, born in evil times of good old Roman blood, with the relics of that greatness which they saw about them; so Caer Vyrddin, Caer Llion, Caer Seint, and many another Caer were inevitably made the scenes of Arthur's splendour and great exploits." [21]

Geoffrey of Monmouth, there can be little doubt, exploited some local tradition when he placed Arthur's coronation among the imposing mon-

[19] *Mod. Lang. Rev.,* XXX (1935), 204–9. [20] J. Bédier, *Légendes épiques,* 3d ed., IV, 413.
[21] W. J. Gruffydd, *Math Vab Mathonwy,* p. 346.

uments of Caerleon. Similar associations clustering about the awesome remains of Caerwent and Caer Seint in Wales and of Trimontium in Scotland inspired the Breton *conteurs* and were passed on to the French romancers. Nor has it been duly recognized how the border fortress of Dinas Bran, overlooking the valley of the Dee, stimulated the creation of legend, though *Fouke Fitz Warin* bears testimony to the fact. It was seemingly the wonder evoked by these venerable and picturesque ruins which led to the choice of Carlion and Dinasdaron (Dinas Bran) as appropriate sites for Arthur's court and to the localization of romantic adventures at Caruent, the city of Sinadon (Caer Seint near Carnarvon), and the Castle of the Fisher King (Dinas Bran). A different cause, mistaken inference, brought about the placing of Avalon at Glastonbury and of the Castle of Maidens at Edinburgh or Gloucester. Yet there is little room for doubt that these identifications too go back to the twelfth century and were taken quite seriously, so seriously in fact that search was undertaken at Glastonbury for Arthur's bones,[22] and for centuries "Castellum Puellarum" was an official designation of Edinburgh.

What Troy and Colchis and the field of Enna are to the Hellenic tradition, what Verona and Worms and Leire are to the Germanic and Anglo-Saxon epic, what Roncesvaux and St. Guilhem-le-Désert are to the Carolingian cycle, such are these British places for the *Matière de Bretagne*. When one realizes what energies the scholars of Europe and the United States have poured into the discussion of the site of Homer's Troy or the itinerary of Odysseus, and what rich results have attended the researches of Bédier and his predecessors into the topography of the *chansons de geste*, it is surprising to observe how little satisfactory work has been done on the identification of Arthurian places and the study of their traditions. There are, of course, the significant articles of Zimmer and Dr. Brugger, but the latter overemphasize the Scottish and Breton localities and tend to neglect the Welsh, equating, for example, Estregales with Strathclyde and Gomeret with Vannes. There is the admirable study of Professor Kenneth Jackson on Nennius' list of Arthur's battles,[23] but unfortunately the results are mainly negative. Snell's book, *King Arthur's Country*, though useful, is amateurish. Loth's handling of the topography of the Tristan legend in Cornwall cannot be accepted.[24] Only the Glastonbury legends have received satisfactory treatment, at the hands of J. Armitage Robinson and Professor Nitze.[25] The Britain of the French and English romances, not to mention the Britain of the earlier Cymric stories, calls for a full, scientific, and yet imaginative monograph, founded on a clear understanding of the historic growth and spread of the tradition. The possibilities of the subject,

[22] *Speculum*, IX (1934), 355–61.   [23] *Mod. Phil.*, XLIII (1945), 44–57.
[24] J. Loth, *Contributions à l'étude des romans de la Table Ronde*, pp. 60–112.
[25] J. A. Robinson, *Two Glastonbury Legends* (Cambridge, 1926). *Perlesvaus*, ed. W. A. Nitze and others, II, 45–72.

I trust, have been shown in the foregoing pages, and a book, illustrated with photographs, early engravings, and water colors, could serve both as an indispensable commentary on the Arthurian texts and as a magic talisman to re-create the wonder of Logres, Lyones, and Gales which our ancestors knew. For it is true, as Kipling wrote, of Britain:

> She is not any common Earth,
> Water or wood or air,
> But Merlin's Isle of Gramarye . . .

And though Chrétien barely mentions Merlin and his natural bent was toward realism, rather than toward gramarye, it is he who gives us the earliest full report on the wonders and enchantments which befell in Britain in the days of King Arthur.

APPENDIX

Names of Arthurian Persons and Places in Chrétien's Four Traditional Romances

IN SELECTING from among the variants of a given name the one which best represents Chrétien's own form I have been guided entirely by considerations of historical origin, whenever that origin can be determined with some assurance. When the origin is uncertain, I have adopted Foerster's reading and have supplied variants. If Wace is the obvious source of a name, as in the case of Anguisseaus, Cadualans, Cadorcaniois, I have preferred the manuscript reading which came closest to Wace's forms—Angusel, Cadualan, Chadorkeneneis. Since it is generally conceded that Chrétien took over these names from Wace, there is the strongest presumption that the reading which comes closest to Wace is that which comes closest to Chrétien. When the name is that of a historic character such as Owein of Cyveilioc, I have preferred again the closest reading, for example, Yvain de Cavaliot. When the name Rinduran occurs in Breton and Cornish documents and no other origin is suggested, I prefer the forms Rindurans, Rinduranz. Where the form Leconuials, though manifestly corrupt, is demonstrably closer than any other reading to what Chrétien must have found in X, I have adopted it. In no instance have I adopted a hypothetical form, but only one which has manuscript authority. But of the variants supplied by the manuscripts I have chosen on principle the reading which shows the least departure from the historic source of the name.

If it be objected that no attention has been paid to manuscript classification as a test of soundness, my reply is twofold. First, Professor Misrahi, after long study of the manuscripts of *Erec,* has concluded that Foerster's stemma is of little value; and even Foerster referred to "dem Wirrwarr der zahllosen, einander widersprechenden Varianten." Secondly, the forms cited above as most certain to approximate what Chrétien wrote come not from one manuscript or a single group in Foerster's stemma. Three appear in B, and one each from H, V, E. Now Foerster pronounced the group to which V and E belong worthless for the establishment of the text. But it is evident from the preceding paragraph that these manuscripts occasionally give the most authentic forms of proper names. Accordingly, I hope my neglect of Foerster's stemmata is justified.

Professor Misrahi has noted that Foerster's readings are not always accurate, and I have relied for *Erec* on the transcripts which Professor Misrahi has kindly placed at my disposal. The verse references are to the following editions: *Erec und Enide,* ed. W. Foerster (Halle, 1890); *Der Karrenritter,* ed. Foerster (Halle, 1899); *Der Löwenritter (Yvain),* ed. Foerster (Halle, 1887); *Der Percevalroman (Li Contes del Graal),* ed. A. Hilka (Halle, 1932).

Agravain. *Graal,* vss. 4768, 8139. Brother of Gauvain. Possibly a metathesized form of Garravain, *Erec,* vs. 1710. Garravain is in all probability a variant of Gorvain, and Gorvain in turn a derivative, as M. Lot maintained (*Romania,* XXIV, 326), of Welsh Gwrvan; and Gwrvan's epithet Gwallt-a(d)vwyn, as I showed on pp. 149–51, is the original of the name Gauvain. Thus Agravain and Gauvain would both be sons of Loth, and therefore brothers.

Aguisiez. *See* Anguisseaus.

Alier. *Yvain,* vs. 2939. A count who made war on "la Dame de Noiroison." Origin unknown.

Amauguins. *Erec,* vs. 318 (variants Amaguins, Amaugis); vs. 1726 (variants Amaugins, Amaingins, Et Maugons). King, and knight of the Round Table. Probably identical with King Amangon or Mangon, whose name seems to be a corruption of Welsh Manawydan, assimilated to the French noun *mangon.* Cf. *Elucidation,* ed. A. W. Thompson, pp. 47–49 and *supra,* pp. 244–50.

Anguingeron. *Graal,* vs. 2004 (many variants). Seneschal of Clamadeu. Origin unknown.

Anguisseaus. *Erec,* vs. 1970 (variants Aguiflez, Aguisies, Aguisiez, Agousles, Anguissans). King of Escoce. From Wace, ed. Arnold, vs. 10249: "D'Escoce i vint reis Augusel [variant Angusel]." Wace took the name from Geoffrey's Anguselus, "rex Albaniae, quae nunc Scotia dicitur." Faral, *Légende arthurienne,* III, 243. Geoffrey's form seems to be a diminutive formed on the common Scottish and Irish name Angus. Cf. also *ibid.,* II, 263; III, 237.

Ares. *Erec,* vss. 1528, 1728 (variants Yres, Areins). Father of Tor or Estor. Origin unknown.

Artur, Arthur, Artu. King of Britain, son of Uterpandragon. From Welsh Arthur, which is generally derived from the Roman name Artorius.

Avalon. *Erec,* vs. 1955. Island of which Guigamor was lord. From Welsh "ynis Avallach," probably influenced by Breton place names, Bothavalon and Avaellon. *Zts. f. franz. Sprache u. Lit.,* XII, "Abhandlungen," 248 f. The Welsh Isle of Avallach owed its name to Avallach, father of Modron, and Modron was the original of Morgain la Fée, the mistress of Guigamor and frequently represented as lady of the isle of Avalon. *Romanic Review,* XXIX, 176 f. *PMLA,* LVI, 920.

Ban. *Erec,* vs. 1975 (variants Bauz, Braus); *Graal,* vs. 467. King of Gomeret. A scribal corruption of Bran, derived from Welsh Bran, who held his court in Gwynedd, AF. Goynet. Cf. *supra,* pp. 74, 348–51.

Baudemaguz. *Charrette,* vss. 656, 3157 etc. (variants Bademaguz, Bondemaguz). King of Goirre, father of Meleagant. A compound name. The names of the two Welsh brothers, King Bran and Manawydan, were linked. The latter became French Mangon, Norman Mangun, by assimilation to the common noun, *mangon* or *mangun.* The French preposition *de* was inserted by misunderstanding the latter as a place name. Thus we have a hypothetical Brandemangun. Scribal corruption produced Bandemagun, and further corruption and an effort to form a nominative would give Baudemaguz, Bondemaguz. For evidence cf. Chap. XL.

Bedoier. *Erec,* vs. 1735 (variants Bedoins, Bediens). The constable. Wace, ed. Arnold, vs. 10157 etc. Bedoer, Arthur's *buteillier.* Geoffrey, "Beduerus pincerna." Faral, III, 244. From Welsh Beduir, Bedwyr, warrior of Arthur. Malory, *Morte d'Arthur*, Everyman ed., I, xviii; *Aberystwyth Studies*, VIII, 56; Loth, *Mabinogion*, 2d ed., Index s.v. *Bedwyr ab Bedrawt*.

Belrepeire. *Graal*, vs. 2386 etc. Castle of Blancheflor. In *Enfances Gauvain*, vs. 254, the castle of Gauvain's mother Morchades.

Bilis. *Erec*, vss. 1994, 1997, 2003 (variants Bilins, Belins, Bylis). Dwarf-king of the Antipodes. From Welsh Beli. Cf. *supra*, pp. 142 f.; *Mod. Phil.*, XXXVIII, 289–99; *PMLA*, LVI, 917–24.

Blancheflor. *Graal*, vss. 2417, 2912. Perceval's ladylove, chatelaine of Belrepeire. A common name in O.F. literature. Possibly attached to the heroine since somewhat similar stories are told of Floree in *Livre d'Artus* and Florence in *Artus de la Petite Bretagne*. Cf. *supra*, pp. 369 f.

Bleobleheris. *Erec*, vs. 1714 (variants Blioberis, Blios Blieris, Bleoberis, Bleos Blieris, Blioble Heri). Knight of Arthur's. Probably a scribal corruption of Bleheris. In *Elucidation* (ed. A. W. Thompson, vs. 162) Blihos Bliheris is a knight overcome by Gauvain and sent to Arthur's court. He knew such excellent tales that no one could tire of listening to him. The name is that of the famous *conteur* Bleheris, and has been mistakenly tacked on to a knight. Cf. *ibid.*, pp. 79–81; *Romania*, LIII, 91 f.; *Romanic Review*, XXXIII, 173. It is generally agreed that Bleheri is the French form of the Welsh name Bleddri.

Brandes. *Erec*, vs. 1935 (variants Brandains, Branles, Bradeus). Count of Gloescestre. Probably a corruption of "Bran, dus de Gloescestre." Compare Brandus des Illes in the *Vulgate Lancelot*, whose name seems to resolve itself into "Bran, dus des Illes." Newstead, *Bran the Blessed in Arthurian Romance*, pp. 146–50.

Brandigan. *Erec*, vss. 5389, 6271. Castle of King Eurain. The name Bran once more, taken for a place name, with a termination added on the analogy of Caradigan. Cf. *supra*, pp. 168–71.

Brangien. *Erec*, vs. 2077. Handmaid of Iseut. In all probability derived from the Welsh name Branwen. G. Schoepperle, *Tristan and Isolt*, II, 272.

Bravain. *Erec*, vs. 1737 (variant Braavains). Knight of Arthur's. Unless this is a scribal error for Gravain (see Agravain above), origin unknown.

Breons. *Erec*, vs. 1745 (variant Bruns). Knight of Arthur's, son of Canodan. Possibly a corruption of Breton Brien.

Briein. *Erec*, vs. 1705 (variant Bruian). Accompanied Esliz, Elis, or Eliz. In all probability identical with Brien, accompanied by Bilis or Belins.

Brien. *Erec*, vss. 1996, 1998 (variants Bliant, Bruiant, Blianz, Brihans). Tall brother of the dwarf king Bilis. The name is Breton Brien, substituted for Welsh Bran. Cf. *supra*, pp. 434 f., and *PMLA*, LVI, 921–24.

Broceliande. *Yvain*, vss. 189, 697. Forest in Brittany. Cf. *supra*, pp. 291 f.; F. Bellamy, *Forêt de Bréchéliant; Beihefte zur Zts. f. rom. Phil.*, LXX, 129–39.

Bruianz. *Erec*, vs. 6730 (variant Brianz). Brianz des Illes appears also in Wauchier (Potvin, *Perceval le Gallois*, vss. 29159, 30720) and in *Perlesvaus* (ed. Nitze, II, 100), and is probably the same as Brandus des Illes in the *Vulgate Lancelot* (Sommer, *Vulgate Version*, III, 151–66) and Perceval's father, who was feared throughout the isles of the sea (*Graal*, vss. 416–19) and who goes back to Welsh Bran. Cf. *supra*, pp. 347–50. Miss Weston suggested that the name had been influenced by that of the historic Brian de Insula. *Mod. Phil.,* XXII, 405 ff.

Brun. *Erec,* vs. 1715 (variant Bron). Brun de Piciez, Penes, or Pecies, brother of Grus, Gran, Granderies, or Grensires. Origin unknown.

Cadoc. *Erec,* vss. 4515, 4545, 4574. Knight of Cardueil. The name Cadoc is of course the Welsh Cadawc or Cadoc. It seems to have been substituted for that of Do or Doon of Cardoil, who appears in the *Vulgate Lancelot* and *Livre d'Artus.* Doon, there is reason to believe, goes back to the Welsh Don. Cf. Chap. XXIII.

Cadorcaniois. *Erec,* vs. 1742 (variants Cadocanois, Cardocaniois). Count. Evidently borrowed from Wace's Mauric Chadorkeneneis, Geoffrey's Mauricius Cadorcanensis.

Cadrez. *Erec,* vs. 1972 (several variants including Cador). Son of King Anguisseaus of Escoce. Origin unknown unless the correct form was Cador, from Welsh Kadwr, but Kadwr had no connection with Anguisseaus or Escoce.

Cadualans. *Erec,* vss. 315, 6816 (several variants, including Cadoualanz, Cadoalans). King, vassal of Arthur. From Wace, ed. Le Roux de Lincy, vss. 14447, 14500, Cadualan, Cadwalan. Geoffrey, Cadvallo, Cadwallo. Faral, *Légende arthurienne,* III, 286–99. Geoffrey's Cadwallo was the historic king of North Wales (616–65). *Ibid.,* II, 320–32. Loth, *Mabinogion,* 2d ed., II, Index s.v. *Cadwallawn ab Cadvan.*

Calogrenant. *Yvain,* vs. 57 etc. Knight of Arthur's. From Cai lo grenant, "Kay the Grumbler." Cf. *supra,* pp. 273–77.

Camalot. *Charrette,* vs. 34 (variants Camehelot, Chamalot). Place where Arthur held court. Ingenious efforts have been made to identify the site of Camalot with places in England (*Romanic Review,* XX, 231–36; *Zts. f. franz. Sprache u. Lit.,* XX, 150; F. J. Snell, *King Arthur's Country,* pp. 50–59; *Perlesvaus,* ed. Nitze, II, 196–98), but I find none of them convincing. The name seems due to three developments. (1) The mythical isle of Avalon (itself developed from the Welsh Avallach) became Cavalon under the influence of the Breton personal name Cavallon, cited in documents of the 11th century. Cf. *Zts. f. franz. Sprache u. Lit.,* XLIX, 396. As a result we have in *Conte del Graal* (vss. 4791, 5316) and in *Meraugis* (vss. 37 etc.) a King of Cavalon, where the evidence shows we should have Avalon. Cf. *supra,* pp. 86, 417 f. (2) Cavalon, in turn, being confused with Carlion (Caerleon in Wales), became the principal seat of Arthur. Thus we find in *Conte del Graal* that the manuscripts offer Carlion as a variant of Cavalon (ed. Hilka, pp. 215, 239), that the continuations refer to Cavalon as being in Wales and as the court of Arthur (*ibid.,* p. 624), and represent him as holding his royal feasts at Cavillon (Potvin, *Perceval le Gallois,* V, vss. 33297, 33631, 33741). (3) Cavalon was corrupted and changed for purposes of rime (as in the *Charrette*) to Camalot. The double origin of Camalot in the isle of Avalon and in Carlion is illustrated by the curious fact that the author of *Perlesvaus* distinguishes two Camaalots, one the "Vaus de Kamaalot," situated in "la plus sauvaje isle . . . devers Occident," the other, "dont cil conteor content," being the place where King Arthur often held court. *Perlesvaus,* ed. Nitze, ll. 457, 461, 7277–87. The first must be identical with the "vaus d'Avaron," which are described in Boron's *Joseph* (vss.

3219–21) as "en la terre vers Occident, ki est sauvage durement"; in other words, Avalon. The second represents the confusion with Carlion, which, as early as Geoffrey of Monmouth's *Historia,* is represented as Arthur's capital.

Canodan. *Erec,* vs. 1745. Father of Breons. Origin unknown.

Caradigan. *Erec,* vs. 28 etc. Cardigan in Wales. From Welsh Ceredigiaun. Cf. *supra,* pp. 29, 75.

Carahes. *Erec,* vs. 1727 (variants Guerrees, Carabes, Karades). Probably a variant of Gaharies, Gaheriez, brother of Gauvain (*Erec,* vs. 1725, *Graal,* vs. 8141). If so, from Welsh Gware, influenced by the Breton place name Cahares, modern Carhaix.

Carduel. *Erec,* vs. 4515 (variants Cabriol, Cardueil, Carboil); vs. 4574 (variants Cabruel, Cardueil, Cabriel); vs. 5282; *Yvain,* vs. 7 (variants Cardoeil, Cardueil, Cardoel, Cardoil); *Graal,* vss. 336, 839. Modern Carlisle in Cumberland. The *d* is probably due to contamination by Breton Kerduel. Snell, *King Arthur's Country,* p. 242. Cf. *supra,* pp. 29, 291.

Carlion. *Charrette,* vs. 32; *Graal,* vss. 4003, 4155, etc. From Welsh Kaer Llyon, modern Caerleon in Monmouthshire. The site of Arthur's coronation, according to Geoffrey and Wace.

Carnant. *See* Caruent.

Carsenefide. *Erec,* vs. 6894 (variants Quissenefide, Tarsenesyde). Enide's mother. The name, like that of her husband (Leconuials), is due to some misunderstanding.

Caruent. *Erec,* vs. 2315 (variants Carnant, Carrant, Charnan, Caruan). From Caer Went, modern Caerwent in Monmouthshire, still famous for its Roman ruins and mentioned along with Caerleon by Gaimar as one of the three renowned cities of Wales. Cf. *supra,* pp. 73 f.

Cavaliot. *See* Yvain de Cavaliot.

Cavalon. *Graal,* vss. 463, 4791, 5316 (variants Escavalon, Quavalon, Carlion). Development of Avalon under the influence of the Breton personal name Cavallon. *See* Camalot.

Caveron. *Erec,* vs. 1721 (variants Cauerrons, Caueres). Lord of Roberdic. Origin unknown.

Cestre. *Yvain,* vs. 2680. Town where Arthur held court. Modern Chester.

Chanpguin. *See* Roche de Sanguin.

Chastel Orguelleus. *Graal,* vss. 4689, 4723. An imaginary castle.

Clamadeu. *Graal,* vs. 2005 etc. (variants Clamades, Clamados). Lord of the Isles, suitor and besieger of Blancheflor. Probably a folk etymology ("Cry to God") for Carado. Cf. *supra,* p. 371, n. 30.

Clarianz. *Graal,* vs. 8269 (variants Clarisans, Clarisant, Clarissanz, Clarissante). Sister of Gauvain, beloved of Guiromelant. A misreading of Elaine, which goes back to Welsh Elen, the name of Clarianz' prototype. Cf. Chap. LXXIX.

Clivelon. *Erec,* vs. 1938 (variants Clivion, Lution). Earldom belonging to Menagormon. Origin unknown.

Coguillanz. *Charrette,* vs. 5812. Lord of Mautirec. Origin unknown.

Coi. *Erec,* vs. 1972 (variant Quoi). Son of Anguisseaus, King of Escoce. Probably same name as Keu, which appears in *Fergus,* ed. Martin, p. 68, as Coi, and in *Yder* frequently as Quoi.

Cornoaille. *Erec*, vs. 6647; *Charrette*, vs. 3906. Modern Cornwall.

Corque. *Erec*, 1965 (variant Corke). Territory of Garras. Probably modern Cork in Ireland.

Cotoatre. *Graal*, vs. 3675. Place. An aphetic form of Escotoatre, Anglo-French name for the Firth of Forth. Cf. *supra*, p. 408.

Danebroc. *Erec*, vss. 2131, 2137 (variants Daneborc, Daneboc, Tenebroc). A castle near which a tourney was held. Modern Edinburgh. An Anglo-French form, probably suggested by a supposed connection with the Danes. The form in *-oc* is confirmed by the rime with Meliadoc, though one would expect Daneborc, as in the lai of *Doon. Romania*, VIII, 61. Cf. *supra* pp. 108–14, and *Zts. f. franz. Sprache u. Lit.*, XLIX, 96, n. 123.

David. *Erec*, vs. 1959. Knight of Tintaguel. From Biblical David.

Dinasdaron. *Graal*, vss. 2732, 2753. Castle in Wales, where Arthur held court. The first element *dinas-* is certainly the Welsh word for castle, fortress. The second element *-daron* is very probably a corruption of Bran. It has been shown by Prof. Newstead (*Bran the Blessed in Arthurian Romance*, pp. 54 f., 95–106, especially p. 97, n.) and also above, pp. 392 f., that the ruinous castle of Dinas Bran in northeastern Wales was the center of traditions known to the Breton *conteurs*.

Do. *Erec*, vss. 1729, 2230; *Graal*, vs. 4721. Father of Giflet or Guiflet. Surely derived from Welsh Don, mother of Gilfaethwy. Cf. *supra*, pp. 160–62.

Dodiniaus. *Erec*, vs. 1700; *Yvain*, vs. 54. Dodinel le Sauvage, a knight of Arthur's. The name is a French diminutive, meaning "Little Simpleton," and probably was in origin a nickname of Perceval. Cf. *supra*, pp. 339 f.

Elis. *Erec*, vs. 1705 (variants Elies, Eslis). The coupling of this name with Briein suggests that it is an aphetic form of Bilis or Belins, the dwarf-king, who is coupled with Brien.

Enide. *Erec*, vs. 2031 etc. Erec's bride. Origin uncertain. Cf. Chap. XII.

Erec. *Erec*, vs. 19 etc. Knight of Arthur's court, son of King Lac. The immediate original of Erec is Breton Guerec, which was substituted for Welsh Gweir, son of Llwch (Welsh *llwch* means "lake"). Cf. Chap. VIII.

Escalibor. *Graal*, vs. 5902. Gauvain's sword. From Irish Caladbolg through Welsh Caledvwlch. Cf. Chap. LXXIII.

Escavalon. *See* Cavalon.

Esclados. *Yvain*, vs. 1970. Esclados li Ros, husband of Laudine. Probably a modification of Caradoc, from Welsh Caradoc; this, in turn, may have been substituted for Irish Curoi. Cf. *supra*, p. 282, n. 18.

Escoce. *Erec*, vss. 1970, 5231. The portion of Scotland north of the Firth of Forth. Cf. Guillaume le Clerc, *Fergus*, ed. E. Martin, p. 107.

Estrangot. *Erec*, vs. 1710 (variants Tangot, Tranglot). Land of Garravain. Probably substitution of the name of a Saracen giant Estragot (E. Langlois, *Table des Noms Propres*) for (D)estregales.

Estregales. *Erec*, vss. 1874, 3881. Realm of King Lac. The *D* of Destregales was mistaken by Chrétien or his source for the preposition *de*, with elision of *e*. Destregales was a French form meaning "right Wales," i.e., southern Wales, and corresponding to Welsh Deheubarth, "right part," applied to southern Wales. Cf. *supra*, pp. 70 f.

Eurain. *Erec,* vs. 5404 etc. (variants Eureus, Enris, Enrins, Uirains, Eurins). King of the castle of Brandigan. A double personality, partly modeled on Bran, partly on Urien, to whom he owes his name, which is elsewhere found corrupted into Urain. Cf. Chap. XXV.

Evroic. *Erec,* vs. 2131. Modern York. Anglo-Norman form based on Anglian Eoforwic.

Fine Posterne. *Erec,* vs. 1952. Land of Graillemers. Popular form of Finisterre. *Zts. f. franz. Sprache u. Lit.,* XLVII, 229.

Gaheriez. *Erec,* vs. 1725; *Graal,* vs. 8141 (variants Gaharies, Gaeriez, etc.). Gauvain's brother. From Welsh Gware Gwallt-euryn, equivalent of Gwri Gwallt-euryn, hero of the *Four Branches of the Mabinogi.* Cf. *supra,* pp. 72, 149–51.

Galegantin. *Erec,* vs. 1738 (variants Galerantins, Galerantis, Galogantins). A Welsh knight of Arthur's. Possibly a scribal corruption of Galvagin (Gauvain) under the influence of the common French name Galeran.

Gales. *Erec,* vs. 6449; *Yvain,* vs. 7; *Graal,* vss. 501, 2753, 4135. Modern Wales. Gales is an Anglo-Norman form, based on Anglo-Saxon *wealas,* nominative plural of *wealh,* meaning "foreigner, Briton."

Gales li Chaus. *Erec,* vs. 1726. Knight of Arthur's. According to Gerbert's continuation of *Graal* (ed. M. Williams, I, vs. 3072) he is said to be Perceval's father, though there is no other support for this identification.

Galoain. *Erec,* vs. 3129 (variant Galuain). A count. The name is apparently a form of Gauvain. Cf. Chap. XIX.

Galvoie. *Graal,* vss. 6602, 8385, 8648. Modern Galloway in southwestern Scotland. Cf. *supra,* pp. 452, 457.

Gandeluz. *Erec,* vs. 1701 (variants Gaudeluz, Candeluz). Knight of Arthur's. Apparently the Breton name Condeloc or Cundeluc, which appears in 9th-century records (*Zts. f. franz. Sprache u. Lit.,* XLIX, 433n.) and in *Fouke Fitz Warin* (ed. L. Brandin, p. 12) as Candelou.

Garin. *Graal,* vs. 5230 etc. A vavasor at whose *ostel* in the castle of Tintagel Gauvain was entertained. Garin son of Bertain, dweller in a Cornish castle, may owe his name, as Windisch (*Das keltische Brittannien,* pp. 174 f.) pointed out, to Geraint son of Erbin, king of Cornwall. But the name was also conspicuous in the Lorrain cycle.

Garras. *Erec,* vs. 1965 (variants Garins, Sarras). King of Corque. Origin unknown.

Garravain d'Estrangot. *Erec,* vs. 1710. Knight of Arthur's. Garravain is probably the same as Agravain (see above) and therefore derived from Welsh Gwrvan.

Gaudin de la Montaingne. *Erec,* 2227. Knight captured by Erec at Danebroc. Gaudin is a French name.

Gauvain. *Erec,* vs. 39 etc. Son of Loth; the best of Arthur's knights. Derived through Galvagin from the epithet Gwallt-a(d)vwyn, attached to Gwrvan. Cf. Chap. XXI.

Gavoie. *See* Galvoie.

Giflet. *Erec,* vss. 317, 1729, 2230; *Graal,* vss. 2883, 4721. One of Arthur's knights, son of Do. From Welsh Gilfaethwy son of Don, prominent in mabinogi of

Math. Cf. *supra,* p. 162, and W. J. Gruffydd, *Math Vab Mathonwy,* pp. 204 f.

Gleodalen. *Erec,* vs. 2005 (variants Glodoalan, Glecidalan etc.). Dwarf-king. Probably the Guidolwyn Gorr (dwarf), mentioned in *Kulhwch.* Cf. *supra,* p. 141.

Gloescestre. *Erec,* vs. 1935 (variants Loecestre, Colescestre etc.). Town belonging to Brandes. Modern Gloucester. From Welsh *Gloyw* and AS. *ceaster.*

Godegrain. *Erec,* vs. 1943 (variant Gondegrain). A count. Origin unknown.

Gohort. *Erec,* vs. 1695 (variants Goort, Goars, Gehort, Ghot, etc.); *Graal,* vss. 1548, 1892. Territory of Gornemant. Origin unknown, unless the combination Gornemant de Gohort is a corruption of Gwrnach Gawr in *Kulhwch,* Gawr meaning "giant." Cf. *supra,* pp. 360–62.

Goirre. *Charrette,* vss. 643, 6141 (variant Gorre). Land of Baudemaguz and his son Meleagant. A corruption of Voirre, in the expression Isle de Voirre, "Isle of Glass." Cf. Chap. XXXII.

Gomeret. *Erec,* vs. 1975; *Graal,* vs. 467. Kingdom of Ban or Braus. A scribal corruption of Goinnet, Anglo-French for Gwynedd, northwestern Wales, where King Bran held court. Cf. *supra,* pp. 348–51.

Gornemant. *See* Gohort.

Gornevein. *Erec,* vs. 1727 (variants Gladorlins, Gordevains, Cadorvains, Gadoins). Knight of Arthur's. Probably the name is a corruption of Gorvain, found in several romances and derived from Welsh Gwrvan. *Romania,* XXIV, 326.

Gorre. *See* Goirre.

Governauz. *Charrette,* vs. 5796 (variants Couert, Convoiteus, Toretas). Lord of Roberdic. In view of uncertainty as to correct form no derivation can be hazarded.

Graillemer. *Erec,* vs. 1952 (variants Graislemiers, Greslemuef, Grailemus, Garlemers). Lord of Fine Posterne, vassal of Arthur's, brother of Guigamor. Renaut de Beaujeu, who borrowed many names from *Erec,* gives Grahelens de Fine Posterne in vs. 5519 of *Le Bel Inconnu,* and this was doubtless the correct form. The lai of *Graelent* (vss. 8, 756) gives the form Graalant Muer. This is Middle Breton for the Old Breton Gradlon Mor, "the Great," the name of a historic king of Cornouaille in the sixth century. As Gralon, this personage still figures in Breton folklore. Cf. Sébillot, *Folklore de France,* I, 384; II, 43–53, 79. Zimmer first made the identification in *Zts. f. franz. Sprache u. Lit.,* XII, 1–7.

Grain. *Erec,* vs. 1727 (variant Greins). Knight of Arthur's. Origin unknown.

Greoreas. *Graal,* vss. 7118, 7141, 7302 (several variants). Wounded knight, healed by Gauvain. Name unexplained. The figure is a parallel to the Maimed King. Cf. *supra,* pp. 433–36.

Grigoras. *Erec,* vs. 2005 (variants Grigoro, Gribalo, Gligorras, Gilgolas). Dwarf-king. Origin unknown.

Gringalet. *See* Guingalet.

Gringaron. *See* Anguingeron.

Gronosis. *Erec,* vs. 1740 (variants Graimoins, Grolius, Ennios). Son of Keu the seneschal. Origin unknown.

Grus. *Erec,* vs. 1716 (variants Grans, Granderies, Grensires). Knight of Arthur's, brother of Brun. Origin unknown.

Guenievre. *Erec,* vs. 125 etc. *Charrette,* vs. 1111 etc. (variants Ganievre, Genivre, Genoivre). Wife of Arthur. From Welsh Gwenhwyvar. Cf. Chap. XXVII.

Guerehes. *Graal,* vs. 8141. Brother of Gauvain and son of Lot. Derived from Gwri Gwallt-euryn, hero of the *Four Branches,* who was confused with Gweir son of Llwch mentioned in *Kulhwch.* Cf. *supra,* pp. 71 f. A man named Guerrehes is recorded in a Breton document of 1163. H. Morice, *Mémoires pour servir de preuves à l'histoire de Bretagne,* I, 588.

Guergesin. *Erec,* vs. 1961 (variants Guerguesin, Guerguelin). Duke of Hautbois. Origin unknown. *Romania,* XXIV (1895), 336.

Guigamor. *Erec,* vs. 1954 (variants Guingas, Guilemers, Guingamars). Lord of Avalon, lover of Morgain la Fée, hero of the lai of *Guingamor.* The common Breton name Guichomar, Guiemar, etc. L. A. Paton, *Fairy Mythology,* pp. 60–73. *Zts. f. franz. Sprache u. Lit.,* XLIX, 202–16.

Guinable. *Charrette,* vs. 215. A count. Origin unknown.

Guingalet. *Erec,* vss. 3955, 3965; *Graal,* vss. 6209, 7316, 7429 (variant Gringalet). Gauvain's horse. Either from Old Welsh *guin-calet,* meaning "white-hardy," or from Keincaled, meaning "handsome-hardy." Cf. Chap. XXII.

Guingambresil. *Graal,* vss. 4749, 4755, etc. (variants Guigambresil etc.). Knight in service of the King of Cavalon; challenger of Gauvain. A compound name, from Gui(n)gamor and Bercilak. Guigamor is a Breton name, applied to the lord of Avalon (see above). Bercilak goes back to the Irish common noun *bachlach,* meaning "churl," frequently applied to Curoi, challenger of Cuchulainn. Cf. Chap. LXXII.

Guiromelant. *Graal,* vss. 8627, 8653 etc. (variants Grinomalanz, Grimolans, Guimelans, etc.). Lord of Orquelenes, lover of Clarianz, and enemy of Gauvain. One suspects that the latter part of the name is due to some connection with Welsh Melwas, but it is difficult to make out a case.

Guivret. *Erec,* vs. 3868 etc. Dwarf-king. The character is based on the Welsh dwarfs, Beli and Guidolwyn (cf. Chap. XX), but the name is probably Breton, being found in place names as Lan-Guivret, Lan Wivret. *Zts. f. franz. Sprache u. Lit.,* XLIX, 452.

Harpin de la Montaingne. *Yvain,* vs. 3857. Giant. Origin unknown.

Honolan. *See* Huberlan.

Huberlan. *Erec,* vs. 1746. An earldom. Probably a mangled form of Northumberlande or Cumberland.

Ignaures. *Charrette,* vs. 5808. Knight present at tourney of Noauz. Cf. E. Levi in *Studi romanzi,* XIV, 159 ff.

Irlande. *Erec,* vs. 2176; *Charrette,* vs. 5729 etc. Anglo-Norman form of Ireland.

Iseut. *Erec,* vs. 424. Mark's wife. From Welsh Essyllt. Thomas, *Tristan,* ed. Bédier, II, 112–15; J. Loth, *Contributions à l'étude des romans de la Table Ronde,* pp. 23 ff.

Kaherdin. *Graal,* vs. 4725. Knight of Arthur's. A curious formation from Kae Hir, Keu the Tall, under the influence of the Turkish Kahedin or Kaardin. *Romania,* LIII, 95. *Zts. f. rom. Phil.,* XLII, 482. Weston, *Legend of Perceval,* I, 272, n. 1.

Karados Briebraz. *Erec,* vs. 1719 (variants Cardos, Caradue). Knight of Arthur's. Through Breton Karadoc(us) Brech Bras from Welsh Caradoc Breich Bras (Arm-strong). Cf. *supra* pp. 49 f., and Chrétien, *Karrenritter,* ed. W. Foerster, p. cxiii; Loth, *Mabinogion,* 2d ed., I, 360, n. 1.

Kerrin. *Erec,* vs. 1985 (variants Quirions, Quarrons, Guermons, Krenus). The old King of Riel. Origin unknown. On this figure cf. *Acta Universitatis Lundensis,* XIII, 54.

Keu. *Erec,* vs. 317 etc. (variants Kai, Kei etc.). Seneschal of Arthur. From Welsh Cai, Kei. Cf. *supra,* pp. 154 f.

Keu d'Estraus. *Erec,* vs. 1725; *Charrette,* vs. 5830. Knight. Probably a double of Keu the seneschal. Estraus is unexplained.

Labigodes. *Erec,* vs. 1741 (variant Laboges). Knight of Arthur's. Origin unknown.

Lac. *Erec,* vs. 19 etc. King of Estregales, father of Erec. Translation of Welsh Lluch, which was both a personal name and a common noun, meaning "lake." Goes back ultimately to Irish god Lug. Cf. *supra,* pp. 55, 71–73.

Lalut. *Erec,* vss. 6249, 6251, 6320 (variants Laluth, Lalit, Lelit). Town where Enide lived. Origin uncertain, unless the word is due to corruption and misunderstanding of "le lac." Cf. *supra,* pp. 107 f.

Lancelot del Lac. *Erec,* vs. 1694. *Charrette,* vs. 3676 etc. Lover of Guenievre. From Welsh Lluch Llauynnauc, Arthur's warrior in Black Book of Carmarthen. Ultimately from Irish Lug Lonnbemnech. Cf. Chap. XXVI.

Landuc. *Yvain,* vs. 2151. Presumably the territory of Laudine. Origin unknown.

Laudine. *Yvain,* vs. 2151. Widow of Esclados and bride of Yvain. Either a corruption of "la dame"—the reading of seven mss.—or corruption of some form of Lothian such as Laudyan. Cf. Chap. LI.

Laudunet. *Yvain,* vs. 2153 (variants Laudonez, Laudinet, etc.). Duke, father of Laudine. A corruption of some form of Lothian, such as Geoffrey's Lodonesia. Faral, *Légende arthurienne,* III, 225. Cf. *supra,* pp. 302 f.

Leconuials. *Erec,* vs. 6896 (variants Liconaus, Licoranz). Father of Enide. Corruption and misunderstanding of "li cons vials," meaning "the old count." Cf. *supra,* pp. 35 f.

Leones. *Charrette,* vs. 1878 (variants Aloens, Looys). Knight of Arthur's. Possibly the Lion or Lioniaus of *Conte del Graal,* who is probably the Llew (meaning "lion") of the mabinogi of *Math.* Cf. *PMLA,* XLV, 432–38, and *supra,* pp. 295 f.

Letron de Prepelesant. *Erec,* vs. 1743 (variants Litons li Perpellosent, Letrons de Prepelesent). Knight of Arthur's. Origin unknown.

Liconaus. *See* Leconuials.

Limors. *Erec,* vss. 4717, 4947, etc. Castle of Count Orguilleus. Originally "li mors," meaning the dead man, a translation of Breton "ar maro," a title applied to Death personified. Cf. Chap. XXIV.

Loenel. *See* Yvain.

Logres. *Charrette,* vs. 1313 etc.; *Graal,* vs. 8639. Modern England. From Welsh Lloegr or Lloegyr. Cf. *Graal,* ed. Hilka, p. 733.

Loholz. *Erec,* vs. 1732 (variants Lohos, Lohous). Son of Arthur. Probably a corruption of Welsh Llacheu, name of Arthur's son. *Romanic Rev.*, III, 179–84; *Romania*, XLIII, 100–102; *Perlesvaus*, ed. Nitze, II, 297 f., 303–6.

Looys. *See* Leones.

Lore. *Graal*, vs. 9227. Lady attendant on Guenievre. Probably an aphetic form of Floree or Florie, name of Gauvain's *amie*. J. L. Weston, *Legend of Gawain*, pp. 46 f. and *supra*, 82–85, 370.

Lot. *Erec*, vs. 1737; *Yvain*, vs. 6267; *Graal*, vss. 8135, 8751. Father of Gauvain. From Welsh Lloch, alternative form of Lluch. Ultimately from Irish Lug. Cf. *supra*, pp. 187–90.

Lucan. *Erec*, vs. 1529. Butler at Arthur's court. Origin unknown.

Lunete. *Yvain*, vs. 2414 etc. Confidante of Laudine. Possibly the equivalent of Aranrot, whose name means "silver wheel," prominent in mabinogi of *Math*. Cf. Chap. L.

Mabonagrain. *Erec*, vs. 6132 etc. Nephew of Eurain. The first two syllables certainly represent Welsh Mabon, and this name goes back to Apollo Maponos in Old Celtic. The element *-agrain* may be due to the addition of the name of Mabon's brother Irain (for Ivain). Cf. *supra*, pp. 175–78.

Maheloas. *Erec*, vs. 1946 (variants Meloaus, Mahalos, Malehoes). Lord of the Isle de Voirre. From Welsh Melwas, a name meaning Prince Youth, and attached to the lord of the "ynys wydrin," i.e. Isle of Glass. Cf. *supra*, pp. 256–59.

Mauduiz li Sages. *Erec*, vs. 1699 (variant Maudus). A knight of Arthur's. Doubtless the same as Malduc(k), an enchanter in *Lanzelet*, styled "der wise." The name probably represents Welsh Madoc, and this in turn may be a substitution for Mabon. *Romania*, XXV, 286; Loth, *Mabinogion*, 2d ed., II, 318, n. 1.

Mautirec. *Charrette*, vs. 5812. Land of Coguillant. Origin unknown.

Meleagant. *Charrette*, vs. 641 etc. Son of Baudemaguz, abductor of Guenievre. From Welsh Melwas, under the influence of classical Meleager. Cf. Chap. XXXI.

Meliadoc. *Erec*, vs. 2132. Knight who heads one side in tourney of Danebroc. A form of Meriadoc, a Breton, Cornish, and Welsh personal name, which seems ultimately to derive from a district Meiriadauc in Denbighshire. *Zts. f. franz. Sprache u. Lit.*, XLIX, 237–39. *Breuddwyd Maxen*, ed. I. Williams (Bangor, 1908), p. xiii.

Meliant de Lis. *Graal*, vs. 4825 etc. Foster son of Tiebaut de Tintaguel and lover of his elder daughter. From Welsh Melwas. Cf. *supra*, pp. 426–29.

Melis. *Erec*, vs. 2132 (variants Melic, Miles). Associated with Meliadoc. Origin unknown.

Menagormon. *Erec*, vs. 1937 (variants Margogorlon, Margengomon, Magergomon). Count of Clivelon. Origin unknown.

Merlin. *Erec*, vs. 6693. Doubtless the famed wizard. Form of Welsh Myrddin, established by Geoffrey and Wace.

Mont Dolereus. *Erec*, vs. 1724; *Graal*, vs. 4724. Castle owned by Yder, goal of an adventure. Geoffrey names Mons Dolorosus as a foundation of Ebraucus. By 1170 identified with the Roman fort on hill near Melrose. Cf. *supra*, p. 110.

Montescleire. *Graal*, vs. 4706. A castle whose mistress desires deliverance. "The

Shining Mountain," probably mythical. Cf. Ulrich von Zatzikhoven, *Lanzelet*, vss. 209–11.

Montrevel. *Erec,* vss. 1339, 1881 (variants Monreuel, Reulein, Reuelin). Castle which Erec gave his father-in-law. Origin uncertain. Brugger pointed out that there were places called Montrevel in the departments of Ain and Isère. *Zts. f. franz. Sprache u. Lit.,* XXVII, "Abhandlungen," 93.

Morgain, Morgue. *Erec,* vss. 1957, 4218, 4220; *Yvain,* vs. 2953 (Morgue la sage). Mistress of Guigamor, sister of Arthur, the famous fay. The name is the Welsh and Breton Morcant, Morgant, properly a masculine name only. This fact had curious results: in *Chanson d'Antioche* Morgan la Fée and her brother Morgant are mentioned; in *Geraint* Morgan Tud is King Arthur's male physician. Cf. *Revue celt.,* XIII, 496 f.; *Romania,* XXVIII, 322 ff. The explanation of this masculine name seems to be that it was substituted for Irish Morrigan in Western Wales, and so passed on to the Bretons. Cf. *Speculum,* XX, 192–202. Morgue is a back formation from Morgain, on the analogy of Eve, Evain. Morgain took over the Welsh traditions of Modron, as well as the Irish legends of Morrigan.

Morhot. *Erec,* vs. 1248. The Irish champion vanquished by Tristan. Whatever the ultimate origin of this name (cf. G. Schoepperle, *Tristan and Isolt,* II, 329), the form which appears in the *Tristramssaga,* Morhaut, has been affected by the Germanic name Moraldus, recorded in Brittany before 1083. H. Morice, *Mémoires pour servir de preuves à l'histoire de Bretagne,* I, 436.

Noauz. *Charrette,* vss. 5389, 5525, 6089 (variants Noax, Nouaus, Vouauz). Place where tourney was held, and from which the Dame took her name. This is almost certainly a case of misunderstanding. According to ms. E (vss. 5665, 5674), Guenievre's messenger bade Lancelot bear himself at the tourney "a noauz," meaning "in a worse manner." This expression Chrétien, or more probably his source, must have taken to mean "at Noauz"!

Noiroison. *Yvain,* vs. 3287 (variants Noroison, Norison, Uoir Reson). Place from which la Dame de Noiroison took her title. Since she shows a certain kinship to Morgain la Fée and Morgain and her sisters took the form of black birds, Noiroison is probably due to a misunderstanding and deformation of "noir oisel." Cf. *supra,* pp. 309–11.

Nut. *Erec,* vss. 1046, 1213, 6819. The father of Yder. From Welsh Nudd, father of Edern. Probably Nudd goes back to the name of the British god Nodens or Nodons. Cf. remarks of Tolkien in R. E. M. and T. V. Wheeler, *Report on Excavation of the Prehistoric, Roman and Post-Roman Site in Lydney Park* (1932), pp. 132–37.

Orcanie. *Graal,* vss. 8889, 9101 etc. A city(?) where Arthur held court. A regular Anglo-Norman form for the Orkney Isles. The connection with Arthur is probably a mistake. Properly Orcanie is the territory which Gauvain inherited from his father Loth and to which therefore he sent a messenger to assemble his *pooir* (vss. 8886 f.). For Loth's connection with Orcanie cf. *supra,* pp. 71 f.

Orguelleus de la Lande. *Erec,* vs. 2175. Opponent of Erec at tourney of Danebroc. *Graal,* vs. 3817 etc. Jealous husband of Lady of the Tent. His Welsh prototype is Arawn in mabinogi of *Pwyll.* Cf. *supra,* pp. 122–26.

Orguelleus de la Roche à l'Estroite Voie. *Graal,* vss. 8646 f. Knight who guarded the Porz de Galvoie. Possibly his Welsh prototype was Havgan, slain by Pwyll at the ford.

Orguelleuse de Logres. *Graal,* vs. 8638. A damsel who guided Gauvain. A parallel figure to the scornful damsel who guided Beaumayns in Malory's Book VII. Her original is probably Liban in *Cuchulainn's Sickbed.* Cf. Chap. LXXVII.

Orguilleus de Limors. *Erec,* vss. 4947, 5070, 6495 (variant Oringle). Count. This person parallels Mabuz, lord of Schatel le Mort, in *Lanzelet,* and goes back to Welsh Mabon. Cf. Chap. XXIV.

Oringle. *See* Orguilleus de Limors.

Orquelenes. *Graal,* vs. 8626 (variants Orcaneles, Siorcanie, Orcanelens, Orquantansis, etc.). City of Guiromelant. Most of the mss. give forms beginning Orcan- or Orquan-; three follow with the adverb *ensi, einsint,* or the corruption *ansis.* I take the original reading of the verse to be something like: "Et s'a Orcan ainsi a non." In *Estoire del S. Graal* (Sommer, *Vulgate Version,* I, 52 f., 73, 77) there is a city Orcaus, which seems to be the same, lying on a river and near a Roche de Sanc, as Orquelenes lies on a river and near the Roche de Sanguin.

Outregales. *See* Estregales.

Pandragon. *See* Uterpandragon.

Peneuris. *Erec,* vs. 5185 (variants Pointurie, Penuris, Peneuril, Penris, Pencoxric). A castle belonging to Guivret's sisters. If Pointurie is the original reading, it may be a misunderstanding of *peinturé,* for Guivret's sisters are related to Morgain, and Morgain's castle was famous for its paintings. Cf. *supra,* pp. 144 f., 157.

Perceval. *Erec,* vs. 1526; *Graal,* vs. 1351 etc. Knight of Arthur's, cousin of the Fisher King. Substitution for Welsh Peredur. Peredur, through similarity of names, seems to have taken over Welsh traditions of Pryderi. Cf. Chap. LIX.

Pilades. *Charrette,* vs. 5825. Knight participating in tourney of Noauz. Doubtless the Greek Pylades.

Pomelegloi. *Charrette,* vss. 5388, 5646 (variants Pomelagoi, Pomagloi, Pomeloi, Pomelesglai). Apparently a place name. Origin unknown.

Quenedic. *Erec,* vs. 1722 (variants Quinedic, Quinodinc). King. Origin unknown.

Quinqueroi. *Graal,* vss. 951, 4127 (variants Guingueroi, Kinkerloi, Kinkenroi etc.). Forest, where the Red Knight dwelt. Not identified.

Quintareus. *Erec,* vs. 1723 (variants Descume Carroux, Descomme Carrous, Decume Raous, de Guivre Catons). Place? Possibly a deformation of "d'escu roux."

Rindurans. *Erec,* vs. 2182 (variants Rainduranz, Riduars, Randuraz). Participant in tourney near Danebroc, son of "la vielle de Tergalo." The name Rinduran occurs in both Breton and Cornish documents. Cf. *Zts. f. franz. Sprache u. Lit.,* XLIX, 479.

Rion. *Graal,* vs. 851. King of the Isles, vanquished by Arthur. Probably the giant king Ritho of Geoffrey, the Rithon of Wace. This figure may go back to a Welsh Rithon or Ritta. Cf. J. Rhys, *Celtic Folklore,* II, 560–64; *Graal,* ed. Hilka, p. 635; *Zts. f. franz. Sprache u. Lit.,* XLIV, "Referate," 45–48.

Roadan. *See* Rotelan.

Robais. *Erec,* vss. 5282, 6414 (variants Rohais, Roal, Roais). Place where Arthur held court. Possibly identical with Rotelan, Roalan, i.e. Rudlan in North Wales.

Roberdic. *Erec,* vs. 1721 (variants Rebedic, Redic, Rebedinc, Rebedas). Fief of Caveron. *Charrette,* vs. 5796 (variants Robediet, Beredinc, Genedic). Fief of Governauz. Unidentified.

Roche de Sanguin. *Graal,* vs. 8817 (variants Chanpguin, Changuin, Camp Guin, Canguin, Champguin). Castle of Ladies. The reading Sanguin seems assured by the context which says that cloths were there dyed "vert et sanguin." There is much evidence that the Castle of Ladies was sometimes localized on the Severn, and that Sabrin was twisted into Sanguin. Cf. *supra,* pp. 451–54.

Rotelan. *Erec,* vss. 1335, 1882 (variants Rodoan, Roalan, Roadan, Rodelen, Rodoalen, etc.). Castle presented by Erec to his father-in-law. Rudlan in North Wales. Cf. *supra,* p. 76.

Sagremor. *Erec,* vss. 1733, 2231, etc.; *Graal,* vss. 4220, 4230, etc. Knight of Arthur's. The name seems to represent a form of the common noun *sicamor,* but why Sagremor should be named after a tree and why he is described as "le Desreé" is unknown.

Sanguin. *See* Roche de Sanguin.

Sanson, Isle de Saint. *Erec,* vs. 1249. Island where Tristan defeated Morhot. Probably the island of this name in the Scilly group is meant, though it lies nowhere near Tintagel. Thomas, *Tristan,* ed. Bédier, II, 119. G. Schoepperle, *Tristan and Isolt,* I, 102–4; II, 366 f.

Scaudone. *Graal,* vs. 298 (variants Vaugonne, Vaucoigne, Valonne, Valbone, Valdonne). Hilka mistakenly gives the reading of ms. H as "descandone," though the *u* is plain. Brugger perceived (*Zts. f. franz. Sprache u. Lit.,* XLV, "Referate," 412n.) that here was a corruption of Snaudone, and compared it with Perceval's statement in Rochat *Perceval* (p. 91): "A Sinadon la fu jo nes." But he wrongly identified the place with Stirling in Scotland. Actually we find Snavdone in *Historia Meriadoci* (ed. J. D. Bruce, p. 1) clearly identified as the Welsh mountain Snowdon, and similar forms occur elsewhere in twelfth- and thirteenth-century documents. *Speculum,* XXII, 527. The "destroit de Scaudone" are therefore the mountain passes of Snowdon, and the locality harmonizes perfectly with Prof. Newstead's evidence (*Romanic Rev.,* XXXVI, 3–31) that Perceval's father was king of North Wales. Chrétien apparently wrote "li destroit desnaudone." The scribe of H changed *n* to *c.* Other scribes mistook *n* for *u,* thought *uau-* represented a form of *val* with vocalized *l,* and wrote Valonne, Valbone, Valdonne. The last form was suggested by the *chansons de geste.* Cf. E. Langlois, *Table des Noms Propres.*

Semiramis. *Charrette,* vs. 5816. Knight who participated in the tourney of Noauz. Evidently an arbitrary use of the name of the historic queen.

Tabriol. *See* Cadoc *and* Carduel.

Taulas. *Erec,* vs. 1729 (variants Tauas, Talas, etc.). Knight of Arthur's. Origin unknown.

Taulas de la Deserte. *Charrette,* vs. 5834 (variant Tallas). Knight who participated in tourney of Noauz. Presumably identical with the other Taulas.

Tenebroc. *See* Danebroc.

Tergalo. *Erec,* vs. 2183 (variants Tergalou, Tregalloi, Tergallon, Tresgeuleu). Place connected with "la vielle," mother of Rindurans. Unidentified.

Thoas. *Charrette,* vs. 5842 (variant Connain). Participant in the tourney of Noauz. Either the Thoas of *Roman de Troie* or the Breton name Conan.

Tiebaut de Tintaguel. *Graal,* vs. 4835 etc. (variants Tybaut, Tibaut, etc.). Rimes with *saut* (4931), *haut* (4991). Foster father of Meliant. An arbitrary substitution for Baut, which in turn is a corruption of Ban and ultimately of Welsh Bran. Cf. *supra,* pp. 427-29.

Tintaguel. *Erec,* vss. 1959, 6518; *Graal,* vss. 4835, 4884. Town where Arthur held court and where Tiebaut dwelt. Famous castle of Tintagel on coast of Cornwall.

Tor(z). *Erec,* vss. 1528, 1728 (variants Corz, Estor, Estus, Hector, Toz). Son of King Ares. Origin unknown. Cf. *Histoire littéraire,* XXXI, 168.

Trae d'Anet. *Graal,* vss. 4828, 4831 (many variants). Knight. Origin unknown.

Trebuchet. *Graal,* vs. 3679 (variants Trabuché, Tribuchet, Trebuchel, Triboet). A smith who lived at the lake above Cotoatre. Origin unknown.

Treverain. *Erec,* vs. 1941 (variants Trauerain, Treueren, Treuarin, Trouerain, Touertins). Earldom(?). Unidentified.

Tristan. *Erec,* vss. 1248, 1713 (variant Tristrans). The lover of Iseut. There is no reason to differentiate "Tristanz qui onques ne rist," since the lover of Iseut was noted for his tragic fate. The name is derived through Welsh Trystan, Drystan, from Pictish Drust(an), a king who reigned about 780. Thomas, *Tristan,* ed. Bédier, II, 105-8. *Beiblatt zur Anglia,* XV, 16-21. *Mod. Phil.,* XXXIII, 231. *Comptes rendus de l'Acad. des Inscriptions,* 1924, p. 128.

Urien. *Erec,* vs. 1706; *Yvain,* vs. 1018 etc.; *Graal,* vs. 8149. Father of Yvain. From Welsh Urien, the name of a famous chief of the North Britons in the latter half of the sixth century, father of Owein. Cf. *supra,* p. 269.

Uterpandragon. *Erec,* vs. 1811; *Yvain,* vs. 663; *Graal,* vss. 445, 8740. Father of Arthur. Probably derived from Geoffrey's Uter Pendragon through Wace. Cf. A. B. Hopkins, *Influence of Wace on Crestien de Troyes,* pp. 109 f.; M Pelan, *Influence du Brut de Wace,* pp. 59-62. Geoffrey may have invented the relationship of Arthur to Uter as a result of misinterpreting a gloss in Nennius. Cf. *Vassar Mediaeval Studies,* pp. 4 f. But that Uthir Pen Dragon existed before Geoffrey's time in Welsh legend seems evident from the reference to him in the archaic poem in the Black Book of Carmarthen. Cf. Malory, *Morte d'Arthur,* Everyman ed., I, xviii; *Revue celt.,* XLIX, 133-35. Loth (*ibid.,* p. 135) says: "Pendragon peut signifier chef des dragons, mais dans le sens de chef des guerriers."

Valdone. *See* Scaudone.

Yder. *Erec,* vs. 313; *Charrette,* vs. 5822. King in Arthur's court. *Erec,* vs. 1046 etc. Son of Nut, who became a member of Arthur's court. *Erec,* vs. 1724. Knight of Mont Dolereus, knight of Arthur's. Though Chrétien probably intended to differentiate the three Yders, there is only one Edern, the son of Nudd, who is associated with Arthur in the Welsh texts. Loth, *Mabinogion,* 2d ed., I, 262, 373. It has been shown above, pp. 77-79, that the obnoxious role which Yder, son of Nut, plays in *Erec* is quite alien to tradition and has been arbitrarily foisted on him. Yder first appears on the Continent as Isdernus on the Modena sculpture. Cf. R. S. and L. H. Loomis, *Arthurian Legends in Medieval Art,* pp. 32–35; *Romanic Review,* XV, 269–71. On other appearances of Yder cf. *Yderroman,* ed. H. Gelzer, pp. liv–lvii, lxx f.

Yguerne. *Graal,* vs. 8748. Wife of Uterpandragon, mother of Arthur. Doubtless derived through Wace's Igerne from Geoffrey's Igerna. No Celtic original for Igerna is known, unless Welsh texts dependent on Geoffrey are correct in giving the name as Eigr or Eigyr. Cf. Geoffrey, *Historia Regum Britanniae,* ed. Griscom, p. 423; *Cymmrodor,* XXIV, 258.

Yonet. *Graal,* vs. 915 etc. (variants Ionet, Yvonet). A squire in Arthur's household. The name is of uncertain derivation. *Zts. f. franz. Sprache u. Lit.,* XLIX, 400–402.

Yvain. *Erec,* vss. 1706, 2230; *Yvain, passim; Graal,* vs. 8152. Son of Urien. Yvain de Loenel, *Erec,* vs. 1707. Yvains li Avoutre, *Erec,* vs. 1708; *Graal,* vss. 8157–59. Though Chrétien distinguishes the three Yvains, there is reason to believe that they were originally one and the same, as in the case of the Yders. Yvain son of Urien is the historic Owein son of Urien, a prince of the North Britons of the late sixth century. The form Yvain is a Breton development since Ivan(us) appears in Breton records of the eleventh century. Cf. *supra,* pp. 269, 273. Yvain de Loenel, as Brugger pointed out in *Mod. Phil.,* XXXVIII, 282–86, probably owed his title to an early association with Loeneis, i.e. Lothian, recorded by Gaimar. Yvain the Bastard was the son of Urien already mentioned since we have a Welsh account of his begetting by Urien on Modron out of wedlock. Cf. Chap. XLV.

Yvain de Cavaliot. *Erec,* vs. 1709. Knight of Arthur's. The name, as Brugger pointed out (*Mod. Phil.,* XXXVIII, 268), represents a corruption of that borne by a celebrated contemporary of Chrétien's, Owein Cyveilioc, Cyveilioc being the territory over which he ruled. Giraldus Cambrensis calls him Oeneus de Keveiliauc and says something of his friendly relations with Henry II. Giraldus, *Opera,* VI, 144 f. He was also noted as a poet. *Cymmrodor,* XXXII, 2 f., 46–57. In *Fouke Fitz Warin* he is "Yweyn Keveyllok, un chevaler hardy e fer." Cf. *Dict. Nat. Biog.,* XIV, 1289 f.

INDEX OF NAMES
AND TITLES

When an author's name is more familiar than the title of his work (e.g. Geoffrey of Monmouth, Malory), references are given under the name. When the author is unknown or unfamiliar (e.g. *Peredur, Fergus*), references will be found under the title. For personal or place names occurring in Chrétien's four traditional poems, consult also the Appendix, pp. 477-92.

INDEX OF SUBJECTS